MICROSOFT®
Office 2003
Brief Concepts and Techniques

WORD 2003   EXCEL 2003   ACCESS 2003   POWERPOINT 2003

Gary B. Shelly
Thomas J. Cashman
Misty E. Vermaat

Contributing Authors
Steven G. Forsythe
Mary Z. Last
Philip J. Pratt
James S. Quasney
Susan L. Sebok

THOMSON
COURSE TECHNOLOGY

COURSE TECHNOLOGY
25 THOMSON PLACE
BOSTON MA 02210

SHELLY
CASHMAN
SERIES®

Australia • Canada • Denmark • Japan • Mexico • New Zealand • Philippines • Puerto Rico • Singapore
South Africa • Spain • United Kingdom • United States

THOMSON

COURSE TECHNOLOGY

Microsoft Office 2003
Brief Concepts and Techniques

Gary B. Shelly
Thomas J. Cashman
Misty E. Vermaat

Executive Editor:
Cheryl Costantini

Senior Product Manager:
Alexandra Arnold

Product Manager:
Erin Runyon

Associate Product Manager:
Reed Cotter

Editorial Assistant:
Selena Coppock

Print Buyer:
Denise Powers

Signing Representative:
Cheryl Costantini

Series Consulting Editor:
Jim Quasney

Director of Production:
Becky Herrington

Production Editor:
Kristen Guevara

Production Assistant:
Jennifer Quiambao

Development Editor:
Ginny Harvey

Copy Editors/Proofreaders:
Ginny Harvey
Nancy Lamm
Lyn Markowicz
Lori Silfen
Lisa Jedlicka
Kim Kosmatka
Marilyn Martin

Interior Design:
Becky Herrington

Cover Design:
Richard Herrera

Illustrators:
Richard Herrera
Andrew Bartel
Ken Russo

Compositors:
Jeanne Black
Andrew Bartel
Kellee LaVars
Kenny Tran
Michelle French

Indexer:
Cristina Haley

Printer:
Banta Menasha

Course Technology reserves the right to revise this publication and make changes from time to time in its content without notice.

ISBN 0-619-20022-7 (perfect bound)
ISBN 0-619-20023-5 (spiral bound)

PHOTO CREDITS: **Microsoft Windows XP** *Project 1, page* WIN 5 Dell computer, monitor, and printer, Courtesy of Dell, Inc.; *page* WIN 6 Dell computer and monitor, Courtesy of Dell, Inc.; **Microsoft PowerPoint 2003** *Project 1, page* PPT 6 notebook computer, Courtesy of PhotoDisc, Inc.

MICROSOFT®
Office 2003
Brief Concepts and Techniques
WORD 2003   EXCEL 2003   ACCESS 2003   POWERPOINT 2003

Contents

Project Two

Creating a Research Paper

MICROSOFT
Office Excel 2003

Project One

Creating a Worksheet
and an Embedded Chart

Project Two

Formulas, Functions, Formatting, and Web Queries

Microsoft Office Access 2003

Project One

Creating and Using a Database

Project Two

Querying a Database Using the Select Query Window

Microsoft Office PowerPoint 2003

Project One

Using a Design Template and Text Slide Layout to Create a Presentation

Appendix A

Microsoft Office Help System

Appendix B

Speech and Handwriting Recognition and Speech Playback

Appendix C

Publishing Office Web Pages to a Web Server

Appendix D

Changing Screen Resolution and Resetting the Word Toolbars and Menus

Appendix E

Microsoft Office Specialist Certification

Preface

The Shelly Cashman Series® offers the finest textbooks in computer education. We are proud of the fact that our series of Microsoft Office 4.3, Microsoft Office 95, Microsoft Office 97, Microsoft Office 2000, and Microsoft Office XP textbooks have been the most widely used books in education. With each new edition of our Office books, we have made significant improvements based on the software and comments made by the instructors and students. The *Microsoft Office 2003* books continue with the innovation, quality, and reliability that you have come to expect from the Shelly Cashman Series.

In this *Microsoft Office 2003* book, you will find an educationally sound, highly visual, and easy-to-follow pedagogy that combines a vastly improved step-by-step approach with corresponding screens. All projects and exercises in this book are designed to take full advantage of the Office 2003 enhancements. The popular Other Ways and More About features offer in-depth knowledge of the Office applications. The new Q&A feature offers students a way to solidify important application concepts. The Learn It Online page presents a wealth of additional exercises to ensure your students have all the reinforcement they need. The project material is developed to ensure that students will see the importance of learning how to use the Office applications for future coursework.

Objectives of This Textbook

Microsoft Office 2003: Brief Concepts and Techniques is intended for a two-credit hour course or a regular semester course that includes a nine-to-ten-week introduction to Office 2003. No experience with a computer is assumed, and no mathematics beyond the high school freshman level is required. The objectives of this book are:

- To teach the fundamentals of Microsoft Office Word 2003, Microsoft Office Excel 2003, Microsoft Office Access 2003, Microsoft Office PowerPoint 2003, and Microsoft Windows XP
- To expose students to practical examples of the computer as a useful tool
- To acquaint students with the proper procedures to create documents, worksheets, databases, and presentations suitable for coursework, professional purposes, and personal use
- To help students discover the underlying functionality of Office 2003 so they can become more productive
- To develop an exercise-oriented approach that allows learning by doing
- To introduce students to new input technologies
- To encourage independent study, and help those who are working alone

The Shelly Cashman Approach

Features of the Shelly Cashman Series *Microsoft Office 2003* books include:

- **Project Orientation:**   Each project in the book presents a practical problem and complete solution in an easy-to-understand approach.
- **Step-by-Step, Screen-by-Screen Instructions:**   Each of the tasks required to complete a project is identified throughout the project. Full-color screens with call outs accompany the steps.
- **Thoroughly Tested Projects:**   Unparalleled quality is ensured because every screen in the book is produced by the author only after performing a step, and then each project must pass Course Technology's award-winning Quality Assurance program.
- **Other Ways Boxes and Quick Reference Summary:**   The Other Ways boxes displayed at the end of most of the step-by-step sequences specify the other ways to do the task completed in the steps. Thus, the steps and the Other Ways box make a comprehensive reference unit.
- **More About and Q&A Features:**   These marginal annotations provide background information, tips, and answers to common questions that complement the topics covered, adding depth and perspective to the learning process.
- **Integration of the World Wide Web:**   The World Wide Web is integrated into the Office 2003 learning experience by (1) More About annotations that send students to Web sites for up-to-date information

and alternative approaches to tasks; (2) a Microsoft Office Specialist Certification Web page so students can prepare for the certification examinations; (3) a Quick Reference Summary Web page that summarizes the ways to complete tasks (mouse, menu, shortcut menu, and keyboard); and (4) the Learn It Online page at the end of each project, which has project reinforcement exercises, learning games, and other types of student activities.

Organization of This Textbook

Microsoft Office 2003: Brief Concepts and Techniques provides basic instruction on how to use the Office 2003 applications. The material is divided into nine projects, one PowerPoint Web feature, five appendices, and a Quick Reference Summary.

Microsoft Windows XP and Office 2003

Project 1 – Introduction to Microsoft Windows XP and Office 2003   In this project, students learn about user interfaces, Windows XP, Windows Explorer, and each Office 2003 application. Topics include using the mouse; minimizing, maximizing, and restoring windows; closing and reopening windows; sizing and scrolling windows; launching and quitting an application; displaying the contents of a folder; expanding and collapsing a folder; creating a folder; selecting and copying a group of files; renaming and deleting a file and a folder; using Windows XP Help; and shutting down Windows XP. Topics pertaining to Microsoft Office 2003 include a brief explanation of Microsoft Office Word 2003; Microsoft Office Excel 2003; Microsoft Office Access 2003; Microsoft Office PowerPoint 2003; Microsoft Office Publisher 2003; Microsoft Office FrontPage 2003; and Microsoft Office Outlook 2003 and examples of how these applications take advantage of the Internet and World Wide Web.

Microsoft Office Word 2003

Project 1 – Creating and Editing a Word Document   In Project 1, students are introduced to Word terminology and the Word window by preparing an announcement. Topics include starting and quitting Word; entering text; checking spelling while typing; saving a document; selecting characters, words, lines, and paragraphs; changing the font and font size of text; centering, right-aligning, bolding, and italicizing text; undoing commands and actions; inserting clip art in a document; resizing a graphic; printing a document; opening a document; correcting errors; and using the Word Help system.

Project 2 – Creating a Research Paper   In Project 2, students use the MLA style of documentation to create a research paper. Topics include changing margins; adjusting line spacing; using a header to number pages; entering text using Click and Type; first-line indenting paragraphs; using the AutoCorrect feature and AutoCorrect Options button; adding a footnote; modifying a style; inserting a symbol automatically; inserting a manual page break; creating a hanging indent; creating a text hyperlink; sorting paragraphs; moving text; using the Paste Options button; finding a synonym; counting and recounting words in a document; checking spelling and grammar at once; e-mailing a document; and using the Research task pane.

Microsoft Office Excel 2003

Project 1 – Creating a Worksheet and Embedded Chart   In Project 1, students are introduced to Excel terminology, the Excel window, speech recognition and speech playback, and the basic characteristics of a worksheet and workbook. Topics include starting and quitting Excel; customizing Excel; entering text and numbers; selecting a range; using the AutoSum button; copying using the fill handle; changing font size and color; formatting in bold; centering across columns; using the AutoFormat command; charting using the ChartWizard; saving and opening a workbook; editing a worksheet; using the AutoCalculate area; and using the Excel Help system.

Project 2 – Formulas, Functions, Formatting, and Web Queries   In Project 2, students use formulas and functions to build a worksheet and learn more about formatting and printing a worksheet. Topics include entering dates and formulas; using functions; verifying formulas; changing fonts; formatting text and numbers; conditional formatting; drawing borders; changing the widths of columns and rows; spell checking; changing sheet names; previewing a worksheet; printing a section of a worksheet; and displaying and printing the formulas in a worksheet. This project also introduces students to accessing real-time data using Web Queries and sending the open workbook as an e-mail attachment directly from Excel.

Microsoft Office Access 2003

Project 1 – Creating and Using a Database   In Project 1, students are introduced to the concept of a database and shown how to use Access 2003 to create a database. Topics include creating a database; creating a table; defining the fields in a table; opening a table; adding records to a table; closing a table; and previewing and printing the contents of a table. Other topics in this project include creating a query using the Simple Query Wizard; using a form to view data; using the Report Wizard to create a report; and using the Access Help system. Students also learn how to design a database to eliminate redundancy.

Project 2 – Querying a Database Using the Select Query Window   In Project 2, students learn to use queries to obtain information from the data in their databases. Topics include creating queries, running queries, saving queries, and printing the results. Specific query topics include displaying only selected fields; using character data in criteria; specifying parameter queries; using wildcards; using numeric data in criteria; using comparison operators; and creating compound criteria. Other related topics include sorting, joining tables, and restricting records in a join. Students also learn to use calculated fields, statistics, and grouping. They also learn how to create top-values queries and how to format fields in queries. Finally, they learn to create and use crosstab queries.

Microsoft Office PowerPoint 2003

Project 1 – Using a Design Template and Text Slide Layout to Create a Presentation   In Project 1, students are introduced to PowerPoint terminology, the PowerPoint window, and the basics of creating a bulleted list presentation. Topics include choosing a design template by using a task pane; creating a title slide and text slides with single and multi-level bulleted lists; changing the font size and font style; ending a slide show with a black slide; saving a presentation; viewing the slides in a presentation; checking a presentation for spelling errors; printing copies of the slides; and using the PowerPoint Help system.

Project 2 – Using the Outline Tab and Clip Art to Create a Slide Show   In Project 2, students create a presentation from an outline, insert clip art, and add animation effects. Topics include creating a slide presentation by indenting paragraphs on the Outline tab; changing slide layouts; inserting clip art; changing clip art size; adding an animation scheme; animating clip art; running an animated slide show; printing audience handouts from an outline; and e-mailing a slide show from within PowerPoint.

Web Feature – Creating a Presentation on the Web Using PowerPoint   In the Web feature, students are introduced to saving a presentation as a Web page. Topics include saving an existing PowerPoint presentation as an HTML file; viewing the presentation as a Web page; editing a Web page through a browser; and viewing the editing changes.

Appendices

The book includes five appendices. Appendix A presents an introduction to the Microsoft Office Help system. Appendix B describes how to use the Office speech and handwriting recognition and speech playback capabilities. Appendix C explains how to publish Web pages to a Web server. Appendix D shows how to change the screen resolution and reset the menus and toolbars. Appendix E introduces students to Microsoft Office Specialist certification.

Microsoft Office 2003 Quick Reference Summary

In Office 2003, you can accomplish a task in a number of ways, such as using the mouse, menu, shortcut menu, and keyboard. The Quick Reference Summary at the back of the book provides a quick reference to each task presented.

End-of-Project Student Activities

A notable strength of the Shelly Cashman Series *Microsoft Office 2003* books is the extensive student activities at the end of each project. Well-structured student activities can make the difference between students merely participating in a class and students retaining the information they learn. The Shelly Cashman Series *Office* books include the activities described on the next page.

- **What You Should Know**   A listing of the tasks completed within a project together with the pages on which the step-by-step, screen-by-screen explanations appear.
- **Learn It Online**   Every project features a Learn It Online page that comprises twelve exercises. These exercises include True/False, Multiple Choice, Short Answer, Flash Cards, Practice Test, Learning Games, Tips and Tricks, Newsgroup usage, Expanding Your Horizons, Search Sleuth, Office Online Training, and Office Marketplace.
- **Apply Your Knowledge**   This exercise usually requires students to open and manipulate a file on the Data Disk that parallels the activities learned in the project. To obtain a copy of the Data Disk, follow the instructions on the inside back cover of this textbook.
- **In the Lab**   Three in-depth assignments per project require students to utilize the project concepts and techniques to solve problems on a computer.
- **Cases and Places**   Five unique real-world case-study situations, including one small-group activity.

Instructor Resources CD-ROM

The Shelly Cashman Series is dedicated to providing you with all of the tools you need to make your class a success. Information on all supplementary materials is available through your Course Technology representative or by calling one of the following telephone numbers: Colleges and Universities, 1-800-648-7450; High Schools, 1-800-824-5179; Private Career Colleges, 1-800-347-7707; Canada, 1-800-268-2222; Corporations with IT Training Centers, 1-800-648-7450; and Government Agencies, Health-Care Organizations, and Correctional Facilities, 1-800-477-3692.

The Instructor Resources for this textbook include both teaching and testing aids. The contents of each item on the Instructor Resources CD-ROM (ISBN 0-619-20048-0) are described below.

INSTRUCTOR'S MANUAL   The Instructor's Manual is made up of Microsoft Word files, which include detailed lesson plans with page number references, lecture notes, teaching tips, classroom activities, discussion topics, projects to assign, and transparency references. The transparencies are available through the Figure Files described below.

LECTURE SUCCESS SYSTEM   The Lecture Success System consists of intermediate files that correspond to certain figures in the book, allowing you to step through the creation of an application in a project during a lecture without entering large amounts of data.

SYLLABUS   Sample syllabi, which can be customized easily to a course, are included. The syllabi cover policies, class and lab assignments and exams, and procedural information.

FIGURE FILES   Illustrations for every figure in the textbook are available in electronic form. Use this ancillary to present a slide show in lecture or to print transparencies for use in lecture with an overhead projector. If you have a personal computer and LCD device, this ancillary can be an effective tool for presenting lectures.

POWERPOINT PRESENTATIONS   PowerPoint Presentations is a multimedia lecture presentation system that provides slides for each project. Presentations are based on project objectives. Use this presentation system to present well-organized lectures that are both interesting and knowledge based. Power-Point Presentations provides consistent coverage at schools that use multiple lecturers.

SOLUTIONS TO EXERCISES   Solutions are included for the end-of-project exercises, as well as the Project Reinforcement exercises.

RUBRICS AND ANNOTATED SOLUTION FILES   The grading rubrics provide a customizable framework for assigning point values to the laboratory exercises. Annotated solution files that correspond to the grading rubrics make it easy for you to compare students' results with the correct solutions whether you receive their homework as hard copy or via e-mail.

TEST BANK & TEST ENGINE   The ExamView test bank includes 110 questions for every project (25 multiple-choice, 50 true/false, and 35 completion) with page number references, and when appropriate, figure references. A version of the test bank you can print also is included. The test bank comes with a copy of the test engine, ExamView, the ultimate tool for your objective-based testing needs. ExamView is a state-of-the-art test builder that is easy to use. ExamView enables you to create paper-, LAN-, or Web-based tests from test banks designed specifically for your Course Technology textbook. Utilize the ultra-efficient QuickTest Wizard to create tests in less than five minutes by taking advantage of Course Technology's question banks, or customize your own exams from scratch.

LAB TESTS/TEST OUT   The Lab Tests/Test Out exercises parallel the In the Lab assignments and are supplied for the purpose of testing students in the laboratory on the material covered in the project or testing students out of the course.

DATA FILES FOR STUDENTS   All the files that are required by students to complete the exercises are included. You can distribute the files on the Instructor Resources CD-ROM to your students over a network, or you can have them follow the instructions on the inside back cover of this book to obtain a copy of the Data Disk.

ADDITIONAL ACTIVITIES FOR STUDENTS   These additional activities consist of Project Reinforcement Exercises, which are true/false, multiple choice, and short answer questions that help students gain confidence in the material learned.

SAM 2003

SAM 2003 helps you energize your class exams and training assignments by allowing students to learn and test important computer skills in an active, hands-on environment.

SAM 2003 ASSESSMENT   With SAM 2003 Assessment, you create powerful interactive exams on critical applications such as Word, Excel, Access, PowerPoint, Outlook, Windows, and the Internet. The exams simulate the application environment, allowing your students to demonstrate their knowledge and think through the skill by performing real-world tasks.

SAM 2003 TRAINING   Invigorate your lesson plan with SAM 2003 Training. Using highly interactive text, graphics, and sound, SAM 2003 Training gives your students the flexibility to learn computer applications by choosing the training method that fits them best.

SAM 2003 ASSESSMENT AND TRAINING   Designed to be used with the Shelly Cashman Series, SAM 2003 Assessment and Training includes built-in page references so students can create study guides that match the Shelly Cashman Series textbooks you use in class. Powerful administrative options allow you to schedule customized exams and assignments, secure your tests, and choose from more than one dozen reports to track testing and learning progress.

Online Content

Course Technology offers textbook-based content for Blackboard, WebCT, and MyCourse 2.1

BLACKBOARD AND WEBCT   As the leading provider of IT content for the Blackboard and WebCT platforms, Course Technology delivers rich content that enhances your textbook to give your students a unique learning experience. Course Technology has partnered with WebCT and Blackboard to deliver our market-leading content through these state-of-the-art online learning platforms.

MYCOURSE 2.1   MyCourse 2.1 is Course Technology's powerful online course management and content delivery system. Completely maintained and hosted by Thomson, MyCourse 2.1 delivers an online learning environment that is completely secure and provides superior performance. MyCourse 2.1 allows nontechnical users to create, customize, and deliver World Wide Web-based courses; post content and assignments; manage student enrollment; administer exams; track results in the online gradebook; and more.

Workbook for Microsoft Office 2003

This highly popular supplement (ISBN 0-619-20028-6) includes a variety of activities that help students recall, review, and master the concepts presented. The *Workbook* complements the end-of-project material with a guided project outline; a self-test consisting of true/false, multiple-choice, short answer, and matching questions; and activities calculated to help students develop a deeper understanding of the information presented.

To the Student... Getting the Most Out of Your Book

Welcome to *Microsoft Office 2003: Brief Concepts and Techniques*. You can save yourself a lot of time and gain a better understanding of the Office 2003 applications if you spend a few minutes reviewing the figures and callouts in this section.

1 Project Orientation

Each project presents a practical problem and shows the solution in the first figure of the project. The project orientation lets you see firsthand how problems are solved from start to finish using application software and computers.

2 Consistent Step-by-Step, Screen-by-Screen Presentation

Project solutions are built using a step-by-step, screen-by-screen approach. This pedagogy allows you to build the solution on a computer as you read through the project. Generally, each step is followed by an italic explanation that indicates the result of the step.

3 More Than Just Step-by-Step

More About and Q&A annotations in the margins of the book and substantive text in the paragraphs provide background information, tips, and answers to common questions that complement the topics covered, adding depth and perspective. When you finish with this book, you will be ready to use the Office applications to solve problems on your own.

4 Other Ways Boxes and Quick Reference Summary

Other Ways boxes that follow many of the step sequences and a Quick Reference Summary at the back of the book explain the other ways to complete the task presented, such as using the mouse, menu, shortcut menu, and keyboard.

5 Emphasis on Getting Help When You Need It

The first project of each application and Appendix A show you how to use all the elements of the Office Help system. Being able to answer your own questions will increase your productivity and reduce your frustrations by minimizing the time it takes to learn how to complete a task.

6 Review

After you successfully step through a project, a section titled What You Should Know summarizes the project tasks with which you should be familiar. Terms you should know for test purposes are bold in the text.

7 Reinforcement and Extension

The Learn It Online page at the end of each project offers reinforcement in the form of review questions, learning games, and practice tests. Also included are Web-based exercises that require you to extend your learning beyond the book.

8 Laboratory Exercises

If you really want to learn how to use the applications, then you must design and implement solutions to problems on your own. Every project concludes with several carefully developed laboratory assignments that increase in complexity.

Shelly Cashman Series – Traditionally Bound Textbooks

The Shelly Cashman Series presents the following computer subjects in a variety of traditionally bound textbooks. For more information, see your Course Technology representative or call 1-800-648-7450. For Shelly Cashman Series information, visit Shelly Cashman Online at **scseries.com**

COMPUTERS	
Computers	Discovering Computers 2005: A Gateway to Information, Web Enhanced, Complete Edition
	Discovering Computers 2005: A Gateway to Information, Web Enhanced, Introductory Edition
	Discovering Computers 2005: A Gateway to Information, Web Enhanced, Brief Edition
	Discovering Computers 2005: Fundamentals Edition
	Teachers Discovering Computers: Integrating Technology in the Classroom 3e
	Exploring Computers: A Record of Discovery 4e
	Study Guide for Discovering Computers 2005: A Gateway to Information, Web Enhanced
	Essential Introduction to Computers 5e (40-page)

WINDOWS APPLICATIONS	
Microsoft Office	Microsoft Office 2003: Essential Concepts and Techniques (5 projects)
	Microsoft Office 2003: Brief Concepts and Techniques (9 projects)
	Microsoft Office 2003: Introductory Concepts and Techniques, (15 projects)
	Microsoft Office 2003: Advanced Concepts and Techniques (12 projects)
	Microsoft Office 2003: Post Advanced Concepts and Techniques (11 projects)
	Microsoft Office XP: Essential Concepts and Techniques (5 projects)
	Microsoft Office XP: Brief Concepts and Techniques (9 projects)
	Microsoft Office XP: Introductory Concepts and Techniques, Windows XP Edition
	Microsoft Office XP: Introductory Concepts and Techniques, Enhanced Edition (15 projects)[1]
	Microsoft Office XP: Advanced Concepts and Techniques (11 projects)
	Microsoft Office XP: Post Advanced Concepts and Techniques (11 projects)
Integration	Integrating Microsoft Office XP Applications and the World Wide Web: Essential Concepts and Techniques
PIM	Microsoft Outlook 2002: Essential Concepts and Techniques
Microsoft Works	Microsoft Works 6: Complete Concepts and Techniques[2] • Microsoft Works 2000: Complete Concepts and Techniques[2]
Microsoft Windows	Microsoft Windows XP: Complete Concepts and Techniques[3]
	Microsoft Windows XP: Brief Concepts and Techniques
	Microsoft Windows 2000: Complete Concepts and Techniques (6 projects)[3]
	Microsoft Windows 2000: Brief Concepts and Techniques (2 projects)
	Microsoft Windows 98: Essential Concepts and Techniques (2 projects)
	Microsoft Windows 98: Complete Concepts and Techniques (6 projects)[3]
	Introduction to Microsoft Windows NT Workstation 4
Word Processing	Microsoft Word 2003[3] • Microsoft Word 2002[3]
Spreadsheets	Microsoft Excel 2003[3] • Microsoft Excel 2002[3]
Database	Microsoft Access 2003[3] • Microsoft Access 2002[3]
Presentation Graphics	Microsoft PowerPoint 2003[3] • Microsoft PowerPoint 2002[3]
Desktop Publishing	Microsoft Publisher 2003[2] • Microsoft Publisher 2002[2]

PROGRAMMING	
Programming	Microsoft Visual Basic.NET: Complete Concepts and Techniques[3] • Microsoft Visual Basic 6: Complete Concepts and Techniques[2] • Programming in QBasic • Java Programming 2e: Complete Concepts and Techniques[3] • Structured COBOL Programming 2e

INTERNET	
Browser	Microsoft Internet Explorer 6: Introductory Concepts and Techniques • Microsoft Internet Explorer 5: An Introduction • Netscape Navigator 6: An Introduction
Web Page Creation and Design	Web Design: Introductory Concepts and Techniques • HTML: Complete Concepts and Techniques 2e[3] Microsoft FrontPage 2003[3] • Microsoft FrontPage 2002[3] • Microsoft FrontPage 2002: Essential Concepts and Techniques • Java Programming: Complete Concepts and Techniques 2e[3] • JavaScript: Complete Concepts and Techniques 2e[2] • Macromedia Dreamweaver MX: Complete Concepts and Techniques[3]

SYSTEMS ANALYSIS	
Systems Analysis	Systems Analysis and Design 5e

DATA COMMUNICATIONS	
Data Communications	Business Data Communications: Introductory Concepts and Techniques 4e

[1]Available running under Windows XP or running under Windows 2000, [2]Also available as an Introductory Edition, which is a shortened version of the complete book, [3]Also available as an Introductory Edition, which is a shortened version of the complete book and also as a Comprehensive Edition, which is an extended version of the complete book

Microsoft **Windows XP and Office 2003**

MICROSOFT
Windows XP and Office 2003

MICROSOFT
Windows XP and Office 2003

Introduction to Microsoft Windows XP and Office 2003

CASE PERSPECTIVE

After weeks of planning, your organization finally installed Microsoft Windows XP Professional on all workstations. As the computer trainer for the upcoming in-house seminar, you realize you should know more about Microsoft Windows XP Professional but have had little time to learn. Since installing Windows XP Professional, many employees have come to you with questions. You have taken the time to answer their questions by sitting down with them at their computers and searching for the answers using the Help and Support feature.

From their questions, you determine that you should customize the seminar to cover the basics of Windows XP Professional, including basic mouse operations, working with windows, launching an application, and searching for answers using Help and Support. Your goal is to become familiar with Microsoft Windows XP Professional in order to teach the seminar more effectively to the participants.

As you read through this project, you will learn how to use the Windows XP operating system to perform basic operating system tasks and become familiar with the Microsoft Office 2003 applications.

MICROSOFT
Windows XP and Office 2003

Introduction to Microsoft Windows XP and Office 2003

Objectives

You will have mastered the material in this project when you can:

- Launch Microsoft Windows XP, log on to the computer, and identify the objects on the desktop
- Perform the basic mouse operations: point, click, right-click, double-click, drag, and right-drag
- Display the Start menu and launch an application program
- Add and remove a desktop icon
- Open, minimize, maximize, restore, and close a window

- Move, size, and scroll a window
- Launch and quit an application using Windows Explorer
- Expand and collapse a folder
- Display the contents of a drive and folder
- Copy, move, rename, and delete files
- Use Help and Support
- Log off from the computer and turn it off

Introduction

An **operating system** is the set of computer instructions, called a computer program, that controls the allocation of computer hardware such as memory, disk devices, printers, and CD and DVD drives, and provides the capability for you to communicate with the computer. The most popular and widely used operating system is **Microsoft Windows**. **Microsoft Windows XP**, the newest version of Microsoft Windows, allows you to easily communicate with and control your computer.

Windows XP is easy to use and can be customized to fit individual needs. Windows XP simplifies the processes of working with documents and applications, transferring data between documents, organizing the manner in which you interact with the computer, and using the computer to access information on the Internet or an intranet. The **Internet** is a worldwide group of connected computer networks that allows public access to information on thousands of subjects and gives users the means to use this information, send messages, and obtain products and services.

Microsoft Windows XP Operating Systems

The Microsoft Windows XP operating systems consist of Microsoft Windows XP Professional and Microsoft Windows XP Home Edition. **Microsoft Windows XP Professional** is the operating system designed for businesses of all sizes and for advanced home computing. In business, Windows XP Professional is commonly used on computer workstations and portable computers. A **workstation** is a computer connected to a server. A **server** is a computer that controls access to the hardware and software on a network and provides a centralized storage area for programs, data, and information. Figure 1-1 illustrates a simple computer network consisting of a server and three computers (called workstations) and a laser printer connected to the server (Figure 1-1).

FIGURE 1-1

More About

Microsoft Windows XP

Microsoft Windows XP combines the best features of Microsoft Windows 98 with the power and reliability of Microsoft Windows 2000. Windows 98, which was designed for use on personal computers, is the most popular operating system for PCs. Windows 2000, designed for use on a computer network, is the most widely used business version of Windows.

Microsoft Windows XP Home Edition contains many of the features of the Microsoft Windows XP Professional operating system but is designed for entertainment and home use. Home Edition allows you to establish in the home a network of computers that share a single Internet connection, share a device such as a printer or a scanner, share files and folders, and play multi-computer games. The network can be created using Ethernet cable or telephone wire, or it can be wireless.

More About

**Microsoft
Windows XP**

A vast amount of information
about Microsoft Windows XP
is available on the Internet.
For additional information
about Microsoft Windows
XP, visit the Windows XP
More About Web Page
(scsite.com/winoff2003/more)
and then click Microsoft
Windows XP.

Microsoft Windows XP Professional

Microsoft Windows XP Professional (called **Windows XP** for the rest of the book) is an operating system that performs every function necessary for you to communicate with and use the computer. Windows XP is called a **32-bit operating system** because it uses 32 bits for addressing and other purposes, which means the operating system can address more than four gigabytes of RAM (random-access memory) and perform tasks faster than older operating systems. A **Windows XP 64-Bit Edition** is also available for individuals solving complex scientific problems, developing high-performance design and engineering applications, or creating 3-D animations.

Windows XP is easy to use and can be customized to fit individual needs. Windows XP simplifies the process of working with documents and applications by transferring data between documents, organizing the manner in which you interact with the computer, and using the computer to access information on the Internet or an intranet. Windows XP is used to run **application programs**, which are programs that perform an application-related function such as word processing. To use the application programs that can be launched under Windows XP, you must know about the Windows XP user interface.

What Is a User Interface?

A **user interface** is the combination of hardware and software that you use to communicate with and control the computer. Through the user interface, you are able to make selections on the computer, request information from the computer, and respond to messages displayed by the computer. Thus, a user interface provides the means for dialogue between you and the computer.

Hardware and software together form the user interface. Among the hardware devices associated with a user interface are the monitor, keyboard, and mouse (Figure 1-2). The **monitor** displays messages and provides information. You respond by entering data in the form of a command or other response using the **keyboard** or **mouse**. Among the responses available to you are ones that specify which application program to run, what document to open, when to print, and where to store data for future use.

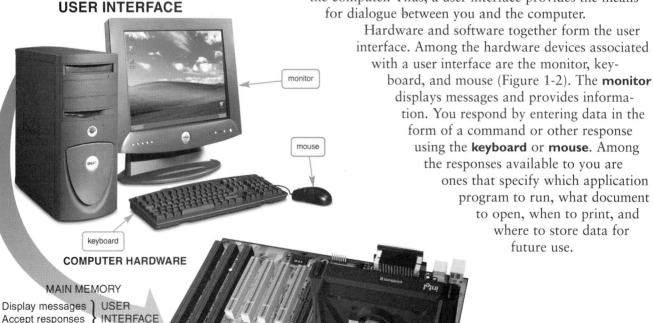

USER INTERFACE

monitor

mouse

keyboard

COMPUTER HARDWARE

MAIN MEMORY

Display messages ⎫ USER
Accept responses ⎬ INTERFACE
Determine actions ⎭ PROGRAMS

COMPUTER SOFTWARE

FIGURE 1-2

The computer software associated with the user interface consists of the programs that engage you in dialogue (Figure 1-2). The computer software determines the messages you receive, the manner in which you should respond, and the actions that occur, based on your responses.

The goal of an effective user interface is to be **user-friendly**, which means the software can be used easily by individuals with limited training. Research studies have indicated that the use of graphics can play an important role in aiding users to interact effectively with a computer. A **graphical user interface**, or **GUI** (pronounced gooey), is a user interface that displays graphics in addition to text when it communicates with the user.

The Windows XP graphical user interface was designed carefully to be easier to set up, simpler to learn, faster, more powerful, and better integrated with the Internet than previous versions of Microsoft Windows.

Launching Microsoft Windows XP

When you turn on the computer, an introductory black screen consisting of the Microsoft Windows XP logo, progress bar, copyright messages (Copyright © 1985–2001 and Microsoft Corporation), and the word, Microsoft, are displayed. The progress bar indicates the progress of the Windows XP operating system launch. After approximately one minute, the Welcome screen displays (Figure 1-3).

More About

The Windows XP Interface

Some older interfaces, called command-line interfaces, required you to type keywords (special words, phrases, or codes the computer understood) or press special keys on the keyboard to communicate with the interface. Today, graphical-user interfaces incorporate colorful graphics, use of the mouse, and Web browser-like features, which make them more user friendly.

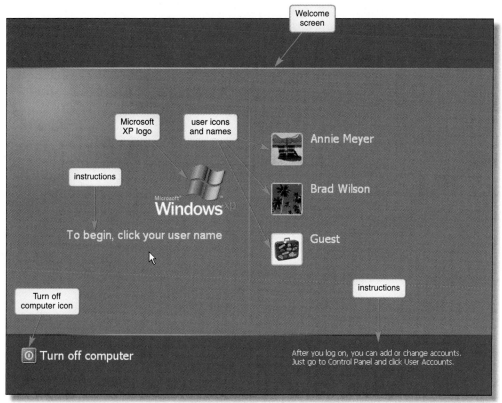

FIGURE 1-3

More About

User Names and Passwords

A unique user name identifies each computer user. In the past, users often entered a variation of their name as the user name. For example, Brad Wilson might have chosen bradwilson or bwilson. Today, most Windows XP users use their first and last names without variation as the user name. A password is a combination of characters that allows a user access to certain computer resources on the network. Passwords should be kept confidential.

More About

Microsoft Mice

For additional information about Microsoft Mice, visit the Microsoft Windows XP More About Web Page (scsite.com/winoff2003/more) and then click Microsoft Mice.

The **Welcome screen** shows the names of every computer user on the computer. On the left side of the Welcome screen, the Microsoft XP logo and the instructions, To begin, click your user name, appear. On the right side of the Welcome screen is a list of the **user icons** and **user names** for all authorized computer users (Annie Meyer, Brad Wilson, and Guest). Clicking the user icon or user name begins the process of logging on to the computer. The list of user icons and names on the Welcome screen on your computer may be different.

At the bottom of the Welcome screen is the Turn off computer icon and the instructions, After you log on, you can add or change accounts. Just go to Control Panel and click User Accounts. Clicking the Turn off computer icon initiates the process of shutting down the computer. The **Control Panel** allows you to create a new user, change or remove an existing user, and change user information. The user information that can be changed consists of the user icon and user name, user password, and account type (Administrator, Limited, and Guest).

The Windows XP User Interface

The Windows XP interface provides the means for dialogue between you and the computer. Part of this dialogue involves requesting information from the computer and responding to messages displayed by the computer. You can request information and respond to messages by using either the mouse or the keyboard.

A **mouse** is a pointing device used with Windows XP that is attached to the computer by a cable. Although it is not required to use Windows XP, Windows XP supports the use of the **Microsoft IntelliMouse** (Figure 1-4). The IntelliMouse contains three buttons: the primary mouse button, the secondary mouse button, and the wheel button between the primary and secondary mouse buttons. Typically, the **primary mouse button** is the left mouse button and the **secondary mouse button** is the right mouse button, although Windows XP allows you to switch them. In this book, the left mouse button is the primary mouse button and the right mouse button is the secondary mouse button. The functions the **wheel button** and wheel perform depend on the software application being used. If the mouse connected to the computer is not an IntelliMouse, it will not have a wheel button between the primary and secondary mouse buttons.

Using the mouse, you can perform the following operations: (1) point; (2) click; (3) right-click; (4) double-click; (5) drag; and (6) right-drag. These operations are demonstrated on the following pages.

More About

The Mouse

The mouse, although invented in the 1960s, was not used widely until the Apple Macintosh computer became available in 1984. Even then, some highbrows called mouse users wimps. Today, the mouse is an indispensable tool for every computer user.

cable

wheel button

primary mouse button

secondary mouse button

IntelliMouse

FIGURE 1-4

Many common tasks, such as logging on to the computer or logging off, are performed by pointing to an item and then clicking the item. **Point** means you move the mouse across a flat surface until the mouse pointer rests on the item of choice. As you move the mouse across a flat surface, the IntelliEye optical sensor on the underside of the mouse senses the movement of the ball on the mouse (Figure 1-5), and the mouse pointer moves across the desktop in the same direction.

Click means you press and release the primary mouse button, which in this book is the left mouse button. In most cases, you must point to an item before you click.

Logging On to the Computer

After launching Windows XP but before working with Windows XP, you must log on to the computer. **Logging on** to the computer opens your user account and makes the computer available for use.

In the following steps, the Brad Wilson icon and the Next button are used to log on to the computer. In a school environment, you will want to log on to the computer by pointing to and clicking *your user icon* on the Welcome screen and typing *your password* in the text box instead of the password shown in the steps.

The following steps illustrate how to log on to the computer by pointing to and clicking your icon on the Welcome screen, typing your password, and then pointing to and clicking the Next button.

optical sensor

FIGURE 1-5

To Log On to the Computer

1

• **Point to the Brad Wilson icon on the Welcome screen by moving the mouse across a flat surface until the mouse pointer rests on the icon.**

Pointing to the Brad Wilson icon displays a yellow border on the icon and dims the other user icons and names (Figure 1-6).

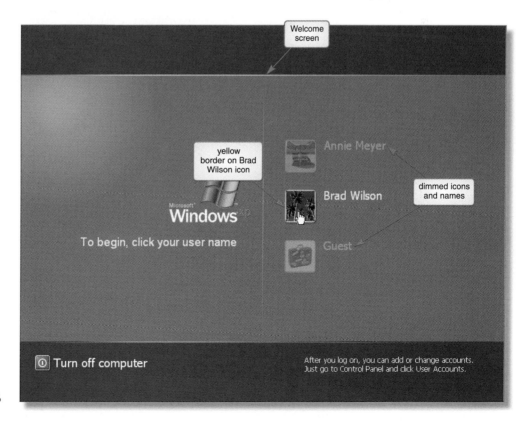

Welcome screen

yellow border on Brad Wilson icon

Annie Meyer

Brad Wilson

dimmed icons and names

Guest

Microsoft
Windows xp
To begin, click your user name

⏻ Turn off computer

After you log on, you can add or change accounts. Just go to Control Panel and click User Accounts.

FIGURE 1-6

2

• **Click the Brad Wilson icon by pressing and releasing the left mouse button, type** lakers **in the Type your password text box, and then point to the Next button.**

Windows XP highlights the Brad Wilson icon and name, displays the Type your password text box containing a series of bullets (••••••) and an insertion point, and the Next and Help buttons (Figure 1-7). A text box is a rectangular area in which you can enter text. The bullets in the text box hide the password entered by the user.

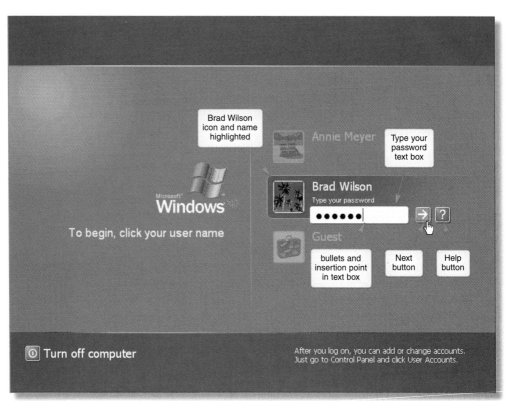

FIGURE 1-7

3

• **Click the Next button.**

The contents of the Welcome screen change to contain the word, Welcome, on the left side of the screen and the user name, user icon, and message, Loading your personal settings..., on the right side. This screen appears momentarily while the user is logged on to the computer and then several items appear on a background called the desktop (Figure 1-8). The background design of the desktop is Bliss, but your computer may display a different design.

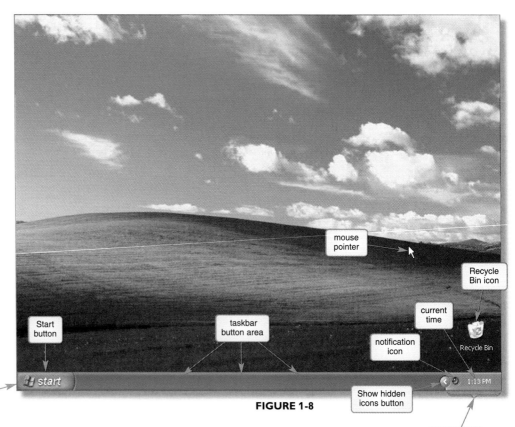

FIGURE 1-8

The items on the desktop in Figure 1-8 include the Recycle Bin icon and its name in the lower-right corner of the desktop and the taskbar across the bottom of the desktop. The Recycle Bin icon (Recycle Bin) allows you to discard unneeded objects. Your computer's desktop may contain more, fewer, or different icons because you can customize the desktop of the computer.

The **taskbar** shown at the bottom of the screen in Figure 1-8 contains the Start button, taskbar button area, and notification area. The **Start button** allows you to launch a program quickly, find or open a document, change the computer's settings, obtain Help, shut down the computer, and perform many more tasks. The **taskbar button area** contains buttons to indicate which windows are open on the desktop. In Figure 1-8, no windows are displayed on the desktop and no buttons appear in the taskbar button area.

The **notification area** contains the Show hidden icons button, one notification icon, and the current time. The **Show hidden icons button** indicates that one or more inactive icons are hidden from view in the notification area. The **notification icon** in the notification area provides quick access to programs on the computer. Other icons that provide information about the status of the computer appear temporarily in the notification area. For example, the Printer icon appears when a document is sent to the printer and is removed when printing is complete. The notification area on your desktop may contain more, fewer, or different icons because the contents of the notification area can change.

The mouse pointer appears on the desktop. On the desktop, the **mouse pointer** is the shape of a block arrow. The mouse pointer allows you to point to objects on the desktop and may change shape when it points to different objects. A shadow may be displayed behind the mouse pointer to make the mouse pointer appear in a three-dimensional form.

When you click an object, such as the Brad Wilson icon (or your icon) or the Next button shown in Figure 1-7, you must point to the object before you click. In the steps that follow, the instruction that directs you to point to a particular item and then click is, Click the particular item. For example, Click the Next button means point to the Next button and then click.

The Windows XP Desktop

Nearly every item on the Windows XP desktop is considered an object. Even the desktop itself is an object. Every **object** has properties. The **properties** of an object are unique to that specific object and may affect what can be done to the object or what the object does. For example, a property of an object may be the color of the object, such as the color of the desktop.

The Windows XP desktop and the objects on the desktop emulate a work area in an office. You may think of the Windows desktop as an electronic version of the top of your desk. You can place objects on the desktop, move the objects around on the desktop, look at them, and then put them aside, and so on. In this project, you will learn how to interact and communicate with the Windows XP desktop.

Displaying the Start Menu

A **menu** is a list of related commands and each **command** on a menu performs a specific action, such as searching for files or obtaining Help. The **Start menu** allows you to access easily the most useful items on the computer. The Start menu contains commands that allow you to connect to and browse the Internet, launch an e-mail program, launch application programs, store and search for documents, customize the computer, and obtain Help on thousands of topics.

The following steps show how to display the Start menu.

To Display the Start Menu

1

• **Point to the Start button on the taskbar.**

The mouse pointer on the Start button causes the color of the Start button to change to light green and displays a ToolTip (Click here to begin) (Figure 1-9). The ToolTip provides instructions for using the Start button.

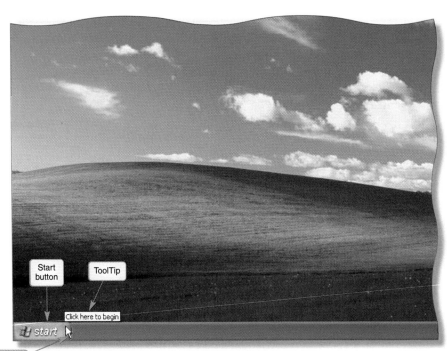

FIGURE 1-9

2

• **Click the Start button.**

The Start menu appears, the color of the Start button changes to dark green, and the Start button becomes recessed (Figure 1-10). The top section of the Start menu contains the user icon and name, the middle section contains two columns of commands, and the bottom section contains two icons (Log Off and Turn Off Computer).

FIGURE 1-10

3

• **Point to All Programs on the Start menu.**

When you point to All Programs, Windows XP highlights the All Programs command on the Start menu by displaying the All Programs command name in white text on a blue background and displays the All Programs submenu (Figure 1-11). A submenu is a menu that appears when you point to a command followed by a right arrow. Whenever you point to a command on a menu or submenu, the command name is highlighted.

FIGURE 1-11

4

• **Point to Accessories on the All Programs submenu.**

When you point to Accessories, Windows XP highlights the Accessories command on the All Programs submenu and displays the Accessories submenu (Figure 1-12). Clicking a command on the Accessories submenu that contains an application name launches that application. For example, to launch Notepad, you would click the Notepad command on the Accessories submenu.

FIGURE 1-12

5

• **Point to an open area of the desktop and then click the open area to close the Start menu, Accessories submenu, and All Programs submenu.**

The Start menu, Accessories submenu, and All Programs submenu close, and the recessed dark green Start button changes to its original light green color (Figure 1-13). The mouse pointer points to the desktop. To close a menu, click any area of the desktop except the menu itself.

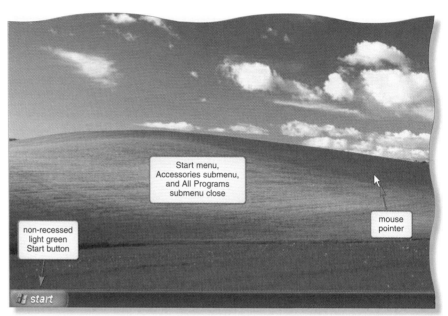

Start menu,
Accessories submenu,
and All Programs
submenu close

mouse
pointer

non-recessed
light green
Start button

start

FIGURE 1-13

The middle section of the Start menu shown in Figure 1-10 on page WIN 12 consists of two columns of commands. Each command is identified by a unique icon and name. Commands may represent an application program, folder, or operation.

The list of commands above the separator line at the top of the left column, called the **pinned items list**, consists of the default Web browser program (Internet Explorer) and default e-mail program (Outlook Express). The list of commands below the separator line, called the **most frequently used programs list**, contains the most frequently used programs. Programs are added to the list when you use them. Currently, three programs (Windows Media Player, Windows Movie Maker, and Windows Messenger) are displayed in the list.

The most frequently used program list can contain up to six programs. If the list contains fewer than six programs when you launch a new program, the program name is added to the list. If the list contains six names when you launch a program that is not on the list, Windows XP replaces a less frequently used program with the new application. The All Programs command appears below the separator line at the bottom of the left column.

A list of commands to access various folders appears above the separator line at the top of the right column (My Documents, My Recent Documents, My Pictures, My Music, and My Computer). If the computer is connected to a network, the My Network Places command may appear below the My Computer command. Below the separator line are other commands. They are commands to customize the computer (Control Panel), connect to the Internet (Connect To), and add printers and fax printers to the computer (Printers and Faxes). Below the separator line at the bottom of the right column are commands to obtain Help (Help and Support), search for documents and folders (Search), and launch programs (Run).

A **right arrow** following a command on the Start menu indicates that pointing to the command will display a submenu. The All Programs command is followed by a green right arrow, and the My Recent Documents and Connect To commands are followed by smaller black arrows. One command (Run) is followed by an **ellipsis** (...) to indicate more information is required to execute the command.

Windows XP provides a number of ways in which to accomplish a particular task. In the remainder of this book, a specific set of steps will illustrate how to accomplish each task. These steps may not be the only way in which the task can be completed. If you can perform the same task using other means, the Other Ways box specifies the methods. In each case, the method shown in the steps is the preferred method, but it is important for you to be aware of all the techniques you can use.

Adding an Icon to the Desktop

Although the Windows XP desktop may contain only the Recycle Bin icon (see Figure 1-8 on page WIN 10), you may want to add additional icons to the desktop. For example, you may want to add the My Computer icon to the desktop so you can view the contents of the computer easily. One method of viewing the contents of the computer is to click the My Computer command on the Start menu to open the My Computer window. If you use My Computer frequently, you may want to place the My Computer icon on the desktop where it is easier to find.

One method of adding the My Computer icon to the desktop is to right-click the My Computer command on the Start menu. **Right-click** means you press and release the secondary mouse button, which in this book is the right mouse button. As directed when using the primary mouse button to click an object, normally you will point to the object before you right-click it. The following steps illustrate how to add the My Computer icon to the desktop.

To Add an Icon to the Desktop

1

• **Click the Start button, point to My Computer on the Start menu, and then press and release the right mouse button.**

Windows XP highlights the My Computer command and displays a shortcut menu containing nine commands (Figure 1-14). Right-clicking an object, such as the My Computer command, displays a shortcut menu that contains commands specifically for use with that object.

FIGURE 1-14

2

• **Point to Show on Desktop on the shortcut menu.**

When you point to Show on Desktop, Windows XP highlights the Show on Desktop command (Figure 1-15).

FIGURE 1-15

3

• **Click Show on Desktop.**

The shortcut menu closes and the My Computer icon is displayed on the desktop (Figure 1-16). The Start menu remains on the desktop.

4

• **Click an open area on the desktop to close the Start menu.**

The Start menu closes.

Other Ways

1. Right-click desktop, click Properties on shortcut menu, click Desktop tab, click Customize Desktop, click icon title, click OK button, click OK button

FIGURE 1-16

Whenever you right-click an object, a shortcut menu is displayed. As you will see, the use of shortcut menus speeds up your work and adds flexibility to your interaction with the computer.

Opening a Window Using a Desktop Icon

Double-click means you quickly press and release the left mouse button twice without moving the mouse. In most cases, you must point to an item before you double-click. The following step shows how to open the My Computer window on the desktop by double-clicking the My Computer icon on the desktop.

To Open a Window Using a Desktop Icon

1

• **Point to the My Computer icon on the desktop and then double-click by quickly pressing and releasing the left mouse button twice without moving the mouse.**

The My Computer window opens and the recessed dark blue My Computer button is displayed in the taskbar button area (Figure 1-17). The My Computer window allows you to view the contents of the computer.

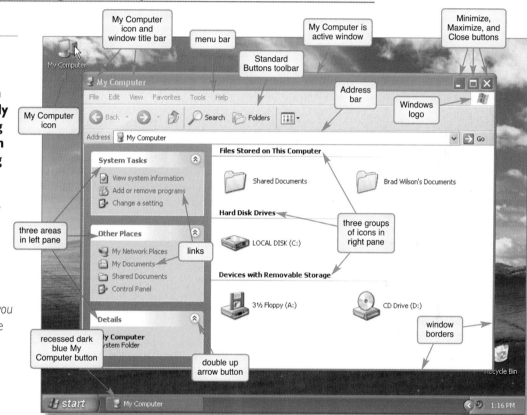

FIGURE 1-17

The My Computer window, the only open window, is the active window. The **active window** is the window you currently are using or that currently is selected. Whenever you click an object that opens a window, such as the My Computer icon, Windows XP will open the window and a recessed dark blue button in the taskbar button area will identify the open window. The recessed dark blue button identifies the active window. The contents of the My Computer window on your computer may be different from the contents of the My Computer window shown in Figure 1-17.

Other Ways

1. Right-click desktop icon, click Open on shortcut menu
2. Press WINDOWS+E

More About

Double-Clicking

Double-clicking is the most difficult mouse skill to learn. Many people have a tendency to move the mouse before they click a second time, even when they do not want to move the mouse. With a little practice, you should find double-clicking without moving the mouse becomes quite natural.

More About

The Contents of the My Computer Window

Because windows can be easily customized, your My Computer window may not resemble the window shown in Figure 1-17. For example, different toolbars may appear below the menu bar, icons may appear smaller, icons may not be grouped, and different areas may be displayed in the left pane of the window.

More About

My Computer

While the trade press and media once poked fun at the My Computer name, Microsoft continues to expand the concept. Windows XP now showcases the My Computer, My Documents, My Pictures, and My Music names by placing them on the Start menu. In addition, the new My Videos folder was added to the operating system. Microsoft contends that beginners find these names easier to understand.

The My Computer Window

The thin blue line, or **window border**, surrounding the My Computer window shown in Figure 1-17 on the previous page determines its shape and size. The **title bar** at the top of the window contains a small icon that is similar to the icon on the desktop, and the **window title** (My Computer) identifies the window. The color of the title bar (dark blue) and the recessed dark blue My Computer button in the taskbar button area indicate that the My Computer window is the active window. The color of the active window on your computer may be different from the color shown in Figure 1-17.

Clicking the icon at the left on the title bar will display the **System menu**, which contains commands to carry out the actions associated with the My Computer window. At the right on the title bar are three buttons (the Minimize button, the Maximize button, and the Close button) that can be used to specify the size of the window or close the window.

The **menu bar**, which is the horizontal bar below the title bar of a window, in Figure 1-17 contains a list of menu names for the My Computer window: File, Edit, View, Favorites, Tools, and Help. The Windows logo appears on the far right of the menu bar.

The Standard buttons toolbar displays below the menu bar. The **Standard Buttons toolbar** allows you to perform often-used tasks more quickly than when you use the menu bar. Each button on the Standard Buttons toolbar contains an icon. Three buttons contain a **text label** (Back, Search, and Folders) that identifies the function of the button. Each button will be explained in detail as it is used. The buttons on the Standard Buttons toolbar on your computer may be different.

Below the Standard Buttons toolbar is the Address bar. The **Address bar** allows you to launch an application, display a document, open another window, and search for information on the Internet. The Address bar shown in Figure 1-17 displays the Address box containing the My Computer icon, window title, down arrow, and the Go button.

The area below the Address bar is divided into two panes. The System Tasks, Other Places, and Details areas are displayed in the left pane. A title identifies each area. A button appears to the right of the title in each area to indicate whether the area is expanded or collapsed. A button identified by a **double up arrow** indicates the area is expanded. A button identified by a **double down arrow** indicates the area is collapsed. When you click the double up arrow button, the area collapses and only the title and the double down arrow button appear. When you click the double down arrow button, the area expands and the entire contents of the area are visible.

All three areas in the left pane are expanded. The **System Tasks area** contains a title (System Tasks) and three tasks (View system information, Add or remove programs, and Change a setting) associated with the My Computer window. The **Other Places area** contains a title (Other Places) and links to four folders (My Network Places, My Documents, Shared Documents, and Control Panel) associated with the My Computer folder. The **Details area** contains a title (Details), the window title (My Computer), and the folder type (System Folder) of the My Computer window. Clicking the double up arrow collapses the area and leaves only the title and arrow button.

Pointing to a task in the System Tasks area or a folder name in the Other Places area underlines the task or folder name and displays the task or folder name in light blue. Underlined text, such as the task and folder names, is referred to as a **hyperlink**, or simply a **link**. Pointing to a link changes the mouse pointer to a hand icon, and clicking a link displays information associated with the link. For example, clicking the Add or remove programs task in the System Tasks area allows you to install or remove application programs, and clicking the My Documents link in the Other Places area opens the My Documents window.

The right pane of the My Computer window contains three groups of icons. The top group, Files Stored on This Computer, contains Shared Documents and Brad Wilson's Documents icons. The **Shared Documents folder** contains documents and folders that are available (shared) to other computer users on the network, and the Brad Wilson's Documents folder contains his personal documents. On your computer, your name will replace the Brad Wilson name in the Brad Wilson's Documents icon.

The middle group, Hard Disk Drives, contains the LOCAL DISK (C:) drive icon. A title to the right of the icon identifies the drive name, LOCAL DISK (C:). The bottom group, Devices with Removable Storage, contains the 3½ Floppy (A:) and CD Drive (D:) icons and labels. The three icons in the Hard Disk Drives and Devices with Removable Storage sections, called **drive icons**, represent a hard disk drive, 3½ floppy disk drive, and a Compact Disc drive. The number of groups in the right pane and the icons in the groups on your computer may be different.

Clicking a drive or folder icon selects the icon in the right pane and displays details about the drive or folder in the areas in the left pane. Double-clicking a drive or folder icon allows you to display the contents of the corresponding drive or folder in the right pane and details about the drive or folder in the areas in the left pane. You may find more, fewer, or different drive and folder icons in the My Computer window on your computer.

Minimizing a Window

Two buttons on the title bar of a window, the Minimize button and the Maximize button, allow you to control the way a window is displayed or is not displayed on the desktop. When you click the **Minimize button** (see Figure 1-18 on the next page), the My Computer window no longer is displayed on the desktop and the recessed dark blue My Computer button in the taskbar button area changes to a non-recessed medium blue button. A minimized window still is open but is not displayed on the screen. To minimize and then redisplay the My Computer window, complete the steps on the next page.

More About

Minimizing Windows

Windows management on the Windows XP desktop is important in order to keep the desktop uncluttered. You will find yourself frequently minimizing windows and then later reopening them with a click of a button in the taskbar button area.

To Minimize and Redisplay a Window

1

• **Point to the Minimize button on the title bar of the My Computer window.**

The mouse pointer points to the Minimize button on the My Computer window title bar, the color of the Minimize button changes to light blue, a ToolTip is displayed below the Minimize button, and the recessed dark blue My Computer button appears on the taskbar (Figure 1-18).

FIGURE 1-18

2

• **Click the Minimize button.**

When you minimize the My Computer window, Windows XP removes the My Computer window from the desktop, the My Computer button changes to a non-recessed button, and the color of the button changes to medium blue (Figure 1-19).

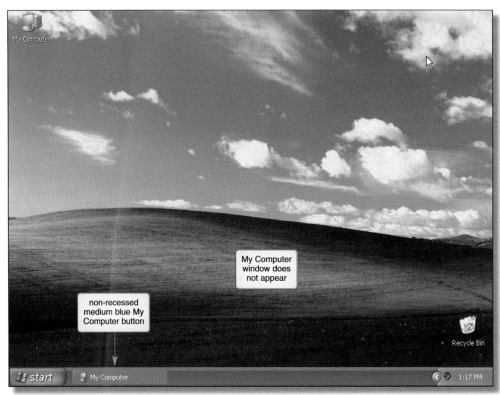

FIGURE 1-19

3

• **Click the My Computer button in the taskbar button area.**

The My Computer window is displayed in the same place with the same size as it was before being minimized, and the My Computer button on the taskbar is recessed (Figure 1-20). With the mouse pointer pointing to the My Computer button, the color of the button is medium blue. Moving the mouse pointer off the button changes its color to dark blue. The My Computer window is the active window because it contains the dark blue title bar.

FIGURE 1-20

Whenever a window is minimized, it is not displayed on the desktop, but a non-recessed dark blue button for the window is displayed in the taskbar button area. Whenever you want a minimized window to display and be the active window, click its button in the taskbar button area.

As you point to many objects, such as a button or command, when you work with Windows XP, Windows XP displays a ToolTip. A **ToolTip** is a short on-screen note associated with the object to which you are pointing. ToolTips display on the desktop for approximately five seconds. Examples of ToolTips are shown in Figure 1-9 on page WIN 12, Figure 1-18 on the previous page, Figure 1-21 on the next page, Figure 1-23 on page WIN 23, and Figure 1-25 on page WIN 24. To reduce clutter on the screen, the ToolTips will not be shown on the remaining screens in this book.

Maximizing and Restoring a Window

Sometimes when information is displayed in a window, the information is not completely visible. One method of displaying the entire contents of a window is to enlarge the window using the **Maximize button**. The Maximize button maximizes a window so the window fills the entire screen, making it easier to see the contents of the window. When a window is maximized, the **Restore Down button** replaces the Maximize button on the title bar. Clicking the Restore Down button will return the window to its size before maximizing. To maximize and restore the My Computer window, complete the steps on the next page.

Other Ways

1. Click icon on left side of title bar, click Minimize, in taskbar button area click taskbar button
2. Right-click title bar, click Minimize, in taskbar button area click taskbar button
3. Press WINDOWS+M

Q&A

Q: Is there another way to maximize a window?

A: Yes. If the window appears on the desktop, double-click its title bar. If the window is not displayed on the desktop, right-click the window's button on the taskbar and then click Maximize on the shortcut menu.

To Maximize and Restore a Window

1

• **Point to the Maximize button on the title bar of the My Computer window.**

The mouse pointer points to the Maximize button on the My Computer window title bar and the color of the Maximize button changes to light blue (Figure 1-21). A ToolTip identifying the button name is displayed below the Maximize button.

FIGURE 1-21

2

• **Click the Maximize button.**

The My Computer window expands so it and the taskbar fill the desktop (Figure 1-22). The Restore Down button replaces the Maximize button, the My Computer button in the taskbar button area does not change, and the My Computer window still is the active window.

FIGURE 1-22

3

• **Point to the Restore Down button on the title bar of the My Computer window.**

The mouse pointer points to the Restore Down button on the My Computer window title bar and the color of the Restore Down button changes to light blue (Figure 1-23). A ToolTip is displayed below the Restore Down button identifying it.

FIGURE 1-23

4

• **Click the Restore Down button.**

The My Computer window returns to the size and position it occupied before being maximized (Figure 1-24). The My Computer button does not change. The Maximize button replaces the Restore Down button.

FIGURE 1-24

More About

Opening and Closing a Window

Windows XP remembers the size of a window when you close the window. When you reopen the window, it will display in the same size you closed it.

When a window is maximized, such as in Figure 1-22 on page WIN 22, you also can minimize the window by clicking the Minimize button. If, after minimizing the window, you click its button in the taskbar button area, the window will return to its maximized size.

Closing a Window

The **Close button** on the title bar of a window closes the window and removes the taskbar button from the taskbar. The following steps show how to close the My Computer window.

To Close a Window

1

• **Point to the Close button on the title bar of the My Computer window.**

The mouse pointer points to the Close button on the My Computer window title bar and the color of the Close button changes to light red (Figure 1-25). A ToolTip is displayed below the Close button.

FIGURE 1-25

2

• **Click the Close button.**

The My Computer window closes and the My Computer button no longer is displayed in the taskbar button area (Figure 1-26).

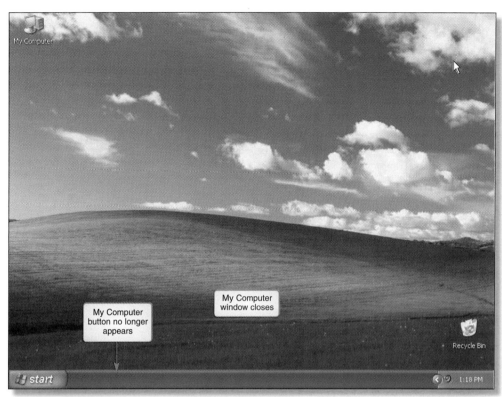

My Computer
window closes

My Computer
button no longer
appears

Recycle Bin

start   1:18 PM

FIGURE 1-26

Other Ways

1. Click icon on left side of title bar, click Close
2. Right-click title bar, click Close on shortcut menu
3. Press ALT+F4

Opening a Window Using the Start Menu

Previously, you opened the My Computer window by double-clicking the My Computer icon on the desktop. Another method of opening a window and viewing the contents of the window is to click a command on the Start menu. The steps on the next page show how to open the My Documents window using the My Documents command on the Start menu.

More About

Opening a Window

Although the preferred method of opening a window in previous Windows versions was double-clicking a desktop icon, using the redesigned Start menu now makes it easier to open those windows.

To Open a Window Using the Start Menu

1

• **Click the Start button on the taskbar and then point to the My Documents command on the Start menu.**

The Start menu is displayed, the Start button is recessed on the taskbar, the color of the button changes to dark green, and the mouse pointer points to the highlighted My Documents command on the Start menu (Figure 1-27).

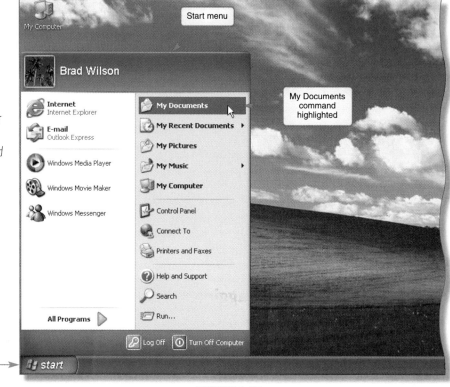

FIGURE 1-27

2

• **Click My Documents on the Start menu.**

The My Documents window opens, the recessed dark blue My Documents button is displayed in the taskbar button area, and the My Documents window is the active window (Figure 1-28). You may find more, fewer, or different folder icons in the right pane on your computer.

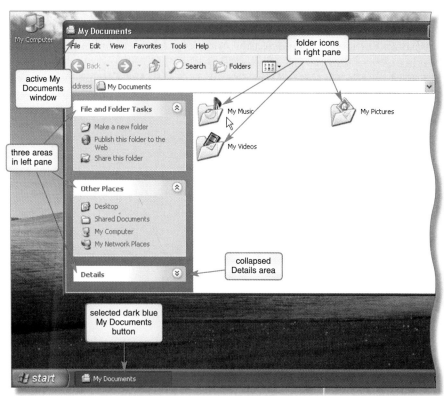

FIGURE 1-28

Other Ways

1. Click Start button, right-click window icon, click Open on shortcut menu

The My Documents Window

The **My Documents window** shown in Figure 1-28 is a central location for the storage and management of documents. The title bar at the top of the My Documents window identifies the window and the color of the title bar (dark blue) and the recessed dark blue My Documents button in the taskbar button area indicate the My Documents window is the active window.

The File and Folders Tasks, Other Places, and Details areas display in the left pane. The **File and Folders Tasks area** contains three tasks (Make a new folder, Publish this folder to the Web, and Share this folder). The **Other Places area** contains links to four folders (Desktop, Shared Documents, My Computer, and My Network Places). The **Details area** is collapsed and only the title and a double down arrow button appear in the area.

The right pane of the My Documents window contains the My Music, My Pictures, and My Videos folders. Clicking a folder icon in the right pane highlights the icon in the right pane and changes the files and folder tasks in the File and Folder Tasks area in the left pane. Double-clicking a folder icon displays the contents of the corresponding folder in the right pane, adds another area to the folder (My Music Tasks area, My Pictures Tasks area, or My Videos Tasks area) in the left pane, and changes the file and folder information in the left pane.

Moving a Window by Dragging

Drag means you point to an item, hold down the left mouse button, move the item to the desired location, and then release the left mouse button. You can move any open window to another location on the desktop by pointing to the title bar of the window and then dragging the window. The following steps illustrate dragging the My Documents window to the center of the desktop.

> **More About**
>
> **Dragging**
>
> Dragging is the second-most difficult mouse skill to learn. You may want to practice dragging a few times so you will be comfortable with it. Do not let dragging become a drag — PRACTICE!!

To Move a Window by Dragging

1

• **Point to the My Documents window title bar (Figure 1-29).**

FIGURE 1-29

2

• **Hold down the left mouse button, move the mouse down so the window moves to the center of the desktop, and then release the left mouse button.**

As you drag the My Documents window, the window moves across the desktop. When you release the left mouse button, the window is displayed in its new location on the desktop (Figure 1-30).

FIGURE 1-30

Expanding an Area

The Details area in the My Documents window is collapsed and a double down arrow button appears to the right of the Details title (see Figure 1-31). Clicking the button or the area title expands the Details area and reveals the window title (My Documents) and folder type (System Folder) in the Details area. Similarly, clicking the double up arrow button or the area title collapses the area so only the area title and double down arrow button appear in the area. The following steps illustrate how to expand the Details area in the left pane of the My Documents window.

To Expand an Area

1

• **Point to the double down arrow button in the Details area.**

The mouse pointer changes to a hand icon and points to the double down arrow button in the Details area and the color of the Details title and button changes to light blue (Figure 1-31).

FIGURE 1-31

2

• **Click the double down arrow button.**

The Details area expands, the window title (My Documents) and folder type (System Folder) is displayed in the area, the double down arrow on the button changes to a double up arrow, a portion of the left pane is not visible, and a scroll bar is displayed in the area (Figure 1-32).

FIGURE 1-32

Q: Is scrolling a window the most efficient way to view objects in a window?

A: No. There are other more efficient methods. You can either maximize a window or size it so that all the objects in the window are visible. It is better to avoid scrolling because scrolling takes time.

A **scroll bar** is a bar that appears when the contents of a pane or window are not completely visible. A vertical scroll bar contains an **up scroll arrow**, a **down scroll arrow**, and a **scroll box** that enable you to view areas that currently are not visible. A vertical scroll bar is displayed along the right side of the left pane in the My Documents window shown in Figure 1-32 on the previous page. In some cases, the vertical scroll bar also may appear along the right side of the right pane in a window.

Scrolling in a Window

Previously, the My Documents window was maximized to display information that was not completely visible in the My Documents window. Another method of viewing information that is not visible in a window is to use the scroll bar.

Scrolling can be accomplished in three ways: (1) click the scroll arrows; (2) click the scroll bar; and (3) drag the scroll box. On the following pages, you will use the scroll bar to scroll the contents of the left pane of the My Documents window. The following steps show how to scroll the left pane using the scroll arrows.

To Scroll Using Scroll Arrows

1

• **Point to the up scroll arrow on the vertical scroll bar.**

The color of the up scroll arrow changes to light blue (Figure 1-33).

FIGURE 1-33

2

• **Click the up scroll arrow two times.**

The left pane scrolls down (the contents in the left pane move up) and displays a portion of the text in the File and Folder Tasks area at the top of the pane that previously was not visible (Figure 1-34). Because the size of the left pane does not change when you scroll, the contents in the left pane will change, as seen in the difference between Figure 1-33 and Figure 1-34.

FIGURE 1-34

3

• **Click the up scroll arrow three more times.**

The scroll box moves to the top of the scroll bar and the remaining text in the File and Folder Tasks area is displayed (Figure 1-35).

FIGURE 1-35

More About

The Scroll Box

Dragging the scroll box is
the most efficient technique
to scroll long distances. In
many application programs,
such as Microsoft Word, as
you scroll using the scroll
box, the page number of the
document appears next to
the scroll box.

More About

**Scrolling
Guidelines**

General scrolling guidelines:
(1) To scroll short distances
(line by line), click the scroll
arrows; (2) To scroll one
screen at a time, click the
scroll bar; and (3) To scroll
long distances, drag the
scroll box.

You can scroll continuously using scroll arrows by pointing to the up or down scroll arrow and holding down the left mouse button. The area being scrolled continues to scroll until you release the left mouse button or you reach the top or bottom of the area. You also can scroll by clicking the scroll bar itself. When you click the scroll bar, the area being scrolled moves up or down a greater distance than when you click the scroll arrows.

The third way in which you can scroll is by dragging the scroll box. When you drag the scroll box, the area being scrolled moves up or down as you drag.

Being able to view the contents of a window by scrolling is an important Windows XP skill because in many cases, the entire contents of a window are not visible.

Sizing a Window by Dragging

As previously mentioned, sometimes when information is displayed in a window, the information is not completely visible. A third method of displaying information that is not visible is to change the size of the window by dragging the border of a window. The following step illustrates changing the size of the My Documents window.

To Size a Window by Dragging

1

• **Position the mouse pointer over the bottom border of the My Documents window until the mouse pointer changes to a two-headed arrow.**

• **Drag the bottom border downward until the Details area on your desktop resembles the Details area shown in Figure 1-36.**

As you drag the bottom border, the My Documents window, vertical scroll bar, and scroll box change size. After dragging, the Details area is visible and the vertical scroll bar no longer is visible (Figure 1-36).

FIGURE 1-36

In addition to dragging the bottom border of a window, you also can drag the other borders (left, right, and top) and any window corner. If you drag a vertical border (left or right), you can move the border left or right. If you drag a horizontal border (top or bottom), you can move the border of the window up or down. If you drag a corner, you can move the corner up, down, left, or right.

Collapsing an Area

The Details area in the My Documents window is expanded and a double up arrow button displays to the right of the Details title (Figure 1-36). Clicking the button or the area title collapses the Details area and removes the window title (My Documents) and folder type (System Folder) from the Details area. The following steps show how to collapse the Details area in the My Documents window.

To Collapse an Area

1

• **Point to the double up arrow button in the Details area.**

The mouse pointer changes to a hand icon, points to the double up arrow button in the Details area, and the color of the Details title and button changes to light blue (Figure 1-37).

FIGURE 1-37

2

• **Click the double up arrow button.**

The Details area collapses and only the Details title and the double down arrow button are displayed (Figure 1-38).

FIGURE 1-38

Resizing a Window

After moving and resizing a window, you may wish to return the window to approximately its original size. To return the My Documents window to about its original size, complete the following steps.

To Resize a Window

1 Position the mouse pointer over the bottom border of the My Documents window border until the mouse pointer changes to a two-headed arrow.

2 Drag the bottom border of the My Documents window up until the window is the same size as shown in Figure 1-28 on page WIN 26 and then release the mouse button.

The My Documents window is approximately the same size as it was before you made it smaller.

Closing a Window

After you have completed work in a window, normally you will close the window. The following steps show how to close the My Documents window.

To Close a Window

1 Point to the Close button on the right of the title bar in the My Documents window.

2 Click the Close button.

The My Documents window closes and the desktop contains no open windows.

Deleting a Desktop Icon by Right-Dragging

The My Computer icon remains on the desktop. In many cases after you have placed an icon on the desktop, you will want to delete the icon. Although Windows XP has many ways to delete desktop icons, one method of removing the My Computer icon from the desktop is to right-drag the My Computer icon to the Recycle Bin icon on the desktop. **Right-drag** means you point to an item, hold down the right mouse button, move the item to the desired location, and then release the right mouse button. When you right-drag an object, a shortcut menu is displayed. The shortcut menu contains commands specifically for use with the object being dragged.

When you delete an icon from the desktop, Windows XP places the item in the **Recycle Bin**, which is an area on the hard disk that contains all the items you have deleted not only from the desktop but also from the hard disk. When the Recycle Bin becomes full, you can empty it. Up until the time you empty the Recycle Bin, you can recover deleted items from the Recycle Bin. The following steps illustrate how to delete the My Computer icon by right-dragging the icon to the Recycle Bin icon.

To Delete a Desktop Icon by Right-Dragging

1

• **Point to the My Computer icon on the desktop, hold down the right mouse button, drag the My Computer icon over the Recycle Bin icon.**

• **Release the right mouse button and then point to Move Here on the shortcut menu.**

The My Computer icon is displayed on the desktop as you drag the icon. When you release the right mouse button, a shortcut menu is displayed on the desktop (Figure 1-39). Pointing to the Move Here command on the shortcut menu highlights the Move Here command.

FIGURE 1-39

Microsoft
Windows XP

2

• **Click Move Here and then point to the Yes button in the Confirm Delete dialog box.**

The shortcut menu closes, and the Confirm Delete dialog box is displayed on the desktop (Figure 1-40). A dialog box is displayed whenever Windows XP needs to supply information to you or wants you to enter information or select among several options. The Confirm Delete dialog box contains a question, a message, and the Yes and No buttons.

3

• **Click the Yes button.**

The Confirm Delete dialog box closes, the My Computer icon no longer is displayed on the desktop, and the My Computer icon now is contained in the Recycle Bin.

FIGURE 1-40

Other Ways

1. Drag icon to Recycle Bin, click Yes button
2. Right-click icon, click Delete, click Yes button

If you click **Move Here** on the shortcut menu shown in Figure 1-39 on the previous page, Windows XP will move the icon from its current location to the new location. If you click Cancel, the operation will be terminated, and the **Cancel command** will reset anything you have done during the operation.

In Figure 1-40, the Confirm Delete dialog box contains the Yes button and the No button. Clicking the Yes button completes the operation and clicking the No button terminates the operation.

Although you can move icons by dragging with the primary (left) mouse button and by right-dragging with the secondary (right) mouse button, it is strongly suggested you right-drag because a shortcut menu appears and, in most cases, you can specify the exact operation you want to occur. When you drag using the left mouse button, a default operation takes place and that operation may not be the operation you intended to perform.

Summary of Mouse and Windows Operations

You have seen how to use the mouse to point, click, right-click, double-click, drag, and right-drag in order to accomplish certain tasks on the desktop. The use of a mouse is an important skill when using Windows XP. In addition, you have learned how to move around and use windows on the Windows XP desktop.

The Keyboard and Keyboard Shortcuts

The **keyboard** is an input device on which you manually key in, or type, data. Figure 1-41 shows the Microsoft Office keyboard designed specifically for use with Microsoft Office and the Internet. The Single Touch pad along the left side of the keyboard contains keys to browse the Internet, copy and paste text, and switch between applications. A scroll wheel allows you to move quickly within a document window. The Hot Keys along the top of the keyboard allow you to launch a Web browser or e-mail program, play multimedia, and adjust the system volume.

FIGURE 1-41

Many tasks you accomplish with a mouse also can be accomplished using a keyboard. To perform tasks using the keyboard, you must understand the notation used to identify which keys to press. This notation is used throughout Windows XP to identify a **keyboard shortcut**.

Keyboard shortcuts consist of (1) pressing a single key (such as press the ENTER key); or (2) pressing and holding down one key and pressing a second key, as shown by two key names separated by a plus sign (such as press CTRL+ESC). For example, to obtain help about Windows XP, you can press the F1 key and to display the Start menu, hold down the CTRL key and then press the ESC key (press CTRL+ESC).

Often, computer users will use keyboard shortcuts for operations they perform frequently. For example, many users find pressing the F1 key to launch Help and Support easier than using the Start menu as shown later in this project. As a user, you probably will find the combination of keyboard and mouse operations that particularly suits you, but it is strongly recommended that generally you use the mouse.

Launching an Application Program

One of the basic tasks you can perform using Windows XP is launching an application program. A **program** is a set of computer instructions that carries out a task on the computer. An **application program** is a set of specific computer instructions that is designed to allow you to accomplish a particular task. For example, a **word processing program** is an application program that allows you to create written documents; a **presentation graphics program** is an application program that allows you to create graphic presentations for display on a computer; and a **Web browser program** is an application program that allows you to search for and display Web pages.

The **default Web browser program** (Internet Explorer) appears in the pinned items list on the Start menu shown in Figure 1-42. Because the default **Web browser** is selected during the installation of the Windows XP operating system, the default Web browser on your computer may be different. In addition, you can easily select another Web browser as the default Web browser. Another frequently used Web browser program is **MSN Explorer**.

Launching an Application Using the Start Menu

The most common activity performed on a computer is launching an application program to accomplish specific tasks. You can launch an application program by using the Start menu. To illustrate the use of the Start menu to launch an application program, the default Web browser program (Internet Explorer) will be launched. The following steps illustrate launching Internet Explorer using the Internet command on the Start menu.

To Launch a Program Using the Start Menu

1

• **Click the Start button on the taskbar and then point to Internet on the pinned items list on the Start menu.**

The Start menu is displayed (Figure 1-42). The pinned items list on the Start menu contains the Internet command to launch the default Web browser program and the name of the default Web browser program (Internet Explorer). The default Web browser program on your computer may be different.

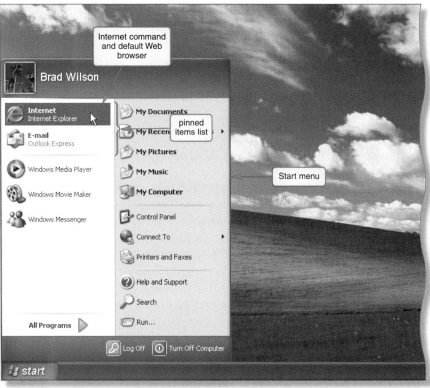

FIGURE 1-42

2

• **Click Internet.**

Windows XP launches the Internet Explorer program by displaying the Welcome to MSN.com – Microsoft Internet Explorer window, displaying the MSN home page in the window, and adding a recessed button on the taskbar (Figure 1-43). The URL for the Web page is displayed in the Address bar. Because you can select the default Web browser and the Web page to display when you launch the Web browser, the Web page that is displayed on your desktop may be different.

3

• **Click the Close button in the Microsoft Internet Explorer window.**

The Microsoft Internet Explorer window closes.

FIGURE 1-43

Other Ways

1. Click Start button, in frequently used program list click Internet Explorer
2. Click Start button, point to All Programs, click Internet Explorer
3. Press CTRL+ESC, press I

Any computer connected to the Internet that contains Web pages you can reference is called a **Web site**. The **MSN.com Web site**, one of millions of Web sites around the world, is stored on a computer operated by Microsoft Corporation and can be accessed using a Web browser. The Welcome to MSN.com **Web page** shown in Figure 1-43 is the first Web page you see when you access the MSN.com Web site and is, therefore, referred to as a **home page**, or **start page.**

After you have launched a Web browser, you can use the program to search for and display additional Web pages located on different Web sites around the world.

In the preceding section, you launched Internet Explorer and then quit the Internet Explorer program by closing the Microsoft Internet Explorer window. In the next section, you will launch the Windows Explorer application program.

Windows Explorer

Windows Explorer is an application program included with Windows XP. It allows you to view the contents of the computer, the hierarchy of drives and folders on the computer, and the files and folders in each folder. In this project, you will use Windows Explorer to (1) expand and collapse drives and folders; (2) display drive and folder contents; (3) launch an application program; (4) copy a file between folders; and (5) rename and then delete a file. These are common operations that you should understand how to perform.

Launching Windows Explorer

As with many other operations, Windows XP offers a variety of ways to launch Windows Explorer. The following steps show how to launch Windows Explorer using the Folders button in the My Computer window.

To Launch Windows Explorer and Maximize Its Window

1

• **Click the Start button on the taskbar and then click My Computer on the Start menu.**

• **Maximize the My Computer window.**

• **If the status bar does not appear at the bottom of the My Computer window, click View on the menu bar and then click Status Bar.**

• **Point to the Folders button on the Standard Buttons toolbar.**

The maximized My Computer window is displayed (Figure 1-44). The status bar is located at the bottom of the window. Pointing to the Folders button on the Standard Buttons toolbar displays a three-dimensional button.

FIGURE 1-44

2

• **Click the Folders button.**

The Folders pane is displayed in place of the left pane in the My Computer window (Figure 1-45).

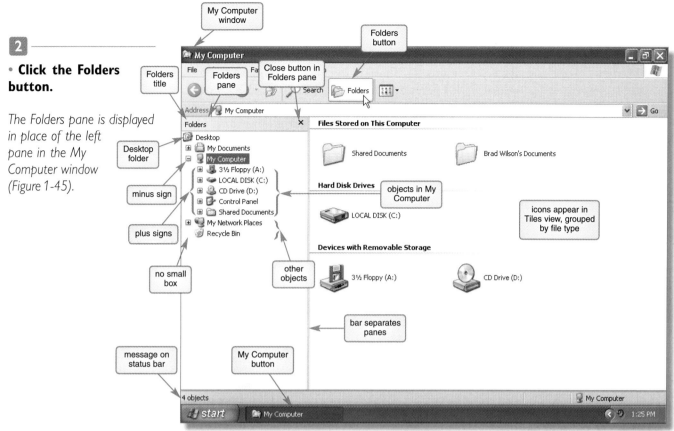

FIGURE 1-45

Clicking the Folders button in the My Computer window selects the Folders button, displays the Folders pane shown in Figure 1-45, and allows you to use Windows Explorer. The **Folders pane** (or **Folder bar**) displays the **hierarchical structure** of folders and drives on the computer. The title bar in the Folders pane contains a title (Folders) and Close button. Clicking the Close button removes the Folders pane from the My Computer window and deselects the Folders button. A bar separates the Folders pane and the right pane of the My Computer window. You can drag the bar left or right to change the size of the Folders pane.

The top level of the hierarchy in the Folders pane is the Desktop. Below the Desktop are the My Documents, My Computer, My Network Places, and Recycle Bin icons. The icons on your computer may be different.

To the left of the My Computer icon is a minus sign in a small box. The **minus sign** indicates that the drive or folder represented by the icon next to it, in this case My Computer, contains additional folders or drives and these folders or drives appear below the icon. Thus, below the My Computer icon are the 3½ Floppy (A:), LOCAL DISK (C:), CD Drive (D:), Control Panel, and Shared Documents icons. Each of these icons has a small box with a plus sign next to it. The **plus sign** indicates that the drive or folder represented by the icon has more folders within it but the folders do not appear in the Folders pane. As you will see shortly, clicking the box with the plus sign will display the folders within the drive or folder represented by the icon. If an item contains no folders, such as the Recycle Bin, no hierarchy exists and no small box is displayed next to the icon.

Other Ways

1. Click Start button, right-click My Computer, click Explore on shortcut menu
2. Right-click Start button or any desktop icon, click Explore on shortcut menu
3. Click Start button, point to All Programs, point to Accessories, click Windows Explorer, click My Computer

More About

Icons

In many cases, you may not recognize a particular icon because hundreds of icons are developed by software vendors to represent their products. Each icon is supposed to be unique and eye-catching. You can purchase thousands of icons on floppy disk or CD-ROM to use to represent the documents you create.

The right pane in the My Computer window illustrated in Figure 1-45 on the previous page contains three groups of icons. The Files Stored on This Computer group contains the Shared Documents icon and Brad Wilson's Documents icon. The Hard Disk Drives group contains the LOCAL DISK (C:) icon. The Devices with Removable Storage group contains the 3½ Floppy (A:) and CD Drive (D:) icons.

The **status bar** appears at the bottom of the window and contains information about the documents, folders, and programs in a window. A message on the left of the status bar located at the bottom of the window indicates the right pane contains four objects.

Windows Explorer displays the drives and folders on the computer in hierarchical structure in the Folders pane. This arrangement allows you to move and copy files and folders using only the Folders pane and the contents of the right pane.

Expanding a Folder

Explorer displays the hierarchy of items in the Folders pane and the contents of drives and folders in the right pane. To expand a drive or folder in the Folders pane, click the plus sign in the small box to the left of the drive or folder icon. Clicking the plus sign expands the hierarchy in the Folders pane. The contents of the right pane remain the same. The following steps show how to expand a folder.

To Expand a Folder

1

• **Point to the plus sign in the small box to the left of the My Documents icon in the Folders pane (Figure 1-46).**

FIGURE 1-46

Windows XP Project 1

2

• **Click the plus sign.**

The hierarchy below the My Documents icon expands to display the My Music folder, My Pictures folder, and My Videos folder (Figure 1-47). The minus sign to the left of the My Documents folder indicates the folder is expanded. No sign to the left of the My Music, My Pictures, and My Videos folders indicates the folders contain no additional folders.

FIGURE 1-47

In Figure 1-47, the My Documents folder is expanded and the right pane still contains the contents of the My Computer folder. Clicking the plus sign next to a folder icon expands the hierarchy but does not change the contents of the right pane.

Expanding a Drive

When a plus sign in a small box displays to the left of a drive icon in the Folders pane, you can expand the drive to show all the folders it contains. The steps on the next page illustrate expanding drive C to view the folders on drive C.

Other Ways

1. Click drive icon in Folders pane
2. Select drive to expand using ARROW keys, press PLUS on numeric keyboard
3. Select drive to expand, press RIGHT ARROW

Q&A

Q: Which views are available when viewing icons in a window?

A: You can display icons in most windows in Thumbnails view, Tiles view, Icons view, List view, or Details view. Filmstrip view is available in the My Picture window. You also can view pictures as a slide presentation in the My Pictures window, any subfolder in the My Pictures window, or any other folder customized as a pictures folder.

To Expand a Drive

1

• **Point to the plus sign in the small box to the left of the LOCAL DISK (C:) icon (Figure 1-48).**

FIGURE 1-48

2

• **Click the plus sign.**

The hierarchy below the LOCAL DISK (C:) icon expands to display the folders contained on LOCAL DISK (C:) (Figure 1-49). The folders are indented below the LOCAL DISK (C:) icon and the minus sign to the left of the LOCAL DISK (C:) icon indicates the drive has been expanded. A folder with a plus sign contains more folders.

FIGURE 1-49

In Figure 1-49, the LOCAL DISK (C:) drive is expanded and the right pane still contains the contents of the My Computer folder. Clicking the plus sign next to a drive icon expands the hierarchy but does not change the contents of the right pane.

When a drive is expanded, the folders contained within the expanded drive display in the Folders pane. You can continue this expansion to view further levels of the hierarchy.

Displaying Files and Folders in Windows Explorer

You can display files and folders in the right pane in several different views. Currently, the files and folders in the My Computer folder display in Tiles view using Large Icons format and are grouped based upon file type. Other folders may display in a different view. The manner in which you display drive or folder contents in the right pane is a matter of personal preference.

Displaying Drive and Folder Contents

Explorer displays the hierarchy of items in the left, or Folders, pane and the contents of drives and folders in the right pane. To display the contents of a drive or folder in the right pane, click the drive or folder icon in the Folders pane. Clicking the icon displays the contents of the drive or folder in the right pane and expands the hierarchy in the Folders pane. The following step shows how to display the contents of the Shared Documents folder.

To Display the Contents of a Folder

1

• **Click the Shared Documents icon in the Folders pane.**

The highlighted Shared Documents name is displayed in the Folders pane, the hierarchy below the Shared Documents icon expands, and the right pane contains the contents of the Shared Documents folder (Figure 1-50). The window title changes to Shared Documents, the Shared Documents button replaces the My Computer button on the taskbar, and the status bar indicates two objects are displayed in the right pane.

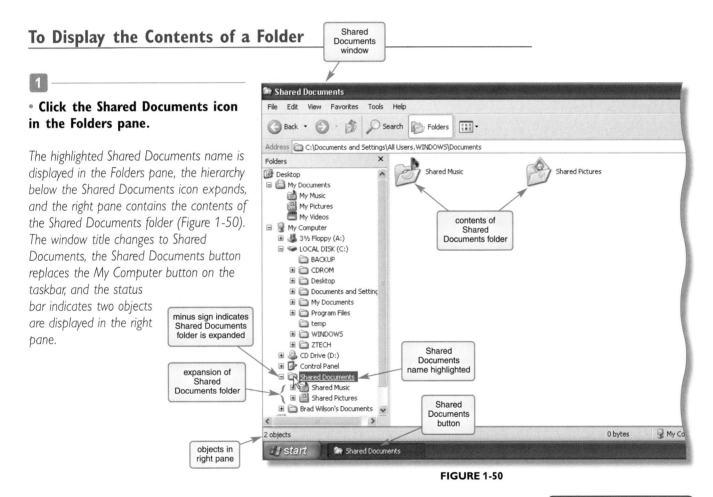

FIGURE 1-50

Other Ways

1. Right-click Shared Documents icon, click Explore on shortcut menu

Whenever files or folders display in the right pane of a window, you can display the contents of the file or folder by double-clicking the icon of the file or folder.

In Figure 1-50 on the previous page, you clicked the Shared Documents icon in the Folders pane and the contents of the Shared Documents folder displayed in the right pane and the hierarchy below the Shared Documents icon expanded. If you click the icon of an expanded drive or folder, the contents of the drive or folder are displayed in the right pane The hierarchy below the icon will not expand because it is already expanded. The step below shows how to display the contents of the expanded LOCAL DISK (C:) drive.

To Display the Contents of an Expanded Drive

1

• **Click the LOCAL DISK (C:) icon in the Folders pane.**

The LOCAL DISK (C:) entry is selected in the Folders pane, the expanded Shared Documents folder collapses, and the contents of the LOCAL DISK (C:) folder are displayed in the right pane (Figure 1-51). Notice that all the folder icons appear first and then the file icons appear. The status bar indicates 21 objects and 8 hidden objects occupy 328 kilobytes and the amount of space that is not being used on the disk is 9.02 gigabytes.

FIGURE 1-51

Launching an Application Program from Windows Explorer

Earlier in this project you launched Internet Explorer from the Start menu (see Figures 1-42 and 1-43 on pages WIN 38 and WIN 39). You also can launch an application program from the right pane of a window. To launch the Internet Explorer program stored in the Program Files folder, complete the following steps.

To Launch an Application Program from Explorer

1

• **Click the plus sign to the left of the Program Files icon in the Folders pane.**

• **Click the Internet Explorer icon in the Folders pane.**

• **Point to the IEXPLORE (Internet Explorer) icon in the right pane of the Internet Explorer window.**

The Program Files and Internet Explorer folders expand, the Internet Explorer folder is selected, the window title changes to Internet Explorer, the Internet Explorer button replaces the LOCAL DISK (C:) button on the taskbar, and the contents of the Internet Explorer folder are displayed in the right pane (Figure 1-52). The status bar indicates 6 objects and 1 hidden object consume 124 kilobytes on drive C.

FIGURE 1-52

2

• **Double-click the IEXPLORE icon.**

Windows launches the Internet Explorer program. The Welcome to MSN.com - Microsoft Internet Explorer window, containing the MSN page, is displayed (Figure 1-53). Because Web pages are modified frequently, the Web page that is displayed on your desktop may be different from the Web page shown in Figure 1-53. The URL for the Web page is displayed in the Address bar.

FIGURE 1-53

Other Ways

1. Right-click IEXPLORE icon, click Open on shortcut menu
2. Click IEXPLORE icon, press ENTER

More About

Launching Programs in Explorer

Usually, people find launching from the Start menu or from a window easier and more intuitive than starting programs from Explorer. In most cases, you will not launch programs from Explorer.

You can use the Internet Explorer program for any purpose you wish, just as if you had launched it from the Start menu. When you are finished with the Internet Explorer program, you should quit the program. The step below shows how to quit the Internet Explorer program.

To Quit an Application Program

1 **Click the Close button on the Welcome to MSN.com - Microsoft Internet Explorer title bar.**

The Welcome to MSN.com - Microsoft Internet Explorer window closes.

Closing Folder Expansions

Sometimes, after you have completed work with expanded folders, you will want to close the expansions while still leaving the Explorer window open. The following steps illustrate how to close the expanded folders shown in Figure 1-52 on page WIN 47.

To Close Expanded Folders

1

• **Click the minus sign to the left of the Internet Explorer icon.**

The expansion of the Internet Explorer folder collapses and the minus sign changes to a plus sign (Figure 1-54). The contents of the right pane do not change.

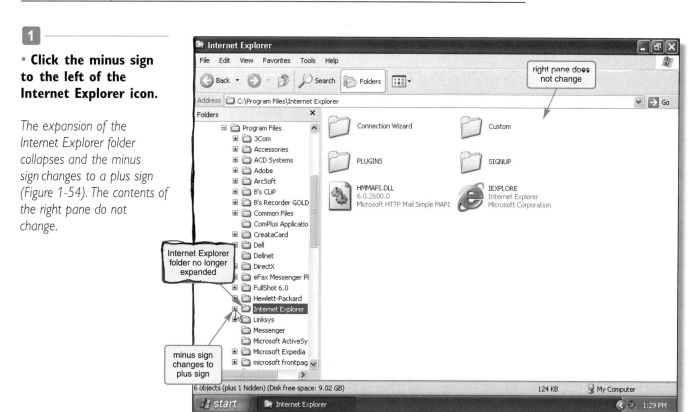

FIGURE 1-54

2

• **Click the minus sign to the left of the Program Files icon.**

The expansion of the Program Files folder collapses, the minus sign changes to a plus sign, the window title changes to Program Files, the Program Files button replaces the Internet Explorer button on the taskbar, and the right pane contains the files and folders in the Program Files folder (Figure 1-55).

FIGURE 1-55

Moving through the Folders pane and right pane is an important skill because you will find that you use Windows Explorer to perform a significant amount of file maintenance on the computer.

Copying, Moving, Renaming, and Deleting Files in Windows Explorer

Three common operations that every student should understand how to perform are copying a file, renaming a file, and deleting a file. On the following pages, you will use Windows Explorer to copy a file from the WINDOWS folder on drive C to the My Pictures folder on drive C, rename a file in the My Pictures folder, and then delete a file in the My Pictures folder.

Copying Files in Windows Explorer

When copying files, the drive and folder containing the files to be copied are called the **source drive** and **source folder**, respectively. The drive and folder to which the files are copied are called the **destination drive** and **destination folder**, respectively. In the following steps, the WINDOWS folder is the source folder, the My Pictures folder is the destination folder, and drive C is both the source drive and the destination drive.

One method of copying files in Windows Explorer is to right-drag a file icon from the right pane to a folder or drive icon in the Folders pane. The following steps show how to copy the Prairie Wind file from the WINDOWS folder (source folder) to the My Pictures folder (destination folder).

To Copy a File in Windows Explorer by Right-Dragging

1

• **Click the WINDOWS icon in the Folders pane.**

• **Scroll the right pane to display the Prairie Wind icon. If the Prairie Wind file is not available, display another icon.**

• **Scroll the Folders pane to display the expanded My Documents folder.**

The contents of the WINDOWS folder, including the Prairie Wind icon, are displayed in the right pane and the My Pictures folder is displayed in the expanded My Documents folder in the Folders pane (Figure 1-56).

FIGURE 1-56

• Right-drag the Prairie Wind icon onto the top of the My Pictures icon.

• Point to Copy Here on the shortcut menu.

The dimmed image of the Prairie Wind icon is displayed as you right-drag the icons onto the top of the My Pictures icon, a shortcut menu is displayed, and the dimmed image no longer is displayed (Figure 1-57).

3

• Click Copy Here.

The Prairie Wind file is copied to the My Pictures folder.

FIGURE 1-57

Q&A

Q: Are copying and moving the same?

A: No! When you copy a file, it will be located in both the place to which it was copied and the place from which it was copied. When you move a file, it will be located in only the location to which it was moved. You will be sorry if you do not know the difference, and a file you thought was copied was moved instead.

You can move files using the techniques just discussed except that you click **Move Here** instead of Copy Here on the shortcut menu (see Figure 1-57). The difference between a move and a copy, as mentioned previously, is that when you move a file, it is placed on the destination drive or in the destination folder and is permanently removed from its current location. When a file is copied, it is placed on the destination drive or in the destination folder as well as remaining stored in its current location.

In general, you should right-drag to copy or move a file instead of dragging a file. If you drag a file from one folder to another on the same drive, Windows XP moves the file. If you drag a file from one folder to another folder on a different drive, Windows XP copies the file. Because of the different ways this is handled, it is strongly suggested you right-drag when moving or copying files.

Displaying the Contents of the My Pictures Folder

After copying a group of files, you might want to examine the folder or drive where the files were copied to ensure they were copied properly. The following step shows how to display the contents of the My Pictures folder.

To Display the Contents of a Folder

1

• **Click the My Pictures icon in the Folders pane.**

The contents of the My Pictures folder, including the Prairie Wind file, are displayed in the right pane (Figure 1-58). If additional files or folders are contained in the My Pictures folder, their icons and titles also are displayed.

FIGURE 1-58

Renaming Files and Folders

In some circumstances, you may want to **rename** a file or a folder. This could occur when you want to distinguish a file in one folder or drive from a copy, or if you decide you need a better name to identify a file. The steps on the next page illustrate how to change the name of the Prairie Wind file in the My Pictures folder to Blue Prairie Wind.

To Rename a File

1

- **Right-click the Prairie Wind icon in the right pane and then point to Rename on the shortcut menu.**

The selected Prairie Wind icon and a shortcut menu are displayed (Figure 1-59).

FIGURE 1-59

2

- **Click Rename.**
- **Type** Blue Prairie Wind **and then press the enter key.**

The file is renamed Blue Prairie Wind (Figure 1-60). Notice that the file in the My Pictures folder is renamed, but the original file in the WINDOWS folder in drive C is not renamed.

Other Ways

1. Right-click icon, press M, type name, press ENTER
2. Click icon, press F2, type name, press ENTER
3. Click icon, on File menu click Rename, type name, press ENTER
4. Select icon, press ALT+F, press M, type name, press ENTER

FIGURE 1-60

Renaming files by this method also can be accomplished in other windows. For example, if you open the My Computer window and then open the My Music window, you can rename any file stored in the My Music window using the technique just presented.

Use caution when renaming files on the hard disk. If you inadvertently rename a file that is associated with certain programs, the programs may not be able to find the file and, therefore, may not execute properly.

Deleting Files in Windows Explorer

A final operation that you may want to perform in Windows Explorer is to delete a file. Exercise extreme caution when deleting a file or files. When you delete a file from a hard drive, the deleted file is stored in the Recycle Bin where you can recover it until you empty the Recycle Bin. If you delete a file from a floppy disk, the file is gone permanently once you delete it.

Assume you have decided to delete the Blue Prairie Wind file from the My Pictures window. The following steps illustrate how to delete the Blue Prairie Wind file.

More About

Deleting Files

Someone proposed that the Delete command be removed from operating systems after an employee, who thought he knew what he was doing, deleted an entire database, which cost the company millions of dollars to replace. You should regard the Delete command as something to be used with extreme caution.

To Delete a File by Right-Dragging to the Recycle Bin

1

• **Scroll the Folders pane to display the Recycle Bin icon.**

• **Right-drag the Blue Prairie Wind icon to the Recycle Bin icon in the Folders pane and then point to Move Here on the shortcut menu.**

The Blue Prairie Wind icon in the right pane is right-dragged to the Recycle Bin icon in the Folders pane and a shortcut menu is displayed (Figure 1-61). The Move Here command is highlighted on the shortcut menu.

FIGURE 1-61

2

• **Click Move Here.**

The Blue Prairie Wind icon is removed from the right pane and moved to the Recycle Bin (Figure 1-62). If you wish to terminate the deleting process before it is complete, you can click the Cancel command on the shortcut menu.

FIGURE 1-62

You can use the methods just specified to delete folders on a floppy disk or a hard disk. Again, you should use extreme caution when deleting files and folders to ensure you do not delete something you may not be able to recover.

Removing the Status Bar

Earlier in this project, you may have used the View command on the menu bar to display the status bar to view information about the folders, programs, and documents in the My Computer window. If you did, you should return the status bar to its original state by removing the status bar. The following steps remove the status bar.

To Remove the Status Bar

1 **Click View on the menu bar.**

2 **Click Status Bar on the View menu.**

The status bar no longer is displayed.

Quitting Windows Explorer

When you have finished working with Windows Explorer, you can quit Windows Explorer by closing the Folders pane or by closing the Windows Explorer (My Pictures) window. The following step shows how to quit Windows Explorer by closing the My Pictures window.

To Quit Windows Explorer

1 **Click the Close button on the My Pictures window title bar.**

Windows XP closes the My Pictures window and quits Windows Explorer.

Using Help and Support

One of the more powerful Windows XP features is Help and Support. **Help and Support** is available when using Windows XP, or when using any application program running under Windows XP. It contains answers to many questions you may ask with respect to Windows XP.

Launching Help and Support

Before you can access the Help and Support Center services, you must launch Help and Support. One method of launching Help and Support uses the Start menu. The following steps show how to launch Help and Support.

To Launch Help and Support

1

• **Click the Start button on the taskbar and then point to Help and Support on the Start menu.**

Windows XP displays the Start menu and highlights the Help and Support command (Figure 1-63).

More About

Windows XP Help and Support

If you purchased an operating system or application program nine years ago, you received at least one, and more often several, heavy thick technical manuals that explained the software. With Windows XP, you receive a booklet with only 34 pages. The Help and Support feature of Windows XP replaces the reams and reams of printed pages in hard-to-understand technical manuals.

FIGURE 1-63

2

• **Click Help and Support and then click the Maximize button on the Help and Support Center title bar.**

The Help and Support Center window opens and maximizes (Figure 1-64). The window contains the Help viewer. The Help viewer includes the navigation toolbar, Search text box and Set search options link, and table of contents. The table of contents contains four areas (Pick a Help topic, Ask for assistance, Pick a task, and Did you know?).

FIGURE 1-64

Other Ways

1. Press F1
2. Press CTRL+ESC, press H
3. Press WINDOWS+F1

The Help and Support Center title bar shown in Figure 1-64 contains a Minimize button, Restore Down button, and Close button. You can minimize or restore the Help and Support Center window as needed and also close the Help and Support Center window.

The navigation toolbar is displayed below the title bar. The **navigation toolbar** allows you to navigate through Help topics and pages, browse and save Help topics and pages, view previously saved Help topics and pages, get online support for questions and problems, and customize the Help viewer. An icon identifies each button on the navigation toolbar. Six buttons contain a text label (Back, Index, Favorites, History, Support, and Options). The buttons on the navigation toolbar on your computer may be different.

The area below the navigation toolbar contains the Search text box and Start searching button used to search for Help, the Set search options link to set the criteria for searching the Help and Support Center, and the window's title (Help and Support Center).

The **table of contents** contains four areas. The **Pick a Help topic area** contains four category groups. A unique icon identifies each group. Clicking a category in a group displays a list of subcategories and Help topics related to the category.

The **Ask for assistance area** contains two tasks. The first task (**Remote Assistance**) allows an individual at another computer to connect and control your computer while helping to solve a problem. The second task (**Windows XP newsgroups**) allows you to obtain Help from product support experts or discuss your questions with other Windows XP users in newsgroups.

The **Pick a task area** contains four tasks. The first task (**Windows Update**) allows you to access a catalog of items such as device drivers, security fixes, critical updates, the latest Help files, and Internet products that you can download to keep your computer up-to-date. The second task (**compatible hardware and software**) allows you to search for hardware and software that are compatible with Windows XP. The third task (**System Restore**) allows you to store the current state of your computer and restore your computer to that state without losing important information. The fourth task (**Tools**) contains a collection of eight helpful tools to keep your computer running smoothly. The **Did you know? area** is updated daily with helpful tips for using Windows XP.

Browsing for Help Topics in the Table of Contents

After launching Help and Support, the next step is to find the Help topic in which you are interested. Assume you want to know more about finding information using the Help and Support Center. The following steps illustrate how to use the table of contents to find a Help topic that describes how to find what you need in the Help and Support Center.

To Browse for Help Topics in the Table of Contents

1

• **Point to Windows basics in the Pick a Help topic area.**

The mouse pointer changes to a hand icon when positioned on the Windows basics category, and the category is underlined (Figure 1-65).

FIGURE 1-65

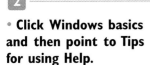

2

• **Click Windows basics and then point to Tips for using Help.**

The navigation pane and topic pane are displayed in the Help and Support Center window (Figure 1-66). The Windows basics area in the navigation pane contains five categories and the underlined Tips for using Help category. The See Also area contains four Help topics. The topic pane contains the Help and Support toolbar and the Windows basics page.

FIGURE 1-66

3

• **Click Tips for using Help and then point to Find what you need in Help and Support Center in the topic pane.**

Windows XP highlights the Tips for using Help category in the Windows basics area, displays the Tips for using Help page in the topic pane, and underlines the Find what you need in Help and Support Center task (Figure 1-67). The Add to Favorites button and Print button on the Help and Support Center toolbar are dimmed to indicate the page cannot be added to the favorites list or printed.

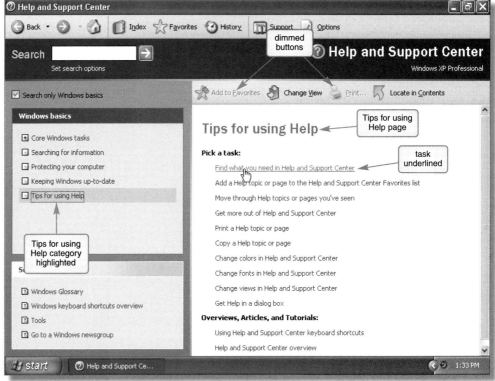

FIGURE 1-67

4

• **Click Find what you need in Help and Support Center and then read the information in the To find what you need in Help and Support Center topic in the topic pane.**

Windows XP removes the dotted rectangle surrounding the Tips for using Help category in the Windows basics area and displays the To find what you need in Help and Support Center topic in the topic pane (Figure 1-68). Clicking the Related Topics link displays a list of related Help topics.

FIGURE 1-68

The check mark in the Search only Windows basics check box shown in Figure 1-66 indicates topics in the Windows basics category will be searched.

In the Windows basics area, the **plus sign** in the small box to the left of the Core Windows tasks category indicates the category contains subcategories but the subcategories do not appear in the area. Clicking the box with the plus sign displays a list of subcategories below the Core Windows category. A **bullet** in a small box indicates a category. Clicking the bullet within a small box displays a list of tasks in the topic pane.

Each of the four Help topics in the See Also area is identified by a question mark in a document icon. The **question mark** indicates a Help topic without further subdivision.

The Help and Support Center toolbar in the topic pane shown in Figure 1-66 contains four buttons. An icon and text label identify each button on the toolbar. The buttons allow you to add a Help topic to the favorites list, display only the Help and Support Center toolbar and topic pane in the Help and Support Center window, print a Help topic in the topic pane, and locate a Help topic in the topic pane in the table of contents.

Using the Help and Support Center Index

A second method of finding answers to your questions about Windows XP is to use the Help and Support Center Index. The **Help and Support Center Index** contains a list of index entries, each of which references one or more Help topics. Assume you want more information about home networking. The steps on the next page illustrate how to learn more about home networking.

To Search for Help Topics Using the Index

1

• **Click the Index button on the navigation toolbar, type** home networking **in the Type in the keyword to find text box, and then point to overview in the list box.**

The Index area, containing a text box, list box, and Display button, is displayed in the navigation pane and the Index page is displayed in the topic pane (Figure 1-69). When you type an entry in the text box, the list of index entries in the list box automatically scrolls and the entry you type is highlighted in the list. Several entries appear indented below the home networking entry.

FIGURE 1-69

2

• **Click overview in the list and then point to the Display button.**

Windows XP displays the overview entry in the text box and highlights the overview entry in the list (Figure 1-70). The yellow outline surrounding the Display button indicates the button is recessed.

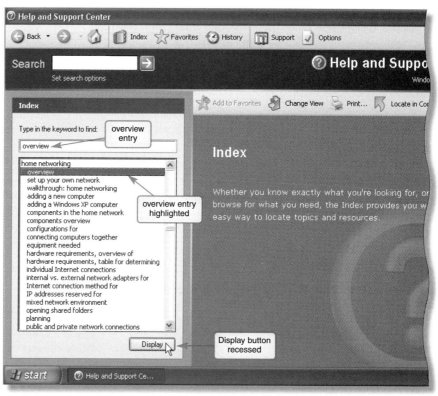

FIGURE 1-70

3

• **Click the Display button.**

The Home or small office network overview topic is displayed in the topic pane (Figure 1-71). The topic contains an overview of home and small office networks. Additional information is available by using the vertical scroll bar in the topic pane.

FIGURE 1-71

In Figure 1-71, the workgroup and server links are underlined and displayed in green font to indicate that clicking the link will display its definition. To remove the definition, click anywhere off the definition. Although not visible in Figure 1-71, other links, such as the Related Topics link, appear at the bottom of the page, underlined, and in blue font. Clicking the Related Topics link displays a pop-up window that contains topics related to the home or small office network overview.

After using the Help and Support Center, normally you will close the Help and Support Center. The following step shows how to close the Help and Support Center.

Other Ways

1. Press ALT+N, type keyword, press DOWN ARROW until topic is highlighted, press ALT+D (or ENTER)

To Close the Help and Support Center

1 **Click the Close button on the title bar of the Help and Support Center window.**

Windows XP closes the Help and Support Center window.

Logging Off and Turning Off the Computer

After completing your work with Windows XP, you should close your user account by logging off from the computer. Logging off from the computer closes any open applications, allows you to save any unsaved documents, ends the Windows XP session, and makes the computer available for other users. Perform the steps on the next page to log off from the computer.

Q: Why is it important to log off the computer?

A: It is important to log off the computer so you do not lose your work. Some users of Windows XP have turned off their computers without following the log off procedure only to find data they thought they had stored on disk was lost.

To Log Off from the Computer

1

• **Click the Start button on the taskbar and then point to Log Off on the Start menu.**

Windows XP displays the Start menu and highlights the Log Off command (Figure 1-72).

FIGURE 1-72

2

• **Click Log Off.**
• **Point to the Log Off button in the Log Off Windows dialog box.**

Windows XP displays the Log Off Windows dialog box (Figure 1-73). The dialog box contains three buttons (Switch User, Log Off, and Cancel). Pointing to the Log Off button changes the color of the button to light orange and displays the Log Off balloon. The balloon contains the balloon name, Log Off, and the text, Closes your programs and ends your Windows session. The Cancel button is hidden behind the balloon.

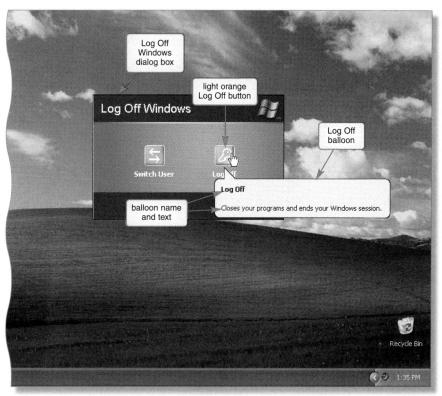

FIGURE 1-73

3

• **Click the Log Off button.**

Windows XP logs off from the computer and displays the Welcome screen (Figure 1-74). A message is displayed below the Brad Wilson name on the Welcome screen to indicate the user has unread e-mail messages. Your user name will be displayed instead of the Brad Wilson name on the Welcome screen.

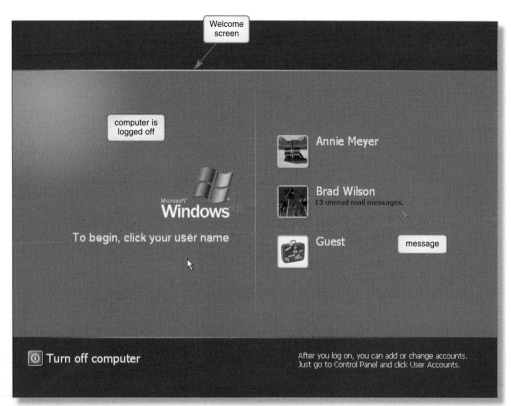

FIGURE 1-74

Other Ways

1. Press CTRL+ESC, press L, press L

While Windows XP is logging off, a blue screen containing the word, Welcome, appears on the desktop and the messages, Logging off..., and Saving your settings..., appear on the screen momentarily. The blue screen closes and the Welcome screen (Figure 1-74) appears on the desktop. At this point, another user can log on.

If you accidentally click Log Off on the Start menu as shown in Figure 1-72 and you do not want to log off, click the Cancel button in the Log Off Windows dialog box to return to normal Windows XP operation.

After logging off, you also may want to turn off the computer using the **Turn off computer link** on the Welcome screen. Turning off the computer shuts down Windows XP so you can turn off the power to the computer. Many computers turn the power off automatically. The steps on the next page illustrate how to turn off the computer. If you are not sure about turning off the computer, simply read the steps.

To Turn Off the Computer

1

• **Point to the Turn off computer link on the Welcome screen.**

Pointing to the Turn off computer link underlines the Turn off computer link (Figure 1-75).

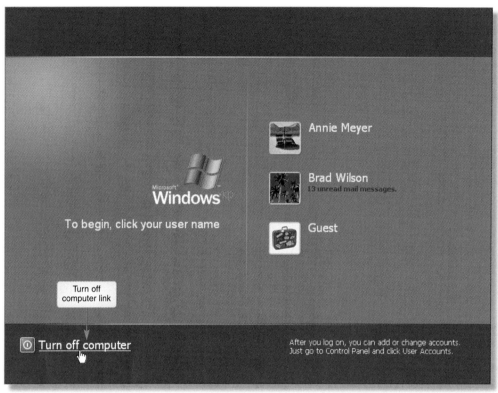

FIGURE 1-75

2

• **Click Turn off computer.**

The Welcome screen darkens and the Turn off computer dialog box is displayed (Figure 1-76). The dialog box contains four buttons (Stand By, Turn Off, Restart, and Cancel). The buttons allow you to perform different operations, such as placing the computer in stand by mode (Stand By), shutting down Windows XP (Turn Off), restarting the computer (Restart), and canceling the process of shutting down Windows XP (Cancel).

FIGURE 1-76

3

• **Point to the Turn Off button in the Turn off computer dialog box.**

The color of the Turn Off button changes to light red and the Turn Off balloon is displayed (Figure 1-77). The balloon contains the balloon name, Turn Off, and the text, Shuts down Windows so that you can safely turn off the computer.

4

• **Click the Turn Off button.**

Windows XP is shut down.

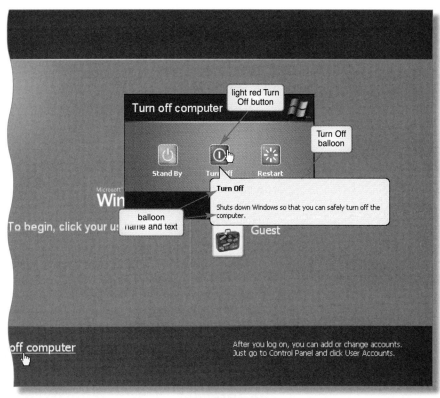

FIGURE 1-77

Other Ways

1. Press CTRL+ESC, press U, use ARROW keys to select Turn Off, press ENTER
2. Press ALT+F4, use ARROW keys to select Turn Off, press ENTER

While Windows XP is shutting down, a blue screen containing the word, Welcome, is displayed on the desktop and the message, Windows is shutting down…, appears momentarily. At this point, you can turn off the computer. When shutting down Windows XP, you should never turn off the computer before these messages appear.

If you accidentally click Turn off computer on the Welcome screen as shown in Figure 1-75 on page WIN 66 and you do not want to shut down Windows XP, click the Cancel button in the Turn off computer dialog box shown in Figure 1-76 to return to normal Windows XP operation.

What Is Microsoft Office 2003?

Microsoft Office 2003 is a collection of the more popular Microsoft application software products and is available in Standard, Small Business, Professional, Student and Teacher, and Developer editions. The **Microsoft Office Professional Edition 2003** includes the five basic applications, which are Microsoft Office Word 2003, Microsoft Office Excel 2003, Microsoft Office Access 2003, Microsoft Office PowerPoint 2003, and Microsoft Office Outlook 2003. Office allows you to work more efficiently, communicate more effectively, and improve the appearance of each document you create.

Office contains a collection of media files (art, sound, animation, and movies) that you can use to enhance documents. **Microsoft Clip Organizer** allows you to organize the media files on your computer and search for specific files, as well as search for and organize media files located on the Internet. Clip art and media files are accessible from the Microsoft Office Online Web site and contains thousands of additional media files.

With the **Office Speech Recognition** software installed and a microphone, you can speak the names of toolbar buttons, menus, and menu commands, and list items, screen alerts, and dialog box controls, such as OK and Cancel. You also can dictate text and numbers to insert them as well as delete them. If you have speakers, you can instruct the computer to speak a document or worksheet to you. In addition, you can translate a word, phrase, or an entire document from English into Japanese, Chinese, French, Spanish, or German.

Menus and toolbars adjust to the way in which you work. As Office detects which commands you use more frequently, these commands are displayed at the top of the menu, and the infrequently used commands are placed in reserve. A button at the bottom of the menu allows you to expand the menu in order to view all its commands. More frequently used buttons on a toolbar appear on the toolbar, while less frequently used buttons are not displayed.

In addition, Office integrates its applications with the power of the Internet so you can share information, communicate and collaborate on projects over long distances, and conduct online meetings.

The Internet, World Wide Web, and Intranets

Office allows you to take advantage of the Internet, the World Wide Web, and intranets. The **Internet** is a worldwide network of thousands of computer networks and millions of commercial, educational, government, and personal computers. The **World Wide Web** is an easy-to-use graphical interface for exploring the Internet. The World Wide Web consists of many individual Web sites. A **Web site** consists of a single **Web page** or multiple Web pages linked together. The first Web page in the Web site is called the **home page** and a unique address, called a **Uniform Resource Locator** (**URL**), identifies each Web page. Web sites are located on computers called Web servers.

A software tool, called a **browser**, allows you to locate and view a Web page. One method of viewing a Web page is to use the browser to enter the URL for the Web page. A widely used browser, called **Internet Explorer**, is included with Office. Another method of viewing a Web page is clicking a hyperlink. A **hyperlink** is colored or underlined text or a graphic that, when clicked, connects to another Web page.

An **intranet** is a special type of Web site that is available only to the users of a particular type of computer network, such as a network used within a company or organization for internal communication. Like the Internet, hyperlinks are used within an intranet to access documents, pages, and other destinations on the intranet.

Office and the Internet

Office was designed in response to customer requests to streamline the process of information sharing and collaboration within their organizations. Organizations that, in the past, made important information available only to a select few, now want their information accessible to a wider range of individuals who are using tools such as Office and Internet Explorer. Office allows users to utilize the Internet or an intranet as a central location to view documents, manage files, and work together.

Each of the Office applications makes publishing documents on a Web server as simple as saving a file on a hard disk. Once the file is placed on the Web server, users can view and edit the documents, and conduct Web discussions and live online meetings.

An explanation of each Office application along with how it is used to access an intranet or the Internet is given on the following pages.

Microsoft Office Word 2003

Microsoft Office Word 2003 is a full-featured word processing program that allows you to create many types of personal and business communications, including announcements, letters, resumes, business documents, and academic reports, as well as other forms of written documents. Figure 1-78 illustrates the top portion of the announcement that students create in Project 1 of the Word section of this book. The steps to create the announcement also are shown in Project 1 of the Word section of this book.

Grand Prix Announcement - Microsoft Word window

top portion of announcement

FIGURE 1-78

The Word AutoCorrect, Spelling, and Grammar features allow you to proofread documents for errors in spelling and grammar by identifying the errors and offering corrections as you type. As you create a specific document, such as a business letter or resume, Word provides wizards, which ask questions and then use your answers to format the document before you type the text of the document.

Word automates many often-used tasks and provides you with powerful desktop publishing tools to use as you create professional looking brochures, advertisements, and newsletters. The drawing tools allow you to design impressive 3-D effects by including shadows, textures, and curves.

Word makes it easier for you to share documents in order to collaborate on a document. The Send for Review and Markup features allow you to send a document for review and easily track the changes made to the document.

Word and the Internet

Word makes it possible to design and publish Web pages on an intranet or the Internet, insert a hyperlink to a Web page in a word processing document, as well as access other Web pages to search for and retrieve information and pictures from them. Figure 1-79 illustrates the top portion of a cover letter that contains a hyperlink (e-mail address) that allows you to send an e-mail message to the sender.

Clicking the hyperlink starts the Outlook mail program, through which you can send an e-mail message to the author of the cover letter. In Figure 1-80, the Resume and Cover Letter - Message window that allows you to compose a new e-mail message contains the recipient's e-mail address (okamoto@earth.net), subject of the e-mail message (Resume and Cover Letter), and a brief message.

FIGURE 1-79

FIGURE 1-80

Microsoft Office Excel 2003

Microsoft Office Excel 2003 is a spreadsheet program that allows you to organize data, complete calculations, graph data, develop professional looking reports, publish organized data to the Web, access real-time data from Web sites, and make decisions. Figure 1-81 illustrates the Excel window that contains the worksheet and 3-D Column chart created in one of the exercises in Project 1 of the Excel section of this book.

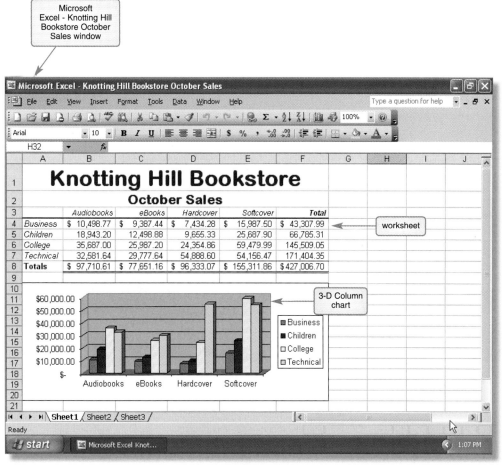

FIGURE 1-81

Excel and the Internet

Using Excel, you can create hyperlinks within a worksheet to access other Office documents on the network, an organization's intranet, or the Internet. You also can save worksheets as static or dynamic Web pages that can be viewed using a browser. Static Web pages cannot be changed by the person viewing them. Dynamic Web pages give the person viewing them in their browser many capabilities to modify them using Excel. In addition, you can create and run queries to retrieve information from a Web page directly into a worksheet.

Figure 1-82 illustrates a worksheet created by running a Web query to retrieve stock market information for two stocks (XM Satellite Radio Holdings Inc. and Sirius Satellite Radio Inc.). The two hyperlinks were created using the Insert Hyperlink button on the Standard toolbar, and the information in the worksheet was obtained from the MSN Money Web site.

The Refresh All button on the External Data toolbar allows you to update the last price of the stocks (Last). Clicking the Refresh All button locates the MSN Money Web site, retrieves current information for the stocks listed in the worksheet, and displays the updated information in the worksheet (Figure 1-83). Notice that the stock prices and information in this worksheet differ from what was displayed in the worksheet shown in Figure 1-82.

FIGURE 1-82

FIGURE 1-83

Microsoft Office Access 2003

Microsoft Office Access 2003 is a comprehensive database management system (DBMS). A **database** is a collection of data organized in a manner that allows access, retrieval, and use of that data. Access allows you to create a database; add, change, and delete data in the database; sort data in the database; retrieve data from the database; and create forms and reports using the data in the database.

The database created in Project 1 of the Access section of this book is displayed in the Microsoft Access - [Client : Table] window illustrated in Figure 1-84. The steps to create this database are shown in Project 1 of Access.

FIGURE 1-84

Access and the Internet

Databases provide a central location to store related pieces of information. Access simplifies the creation of a database with a wizard that quickly can build one of more than a dozen types of databases. You also can transform lists or worksheets into databases using Access wizards. Data access pages permit you to share a database with other computer users on a network, intranet, or over the Internet, as well as allowing the users to view and edit the database. The database shown in Figure 1-85 on the next page contains information (order number, customer number, order date, product number, and quantity) about three orders entered over the Internet using the Internet Explorer browser.

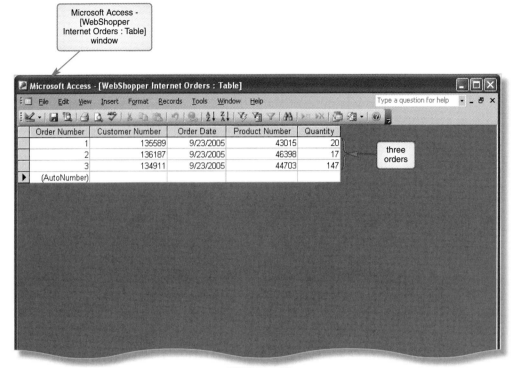

FIGURE 1-85

Figure 1-86 illustrates a simple online order form created to enter order information into the database shown in Figure 1-85. The order form, containing information about order number 4, is displayed in the WebShopper Internet Orders - Microsoft Internet Explorer window.

FIGURE 1-86

Microsoft Office PowerPoint 2003

Microsoft Office PowerPoint 2003 is a complete presentation graphics program that allows you to produce professional looking presentations. PowerPoint provides the flexibility that lets you make informal presentations using overhead transparencies, make electronic presentations using a projection device attached to a personal computer, make formal presentations using 35mm slides or a CD, or run virtual presentations on the Internet.

In PowerPoint, you create a presentation in Normal view. **Normal view** allows you to view the tabs pane, slide pane, and notes pane at the same time. The first slide in the presentation created in one of the exercises in Project 1 of the PowerPoint section of this book appears in the Microsoft PowerPoint - [Rivercrest Community Center] window illustrated in Figure 1-87. The full window contains the Outline tab with the presentation outline, the slide pane displaying the first slide in the presentation, and the notes pane showing a note about the presentation.

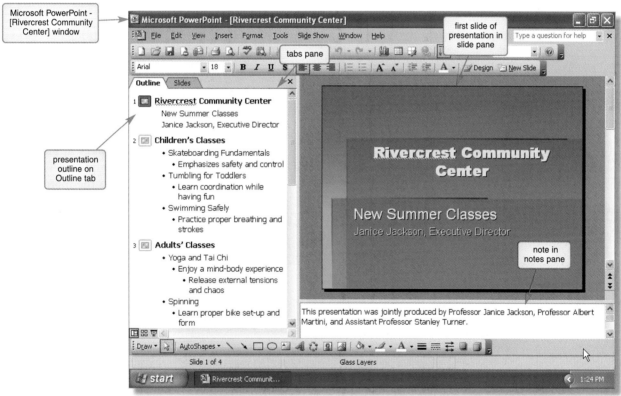

FIGURE 1-87

PowerPoint allows you to create dynamic presentations easily that include multimedia features such as sounds, movies, and pictures. PowerPoint comes with templates that assist you in designing a presentation that you can use to create a slide show. PowerPoint also contains formatting for tables, so that you do not have to create the tables using Excel or Word. The Table Draw tool used in Word to draw tables also is available in PowerPoint.

PowerPoint makes it easier for you to share presentations and collaborate on those presentations. The Send for Review feature and Compare and Merge feature allow you to send a presentation for review and easily merge comments and revisions from multiple reviewers.

PowerPoint and the Internet

PowerPoint allows you to publish presentations on the Internet or an intranet. Figure 1-88 illustrates the first slide in a presentation to be published on the Internet. The slide appears in slide view and contains a title (Computers 4 U), a subtitle (Complete Repairs and Service), and a presenter message (Elliott Dane and Lynn Verone). The additional slides in this presentation do not appear in Figure 1-88.

Figure 1-89 shows the first Web page in a series of Web pages created from the presentation illustrated in Figure 1-88. The Web page appears in the Computers 4 U window in the Internet Explorer browser window. Navigation buttons below the Web page allow you to view additional Web pages in the presentation.

FIGURE 1-88

FIGURE 1-89

The Web Toolbar

The easiest method of navigating an intranet or the Internet is to use the Web toolbar. The Web toolbar allows you to search for and open Office documents that you have placed on an intranet or the Internet. The Web toolbar in the Benjamin Okamoto Cover Letter - Microsoft Word window shown in Figure 1-90 is available in all Office applications except FrontPage. Currently, a Word document (cover letter) is displayed in the window, and the path and file name of the document appear in the text box on the Web toolbar.

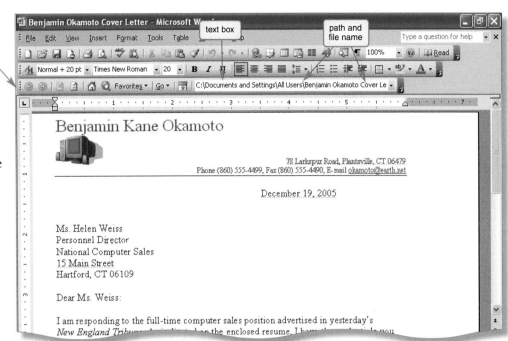

FIGURE 1-90

The buttons and text box on the Web toolbar allow you to jump to Web pages you have viewed previously, cancel a jump to a Web page, update the contents of the current Web page, or replace all other toolbars with the Web toolbar. In addition, you can view the first Web page displayed, search the Web for new Web sites, and add any Web pages you select to the Favorites folder, so you can return to them quickly in the future.

Microsoft Office Publisher 2003

Microsoft Office Publisher 2003 is a desktop publishing program (DTP) that allows you to design and produce professional quality documents (newsletters, flyers, brochures, business cards, Web sites, and so on) that combine text, graphics, and photographs. Desktop publishing software provides a variety of tools, including design templates, graphic manipulation tools, color schemes or libraries, and various page wizards and templates. For large jobs, businesses use desktop publishing software to design publications that are **camera ready**, which means the files are suitable for production by outside commercial printers. Publisher also allows you to locate commercial printers, service bureaus, and copy shops willing to accept customer files created in Publisher.

Publisher allows you to design a unique image, or logo, using one of more than 45 master design sets. This, in turn, permits you to use the same design for all your printed documents (letters, business cards, brochures, and advertisements) and Web pages. Publisher includes 60 coordinated color schemes, more than 10,000 high-quality clip art images, 1,500 photographs, 1,000 Web-art graphics, 175 fonts, 340 animated graphics, and hundreds of unique Design Gallery elements (quotations, sidebars, and so on). If you wish, you also can download additional images from the Microsoft Office Online Web page on the Microsoft Web site.

In the Business Card - Hank Landers - Microsoft Publisher window illustrated in Figure 1-91 on the next page, a business card that was created using the Business Card wizard and the Arcs design set is displayed.

Business Card - Hank
Landers - Microsoft
Publisher - Print
Publication window

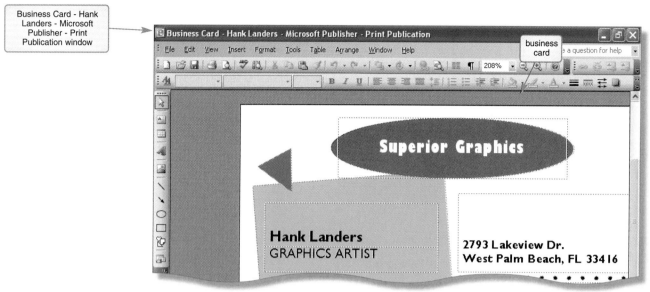

FIGURE 1-91

Superior Graphics -
Microsoft Internet
Explorer window

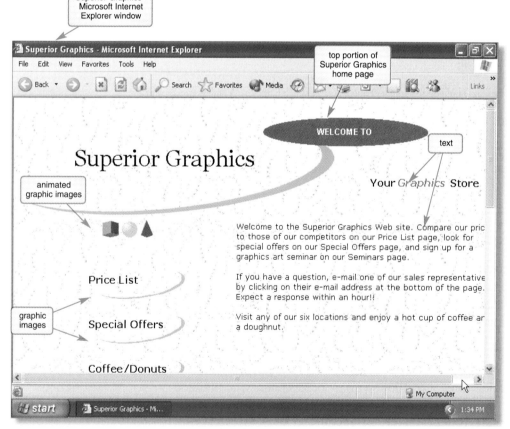

FIGURE 1-92

Publisher and the Internet

Publisher allows you easily to create a multipage Web site with custom color schemes, photo images, animated images, and sounds. Figure 1-92 illustrates the Superior Graphics - Microsoft Internet Explorer window displaying the top portion of the home page in a Web site created using the Web page wizard and Arcs design set.

The home page in the Superior Graphics Web site contains text, graphic images, animated graphic images, and displays using the same design set (Arcs) as the business card illustrated in Figure 1-91.

Microsoft Office FrontPage 2003

Microsoft Office FrontPage 2003 is a Web page authoring and site management program that lets you create and manage professional looking Web sites on the Internet or an intranet. You can create and edit Web pages without knowing HyperText Markup Language (HTML), view the pages and files in the Web site and control their organization, manage existing Web sites, import and export files, and diagnose and correct problems. A variety of templates, including the Workgroup Web template that allows you to set up and maintain the basic structure of a workgroup Web, are available to facilitate managing the Web site.

Figure 1-93 illustrates the top portion of a Web page created using FrontPage that contains information about the Shelly Cashman Series developed by Course Technology. It appears in the SCSITE.COM Shelly Cashman Series Student Resources - Microsoft Internet Explorer window.

FIGURE 1-93

Microsoft Office Outlook 2003

Microsoft Office Outlook 2003 is a powerful communications and scheduling program that helps you communicate with others, keep track of your contacts, and organize your busy schedule. Outlook allows you to send and receive electronic mail and permits you to engage in real-time messaging with family, friends, or coworkers using instant messaging. Outlook also provides you with the means to organize your contacts. Users easily can track e-mail messages, meetings, and notes with a particular contact. Outlook's Calendar, Contacts, Tasks, and Notes components aid in this organization. Contact information readily is available from the Outlook Calendar, Mail, Contacts, and Task components by accessing the Find a Contact feature. **Personal information management** (**PIM**) programs such as Outlook provide a way for individuals and workgroups to organize, find, view, and share information easily.

Figure 1-94 on the next page shows the Outlook Today - Microsoft Outlook window with the Navigation Pane on the left side of the window and the **Outlook Today page** on the right side of the window. The Outlook Today page contains the current date (Friday, September 23, 2005); the Calendar area with the currently scheduled events; the Tasks area with a list of tasks to perform; and the Messages area that summarizes the users e-mail messages by folder. You can customize this page by clicking the Customize Outlook Today button in the upper-right corner of the Outlook Today page.

The **Navigation Pane** is a new feature in Outlook. It is set up to help you navigate Outlook while using any of the components. It comprises one or more panes and two sets of buttons. Although the two sets of buttons remain constant, the area of the Navigation Pane above the buttons changes depending on the active component (Mail, Calendar, Contacts, or Tasks). In Figure 1-94, the expanded Mail pane displays the Favorite Folders pane and the All Mail Folders pane. Clicking a button in the Navigation Pane displays the contents of the component's folder with its associated panes in the Outlook window.

FIGURE 1-94

FIGURE 1-95

Outlook allows you to click the Mail button in the Navigation Pane to view e-mail messages, click the Calendar button to schedule activities (events, appointments, and meetings), click the Contacts button to maintain a list of contacts and e-mail addresses, and click the Tasks button to view a detailed list of tasks.

When you click the Inbox icon in the Mail pane, the Inbox - Microsoft Outlook window is displayed and the contents of the Inbox folder (your e-mail messages) and the Reading Pane are displayed in the window (Figure 1-95).

The Inbox message pane contains two e-mail messages. The second e-mail message is highlighted. The contents of the highlighted e-mail message are displayed in the Reading Pane.

The Microsoft Office 2003 Help System

At any time while you are using one of the Office applications, you can interact with the **Microsoft Office 2003 Help system** for that application and display information on any topic associated with the application. Several categories of help are available to you. One of the easiest methods to obtain help is to use the Type a question for help box. The **Type a question for help box** on the right side of the menu bar lets you type free-form questions, such as how do I save or how do I create a Web page, or you can type terms, such as template, smart tags, or speech. The Help system responds by displaying a list of topics relating to the question or term in the Search Results task pane. The Type a question for help box that appears in the Grand Prix Announcement – Microsoft Word window is illustrated in Figure 1-96.

FIGURE 1-96

When you type the question, How do I check Spelling, in the Type a question for help box shown in Figure 1-96, the Help system displays a list of topics relating to the question. Clicking a topic in the list opens a Help window that provides Help information about spell checking. Detailed instructions for using the Type a question for help box and the other categories of Help are explained in Appendix A of this book.

Project Summary

Project 1 illustrated the Microsoft Windows XP graphical user interface and the Microsoft Office 2003 applications. You started Windows XP, learned the components of the desktop and the six mouse operations. You opened, closed, moved, resized, minimized, maximized, and scrolled a window. You used Windows Explorer to copy a file, display the contents of a folder, expand and collapse a folder, and then rename and delete a file. You obtained help about using Microsoft Windows XP and shut down Windows XP.

Brief explanations of the Word, Excel, Access, PowerPoint, Publisher, FrontPage, and Outlook applications and examples of how these applications interact with the Internet were given. With this introduction, you now are ready to begin a more in-depth study of each Office application explained in this book.

 If you have a SAM user profile, you may have access to hands-on instruction, practice, and assessment of the skills covered in this project. Log in to your SAM account and go to your assignments page to see what your instructor has assigned.

What You Should Know

Having completed this project, you should be able to perform the tasks below. The tasks are listed in the same order they were presented in this project. For a list of the buttons, menus, toolbars, and commands introduced in this project, see the Quick Reference Summary at the back of this book and refer to the Page Number column.

1. Log On to the Computer   (WIN 9)
2. Display the Start Menu   (WIN 12)
3. Add an Icon to the Desktop   (WIN 15)
4. Open a Window Using a Desktop Icon (WIN 17)
5. Minimize and Redisplay a Window   (WIN 20)
6. Maximize and Restore a Window   (WIN 22)
7. Close a Window   (WIN 24, WIN 35)
8. Open a Window Using the Start Menu (WIN 26)
9. Move a Window by Dragging   (WIN 27)
10. Expand an Area   (WIN 29)
11. Scroll Using Scroll Arrows   (WIN 30)
12. Size a Window by Dragging   (WIN 32)
13. Collapse an Area   (WIN 33)
14. Resize a Window   (WIN 34)
15. Delete a Desktop Icon by Right-Dragging (WIN 35)
16. Launch a Program Using the Start Menu (WIN 38)
17. Launch Windows Explorer and Maximize Its Window   (WIN 40)
18. Expand a Folder   (WIN 42)
19. Expand a Drive   (WIN 44)
20. Display the Contents of a Folder   (WIN 45, WIN 53)
21. Display the Contents of an Expanded Drive (WIN 46)
22. Launch an Application Program from Explorer (WIN 47)
23. Quit an Application Program   (WIN 48)
24. Close Expanded Folders   (WIN 49)
25. Copy a File in Windows Explorer by Right-Dragging   (WIN 51)
26. Display the Contents of a Folder (WIN 53)
27. Rename a File   (WIN 54)
28. Delete a File by Right-Dragging to the Recycle Bin   (WIN 55)
29. Remove the Status Bar   (WIN 56)
30. Quit Windows Explorer   (WIN 57)
31. Launch Help and Support   (WIN 57)
32. Browse for Help Topics in the Table of Contents (WIN 59)
33. Search for Help Topics Using the Index (WIN 62)
34. Close the Help and Support Center   (WIN 63)
35. Log Off from the Computer   (WIN 64)
36. Turn Off the Computer   (WIN 66)

Learn It Online

Instructions: To complete the Learn It Online exercises, start your browser, click the Address bar, and then enter the Web address scsite.com/winoff2003/learn. When the Window XP Learn It Online page is displayed, follow the instructions in the exercises below. Each exercise has instructions for printing your results, either for your own records or for submission to your instructor.

1 Project Reinforcement TF, MC, and SA

Below Windows XP Project 1, click the Project Reinforcement link. Print the quiz by clicking Print on the File menu for each page. Answer each question.

2 Flash Cards

Below Windows XP Project 1, click the Flash Cards link and read the instructions. Type 20 (or a number specified by your instructor) in the Number of playing cards text box, type your name in the Enter your Name text box, and then click the Flip Card button. When the flash card is displayed, read the question and then click the ANSWER box arrow to select an answer. Flip through Flash Cards. If your score is 15 (75%) correct or greater, click Print on the File menu to print your results. If your score is less than 15 (75%) correct, then redo this exercise by clicking the Replay button.

3 Practice Test

Below Windows XP Project 1, click the Practice Test link. Answer each question, enter your first and last name at the bottom of the page, and then click the Grade Test button. When the graded practice test is displayed on your screen, click Print on the File menu to print a hard copy. Continue to take practice tests until you score 80% or better.

4 Who Wants To Be a Computer Genius?

Below Windows XP Project 1, click the Computer Genius link. Read the instructions, enter your first and last name at the bottom of the page, and then click the PLAY button. When your score is displayed, click the PRINT RESULTS link to print a hard copy.

5 Wheel of Terms

Below Windows XP Project 1, click the Wheel of Terms link. Read the instructions, and then enter your first and last name and your school name. Click the PLAY button. When your score is displayed, right-click the score and then click Print on the shortcut menu to print a hard copy.

6 Crossword Puzzle Challenge

Below Windows XP Project 1, click the Crossword Puzzle Challenge link. Read the instructions, and then enter your first and last name. Click the SUBMIT button. Work the crossword puzzle. When you are finished, click the Submit button. When the crossword puzzle is redisplayed, click the Print Puzzle button to print a hard copy.

7 Tips and Tricks

Below Windows XP Project 1, click the Tips and Tricks link. Click a topic that pertains to Project 1. Right-click the information and then click Print on the shortcut menu. Construct a brief example of what the information relates to in Windows XP to confirm you understand how to use the tip or trick.

8 Newsgroups

Below Windows XP Project 1, click the Newsgroups link. Click a topic that pertains to Project 1. Print three comments.

9 Expanding Your Horizons

Below Windows XP Project 1, click the Expanding Your Horizons link. Click a topic that pertains to Project 1. Print the information. Construct a brief example of what the information relates to in Windows XP to confirm you understand the contents of the article.

10 Search Sleuth

Below Windows XP Project 1, click the Search Sleuth link. To search for a term that pertains to this project, select a term below the Project 1 title and then use the Google search engine at google.com (or any major search engine) to display and print two Web pages that present information on the term.

11 Windows XP Online Training

Below Windows XP Project 1, click the Windows XP Online Training link. When your browser displays the Microsoft Office Online Web page, click the Windows XP link. Click one of the Windows XP courses that covers one or more of the objectives listed at the beginning of the project on page WIN 4. Print the first page of the course before stepping through it.

12 Office Marketplace

Below Windows XP Project 1, click the Office Marketplace link. When your browser displays the Microsoft Office Online Web page, click the Office Marketplace link. Click a topic that relates to one of the Office 2003 applications. Print the first page.

In the Lab

1 Taking the Windows XP Tour

Instructions: Use a computer to perform the following tasks.

Part 1: *Launching the Windows XP Tour*

1. If necessary, start Microsoft Windows XP and log on to the computer.
2. Click the Start button and then click Help and Support on the Start menu.
3. Click the Maximize button on the Help and Support Center title bar.
4. Click What's new in Windows XP in the navigation pane.
5. Click Taking a tour or tutorial in the navigation pane. The Taking a tour or tutorial page appears in the topic pane.
6. Click Take the Windows XP tour in the topic pane. The Windows XP Tour dialog box appears.
7. If your computer does not have speakers or earphones, proceed to step 8 below. If your computer has speakers or earphones, follow the steps in Part 2.
8. If your computer does not have speakers or earphones, follow the steps in Part 3.

Part 2: *Taking the Windows XP Tour with Sound and Animation*

1. Verify the Play the animated tour that features text, animation, music, and voice narration button is selected in the Windows XP Tour dialog box and then click the Next button.
2. Listen to the voice narration of the introduction to the Windows XP tour.
3. Click the gray Windows XP Basics button and answer the following questions.
   a. What is the narrow band at the bottom of the desktop called? _____
   b. What identifies a shortcut icon? _____
   c. What icons appear on the desktop the first time you launch Windows? _____
   d. What is contained in the notification area? _____
   e. How does Windows keep the taskbar tidy? _____
   f. What does a right-facing arrow on a Start menu command signify? _____
   _____
   g. In which folders are text, image, and music files placed? _____
   _____
   h. What does the Restore Down button do? _____
   i. What appears when a program needs some information from you before it can complete a command?
   _____
   j. What do you use to set up user accounts? _____
   k. Where do you go when you want to interrupt your Windows session and let someone else use the computer? _____
4. Click the Skip Intro button in the lower corner of the desktop to skip the introduction to the Windows XP tour.
5. Click the yellow Best for Business button and listen to the narration.
6. Click the red Safe and Easy Personal Computing button and listen to the narration.
7. Click the green Unlock the World of Digital Media button and listen to the narration.
8. Click the blue The Connected Home and Office button and listen to the narration.

In the Lab

9. Click the red Exit Tour button on the desktop to exit the Windows XP tour.
10. Click the Close button in the Help and Support center window.
11. You have completed this lab assignment.

Part 3: *Taking the Windows XP Tour without Sound or Animation*

1. Click the Play the non-animated tour that features text and images only button in the Windows XP Tour dialog box and then click the Next button.
2. Click the Start Here button to read about the basics of the Windows XP operating system.
3. Scroll the Windows XP Basics window and read the paragraph below the Windows Desktop heading. Click the Next button to display the next topic.
4. Scroll the Windows XP Basics window and read the paragraph below the Icons heading. Answer the following questions.
   a. What icon displays on the desktop the first time you launch Windows? _____
   b. Does deleting a shortcut icon affect the actual program or file? _____
5. Click the Next button to display the next topic. Scroll the Windows XP Basics window and read the paragraphs below the Taskbar heading. Answer the following question.
   a. Where is the notification area located? _____
6. Click the Next button to display the next topic. Scroll the Windows XP Basics window and read the paragraph below the Start Menu heading. Answer the following question.
   a. What does a right-facing arrow mean? _____
7. Click the Next button to display the next topic. Scroll the Windows XP Basics window and read the paragraph below the Files and Folder heading. Answer the following question.
   a. In which folders are text, image, and music files placed?

   _____
8. Click the Next button to display the next topic. Scroll the Windows XP Basics window and read the paragraphs below the Windows heading. Answer the following question.
   a. What appears if a program needs some information from you before it can complete a command?

   _____
9. Click the Next button to display the next topic. Scroll the Windows XP Basics window and read the paragraphs below the Control Panel heading. Answer the following questions.
   a. What Windows feature do you use to customize computer settings? _____
   b. Where is this feature located? _____
10. Click the Next button to display the next topic. Scroll the Windows XP Basics window and read the paragraphs below the Ending Your Session heading. Answer the following question.
    a. What do you do when you want to interrupt your Windows session and let someone else use the computer? _____
11. Click the Next button repeatedly to display the topics in the remaining four sections of the Windows XP tour.
12. Click the Close button in the window to end the tour.
13. Click the Close button in the Help and Support Center window.
14. You have completed this lab assignment.

In the Lab

2 Windows Explorer

Instructions: Use a computer to perform the following tasks.

1. Start Microsoft Windows XP and connect to the Internet.
2. Right-click the Start button on the Windows taskbar, click Explore on the shortcut menu, and then maximize the Start Menu window.
3. If necessary, scroll to the left in the Folders pane so the Start Menu and Programs icons are visible.
4. Click the Programs icon in the Start Menu folder.
5. Double-click the Internet Explorer Shortcut icon in the Contents pane to launch the Internet Explorer application. What is the URL of the Web page that appears in the Address bar in the Microsoft Internet Explorer window? _____
6. Click the URL in the Address bar in the Internet Explorer window to select it. Type scsite.com and then press the ENTER key.
7. Scroll the Web page to display the Browse by Subject area containing the subject categories. Clicking a subject category displays the book titles in that category.
8. Click Operating Systems in the Browse by Subject area.
9. Click the Microsoft Windows XP Comprehensive Concepts and Techniques link.
10. Right-click the Microsoft Windows XP textbook cover image on the Web page, click Save Picture As on the shortcut menu, type Windows XP Cover in the File name box, and then click the Save button in the Save Picture dialog box to save the image in the My Pictures folder.
11. Click the Close button in the Microsoft Internet Explorer window.
12. If necessary, scroll to the top of the Folders pane to make the drive C icon visible.
13. Click the minus sign in the box to the left of the drive C icon. The 3½ Floppy (A:) and My Documents icons should be visible in the Folders pane.
14. Click the plus sign in the box to the left of the My Documents icon.
15. Click the My Pictures folder name in the Folders pane.
16. Right-click the Windows XP Cover icon and then click Properties on the shortcut menu.
    a. What type of file is the Windows XP Cover file? _____
    b. When was the file last modified? _____
    c. With what application does this file open? _____
17. Click the Cancel button in the Windows XP Cover Properties dialog box.
18. Insert a formatted floppy disk in drive A of your computer.
19. Right-drag the Windows XP Cover icon to the 3½ Floppy (A:) icon in the Folders pane. Click Move Here on the shortcut menu. Click the 3½ Floppy (A:) icon in the Folders pane.
    a. Is the Windows XP Cover file stored on drive A? _____
20. Click the Close button in the 3½ Floppy (A:) window.

3 Using the Help and Support Center

Instructions: Use Windows Help and Support to perform the following tasks.

Part 1: Using the Question Mark Button

1. If necessary, launch Microsoft Windows XP and then log on to the computer.
2. Right-click an open area of the desktop to display a shortcut menu.
3. Click Properties on the shortcut menu to display the Display Properties dialog box.
4. Click the Desktop tab in the Display Properties dialog box.
5. Click the Help button on the title bar. The mouse pointer changes to a block arrow with a question mark.
6. Click the list box in the Desktop sheet. A pop-up window displays explaining the list box. Read the information in the pop-up window and then summarize the function of the list box.

_____

7. Click an open area of the Desktop sheet to remove the pop-up window.
8. Click the Help button on the title bar and then click the Customize Desktop button. A pop-up window displays explaining what happens when you click this button. Read the information in the pop-up window and then summarize the function of the button.

_____

9. Click an open area in the Desktop sheet to remove the pop-up window.
10. Click the Help button on the title bar and then click the monitor icon in the Desktop sheet. A pop-up window displays explaining the function of the monitor. Read the information in the pop-up window and then summarize the function of the monitor.

_____

11. Click an open area in the Desktop sheet to remove the pop-up window.
12. Click the Help button on the title bar and then click the Cancel button. A pop-up window displays explaining what happens when you click the button. Read the information in the pop-up window and then summarize the function of the Cancel button.

_____

13. Click an open area in the Desktop sheet to remove the pop-up window.
14. Click the Cancel button in the Display Properties dialog box.

Part 2: Finding What's New in Windows XP

1. Click the Start button and then click Help and Support on the Start menu.
2. Click the Maximize button on the Help and Support Center title bar.
3. Click What's new in Windows XP in the navigation pane.
4. Click What's new topics in the navigation pane. Ten topics display in the topic pane.
5. Click What's new on your desktop in the topic pane.
6. Click Start menu (or the plus sign in the small box preceding Start menu) to expand the entry. Read the information about the Start menu.
7. Click the Using the Start menu link.
8. Click the Print button on the Help and Support toolbar to print the topic. Click the Print button in the Print dialog box.

(continued)

In the Lab

Using Help and Support Center *(continued)*

9. Scroll the topic pane to display the Related Topics link. Click the Related Topics link to display a pop-up window containing three related topics. List the three topics.

_____

_____

10. Click Display a program at the top of the Start menu in the pop-up window.
11. Click the Print button on the Help and Support toolbar to print the topic. Click the Print button in the Print dialog box.

Part 3: *Viewing Windows XP Articles*

1. Click Windows XP articles: Walk through ways to use your PC in the What's new in Windows XP area in the navigation pane. A list of overviews, articles, and tutorials displays in the topic pane.
2. Click Walkthrough: Making music in the topic pane. Read the Making music article in the topic pane. List four ways in which you can use Windows XP musically.

_____

_____

3. Click Play music in the Making Music area. Scroll to display the Display details about a CD area. List the three steps to display details about a CD.

_____

_____

4. Scroll to the top of the window to display the Making Music area.
5. Click Create CDs in the Making Music area. Scroll to display the steps to burn your own CD. List the six steps to burn a CD.

_____

_____

_____

_____

_____

_____

6. Read other articles of interest to you in the Making music area.
7. Click the Close button in the Help and Support Center window.

MICROSOFT OFFICE WORD

MICROSOFT
Office Word 2003

Creating and Editing a Word Document

PROJECT

1

CASE PERSPECTIVE

Racing fans everywhere proclaim the Formula One Grand Prix as the most exhilarating racing competition in the world. Formula One Grand Prix events typically run for three days in a variety of countries including Brazil, Canada, England, Germany, Italy, Spain, and the United States. On the first day of each event, drivers practice on the tracks. Qualifying sessions begin on the second day. The fastest 26 drivers participate in a drivers' parade and then compete in the Formula One Grand Prix race on Sunday. During the race of nearly 200 miles, Formula One cars reach speeds that exceed 220 miles per hour.

When the Formula One Grand Prix season approaches, travel agents begin taking reservations for race packages. Jill Hall is a senior travel agent at Beacon Travel, where you are employed as a summer intern. Jill knows you have learned the guidelines for designing announcements in your marketing classes and has asked you to prepare a one-page flier announcing Beacon's Grand Prix race packages. You decide to use thick, bold characters to emphasize the headline and title. To attract attention to the announcement, you plan to include a large graphic of a Formula One race car. When you show the finished document to Jill, she is quite impressed. After Jill approves the completed flier, she wants you to distribute it to businesses for display on bulletin boards and in window fronts.

As you read through this project, you will learn how to use Word to create, save, and print a document that includes a graphical image.

Creating and Editing a Word Document

Objectives

You will have mastered the material in this project when you can:

- Start and quit Word
- Describe the Word window
- Enter text in a document
- Check spelling as you type
- Save a document
- Format text and paragraphs

- Undo and redo commands or actions
- Insert clip art in a document
- Print a document
- Open a document
- Correct errors in a document
- Use Word's Help to answer questions

What Is Microsoft Office Word 2003?

Microsoft Office Word 2003 is a full-featured word processing program that allows you to create professional looking documents and revise them easily. With Word, you can develop announcements, letters, memos, resumes, reports, fax cover sheets, mailing labels, newsletters, and many other types of documents. Word also provides tools that enable you to create Web pages with ease. From within Word, you can place these Web pages directly on a Web server.

Word has many features designed to simplify the production of documents and make documents look visually appealing. Using Word, you easily can change the shape, size, and color of text. You also can include borders, shading, tables, images, pictures, and Web addresses in documents. With proper hardware, you can dictate or handwrite text instead of typing it in Word. You also can speak instructions to Word.

While you are typing, Word performs many tasks automatically. For example, Word detects and corrects spelling and grammar errors in several languages. Word's thesaurus allows you to add variety and precision to your writing. Word also can format text such as headings, lists, fractions, borders, and Web addresses as you type them. Within Word, you can e-mail a copy of a Word document to an e-mail address.

This latest version of Word has many new features to make you more productive. It supports XML documents, improves readability of documents, supports ink input from devices such as the Tablet PC, provides more control for protecting documents, allows two documents to be compared side by side, and includes the capability to search a variety of reference information.

Project One — Grand Prix Announcement

To illustrate the features of Word, this book presents a series of projects that use Word to create documents similar to those you will encounter in academic and business environments. Project 1 uses Word to produce the announcement shown in Figure 1-1.

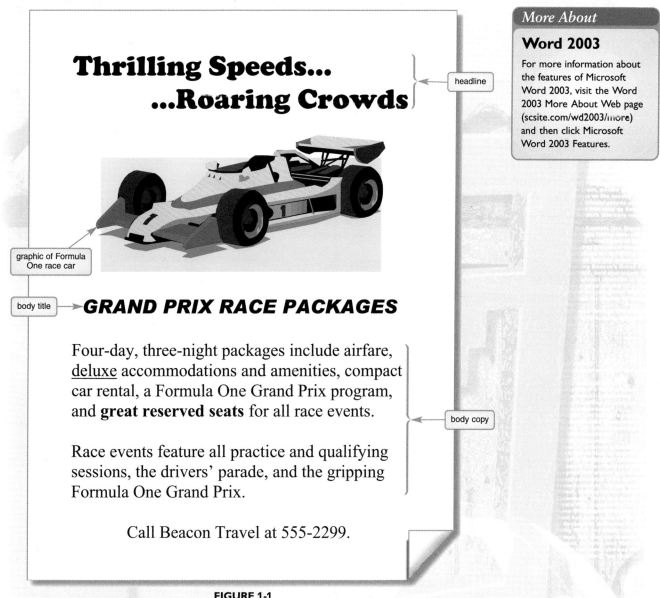

FIGURE 1-1

The announcement informs potential customers about Grand Prix race packages available through Beacon Travel. The announcement begins with a headline in large, thick characters. Below the headline is a graphic of a Formula One race car, followed by the body title, GRAND PRIX RACE PACKAGES. The paragraphs of body copy below the body title briefly discuss the items included in the race packages. Finally, the last line of the announcement lists the telephone number of Beacon Travel.

Starting and Customizing Word

If you are stepping through this project on a computer and you want your screen to match the figures in this book, then you should change your computer's resolution to 800 × 600. For more information about how to change the resolution on your computer, read Appendix D.

To start Word, Windows must be running. The following steps show how to start Word. You may need to ask your instructor how to start Word for your system.

To Start Word

1

• **Click the Start button on the Windows taskbar, point to All Programs on the Start menu, point to Microsoft Office on the All Programs submenu, and then point to Microsoft Office Word 2003 on the Microsoft Office submenu.**

Windows displays the commands on the Start menu above the Start button and then displays the All Programs and Microsoft Office submenus (Figure 1-2).

FIGURE 1-2

2

• **Click Microsoft Office Word 2003.**

Word starts. After a few moments, Word displays a new blank document titled Document1 in the Word window (Figure 1-3). The Windows taskbar displays the Word program button, indicating Word is running.

3

• **If the Word window is not maximized, double-click its title bar to maximize it.**

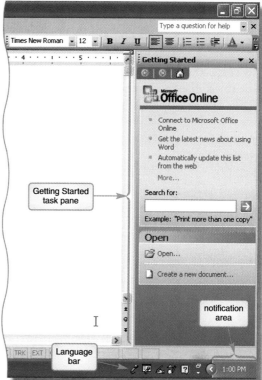

FIGURE 1-3

The screen in Figure 1-3 shows how the Word window looks the first time you start Word after installation on most computers. If the Office Speech Recognition software is installed and active on your computer, then when you start Word the Language bar is displayed on the screen. The **Language bar** contains buttons that allow you to speak commands and dictate text. It usually is located on the right side of the Windows taskbar next to the notification area, and it changes to include the speech recognition functions available in Word. In this book, the Language bar is closed because it takes up computer resources and with the Language bar active, the microphone can be turned on accidentally by clicking the Microphone button, causing your computer to act in an unstable manner. For additional information about the Language bar, see page WD 16 and Appendix B.

As shown in Figure 1-3, Word may display a task pane on the right side of the screen. A **task pane** is a separate window that enables users to carry out some Word tasks more efficiently. When you start Word, it automatically may display the Getting Started task pane, which is a task pane that allows you to search for Office-related topics on the Microsoft Web site, open files, or create new documents. In this book, the Getting Started task pane is closed to allow the maximum typing area in Word.

After installation, Word displays the toolbar buttons on a single row. A **toolbar** contains buttons and boxes that allow you to perform frequent tasks quickly. For more efficient use of the buttons, the toolbars should be displayed on two separate rows instead of sharing a single row.

The steps on the next page show how to customize the Word window by closing the Language bar, closing the Getting Started task pane, and displaying the toolbar buttons on two separate rows.

Other Ways

1. Double-click Word icon on desktop
2. Click Microsoft Office Word 2003 on Start menu
3. Click Start button, point to All Programs on Start menu, click New Office Document, click General tab, double-click Blank Document icon

More About

Task Panes

When you first start Word, a small window called a task pane may be displayed docked on the right side of the screen. You can drag a task pane title bar to float the pane in your work area or dock it on either the left or right side of a screen, depending on your personal preference.

To Customize the Word Window

1

• **To close the Language bar, right-click it to display a shortcut menu with a list of commands.**

The Language bar shortcut menu appears (Figure 1-4).

FIGURE 1-4

2

• **Click Close the Language bar on the shortcut menu.**

• **If the Getting Started task pane is displayed, click the Close button in the upper-right corner of the task pane.**

The Language bar disappears. Word removes the Getting Started task pane from the screen (Figure 1-5).

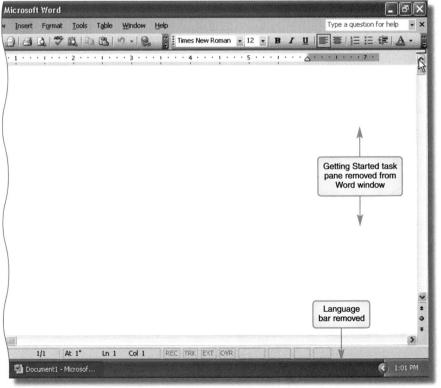

FIGURE 1-5

3

• **If the toolbar buttons are displayed on one row, click the Toolbar Options button.**

Word displays the Toolbar Options list, which shows the buttons that do not fit on the toolbars when they are displayed on one row (Figure 1-6).

FIGURE 1-6

4

• **Click Show Buttons on Two Rows in the Toolbar Options list.**

• **If your screen differs from Figure 1-7, click the Normal View button on the horizontal scroll bar.**

Word displays the toolbars on two separate rows (Figure 1-7). The Toolbar Options list now is empty because all of the buttons fit on the toolbars when they display on two rows.

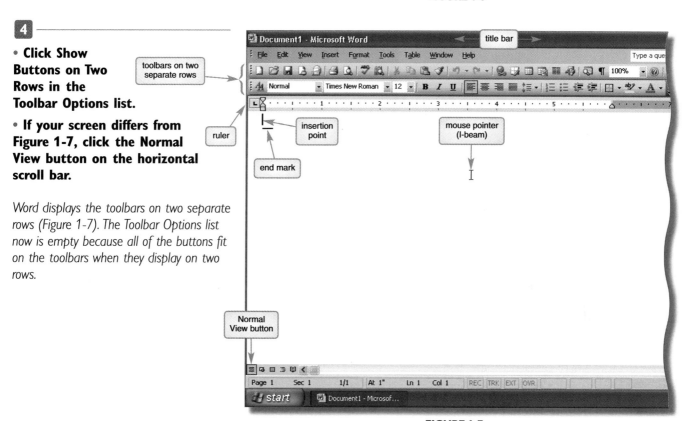

FIGURE 1-7

As an alternative to Steps 3 and 4 above, you can point to the beginning of the second toolbar (Figure 1-6), and when the mouse pointer changes to a four-headed arrow, drag the toolbar down to create two rows of toolbars.

Each time you start Word, the Word window appears the same way it did the last time you used Word. If the toolbar buttons are displayed on one row, then they will be displayed on one row the next time you start Word.

As you work through creating a document, you will find that certain Word operations automatically display a task pane. In addition to the Getting Started task pane shown in Figure 1-4, Word provides 13 other task panes. Some of the more important ones are the Help, Clip Art, Clipboard, and Research task panes. These task panes are discussed as they are used throughout the book.

At any point while working with Word, you can open or close a task pane by clicking View on the menu bar and then clicking Task Pane. To display a different task pane, click the Other Task Panes button to the left of the Close button on the task pane title bar (Figure 1-4 on page WD 8) and then click the desired task pane in the list. The Back and Forward buttons below the task pane title bar allow you to switch among task panes you have opened during a Word session. The Home button causes Word to display the Getting Started task pane.

The Word Window

The Word window consists of a variety of components to make your work more efficient and documents more professional. The following sections discuss these components, which are identified in either Figure 1-7 on the previous page or Figure 1-8.

Document Window

The **document window** displays text, tables, graphics, and other items as you type or insert them in a document. Only a portion of a document, however, appears on the screen at one time. You view the portion of the document displayed on the screen through a document window (Figure 1-8).

FIGURE 1-8

A document window contains several elements commonly found in other application software, as well as some elements unique to Word. The main elements of the Word document window are the insertion point, end mark, mouse pointer, rulers, scroll bars, and status bar.

INSERTION POINT   The **insertion point** (Figure 1-7 on page WD 9) is a blinking vertical bar that indicates where text will be inserted as you type. As you type, the insertion point moves to the right and, when you reach the end of a line, it moves downward to the beginning of the next line. You also insert graphics, tables, and other items at the location of the insertion point.

END MARK   The **end mark** (Figure 1-7) is a short horizontal line that indicates the end of the document. Each time you begin a new line, the end mark moves downward.

MOUSE POINTER   The **mouse pointer** becomes different shapes depending on the task you are performing in Word and the pointer's location on the screen (Figure 1-7). The mouse pointer in Figure 1-7 has the shape of an I-beam. Other mouse pointer shapes are described as they appear on the screen during this and subsequent projects.

RULERS   At the top edge of the document window is the horizontal ruler (Figure 1-8). You use the **horizontal ruler**, usually simply called the **ruler**, to set tab stops, indent paragraphs, adjust column widths, and change page margins.

An additional ruler, called the **vertical ruler**, sometimes is displayed at the left edge of the Word window when you perform certain tasks. The purpose of the vertical ruler is discussed in a later project. If your screen displays a vertical ruler, click View on the menu bar and then click Normal.

SCROLL BARS   By using the **scroll bars**, you display different portions of your document in the document window (Figure 1-8). At the right edge of the document window is a vertical scroll bar. At the bottom of the document window is a horizontal scroll bar. On both the vertical and horizontal scroll bars, the position of the **scroll box** reflects the location of the portion of the document that is displayed in the document window.

On the left edge of the horizontal scroll bar are five buttons that change the view of a document. On the bottom of the vertical scroll bar are three buttons you can use to scroll through a document. These buttons are discussed as they are used in later projects.

STATUS BAR   The **status bar** displays at the bottom of the document window, above the Windows taskbar (Figure 1-8). The status bar presents information about the location of the insertion point and the progress of current tasks, as well as the status of certain commands, keys, and buttons.

From left to right, Word displays the following information on the status bar in Figure 1-8: the page number, the section number, the page containing the insertion point followed by the total number of pages in the document, the position of the insertion point in inches from the top of the page, the line number and column number of the insertion point, and then several status indicators.

You use the **status indicators** to turn certain keys or modes on or off. Word displays the first four status indicators (REC, TRK, EXT, and OVR) darkened when they are on and dimmed when they are off. For example, the dimmed OVR indicates overtype mode is off. To turn these four status indicators on or off, double-click the status indicator on the status bar. Each of these status indicators is discussed as it is used in the projects.

The remaining status indicators display icons as you perform certain tasks. For example, when you begin typing in the document window, Word displays a Spelling and Grammar Status icon. When Word is saving your document, it displays a Background Save icon. When you print a document, Word displays a Background Print icon. If you perform a task that requires several seconds (such as saving a document), the status bar usually displays a message informing you of the progress of the task.

Menu Bar and Toolbars

The menu bar and toolbars display at the top of the screen just below the title bar (Figure 1-9).

FIGURE 1-9

MENU BAR The **menu bar** is a special toolbar that displays the Word menu names. Each menu name represents a menu. A **menu** contains a list of commands you use to perform tasks such as retrieving, storing, printing, and formatting data in a document.

When you point to a menu name on the menu bar, the area of the menu bar containing the name is displayed as a selected button. Word shades selected buttons in light orange and surrounds them with a blue outline.

To display a menu, click the menu name on the menu bar. For example, to display the Edit menu, click the Edit menu name on the menu bar. When you click a menu name on the menu bar, Word initially displays a **short menu** listing your most recently used commands (Figure 1-10a). If you wait a few seconds or click the arrows at the bottom of the short menu, it expands into a full menu. A **full menu** lists all the commands associated with a menu (Figure 1-10b). You also can display a full menu immediately by double-clicking the menu name on the menu bar.

FIGURE 1-10

(a) Short Menu   **(b) Full Menu**

In this book, when you display a menu, use one of the following techniques to ensure that Word always displays a full menu:

1. Click the menu name on the menu bar and then wait a few seconds.
2. Click the menu name on the menu bar and then click the arrows at the bottom of the short menu.
3. Click the menu name on the menu bar and then point to the arrows at the bottom of the short menu.
4. Double-click the menu name on the menu bar.

Both short and full menus may display some dimmed commands. A **dimmed command** appears gray, or dimmed, instead of black, which indicates it is not available for the current selection. A command with medium blue shading in the rectangle to its left on a full menu is called a **hidden command** because it does not appear on a short menu. As you use Word, it automatically personalizes the short menus for you based on how often you use commands. That is, as you use hidden commands on the full menu, Word *unhides* them and places them on the short menu.

Some commands have an arrow at the right edge of the menu. If you point to this arrow, Word displays a **submenu**, which is a list of additional commands associated with the selected command.

TOOLBARS   Word has many predefined, or built-in, toolbars. A toolbar contains buttons, boxes, and menus that allow you to perform tasks more quickly than using the menu bar. For example, to print a document, you can click the Print button on a toolbar instead of navigating through the File menu to reach the Print command.

Each button on a toolbar displays an image to help you remember its function. Also, when you position the mouse pointer on, or point to, a button or box, Word displays the name of the button or box in a ScreenTip. A **ScreenTip** is a short on-screen note associated with the object to which you are pointing.

Two built-in toolbars are the Standard toolbar and the Formatting toolbar. Figure 1-11a shows the **Standard toolbar** and identifies its buttons and boxes. Figure 1-11b shows the **Formatting toolbar**. Each of these buttons and boxes will be explained in detail when it is used in this book.

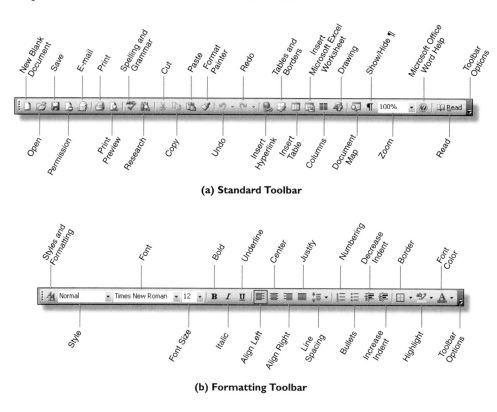

(a) Standard Toolbar

(b) Formatting Toolbar

FIGURE 1-11

When you first install Word, the buttons on both the Standard and Formatting toolbars are preset to display on the same row immediately below the menu bar (Figure 1-12a). Unless the resolution of your display device is greater than 800 × 600, many of the buttons that belong to these toolbars are hidden when the two toolbars share one row. The buttons that display on the toolbar are the more frequently used buttons. Hidden buttons display in the Toolbar Options list (Figure 1-12b). You can display all the buttons on either toolbar by double-clicking the **move handle**, which is the vertical dotted line on the left edge of the toolbar.

As an alternative, you can instruct Word to display the buttons on the Standard and Formatting toolbars on separate rows, one below the other, by clicking the Show Buttons on Two Rows command in the Toolbar Options list (Figure 1-12b). In this book, the Standard and Formatting toolbars are shown on separate rows so that all buttons are displayed on a screen with the resolution set to 800 × 600 (Figure 1-12c).

In the previous figures, the Standard and Formatting toolbars are docked. A **docked toolbar** is a toolbar that is attached to an edge of the Word window. Depending on the task you are performing, Word may display additional toolbars on the screen. These additional toolbars either are docked or floating in the Word window. A **floating toolbar** is not attached to an edge of the Word window; that is, it appears in the middle of the Word window. You can rearrange the order of docked toolbars and can move floating toolbars anywhere in the Word window. Later in this book, steps are presented that show you how to float a docked toolbar or dock a floating toolbar.

(a) Standard and Formatting Toolbars on One Row

(b) Toolbar Options List

(c) Standard and Formatting Toolbars on Two Rows

FIGURE 1-12

Resetting Menus and Toolbars

Each project in this book begins with the menus and toolbars appearing as they did at the initial installation of the software. If you are stepping through this project on a computer and you want your menus and toolbars to match the figures in this book, then you should reset your menus and toolbars. For more information about how to reset menus and toolbars, read Appendix D.

More About

Speech Recognition

If Office Speech Recognition software is installed on your computer, you can speak instructions to Word including toolbar button names, menu names and commands, and items in dialog boxes and task panes. You also can dictate so Word writes exactly what you say. The microphone picks up others' voices and background sounds, so speech recognition is most effective when used in a quiet environment.

Speech Recognition

With the **Office Speech Recognition software** installed and a microphone, you can speak the names of toolbar buttons, menus, menu commands, list items, alerts, and dialog box controls, such as OK and Cancel. You also can dictate text, such as words and sentences. To indicate whether you want to speak commands or dictate text, you use the Language bar. The Language bar can be in one of four states: (1) **restored**, which means it is displayed somewhere in the Word window (Figure 1-13a); (2) **minimized**, which means it is displayed on the Windows taskbar (Figure 1-13b); (3) **hidden**, which means you do not see it on the screen but it will be displayed the next time you start your computer; or (4) **closed**, which means it is hidden permanently until you enable it. If the Language bar is hidden and you want it to be displayed, then do the following:

1. Right-click an open area on the Windows taskbar at the bottom of the screen.
2. Point to Toolbars and then click Language bar on the Toolbars submenu.

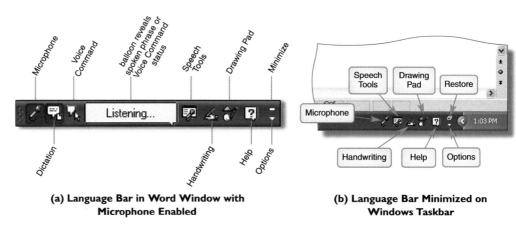

(a) Language Bar in Word Window with Microphone Enabled

(b) Language Bar Minimized on Windows Taskbar

FIGURE 1-13

If the Language bar command is dimmed on the Toolbars submenu or if the Speech command is dimmed on the Tools menu, the Office Speech Recognition software is not installed.

In this book, the Language bar does not appear in the figures. If you want to close the Language bar so that your screen is identical to what you see in the book, right-click the Language bar and then click Close the Language bar on the shortcut menu. Additional information about the speech recognition capabilities of Word is available in Appendix B.

Q: What font size should I use in an announcement?

A: An announcement usually is posted on a bulletin board. Thus, its font size should be as large as possible so that all potential readers easily can see the announcement.

Entering Text

Characters that display on the screen are a specific shape, size, and style. The **font**, or typeface, defines the appearance and shape of the letters, numbers, and special characters. The preset, or **default**, font is Times New Roman (Figure 1-14). **Font size** specifies the size of the characters and is determined by a measurement system called points. A single **point** is about 1/72 of one inch in height. Thus, a character with a font size of 12 is about 12/72 or 1/6 of one inch in height. On most computers, the default font size in Word is 12.

If more of the characters in your document require a larger font size than the default, you easily can change the font size before you type. In Project 1, many of the characters in the body copy of the announcement are a font size of 22. The following steps show how to increase the font size before you begin typing text.

To Increase the Font Size before Typing

1

• **Click the Font Size box arrow on the Formatting toolbar.**

Word displays a list of available font sizes in the Font Size list (Figure 1-14). The available font sizes depend on the current font, which is Times New Roman.

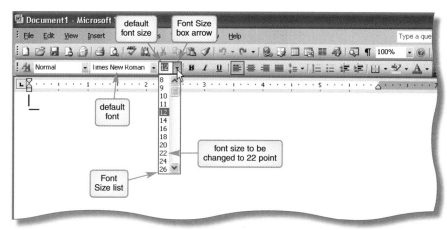

FIGURE 1-14

2

• **Click 22 in the Font Size list.**

The font size for characters to be entered in this document changes to 22 (Figure 1-15). The size of the insertion point increases to reflect the new font size.

FIGURE 1-15

The new font size takes effect immediately in the document. Word uses this font size for characters you enter in this announcement.

Typing Text

To enter text in a document, you type on the keyboard or speak into the microphone. The example on the next page illustrates the steps required to type both lines of the headline in the announcement. By default, Word positions these lines at the left margin. In a later section, this project will show how to make all of the characters in the headline larger and thicker, and how to position the second line of the headline at the right margin.

The steps on the next page show how to begin typing text in the announcement.

Other Ways

1. On Format menu click Font, click Font tab, select desired font size in Size list, click OK button
2. Right-click paragraph mark above end mark, click Font on shortcut menu, click Font tab, select desired font size in Size list, click OK button
3. Press CTRL+SHIFT+P, type desired font size, press ENTER
4. Press CTRL+SHIFT+> repeatedly
5. In Voice Command mode, say "Font Size, [select font size]"

To Type Text

1

• **Type** Thrilling Speeds **and then press the** PERIOD **(.) key three times. If you make an error while typing, press the** BACKSPACE **key until you have deleted the text in error and then retype the text correctly.**

As you type, the insertion point moves to the right (Figure 1-16).

FIGURE 1-16

2

• **Press the** ENTER **key.**

Word moves the insertion point to the beginning of the next line (Figure 1-17). Notice the status bar indicates the current position of the insertion point. That is, the insertion point currently is on line 2 column 1.

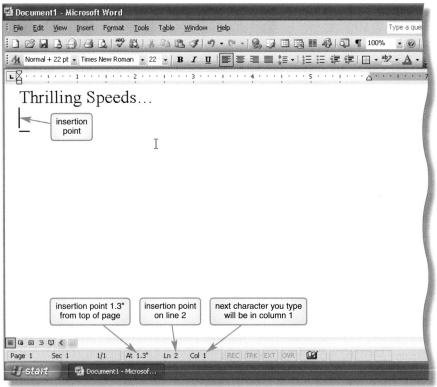

FIGURE 1-17

3

• **Press the PERIOD key three times.**

• **Type** Roaring Crowds **and then press the ENTER key.**

The headline is complete (Figure 1-18). The insertion point is on line 3.

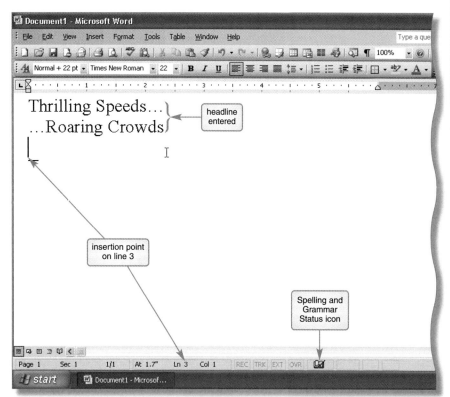

FIGURE 1-18

Other Ways

1. In Dictation mode, say "Thrilling Speeds, Period, Period, Period, New Line, Period, Period, Period, Roaring Crowds, New Line"

When you begin entering text in a document, the **Spelling and Grammar Status icon** appears at the right of the status bar (Figure 1-18). As you type, the Spelling and Grammar Status icon shows an animated pencil writing on paper, which indicates Word is checking for possible errors. When you stop typing, the pencil changes to either a red check mark or a red X. In Figure 1-18, the Spelling and Grammar Status icon contains a red check mark.

In general, if all of the words you have typed are in Word's dictionary and your grammar is correct, the Spelling and Grammar Status icon contains a red check mark. If you type a word not in the dictionary (because it is a proper name or misspelled), a red wavy underline appears below the word. If you type text that may be incorrect grammatically, a green wavy underline appears below the text. When Word flags a possible spelling or grammar error, it also changes the red check mark on the Spelling and Grammar Status icon to a red X. As you enter text in a document, your Spelling and Grammar Status icon may show a red X instead of a red check mark. Later, this project will show how to check the spelling of these flagged words. At that time, the red X returns to a red check mark.

More About

Entering Text

In the days of typewriters, the letter l was used for both the letter l and the numeral one. Keyboards, however, have both a numeral one and the letter l. Keyboards also have both a numeral zero and the letter o. Be careful to press the correct keyboard character when creating a word processing document.

Microsoft Office
Word 2003

Entering Blank Lines in a Document

To enter a blank line in a document, press the ENTER key without typing any text on the line. The following example shows how to enter three blank lines below the headline.

To Enter Blank Lines in a Document

• **Press the ENTER key three times.**

Word inserts three blank lines in the document below the headline (Figure 1-19).

FIGURE 1-19

Displaying Formatting Marks

To indicate where in a document you press the ENTER key or SPACEBAR, you may find it helpful to display formatting marks. A **formatting mark**, sometimes called a **nonprinting character**, is a character that Word displays on the screen but is not visible on a printed document. For example, the paragraph mark (¶) is a formatting mark that indicates where you pressed the ENTER key. A raised dot (•) shows where you pressed the SPACEBAR. Other formatting marks are discussed as they appear on the screen.

More About

Hidden Text

When you display formatting marks, Word also displays hidden text. Text formatted as hidden shows on the screen but does not print. Hidden text is useful if you want to write a note to yourself in a document. To format text as hidden, select the text, click Format on the menu bar, click Font, click the Font tab, place a check mark in the Hidden check box, and then click the OK button.

Depending on settings made during previous Word sessions, the Word screen already may display formatting marks (Figure 1-20). The following step shows how to display formatting marks, if they are not displayed already on the screen.

To Display Formatting Marks

1

• **If it is not selected already, click the Show/Hide ¶ button on the Standard toolbar.**

Word displays formatting marks on the screen (Figure 1-20). The Show/Hide ¶ button is selected. That is, the button is light orange and surrounded with a blue outline.

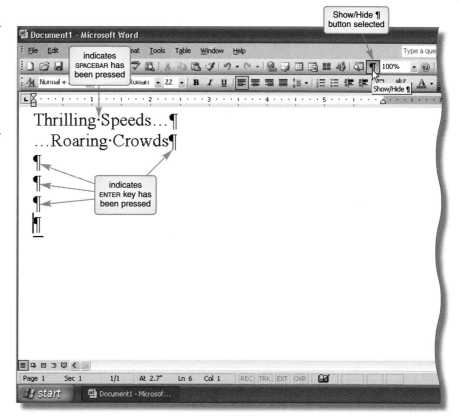

FIGURE 1-20

Notice several changes to the Word document window (Figure 1-20). A paragraph mark appears at the end of each line to indicate you pressed the ENTER key. Each time you press the ENTER key, Word creates a new paragraph. The size of paragraph marks is 22 point because the font size was changed earlier in the project. Between each word, a raised dot appears, indicating you pressed the SPACEBAR. Finally, the Show/Hide ¶ button changes from blue to light orange and has a blue outline, which indicates it is selected.

If you feel the formatting marks clutter the screen, you can hide them by clicking the Show/Hide ¶ button again. It is recommended that you display formatting marks; therefore, the document windows presented in this book show the formatting marks.

Microsoft Office
Word 2003

Entering More Text

Every character in the body title (GRAND PRIX RACE PACKAGES) of the announcement is in capital letters. The next step is to enter this body title in all capital letters in the document window, as explained below.

To Type More Text

1 **Press the CAPS LOCK key on the keyboard to turn on capital letters. Verify the caps lock indicator is lit on the keyboard.**

2 **Type** GRAND PRIX RACE PACKAGES **and then press the CAPS LOCK key to turn off capital letters.**

3 **Press the ENTER key twice.**

Word displays the body title on line 6 (Figure 1-21). Depending on your Word settings, your screen may not display the smart tag indicator below the word, RACE.

FIGURE 1-21

Using Wordwrap

Wordwrap allows you to type words in a paragraph continually without pressing the ENTER key at the end of each line. When the insertion point reaches the right margin, Word automatically positions the insertion point at the beginning of the next line. As you type, if a word extends beyond the right margin, Word also automatically positions that word on the next line with the insertion point.

As you type text in the document window, do not press the ENTER key when the insertion point reaches the right margin. Word creates a new paragraph each time you press the ENTER key. Thus, press the ENTER key only in these circumstances:

1. To insert blank lines in a document
2. To begin a new paragraph
3. To terminate a short line of text and advance to the next line
4. In response to certain Word commands

The following step illustrates wordwrap.

To Wordwrap Text as You Type

1

• **Type** Four-day, three-night packages include airfare, deluxe **and then press the** SPACEBAR.

The word, deluxe, wraps to the beginning of line 9 because it is too long to fit on line 8 (Figure 1-22). Your document may wordwrap differently depending on the type of printer you are using.

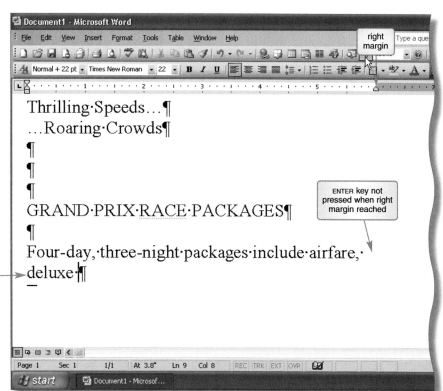

the word, deluxe, could not fit on line 8, so it wrapped to beginning of line 9

ENTER key not pressed when right margin reached

FIGURE 1-22

Entering Text that Scrolls the Document Window

As you type more lines of text than Word can display in the document window, Word **scrolls** the top portion of the document upward off the screen. Although you cannot see the text once it scrolls off the screen, it remains in the document. As previously discussed, the document window allows you to view only a portion of your document at one time (Figure 1-8 on page WD 10).

The following step shows how Word scrolls text through the document window.

To Enter Text that Scrolls the Document Window

1

• **Type** accommodations and amenities, compact car rental, a Formula One Grand Prix program, and great reserved seats for all race events.

• **Press the ENTER key twice.**

Word scrolls the headline off the top of the screen (Figure 1-23). Your screen may scroll differently depending on the type of monitor you are using.

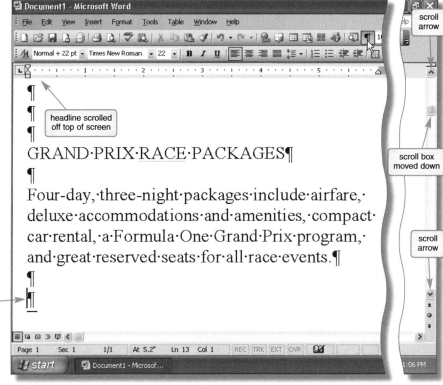

FIGURE 1-23

When Word scrolls text off the top of the screen, the scroll box on the vertical scroll bar at the right edge of the document window moves downward (Figure 1-23). The scroll box indicates the current relative location of the portion of the document that is displayed in the document window. You may use either the mouse or the keyboard to scroll to a different location in a document.

With the mouse, you can use the scroll arrows or the scroll box on the scroll bar to display a different portion of the document in the document window, and then click the mouse to move the insertion point to that location. Table 1-1 explains various techniques for using the scroll bar to scroll vertically with the mouse.

Table 1-1 Using the Scroll Bar to Scroll with the Mouse	
SCROLL DIRECTION	**MOUSE ACTION**
Up	Drag the scroll box upward.
Down	Drag the scroll box downward.
Up one screen	Click anywhere above the scroll box on the vertical scroll bar.
Down one screen	Click anywhere below the scroll box on the vertical scroll bar.
Up one line	Click the scroll arrow at the top of the vertical scroll bar.
Down one line	Click the scroll arrow at the bottom of the vertical scroll bar.

When you use the keyboard to scroll, the insertion point automatically moves when you press the appropriate keys. Table 1-2 outlines various techniques to scroll through a document using the keyboard.

Table 1-2 Scrolling with the Keyboard	
SCROLL DIRECTION	**KEY(S) TO PRESS**
Left one character	LEFT ARROW
Right one character	RIGHT ARROW
Left one word	CTRL+LEFT ARROW
Right one word	CTRL+RIGHT ARROW
Up one line	UP ARROW
Down one line	DOWN ARROW
To end of a line	END
To beginning of a line	HOME
Up one paragraph	CTRL+UP ARROW
Down one paragraph	CTRL+DOWN ARROW
Up one screen	PAGE UP
Down one screen	PAGE DOWN
To top of document window	ALT+CTRL+PAGE UP
To bottom of document window	ALT+CTRL+PAGE DOWN
To beginning of a document	CTRL+HOME
To end of a document	CTRL+END

Checking Spelling and Grammar as You Type

As you type text in the document window, Word checks your typing for possible spelling and grammar errors. If a word you type is not in the dictionary, a red wavy underline appears below the word. Similarly, if text you type contains a possible grammar error, a green wavy underline appears below the text. In both cases, the Spelling and Grammar Status icon on the status bar shows a red X, instead of a check mark. Although you can check the entire document for spelling and grammar errors at once, you also can check these flagged errors immediately.

To verify that the check spelling as you type feature is enabled, right-click the Spelling and Grammar Status icon on the status bar and then click Options on the shortcut menu. When Word displays the Spelling & Grammar dialog box, be sure Check spelling as you type has a check mark and Hide spelling errors in this document does not have a check mark.

When a word is flagged with a red wavy underline, it is not in Word's dictionary. To display a list of suggested corrections for a flagged word, you right-click the word. A flagged word, however, is not necessarily misspelled. For example, many names, abbreviations, and specialized terms are not in Word's main dictionary. In these cases, you tell Word to ignore the flagged word. As you type, Word also detects duplicate words. For example, if your document contains the phrase, to the the store, Word places a red wavy underline below the second occurrence of the word, the.

In the example on the next page, the word, feature, has been misspelled intentionally as feture to illustrate Word's check spelling as you type. If you are doing this project on a personal computer, your announcement may contain different misspelled words, depending on the accuracy of your typing.

To Check Spelling and Grammar as You Type

1

• **Type** Race events feture **and then press the SPACEBAR.**

• **Position the mouse pointer in the flagged word (feture, in this case).**

Word flags the misspelled word, feture, by placing a red wavy underline below it (Figure 1-24). The Spelling and Grammar Status icon on the status bar now contains a red X, indicating Word has detected a possible spelling or grammar error.

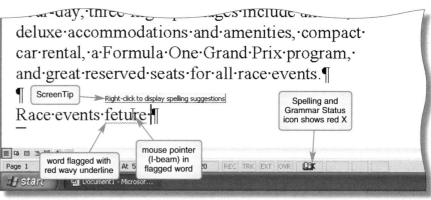

FIGURE 1-24

2

• **Right-click the flagged word, feture.**

Word displays a shortcut menu that lists suggested spelling corrections for the flagged word (Figure 1-25).

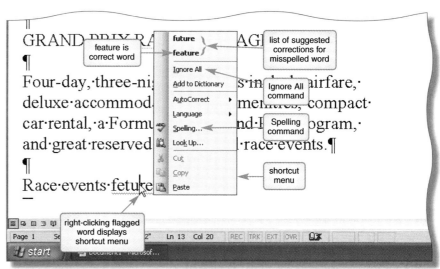

FIGURE 1-25

3

• **Click feature on the shortcut menu.**

Word replaces the misspelled word with the word selected on the shortcut menu (Figure 1-26). The Spelling and Grammar Status icon once again contains a red check mark.

GRAND·PRIX·RACE·PACKAGES¶

¶

Four-day,·three-night·packages·include·airfare,·
deluxe·accommodations·and·amenities,·compact·
car·rental,·a·Formula·One·Grand·Prix·program,·
and·great·reserved·seats·for·all·race·events.¶

¶

Race·events·feature·¶

Spelling and Grammar Status icon shows red check mark

flagged word replaced with selected word

Page 1   Ln 13 Col 20   REC TRK EXT OVR

FIGURE 1-26

Other Ways

1. Double-click Spelling and Grammar Status icon on status bar, click correct word on shortcut menu
2. In Voice Command mode, say "Spelling and Grammar"

If a flagged word actually is spelled correctly and, for example, is a proper name, you can right-click it and then click Ignore All on the shortcut menu (Figure 1-25). If, when you right-click the misspelled word, your desired correction is not in the list on the shortcut menu, you can click outside the shortcut menu to close the menu and then retype the correct word, or you can click Spelling on the shortcut menu to display the Spelling dialog box. Project 2 discusses the Spelling dialog box.

If you feel the wavy underlines clutter the document window, you can hide them temporarily until you are ready to check for spelling and grammar errors. To hide spelling errors, right-click the Spelling and Grammar Status icon on the status bar and then click Hide Spelling Errors on the shortcut menu. To hide grammar errors, right-click the Spelling and Grammar Status icon on the status bar and then click Hide Grammatical Errors on the shortcut menu.

The next step is to type the remainder of text in the announcement, as described in the following steps.

To Enter More Text

1 Press the END key to move the insertion point to the end of the line.

2 Type all practice and qualifying sessions, the drivers' parade, and the gripping Formula One Grand Prix.

3 Press the ENTER key twice.

4 Type Call Beacon Travel at 555-2299.

The text of the announcement is complete (Figure 1-27).

FIGURE 1-27

Saving a Document

As you create a document in Word, the computer stores it in memory. If the computer is turned off or if you lose electrical power, the document in memory is lost. Hence, if you plan to use the document later, you must save it on disk.

A saved document is called a **file**. A **file name** is the name assigned to a file when it is saved. This project saves the announcement with the file name, Grand Prix Announcement. Depending on your Windows settings, the file type .doc may display immediately after the file name. The file type **.doc** indicates the file is a Word document.

The following steps illustrate how to save a document on a floppy disk in drive A using the Save button on the Standard toolbar.

To Save a New Document

1

• **With a formatted floppy disk in drive A, click the Save button on the Standard toolbar.**

Word displays the Save As dialog box (Figure 1-28). The first line from the document (Thrilling Speeds) is selected in the File name text box as the default file name. You can change this selected file name by immediately typing the new name.

FIGURE 1-28

2

• **Type** Grand Prix Announcement **in the File name text box. Do not press the ENTER key after typing the file name.**

The file name, Grand Prix Announcement, replaces the text, Thrilling Speeds, in the File name text box (Figure 1-29).

FIGURE 1-29

3

• **Click the Save in box arrow.**

*Word displays a list of the available drives and folders in which you can save the document (Figure 1-30). A **folder** is a specific location on a disk. Your list may differ depending on your computer's configuration.*

FIGURE 1-30

4

• **Click 3½ Floppy (A:) in the Save in list.**

Drive A becomes the new save location (Figure 1-31). The Save As dialog box now shows names of existing files stored on the floppy disk in drive A. In Figure 1-31, the list is empty because no Word files currently are stored on the floppy disk in drive A.

FIGURE 1-31

5

• **Click the Save button in the Save As dialog box.**

Word saves the document on the floppy disk in drive A with the file name, Grand Prix Announcement (Figure 1-32). Although the announcement is saved on a floppy disk, it also remains in main memory and on the screen.

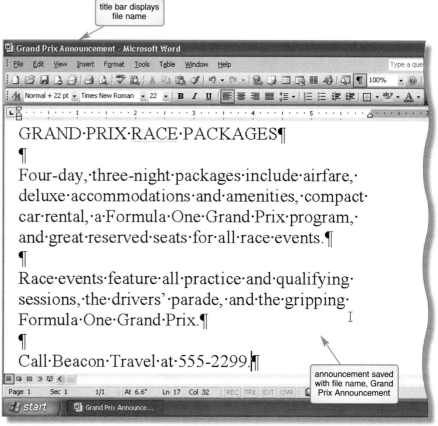

title bar displays file name

announcement saved with file name, Grand Prix Announcement

FIGURE 1-32

Other Ways

1. On File menu click Save As, type file name, select drive or folder using either the Save in list or the My Computer icon, click Save button in dialog box
2. Press CTRL+S, type file name, select location in Save in list, click Save button in dialog box
3. In Voice Command mode, say "File, Save As, [type file name], Save In, [select folder], Save"

More About

Saving

Word allows you to save a document in more than 10 different file formats. Choose the file format by clicking the Save as type box arrow at the bottom of the Save As dialog box (Figure 1-31 on the previous page). Word Document is the default file format. When you save a document, use meaningful file names. A file name can be up to 255 characters, including spaces. The only invalid characters are the backslash (\), slash (/), colon (:), asterisk (*), question mark (?), quotation mark ("), less than symbol (<), greater than symbol (>), and vertical bar (|).

While Word is saving the document, it displays a message on the status bar indicating the progress of the save. After the save operation is complete, Word changes the name of the document on the title bar from Document1 to Grand Prix Announcement (Figure 1-32).

You can use the seven buttons at the top of the Save As dialog box (Figure 1-30 on the previous page) and the five icons along the left edge to change the save location and other tasks. Table 1-3 lists the function of the buttons and icons in the Save As dialog box.

When you click the Tools button in the Save As dialog box, Word displays the Tools menu. The Save Options command on the Tools menu allows you to save a backup copy of the document, create a password to limit access to the document, and carry out other functions that are discussed later.

BUTTON OR ICON	BUTTON OR ICON NAME	FUNCTION
Table 1-3	Save As Dialog Box Buttons and Icons	
	Default File Location	Displays contents of default file location
	Up One Level	Displays contents of folder one level up from current folder
	Search the Web	Starts Web browser and displays search engine
	Delete	Deletes selected file or folder
	Create New Folder	Creates new folder
	Views	Changes view of files and folders
Tools	Tools	Lists commands to print or modify file names and folders
My Recent Documents	My Recent Documents	Displays contents of My Recent Documents in Save in list (you cannot save to this location)

BUTTON OR ICON	BUTTON OR ICON NAME	FUNCTION
Table 1-3	Save As Dialog Box Buttons and Icons	
Desktop	Desktop	Displays contents of Windows desktop folder in Save in list to save quickly to the Windows desktop
My Documents	My Documents	Displays contents of My Documents in Save in list to save quickly to the My Documents folder
My Computer	My Computer	Displays contents of My Computer in Save in list to save quickly to another drive on the computer
My Network Places	My Network Places	Displays contents of My Network Places in Save in list to save quickly to My Network Places

Formatting Paragraphs and Characters in a Document

The text for Project 1 now is complete. The next step is to format the paragraphs and characters in the announcement.

Paragraphs encompass the text up to and including a paragraph mark (¶). **Paragraph formatting** is the process of changing the appearance of a paragraph. For example, you can center or indent a paragraph.

Characters include letters, numbers, punctuation marks, and symbols. **Character formatting** is the process of changing the way characters appear on the screen and in print. You use character formatting to emphasize certain words and improve readability of a document. For example, you can italicize or underline characters.

In many cases, you apply both paragraph and character formatting to the same text. For example, you may center a paragraph (paragraph formatting) and bold the characters in a paragraph (character formatting).

With Word, you can format paragraphs and characters before you type, or you can apply new formats after you type. Earlier, this project showed how to change the font size (character formatting) before you typed any text. This section shows how to format existing text.

Q: What is the difference between character formatting and paragraph formatting?

A: Character formatting includes changing the font, font style, font size; adding an underline, color, strikethrough, shadow, or outline; embossing; engraving; making a superscript or subscript; and changing the case of the letters. Paragraph formatting includes alignment; indentation; and spacing above, below, and in between lines.

Figure 1-33a shows the announcement before formatting its paragraphs and characters. Figure 1-33b shows the announcement after formatting. As you can see from the two figures, a document that is formatted is easier to read and looks more professional.

(a) Unformatted Document

(b) Formatted Document

FIGURE 1-33

Selecting and Formatting Paragraphs and Characters

To format a single paragraph, move the insertion point in the paragraph and then format the paragraph. That is, you do not need to select a single paragraph to format it. To format *multiple* paragraphs, however, you first must select the paragraphs you want to format and then format them. In the same manner, to format a single word, position the insertion point in the word and then format the word. To format multiple characters or words, however, you first must select the characters or words to be formatted and then format the selection.

Selected text is highlighted text. If your screen normally displays dark letters on a light background, then selected text displays light letters on a dark background.

Selecting Multiple Paragraphs

The first formatting step in this project is to change the font size of the characters in the headline. The headline consists of two separate lines, each ending with a paragraph mark. As previously discussed, Word creates a new paragraph each time you press the ENTER key. Thus, the headline actually is two separate paragraphs.

To change the font size of the characters in the headline, you first must **select** (highlight) both paragraphs in the headline, as shown in the following steps.

To Select Multiple Paragraphs

1

• **Press CTRL+HOME; that is, press and hold down the CTRL key, press the HOME key, and then release both keys.**

• **Move the mouse pointer to the left of the first paragraph to be selected until the mouse pointer changes to a right-pointing block arrow.**

CTRL+HOME is a keyboard shortcut that positions the insertion point at the top of the document. The mouse pointer changes to a right-pointing block arrow when positioned to the left of a paragraph (Figure 1-34).

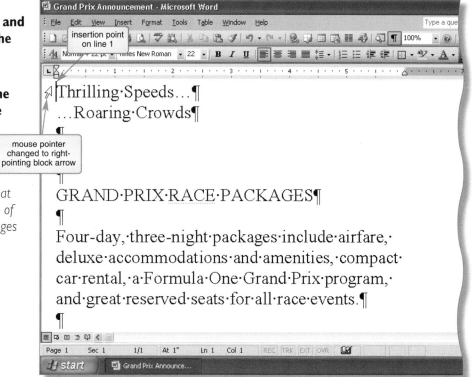

FIGURE 1-34

Microsoft Office
Word 2003

2

• **Drag downward until both paragraphs are selected.**

Word selects (highlights) both of the paragraphs (Figure 1-35). Dragging is the process of holding down the mouse button while moving the mouse and then releasing the mouse button.

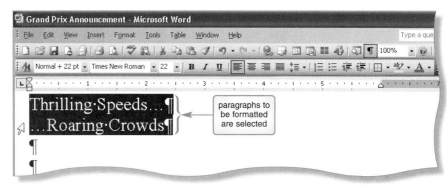

paragraphs to be formatted are selected

FIGURE 1-35

Changing the Font Size of Text

The next step is to increase the font size of the characters in the selected headline. Recall that the font size specifies the size of the characters. Earlier, this project showed how to change the font size to 22 for characters typed in the entire announcement. To give the headline more impact, it has a font size larger than the body copy. The following steps show how to increase the font size of the headline from 22 to 36 point.

To Change the Font Size of Text

1

• **With the text selected, click the Font Size box arrow on the Formatting toolbar.**

Word displays a list of available font sizes (Figure 1-36). Available font sizes vary depending on the current font and the printer driver.

text still selected

Font Size box arrow

Font Size list

FIGURE 1-36

2

• **Click the down scroll arrow on the Font Size scroll bar until 36 appears in the list (Figure 1-37).**

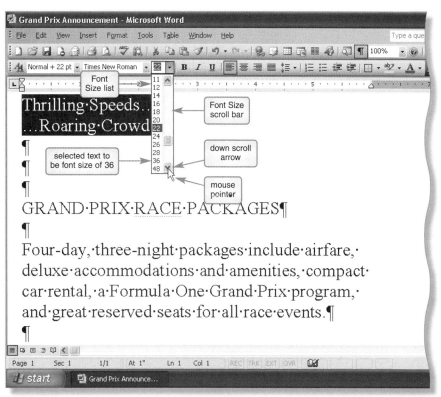

FIGURE 1-37

3

• **Click 36 in the Font Size list.**

Word increases the font size of the headline to 36 (Figure 1-38). The Font Size box on the Formatting toolbar displays 36, indicating the selected text has a font size of 36. Notice that when the mouse pointer is positioned in selected text, its shape is a left-pointing block arrow.

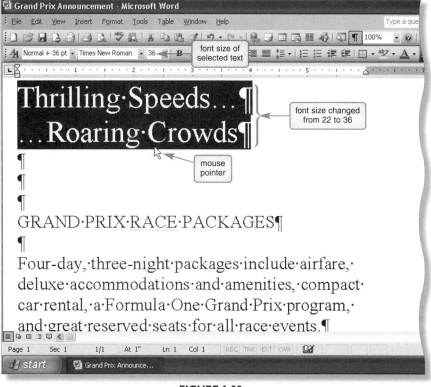

FIGURE 1-38

Other Ways

1. On Format menu click Font, click Font tab, select desired font size in Size list, click OK button
2. Right-click selected text, click Font on shortcut menu, click Font tab, select desired font size in Size list, click OK button
3. Press CTRL+SHIFT+P, type desired font size, press ENTER
4. In Voice Command mode, say "Font Size, [select font size]"

Changing the Font of Text

As mentioned earlier in this project, the default font in Word is Times New Roman. Word, however, provides many other fonts to add variety to your documents. The following steps show how to change the font of the headline in the announcement from Times New Roman to Cooper Black.

To Change the Font of Text

1

• **With the text selected, click the Font box arrow on the Formatting toolbar and then scroll through the Font list until Cooper Black (or a similar font) is displayed.**

Word displays a list of available fonts (Figure 1-39). Your list of available fonts may differ, depending on the type of printer you are using.

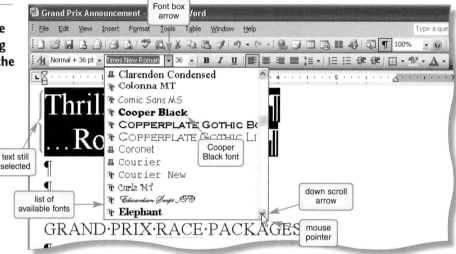

FIGURE 1-39

2

• **Click Cooper Black (or a similar font).**

Word changes the font of the selected text to Cooper Black (Figure 1-40).

FIGURE 1-40

Right-Align a Paragraph

The default alignment for paragraphs is **left-aligned**, that is, flush at the left margin of the document with uneven right edges. In Figure 1-41, the Align Left button is selected to indicate the paragraph containing the insertion point is left-aligned.

The second line of the headline, however, is to be **right-aligned**, that is, flush at the right margin of the document with uneven left edges. Recall that the second line of the headline is a paragraph, and paragraph formatting does not require you to select the paragraph prior to formatting. Just position the insertion point in the paragraph to be formatted and then format it accordingly.

The following steps show how to right-align the second line of the headline.

To Right-Align a Paragraph

1

• **Click somewhere in the paragraph to be right-aligned.**

Word positions the insertion point at the location you clicked (Figure 1-41).

FIGURE 1-41

2

• **Click the Align Right button on the Formatting toolbar.**

The second line of the headline now is right-aligned (Figure 1-42). Notice that you did not have to select the paragraph before right-aligning it. Formatting a single paragraph requires only that the insertion point be positioned somewhere in the paragraph.

FIGURE 1-42

When a paragraph is right-aligned, the Align Right button on the Formatting toolbar is selected. If, for some reason, you wanted to return the paragraph to left-aligned, you would click the Align Left button on the Formatting toolbar.

Other Ways

1. On Format menu click Paragraph, click Indents and Spacing tab, click Alignment box arrow, click Right, click OK button
2. Right-click paragraph, click Paragraph on shortcut menu, click Indents and Spacing tab, click Alignment box arrow, click Right, click OK button
3. Press CTRL+R
4. In Voice Command mode, say "Align Right"

Microsoft Office
Word 2003

Center a Paragraph

The body title currently is left-aligned (Figure 1-42 on the previous page). The following step shows how to **center** the paragraph, that is, position its text horizontally between the left and right margins on the page.

To Center a Paragraph

1

• **Click somewhere in the paragraph to be centered.**

• **Click the Center button on the Formatting toolbar.**

Word centers the body title between the left and right margins (Figure 1-43). The Center button on the Formatting toolbar is selected, which indicates the paragraph containing the insertion point is centered.

FIGURE 1-43

When a paragraph is centered, the Center button on the Formatting toolbar is selected. If, for some reason, you wanted to return the paragraph to left-aligned, you would click the Align Left button on the Formatting toolbar.

More About

Centering

The Center button on the Formatting toolbar centers text horizontally between the left and right margins. You also can center text vertically between the top and bottom margins. To do this, click File on the menu bar, click Page Setup, click the Layout tab, click the Vertical alignment box arrow, click Center in the list, and then click the OK button.

Undoing, Redoing, and Repeating Commands or Actions

Word provides an Undo button on the Standard toolbar that you can use to cancel your recent command(s) or action(s). For example, if you format text incorrectly, you can undo the format and try it again. If, after you undo an action, you decide you did not want to perform the undo, you can use the Redo button to redo the undo. Word prevents you from undoing or redoing some actions, such as saving or printing a document.

The following steps show how to undo the center format to the body title using the Undo button and then re-center it using the Redo button.

To Undo and Redo an Action

1

• **Click the Undo button on the Standard toolbar.**

Word returns the body title to its formatting before you issued the center command (Figure 1-44). That is, Word left-aligns the body title.

2

• **Click the Redo button on the Standard toolbar.**

Word reapplies the center format to the body title (shown in Figure 1-43).

FIGURE 1-44

You also can cancel a series of prior actions by clicking the Undo button arrow on the Standard toolbar (Figure 1-44) to display the list of undo actions and then dragging through the actions you wish to undo.

Whereas the Undo command cancels an action you did not want to perform, Word also provides a **Repeat command** on the Edit menu, which duplicates your last command so you can perform it again. For example, if you centered a paragraph and wish to format another paragraph the exact same way, you could click in the second paragraph to format, click Edit on the menu bar, and then click Repeat Paragraph Alignment. The text listed after Repeat varies, depending on your most recent action. If the action cannot be repeated, Word displays the text, Can't Repeat, on the Edit menu.

Selecting a Line and Formatting It

The characters in the body title, GRAND PRIX RACE PACKAGES, are to be a different font, larger font size, and italicized. To make these changes, you must select the line of text containing the body title, as shown in the following step.

To Select a Line

1

• **Move the mouse pointer to the left of the line to be selected (in this case, GRAND PRIX RACE PACKAGES) until it changes to a right-pointing block arrow and then click.**

Word selects the entire line to the right of the mouse pointer (Figure 1-45).

FIGURE 1-45

The next step is to change the font of the selected characters from Times New Roman to Arial Black and increase the font size of the selected characters from 22 to 24, as explained below.

To Format a Line of Text

1 **With the text selected, click the Font box arrow on the Formatting toolbar and then scroll to Arial Black (or a similar font) in the list. Click Arial Black (or a similar font).**

2 **With the text selected, click the Font Size box arrow on the Formatting toolbar and then click 24 in the list.**

Word changes the characters in the body title to 24-point Arial Black (Figure 1-46).

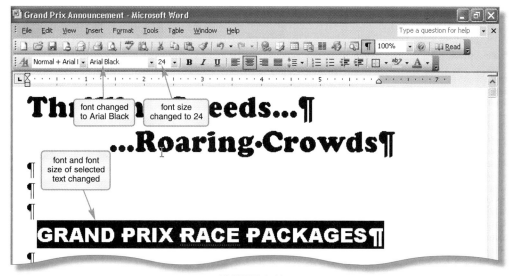

FIGURE 1-46

More About

Fonts

With some fonts, the formatting marks are not displayed on the screen properly. For example, the raised dot in each space may be displayed behind a character instead of in the space between two characters, causing the characters to look incorrect. Notice in Figure 1-46 that the formatting marks in the body title run into the characters. Recall that formatting marks do not print. Thus, the line will print fine.

Italicizing Text

Italicized text has a slanted appearance. The following step shows how to italicize the selected characters in the body title.

To Italicize Text

1

• **With the text still selected, click the Italic button on the Formatting toolbar.**

Word italicizes the text (Figure 1-47). The Italic button on the Formatting toolbar is selected.

FIGURE 1-47

When the selected text is italicized, the Italic button on the Formatting toolbar is selected. If, for some reason, you wanted to remove the italic format from the selected text, you would click the Italic button a second time, or you immediately could click the Undo button on the Standard toolbar.

Other Ways

1. On Format menu click Font, click Font tab, click Italic in Font style list, click OK button
2. Right-click selected text, click Font on shortcut menu, click Font tab, click Italic in Font style list, click OK button
3. Press CTRL+I
4. In Voice Command mode, say "Italic"

Underlining Text

The next step is to underline a word in the first paragraph below the body title. **Underlined** text prints with an underscore (_) below each character. Underlining is used to emphasize or draw attention to specific text.

As with a single paragraph, if you want to format a single word, you do not need to select the word. Simply position the insertion point somewhere in the word and apply the desired format. The following step shows how to underline a word.

To Underline a Word

1

- **Click somewhere in the word to be underlined (deluxe, in this case).**
- **Click the Underline button on the Formatting toolbar.**

Word underlines the word containing the insertion point (Figure 1-48). The Underline button on the Formatting toolbar is selected.

FIGURE 1-48

When the text containing the insertion point is underlined, the Underline button on the Formatting toolbar is selected. If, for some reason, you wanted to remove the underline from the text, you would click the Underline button a second time, or you immediately could click the Undo button on the Standard toolbar.

In addition to the basic underline shown in Figure 1-48, Word has many decorative underlines that are available through the Font dialog box. For example, you can use double underlines, dotted underlines, and wavy underlines. In the Font dialog box, you also can change the color of an underline and instruct Word to underline only the words and not the spaces between the words. To display the Font dialog box, click Format on the menu bar and then click Font.

Scrolling

The next text to format is in the lower portion of the announcement, which currently is not showing in the document window. To continue formatting the document, scroll down so the lower portion of the announcement is displayed in the document window, as shown in the following step.

To Scroll through a Document

1

• **Click the down scroll arrow on the vertical scroll bar nine times.**

Word scrolls through the document (Figure 1-49). Depending on your monitor type, your screen may scroll differently.

FIGURE 1-49

Other Ways

1. See Tables 1-1 and 1-2 on pages WD 24 and WD 25
2. In Dictation mode, say key name(s) in Table 1-2

Selecting a Group of Words

The next step is to bold the words, great reserved seats, in the announcement. To do this, you first must select this group of words. The following steps show how to select a group of words.

To Select a Group of Words

1

• **Position the mouse pointer immediately to the left of the first character of the text to be selected (in this case, the g in great).**

The mouse pointer's shape is an I-beam when positioned in unselected text in the document window (Figure 1-50).

Four-dight packages·include·airfare,·
deluxetions·and·amenities,·compact·
car·rental,·a·Formula·One·Grand·Prix·program,·
and·great·reserved·seats·for·all·race·events.¶
¶

FIGURE 1-50

Microsoft Office
Word 2003

2

• **Drag the mouse pointer through the last character of the text to be selected (in this case, the second s in seats).**

Word selects the phrase, great reserved seats (Figure 1-51).

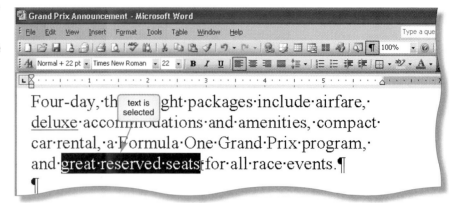

FIGURE 1-51

Bolding Text

Bold characters display somewhat thicker and darker than those that are not bold. The following step shows how to bold the selected phrase, great reserved seats.

To Bold Text

1

• **With the text selected, click the Bold button on the Formatting toolbar.**

• **Click inside the selected text to remove the selection (highlight).**

Word formats the selected text in bold and positions the insertion point inside the bold text (Figure 1-52). The Bold button on the Formatting toolbar is selected.

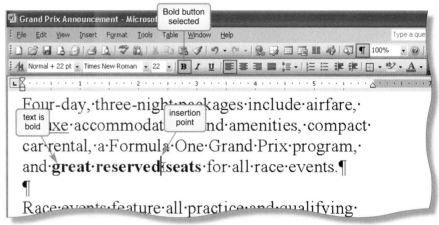

FIGURE 1-52

When you click in the document, Word positions the insertion point at the location you clicked and removes the selection (highlight) from the screen. If you click inside the selection, the Formatting toolbar displays the formatting characteristics of the characters and paragraphs containing the insertion point. For example, at the location of the insertion point, the characters are a 22-point Times New Roman bold font, and the paragraph is left-aligned.

When the selected text is bold, the Bold button on the Formatting toolbar is selected. If, for some reason, you wanted to remove the bold format from the selected text, you would click the Bold button a second time, or you immediately could click the Undo button on the Standard toolbar.

The next step is to center the last line of the announcement, as described in the following steps.

To Center a Paragraph

1 Click somewhere in the paragraph to be centered (in this case, the last line of the announcement).

2 Click the Center button on the Formatting toolbar.

Word centers the last line of the announcement (Figure 1-53).

More About

Toolbar Buttons

Many of the buttons on the Formatting toolbar are toggles; that is, click them once to format the selected text, and click them again to remove the format from the selected text. For example, clicking the Bold button bolds selected text; clicking the Bold button again removes the bold format.

FIGURE 1-53

The formatting for the announcement now is complete.

Inserting Clip Art in a Word Document

Files containing graphical images, also called **graphics**, are available from a variety of sources. Word includes many predefined graphics, called **clip art**, that you can insert in a document. Clip art is located in the **Clip Organizer**, which contains a collection of clips, including clip art, as well as photographs, sounds, and video clips.

More About

Graphics

If you have a scanner or digital camera attached to your computer, Word can insert a graphic directly from these devices. You also can scan a graphic into a file and then insert the scanned file into the Word document.

Inserting Clip Art

The next step in the project is to insert clip art of a race car in the announcement between the headline and the body title. Recall that Word has 14 task panes, some of which automatically appear as you perform certain operations. When you use the Clip Art command, Word automatically displays the Clip Art task pane. The following steps show how to use the Clip Art task pane to insert clip art in a document.

To Insert Clip Art in a Document

1

• **To position the insertion point where you want the clip art to be located, press CTRL+HOME and then press the DOWN ARROW key three times.**

• **Click Insert on the menu bar.**

Word positions the insertion point on the second paragraph mark below the headline, and displays the Insert menu (Figure 1-54). Remember that a short menu initially displays, which expands into a full menu after a few seconds.

FIGURE 1-54

2

• **Point to Picture on the Insert menu.**

Word displays the Picture submenu (Figure 1-55). As discussed earlier, when you point to a command that has a small arrow to its right, Word displays a submenu associated with that command.

FIGURE 1-55

3

- **Click Clip Art on the Picture submenu.**

- **If the Search for text box contains text, drag through the text to select it.**

- **Type** race car **in the Search for text box.**

Word displays the Clip Art task pane at the right edge of the Word window (Figure 1-56). Recall that a task pane is a separate window that enables you to carry out some Word tasks more efficiently. When you click the Go button, Word searches the Clip Organizer for clips that match the description you type in the Search for text box.

FIGURE 1-56

4

- **Click the Go button.**

Word displays a list of clips that match the description, race car (Figure 1-57). If you are connected to the Web, the Clip Art task pane displays clips from the Web, as well as those installed on your hard disk.

FIGURE 1-57

Microsoft Office
Word 2003

 5

• **Click the image to be inserted in the document (in this case, the Formula One race car).**

Word inserts the clip art in the document at the location of the insertion point (Figure 1-58). In the Clip Art task pane, the selected clip art has a box arrow at its right edge.

 6

• **Click the Close button on the Clip Art task pane title bar.**

Word removes the Clip Art task pane from the screen.

FIGURE 1-58

Other Ways

1. In Voice Command mode, say "Insert, Picture, Clip Art"

The clip art in the announcement is part of a paragraph. Because that paragraph is left-aligned, the clip art also is left-aligned. Notice the Align Left button on the Formatting toolbar is selected (Figure 1-58). You can use any of the paragraph alignment buttons on the Formatting toolbar to reposition the clip art. The following step shows how to center a graphic that is part of a paragraph.

More About

Clip Art

If you are not connected to the Web, Word displays clip art from your hard disk. If you are connected to the Web, Word displays clip art from your hard disk and also from Microsoft's Web site. Your results may differ from those shown in the preceding steps if you are not connected to the Web. When clip art images display in the Clip Art task pane, Web clips are identified by a small globe displayed in their lower-left corner (Figure 1-58).

To Center a Paragraph Containing a Graphic

1 **With the insertion point on the paragraph mark containing the clip art, click the Center button on the Formatting toolbar.**

Word centers the paragraph, which also centers the graphic in the paragraph (Figure 1-59).

FIGURE 1-59

More About

Clip Art Packages

For more information about the clip art available for purchase, visit the Word 2003 More About Web page (scsite.com/wd2003/more) and then click Clip Art.

Resizing a Graphic

The clip art in this announcement is to be a larger size. Once you have inserted a graphic in a document, you easily can change its size. **Resizing** includes both enlarging and reducing the size of a graphic. To resize a graphic, you first must select it. Thus, the following step shows how to select a graphic.

Q&A

Q: Where should a graphic be positioned in an announcement?

A: Emphasize a graphic by placing it at the optical center of the page. To determine optical center, divide the page in half horizontally and vertically. The optical center is located one third of the way up the vertical line from the point of intersection of the two lines.

To Select a Graphic

1

• **Click anywhere in the graphic.**

• **If your screen does not display the Picture toolbar, click View on the menu bar, point to Toolbars, and then click Picture.**

*Word selects the graphic (Figure 1-60). A selected graphic is displayed surrounded by a **selection rectangle**, which has small squares, called **sizing handles**, at each corner and middle location. You use the sizing handles to change the size of the graphic. When a graphic is selected, the Picture toolbar automatically should appear on the screen.*

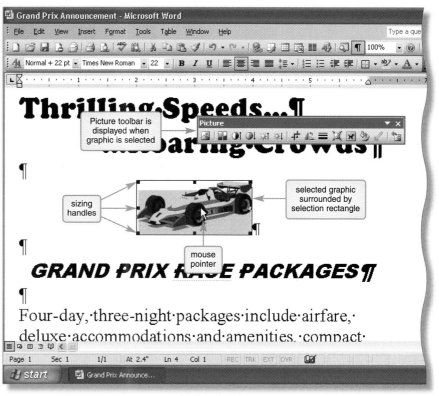

FIGURE 1-60

The following steps show how to resize the graphic just inserted and selected.

To Resize a Graphic

1

• **With the graphic still selected, point to the upper-right corner sizing handle.**

The mouse pointer shape changes to a two-headed arrow when it is on a sizing handle (Figure 1-61). To resize a graphic, you drag the sizing handle(s) until the graphic is the desired size.

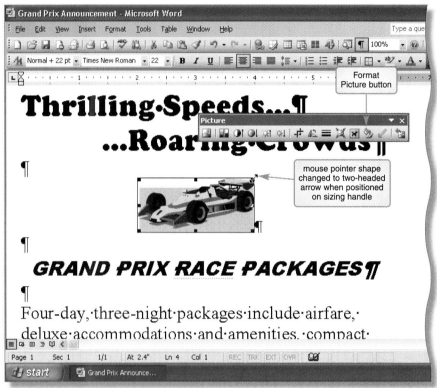

FIGURE 1-61

2

• **Drag the sizing handle diagonally outward until the dotted selection rectangle is positioned approximately as shown in Figure 1-62.**

When you drag a corner sizing handle, the proportions of the graphic remain intact.

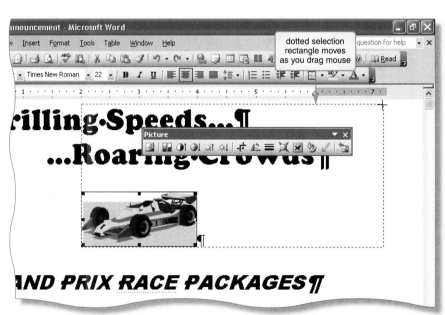

FIGURE 1-62

3

• **Release the mouse button. Press**
CTRL+HOME.

*Word resizes the graphic (Figure 1-63).
When you click outside of a graphic or
press a key to scroll through a document,
Word deselects the graphic. The Picture
toolbar disappears from the screen when
you deselect a graphic.*

FIGURE 1-63

Instead of resizing a selected graphic by dragging a sizing handle with the
mouse, you also can use the Format Picture dialog box to resize a graphic by clicking
the Format Picture button on the Picture toolbar (Figure 1-61) and then clicking the
Size tab. In the Size sheet, you can enter exact height and width measurements. If
you have a precise measurement for a graphic, use the Format Picture dialog box;
otherwise, drag the sizing handles to resize a graphic.

Sometimes, you might resize a graphic and realize it is the wrong size. In this
case, you may want to return the graphic to its original size and start again. To
restore a resized graphic to its exact original size, click the graphic to select it and
then click the Format Picture button on the Picture toolbar to display the Format
Picture dialog box. Click the Size tab, click the Reset button, and then click the OK
button.

Saving an Existing Document with the Same File Name

The announcement for Project 1 now is complete. To transfer the modified
document with the formatting changes and graphic to the floppy disk in drive A,
you must save the document again. When you saved the document the first time, you
assigned a file name to it (Grand Prix Announcement). When you use the procedure
on the next page, Word automatically assigns the same file name to the document
each time you subsequently save it.

Other Ways

1. Click Format Picture
   button on Picture toolbar,
   click Size tab, enter
   desired height and width,
   click OK button
2. On Format menu click
   Picture, click Size tab,
   enter desired height and
   width, click OK button
3. In Voice Command mode,
   say "Format, Picture"

More About

**The Picture
Toolbar**

The Picture toolbar is a
floating toolbar. Thus, you can
drag its title bar to move the
toolbar to a different location
on the screen.

To Save an Existing Document with the Same File Name

1

• **Click the Save button on the Standard toolbar.**

Word saves the document on a floppy disk inserted in drive A using the currently assigned file name, Grand Prix Announcement (Figure 1-64).

FIGURE 1-64

While Word is saving the document, the Background Save icon appears near the right edge of the status bar. When the save is complete, the document remains in memory and on the screen.

If, for some reason, you want to save an existing document with a different file name, click Save As on the File menu to display the Save As dialog box. Then, fill in the Save As dialog box as discussed in Steps 2 through 5 on pages WD 28 through WD 30.

Printing a Document

The next step is to print the document you created. A printed version of the document is called a **hard copy** or **printout**. The following steps show how to print the announcement created in this project.

To Print a Document

1

• **Ready the printer according to the printer instructions.**

• **Click the Print button on the Standard toolbar.**

The mouse pointer briefly changes to an hourglass shape as Word prepares to print the document. While the document is print-ing, a printer icon appears in the notification area on the Windows taskbar (Figure 1-65).

2

• **When the printer stops printing the document, retrieve the printout, which should look like Figure 1-1 on page WD 5.**

FIGURE 1-65

When you use the Print button to print a document, Word prints the entire document automatically. You then may distribute the printout or keep it as a permanent record of the document.

If you wanted to print multiple copies of the document, display the Print dialog box by clicking File on the menu bar and then clicking Print. In addition to the number of copies, the Print dialog box has several printing options.

If you wanted to cancel your job that is printing or one you have waiting to be printed, double-click the printer icon on the taskbar (Figure 1-65). In the printer window, click the job to be canceled and then click Cancel on the Document menu.

Other Ways

1. On File menu click Print, click OK button
2. Press CTRL+P, press ENTER
3. In Voice Command mode, say "Print"

Q&A

Q: How can I save ink, print faster, or decrease printer overrun errors?

A: Print a draft. Click File on the menu bar, click Print, click the Options button, place a check mark in the Draft output check box, and then click the OK button in each dialog box.

Quitting Word

After you create, save, and print the announcement, Project 1 is complete. The following steps show how to quit Word and return control to Windows.

To Quit Word

1

• **Position the mouse pointer on the Close button on the right side of the title bar (Figure 1-66).**

2

• **Click the Close button.**

The Word window closes.

FIGURE 1-66

Other Ways

1. On File menu click Exit
2. Right-click Microsoft Word button on Windows taskbar, click Close on shortcut menu
3. Press ALT+F4
4. In Voice Command mode, say "File, Exit"

When you quit Word, a dialog box may display asking if you want to save the changes. This occurs if you made changes to the document since the last save. Clicking the Yes button in the dialog box saves the changes; clicking the No button ignores the changes; and clicking the Cancel button returns to the document. If you did not make any changes since you saved the document, this dialog box usually is not displayed.

Starting Word and Opening a Document

Once you have created and saved a document, you often will have reason to retrieve it from disk. For example, you might want to revise the document or print it again. Earlier, you saved the Word document created in Project 1 on a floppy disk using the file name, Grand Prix Announcement.

The following steps, which assume Word is not running, show how to open the Grand Prix Announcement file from a floppy disk in drive A.

To Open a Document

1

• **With your floppy disk in drive A, click the Start button on the Windows taskbar, point to All Programs on the Start menu, point to Microsoft Office on the All Programs submenu, and then click Microsoft Office Word 2003 on the Microsoft Office submenu.**

Word starts. The Open area of the Getting Started task pane lists up to four of the most recently used files (Figure 1-67).

FIGURE 1-67

2

• **Click Grand Prix Announcement in the Getting Started task pane.**

Word opens the document, Grand Prix Announcement, from the floppy disk in drive A and displays it in the Word window (Figure 1-68). The Getting Started task pane closes.

file name
on title bar

Grand Prix
Announcement
document is displayed
in document window

FIGURE 1-68

If you want to open a document other than one of the four most recently opened ones, click the Open button on the Standard toolbar or the More link in the Getting Started task pane. Clicking the Open button or the More link displays the Open dialog box, which allows you to navigate to a document stored on disk.

Correcting Errors

After creating a document, you often will find you must make changes to it. For example, the document may contain an error or new circumstances may require you add text to the document.

Types of Changes Made to Documents

The types of changes made to documents normally fall into one of the three following categories: additions, deletions, or modifications.

ADDITIONS Additional words, sentences, or paragraphs may be required in a document. Additions occur when you omit text from a document and want to insert it later. For example, the travel agency may decide to add breakfast as part of its Grand Prix race packages.

DELETIONS Sometimes, text in a document is incorrect or is no longer needed. For example, the travel agency may stop including car rental in their Grand Prix race packages. In this case, you would delete the words, compact car rental, from the announcement.

MODIFICATIONS If an error is made in a document or changes take place that affect the document, you might have to revise a word(s) in the text. For example, the travel agency might change the Grand Prix race packages from four-day, three-night to five-day, four-night.

Inserting Text in an Existing Document

Word inserts text to the left of the insertion point. The text to the right of the insertion point moves to the right and downward to fit the new text. The following steps show how to insert the word, fun, to the left of the word, drivers', in the announcement.

To Insert Text in an Existing Document

1

• **Scroll through the document and then click to the left of the location of text to be inserted (in this case, the d in drivers').**

Word positions the insertion point at the clicked location (Figure 1-69).

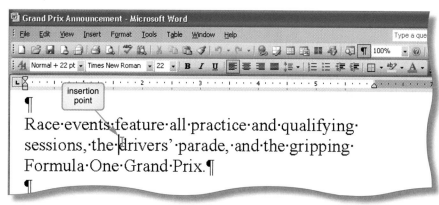

FIGURE 1-69

2

• **Type** fun **and then press the SPACEBAR.**

Word inserts the word, fun, to the left of the insertion point (Figure 1-70).

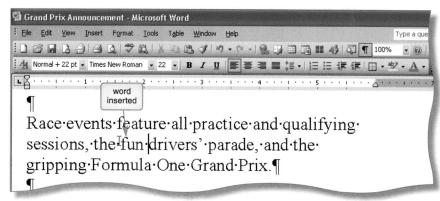

FIGURE 1-70

In Word, the default typing mode is insert mode. In **insert mode**, as you type a character, Word inserts the character and moves all the characters to the right of the typed character one position to the right. You can change to overtype mode by double-clicking the OVR status indicator on the status bar (Figure 1-8 on page WD 10). In **overtype mode**, Word replaces characters to the right of the insertion point. Double-clicking the OVR status indicator again returns Word to insert mode.

More About

**The Clipboard
Task Pane**

If you click the Cut button
(or Copy button) twice in a
row, Word displays the
Clipboard task pane. You use
the Clipboard task pane to
copy and paste items within a
document or from one Office
document to another. To
close the Clipboard task
pane, click the Close button
on the task pane title bar.

Deleting Text from an Existing Document

It is not unusual to type incorrect characters or words in a document. As discussed earlier in this project, you can click the Undo button on the Standard toolbar to immediately undo a command or action — this includes typing. Word also provides other methods of correcting typing errors.

To delete an incorrect character in a document, simply click next to the incorrect character and then press the BACKSPACE key to erase to the left of the insertion point, or press the DELETE key to erase to the right of the insertion point.

To delete a word or phrase you first must select the word or phrase. The following steps show how to select the word, fun, that was just added in the previous steps and then delete the selection.

To Select a Word

1

• **Position the mouse pointer somewhere in the word to be selected (in this case, fun), as shown in Figure 1-71.**

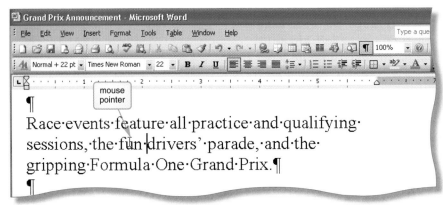

FIGURE 1-71

2

• **Double-click the word to be selected.**

The word, fun, is selected (Figure 1-72).

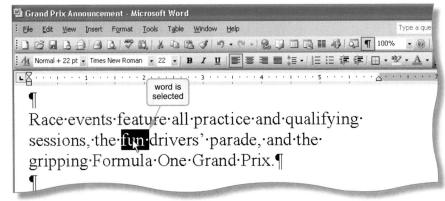

FIGURE 1-72

Other Ways

1. Drag through the word
2. With insertion point at beginning of desired word, press CTRL+SHIFT+RIGHT ARROW
3. With insertion point at beginning of desired word, in Voice Command mode, say "Select Word"

The next step is to delete the selected text.

To Delete Text

1

• **With the text selected, press the DELETE key.**

Word deletes the selected word from the document (Figure 1-73).

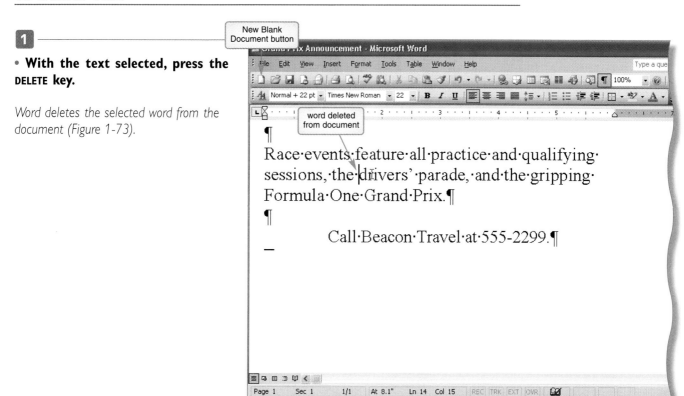

New Blank Document button

word deleted from document

FIGURE 1-73

Closing the Entire Document

Sometimes, everything goes wrong. If this happens, you may want to close the document entirely and start over. You also may want to close a document when you are finished with it so you can begin your next document.

To Close the Entire Document and Start Over

1. Click File on the menu bar and then click Close.
2. If Word displays a dialog box, click the No button to ignore the changes since the last time you saved the document.
3. Click the New Blank Document button (Figure 1-73) on the Standard toolbar.

You also can close the document by clicking the Close button at the right edge of the menu bar.

More About

**The Word Help
System**

The best way to become
familiar with the Word Help
system is to use it. Appendix
A includes detailed information on the Word Help system and exercises that will
help you gain confidence in
using it.

Word Help System

At anytime while you are using Word, you can get answers to questions through the **Word Help system**. You activate the Word Help system by using the Type a question for help box on the menu bar, the Microsoft Office Word Help button on the Standard toolbar, or the Help menu (Figure 1-74). Used properly, this form of online assistance can increase your productivity and reduce your frustrations by min-imizing the time you spend learning how to use Word.

The following section shows how to obtain answers to your questions using the Type a question for help box. Additional information about using the Word Help system is available in Appendix A.

Using the Type a Question for Help Box

Through the Type a question for help box on the right side of the menu bar (Figure 1-66 on page WD 54), you type free-form questions, such as *how do I save* or *how do I create a Web page*, or you type terms, such as *copy*, *save*, or *format*. Word responds by displaying a list of topics related to the word or phrase you typed. The following steps show how to use the Type a question for help box to obtain information about shortcut keys.

To Use the Type a Question for Help Box

1

• **Click the Type a question for help box on the right side of the menu bar and then type** shortcut keys **(Figure 1-74).**

FIGURE 1-74

2

• Press the ENTER key.

• When Word displays the Search Results task pane, if necessary, scroll to display the topic, About shortcut keys.

• Click About shortcut keys.

• If the Microsoft Office Help window has an Auto Tile button, click it so the Word window and Help window display side-by-side.

Word displays the Search Results task pane with a list of topics relating to the phrase, shortcut keys. When the About shortcut keys link is clicked, Word opens the Microsoft Office Word Help window on the right side of the screen (Figure 1-75).

FIGURE 1-75

3

• Click the Show All link on the right side of the Microsoft Office Word Help window to expand the links in the window.

• Double-click the Microsoft Office Word Help window title bar to maximize the window.

The links in the Microsoft Office Word Help window are expanded and the window is maximized (Figure 1-76).

4

• Click the Close button on the Microsoft Office Word Help window title bar.

• Click the Close button on the Search Results task pane.

Word closes the Microsoft Office Word Help window. The Word document window again is active.

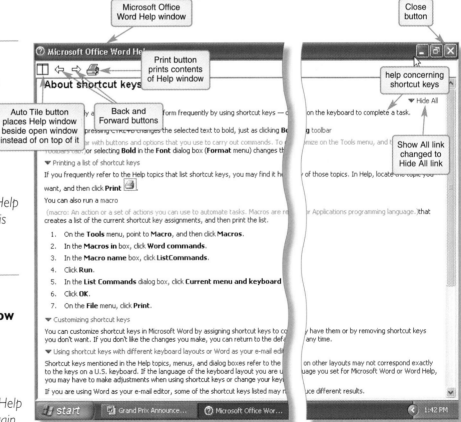

FIGURE 1-76

Use the buttons in the upper-left corner of the Microsoft Office Word Help window (Figure 1-76 on the previous page) to navigate through the Help system, change the display, or print the contents of the window.

You can use the Type a question for help box to search for Help about any topic concerning Word. As you enter questions and terms in the Type a question for help box, Word adds them to the Type a question for help list. Thus, if you click the Type a question for help box arrow, Word displays a list of previously typed questions and terms.

More About

Certification

The Microsoft Office Specialist Certification program provides an opportunity for you to obtain a valuable industry credential - proof that you have the Word 2003 skills required by employers. For more information, see Appendix E or visit the Word 2003 Certification Web page (scsite.com/wd2003/cert).

Quitting Word

The final step in this project is to quit Word.

To Quit Word

1 Click the Close button on the right side of the Word title bar (Figure 1-66 on page WD 54).

2 If Word displays a dialog box, click the No button to ignore the changes since the last time you saved the document.

The Word window closes.

Project Summary

In creating the Grand Prix Announcement document in this project, you gained a broad knowledge of Word. First, you were introduced to starting Word. You learned about the Word window. Before entering any text in the document, you learned how to change the font size. You then learned how to type in the Word document window. The project showed how to use Word's check spelling as you type feature.

Once you saved the document, you learned how to format its paragraphs and characters. Then, the project showed how to insert and resize a clip art image. You also learned how to save the document again, print it, and then quit Word. You learned how to open a document, and insert, delete, and modify text. Finally, you learned how to use the Word Help system to answer questions.

If you have a SAM user profile, you may have access to hands-on instruction, practice, and assessment of the skills covered in this project. Log in to your SAM account and go to your assignments page to see what your instructor has assigned.

What You Should Know

Having completed this project, you should be able to perform the tasks below. The tasks are listed in the same order they were presented in this project. For a list of the buttons, menus, toolbars, and commands introduced in this project, see the Quick Reference Summary at the back of this book and refer to the Page Number column.

1. Start Word   (WD 6)
2. Customize the Word Window   (WD 8)
3. Increase the Font Size before Typing   (WD 17)
4. Type Text   (WD 18)
5. Enter Blank Lines in a Document   (WD 20)
6. Display Formatting Marks   (WD 21)
7. Type More Text   (WD 22)
8. Wordwrap Text as You Type   (WD 23)
9. Enter Text that Scrolls the Document Window (WD 24)
10. Check Spelling and Grammar as You Type (WD 26)
11. Enter More Text   (WD 27)
12. Save a New Document   (WD 28)
13. Select Multiple Paragraphs   (WD 33)
14. Change the Font Size of Text   (WD 34)
15. Change the Font of Text   (WD 36)
16. Right-Align a Paragraph   (WD 37)
17. Center a Paragraph   (WD 38)
18. Undo and Redo an Action   (WD 39)
19. Select a Line   (WD 40)
20. Format a Line of Text   (WD 40)
21. Italicize Text   (WD 41)
22. Underline a Word   (WD 42)
23. Scroll through a Document   (WD 43)
24. Select a Group of Words   (WD 43)
25. Bold Text   (WD 44)
26. Center a Paragraph   (WD 45)
27. Insert Clip Art in a Document   (WD 46)
28. Center a Paragraph Containing a Graphic (WD 48)
29. Select a Graphic   (WD 49)
30. Resize a Graphic   (WD 50)
31. Save an Existing Document with the Same File Name   (WD 52)
32. Print a Document   (WD 53)
33. Quit Word   (WD 54, WD 62)
34. Open a Document   (WD 55)
35. Insert Text in an Existing Document   (WD 57)
36. Select a Word   (WD 58)
37. Delete Text   (WD 59)
38. Close the Entire Document and Start Over (WD 59)
39. Use the Type a Question for Help Box   (WD 60)

Learn It Online

Instructions: To complete the Learn It Online exercises, start your browser, click the Address bar, and then enter the Web address scsite.com/wd2003/learn. When the Word 2003 Learn It Online page is displayed, follow the instructions in the exercises below. Each exercise has instructions for printing your results, either for your own records or for submission to your instructor.

1 Project Reinforcement TF, MC, and SA

Below Word Project 1, click the Project Reinforcement link. Print the quiz by clicking Print on the File menu for each page. Answer each question.

Flash Cards

Below Word Project 1, click the Flash Cards link and read the instructions. Type 20 (or a number specified by your instructor) in the Number of playing cards text box, type your name in the Enter your Name text box, and then click the Flip Card button. When the flash card is displayed, read the question and then click the ANSWER box arrow to select an answer. Flip through Flash Cards. If your score is 15 (75%) correct or greater, click Print on the File menu to print your results. If your score is less than 15 (75%) correct, then redo this exercise by clicking the Replay button.

3 Practice Test

Below Word Project 1, click the Practice Test link. Answer each question, enter your first and last name at the bottom of the page, and then click the Grade Test button. When the graded practice test is displayed on your screen, click Print on the File menu to print a hard copy. Continue to take practice tests until you score 80% or better.

4 Who Wants To Be a Computer Genius?

Below Word Project 1, click the Computer Genius link. Read the instructions, enter your first and last name at the bottom of the page, and then click the PLAY button. When your score is displayed, click the PRINT RESULTS link to print a hard copy.

5 Wheel of Terms

Below Word Project 1, click the Wheel of Terms link. Read the instructions, and then enter your first and last name and your school name. Click the PLAY button. When your score is displayed, right-click the score and then click Print on the shortcut menu to print a hard copy.

6 Crossword Puzzle Challenge

Below Word Project 1, click the Crossword Puzzle Challenge link. Read the instructions, and then enter your first and last name. Click the SUBMIT button. Work the crossword puzzle. When you are finished, click the Submit button. When the crossword puzzle is redisplayed, click the Print Puzzle button to print a hard copy.

7 Tips and Tricks

Below Word Project 1, click the Tips and Tricks link. Click a topic that pertains to Project 1. Right-click the information and then click Print on the shortcut menu. Construct a brief example of what the information relates to in Word to confirm you understand how to use the tip or trick.

8 Newsgroups

Below Word Project 1, click the Newsgroups link. Click a topic that pertains to Project 1. Print three comments.

9 Expanding Your Horizons

Below Word Project 1, click the Expanding Your Horizons link. Click a topic that pertains to Project 1. Print the information. Construct a brief example of what the information relates to in Word to confirm you understand the contents of the article.

10 Search Sleuth

Below Word Project 1, click the Search Sleuth link. To search for a term that pertains to this project, select a term below the Project 1 title and then use the Google search engine at google.com (or any major search engine) to display and print two Web pages that present information on the term.

11 Word Online Training

Below Word Project 1, click the Word Online Training link. When your browser displays the Microsoft Office Online Web page, click the Word link. Click one of the Word courses that covers one or more of the objectives listed at the beginning of the project on page WD 4. Print the first page of the course before stepping through it.

12 Office Marketplace

Below Word Project 1, click the Office Marketplace link. When your browser displays the Microsoft Office Online Web page, click the Office Marketplace link. Click a topic that relates to Word. Print the first page.

Apply Your Knowledge

1 Checking Spelling and Grammar, Modifying Text, and Formatting a Document

Instructions: Start Word. Open the document, Apply 1-1 Paris Announcement Unformatted, on the Data Disk. See the inside back cover of this book for instructions for downloading the Data Disk or see your instructor for information about accessing files required in this book.

The document on the Data Disk is an unformatted announcement that contains some spelling errors. You are to fix the spelling mistakes, modify text, format paragraphs and characters, and insert clip art in the announcement, so it looks like Figure 1-77 on the next page.

1. Correct each spelling and grammar error by right-clicking the flagged word and then clicking the appropriate correction on the shortcut menu, so the announcement text matches Figure 1-77 on the next page. The unformatted announcement on the Data Disk contains several spelling errors (red wavy underline) and grammar errors (green wavy underline). Word may flag some proper names that are spelled correctly. In these cases, click Ignore Once or Ignore All on the shortcut menu. If your screen does not display the wavy underlines, right-click the Spelling and Grammar Status icon on the status bar and be sure Hide Spelling Errors and Hide Grammatical Errors do not have check marks beside them. If they do, remove the check mark(s) by the appropriate command. If your screen still does not display the wavy underlines, right-click the Spelling and Grammar Status icon on the status bar, click Options on the shortcut menu, click the Recheck Document button, and then click the OK button.
2. At the end of the first sentence of body copy, change the period to an exclamation point. The sentence should read: See Paris this spring – on a shoestring!
3. Delete the word, morning, in the first sentence of the second paragraph of body copy.
4. Insert the word, event, between the text, Discount tickets, in the second sentence of the second paragraph of body copy. The text should read: Discount event tickets…
5. Change the font and font size of the first line of the headline to 72-point Lucida Calligraphy, or a similar font.
6. Change the font and font size of the second line of the headline to 48-point Lucida Calligraphy, or a similar font.
7. Right-align the second line of the headline.
8. Change the font size of the two paragraphs of body copy to 20 point.
9. Change the font and font size of the last line of the announcement to 24-point Arial.
10. Italicize the word, shoestring, in the first paragraph of body copy.
11. Bold the phrase, unbelievably low price, in the same paragraph.
12. Underline the telephone number in the last line of the announcement.
13. Italicize the text in the last line of the announcement.
14. Center the last line of the announcement.
15. Insert the clip art between the first and second lines of the headline. Use the search text, Paris, to locate this, or a similar, clip art image. Center the clip art.
16. Click File on the menu bar and then click Save As. Save the document using Apply 1-1 Paris Announcement Formatted as the file name.
17. Print the revised document, shown in Figure 1-77.

(continued)

Apply Your Knowledge

Checking Spelling and Grammar, Modifying Text, and Formatting a Document *(continued)*

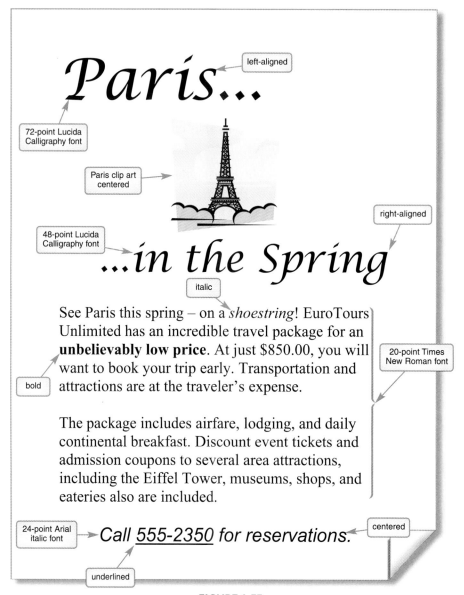

FIGURE 1-77

In the Lab

1 Creating an Announcement with Clip Art

Problem: You work part-time for the events coordinator at Memorial Hall. She has asked you to prepare an announcement for the upcoming annual charity costume ball. First, you prepare the unformatted announcement shown in Figure 1-78a, and then you format it so it looks like Figure 1-78b on the next page. *Hint:* Remember, if you make a mistake while formatting the announcement, you can click the Undo button on the Standard toolbar to undo your last action.

1. Before entering any text, change the font size from 12 to 20.
2. Display formatting marks on the screen.
3. Type the unformatted announcement shown in Figure 1-78a. If Word flags any misspelled words as you type, check the spelling of these words and correct them.
4. Save the document on a floppy disk with Lab 1-1 Costume Ball Announcement as the file name.

Come One...
...Come All

Charity Costume Ball

Mark your calendar for a fun-filled gala on Saturday, August 6, at 8:00 p.m. at Memorial Hall. Tickets are $50.00 per couple, with dinner prepared by Chef Jeffery Vincent of Le Chic and live entertainment by The Class Act. All proceeds go to charity.

As in past years, this event includes prizes for the best costumes, door prizes, a silent auction, and the traditional unmasking at midnight. Have an enjoyable evening while promoting a good cause.

Call 555-6344 for reservations.

(a) Unformatted Document

FIGURE 1-78

5. Change the font of both lines of the headline to Cooper Black, or a similar font. Change the font size from 20 to 48.
6. Right-align the second line of the headline.
7. Center the body title line.

(continued)

In the Lab

Creating an Announcement with Clip Art *(continued)*

8. Change the font of the body title line to Harrington, or a similar font. Change the font size to 36. Bold the body title line.
9. In the first paragraph of the body copy, bold the text, fun-filled.
10. In the same paragraph, italicize the word, live.
11. In the same paragraph, underline the word, All.
12. Center the last line of the announcement.
13. Insert the clip art of a mask between the headline and the body title line. Search for the text, mask, in the Clip Art task pane to locate this, or a similar, graphic.
14. Center the clip art.
15. Save the announcement again with the same file name.
16. Print the formatted announcement, as shown in Figure 1-78b.

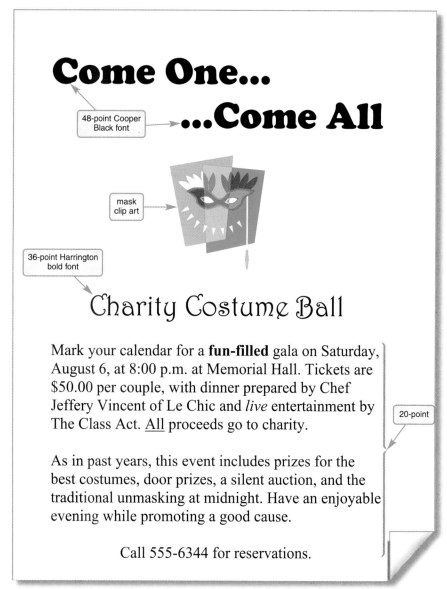

(b) Formatted Document

FIGURE 1-78

2 Creating an Announcement with Resized Clip Art

Problem: Your boss at Southside Physicians Group has requested that you prepare an announcement for the upcoming Public Health Clinic. You prepare the announcement shown in Figure 1-79. *Hint:* Remember, if you make a mistake while formatting the announcement, you can click the Undo button on the Standard toolbar to undo your last action.

1. Before entering any text, change the font size from 12 to 20.
2. Display formatting marks on the screen.

In the Lab

3. Create the announcement shown in Figure 1-79. Enter the text of the document first without the clip art and unformatted; that is, without any bold, underlined, italicized, right-aligned, or centered text. If Word flags any misspelled words as you type, check the spelling of these words and correct them.

4. Save the document on a floppy disk with Lab 1-2 Health Clinic Announcement as the file name.

5. Change the font of both lines of the headline to Brush Script MT, or a similar font. Change the font size from 20 to 48.

6. Right-align the second line of the headline.

7. Center the body title line.

8. Change the font and font size of the body title line to 28-point Bookman Old Style. Bold the body title line.

9. Underline the word, free, in the first paragraph of the body copy.

10. In the next paragraph, italicize these words: Qualified, licensed physicians and nurse practitioners.

FIGURE 1-79

11. Center the last line of the announcement.

12. Insert the clip art between the headline and the body title line. Search for the text, medicine, in the Clip Art task pane to locate this, or a similar, graphic. Center the graphic.

13. Enlarge the graphic. If you make the graphic too large, the announcement may flow onto two pages. If this occurs, reduce the size of the graphic so the announcement fits on a single page. *Hint:* Use Help to learn about print preview, which is a way to see the page before you print it. To exit print preview and return to the document window, click the Close button on the Print Preview toolbar.

14. Save the announcement again with the same file name.

15. Print the announcement.

In the Lab

3 Creating an Announcement with Resized Clip Art, a Bulleted List, and Color

Problem: The owner of Zachary Sports Complex has requested that each student in your class prepare an announcement advertising the sports complex. The student that creates the winning announcement will receive a complimentary membership. You prepare the announcement shown in Figure 1-80. *Hint:* Remember, if you make a mistake while formatting the announcement, you can click the Undo button on the Standard toolbar to undo your last action.

1. Type the announcement shown in Figure 1-80, using the fonts and font sizes indicated in the figure. Check spelling as you type.
2. Save the document on a floppy disk with Lab 1-3 Training Camp Announcement as the file name.
3. Change the font color of the headline to red, the body title to blue, and the last line of the announcement to green. *Hint:* Use Help to learn how to change the font color of text.
4. Add a brown double underline below the text, Space is limited. *Hint:* Use Help to learn how to add a decorative underline to text.
5. Add bullets to the three paragraphs of body copy. *Hint:* Use Help to learn how to add bullets to a list of paragraphs.

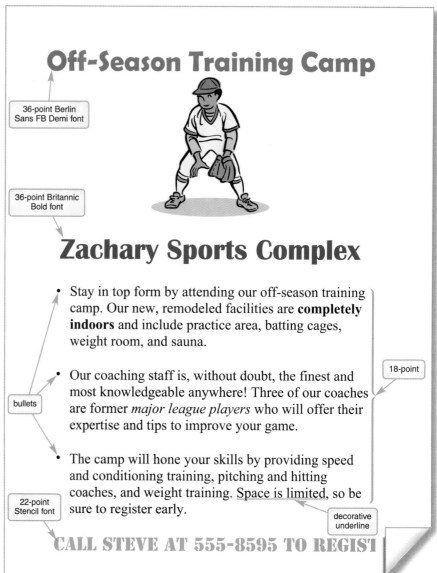

FIGURE 1-80

6. Insert clip art of a baseball player between the headline and the body title line. If you have access to the Web, select the clip art from the Web. Otherwise, select the clip art from the hard disk. In the Clip Art task pane, images from the Web display an icon of a small globe in their lower-left corner.
7. Enlarge the graphic of the baseball player. If you make the graphic too large, the announcement may flow onto two pages. If this occurs, reduce the size of the graphic so the announcement fits on a single page. *Hint:* Use Help to learn about print preview, which is a way to see the page before you print it. To exit print preview and return to the document window, click the Close button on the Print Preview toolbar.
8. Save the announcement again with the same file name.
9. Print the announcement.

Cases and Places

The difficulty of these case studies varies:
■ are the least difficult and ■■ are more difficult. The last exercise is a group exercise.

1 ■ You have been assigned the task of preparing an announcement for The Gridiron Club. The announcement is to contain clip art related to football. Use the following text: first line of headline – Gridiron Club…; second line of headline – …Tailgate Party; body title – GO TROJANS!; first paragraph of body copy – Join us on Friday, October 28, for a pre-game tailgate party. Help us celebrate our beloved Trojans' undefeated season! The Gridiron Club will provide grills, brats, hamburgers, hot dogs, and buns. Please bring a side dish to share and your own nonalcoholic beverages.; second paragraph of body copy – The party starts at 5:30 p.m. in the parking lot by the Administration Center. Kick-off for the first playoff game is at 7:00 p.m.; last line – Call 555-1995 for more information. Use the concepts and techniques presented in this project to create and format this announcement. Be sure to check spelling and grammar in the announcement.

2 ■ You have been assigned the task of preparing an announcement for an upcoming camp at the Sherman Planetarium. The announcement is to contain clip art of a telescope. Use the following text: first line of headline – Reach for…; second line of headline – …the Stars; body title – Space, Stars, and Skies Camp; first paragraph of body copy – Have you always been fascinated by the planets, stars, and space travel? Enroll in our Space, Stars, and Skies Camp to learn more about the cosmos. The camp will meet June 6 through June 9 from 8:30 a.m. until 12:30 p.m. at the Sherman Planetarium.; second paragraph of body copy – Our facilities include simulators, lecture halls, virtual rooms, and a planetarium. Learn about space travel from our staff, two of whom are former astronauts.; third paragraph of body copy – Register early to reserve your seat. Space is limited to 25 participants.; last line – Call 555-9141 to register. Use the concepts and techniques presented in this project to create and format this announcement. Be sure to check spelling and grammar in the announcement.

3 ■■ Your boss at Cornucopia Health Foods has asked you to prepare an announcement for a grand opening. You are to include appropriate clip art. He gives you the following information for the announcement. The doors of its newest store will open in Centerbrook Mall at 9:00 a.m. on Monday, September 26. You will find great deals throughout the store. Discount coupons and free samples will be distributed all day. The first 50 customers at the register will receive a free bottle of vitamin C tablets. Cornucopia Health Foods offers a huge selection of health food and organics. Tofu, carob, soy products, herbal teas, vitamin supplements, and organically grown produce are just a few items in our extensive product line. The store's slogan is as follows: Cornucopia ~ good food for good health! Use the concepts and techniques presented in this project to create the announcement. Change the color of text in the headline, body title, and last line of the announcement. Use a decorative underline in the announcement. Add bullets to the paragraphs of the body copy. Be sure to check spelling and grammar in the announcement.

Cases and Places

4 ◼◼ You have been assigned the task of preparing an announcement for Stone Bay Apartments advertising an apartment for rent. You are to include appropriate clip art. These details have been provided. Stone Bay Apartments has a two-bedroom apartment available for rent now. This upper-level unit has an eat-in kitchen, central air, and a large living room with southern exposure. Rent is $925.00 a month. Utilities are included in rent. Pets are welcome. Interested parties should call 555-8265 to arrange a showing. Stone Bay Apartments provide amenities galore, including laundry facilities, garage parking, clubhouse, pool, and tennis courts. We are located close to Lake Park Mall, grocery stores, restaurants, and Victor Community College. Use the concepts and techniques presented in this project to create the announcement. Change the color of text in the headline, body title, and last line of the announcement. Use a decorative underline in the announcement. Add bullets to some of the paragraphs of the body copy. Be sure to check spelling and grammar in the announcement.

5 ◼◼ **Working Together** Schools, churches, libraries, grocery stores, and other public places have bulletin boards for announcements and other postings. Often, these bulletin boards have so many announcements that some go unnoticed. Look at a bulletin board at one of the locations mentioned above and find a posted announcement that you think might be overlooked. Copy the text from the announcement and distribute it to each team member. Each member then independently should use this text, together with the techniques presented in this project, to create an announcement that would be more likely to catch a reader's eye. Be sure to check spelling and grammar. As a group, critique each announcement and have each member redesign their announcement based on the group's recommendations. Hand in printouts of each team member's original and final announcements.

Creating a Research Paper

PROJECT

2

CASE PERSPECTIVE

Suzy Zhao is a full-time college student, majoring in Finance. Mr. Ortiz, the instructor in her introductory computer class, has assigned a short research paper that should contain a minimum of 325 words. The paper must discuss some aspect of computer security. It also must be written according to the MLA documentation style, which specifies guidelines for report preparation. The paper is to contain one footnote and three references — one of which must be obtained from the World Wide Web. Finally, all students are to submit their papers electronically via e-mail to Mr. Ortiz.

When Suzy graduates from college, she plans to work in the banking sector. She is interested in ways to ensure that users are legitimate before allowing them access to a computer. Suzy recently read a short article about computer security that mentioned computers can use biometrics to authenticate a person's identity by verifying a personal characteristic. Examples include fingerprints, hand geometry, facial features, voice, signatures, and eye patterns. Suzy decides to write her research paper about biometrics. She intends to review computer magazines at the school's library, surf the Internet, and e-mail a few biometrics vendors for information about their products. She also plans to use the Internet to obtain the guidelines for the MLA style of documentation. Suzy knows that you are a computer major and quite skilled at searching the Internet. She asks you to assist her with the Web searches. You immediately agree to help your friend.

As you read through this project, you will learn how to use Word to create a research paper and e-mail a copy of the finished paper.

Creating a Research Paper

Objectives

You will have mastered the material in this project when you can:

- Describe the MLA documentation style for research papers
- Change the margin settings and line spacing in a document
- Use a header to number pages of a document
- Apply formatting using shortcut keys
- Modify paragraph indentation
- Add a footnote to a document

- Count the words in a document
- Insert a manual page break
- Create a hyperlink
- Sort selected paragraphs
- Proof and revise a document
- Display the Web page associated with a hyperlink
- E-mail a copy of a document
- Use the Research task pane to locate information

Introduction

In both academic and business environments, you will be asked to write reports. Business reports range from proposals to cost justifications to five-year plans to research findings. Academic reports focus mostly on research findings. Whether you are writing a business report or an academic report, you should follow a standard style when preparing it.

Many different styles of documentation exist for report preparation, depending on the nature of the report. Each style requires the same basic information; the differences among styles relates to how the information is presented. For example, one documentation style may use the term bibliography, whereas another uses references, and yet a third prefers works cited. Two popular documentation styles for research papers are the **Modern Language Association of America** (**MLA**) and **American Psychological Association** (**APA**) styles. This project uses the MLA documentation style.

Project 2 — Biometrics Research Paper

Project 2 illustrates the creation of a short research paper about biometrics. As shown in Figure 2-1, the paper follows the MLA documentation style. The first two pages present the research paper, and the third page alphabetically lists the works cited.

Zhao 3

Works Cited

Carter, Donnell W., and Louis C. Juarez. *Securing Confidential Data Entered into a Computer.*
Boston: Thomas Publishing, 2005.

Computers and Biometrics. Shelly Cashman Series®. Course Technology. 3 Oct. 2005.
http://www.scsite.com/wd2003/pr2/wc.htm.

Schmidt, Karl J. "Biometrics and Authenticating Computer Users." *Computers and the Internet*
Aug. 2005: 54-62.

> paragraphs in alphabetical order

Zhao 2

Law enforcement, surveillance systems, airports, day-care centers, financial institutions,
the military, and other organizations that deal with highly sensitive data use other types of
biometrics. A face recognition system captures a live face image and compares it with a stored
image. A hand geometry system measures the shape and size of a person's hand (*Computers and
Biometrics*). A voice verification system compares a person's live speech with his or her stored
voice pattern. A signature verification system recognizes the shape of a handwritten signature, as
well as measures the pressure exerted and the motion used to write the signature. Finally, an iris
recognition system reads patterns in the iris of the eye.

> parenthetical citation

Suzy Zhao

Mr. Ortiz

Information Systems 101

October 13, 2005

Biometrics

> header contains last name followed by page number → Zhao 1

> parenthetical citation

Biometrics is the technology of authenticating a person's identity by verifying a personal
characteristic. Biometric devices grant users access to programs, systems, or rooms by analyzing
some biometric identifier (Schmidt 54-62). A biometric identifier is a physical or behavioral
characteristic. Examples include fingerprints, facial features, hand geometry, voice patterns,
signatures, and eye patterns.

A biometric device translates a personal characteristic into a digital code that is compared
with a digital code stored in the computer. If the digital code in the computer does not match the
personal characteristic's code, the computer denies access to the individual.

The most widely used biometric device today is a fingerprint scanner. A fingerprint
scanner captures curves and indentations of a fingerprint. With the cost of fingerprint scanners
less than $100, experts believe this technology will become the home user's authentication
device for e-commerce transactions. To conduct a credit-card transaction, the Web site would
require users to hold a finger on the scanner. External fingerprint scanners usually plug into a
parallel or USB port.[1] Businesses use fingerprint scanners to authenticate users before they can
access a personal computer. Grade schools use fingerprint scanners as an alternative to lunch
money. Students' account balances adjust for each lunch purchased.

> superscripted note reference mark

---

[1] According to Carter and Juarez, newer keyboards and notebook computers have a
fingerprint scanner built into them (42-53).

> explanatory note positioned as footnote

More About

MLA and APA

The MLA documentation style is the standard in the humanities, and the APA style is preferred in the social sciences. For more information about the MLA and APA guidelines, visit the Word 2003 More About Web page (scsite.com/wd2003/more) and then click MLA or APA, respectively.

FIGURE 2-1

MLA Documentation Style

When writing papers, you should adhere to some style of documentation. The research paper in this project follows the guidelines presented by the MLA. To follow the MLA style, double-space text on all pages of the paper using one-inch top, bottom, left, and right margins. Indent the first word of each paragraph one-half inch from the left margin. At the right margin of each page, place a page number one-half inch from the top margin. On each page, precede the page number by your last name.

The MLA style does not require a title page. Instead, place your name and course information in a block at the left margin beginning one inch from the top of the page. Center the title one double-space below your name and course information.

In the body of the paper, place author references in parentheses with the page number(s) of the referenced information. The MLA style uses in-text **parenthetical citations** instead of noting each source at the bottom of the page or at the end of the paper. In the MLA style, notes are used only for optional explanatory notes.

If used, explanatory notes elaborate on points discussed in the body of the paper. Use a superscript (raised number) to signal that an explanatory note exists, and also sequence the notes. Position explanatory notes either at the bottom of the page as footnotes or at the end of the paper as endnotes. Indent the first line of each explanatory note one-half inch from the left margin. Place one space following the superscripted number before beginning the note text. Double-space the note text. At the end of the note text, you may list bibliographic information for further reference.

The MLA style uses the term **works cited** for the bibliographical references. The works cited page alphabetically lists works that are referenced directly in the paper. List works by each author's last name, or, if the author's name is not available, by the title of the work. Italicize or underline the title of the work. Place the works cited on a separate numbered page. Center the title, Works Cited, one inch from the top margin. Double-space all lines. Begin the first line of each entry at the left margin, indenting subsequent lines of the same entry one-half inch from the left margin.

Starting and Customizing Word

To start and customize Word, Windows must be running. If you are stepping through this project on a computer and you want your screen to match the figures in this book, then you should change your computer's resolution to 800 × 600 and reset the toolbars and menus. For information about changing the resolution and resetting toolbars and menus, read Appendix D.

The next steps show how to start Word and customize the Word window. You may need to ask your instructor how to start Word for your system.

More About

Titles of Works

Titles of books, periodicals, and Web sites typically are underlined when a research paper is submitted in printed form. Some instructors require that Web addresses be hyperlinks for online access. Word formats hyperlinks with an underline. To distinguish hyperlinks from titles, the MLA allows titles to be italicized, if approved by the instructor.

Q: How does the APA style differ from the MLA style?

A: In the APA style, double-space all pages of the paper with 1.5" top, bottom, left, and right margins. Indent the first word of each paragraph .5" from the left margin. In the upper-right margin of each page, place a running head that consists of the page number double-spaced below a summary of the paper title.

To Start and Customize Word

1 Click the Start button on the Windows taskbar, point to All Programs on the Start menu, point to Microsoft Office on the All Programs submenu, and then click Microsoft Office Word 2003 on the Microsoft Office submenu.

2 If the Word window is not maximized, double-click its title bar to maximize it.

3 If the Language bar appears, right-click it and then click Close the Language bar on the shortcut menu.

4 If the Getting Started task pane is displayed in the Word window, click its Close button.

5 If the Standard and Formatting toolbar buttons are displayed on one row, click the Toolbar Options button and then click Show Buttons on Two Rows in the Toolbar Options list.

6 If your screen differs from Figure 2-2 on the next page, click View on the menu bar and then click Normal.

7 If your zoom percent is not 100 (shown in Figure 2-2), click View on the menu bar, click Zoom on the View menu, click 100%, and then click the OK button.

Word starts and, after a few moments, displays an empty document titled Document1 in the Word window (shown in Figure 2-2).

Displaying Formatting Marks

As discussed in Project 1, it is helpful to display formatting marks that indicate where in the document you pressed the ENTER key, SPACEBAR, and other keys. The following step discusses how to display formatting marks.

To Display Formatting Marks

1 If the Show/Hide ¶ button on the Standard toolbar is not selected already, click it.

Word displays formatting marks in the document window, and the Show/Hide ¶ button on the Standard toolbar is selected (shown in Figure 2-2).

Changing the Margins

Word is preset to use standard 8.5-by-11-inch paper, with 1.25-inch left and right margins and 1-inch top and bottom margins. These margin settings affect every page in the document.

Periodically, you may want to change the default margin settings. The MLA documentation style, for example, requires one-inch top, bottom, left, and right margins throughout the paper. Thus, the steps on the next page show how to change the margin settings for a document when the window is in normal view. To verify the document window is in normal view, click View on the menu bar and then click Normal.

More About

Writing Papers

The Web contains numerous sites with information, tips, and suggestions about writing research papers. College professors and fellow students develop many of these Web sites. For links to Web sites about writing research papers, visit the Word 2003 More About Web page (scsite.com/wd2003/more) and then click one of the Writing Research Papers links.

More About

Changing Margins

In print layout view, you can change margin settings using the horizontal and vertical rulers. Current margin settings are shaded in gray. The margin boundary is located where the gray meets the white. To change a margin setting, drag the margin boundary on the ruler. To see the numeric margin settings, hold down the ALT key while dragging the margin boundary on the ruler.

To Change the Margin Settings

1

• **Click File on the menu bar (Figure 2-2).**

FIGURE 2-2

2

• **Click Page Setup on the File menu.**

• **When Word displays the Page Setup dialog box, if necessary, click the Margins tab.**

Word displays the current margin settings in the text boxes of the Page Setup dialog box (Figure 2-3).

FIGURE 2-3

3

• **With 1" selected in the Top text box, press the TAB key twice to select 1.25" in the Left text box.**

• **Type** 1 **and then press the TAB key.**

• **Type** 1 **in the Right text box.**

The new left and right margin settings are 1 inch (Figure 2-4). Instead of typing margin values, you can click the text box arrows to increase or decrease the number in the text box.

4

• **Click the OK button in the Page Setup dialog box.**

Word changes the left and right margins.

FIGURE 2-4

The new margin settings take effect immediately in the document. Word uses these margins for the entire document.

When you change the margin settings in the text boxes in the Page Setup dialog box, the Preview area (Figure 2-4) does not adjust to reflect a changed margin setting until the insertion point leaves the respective text box. That is, you must press the TAB or ENTER key or click another text box if you want to view a changed margin setting in the Preview area.

Adjusting Line Spacing

Line spacing is the amount of vertical space between lines of text in a document. By default, Word single-spaces between lines of text and automatically adjusts line height to accommodate various font sizes and graphics.

The MLA documentation style requires that you **double-space** the entire paper; that is, one blank line should be between each line of text. The steps on the next page show how to adjust the line spacing from single to double.

Other Ways

1. In print layout view, drag margin boundary(s) on ruler
2. In Voice Command mode, say "File, Page Setup, Margins, Left, [type left margin setting], Tab, [type right margin setting], OK"

More About

The Page Setup Dialog Box

A document printed in portrait orientation is taller than it is wide. A document printed in landscape orientation is wider than it is tall. If you want to change the orientation of a printout from portrait to landscape, click Landscape in the Orientation area in the Page Setup dialog box (Figure 2-4).

To Double-Space Text

1

• **Click the Line Spacing button arrow on the Formatting toolbar.**

Word displays a list of line spacing options (Figure 2-5).

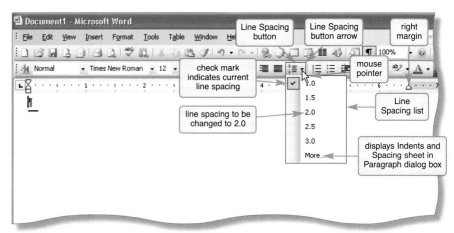

FIGURE 2-5

2

• **Click 2.0 in the Line Spacing list.**

Word changes the line spacing to double at the location of the insertion point (Figure 2-6).

FIGURE 2-6

Other Ways

1. On Format menu click Paragraph, click Indents and Spacing tab, click Line spacing box arrow, click Double, click OK button
2. Right-click paragraph, click Paragraph on shortcut menu, click Indents and Spacing tab, click Line spacing box arrow, click Double, click OK button
3. Press CTRL+2
4. In Voice Command mode, say "Line Spacing, [select 2]"

More About

Line Spacing

If the top of characters or a graphic is chopped off, then line spacing may be set to Exactly in the Paragraph dialog box. To remedy the problem, change the line spacing to Single (1.0), 1.5, Double (2.0), 2.5, 3.0, or At least, all of which accommodate the largest font or graphic.

Notice when line spacing is double (Figure 2-6), the end mark displays one blank line below the insertion point.

The Line Spacing list (Figure 2-5) contains a variety of settings for the line spacing. The default, 1 (for single), and the options 1.5, 2 (for double), 2.5, and 3 (for triple) instruct Word to adjust line spacing automatically to accommodate the largest font or graphic on a line. For additional line spacing options, click More in the Line Spacing list and then click the Line spacing box arrow in the Indents and Spacing sheet in the Paragraph dialog box.

If you wanted to apply the most recently set line spacing to the current or selected paragraphs, you would click the Line Spacing button instead of the Line Spacing button arrow.

To change the line spacing of existing text, select the text first and then change the line spacing. For example, to change an existing paragraph to double-spacing, triple-click the paragraph to select it, click the Line Spacing button arrow on the Formatting toolbar, and then click 2.0 in the list.

Using a Header to Number Pages

In Word, you easily can number pages by clicking Insert on the menu bar and then clicking Page Numbers. Using the Page Numbers command, you can specify the location (top or bottom of the page) and alignment (right, left, or centered) of the page numbers.

The MLA style requires that your last name display to the left of the page number on each page. The Page Numbers command, however, does not allow you to enter text along with the page number. Thus, to place your name to the left of the page number, you must create a header that contains the page number.

Headers and Footers

A **header** is text you want printed at the top of each page in a document. A **footer** is text you want printed at the bottom of every page. In Word, headers print in the top margin one-half inch from the top of every page, and footers print in the bottom margin one-half inch from the bottom of each page, which meets the MLA style. Headers and footers can include text and graphics, as well as the page number, total number of pages, current date, and current time.

In this project, you are to precede the page number with your last name placed one-half inch from the top of each page. Your last name and the page number should print right-aligned; that is, at the right margin.

To create the header, first you display the header area in the document window. Then, you can enter the header text into the header area. The procedures on the following pages show how to create the header with page numbers, according to the MLA documentation style.

To Display the Header Area

1

• **Click View on the menu bar (Figure 2-7).**

FIGURE 2-7

2

• **Click Header and Footer on the View menu.**

• **If your zoom percent is not 100, click View on the menu bar, click Zoom on the View menu, click 100%, and then click the OK button.**

Word switches from normal view to print layout view and displays the Header and Footer toolbar (Figure 2-8). You type header text in the header area.

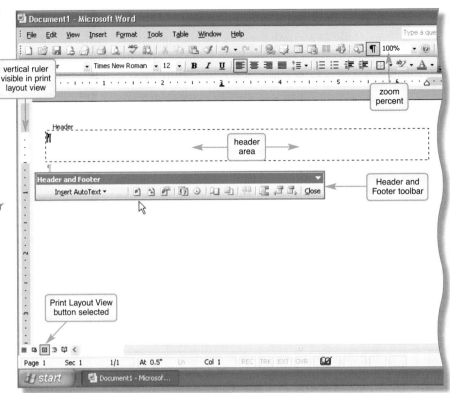

FIGURE 2-8

1. If header already exists, click Print Layout View button on horizontal scroll bar, double-click header area
2. In Voice Command mode, say "View, Header and Footer"

The Header and Footer toolbar initially floats in the document window. To move a floating toolbar, drag its title bar. You can **dock**, or attach, a floating toolbar above or below the Standard and Formatting toolbars by double-clicking the floating toolbar's title bar. To move a docked toolbar, drag its move handle. Recall that the move handle is the vertical dotted bar to the left of the first button on a docked toolbar. If you drag a floating toolbar to an edge of the window, the toolbar snaps to the edge of the window. If you drag a docked toolbar to the middle of the window, the toolbar floats in the Word window.

The header area does not display on the screen when the document window is in normal view because it tends to clutter the screen. To see the header in the document window with the rest of the text, you can display the document in print preview, which is discussed in a later project, or you can switch to print layout view. When you click the Header and Footer command on the View menu, Word automatically switches to **print layout view**, which displays the document exactly as it will print. In print layout view, the Print Layout View button on the horizontal scroll bar is selected (Figure 2-8).

Entering Text Using Click and Type

When in print layout view, you can use **Click and Type** to format and enter text, graphics, and other items. To use Click and Type, you double-click a blank area of the document window. Word automatically formats the item you enter according to the location where you double-click. The next steps show how to use Click and Type to right-align and then type the last name into the header area.

More About

Click and Type

Click and Type is not available in normal view, in a bulleted or numbered list, or in a document formatted as multiple columns. In print layout view, use the ruler to click at a specific location in the document (e.g., 2 inches from the top or bottom).

To Click and Type

1

• **Position the mouse pointer at the right edge of the header area to display a right-align icon next to the I-beam.**

As you move the Click and Type pointer around the window, the icon changes to represent formatting that will be applied if you double-click at that location (Figure 2-9).

FIGURE 2-9

2

• **Double-click.**

• **Type** Zhao **and then press the SPACEBAR.**

Word displays the last name, Zhao, right-aligned in the header area (Figure 2-10).

FIGURE 2-10

Entering a Page Number into the Header

The next task is to enter the page number into the header area, as shown in the following steps.

To Enter a Page Number

1

• **Click the Insert Page Number button on the Header and Footer toolbar.**

Word displays the page number 1 in the header area (Figure 2-11).

FIGURE 2-11

2

• **Click the Close Header and Footer button on the Header and Footer toolbar.**

Word closes the Header and Footer toolbar and returns the screen to normal view (Figure 2-12).

vertical ruler is not displayed in normal view

header is not displayed in normal view

FIGURE 2-12

Word does not display the header on the screen in normal view. Although it disappears from the screen when you switch from print layout view to normal view, the header still is part of the document. To view the header, you can click View on the menu bar and then click Header and Footer; you can switch to print layout view; or you can display the document in print preview. Project 3 discusses print layout view and print preview.

Figure 2-13 identifies the buttons on the Header and Footer toolbar. Just as the Insert Page Number button on the Header and Footer toolbar inserts the page number into the document, three other buttons on the Header and Footer toolbar insert items into the document. The Insert Number of Pages button inserts the total number of pages in the document; the Insert Date button inserts the current date; and the Insert Time button inserts the current time.

To edit an existing header, you can follow the same procedure that you use to create a new header. That is, click View on the menu bar and then click Header and Footer to display the header area. If you have multiple headers, click the Show Next button on the Header and Footer toolbar until the appropriate header displays in the header area. Edit the header as you would any Word text and then click the Close Header and Footer button on the Header and Footer toolbar.

To create a footer, click View on the menu bar, click Header and Footer, click the Switch Between Header and Footer button on the Header and Footer toolbar, and then follow the same procedure as you would to create a header.

Later projects explain other buttons on the Header and Footer toolbar.

FIGURE 2-13

Typing the Body of a Research Paper

The body of the research paper in this project encompasses the first two pages of the research paper. You will type the body of the research paper and then modify it later in the project, so it matches Figure 2-1 on page WD 75.

As discussed earlier in this project, the MLA style does not require a separate title page for research papers. Instead, place your name and course information in a block at the top of the page at the left margin. The next steps describe how to begin typing the body of the research paper.

To Enter Name and Course Information

1 **Type** `Suzy Zhao` **and then press the ENTER key.**

2 **Type** `Mr. Ortiz` **and then press the ENTER key.**

3 **Type** `Information Systems 101` **and then press the ENTER key.**

4 **Type** `October 13, 2005` **and then press the ENTER key.**

Word displays the student name on line 1, the instructor name on line 2, the course name on line 3, and the paper due date on line 4 (Figure 2-14). Depending on your Word settings, the smart tag indicator may not appear below the date on the screen.

Q&A

Q: Does the APA style require a title page?

A: Yes, a separate title page is required instead of placing name and course information on the paper's first page. The running head (header), which contains a brief summary of the title and the page number, also is on the title page.

More About

Smart Tags

Word notifies you of a smart tag by displaying a smart tag indicator, such as the purple dotted underline shown in Figure 2-14. You then can use the smart tag to perform tasks more efficiently. For example, you can schedule an appointment on the under-lined date in Outlook Calendar. Smart tags are discussed later in this project.

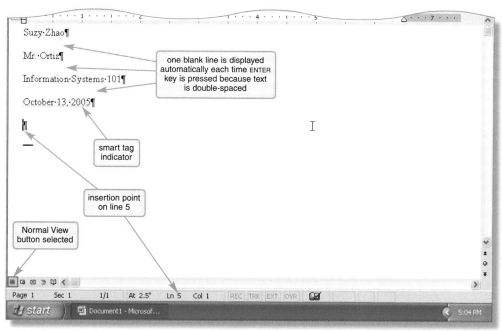

FIGURE 2-14

Notice in Figure 2-14 that the insertion point currently is on line 5. Each time you press the ENTER key, Word advances two lines on the screen. The line counter on the status bar is incremented by only one, however, because earlier you set line spacing to double.

If you watch the screen as you type, you may have noticed that as you typed the first few characters in the month, Octo, Word displayed the **AutoComplete tip**, October, above the characters. To save typing, you could press the ENTER key while the AutoComplete tip appears, which instructs Word to place the text of the AutoComplete tip at the location of your typing.

Applying Formatting Using Shortcut Keys

The next step is to enter the title of the research paper centered between the page margins. As you type text, you may want to format paragraphs and characters as you type them, instead of typing the text and then formatting it later. In Project 1, you typed the entire document, selected the text to be formatted, and then applied the desired formatting using toolbar buttons. When your fingers are already on the keyboard, it often is more efficient to use **shortcut keys**, or keyboard key combinations, to format text as you type it.

The following steps show how to center a paragraph using the shortcut keys CTRL+E and then left-align a paragraph using the shortcut keys CTRL+L. (Recall from Project 1 that a notation such as CTRL+E means to press the letter e on the keyboard while holding down the CTRL key.)

To Format Text Using Shortcut Keys

1

• **Press CTRL+E.**

• **Type** Biometrics **and then press the ENTER key.**

Word centers the title between the left and right margins (Figure 2-15). The paragraph mark and insertion point are centered because the formatting specified in the previous paragraph is carried forward to the next paragraph.

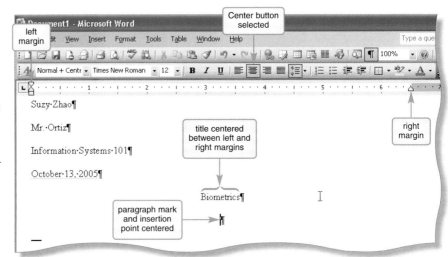

FIGURE 2-15

2

• **Press CTRL+L.**

Word positions the paragraph mark and the insertion point at the left margin (Figure 2-16). The next text you type will be left-aligned.

FIGURE 2-16

Word has many shortcut keys for your convenience while typing. Table 2-1 lists the common shortcut keys for formatting characters. Table 2-2 lists common shortcut keys for formatting paragraphs.

Table 2-1 Shortcut Keys for Formatting Characters	
CHARACTER FORMATTING TASK	**SHORTCUT KEYS**
All capital letters	CTRL+SHIFT+A
Bold	CTRL+B
Case of letters	SHIFT+F3
Decrease font size	CTRL+SHIFT+<
Decrease font size 1 point	CTRL+[
Double-underline	CTRL+SHIFT+D
Increase font size	CTRL+SHIFT+>
Increase font size 1 point	CTRL+]
Italic	CTRL+I
Remove character formatting (plain text)	CTRL+SPACEBAR
Small uppercase letters	CTRL+SHIFT+K
Subscript	CTRL+=
Superscript	CTRL+SHIFT+PLUS SIGN
Underline	CTRL+U
Underline words, not spaces	CTRL+SHIFT+W

Table 2-2 Shortcut Keys for Formatting Paragraphs	
PARAGRAPH FORMATTING TASK	**SHORTCUT KEYS**
1.5 line spacing	CTRL+5
Add/remove one line above	CTRL+0 (zero)
Center paragraph	CTRL+E
Decrease paragraph indent	CTRL+SHIFT+M
Double-space lines	CTRL+2
Hanging indent	CTRL+T
Increase paragraph indent	CTRL+M
Justify paragraph	CTRL+J
Left-align paragraph	CTRL+L
Remove hanging indent	CTRL+SHIFT+T
Remove paragraph formatting	CTRL+Q
Right-align paragraph	CTRL+R
Single-space lines	CTRL+1

Saving the Research Paper

You now should save the research paper. For a detailed example of the procedure summarized below, refer to pages WD 28 through WD 30 in Project 1.

To Save a Document

1 Insert a floppy disk into drive A.

2 Click the Save button on the Standard toolbar.

3 Type Biometrics Paper in the File name text box.

4 Click the Save in box arrow and then click 3½ Floppy (A:).

5 Click the Save button in the Save As dialog box.

Word saves the document with the file name, Biometrics Paper (shown in Figure 2-17 on the next page).

Indenting Paragraphs

According to the MLA style, the first line of each paragraph in the research paper is to be indented one-half inch from the left margin. You can instruct Word to indent just the first line of a paragraph, called **first-line indent**, using the horizontal ruler. The left edge of the horizontal ruler contains two triangles above a square. The **First Line Indent marker** is the top triangle at the 0" mark on the ruler (Figure 2-17). The bottom triangle is discussed later in this project. The small square at the 0" mark is the Left Indent marker. The **Left Indent marker** allows you to change the entire left margin, whereas the First Line Indent marker indents only the first line of the paragraph.

More About

Shortcut Keys

To print a complete list of shortcut keys in Word, type keyboard shortcuts in the Type a question for help box on the right side of the menu bar. In the Search Results task pane, click the Keyboard shortcuts link. In the upper-right corner of the Office Word Help window, click the Show All link. Click the Print button in the Help window and then click the Print button in the Print dialog box.

More About

First-Line Indent

Some users may find it confusing to use the ruler to indent paragraphs. In this case, you can use the Paragraph dialog box to first-line indent a paragraph. To do this, click Format on the menu bar, click Paragraph, click the Indents and Spacing tab, click the Special box arrow, click First line, and then click the OK button.

Microsoft Office
Word 2003

The following steps show how to first-line indent paragraphs in the research paper.

To First-Line Indent Paragraphs

1

• **If the horizontal ruler is not displayed on your screen, click View on the menu bar and then click Ruler.**

• **With the insertion point on the paragraph mark in line 6, point to the First Line Indent marker on the ruler (Figure 2-17).**

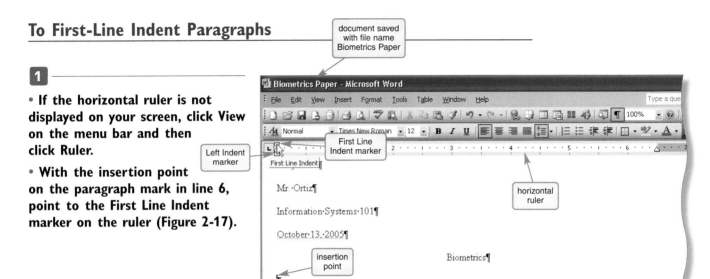

FIGURE 2-17

2

• **Drag the First Line Indent marker to the .5" mark on the ruler.**

As you drag the mouse, Word displays a vertical dotted line in the document window, indicating the proposed location of the first line of the paragraph (Figure 2-18).

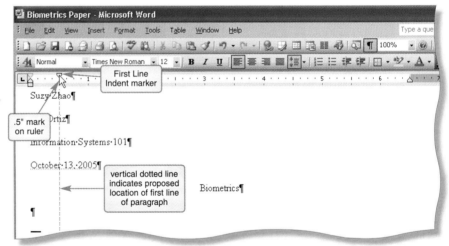

FIGURE 2-18

3

• **Release the mouse button.**

Word displays the First Line Indent marker at the .5" mark on the ruler, or one-half inch from the left margin (Figure 2-19). The paragraph mark containing the insertion point in the document window also moves one-half inch to the right.

FIGURE 2-19

4

• **Type the first paragraph of the research paper body, as shown in Figure 2-20.**

• **Press the ENTER key.**

• **Type** A biometric device translates a personal characteristic into a digital code that is compared with a digital code stored in the computer.

Word automatically indents the first line of the second paragraph by one-half inch (Figure 2-20).

FIGURE 2-20

Recall that each time you press the ENTER key, the paragraph formatting in the previous paragraph is carried forward to the next paragraph. Thus, once you set the first-line indent, its format carries forward automatically to each subsequent paragraph you type.

Using Word's AutoCorrect Feature

As you type, you may make typing, spelling, capitalization, or grammar errors. For this reason, Word provides an **AutoCorrect** feature that automatically corrects these kinds of errors as you type them in the document. For example, if you type the text, ahve, Word automatically changes it to the correct spelling, have, when you press the SPACEBAR or a punctuation mark key such as a period or comma.

Word has predefined many commonly misspelled words, which it automatically corrects for you. In the following steps the word, the, is misspelled intentionally as teh to illustrate the AutoCorrect as you type feature.

Other Ways

1. On Format menu click Paragraph, click Indents and Spacing tab, click Special box arrow, click First line, click OK button
2. Right-click paragraph, click Paragraph on shortcut menu, click Indents and Spacing tab, click Special box arrow, click First line, click OK button
3. Press TAB key at beginning of paragraph
4. In Voice Command mode, say "Format, Paragraph, Indents and Spacing, Special, First line, OK"

To AutoCorrect as You Type

1

• **Press the SPACEBAR.**

• **Type the beginning of the next sentence, misspelling the word, the, as follows:** If the digital code in the computer does not match teh **(Figure 2-21).**

FIGURE 2-21

2

• **Press the SPACEBAR.**

• **Type the rest of the sentence:** personal characteristic's code, the computer denies access to the individual.

As soon as the SPACEBAR is pressed, Word's AutoCorrect feature detects the misspelling and corrects the misspelled word (Figure 2-22).

FIGURE 2-22

More About

AutoCorrect

You can add entries to the AutoCorrect list while checking spelling. Right-click the word flagged with the red wavy underline. Point to AutoCorrect on the shortcut menu and then click the correction you want added to the AutoCorrect list.

Word has a list of predefined typing, spelling, capitalization, and grammar errors that AutoCorrect detects and corrects. If you do not like a change that Word automatically makes in a document and you immediately notice the automatic correction, you can undo the change by clicking the Undo button on the Standard toolbar; clicking Edit on the menu bar and then clicking Undo; or pressing CTRL+Z.

If you do not immediately notice the change, you still can undo a correction automatically made by Word through the AutoCorrect Options button. When you position the mouse pointer on text that Word automatically corrected, a small blue box appears below the text. If you point to the small blue box, Word displays the AutoCorrect Options button. When you click the **AutoCorrect Options button**, Word displays a menu that allows you to undo a correction or change how Word handles future automatic corrections of this type. The following steps show how to use the AutoCorrect Options button and menu.

To Use the AutoCorrect Options Button

1

• **Position the mouse pointer at the beginning of the text automatically corrected by Word (in this case, the t in the).**

Word displays a small blue box below the automatically corrected word (Figure 2-23).

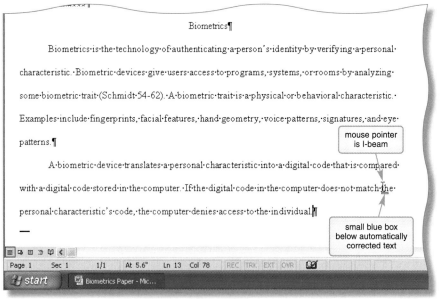

FIGURE 2-23

2

• **Point to the small blue box to display the AutoCorrect Options button.**

• **Click the AutoCorrect Options button.**

Word displays the AutoCorrect Options menu (Figure 2-24).

3

• **Press the ESCAPE key to remove the AutoCorrect Options menu from the screen.**

When you move the mouse pointer, the AutoCorrect Options button disappears from the screen, or you can press the ESCAPE key a second time to remove the AutoCorrect Options button from the screen.

FIGURE 2-24

In addition to the predefined list of AutoCorrect spelling, capitalization, and grammar errors, you can create your own AutoCorrect entries to add to the list. For example, if you tend to type the word, computer, as comptuer, you should create an AutoCorrect entry for it, as shown in these steps.

To Create an AutoCorrect Entry

More About

AutoCorrect Options

The small blue box that appears below the auto-matically corrected text (Figure 2-23) is another type of smart tag indicator. Smart tags are discussed later in this project.

1

• **Click Tools on the menu bar (Figure 2-25).**

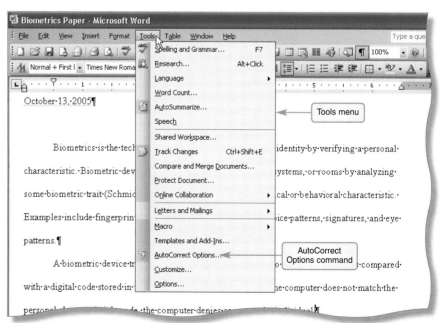

FIGURE 2-25

2

• **Click AutoCorrect Options on the Tools menu.**

• **When Word displays the AutoCorrect dialog box, type** comptuer **in the Replace text box.**

• **Press the TAB key and then type** computer **in the With text box.**

In the AutoCorrect dialog box, the Replace text box contains the misspelled word, and the With text box contains its correct spelling (Figure 2-26).

3

• **Click the Add button in the AutoCorrect dialog box. (If your dialog box displays a Replace button instead, click it and then click the Yes button in the Microsoft Office Word dialog box.)**

• **Click the OK button.**

Word adds the entry alphabetically to the list of words to correct automatically as you type.

FIGURE 2-26

In addition to creating AutoCorrect entries for words you commonly misspell or mistype, you can create entries for abbreviations, codes, and so on. For example, you could create an AutoCorrect entry for asap, indicating that Word should replace this text with the phrase, as soon as possible.

If, for some reason, you do not want Word to correct automatically as you type, you can turn off the Replace text as you type feature by clicking Tools on the menu bar, clicking AutoCorrect Options, clicking the AutoCorrect tab (Figure 2-26), clicking the Replace text as you type check box to remove the check mark, and then clicking the OK button.

The AutoCorrect sheet (Figure 2-26) contains other check boxes that correct capitalization errors if the check boxes are selected. If you type two capital letters in a row, such as TH, Word makes the second letter lowercase, Th. If you begin a sentence with a lowercase letter, Word capitalizes the first letter of the sentence. If you type the name of a day in lowercase, such as tuesday, Word capitalizes the first letter of the day, Tuesday. If you leave the CAPS LOCK key on and begin a new sentence such as aFTER, Word corrects the typing, After, and turns off the CAPS LOCK key.

Sometimes you do not want Word to AutoCorrect a particular word or phrase. For example, you may use the code WD. in your documents. Because Word automatically capitalizes the first letter of a sentence, the character you enter following the period will be capitalized (in the previous sentence, it would capitalize the letter i in the word, in). To allow the code WD. to be entered into a document and still leave the AutoCorrect feature turned on, you should set an exception. To set an exception to an AutoCorrect rule, click Tools on the menu bar, click AutoCorrect Options, click the AutoCorrect tab, click the Exceptions button in the AutoCorrect sheet (Figure 2-26), click the appropriate tab in the AutoCorrect Exceptions dialog box, type the exception entry in the text box, click the Add button, click the Close button in the AutoCorrect Exceptions dialog box, and then click the OK button in the AutoCorrect dialog box.

The next step is to continue typing text in the body of the research paper, up to the location of the footnote, as described below.

To Enter More Text

1 Press the ENTER key.

2 Type the first five sentences in the third paragraph of the paper as shown in Figure 2-27.

Word displays the first five sentences in the third paragraph in the document window (Figure 2-27).

FIGURE 2-27

Adding Footnotes

As discussed earlier in this project, explanatory notes are optional in the MLA documentation style. They are used primarily to elaborate on points discussed in the body of a research paper. The MLA style specifies that a superscript (raised number) be used for a **note reference mark** to signal that an explanatory note exists either at the bottom of the page as a **footnote** or at the end of the document as an **endnote**.

Word, by default, places notes at the bottom of each page as footnotes. In Word, **note text** can be any length and format. Word automatically numbers notes sequentially by placing a note reference mark in the body of the document and also to the left of the note text. If you insert, rearrange, or remove notes, Word renumbers any subsequent note reference marks according to their new sequence in the document.

Q: Should I footnote sources in a research paper?

A: Both the MLA and APA guidelines suggest the use of in-text parenthetical citations, instead of footnoting each source of material in a paper. These parenthetical acknowledgments guide the reader to the end of the paper for complete information on the source.

The following steps show how to add a footnote to the research paper.

To Add a Footnote

1

• **With the insertion point positioned as shown in Figure 2-28, click Insert on the menu bar and then point to Reference (Figure 2-28).**

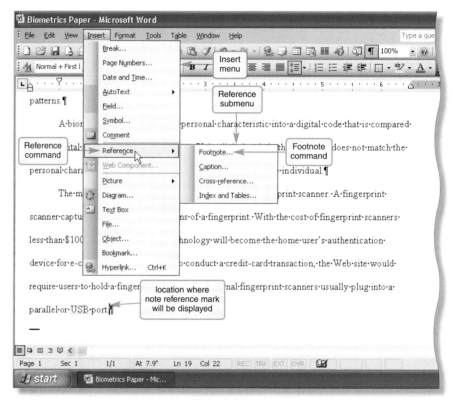

FIGURE 2-28

2

• **Click Footnote on the Reference submenu.**

Word displays the Footnote and Endnote dialog box (Figure 2-29). If you wanted to create endnotes instead of footnotes, you would click Endnotes in the Footnote and Endnote dialog box.

FIGURE 2-29

3

- **Click the Insert button in the Footnote and Endnote dialog box.**

Word opens a note pane in the lower portion of the Word window with the note reference mark (a superscripted 1) positioned at the left margin of the note pane (Figure 2-30). Word also displays the note reference mark in the document window at the location of the insertion point. Note reference marks are, by default, superscripted; that is, raised above other letters.

FIGURE 2-30

4

- **Type** According to Carter and Juarez, newer keyboards and notebook computers have a fingerprint scanner built into them (42-53).

Word displays the note text in the note pane (Figure 2-31).

FIGURE 2-31

The footnote is not formatted according to the MLA requirements. Thus, the next step is to modify the style of the footnote.

Modifying a Style

A **style** is a named group of formatting characteristics that you can apply to text. Word has many built-in, or predefined, styles that you may use to format text. The formats defined by these styles include character formatting, such as the font and font size; paragraph formatting, such as line spacing and text alignment; table formatting; and list formatting.

Whenever you create a document, Word formats the text using a particular style. The underlying style, called the **base style**, for a new Word document is the Normal style. For a new installation of Word 2003, the **Normal style** most likely uses 12-point Times New Roman font for characters and single-spaced, left-aligned paragraphs. As you type, you can apply different predefined styles to the text or you can create your own styles. A later project discusses applying and creating styles.

Other Ways

1. In Voice Command mode, say "Insert, Reference, Footnote, Insert, Dictation, [note text]"

More About

Styles

To view the list of styles associated with the current document, click the Style box arrow on the Formatting toolbar or display the Styles and Formatting task pane by clicking the Styles and Formatting button on the Formatting toolbar. To apply a style, click the desired style name in the Style list or in the Styles and Formatting task pane.

When the insertion point is in the note text area, the entered note text is formatted using the Footnote Text style. The Footnote Text style defines characters as 10-point Times New Roman and paragraphs as single-spaced and left-aligned.

You could change the paragraph formatting of the footnote text to first-line indent and double-spacing as you did for the text in the body of the research paper. Then, you would change the font size from 10 to 12 point. If you use this technique, however, you will need to change the format of the footnote text for each footnote you enter into the document.

A more efficient technique is to modify the format of the Footnote Text style to first-line indent and double-spaced paragraphs and a 12-point font size. By changing the formatting of the Footnote Text style, every footnote you enter into the document will use the formats defined in this style. The following steps show how to modify the Footnote Text style.

To Modify a Style

1

• **Right-click the note text in the note pane.**

Word displays a shortcut menu related to footnotes (Figure 2-32).

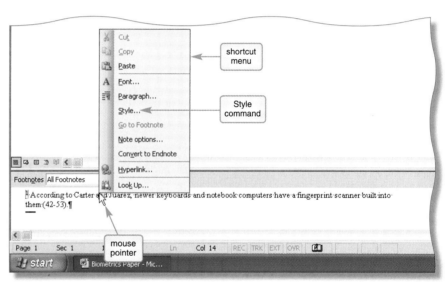

FIGURE 2-32

2

• **Click Style on the shortcut menu.**

• **When Word displays the Style dialog box, if necessary, click Footnote Text in the Styles list.**

The Preview area of the Style dialog box shows the formatting associated with the selected style (Figure 2-33). The selected style is Footnote Text.

FIGURE 2-33

3

• **Click the Modify button in the Style dialog box.**

• **When Word displays the Modify Style dialog box, click the Font Size box arrow in the Formatting area and then click 12 in the Font Size list.**

• **Click the Double Space button in the Modify Style dialog box.**

In the Modify Style dialog box, the font size for the Footnote Text style is changed to 12, and paragraph spacing is changed to double (Figure 2-34). The first-line indent still must be set.

FIGURE 2-34

4

• **Click the Format button in the Modify Style dialog box.**

Word displays the Format button menu above the Format button (Figure 2-35).

FIGURE 2-35

5

• **Click Paragraph on the Format button menu.**

• **When Word displays the Paragraph dialog box, click the Special box arrow and then click First line.**

In the Paragraph dialog box, Word displays First line in the Special box (Figure 2-36). Notice the default first-line indent is 0.5".

FIGURE 2-36

6

• **Click the OK button in the Paragraph dialog box.**

Word modifies the Footnote Text style to first-line indented paragraphs and closes the Paragraph dialog box (Figure 2-37). The Modify Style dialog box is visible again.

7

• **Click the OK button in the Modify Style dialog box.**

• **When Word closes the Modify Style dialog box, click the Apply button in the Style dialog box.**

Word displays the note text using the modified Footnote Text style, that is, the font size of the note text is changed to 12, the line spacing for the note is set to double, and the first line of the note is indented by one-half inch (Figure 2-38).

FIGURE 2-37

1. Click Styles and Formatting button on Formatting toolbar, right-click style name in Pick formatting to apply list, click Modify
2. In Voice Command mode, say "Context menu, Style, Modify, Font Size, [select font size], Double Space, Format, Paragraph, Special, First line, OK, OK, Apply"

FIGURE 2-38

Any future footnotes entered into the document will use a 12-point font with the paragraphs first-line indented and double-spaced. The footnote now is complete. The next step is to close the note pane.

To Close the Note Pane

1

• **Position the mouse pointer on the Close button in the note pane (Figure 2-39).**

2

• **Click the Close button to remove the note pane from the document window.**

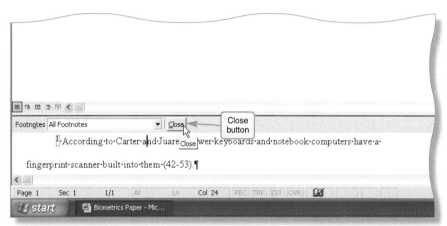

FIGURE 2-39

When Word closes the note pane and returns to the document window, the note text disappears from the screen. Although the note text still exists, it usually is not visible as a footnote in normal view. If, however, you position the mouse pointer on the note reference mark, the note text displays above the note reference mark as a ScreenTip. To remove the ScreenTip, move the mouse pointer.

If you want to verify that the note text is positioned correctly on the page, you must switch to print layout view or display the document in print preview. Project 3 discusses print preview and print layout view.

To delete a note, select the note reference mark in the document window (not in the note pane) by dragging through the note reference mark and then click the Cut button on the Standard toolbar. Another way to delete a note is to click immediately to the right of the note reference mark in the document window and then press the BACKSPACE key twice, or click immediately to the left of the note reference mark in the document window and then press the DELETE key twice.

To move a note to a different location in a document, select the note reference mark in the document window (not in the note pane), click the Cut button on the Standard toolbar, click the location where you want to move the note, and then click the Paste button on the Standard toolbar. When you move or delete notes, Word automatically renumbers any remaining notes in the correct sequence.

You edit note text using the note pane that is displayed at the bottom of the Word window. To display the note text in the note pane, double-click the note reference mark in the document window, or click View on the menu bar and then click Footnotes. In the note pane, you can edit the note as you would any Word text. When finished editing the note text, click the Close button in the note pane.

If you want to change the format of note reference marks in footnotes or endnotes (i.e., from 1, 2, 3, to A, B, C), click Insert on the menu bar, point to Reference, and then click Footnote. When Word displays the Footnote and Endnote dialog box, click the Number format box arrow, click the desired number format in the list, and then click the OK button.

More About

Notes

To convert existing footnotes to endnotes, click Insert on the menu bar, point to Reference, and then click Footnote. Click the Convert button in the Footnote and Endnote dialog box. Make sure the Convert all footnotes to endnotes option button is selected and then click the OK button. Click the Close button in the Footnote and Endnote dialog box.

Using Word Count

Often when you write papers, you are required to compose the papers with a minimum number of words. The minimum requirement for the research paper in this project is 325 words. Word provides a command that displays the number of words, as well as the number of pages, characters, paragraphs, and lines in the current document. The following steps show how to use word count and display the Word Count toolbar, which allows you easily to recount words as you type more text.

To Count Words

 1

• **Click Tools on the menu bar (Figure 2-40).**

FIGURE 2-40

2

• **Click Word Count on the Tools menu.**

• **When Word displays the Word Count dialog box, if necessary, click Include footnotes and endnotes to place a check mark in the check box.**

• **Click the Show Toolbar button in the Word Count dialog box.**

In the Word Count dialog box, the number of pages, words, characters, paragraphs, and lines is displayed (Figure 2-41). The Word Count toolbar is displayed floating in the Word window.

FIGURE 2-41

3

• **Click the Close button in the Word Count dialog box.**

Word removes the Word Count dialog box from the screen, but the Word Count toolbar remains on the screen (Figure 2-42). Your Word Count toolbar may be displayed at a different location on the screen.

Other Ways

1. Click Recount button on Word Count toolbar
2. On File menu click Properties, click Statistics tab, click OK button
3. In Voice Command mode, say "Tools, Word Count, Include footnotes and endnotes, Show Toolbar, Close"

FIGURE 2-42

The Word Count toolbar floats on the screen. As discussed earlier in this project, you can move a floating toolbar by dragging its title bar.

The Word Count dialog box (Figure 2-41) presents a variety of statistics about the current document, including number of pages, words, characters, paragraphs, and lines. You can choose to have note text included or not included in these statistics. If you want statistics on only a section of the document, select the section and then issue the Word Count command.

At anytime, you can recount the number of words in a document by clicking the Recount button on the Word Count toolbar.

More About

Word Count

You also can display statistics about a document by clicking File on the menu bar, clicking Properties, and then clicking the Statistics tab. This information, however, does not include words and characters in the footnotes or endnotes.

Automatic Page Breaks

As you type documents that exceed one page, Word automatically inserts page breaks, called **automatic page breaks** or **soft page breaks**, when it determines the text has filled one page according to paper size, margin settings, line spacing, and other settings. If you add text, delete text, or modify text on a page, Word recomputes the location of automatic page breaks and adjusts them accordingly.

Word performs page recomputation between the keystrokes, that is, in between the pauses in your typing. Thus, Word refers to the automatic page break task as **background repagination**. In normal view, automatic page breaks display on the Word screen as a single dotted horizontal line. The following step illustrates Word's automatic page break feature.

To Page Break Automatically

1

• **With the insertion point positioned as shown in Figure 2-42, press the SPACEBAR and then type the last three sentences of the third paragraph of the paper, as shown in Figure 2-43.**

• **Press the ENTER key and then type the fourth paragraph. Italicize the text in the parenthetical citation.**

• **Drag the title bar of the Word Count toolbar to the location shown in Figure 2-43.**

As you type, Word places an automatic page break between the third and fourth paragraphs in the paper (Figure 2-43). The status bar now displays Page 2 as the current page.

FIGURE 2-43

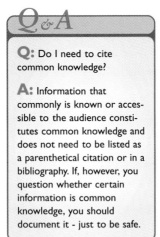

Your page break may occur at a different location, depending on the type of printer connected to the computer.

The header, although not shown in normal view, contains the name Zhao followed by the page number 2. If you wanted to view the header, click View on the menu bar and then click Header and Footer. Then, click the Close Header and Footer button on the Header and Footer toolbar to return to normal view.

Recounting Words in a Document

Now that the last paragraph of the body of the paper is typed, you want to recount the number of words to see if you have met the minimum requirement of 325 words. The following steps show how to use the Word Count toolbar to recount words in a document.

To Recount Words

1

• **Click the Recount button on the Word Count toolbar.**

The Word Count toolbar displays the number of words in the document (Figure 2-44). You now close the Word Count toolbar because the research paper contains the required minimum of 325 words.

2

• **Click the Close button on the Word Count toolbar.**

Word removes the Word Count toolbar from the screen.

FIGURE 2-44

Creating an Alphabetical Works Cited Page

According to the MLA style, the **works cited page** is a bibliographical list of works that are referenced directly in a research paper. You place the list on a separate numbered page with the title, Works Cited, centered one inch from the top margin. The works are to be alphabetized by the author's last name or, if the work has no author, by the work's title. The first line of each entry begins at the left margin. Indent subsequent lines of the same entry one-half inch from the left margin.

The first step in creating the works cited page is to force a page break so the works cited display on a separate page.

Manual Page Breaks

The works cited are to display on a separate numbered page. Thus, you must insert a manual page break following the body of the research paper. A **manual page break**, or **hard page break**, is one that you force into the document at a specific location. Word displays a manual page break on the screen as a horizontal dotted line, separated by the words, Page Break. Word never moves or adjusts manual page breaks; however, Word adjusts any automatic page breaks that follow a manual page break. Word inserts manual page breaks just before the location of the insertion point.

The following step shows how to insert a manual page break after the body of the research paper.

To Page Break Manually

1

- **With the insertion point at the end of the body of the research paper, press the ENTER key.**
- **Then, press CTRL+ENTER.**

The shortcut keys, CTRL+ENTER, instruct Word to insert a manual page break immediately above the insertion point and position the insertion point immediately below the manual page break (Figure 2-45). The status bar indicates the insertion point now is on page 3.

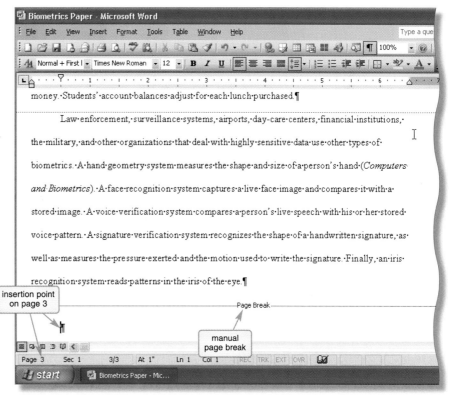

FIGURE 2-45

Word displays the manual page break as a horizontal dotted line with the words, Page Break, in the middle of the line. The header, although not shown in normal view, contains the name Zhao followed by the page number 3. If you wanted to view the header, click View on the menu bar and then click Header and Footer. Then, click the Close Header and Footer button on the Header and Footer toolbar to return to normal view.

If, for some reason, you wanted to remove a manual page break from a document, you must first select the page break by double-clicking it. Then, press the DELETE key; or click the Cut button on the Standard toolbar; or right-click the selection and then click Cut on the shortcut menu.

Q&A

Q: Are bibliographical references presented similarly in the MLA and APA styles?

A: The MLA documentation style uses the title, Works Cited, for the page containing bibliographical references, whereas the APA style uses the title, References. APA guidelines for preparing the reference list entries differ significantly from the MLA style. Refer to an APA handbook or the Web for specifics.

Centering the Title of the Works Cited Page

The works cited title is to be centered between the margins of the paper. If you simply click the Center button on the Formatting toolbar, the title will not be centered properly. Instead, it will be one-half inch to the right of the center point because earlier you set first-line indent at one-half inch. That is, Word indents the first line of every paragraph one-half inch.

To properly center the title of the works cited page, you must move the First Line Indent marker back to the left margin before clicking the Center button, as described in the following steps.

To Center the Title of the Works Cited Page

1 **Drag the First Line Indent marker to the 0" mark on the ruler, which is at the left margin.**

2 **Click the Center button on the Formatting toolbar.**

3 **Type** Works Cited **as the title.**

4 **Press the ENTER key.**

5 **Because your fingers already are on the keyboard, press CTRL+L to left-align the paragraph mark.**

Word centers the title properly, and the insertion point is left-aligned (Figure 2-46).

Q&A

Q: Do I need to credit sources in a research paper?

A: Yes, you must acknowledge sources of information. Citing sources is a matter of ethics and honesty. Use caution when summarizing or paraphrasing a source. Do not plagiarize, which includes using someone else's words or ideas and claiming them as your own.

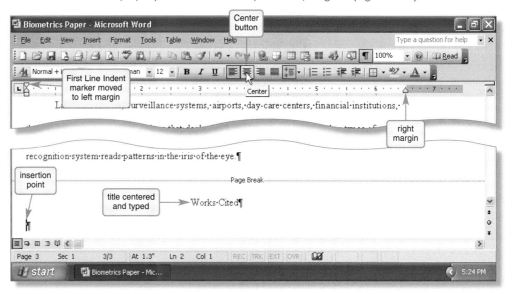

FIGURE 2-46

More About

Hanging Indent

Some users may find it confusing to use the ruler to indent paragraphs. In this case, you can use the Paragraph dialog box to format a paragraph with a hanging indent. To do this, click Format on the menu bar, click Paragraph, click the Indents and Spacing tab, click the Special box arrow, click Hanging, and then click the OK button.

Creating a Hanging Indent

On the works cited page, the first line of each entry begins at the left margin. Subsequent lines in the same paragraph are to be indented one-half inch from the left margin. In essence, the first line hangs to the left of the rest of the paragraph; thus, this type of paragraph formatting is called a **hanging indent**.

One method of creating a hanging indent is to use the horizontal ruler. The **Hanging Indent marker** is the bottom triangle at the 0" mark on the ruler (Figure 2-47). The next steps show how to create a hanging indent using the horizontal ruler.

To Create a Hanging Indent

1

• **With the insertion point in the paragraph to format, point to the Hanging Indent marker on the ruler (Figure 2-47).**

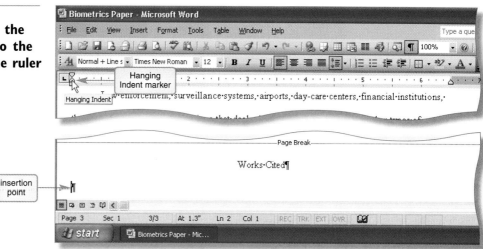

FIGURE 2-47

2

• **Drag the Hanging Indent marker to the .5" mark on the ruler.**

The Hanging Indent marker and Left Indent marker display one-half inch from the left margin (Figure 2-48). When you drag the Hanging Indent marker, the Left Indent marker moves with it. The insertion point in the document window remains at the left margin because only subsequent lines in the paragraph are to be indented.

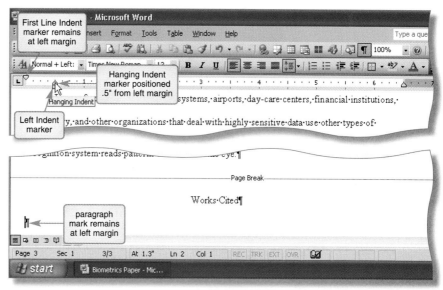

FIGURE 2-48

The next step is to enter the works in the works cited. As you type the works, Word will format them with a hanging indent. The following steps describe how to type the first two works in the works cited.

To Enter Works Cited Paragraphs

1 **Type** Schmidt, Karl J. "Biometrics and Authenticating Computer Users."

2 **Press the SPACEBAR. Press CTRL+I to turn on the italic format. Type** Computers and the Internet **and then press CTRL+I to turn off the italic format.**

3 **Press the SPACEBAR. Type** Aug. 2005: 54-62.

4 Press the ENTER key.

5 **Type** Carter, Donnell W., and Louis C. Juarez.

6 **Press the SPACEBAR. Press CTRL+I to turn on the italic format. Type** Securing Confidential Data Entered into a Computer. **Press CTRL+I to turn off the italic format.**

7 **Press the SPACEBAR. Type** Boston: Thomas Publishing, 2005.

8 **Press the ENTER key.**

Word displays two of the works cited paragraphs in the document window (Figure 2-49).

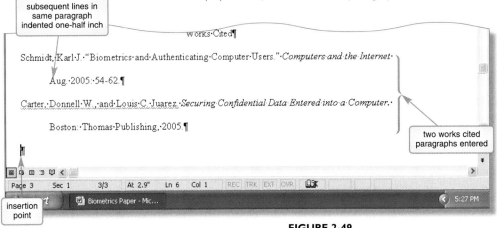

subsequent lines in same paragraph indented one-half inch

two works cited paragraphs entered

insertion point

FIGURE 2-49

When Word wraps the text in each works cited paragraph, it automatically indents the second line of the paragraph by one-half inch. When you press the ENTER key at the end of the first paragraph of text, the insertion point returns automatically to the left margin for the next paragraph. Recall that each time you press the ENTER key, Word carries forward the paragraph formatting from the previous paragraph to the next paragraph.

Inserting Arrows, Faces, and Other Symbols Automatically

As discussed earlier in this project, Word has predefined many commonly misspelled words, which it automatically corrects for you as you type. In addition to words, this built-in list of **AutoCorrect entries** also contains some commonly used symbols. For example, to insert a smiling face in a document, you type :) and Word automatically changes it to ☺. Table 2-3 lists the characters you type to insert arrows, faces, and other symbols in a Word document.

You also can enter the first four symbols in Table 2-3 and other symbols by clicking Insert on the menu bar, clicking Symbol, clicking the Special Characters tab, clicking the desired symbol in the Character list, clicking the Insert button, and then clicking the Close button in the Symbol dialog box.

As discussed earlier in this project, if you do not like a change that Word automatically makes in a document and you immediately notice the automatic correction, you can undo the change by clicking the Undo button on the Standard toolbar; clicking Edit on the menu bar and then clicking Undo; or pressing CTRL+Z.

If you do not immediately notice the change, you can undo a correction automatically made by Word using the AutoCorrect Options button. Figures 2-23 and 2-24 on pages WD 90 and WD 91 illustrated how to display and use the AutoCorrect Options button.

Table 2-3	Word's Automatic Symbols	
TO DISPLAY	**DESCRIPTION**	**TYPE**
©	copyright symbol	(c)
®	registered trademark symbol	(r)
™	trademark symbol	(tm)
…	ellipsis	...
☺	smiling face	:) or :-)
☺	indifferent face	:| or :-|
☹	frowning face	:(or :-(
→	thin right arrow	-->
←	thin left arrow	<
→	thick right arrow	==>
←	thick left arrow	<==
⇔	double arrow	<=>

The next step in the research paper is to enter text that uses the registered trademark symbol. The following steps show how to insert automatically the registered trademark symbol in the research paper.

To Insert a Symbol Automatically

1

• **With the insertion point positioned as shown in Figure 2-49, press CTRL+I to turn on the italic format.**

• **Type** Computers and Biometrics.

• **Press CTRL+I to turn off the italic format.**

• **Press the SPACEBAR.**

• **Type** Shelly Cashman Series(r **as shown in Figure 2-50.**

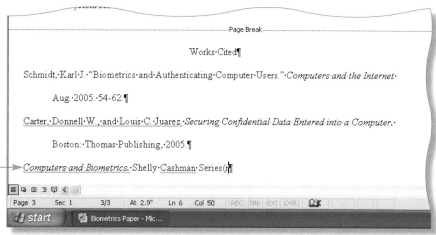

FIGURE 2-50

2

• **Press the RIGHT PARENTHESIS key.**

Word automatically converts the typed (r) to ®, the registered trademark symbol (Figure 2-51).

3

• **Press the PERIOD key.**

• **Press the SPACEBAR.**

• **Type** Course Technology. 3 Oct. 2005.

• **Press the SPACEBAR.**

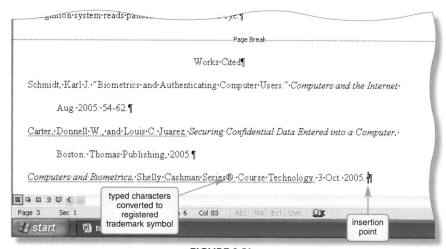

FIGURE 2-51

Other Ways

1. On Insert menu click Symbol, click Special Characters tab, click Registered in Character list, click Insert button, click Close button
2. In Dictation mode, say "Right Parenthesis, R, Left Parenthesis"

Creating a Hyperlink

A **hyperlink** is a shortcut that allows a user to jump easily and quickly to another location in the same document or to other documents or Web pages. **Jumping** is the process of following a hyperlink to its destination. For example, by clicking a hyperlink in the document window while pressing the CTRL key (called **CTRL+clicking**), you jump to another document on your computer, on your network, or on the World Wide Web. When you close the hyperlink destination page or document, you return to the original location in your Word document. In Word, you can create a hyperlink simply by typing the address of the file or Web page to which you want to link and then pressing the SPACEBAR or the ENTER key.

In this project, one of the works cited is from a Web page on the Internet. When someone displays your research paper on the screen, you want him or her to be able to CTRL+click the Web address in the work to jump to the associated Web page for more information.

To create a hyperlink to a Web page in a Word document, you do not have to be connected to the Internet. The following steps show how to create a hyperlink as you type.

To Create a Hyperlink

1

• **With the insertion point positioned as shown in Figure 2-51 on the previous page, type** `http://www.scsite.com/ wd2003/pr2/wc.htm.`

Word does not format the entry as a hyperlink until you press the ENTER key or SPACEBAR (Figure 2-52).

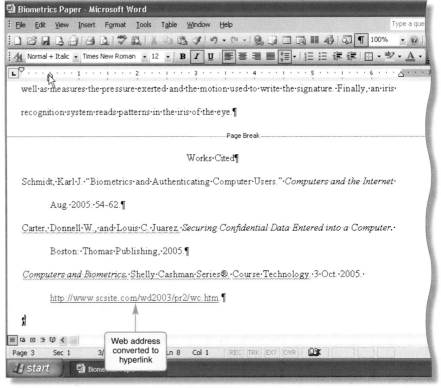

FIGURE 2-52

2

• **Press the ENTER key.**

As soon as you press the ENTER key after typing the Web address, Word formats it as a hyperlink (Figure 2-53). That is, the Web address is underlined and colored blue.

Other Ways

1. Select text, click Insert Hyperlink button on Standard toolbar, click Existing File or Web Page in the Link to bar, type Web address in Address text box, click OK button
2. Right-click selected text, click Hyperlink on short-cut menu, click Existing File or Web Page in the Link to bar, type Web address in Address text box, click OK button

FIGURE 2-53

Later, this project will show how to jump to the hyperlink just created.

Sorting Paragraphs

The MLA style requires that the works cited be listed in alphabetical order by the first character in each work. In Word, you can arrange paragraphs in alphabetic, numeric, or date order based on the first character in each paragraph. Ordering characters in this manner is called **sorting**.

The following steps show how to sort the works cited paragraphs alphabetically.

More About

Hyperlinks

If Word does not convert Web addresses to hyperlinks automatically, click Tools on the menu bar, click AutoCorrect Options, click the AutoFormat As You Type tab, select the Internet and network paths with hyperlinks check box, and then click the OK button.

To Sort Paragraphs

1

- **Select all the works cited paragraphs by pointing to the left of the first paragraph and then dragging down.**
- **Click Table on the menu bar.**

Word displays the Table menu (Figure 2-54). All of the paragraphs to be sorted are selected.

FIGURE 2-54

2

- **Click Sort on the Table menu.**

Word displays the Sort Text dialog box (Figure 2-55). In the Sort by area, Ascending, the default, is selected. The term, ascending, means to sort in alphabetic, numeric, or earliest to latest date order.

FIGURE 2-55

3

• **Click the OK button in the Sort Text dialog box.**

• **Click inside the selected text to remove the selection.**

Word sorts the works cited paragraphs alphabetically (Figure 2-56).

FIGURE 2-56

Other Ways

1. In Voice Command mode, say "Table, Sort, OK"

If you accidentally sort the wrong paragraphs, you can undo a sort by clicking the Undo button on the Standard toolbar.

In the Sort Text dialog box (Figure 2-55 on the previous page), the default sort order is Ascending. By default, Word orders in **ascending sort order**, which means from the beginning of the alphabet to the end of the alphabet, smallest number to the largest number, or earliest date to the most recent date. For example, if the first character of each paragraph to be sorted is a letter, Word sorts the selected paragraphs alphabetically.

You also can sort in descending order by clicking Descending in the Sort Text dialog box. **Descending sort order** means sorting from the end of the alphabet to the beginning of the alphabet, the largest number to the smallest number, or the most recent date to the earliest date.

Q & A

Q: How should I go about proofreading a research paper?

A: Ask yourself these questions: Is the purpose clear? Does the title suggest the topic? Does the paper have an introduction, body, and conclusion? Is the thesis clear? Does each paragraph in the body relate to the thesis? Is the conclusion effective? Are all sources acknowledged?

Proofing and Revising the Research Paper

As discussed in Project 1, once you complete a document, you might find it necessary to make changes to it. Before submitting a paper to be graded, you should proofread it. While **proofreading**, you look for grammatical errors and spelling errors. You want to be sure the transitions between sentences flow smoothly and the sentences themselves make sense. To assist you with the proofreading effort, Word provides several tools. The following pages discuss these tools.

Going to a Specific Location in a Document

Often, you would like to bring a certain page, footnote, or other object into view in the document window. To accomplish this, you could scroll through the document to find a desired page, footnote, or item. Instead of scrolling through the document, however, Word provides an easier method of going to a specific location via the Select Browse Object menu.

The next steps show how to go to the top of page two in the research paper using the Select Browse Object menu.

To Browse by Page

1

• **Click the Select Browse Object button on the vertical scroll bar.**

• **When Word displays the Select Browse Object menu, position the mouse pointer on the Browse by Page icon.**

When you point to an icon on the Select Browse Object menu, Word displays the associated command name at the bottom of the menu (Figure 2-57).

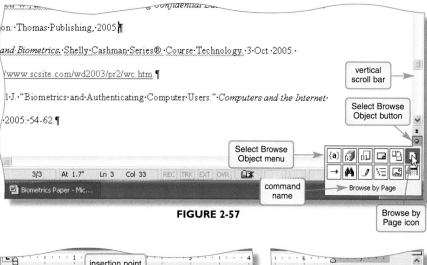

FIGURE 2-57

2

• **Click the Browse by Page icon.**

• **Position the mouse pointer on the Previous Page button on the vertical scroll bar.**

Word closes the Select Browse Object menu and displays the top of page 3 at the top of the document window (Figure 2-58).

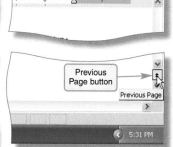

FIGURE 2-58

3

• **Click the Previous Page button.**

Word places the top of page 2 (the previous page) at the top of the document window (Figure 2-59).

Other Ways

1. Double-click page indicator on status bar (Figure 2-59), click Page in Go to what list, type page number in Enter page number text box, click Go To button, click Close button
2. On Edit menu click Go To, and then proceed as described in 1 above starting with click Page in Go to what list
3. Press CTRL+G, and then proceed as described in 1 above starting with click Page in Go to what list

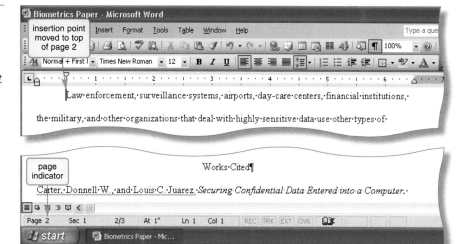

FIGURE 2-59

Depending on the icon you click on the Select Browse Object menu, the function of the buttons above and below the Select Browse Object button on the vertical scroll bar changes. When you select Browse by Page, the buttons become Previous Page and Next Page buttons. If you select Browse by Footnote, however, the buttons become Previous Footnote and Next Footnote buttons, and so on.

Moving Text

While proofreading the research paper, you realize that text in the fourth paragraph would flow better if the third sentence was moved so it followed the first sentence. That is, you want to move the third sentence so it is the second sentence in the fourth paragraph.

To move text, such as words, characters, sentences, or paragraphs, you first select the text to be moved and then use drag-and-drop editing or the cut-and-paste technique to move the selected text. With **drag-and-drop editing**, you drag the selected item to the new location and then insert, or *drop*, it there. **Cutting** involves removing the selected item from the document and then placing it on the Clipboard. The **Clipboard** is a temporary Windows storage area. **Pasting** is the process of copying an item from the Clipboard into the document at the location of the insertion point. The next steps demonstrate drag-and-drop editing.

To drag-and-drop a sentence in the research paper, first select a sentence as shown in the next step.

To Select a Sentence

1

• **Position the mouse pointer (an I-beam) in the sentence to be moved (shown in Figure 2-60).**

• **Press and hold down the CTRL key. While holding down the CTRL key, click the sentence.**

• **Release the CTRL key.**

Word selects the entire sentence (Figure 2-60). Notice that Word includes the space following the period in the selection.

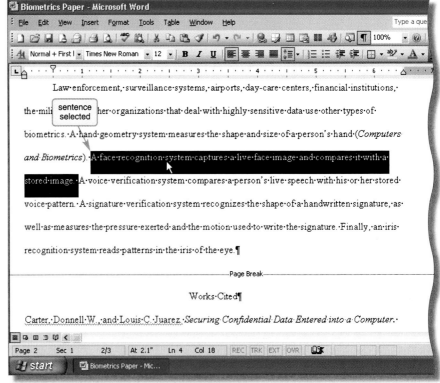

FIGURE 2-60

In the previous steps and throughout Projects 1 and 2, you have selected text. Table 2-4 summarizes the techniques used to select various items with the mouse.

Table 2-4 Techniques for Selecting Items with the Mouse	
ITEM TO SELECT	MOUSE ACTION
Block of text	Click at beginning of selection, scroll to end of selection, position mouse pointer at end of selection, hold down SHIFT key and then click; or drag through the text
Character(s)	Drag through character(s)
Document	Move mouse to left of text until mouse pointer changes to a right-pointing block arrow and then triple-click
Graphic	Click the graphic
Line	Move mouse to left of line until mouse pointer changes to a right-pointing block arrow and then click
Lines	Move mouse to left of first line until mouse pointer changes to a right-pointing block arrow and then drag up or down
Paragraph	Triple-click paragraph; or move mouse to left of paragraph until mouse pointer changes to a right-pointing block arrow and then double-click
Paragraphs	Move mouse to left of paragraph until mouse pointer changes to a right-pointing block arrow, double-click and then drag up or down
Sentence	Press and hold down CTRL key and then click sentence
Word	Double-click the word
Words	Drag through words

More About

Selecting Text

In Word, you can select nonadjacent text. This is helpful when you are formatting multiple items the same way. To select items that are not next to each other (nonadjacent), do the following. Select the first item, such as a word or paragraph, as usual. Press and hold down the CTRL key. While holding down the CTRL key, select any additional items. All selected items are displayed highlighted on the screen.

With the sentence to be moved selected, you can use drag-and-drop editing to move it. You should be sure that drag-and-drop editing is enabled by clicking Tools on the menu bar, clicking Options, clicking the Edit tab, verifying the Drag-and-drop text editing check box is selected, and then clicking the OK button.

The following steps show how to move the selected sentence so it becomes the second sentence in the paragraph.

To Move Selected Text

1

• **With the mouse pointer in the selected text, press and hold down the mouse button.**

When you begin to drag the selected text, the insertion point changes to a dotted insertion point (Figure 2-61).

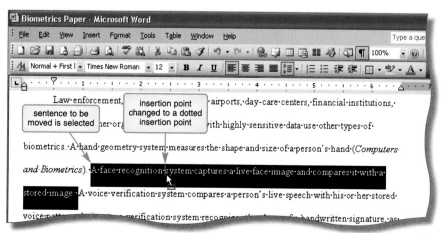

FIGURE 2-61

2

• **Drag the dotted insertion point to the location where the selected text is to be moved, as shown in Figure 2-62.**

The dotted insertion point follows the space after the first sentence in the paragraph (Figure 2-62).

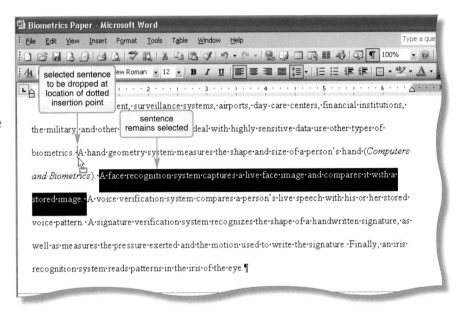

FIGURE 2-62

3

• **Release the mouse button. Click outside the selected text to remove the selection.**

Word moves the selected text to the location of the dotted insertion point (Figure 2-63).

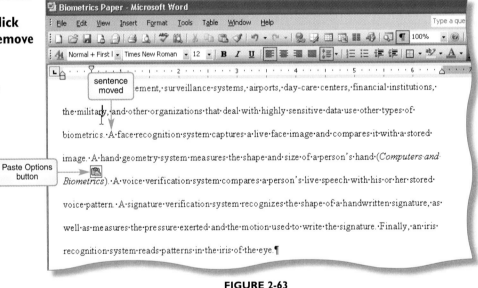

FIGURE 2-63

If you accidentally drag selected text to the wrong location, you can click the Undo button on the Standard toolbar.

You can use drag-and-drop editing to move any selected item. That is, you can select words, sentences, phrases, and graphics and then use drag-and-drop editing to move them.

When you drag-and-drop text, Word automatically displays a Paste Options button near the location of the drag-and-dropped text (Figure 2-63). If you click the **Paste Options button,** a menu is displayed that allows you to change the format of the text that was moved. The next steps show how to display the Paste Options menu.

To Display the Paste Options Menu

1

• **Click the Paste Options button.**

Word displays the Paste Options menu (Figure 2-64).

2

• **Press the ESCAPE key to remove the Paste Options menu from the window.**

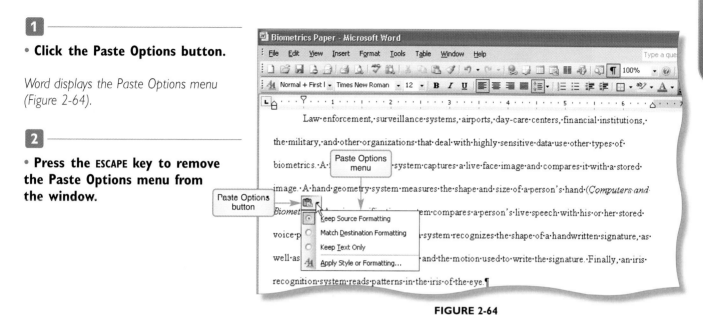

FIGURE 2-64

Other Ways

1. In Voice Command mode, say "Paste Options, Escape"

Smart Tags

A **smart tag** is a button that automatically appears on the screen when Word performs a certain action. In this project, you used two smart tags: AutoCorrect Options (Figures 2-23 and 2-24 on pages WD 90 and WD 91) and Paste Options (Figure 2-64). In addition to AutoCorrect Options and Paste Options, Word provides other smart tags. Table 2-5 summarizes the smart tags available in Word.

BUTTON	NAME	MENU FUNCTION
(icon)	AutoCorrect Options	Undoes an automatic correction, stops future automatic corrections of this type, or displays the AutoCorrect Options dialog box
(icon)	Paste Options	Specifies how moved or pasted items should display, e.g., with original formatting, without formatting, or with different formatting
(icon)	Smart Tag Actions	
	• Person name	Adds this name to Outlook Contacts folder, sends an e-mail, or schedules a meeting in Outlook Calendar with this person
	• Date or time	Schedules a meeting in Outlook Calendar at this date or time or displays your calendar
	• Address	Adds this address to Outlook Contacts folder or displays a map or driving directions
	• Place	Adds this place to Outlook Contacts folder or schedules a meeting in Outlook Calendar at this location

Table 2-5 Smart Tags in Word

More About

Smart Tags

If your screen does not display smart tag indicators, click Tools on the menu bar, click AutoCorrect Options, click the Smart Tags tab, select the Label text with smart tags check box, and then click the OK button. If AutoCorrect Options buttons do not appear on your screen, click Tools on the menu bar, click AutoCorrect Options, click the AutoCorrect tab, select the Show AutoCorrect Options buttons check box, and then click the OK button.

More About

Smart Tag Actions

The commands in the Smart Tag Actions menu vary depending on the smart tag. For example, the Smart Tag Actions menu for a date includes commands that allow you to schedule a meeting in Outlook Calendar or display your Outlook Calendar. The Smart Tag Actions menu for an address includes commands for displaying a map of the address or driving directions to or from the address.

With the AutoCorrect Options and Smart Tag Actions, Word notifies you that the smart tag is available by displaying a **smart tag indicator** on the screen. The smart tag indicator for the AutoCorrect Options smart tag is a small blue box. The smart tag indicator for Smart Tag Actions is a purple dotted underline, as shown in Figure 2-14 on page WD 85. To display a smart tag button, you point to the smart tag indicator.

Clicking a smart tag button displays a menu that contains commands relative to the action performed at the location of the smart tag. For example, if you want to add a name in your Word document to the Outlook Contacts folder, point to the purple dotted line below the name to display the Smart Tag Actions button, click the Smart Tag Actions button to display the Smart Tag Actions menu, and then click Add to Contacts on the Smart Tag Actions menu to display the Contact window in Outlook.

Finding and Replacing Text

While proofreading the paper, you notice that it contains the word, trait, in the first paragraph (Figure 2-65). You prefer to use the word, identifier. Therefore, you wish to change all occurrences of trait to identifier. To do this, you can use Word's find and replace feature, which automatically locates each occurrence of a word or phrase and then replaces it with specified text, as shown in these steps.

To Find and Replace Text

1

• **Press CTRL+HOME to position the insertion point at the top of the document.**

• **Double-click the status bar anywhere to the left of the status indicators.**

• **When Word displays the Find and Replace dialog box, click the Replace tab.**

• **Type** trait **in the Find what text box.**

• **Press the TAB key. Type** identifier **in the Replace with text box.**

Word displays entered text in the Find and Replace dialog box (Figure 2-65).

FIGURE 2-65

2

• **Click the Replace All button in the Find and Replace dialog box.**

A Microsoft Office Word dialog box displays indicating the total number of replacements made (Figure 2-66). The word, identifier, displays in the document instead of the word, trait.

3

• **Click the OK button in the Microsoft Office Word dialog box.**
• **Click the Close button in the Find and Replace dialog box.**

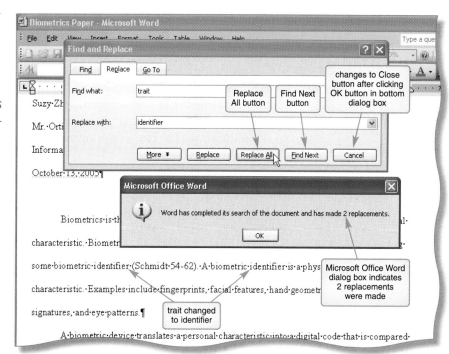

FIGURE 2-66

The Replace All button replaces all occurrences of the Find what text with the Replace with text. In some cases, you may want to replace only certain occurrences of a word or phrase, not all of them. To instruct Word to confirm each change, click the Find Next button in the Find and Replace dialog box (Figure 2-65), instead of the Replace All button. When Word locates an occurrence of the text, it pauses and waits for you to click either the Replace button or the Find Next button. Clicking the Replace button changes the text; clicking the Find Next button instructs Word to disregard the replacement and look for the next occurrence of the Find what text.

If you accidentally replace the wrong text, you can undo a replacement by clicking the Undo button on the Standard toolbar. If you used the Replace All button, Word undoes all replacements. If you used the Replace button, Word undoes only the most recent replacement.

Finding Text

Sometimes, you may want only to find text, instead of finding *and* replacing text. To search for just a single occurrence of text, you would follow these steps.

To Find Text

1. Click the Select Browse Object button on the vertical scroll bar and then click the Find icon on the Select Browse Object menu; or click Edit on the menu bar and then click Find; or press CTRL+F.
2. Type the text to locate in the Find what text box and then click the Find Next button. To edit the text, click the Cancel button in the Find and Replace dialog box; to find the next occurrence of the text, click the Find Next button.

Other Ways

1. Click Select Browse Object button on vertical scroll bar, click Find icon, click Replace tab, type Find what text, type Replace with text, click Replace All button, click Close button
2. On Edit menu click Replace and then proceed as described in 1 above starting with type Find what text
3. Press CTRL+H, and then proceed as described in 1 above starting with type Find what text
4. In Voice Command mode, say "Select Browse Object, Find, Replace, [type text to find], Tab, [type text to replace], OK, OK, Close"

More About

Finding

To search for formatting or special characters, click the More button in the Find dialog box. To find formatting, use the Format button in the Find dialog box. To find a special character, use the Special button.

Finding and Inserting a Synonym

When writing, you may discover that you used the same word in multiple locations or that a word you used was not quite appropriate. In these instances, you will want to look up a **synonym**, or word similar in meaning, to the duplicate or inappropriate word. A **thesaurus** is a book of synonyms. Word provides synonyms and a thesaurus for your convenience.

In this project, you would like a synonym for the word, give, in the first paragraph of the research paper. The following steps show how to find an appropriate synonym.

To Find and Insert a Synonym

1

- **Right-click the word for which you want to find a synonym (give, in this case).**

- **Point to Synonyms on the shortcut menu.**

Word displays a list of synonyms for the word that you right-clicked (Figure 2-67).

2

- **Click the synonym you want (grant) on the Synonyms submenu.**

Word replaces the word, give, in the document with the word, grant (Figure 2-68).

FIGURE 2-67

FIGURE 2-68

If the synonyms list on the shortcut menu does not display an appropriate word, you can display the thesaurus in the Research task pane by clicking Thesaurus on the Synonyms submenu (Figure 2-67). The Research task pane displays a complete thesaurus, in which you can look up synonyms for various meanings of a word. You also can look up an **antonym**, or word with an opposite meaning. The Research task pane is discussed later in this project.

Checking Spelling and Grammar at Once

As discussed in Project 1, Word checks spelling and grammar as you type and places a wavy underline below possible spelling or grammar errors. Project 1 illustrated how to check these flagged words immediately. As an alternative, you can wait and check the entire document for spelling and grammar errors at once.

The following steps illustrate how to check spelling and grammar in the Biometrics Paper at once. In the following example the word, hand, has been misspelled intentionally as han to illustrate the use of Word's check spelling and grammar at once feature. If you are completing this project on a personal computer, your research paper may contain different misspelled words, depending on the accuracy of your typing.

To Check Spelling and Grammar at Once

1

• **Press CTRL+HOME to move the insertion point to the beginning of the document.**

• **Click the Spelling and Grammar button on the Standard toolbar.**

Word displays the Spelling and Grammar dialog box (Figure 2-69). The spelling and grammar check begins at the location of the insertion point, which, in this case, is at the beginning of the document. Word did not find the misspelled word, han, in its dictionary. The Suggestions list displays suggested corrections for the flagged word.

FIGURE 2-69

2

• **Click the Change button in the Spelling and Grammar dialog box.**

Word corrects the misspelled word and then continues the spelling and grammar check until it finds the next error or reaches the end of the document. In this case, it flags an error on the Works Cited page (Figure 2-70). The entry is correct, so you instruct Word to ignore it.

FIGURE 2-70

3

• **Click the Ignore Once button.**

• **Click the Ignore Once button for the next grammar error that Word flags on the Works Cited page.**

Word continues the spelling and grammar check and does not find Cashman in its dictionary (Figure 2-71). Cashman is a proper name and is spelled correctly.

4

• **Click the Ignore All button.**

• **Click the Ignore Once button for each remaining grammar error that Word flags on the Works Cited page.**

• **When the spelling and grammar check is done and Word displays a dialog box, click its OK button.**

FIGURE 2-71

Other Ways

1. On Tools menu click Spelling and Grammar
2. Right-click flagged word, click Spelling (or Grammar) on shortcut menu
3. Press F7
4. In Voice Command mode, say "Spelling and Grammar"

Your document no longer displays red and green wavy underlines below words and phrases. In addition, the red X on the Spelling and Grammar Status icon has returned to a red check mark.

Saving Again and Printing the Document

The document now is complete. You should save the research paper again and print it, as described in the following steps.

To Save a Document Again and Print It

1 **Click the Save button on the Standard toolbar.**

2 **Click the Print button on the Standard toolbar.**

Word saves the research paper with the same file name, Biometrics Paper. The completed research paper prints as shown in Figure 2-1 on page WD 75.

Working with Main and Custom Dictionaries

As shown in the previous steps, Word often flags proper names as errors because these names are not in its main dictionary. To prevent Word from flagging proper names as errors, you can add the names to the custom dictionary. To add a correctly spelled word to the custom dictionary, click the Add to Dictionary button in the Spelling and Grammar dialog box (Figure 2-71) or right-click the flagged word and then click Add to Dictionary on the shortcut menu. Once you have added a word to the custom dictionary, Word no longer will flag it as an error. To view or modify the list of words in a custom dictionary, you would follow these steps.

To View or Modify Entries in a Custom Dictionary

1. Click Tools on the menu bar and then click Options.
2. Click the Spelling & Grammar tab in the Options dialog box.
3. Click the Custom Dictionaries button.
4. When Word displays the Custom Dictionaries dialog box, place a check mark next to the dictionary name to view or modify. Click the Modify button. (In this dialog box, you can add or delete entries to and from the selected custom dictionary.)
5. When finished viewing and/or modifying the list, click the OK button in the dialog box.
6. Click the OK button in the Custom Dictionaries dialog box.
7. If the Suggest from main dictionary only check box is selected in the Spelling & Grammar sheet in the Options dialog box, remove the check mark. Click the OK button in the Options dialog box.

If you have multiple custom dictionaries, you can specify which one Word should use when checking spelling. The following steps describe how to set the default custom dictionary.

To Set the Default Custom Dictionary

1. Click Tools on the menu bar and then click Options.
2. Click the Spelling & Grammar tab in the Options dialog box.
3. Click the Custom Dictionaries button.
4. When the Custom Dictionaries dialog box displays, place a check mark next to the desired dictionary name. Click the Change Default button.
5. Click the OK button in the Custom Dictionaries dialog box.
6. If the Suggest from main dictionary only check box is selected in the Spelling & Grammar dialog box, remove the check mark. Click the OK button in the Spelling & Grammar dialog box.

More About

Certification

The Microsoft Office Specialist Certification program provides an opportunity for you to obtain a valuable industry credential - proof that you have the Word 2003 skills required by employers. For more information, see Appendix E or visit the Word 2003 Certification Web page (scsite.com/wd2003/cert).

Navigating to a Hyperlink

Recall that a requirement of this research paper is that one of the works be a Web page and be formatted as a hyperlink. The following steps show how to check the hyperlink in the document.

To Navigate to a Hyperlink

1

• **Display the third page of the research paper in the document window and then position the mouse pointer in the hyperlink.**

When you position the mouse pointer in a hyperlink in a Word document, a ScreenTip is displayed above the hyperlink (Figure 2-72).

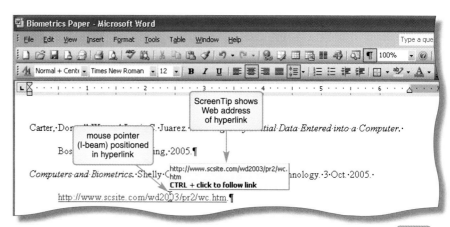

FIGURE 2-72

2

• **While holding down the CTRL key, click the hyperlink. Release the CTRL key.**

If you currently are not connected to the Web, Word connects you using your default browser. The www.scsite.com/wd2003/ pr2/wc.htm Web page is displayed in a browser window (Figure 2-73).

3

• **Close the browser window.**

• **If necessary, click the Microsoft Word program button on the taskbar to redisplay the Word window.**

• **Press CTRL+HOME.**

Word displays the first page of the research paper on the screen.

FIGURE 2-73

The hyperlink in the document changes color, which indicates you CTRL+clicked the hyperlink to display its associated Web page.

E-Mailing a Copy of the Research Paper

Your instructor, Mr. Ortiz, has requested you e-mail him a copy of your research paper so he can verify your hyperlink. The following steps show how to e-mail the document from within Word if you use Outlook as your e-mail program.

To E-Mail a Document

1

• **Click the E-mail button on the Standard toolbar.**

• **Fill in the To text box with Mr. Ortiz's e-mail address and the Introduction text box as shown in Figure 2-74.**

Word displays certain buttons and boxes from the e-mail editor inside the Word window. The file name is displayed automatically in the Subject text box.

2

• **Click the Send a Copy button.**

The document is e-mailed to the recipient named in the To text box.

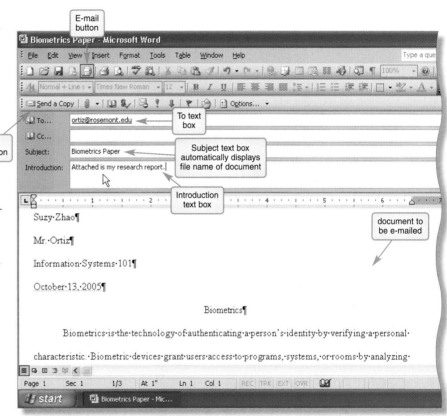

FIGURE 2-74

If you want to cancel the e-mail operation, click the E-mail button again.

In the steps above, the Word document becomes part of the e-mail message. If you wanted to send the Word document as an attachment to the e-mail message instead, do the following.

To E-Mail a Document as an Attachment

1. Click File on the menu bar, point to Send To, and then click Mail Recipient (as Attachment).
2. Fill in the text boxes.
3. Click the Send button.

Other Ways

1. On File menu point to Send To, on Send To submenu click Mail Recipient
2. In Voice Command mode, say "E-mail"

Microsoft Office
Word 2003

More About

The Research Task Pane

Other Office applications, such as Excel and PowerPoint, also use the Research task pane. Internet Explorer uses it, too. Thus, once you learn how to use the Research task pane in Word, you will be able to use it in many other programs.

Using the Research Task Pane

From within Word, you can search through various forms of online reference information. Earlier, this project discussed the Research task pane with respect to looking up a synonym in a thesaurus. Other services available in the Research task pane include the Microsoft Encarta English dictionary, bilingual dictionaries, the Microsoft Encarta Encyclopedia (with a Web connection), and Web sites that provide information such as stock quotes, news articles, and company profiles.

After reading a document you create, you might want to know the meaning of a certain word. For example, in the research paper, you might want to look up the definition of the word, e-commerce. The following step shows how to use the Research task pane to look up the definition of a word.

To Use the Research Task Pane to Locate Information

1

• **While holding down the ALT key, click the word for which you want a definition (in this case, e-commerce). Release the ALT key.**

• **If the Research task pane does not display the definition of the ALT+CLICKED word, click the Search for box arrow and then click All Reference Books.**

Word displays the Research task pane with the ALT+CLICKED word in the Search for text box (Figure 2-75). The Research button on the Standard toolbar is selected and the insertion point is in the ALT+CLICKED word. The contents of your reference book entry in the Research task pane may be different.

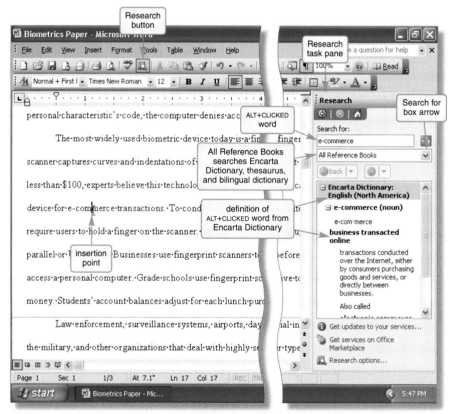

FIGURE 2-75

Other Ways

1. On Tools menu click Research
2. Right-click selected word, click Look Up on shortcut menu
3. In Voice Command mode, say "Tools, Research"

After you have looked up information in the Research task pane, you either can close the task pane or you can insert certain pieces of the information into the document. The next steps illustrate the procedure of copying information displayed in the Research task pane and inserting the copied text in a Word document.

To Insert Text from the Research Task Pane in a Word Document

1

• **In the Research task pane, double-click the word, Internet.**

• **Right-click the selected word.**

The word, Internet, is selected in the Research task pane and a shortcut menu is displayed (Figure 2-76).

FIGURE 2-76

2

• **Click Copy on the shortcut menu to copy the selected text to the Clipboard.**

• **Drag through the word, e-commerce, in the research paper.**

• **Right-click the selected text in the document (Figure 2-77).**

The word, e-commerce, is selected in the document and a shortcut menu is displayed.

FIGURE 2-77

3

• **Click Paste on the shortcut menu.**

• **If necessary, press the SPACEBAR to insert a space after the inserted word.**

• **Click the Close button in the Research task pane.**

Word removes the selected word, e-commerce, and inserts the word, Internet, in its place (Figure 2-78).

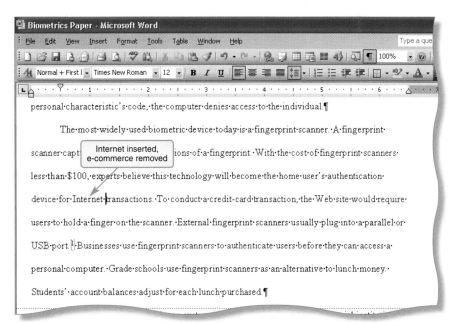

FIGURE 2-78

More About

Quick Reference

For a table that lists how to complete the tasks covered in this book using the mouse, menu, shortcut menu, and keyboard, see the Quick Reference Summary at the back of this book, or visit the Word 2003 Quick Reference Web page (scsite.com/wd2003/qr).

When using Word to insert material from the Research task pane or any other online reference, be very careful not to plagiarize, or copy other's work and use it as your own. Not only is plagiarism unethical, but it is considered an academic crime that can have severe punishments such as failing a course or being expelled from school.

The final step in this project is to quit Word, as described below.

To Quit Word

1 **Click the Close button in the Word window.**

2 **If Word displays a dialog box, click the No button.**

The Word window closes.

Project Summary

In creating the Biometrics Paper in this project, you learned how to use Word to enter and format a research paper using the MLA documentation style. You learned how to change margin settings, adjust line spacing, create headers with page numbers, enter text using Click and Type, and first-line indent paragraphs. You learned how to use Word's AutoCorrect feature. Then, you added a footnote in the research paper and modified the Footnote Text style. You also learned how to count words in a document. In creating the Works Cited page, you learned how to insert a manual page break, create a hanging indent, create a hyperlink, and sort paragraphs.

Once you finished typing text into the entire paper, you learned how to browse through a Word document, move text, and find and replace text. You looked up a synonym for a word and checked spelling and grammar in the entire document. Finally, you navigated to a hyperlink, e-mailed a copy of a document, and looked up information using the Research task pane.

 If you have a SAM user profile, you may have access to hands-on instruction, practice, and assessment of the skills covered in this project. Log in to your SAM account and go to your assignments page to see what your instructor has assigned.

What You Should Know

Having completed this project, you should be able to perform the tasks below. The tasks are listed in the same order they were presented in this project. For a list of the buttons, menus, toolbars, and commands introduced in this project, see the Quick Reference Summary at the back of this book and refer to the Page Number column.

1. Start and Customize Word   (WD 77)
2. Display Formatting Marks   (WD 77)
3. Change the Margin Settings   (WD 78)
4. Double-Space Text   (WD 80)
5. Display the Header Area   (WD 81)
6. Click and Type   (WD 83)
7. Enter a Page Number   (WD 83)
8. Enter Name and Course Information   (WD 85)
9. Format Text Using Shortcut Keys   (WD 86)
10. Save a Document   (WD 87)
11. First-Line Indent Paragraphs   (WD 88)
12. AutoCorrect as You Type   (WD 89)
13. Use the AutoCorrect Options Button   (WD 90)
14. Create an AutoCorrect Entry   (WD 91)
15. Enter More Text   (WD 93)
16. Add a Footnote   (WD 94)
17. Modify a Style   (WD 96)
18. Close the Note Pane   (WD 99)
19. Count Words   (WD 100)
20. Page Break Automatically   (WD 101)
21. Recount Words   (WD 102)
22. Page Break Manually   (WD 103)
23. Center the Title of the Works Cited Page (WD 104)
24. Create a Hanging Indent   (WD 105)
25. Enter Works Cited Paragraphs   (WD 105)
26. Insert a Symbol Automatically   (WD 107)
27. Create a Hyperlink   (WD 108)
28. Sort Paragraphs   (WD 109)
29. Browse by Page   (WD 111)
30. Select a Sentence   (WD 112)
31. Move Selected Text   (WD 113)
32. Display the Paste Options Menu   (WD 115)
33. Find and Replace Text   (WD 116)
34. Find Text   (WD 117)
35. Find and Insert a Synonym   (WD 118)
36. Check Spelling and Grammar at Once (WD 119)
37. Save a Document Again and Print It   (WD 121)
38. View or Modify Entries in a Custom Dictionary (WD 121)
39. Set the Default Custom Dictionary   (WD 121)
40. Navigate to a Hyperlink   (WD 122)
41. E-Mail a Document   (WD 123)
42. E-Mail a Document as an Attachment (WD 123)
43. Use the Research Task Pane to Locate Information   (WD 124)
44. Insert Text from the Research Task Pane in a Word Document   (WD 125)
45. Quit Word   (WD 126)

Learn It Online

Instructions: To complete the Learn It Online exercises, start your browser, click the Address bar, and then enter the Web address scsite.com/wd2003/learn. When the Word 2003 Learn It Online page is displayed, follow the instructions in the exercises below. Each exercise has instructions for printing your results, either for your own records or for submission to your instructor.

1 Project Reinforcement TF, MC, and SA

Below Word Project 2, click the Project Reinforcement link. Print the quiz by clicking Print on the File menu for each page. Answer each question.

2 Flash Cards

Below Word Project 2, click the Flash Cards link and read the instructions. Type 20 (or a number specified by your instructor) in the Number of playing cards text box, type your name in the Enter your Name text box, and then click the Flip Card button. When the flash card is displayed, read the question and then click the ANSWER box arrow to select an answer. Flip through Flash Cards. If your score is 15 (75%) correct or greater, click Print on the File menu to print your results. If your score is less than 15 (75%) correct, then redo this exercise by clicking the Replay button.

3 Practice Test

Below Word Project 2, click the Practice Test link. Answer each question, enter your first and last name at the bottom of the page, and then click the Grade Test button. When the graded practice test is displayed on your screen, click Print on the File menu to print a hard copy. Continue to take practice tests until you score 80% or better.

4 Who Wants To Be a Computer Genius?

Below Word Project 2, click the Computer Genius link. Read the instructions, enter your first and last name at the bottom of the page, and then click the PLAY button. When your score is displayed, click the PRINT RESULTS link to print a hard copy.

5 Wheel of Terms

Below Word Project 2, click the Wheel of Terms link. Read the instructions, and then enter your first and last name and your school name. Click the PLAY button. When your score is displayed, right-click the score and then click Print on the shortcut menu to print a hard copy.

6 Crossword Puzzle Challenge

Below Word Project 2, click the Crossword Puzzle Challenge link. Read the instructions, and then enter your first and last name. Click the SUBMIT button. Work the crossword puzzle. When you are finished, click the Submit button. When the crossword puzzle is redisplayed, click the Print Puzzle button to print a hard copy.

7 Tips and Tricks

Below Word Project 2, click the Tips and Tricks link. Click a topic that pertains to Project 2. Right-click the information and then click Print on the shortcut menu. Construct a brief example of what the information relates to in Word to confirm you understand how to use the tip or trick.

8 Newsgroups

Below Word Project 2, click the Newsgroups link. Click a topic that pertains to Project 2. Print three comments.

9 Expanding Your Horizons

Below Word Project 2, click the Expanding Your Horizons link. Click a topic that pertains to Project 2. Print the information. Construct a brief example of what the information relates to in Word to confirm you understand the contents of the article.

10 Search Sleuth

Below Word Project 2, click the Search Sleuth link. To search for a term that pertains to this project, select a term below the Project 2 title and then use the Google search engine at google.com (or any major search engine) to display and print two Web pages that present information on the term.

11 Word Online Training

Below Word Project 2, click the Word Online Training link. When your browser displays the Microsoft Office Online Web page, click the Word link. Click one of the Word courses that covers one or more of the objectives listed at the beginning of the project on page WD 74. Print the first page of the course before stepping through it.

12 Office Marketplace

Below Word Project 2, click the Office Marketplace link. When your browser displays the Microsoft Office Online Web page, click the Office Marketplace link. Click a topic that relates to Word. Print the first page.

Apply Your Knowledge

1 Revising a Document

Instructions: Start Word. Open the document, Apply 2-1 Authentication Paragraph, on the Data Disk. See the inside back cover of this book for instructions for downloading the Data Disk or see your instructor for information about accessing the files in this book.

The document on the Data Disk is a paragraph of text. You are to revise the paragraph as follows: move a sentence; change the format of the moved sentence; change paragraph indentation, change line spacing, change margin settings, replace all occurrences of the word, memorized, with the word, remembered; add a sentence; remove an automatic hyperlink format, and modify the header. The revised paragraph is shown in Figure 2-79.

Perform the following tasks:

1. Select the first sentence of the paragraph. Use drag-and-drop editing to move this sentence to the end of the paragraph, so it is the last sentence in the paragraph.
2. Click the Paste Options button that displays to the right of the moved sentence. Remove the italic format from the moved sentence by clicking Keep Text Only on the shortcut menu.
3. Use first-line indent to indent the first line of the paragraph.

Revised Authentication Paragraph
10/17/2005 12:35:34 PM

Three common types of authentication are remembered information, biometric devices, and possessed objects. With remembered information, the user enters a word or series of characters that match an entry in the computer's security file. Examples of remembered information are passwords, user IDs, and logon codes. A password is confidential, usually known only by the user and possibly the system administrator. A user ID typically identifies the user, and a logon code identifies an application program. A possessed object is any item the user must carry to access the computer facility. Some examples are keys, badges, and cards. Possessed objects often are used together with a personal identification number (PIN), which is a numeric password. For more information about passwords, visit www.scsite.com/dc2003/apply.htm and click Apply It #1 below Chapter 11.

FIGURE 2-79

4. Change the line spacing of the paragraph from single to double.
5. Change the left and right margins of the document to .75".
6. Use the Find and Replace dialog box to replace all occurrences of the word, memorized, with the word, remembered.
7. Use Word's thesaurus to change the word, usually, to the word, typically, in the sentence that starts, A user ID usually...
8. At the end of the paragraph, press the SPACEBAR and then type this sentence: For more information about passwords, visit www.scsite.com/dc2003/apply.htm and click Apply It #1 below Chapter 11.
9. Remove the hyperlink automatic format from the Web address by positioning the mouse pointer at the beginning of the Web address (that is, the w in www), pointing to the small blue box below the w, clicking the AutoCorrect Options button, and then clicking Undo Hyperlink on the shortcut menu.
10. Display the header on the screen. Change the alignment of the text in the header from left to centered. Insert the word, Revised, in the text so it reads: Revised Authentication Paragraph. On the second line of the header, insert and center the current date and the current time using buttons on the Header and Footer toolbar. Place one space between the current date and current time.
11. Click File on the menu bar and then click Save As. Save the document using the file name, Apply 2-1 Revised Authentication Paragraph.
12. Print the revised paragraph, shown in Figure 2-79.
13. Use the Research task pane to look up the definition of the word, passwords, in the third sentence of the paragraph. Handwrite the definition on your printout.

In the Lab

1 Preparing a Short Research Paper

Problem: You are a college student currently enrolled in an introductory computer class. Your assignment is to prepare a short research paper (350-400 words) about a computer component. The requirements are that the paper be presented according to the MLA documentation style and have three references. One of the three references must be from the Web and formatted as a hyperlink on the Works Cited page. You prepare the paper shown in Figure 2-80, which discusses the system unit.

Marks 1

Nicholas Marks

Ms. White

Computer Literacy 100

August 6, 2005

The System Unit

The system unit is a case that houses the electronic components of the computer used to process data. Although many system units resemble a box, they are available in many shapes and sizes. The case of the system unit, sometimes called a chassis, is made of metal or plastic and protects the internal electronic components from damage. All computers have a system unit (Alvarez 102).

Components of the system unit include the processor, memory modules, adapter cards, drive bays, power supply, ports, and connectors. The processor interprets and carries out the basic instructions that operate a computer. A memory module houses memory chips. An adapter card is a circuit board that provides connections and functions not built into the motherboard.[1] A drive bay holds a disk drive. The power supply allows electricity to travel into a computer.

On a personal computer, the electronic components and most storage devices reside inside the system unit. Other devices, such as a keyboard, mouse, microphone, monitor, printer, speakers, scanner, and digital camera, normally occupy space outside the system unit (*How to Use a Computer*). On a desktop personal computer, the system unit usually is a device separate from the monitor and keyboard. Some system units sit on top of a desk. Other models, called tower models, can stand vertically on the floor.

_____

[1] According to Wilson, four adapter cards most commonly found in desktop personal computers today are sound cards, modem cards, video cards, and network cards (18-32).

FIGURE 2-80a

In the Lab

Marks 2

To conserve space, an all-in-one computer houses the system unit in the same physical case as the monitor. On notebook computers, the keyboard and pointing device often occupy the area on the top of the system unit. The display attaches to the system unit by hinges. The system unit on a PDA (personal digital assistant) or handheld computer usually consumes the entire device. On these small mobile devices, the display is part of the system unit, too.

FIGURE 2-80b

Marks 3

Works Cited

Alvarez, Juan. *Understanding Computer Basics: Stepping Toward Literacy*. Chicago: Martin
    Publishing, 2005.

How to Use a Computer. Shelly Cashman Series®. Course Technology. 3 Aug. 2005.
    www.scsite.com/wd2003/pr2/wc1.htm.

Wilson, Tracey M. "Personal Computers and their Applications." *Computing and Information*
    Systems Weekly May 2005: 18-32.

FIGURE 2-80c

Instructions:

1. If necessary, display formatting marks on the screen.
2. Change all margins to one inch.
3. Adjust line spacing to double.
4. Create a header to number pages.
5. Type the name and course information at the left margin. Center and type the title.
6. Set first-line indent for paragraphs in the body of the research paper.
7. Type the body of the paper as shown in Figure 2-80a and Figure 2-80b. Add the footnote as shown in Figure 2-80a. At the end of the body of the research paper, press the ENTER key and then insert a manual page break.
8. Create the works cited page (Figure 2-80c).
9. Check the spelling of the paper at once.
10. Save the document on a floppy disk using Lab 2-1 System Unit Paper as the file name.
11. Use the Select Browse Object button to go to page 3. If you have access to the Web, CTRL+click the hyperlink to test it.
12. Print the research paper. Handwrite the number of words, paragraphs, and characters in the research paper above the title of your printed research paper.

2 Preparing a Research Report with a Footnote(s)

Problem: You are a college student currently enrolled in an introductory computer class. Your assignment is to prepare a short research paper in any area of interest to you. The requirements are that the paper be presented according to the MLA documentation style, contain at least one explanatory note positioned as a footnote, and have three references. One of the three references must be from the Internet and formatted as a hyperlink on the works cited page. You decide to prepare a paper about employee monitoring (Figure 2-81).

Mills 1

Francis Mills

Mr. Rugenstein

Information Systems 101

August 27, 2005

Employee Monitoring

Employee monitoring involves the use of computers to observe, record, and review an employee's use of a computer, including communications such as e-mail, keyboard activity (used to measure productivity), and Web sites visited. Many computer programs exist that easily allow employers to monitor employees.[1] Further, it is legal for employers to use these programs.

A frequently debated issue is whether an employer has the right to read employee e-mail messages. Actual policies vary widely. Some companies declare that they will review e-mail messages regularly; others state that e-mail messages are private. If a company does not have a formal e-mail policy, it can read e-mail messages without employee notification. One recent survey discovered that more than 73 percent of companies search and/or read employee files, voice mail, e-mail messages, Web connections, and other networking communications. Another claimed that 25 percent of companies have fired employees for misusing communications technology.

Currently, no privacy laws exist relating to employee e-mail (*Privacy Laws and Personal Data*). The 1986 Electronic Communications Privacy Act provides the same right of privacy protection that covers the postal delivery service and telephone companies to various forms of

---

[1] According to Lang, software currently is being developed that can track and record what employees are doing while they work, using a digital video camera with real-time image recognition (33-45).

FIGURE 2-81a

Mills 2

electronic communications, such as e-mail, voice mail, and cellular telephones. The Electronic Communications Privacy Act, however, does not cover communications within a company. This is because any piece of mail sent from an employer's computer is considered company property. Several lawsuits have been filed against employers because many people believe that such internal employee communications should be private (Slobovnik and Stuart 144-160).

FIGURE 2-81b

Instructions Part 1:   Perform the following tasks to create the research paper:

1. If necessary, display formatting marks on the screen. Change all margin settings to one inch. Adjust line spacing to double. Create a header to number pages. Type the name and course information at the left margin. Center and type the title. Set first-line indent for paragraphs in the body of the research paper.

2. Type the body of the paper as shown in Figure 2-81a and Figure 2-81b. Add the footnote as shown in Figure 2-81a. Change the Footnote Text style to the format specified in the MLA style. At the end of the body of the research paper, press the ENTER key once and insert a manual page break.

3. Create the works cited page. Enter the works cited shown below as separate paragraphs. Format the works according to the MLA documentation style and then sort the works cited paragraphs.
    (a) Slobovnik, Victor W., and Janel K. Stuart. Workplace Challenges. Dallas: Techno-Cyber Publishing, 2005.
    (b) Privacy Laws and Personal Data. Shelly Cashman Series®. Course Technology. 3 Aug. 2005. www.scsite.com/wd2003/pr2/wc2.htm.
    (c) Lang, Stefanie. "The New Invasion: Employee Monitoring and Privacy Issues." Technology Issues Aug. 2005: 33-45.

4. Check the spelling of the paper.

5. Save the document on a floppy disk using Lab 2-2 Employee Monitoring Paper as the file name.

6. If you have access to the Web, CTRL+click the hyperlink to test it.

7. Print the research paper. Handwrite the number of words, including the footnotes, in the research paper above the title of your printed research paper.

Instructions Part 2:   Perform the following tasks to modify the research paper:

1. Use Word to find a synonym of your choice for the word, issue, in the first sentence of the second paragraph.

2. Change all occurrences of the word, employers, to the word, companies.

3. Insert a second footnote at the end of the fourth sentence in the last paragraph of the research paper. Use the following footnote text: Some companies even use automated software that searches e-mail messages for derogatory language. One unidentified woman, for example, was fired for using her office e-mail to complain about her boss.

4. In the first footnote, find the word, developed, and change it to the word, written.

5. Save the document on a floppy disk using Lab 2-2 Employee Monitoring Paper - Part 2 as the file name.

6. Print this revised research paper that has notes positioned as footnotes. Handwrite the number of words, including the footnotes, in the research paper above the title of the printed research paper.

Instructions Part 3:   Perform the following tasks to modify the research paper created in Part 2:

1. Convert the footnotes to endnotes. Recall that endnotes display at the end of a document. Switch to print layout view to see the endnotes. *Hint:* Use Help to learn about print layout view and converting footnotes to endnotes.

2. Modify the Endnote text style to 12-point font, double-spaced text with a first-line indent. Insert a page break so the endnotes are placed on a separate, numbered page. Center the title, Endnotes, double-spaced above the notes.

3. Change the format of the note reference marks to capital letters (A, B, etc.). *Hint:* Use Help to learn about changing the number format of note reference marks.

4. Save the document on a floppy disk using Lab 2-2 Employee Monitoring Paper - Part 3 as the file name.

5. Print the revised research paper with notes positioned as endnotes. Handwrite the number of words, including the endnotes, in the research paper above the title of the printed research paper.

In the Lab

3 Composing a Research Paper from Notes

Problem: You have drafted the notes shown in Figure 2-82. Your assignment is to prepare a short research paper from these notes.

Instructions: Perform the following tasks:

1. Review the notes in Figure 2-82 and then rearrange and reword them. Embellish the paper as you deem necessary. Present the paper according to the MLA documentation style. Create an AutoCorrect entry that automatically corrects the spelling of the misspelled word, softare, to the correct spelling, software. Add a footnote that refers the reader to the Web for more information. Create the works cited page from the listed sources. Be sure to sort the works.

2. Check the spelling and grammar of the paper. Save the document on a floppy disk using Lab 2-3 Computer Software Paper as the file name.

3. Use the Research task pane to look up a definition. Copy and insert the definition into the document as a footnote. Be sure to quote the definition and cite the source.

4. Print the research paper. Hand-write the number of words, including the footnotes, in the research paper above the title of the printed research paper. Circle the definition inserted into the document from the Research task pane.

5. Use Word to e-mail the research paper to your instructor, if your instructor gives you permission to do so.

Software, also called a program, is a series of instructions that tells the computer hardware what to do and how to do it. Two categories of software are system software and application software.

System software (source: "The Future of Application Software," an article on page 39-55 in the May 2005 issue of Computers and Peripherals, authors James A. Naylor and Joseph I. Vincent.)
- System software is an interface between the application software, the user, and the computer's hardware.
- An operating system is a popular type of system software. Microsoft Windows is an operating system that has a graphical user interface. Users interact with software through its user interface.
- System software consists of the programs that control or maintain the operations of the computer and its devices.

Application software (source: a Web site titled Guide to Application Software, sponsored by the Shelly Cashman Series® at Course Technology, site visited on October 3, 2005, Web address is www.scsite.com/wd2003/pr2/wc3.htm)
- Application software consists of programs that perform specific tasks for users. Examples are word processing software, spreadsheet software, database software, presentation graphics software, and Web browsers.
- Database software - store data in an organized fashion, and retrieve, manipulate, and display that data in a variety of formats.
- Word processing software - create documents such as letters, reports, and brochures.
- Spreadsheet software - calculate numbers arranged in rows and columns.
- Web browser - connect to the Internet to access and view Web pages.
- Presentation graphics software - create documents called slides that add visual appeal to presentations.
- Other types of application software are available that enable users to perform a variety of tasks, including personal information management, project management, accounting, desktop publishing, photo and video editing, personal finance, tax preparation, reference, education, entertainment, and communications.

Software suites (source: Hardware and Software Made Simple, a book published by Cyber Press Publishing in New York, 2005, written by Nanette Allen and Clint Muhr.)
- When installing the software suite, you install the entire collection of programs at once instead of installing each one individually. Business software suites typically include word processing, spreadsheet, e-mail, and presentation graphics programs.
- Software vendors often bundle and sell individual programs together as a single package called a software suite. This costs much less than buying the applications individually.
- Two widely used business software suites are Microsoft Office and Sun StarOffice.

FIGURE 2-82

Cases and Places

The difficulty of these case studies varies:
■ are the least difficult and ■■ are more difficult. The last exercise is a group exercise.

1 ■ This project discussed the requirements of the MLA documentation style on page WD 76 and in several More About boxes dispersed throughout the project. Using the material presented in this project, write a short research paper (400-450 words) that describes the requirements of the MLA documentation style. Include at least two references and one explanatory note positioned as a footnote. Add an AutoCorrect entry to correct a word you commonly mistype. Use the concepts and techniques presented in this project to format the paper. Type the paper with the Word screen in normal view. Switch to print layout view to proof the paper.

2 ■■ The ever-increasing presence of computers in everyone's lives has generated an awareness of the need to address computing requirements for those who have or may develop physical limitations. The Americans with Disabilities Act (ADA) requires any company with 15 or more employees to make reasonable attempts to accommodate the needs of physically challenged workers. Whether at work or at home, you may find it necessary to acquire devices that address physical limitations. Using Word's Research task pane, the school library, other textbooks, magazines, the Internet, friends and family, or other resources, research the types of input and/or output devices designed for physically challenged computer users. Then, prepare a brief research paper (400-450 words) that discusses your findings. Include at least one explanatory note and two references, one of which must be a Web site on the Internet. Use the concepts and techniques presented in this project to format the paper.

3 ■■ Computers process input (data) into output (information). A computer often holds data, information, and instructions in storage for future use. Most computers today also can communicate with other computers. Computers perform input, output, storage, and communications operations with amazing speed, reliability, consistency, and accuracy. Using Word's Research task pane, the school library, other textbooks, the Internet, magazines, or other resources, research one of the following computer operations: input, output, storage, or communications. Then, prepare a brief research paper (400-450 words) that discusses how the computer operation works and/or the types of devices used for that activity. Include at least one explanatory note and two references, one of which must be a Web site on the Internet. Use the concepts and techniques presented in this project to format the paper.

4 ■■ A programming language is a set of words, symbols, and codes that enables a programmer to communicate instructions to a computer. Just as humans speak a variety of languages (English, Spanish, French, and so on), programmers use a variety of programming languages and program development tools to write computer programs. Using Word's Research task pane, the school library, other textbooks, the Internet, magazines, interviews with programmers, or other resources, research the types of programming languages or program development tools on the market today. Then, prepare a brief research paper (400-450 words) that discusses one or more programming languages or program development tools. Include at least one explanatory note and two references, one of which must be a Web site on the Internet. Use the concepts and techniques presented in this project to format the paper.

Cases and Places

5 ■■ **Working Together** PDAs are one of the more popular lightweight mobile devices in use today. A PDA (personal digital assistant) can provide a variety of personal information management functions including calendar, appointment book, address book, calculator, and notepad, as well as access to the Internet and telephone capabilities. Many different PDAs are on the market. Each team member is to research the features, price, and accessories of one type of PDA by looking through newspapers, magazines, searching the Web, and/or visiting an electronics or computer store. Each team member is to write a minimum of 200 words summarizing his or her findings. Each team member also is to write at least one explanatory note and supply his or her reference for the works cited page. Then, the team should meet as a group to compose a research paper that includes all team members' write-ups. Start by copying and pasting the text into a single document and then write an introduction and conclusion as a group. Use the concepts and techniques presented in this project to format the paper according to the MLA documentation style. Set the default dictionary. If Word flags any of your last names as an error, add the name(s) to the custom dictionary. Hand in printouts of each team member's original write-up, as well as the final research paper.

Creating a Worksheet and an Embedded Chart

P R O J E C T

1

CASE PERSPECTIVE

In the late 1970s, Extreme Blading pioneered the sport of inline skating as an off-season training tool for hockey players. The sport quickly caught on with fitness enthusiasts, aggressive skaters, and the population in general. Today, nearly 50 million inline skaters participate in the activity worldwide and the sport continues to grow.

The Extreme Blading product line includes a variety of skates, including inline, quad, and custom models for all age levels, as well as a complete line of protective gear and other accessories.

For years, the company sold their goods via direct mail, telesales, and company-owned outlets in major cities across the country. Thanks to the popularity of personal computers and the World Wide Web, the company added an e-commerce Web site last year. This new sales channel has given the company access to more than 600 million people worldwide and has resulted in a significant increase in sales.

Sales continued to grow during the first half of this year, thus driving senior management to ask their financial analyst, Maria Lopez, to develop a better sales tracking system. As a first step, Maria has asked you to prepare an easy-to-read worksheet that shows product sales for the second quarter by sales channel (Figure 1-1 on page EX 5). In addition, Maria has asked you to create a chart showing second quarter sales, because the president of the company likes to have a graphical representation of sales that allows her quickly to identify stronger and weaker product groups by sales channel.

As you read through this project, you will learn how to use Excel to create, save, and print a financial report that includes a 3-D Column chart.

Creating a Worksheet and an Embedded Chart

PROJECT

1

Objectives

You will have mastered the material in this project when you can:

- Start and Quit Excel
- Describe the Excel worksheet
- Enter text and numbers
- Use the AutoSum button to sum a range of cells
- Copy a cell to a range of cells using the fill handle
- Format a worksheet
- Create a 3-D Clustered column chart
- Save a workbook and print a worksheet
- Open a workbook
- Use the AutoCalculate area to determine statistics
- Correct errors on a worksheet
- Use the Excel Help system to answer questions

What Is Microsoft Office Excel 2003?

Microsoft Office Excel 2003 is a powerful spreadsheet program that allows users to organize data, complete calculations, make decisions, graph data, develop professional looking reports (Figure 1-1), publish organized data to the Web, and access real-time data from Web sites. The four major parts of Excel are:

- **Worksheets** Worksheets allow users to enter, calculate, manipulate, and analyze data such as numbers and text. The term worksheet means the same as spreadsheet.
- **Charts** Excel can draw a variety of charts.
- **Lists** Lists organize and store data. For example, once a user enters data into a worksheet, Excel can sort the data, search for specific data, and select data that satisfies defined criteria.
- **Web Support** Web support allows users to save Excel worksheets or parts of a worksheet in HTML format, so a user can view and manipulate the worksheet using a browser. Excel Web support also provides access to real-time data, such as stock quotes, using Web queries.

This latest version of Excel makes it much easier to create and manipulate lists of data. It also offers industry-standard XML support that simplifies the sharing of data within and outside an organization; improved statistical functions; smart documents that automatically fill with data; information rights management; allows two workbooks to be compared side by side; and includes the capability of searching a variety of reference information.

FIGURE 1-1

Project One — Extreme Blading Second Quarter Sales

The first step in creating an effective worksheet is to make sure you understand what is required. The person or persons requesting the worksheet should supply their requirements in a requirements document. A **requirements document** includes a needs statement, source of data, summary of calculations, and any other special requirements for the worksheet, such as charting and Web support. Figure 1-2 on the next page shows the requirements document for the new worksheet to be created in this project.

After carefully reviewing the requirements document, the next step is to design a solution or draw a sketch of the worksheet based on the requirements, including titles, column and row headings, location of data values, and the 3-D Column chart, as shown in Figure 1-3 on the next page. The dollar signs, 9s, and commas that you see in the sketch of the worksheet indicate formatted numeric values.

More About

Worksheet Development Cycle

Spreadsheet specialists do not sit down and start entering text, formulas, and data into a blank Excel worksheet as soon as they have a spreadsheet assignment. Instead, they follow an organized plan, or methodology, that breaks the development cycle into a series of tasks. The recommended methodology for creating worksheets includes (1) analyze requirements (supplied in a requirements document); (2) design solution; (3) validate design; (4) implement design; (5) test solution; and (6) document solution.

REQUEST FOR NEW WORKSHEET

Date Submitted:	May 2, 2005
Submitted By:	Maria Lopez
Worksheet Title:	Second Quarter Sales
Needs:	An easy-to-read worksheet that shows Extreme Blading's second quarter sales for each of the product groups (Inline Skates, Quad Skates, Custom Skates, and Accessories) by sales channel (Direct Mail, Outlets, Telesales, and Web). The worksheet also should include total sales for each product group, total sales for each sales channel, and total company sales for the second quarter.
Source of Data:	The data for the worksheet is available at the end of the second quarter from the chief financial officer (CFO) of Extreme Blading.
Calculations:	The following calculations must be made for the worksheet: (a) total second quarter sales for each of the four product groups; (b) total second quarter sales for each of the four sales channels; and (c) total second quarter sales for the company.
Chart Requirements:	Below data in the worksheet, construct a 3-D Clustered column chart that compares the total sales for each product group within each sales channel.

Approvals

Approval Status:	X	Approved
		Rejected
Approved By:		Sylvia Strong
Date:		May 5, 2005
Assigned To:		J. Quasney, Spreadsheet Specialist

requirements document

FIGURE 1-2

sketch of worksheet

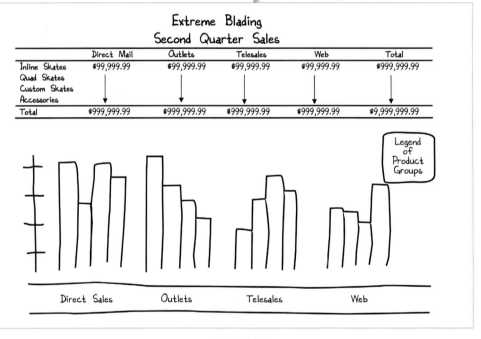

FIGURE 1-3

With a good understanding of the requirements document and a sketch of the worksheet, the next step is to use Excel to create the worksheet and chart.

Starting and Customizing Excel

If you are stepping through this project on a computer and you want your screen to match the figures in this book, then you should change your computer's resolution to 800 × 600. For more information on how to change the resolution on your computer, see Appendix D. The following steps show how to start Excel.

To Start Excel

1

• **Click the Start button on the Windows taskbar, point to All Programs on the Start menu, point to Microsoft Office on the All Programs submenu, and then point to Microsoft Office Excel 2003 on the Microsoft Office submenu.**

Windows displays the Start menu, the All Programs submenu, and the Microsoft Office submenu (Figure 1-4).

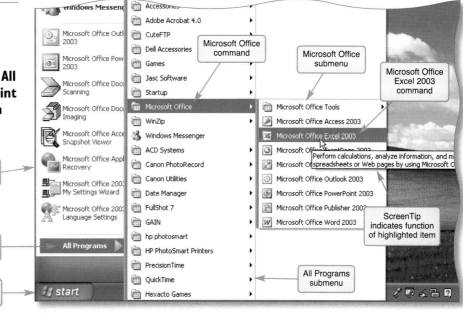

FIGURE 1-4

2

• **Click Microsoft Office Excel 2003.**

Excel starts. After several seconds, Excel displays a blank workbook titled Book1 in the Excel window (Figure 1-5).

3

• **If the Excel window is not maximized, double-click its title bar to maximize it.**

Other Ways

1. Double-click Excel icon on desktop
2. Click Microsoft Office Excel 2003 on Start menu
3. Click Start button, point to All Programs, click New Office Document, click General tab, double-click Blank Workbook icon

FIGURE 1-5

The screen shown in Figure 1-5 on the previous page illustrates how the Excel window looks the first time you start Excel after installation on most computers. If the Office Speech Recognition software is installed and active on your computer, then when you start Excel, the Language bar is displayed on the screen. The **Language bar** contains buttons that allow you to speak commands and dictate text. It usually is located on the right side of the Windows taskbar next to the notification area, and it changes to include the speech recognition functions available in Excel. In this book, the Language bar is closed because it takes up computer resources and with the Language bar active, the microphone can be turned on accidentally by clicking the Microphone button causing your computer to act in an unstable manner. For additional information about the Language bar, see page EX 15 and Appendix B.

As shown in Figure 1-5, Excel displays a task pane on the right side of the screen. A **task pane** is a separate window that enables users to carry out some Excel tasks more efficiently. When you start Excel, it displays the Getting Started task pane, which is a small window that provides commonly used links and commands that allow you to open files, create new files, or search Office-related topics on the Microsoft Web site. In this book, the Getting Started task pane is hidden to allow the maximum number of columns to appear in Excel.

At startup, Excel also displays two toolbars on a single row. A **toolbar** contains buttons, boxes, and menus that allow you to perform tasks quickly. To allow for more efficient use of the buttons, the toolbars should appear on two separate rows, instead of sharing a single row. The following steps show how to close the Language bar, close the Getting Started task pane, and instruct Excel to display the toolbars on two separate rows.

More About

Task Panes

You can drag a task pane title bar to float the pane in your work area or dock it on either the left or right side of a screen, depending on your personal preference.

To Customize the Excel Window

1

• **Right-click the Language bar.**

The Language bar shortcut menu appears (Figure 1-6).

FIGURE 1-6

• **Click Close the Language bar.**

• **Click the Getting Started task pane Close button in the upper-right corner of the task pane.**

• **If the toolbars are positioned on the same row, click the Toolbar Options button.**

The Language bar disappears. Excel closes the Getting Started task pane and displays additional columns. Excel also displays the Toolbar Options list showing the buttons that do not fit on the toolbars when toolbars appear on one row (Figure 1-7).

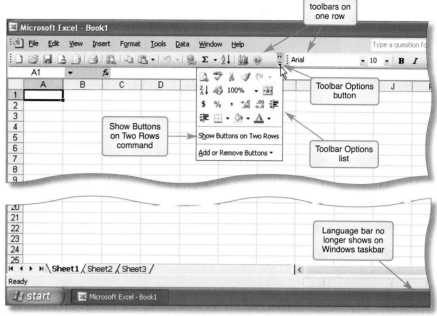

FIGURE 1-7

• **Click Show Buttons on Two Rows.**

Excel displays the toolbars on two separate rows (Figure 1-8). With the toolbars on two separate rows, all of the buttons fit on the two toolbars.

FIGURE 1-8

As you work through creating a worksheet, you will find that certain Excel operations cause Excel to display a task pane. Excel provides eleven task panes, in addition to the Getting Started task pane shown in Figure 1-6. Some of the more important ones are the Clipboard task pane, the Excel Help task pane, and the Clip Art task pane. Throughout the book, these task panes are discussed when they are used.

At any point while working with an Excel worksheet, you can open or close a task pane by clicking the Task Pane command on the View menu. You can activate additional task panes by clicking the Other Task Panes button to the left of the Close button on the task pane title bar (Figure 1-6) and then selecting a task pane in the Other Task Panes list. The Back and Forward buttons below the task pane title bar allow you to switch between task panes that you opened during a session.

The Excel Worksheet

When Excel starts, it creates a new blank workbook, called Book1. The **workbook** (Figure 1-9 on the next page) is like a notebook. Inside the workbook are sheets, each of which is called a **worksheet**. Excel opens a new workbook with three worksheets.

More About

The Excel Help System

Need Help? It is no further away than the Type a question for help box on the menu bar in the upper-right corner of the window. Click the box that contains the text, Type a question for help (Figure 1-8), type help, and then press the ENTER key. Excel responds with a list of topics you can click to learn about obtaining help on any Excel-related topic. To find out what is new in Excel 2003, type what is new in Excel in the Type a question for help box.

If necessary, you can add additional worksheets to a maximum of 255. Each worksheet has a sheet name that appears on a **sheet tab** at the bottom of the workbook. For example, Sheet1 is the name of the active worksheet displayed in the Book1 workbook. If you click the sheet tab labeled Sheet2, Excel displays the Sheet2 worksheet. This project uses only the Sheet1 worksheet.

The Worksheet

The worksheet is organized into a rectangular grid containing vertical columns and horizontal rows. A column letter above the grid, also called the **column heading**, identifies each column. A row number on the left side of the grid, also called the **row heading**, identifies each row. With the screen resolution set to 800 × 600 and the Excel window maximized, Excel displays 12 columns (A through L) and 23 rows (1 through 23) of the worksheet on the screen, as shown in Figure 1-9.

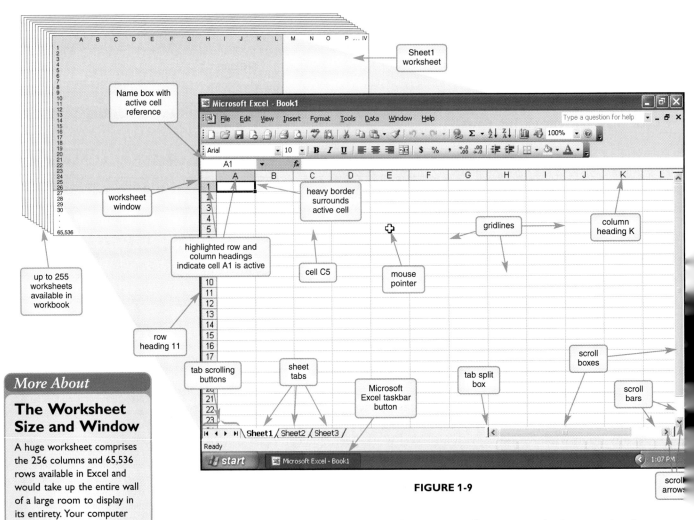

FIGURE 1-9

More About

The Worksheet Size and Window

A huge worksheet comprises the 256 columns and 65,536 rows available in Excel and would take up the entire wall of a large room to display in its entirety. Your computer screen, by comparison, is a small window that allows you to view only a minute area of the worksheet at one time. While you cannot see the entire worksheet, you can move the window over the worksheet to view any part of it.

The intersection of each column and row is a cell. A **cell** is the basic unit of a worksheet into which you enter data. Each worksheet in a workbook has 256 columns and 65,536 rows for a total of 16,777,216 cells. The column headings begin with A and end with IV. The row headings begin with 1 and end with 65,536. Only a small fraction of the active worksheet appears on the screen at one time.

A cell is referred to by its unique address, or **cell reference**, which is the coordinates of the intersection of a column and a row. To identify a cell, specify the column letter first, followed by the row number. For example, cell reference C5 refers to the cell located at the intersection of column C and row 5 (Figure 1-9).

One cell on the worksheet, designated the **active cell**, is the one into which you can enter data. The active cell in Figure 1-9 is A1. The active cell is identified in three ways. First, a heavy border surrounds the cell; second, the active cell reference shows immediately above column A in the Name box; and third, the column heading A and row heading 1 are highlighted so it is easy to see which cell is active (Figure 1-9).

The horizontal and vertical lines on the worksheet itself are called **gridlines**. Gridlines make it easier to see and identify each cell in the worksheet. If desired, you can turn the gridlines off so they do not show on the worksheet, but it is recommended that you leave them on for now.

The mouse pointer in Figure 1-9 has the shape of a block plus sign. The mouse pointer appears as a block plus sign whenever it is located in a cell on the worksheet. Another common shape of the mouse pointer is the block arrow. The mouse pointer turns into the block arrow whenever you move it outside the worksheet or when you drag cell contents between rows or columns. The other mouse pointer shapes are described when they appear on the screen.

Worksheet Window

You view the portion of the worksheet displayed on the screen through a **worksheet window** (Figure 1-9). Below and to the right of the worksheet window are **scroll bars**, **scroll arrows**, and **scroll boxes** that you can use to move the worksheet window around to view different parts of the active worksheet. To the right of the sheet tabs at the bottom of the screen is the tab split box. You can drag the **tab split box** to increase or decrease the view of the sheet tabs (Figure 1-9). When you decrease the view of the sheet tabs, you increase the length of the horizontal scroll bar, and vice versa.

The menu bar, Standard toolbar, Formatting toolbar, and formula bar appear at the top of the screen, above the worksheet window and below the title bar.

Menu Bar

The **menu bar** is a special toolbar that includes the menu names as shown in Figure 1-10a on the next page. Each **menu name** represents a menu. A **menu** is a list of commands that you can use to retrieve, store, print, and manipulate data on the worksheet. When you point to a menu name on the menu bar, the area of the menu bar containing the name changes to a button. To display a menu, such as the Edit menu, click the Edit menu name on the menu bar (Figures 1-10b and 1-10c on the next page). If you point to a menu command with an arrow to its right, Excel displays a **submenu** from which you can choose a command.

More About

The Mouse Pointer

The mouse pointer can change to one of more than 15 different shapes, such as a block arrow, cross hair, or chart symbol, depending on the task you are performing in Excel and the mouse pointer's location on the screen.

Q&A

Q: Can the Excel window or viewing area be increased to show more of the worksheet?

A: Yes. Two ways exist to increase what you can see in the viewing area: (1) on the View menu, click Full Screen; and (2) change to a higher resolution. See Appendix D for information about how to change to a higher resolution.

(a) **Menu Bar and Toolbars**

(b) **Short Menu**

(c) **Full Menu**

FIGURE 1-10

When you click a menu name on the menu bar, Excel displays a **short menu** listing the most recently used commands (Figure 1-10b). If you wait a few seconds or click the arrows at the bottom of the short menu, Excel displays the full menu. The **full menu** lists all of the commands associated with a menu (Figure 1-10c). You also can display a full menu immediately by double-clicking the menu name on the menu bar. In this book, use one of the following techniques to ensure that Excel always displays the full menu.

1. Click the menu name on the menu bar and then wait a few seconds.
2. Click the menu name on the menu bar and then click the arrows at the bottom of the short menu.
3. Click the menu name on the menu bar and then point to the arrows at the bottom of the short menu.
4. Double-click the menu name on the menu bar.

Both short and full menus display some dimmed commands. A **dimmed command** appears gray, or dimmed, instead of black, which indicates it is not available for the current selection. A command with medium blue shading to the left of it on a full menu is called a **hidden command** because it does not appear on a short menu. As you use Excel, it automatically personalizes the short menus for you based on how often you use commands. That is, as you use hidden commands, Excel *unhides* them and places them on the short menu.

The menu bar can change to include other menu names depending on the type of work you are doing in Excel. For example, if you are working with a chart sheet rather than a worksheet, Excel displays the Chart menu bar with menu names that reflect charting commands.

Standard Toolbar and Formatting Toolbar

The Standard toolbar and the Formatting toolbar (Figure 1-11) contain buttons and boxes that allow you to perform frequent tasks more quickly than when using the menu bar. For example, to print a worksheet, you click the Print button on the Standard toolbar. Each button has a picture on the button face to help you remember the button's function. Also, when you move the mouse pointer over a button or box, Excel displays the name of the button or box below it in a **ScreenTip**.

Figures 1-11a and 1-11b illustrate the Standard and Formatting toolbars and describe the functions of the buttons. Each of the buttons and boxes will be explained in detail when they are used.

> **More About**
>
> **Toolbars**
>
> You can move a toolbar to any location on the screen. Drag the move handle (Figure 1-12a on the next page) to the desired location. Once the toolbar is in the window area, drag the title bar to move it. Each side of the screen is called a dock. You can drag a toolbar to a dock so it does not clutter the window.

(a) Standard Toolbar

(b) Formatting Toolbar

FIGURE 1-11

When you first install Excel, both the Standard and Formatting toolbars are preset to display on the same row (Figure 1-12a on the next page), immediately below the menu bar. Unless the resolution of your display device is greater than 800 × 600, many of the buttons that belong on these toolbars are hidden. Hidden buttons appear in the Toolbar Options list (Figure 1-12b on the next page). In this mode, you also can display all the buttons on either toolbar by double-clicking the **move handle** on the left of each toolbar (Figure 1-12a).

> **More About**
>
> **Resetting Toolbars**
>
> If your toolbars have a different set of buttons than shown in Figure 1-11, it probably means that a previous user added or deleted buttons. To reset the toolbars to their default, see Appendix D.

(a) Standard and Formatting Toolbars on One Row

(b) Toolbar Options List

(c) Standard and Formatting Toolbars on Two Rows

FIGURE 1-12

In this book, the Standard and Formatting toolbars are shown on two rows, one below the other, so that all buttons appear on a screen with the resolution set to 800 × 600 (Figure 1-12c). You can show the two toolbars on two rows by clicking the Show Buttons on Two Rows command in the Toolbar Options list (Figure 1-12b).

Formula Bar

The formula bar appears below the Standard and Formatting toolbars (Figure 1-13). As you type, Excel displays the entry in the **formula bar**. Excel also displays the active cell reference in the Name box on the left side of the formula bar.

Status Bar

The status bar is located immediately above the Windows taskbar at the bottom of the screen (Figure 1-13). The **status bar** displays a brief description of the command selected (highlighted) on a menu, the function of the button the mouse pointer is pointing to, or the mode of Excel. **Mode indicators**, such as Enter and Ready, appear on the status bar and specify the current mode of Excel. When the mode is **Ready**, Excel is ready to accept the next command or data entry. When the mode indicator reads **Enter**, Excel is in the process of accepting data through the keyboard into the active cell.

In the middle of the status bar is the AutoCalculate area. The **AutoCalculate area** can be used in place of a calculator or formula to view the sum, average, or other types of totals of a group of numbers on the worksheet. The AutoCalculate area is discussed in detail later in this project.

Keyboard indicators, such as CAPS (Caps Lock), NUM (Num Lock), and SCRL (Scroll), show which keys are engaged. Keyboard indicators appear in the small rectangular boxes on the right side of the status bar (Figure 1-13).

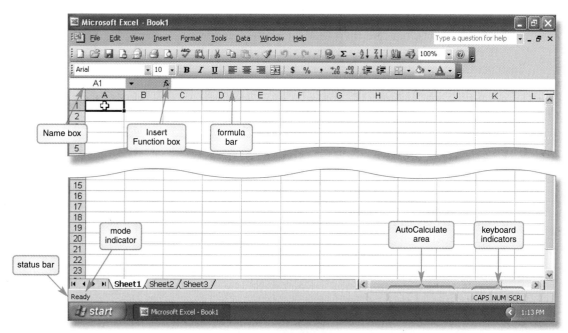

FIGURE 1-13

Speech Recognition and Speech Playback

With the **Office Speech Recognition software** installed and a microphone, you can speak the names of toolbar buttons, menus, menu commands, list items, alerts, and dialog box controls, such as OK and Cancel. You also can dictate cell entries, such as text and numbers. To indicate whether you want to speak commands or dictate cell entries, you use the Language bar. The Language bar can be in one of four states: (1) **restored**, which means it is displayed somewhere in the Excel window (Figure 1-14a); (2) **minimized**, which means it is displayed on the Windows taskbar (Figure 1-14b); (3) **hidden**, which means you do not see it on the screen but it will be displayed the next time you start your computer; (4) **closed**, which means it is hidden permanently until you enable it. If the Language bar is hidden or closed and you want it to display, then do the following:

1. Right-click an open area on the Windows taskbar at the bottom of the screen.
2. Point to Toolbars on the shortcut menu and then click Language bar on the Toolbars submenu.

(a) Language Bar in Excel Window with Microphone Enabled

(b) Language Bar Minimized on Windows Taskbar

FIGURE 1-14

If the Language bar command is dimmed on the Toolbars submenu or if the Speech command is dimmed on the Tools menu, the Office Speech Recognition software is not installed.

In this book, the Language bar does not appear in the figures. If you want to close the Language bar so that your screen is identical to what you see in the book, right-click the Language bar and then click Close the Language bar on the shortcut menu.

If you have speakers, you can use the **speech playback** functions of Excel to instruct the computer to read a worksheet to you. By selecting the appropriate option, you can have the worksheet read in a male or female voice. Additional information about the speech recognition and speech playback capabilities of Excel is available in Appendix B.

More About

Selecting a Cell

You can select any cell by entering its cell reference, such as b4, in the Name box on the left side of the formula bar.

Selecting a Cell

To enter data into a cell, you first must select it. The easiest way **to select a cell** (make it active) is to use the mouse to move the block plus sign mouse pointer to the cell and then click.

An alternative method is to use the arrow keys that are located just to the right of the typewriter keys on the keyboard. An arrow key selects the cell adjacent to the active cell in the direction of the arrow on the key.

You know a cell is selected, or active, when a heavy border surrounds the cell and the active cell reference appears in the Name box on the left side of the formula bar. Excel also changes the active cell's column heading and row heading to a gold color.

Q&A

Q: What is the maximum allowable length of a text entry?

A: A text entry in a cell can contain from 1 to 32,767 characters. Although text entries primarily are used to identify parts of a worksheet, some worksheet applications use text entries as data that you dissect, string together, and manipulate using text functions.

Entering Text

In Excel, any set of characters containing a letter, hyphen (as in a telephone number), or space is considered text. **Text** is used to place titles, such as worksheet titles, column titles, and row titles, on the worksheet. For example, as shown in Figure 1-15, the worksheet title, Extreme Blading, identifies the worksheet created in Project 1. The worksheet subtitle, Second Quarter Sales, identifies the type of report. The column titles in row 3 (Direct Mail, Outlets, Telesales, Web, and Total) identify the numbers in each column. The row titles in column A (Inline Skates, Quad Skates, Custom Skates, Accessories, and Total) identify the numbers in each row.

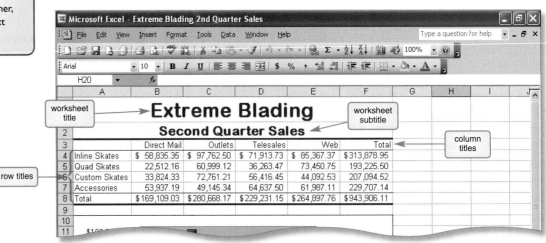

FIGURE 1-15

Entering the Worksheet Titles

The following steps show how to enter the worksheet titles in cells A1 and A2. Later in this project, the worksheet titles will be formatted so they appear as shown in Figure 1-15.

To Enter the Worksheet Titles

1

• **Click cell A1.**

Cell A1 becomes the active cell and a heavy border surrounds it (Figure 1-16).

FIGURE 1-16

2

• **Type** Extreme Blading **in cell A1 and then point to the Enter box in the formula bar.**

Excel displays the title in the formula bar and in cell A1 (Figure 1-17). When you begin typing a cell entry, Excel displays two additional boxes in the formula bar: the Cancel box and the Enter box.

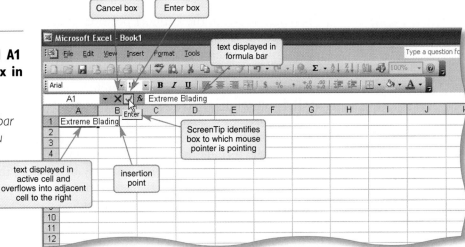

FIGURE 1-17

3

• **Click the Enter box to complete the entry.**

Excel enters the worksheet title in cell A1 (Figure 1-18).

FIGURE 1-18

4

• **Click cell A2 to select it. Type** Second Quarter Sales **as the cell entry. Click the Enter box to complete the entry.**

Excel enters the worksheet subtitle in cell A2 (Figure 1-19).

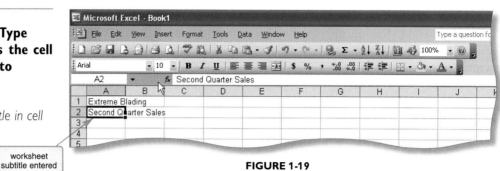

worksheet subtitle entered into cell A2

FIGURE 1-19

In Figure 1-17 on the previous page, the text in cell A1 is followed by the insertion point. The **insertion point** is a blinking vertical line that indicates where the next typed character will appear. In Steps 3 and 4, clicking the **Enter box** completes the entry. Clicking the **Cancel box** cancels the entry.

When you complete a text entry into a cell, a series of events occurs. First, Excel positions the text left-aligned in the cell. **Left-aligned** means the cell entry is positioned at the far left in the cell. Therefore, the E in the worksheet title, Extreme Blading, begins in the leftmost position of cell A1.

Second, when the text is longer than the width of a column, Excel displays the overflow characters in adjacent cells to the right as long as these adjacent cells contain no data. In Figure 1-19, the width of cell A1 is approximately 9 characters. The text consists of 15 characters. Therefore, Excel displays the overflow characters from cell A1 in cell B1, because cell B1 is empty. If cell B1 contained data, Excel would hide the overflow characters, so that only the first 9 characters in cell A1 would appear on the worksheet. Excel stores the overflow characters in cell A1 and displays them in the formula bar whenever cell A1 is the active cell.

Third, when you complete an entry by clicking the Enter box, the cell in which the text is entered remains the active cell.

Correcting a Mistake while Typing

If you type the wrong letter and notice the error before clicking the Enter box or pressing the ENTER key, use the BACKSPACE key to delete all the characters back to and including the incorrect letter. To cancel the entire entry before entering it into the cell, click the Cancel box in the formula bar or press the ESC key. If you see an error in a cell after entering the text, select the cell and retype the entry. Later in this project, additional error-correction techniques are discussed.

AutoCorrect

The **AutoCorrect feature** of Excel works behind the scenes, correcting common mistakes when you complete a text entry in a cell. AutoCorrect makes three types of corrections for you:

1. Corrects two initial capital letters by changing the second letter to lowercase.
2. Capitalizes the first letter in the names of days.
3. Replaces commonly misspelled words with their correct spelling. For example, it will change the misspelled word *recieve* to *receive* when you complete the entry. AutoCorrect will correct the spelling of hundreds of commonly misspelled words automatically.

Entering Column Titles

To enter the column titles in row 3, select the appropriate cell and then enter the text, as described in the following steps.

To Enter Column Titles

1

• **Click cell B3.**

Cell B3 becomes the active cell. The active cell reference in the Name box changes from A2 to B3 (Figure 1-20).

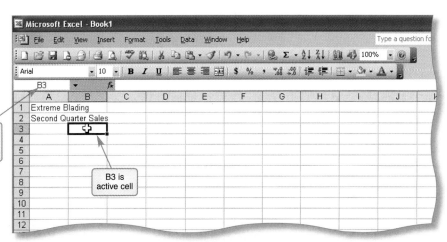

FIGURE 1-20

2

• **Type** Direct Mail **in cell B3.**

Excel displays Direct Mail in the formula bar and in cell B3 (Figure 1-21).

FIGURE 1-21

3

• **Press the RIGHT ARROW key.**

Excel enters the column title, Direct Mail, in cell B3 and makes cell C3 the active cell (Figure 1-22).

FIGURE 1-22

4

• **Repeat Steps 2 and 3 for the remaining column titles in row 3; that is, enter** Outlets **in cell C3,** Telesales **in cell D3,** Web **in cell E3, and** Total **in cell F3 (complete the last entry in cell F3 by clicking the Enter box in the formula bar).**

Excel displays the column titles left-aligned as shown in Figure 1-23.

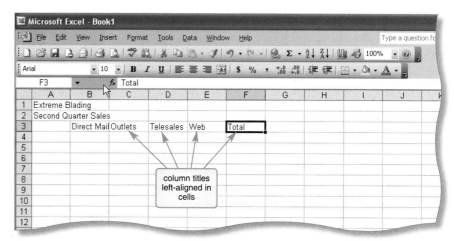

FIGURE 1-23

If the next entry is in an adjacent cell, use the arrow keys to complete the entry in a cell. When you press an arrow key to complete an entry, the adjacent cell in the direction of the arrow (up, down, left, or right) becomes the active cell. If the next entry is in a nonadjacent cell, complete an entry by clicking the next cell in which you plan to enter data. You also can click the Enter box or press the ENTER key and then click the appropriate cell for the next entry.

Entering Row Titles

The next step in developing the worksheet in Project 1 is to enter the row titles in column A. This process is similar to entering the column titles and is described in the following steps.

To Enter Row Titles

1

• **Click cell A4. Type** Inline Skates **and then press the DOWN ARROW key.**

Excel enters the row title, Inline Skates, in cell A4, and cell A5 becomes the active cell (Figure 1-24).

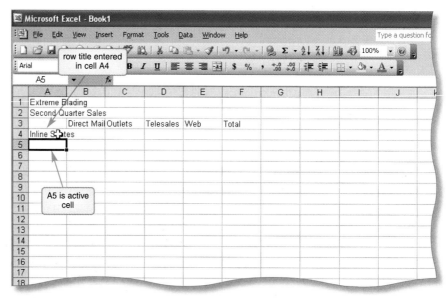

FIGURE 1-24

2

• **Repeat Step 1 for the remaining row titles in column A; that is, enter** Quad Skates **in cell A5,** Custom Skates **in cell A6,** Accessories **in cell A7, and** Total **in cell A8.**

Excel displays the row titles as shown in Figure 1-25.

FIGURE 1-25

When you enter text, Excel automatically left-aligns the text in the cell. Excel treats any combination of numbers, spaces, and nonnumeric characters as text. For example, the following entries are text:

401AX21, 921-231, 619 321, 883XTY

You can change the text alignment in a cell by realigning it. Several alignment techniques are discussed later in the project.

Entering Numbers

In Excel, you can enter numbers into cells to represent amounts. A **number** can contain only the following characters:

0 1 2 3 4 5 6 7 8 9 + - ( ) , / . $ % E e

If a cell entry contains any other keyboard character (including spaces), Excel interprets the entry as text and treats it accordingly. The use of the special characters is explained when they are used in the project.

The Extreme Blading Second Quarter numbers used in Project 1 are summarized in Table 1-1. These numbers, which represent second quarter sales for each of the sales channels and product groups, must be entered in rows 4, 5, 6, and 7. The steps on the next page enter the numbers in Table 1-1 one row at a time.

More About

Entering Numbers as Text

Sometimes, you will want Excel to treat numbers, such as Zip codes and telephone numbers, as text. To enter a number as text, start the entry with an apostrophe (').

Table 1-1 Extreme Blading Second Quarter Data			
	Direct Mail	**Outlets**	**Telesales**	**Web**
Inline Skates	58835.35	97762.50	71913.73	85367.37
Quad Skates	22512.16	60999.12	36263.47	73450.75
Custom Skates	33824.33	72761.21	56416.45	44092.53
Accessories	53937.19	49145.34	64637.50	61987.11

To Enter Numbers

1

• **Click cell B4.**

• **Type** 58835.35 **and then press the** RIGHT ARROW **key.**

Excel enters the number 58835.35 in cell B4 and changes the active cell to cell C4 (Figure 1-26).

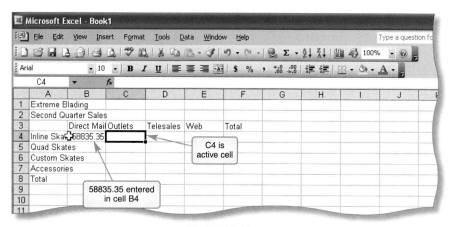

FIGURE 1-26

2

• **Enter** 97762.50 **in cell C4,** 71913.73 **in cell D4, and** 85367.37 **in cell E4.**

Row 4 now contains the second quarter sales by sales channel for the Inline Skates product group (Figure 1-27). The numbers in row 4 are right-aligned, which means Excel displays the cell entry to the far right in the cell.

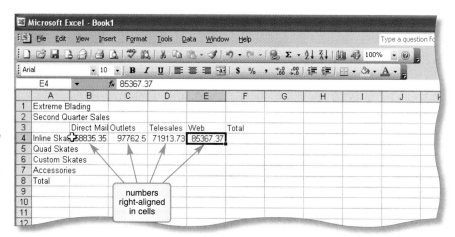

FIGURE 1-27

3

• **Click cell B5.**

• **Enter the remaining second quarter sales provided in Table 1-1 on the previous page for each of the three remaining product groups in rows 5, 6, and 7.**

Excel displays the second quarter sales as shown in Figure 1-28.

FIGURE 1-28

When the numbers are entered into the cells in column B, Excel only partially displays the row titles in column A. When the worksheet is formatted later in the project, the row titles will appear in their entirety.

Steps 1 through 3 complete the numeric entries. As shown in Figure 1-28, Excel does not display trailing zeros in cells C4 and D7. You are not required to type dollar signs, commas, or trailing zeros. When you enter a dollar value that has cents, however, you must add the decimal point and the numbers representing the cents. Later in this project, the numbers will be formatted to use dollar signs, commas, and trailing zeros to improve the appearance and readability of the numbers.

Calculating a Sum

The next step in creating the worksheet is to determine the total second quarter sales for the Direct Mail sales channel in column B. To calculate this value in cell B8, Excel must add, or sum, the numbers in cells B4, B5, B6, and B7. Excel's **SUM function**, which adds all of the numbers in a range of cells, provides a convenient means to accomplish this task.

A **range** is a series of two or more adjacent cells in a column or row or a rectangular group of cells. For example, the group of adjacent cells B4, B5, B6, and B7 is called a range. Many Excel operations, such as summing numbers, take place on a range of cells.

The following steps show how to sum the numbers in column B.

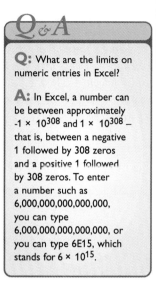

Q: What are the limits on numeric entries in Excel?

A: In Excel, a number can be between approximately -1×10^{308} and 1×10^{308} — that is, between a negative 1 followed by 308 zeros and a positive 1 followed by 308 zeros. To enter a number such as 6,000,000,000,000,000, you can type 6,000,000,000,000,000, or you can type 6E15, which stands for 6×10^{15}.

To Sum a Column of Numbers

1

• **Click cell B8.**

Cell B8 becomes the active cell (Figure 1-29).

FIGURE 1-29

2

• **Click the AutoSum button on the Standard toolbar.**

*Excel responds by displaying =SUM(B4:B7) in the formula bar and in the active cell B8 (Figure 1-30). Excel displays a ScreenTip below the active cell. The B4:B7 within parentheses following the function name SUM is Excel's way of identifying that the SUM function will add the numbers in the range B4 through B7. Excel also surrounds the proposed cells to sum with a moving border, called a **marquee**.*

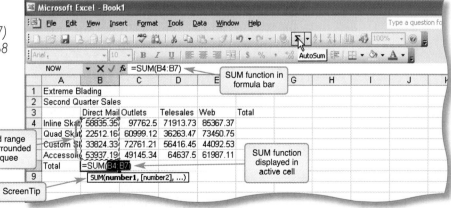

FIGURE 1-30

3

• **Click the AutoSum button a second time.**

Excel enters the sum of the second quarter sales for the Direct Mail sales channel in cell B8 (Figure 1-31). The SUM function assigned to cell B8 appears in the formula bar when cell B8 is the active cell.

FIGURE 1-31

Other Ways

1. Click Insert Function button in formula bar, select SUM in Select a function list, click OK button, select range, click OK button
2. On Insert menu click Function, select SUM in Select a function list, click OK button, select range, click OK button
3. Press ALT+EQUAL SIGN (=) twice
4. In Voice Command mode, say "AutoSum, Sum, Enter"

When you enter the SUM function using the AutoSum button, Excel automatically selects what it considers to be your choice of the range to sum. When proposing the range to sum, Excel first looks for a range of cells with numbers above the active cell and then to the left. If Excel proposes the wrong range, you can correct it by dragging through the correct range before clicking the AutoSum button a second time. You also can enter the correct range by typing the beginning cell reference, a colon (:), and the ending cell reference.

If you click the AutoSum button arrow on the right side of the AutoSum button, Excel displays a list of often used functions from which you can choose. The list includes functions that allow you to determine the average, the minimum value, or the maximum value of a range of numbers.

Using the Fill Handle to Copy a Cell to Adjacent Cells

Excel also must calculate the totals for Outlets in cell C8, Telesales in cell D8, and for Web in cell E8. Table 1-2 illustrates the similarities between the entry in cell B8 and the entries required to sum the totals in cells C8, D8, and E8.

Table 1-2 Sum Function Entries in Row 8		
CELL	**SUM FUNCTION ENTRIES**	**REMARK**
B8	=SUM(B4:B7)	Sums cells B4, B5, B6, and B7
C8	=SUM(C4:C7)	Sums cells C4, C5, C6, and C7
D8	=SUM(D4:D7)	Sums cells D4, D5, D6, and D7
E8	=SUM(E4:E7)	Sums cells E4, E5, E6, and E7

To place the SUM functions in cells C8, D8, and E8, follow the same steps shown previously in Figures 1-29 through 1-31. A second, more efficient method is to copy the SUM function from cell B8 to the range C8:E8. The cell being copied is called the **source area** or **copy area**. The range of cells receiving the copy is called the **destination area** or **paste area**.

Although the SUM function entries in Table 1-2 are similar, they are not exact copies. The range in each SUM function entry uses cell references that are one column to the right of the previous column. When you copy cell references, Excel automatically adjusts them for each new position, resulting in the SUM function entries illustrated in Table 1-2. Each adjusted cell reference is called a **relative reference**.

The easiest way to copy the SUM formula from cell B8 to cells C8, D8, and E8 is to use the fill handle. The **fill handle** is the small black square located in the lower-right corner of the heavy border around the active cell. The following steps show how to use the fill handle to copy cell B8 to the adjacent cells C8:E8.

To Copy a Cell to Adjacent Cells in a Row

1

• **With cell B8 active, point to the fill handle.**

The mouse pointer changes to a cross hair (Figure 1-32).

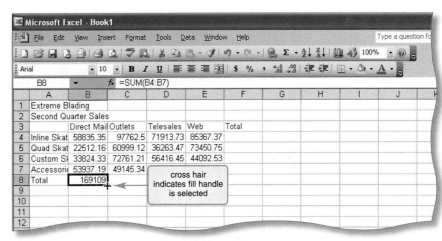

FIGURE 1-32

2

• **Drag the fill handle to select the destination area, range C8:E8. Do not release the mouse button.**

Excel displays a shaded border around the destination area, range C8:E8, and the source area, cell B8 (Figure 1-33).

FIGURE 1-33

3

• **Release the mouse button.**

Excel copies the SUM function in cell B8 to the range C8:E8 (Figure 1-34). In addition, Excel calculates the sums and enters the results in cells C8, D8, and E8. The Auto Fill Options button appears to the right and below the destination area.

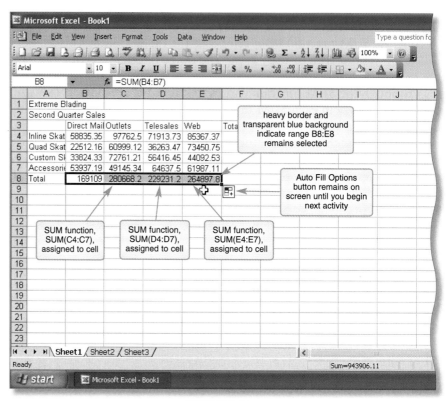

FIGURE 1-34

Once the copy is complete, Excel continues to display a heavy border and transparent blue background around cells B8:E8. The heavy border and transparent blue background are called **see-through view** and indicates a selected range. Excel does not display the transparent blue background around cell B8, the first cell in the range, because it is the active cell. If you click any cell, Excel will remove the heavy border and transparent blue background of the see-through view.

When you copy one range to another, Excel displays an Auto Fill Options button to the right and below the destination area (Figure 1-34). The Auto Fill Options button allows you to choose whether you want to copy the values from the source area to the destination area with formatting, without formatting, or only copy the format. To view the available fill options, click the Auto Fill Options button. The Auto Fill Options button disappears when you begin another activity.

Determining Multiple Totals at the Same Time

The next step in building the worksheet is to determine total second quarter sales for each product group and total second quarter sales for the company in column F. To calculate these totals, you can use the SUM function much as you used it to total the sales by sales channel in row 8. In this example, however, Excel will determine totals for all of the rows at the same time. The following steps illustrate this process.

To Determine Multiple Totals at the Same Time

1

• **Click cell F4.**

Cell F4 becomes the active cell (Figure 1-35).

FIGURE 1-35

2

• **With the mouse pointer in cell F4 and in the shape of a block plus sign, drag the mouse pointer down to cell F8.**

Excel highlights the range F4:F8 with a see-through view (Figure 1-36).

FIGURE 1-36

3

• **Click the AutoSum button on the Standard toolbar.**

Excel assigns the appropriate SUM functions to cells F4, F5, F6, F7, and F8, and then calculates and displays the sums in the respective cells (Figure 1-37).

4

• **Select cell A9 to deselect the range F4:F8.**

FIGURE 1-37

If each cell in a selected range is next to a row of numbers, Excel assigns the SUM function to each cell when you click the AutoSum button. Thus, as shown in the previous steps, each of the five cells in the selected range is assigned a SUM function with a different range, based on its row. This same procedure could have been used earlier to sum the columns. That is, instead of clicking cell B8, clicking the AutoSum button twice, and then copying the SUM function to the range C8:E8, the range B8:E8 could have been selected and then the AutoSum button clicked once, which would have assigned the SUM function to the entire range.

More About

Summing Columns and Rows

A more efficient way to determine the totals in row 8 and column F in Figure 1-37 is to select the range (B4:F8) and then click the AutoSum button on the Standard toolbar.

Formatting the Worksheet

The text, numeric entries, and functions for the worksheet now are complete. The next step is to format the worksheet. You **format** a worksheet to emphasize certain entries and make the worksheet easier to read and understand.

Figure 1-38a shows the worksheet before formatting. Figure 1-38b shows the worksheet after formatting. As you can see from the two figures, a worksheet that is formatted not only is easier to read, but also looks more professional.

(a) Before Formatting

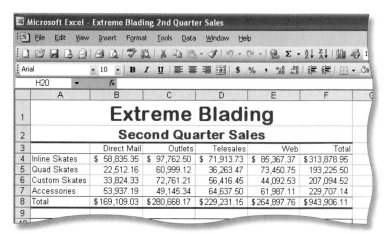

(b) After Formatting

FIGURE 1-38

To change the unformatted worksheet in Figure 1-38a to the formatted worksheet in Figure 1-38b, the following tasks must be completed:

1. Change the font type, change the font style to bold, increase the font size, and change the font color of the worksheet titles in cells A1 and A2.
2. Center the worksheet titles in cells A1 and A2 across columns A through F.
3. Format the body of the worksheet. The body of the worksheet, range A3:F8, includes the column titles, row titles, and numbers. Formatting the body of the worksheet changes the numbers to use a dollars-and-cents format, with dollar signs in the first row (row 4) and the total row (row 8); adds underlining that emphasizes portions of the worksheet; and modifies the column widths to make the text and numbers readable.

The remainder of this section explains the process required to format the worksheet. Although the format procedures are explained in the order described above, you should be aware that you can make these format changes in any order.

Font Type, Style, Size, and Color

The characters that Excel displays on the screen are a specific font type, style, size, and color. The **font type**, or font face, defines the appearance and shape of the letters, numbers, and special characters. Examples of font types include Times New Roman, Arial, and Courier. **Font style** indicates how the characters are formatted. Common font styles include regular, bold, underline, or italic. The **font size** specifies the size of the characters on the screen. Font size is gauged by a measurement system called points. A single point is about 1/72 of one inch in height. Thus, a character with a **point size** of 10 is about 10/72 of one inch in height. The **font color** defines the color of the characters. Excel can display characters in a wide variety of colors, including black, red, orange, and blue.

When Excel begins, the preset font type for the entire workbook is Arial, with a font size and font style of 10-point regular black. Excel allows you to change the font characteristics in a single cell, a range of cells, the entire worksheet, or the entire workbook.

Changing the Font Type

Different font types often are used in a worksheet to make it more appealing to the reader. The following steps show how to change the worksheet title font type from Arial to Arial Rounded MT Bold.

To Change the Font Type

1

• **Click cell A1 and then point to the Font box arrow on the Formatting toolbar.**

Cell A1 is the active cell (Figure 1-39).

FIGURE 1-39

2

• **Click the Font box arrow and then point to Arial Rounded MT Bold.**

Excel displays the Font list with Arial Rounded MT Bold highlighted (Figure 1-40).

FIGURE 1-40

3

• **Click Arial Rounded MT Bold.**

Excel changes the font type of cell A1 from Arial to Arial Rounded MT Bold (Figure 1-41).

FIGURE 1-41

Because many applications supply additional font types beyond what comes with the Windows operating system, the number of font types available on your computer will depend on the applications installed. This book only uses font types that come with the Windows operating system.

Bolding a Cell

You **bold** an entry in a cell to emphasize it or make it stand out from the rest of the worksheet. The following step shows how to bold the worksheet title in cell A1.

To Bold a Cell

• **With cell A1 active, click the Bold button on the Formatting toolbar.**

Excel changes the font style of the worksheet title, Extreme Blading, to bold. With the mouse pointer pointing to the Bold button, Excel displays a ScreenTip immediately below the Bold button to identify the function of the button (Figure 1-42).

FIGURE 1-42

When the active cell is bold, Excel displays the Bold button on the Formatting toolbar with a transparent gold background (Figure 1-42). If you point to the Bold button and the active cell is already bold, then Excel displays the button with a transparent red background. Clicking the Bold button a second time removes the bold font style.

Increasing the Font Size

Increasing the font size is the next step in formatting the worksheet title. You increase the font size of a cell so the entry stands out and is easier to read. The following steps illustrate how to increase the font size of the worksheet title in cell A1.

To Increase the Font Size of a Cell Entry

1

• **With cell A1 selected, click the Font Size box arrow on the Formatting toolbar.**

Excel displays the Font Size list as shown in Figure 1-43.

FIGURE 1-43

2

• **Click 24 in the Font Size list.**

The font size of the characters in cell A1 increase from 10 point to 24 point (Figure 1-44). The increased font size makes the worksheet title easier to read.

FIGURE 1-44

An alternative to clicking a font size in the Font Size list is to click the Font Size box, type the font size, and then press the ENTER key. This procedure allows you to assign a font size not available in the Font Size list to a selected cell entry. With cell A1 selected (Figure 1-44), the Font Size box shows that the new font size is 24 and the transparent gold Bold button shows that the font style is bold.

Changing the Font Color of a Cell Entry

The next step is to change the color of the font in cell A1 from black to violet. The steps on the next page show how to change the font color of a cell entry.

Other Ways

1. On Format menu click Cells, click Font tab, select font size in Size box, click OK button
2. Right-click cell, click Format Cells on shortcut menu, click Font tab, select font size in Size box, click OK button
3. In Voice Command mode, say "Font Size, [desired font size]"

To Change the Font Color of a Cell Entry

1

• **With cell A1 selected, click the Font Color button arrow on the Formatting toolbar.**

Excel displays the Font Color palette (Figure 1-45).

FIGURE 1-45

2

• **Click Violet (column 7, row 3) on the Font Color palette.**

The font in the worksheet title in cell A1 changes from black to violet (Figure 1-46).

FIGURE 1-46

Other Ways

1. On Format menu click Cells, click Font tab, click Color box arrow, select color on Color palette, click OK button
2. Right-click cell, click Format Cells on shortcut menu, click Font tab, click Color box arrow, select color on Color palette, click OK button
3. In Voice Command mode, say "Font Color, [desired color]"

As shown in Figure 1-45, you can choose from 40 different font colors on the Font Color palette. Your Font Color palette may have more or fewer colors, depending on color settings of your operating system. When you choose a color on the Font Color palette, Excel changes the Font Color button on the Formatting toolbar to the chosen color. Thus, to change the font color of the cell entry in another cell to the same color, you only need to select the cell and then click the Font Color button.

Centering a Cell Entry across Columns by Merging Cells

The final step in formatting the worksheet title is to center it across columns A through F. Centering a worksheet title across the columns used in the body of the worksheet improves the worksheet's appearance. To do this, the six cells in the range A1:F1 are combined, or merged, into a single cell that is the width of the columns in the body of the worksheet. **Merging cells** involves creating a single cell by combining two or more selected cells. The following steps illustrate how to center the worksheet title across columns by merging cells.

To Center a Cell Entry across Columns by Merging Cells

1

• **With cell A1 selected, drag to cell F1.**

Excel highlights the selected cells (Figure 1-47).

FIGURE 1-47

2

• **Click the Merge and Center button on the Formatting toolbar.**

Excel merges the cells A1 through F1 to create a new cell A1 and centers the contents of cell A1 across columns A through F (Figure 1-48). After the merge, cells B1 through F1 no longer exist on the worksheet.

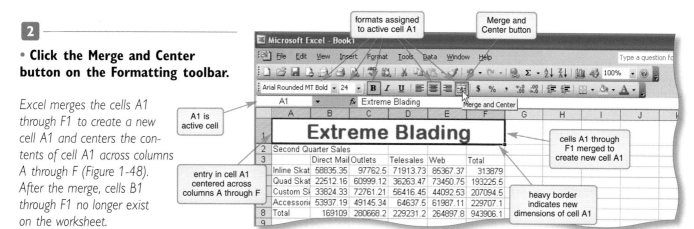

FIGURE 1-48

Excel not only centers the worksheet title across the range A1:F1, but it also merges cells A1 through F1 into one merged cell, cell A1. For the Merge and Center button to work properly, all the cells except the leftmost cell in the selected range must be empty.

The opposite of merging cells is **splitting a merged cell**. After you have merged multiple cells to create one merged cell, you can unmerge, or split, the merged cell to display the original cells on the worksheet. You split a merged cell by selecting it and clicking the Merge and Center button. For example, if you click the Merge and Center button a second time in Step 2, it will split the merged cell A1 to cells A1, B1, C1, D1, E1, and F1.

Most formats assigned to a cell will appear on the Formatting toolbar when the cell is selected. For example, with cell A1 selected in Figure 1-48, Excel displays the font type and font size of the active cell in their appropriate boxes. Transparent gold buttons on the Formatting toolbar indicate other assigned formatting. To determine if less frequently used formats are assigned to a cell, right-click the cell, click Format Cells on the shortcut menu, and then click each of the tabs in the Format Cells dialog box.

Formatting the Worksheet Subtitle

The worksheet subtitle in cell A2 is to be formatted the same as the worksheet title in cell A1, except that the font size should be 16 rather than 24. The steps on the next page show how to format the worksheet subtitle in cell A2.

To Format the Worksheet Subtitle

1 Select cell A2.

2 Click the Font box arrow on the Formatting toolbar and then click Arial Rounded MT Bold.

3 Click the Bold button on the Formatting toolbar.

4 Click the Font Size box arrow on the Formatting toolbar and then click 16.

5 Click the Font Color button on the Formatting toolbar.

6 Select the range A2:F2 and then click the Merge and Center button on the Formatting toolbar.

Excel displays the worksheet subtitle in cell A2 as shown in Figure 1-49.

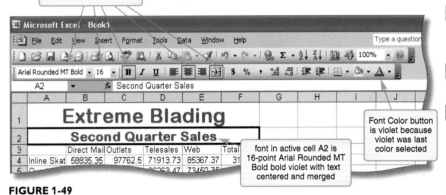

buttons and boxes on Formatting toolbar identify formats assigned to active cell A2

font in active cell A2 is 16-point Arial Rounded MT Bold bold violet with text centered and merged

Font Color button is violet because violet was last color selected

FIGURE 1-49

With cell A2 selected, the buttons and boxes on the Formatting toolbar describe the formats assigned to cell A2. The steps used to format the worksheet subtitle in cell A2 were the same as the steps used to assign the formats to the worksheet title in cell A1, except for the step that assigned violet as the font color. The step to change the font color of the worksheet subtitle in cell A2 used only the Font Color button, rather than the Font Color button arrow. Recall that, when you choose a color on the Font Color palette, Excel assigns the last font color used (in this case, violet) to the Font Color button.

Using AutoFormat to Format the Body of a Worksheet

Excel has customized autoformats that allow you to format the body of the worksheet to give it a professional look. An **autoformat** is a built-in collection of formats such as font style, font color, borders, and alignment, which you can apply to a range of cells. The following steps format the range A3:F8 using the AutoFormat command on the Format menu.

To Use AutoFormat to Format the Body of a Worksheet

1

• Select cell A3, the upper-left corner cell of the rectangular range to format.

• Drag the mouse pointer to cell F8, the lower-right corner cell of the range to format.

Excel highlights the range to format with a heavy border and transparent blue background (Figure 1-50).

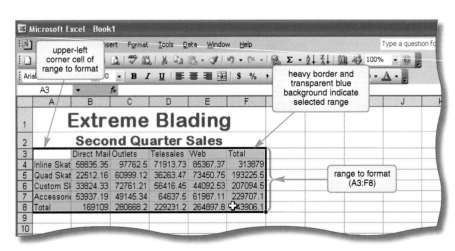

upper-left corner cell of range to format

heavy border and transparent blue background indicate selected range

range to format (A3:F8)

FIGURE 1-50

2

• **Click Format on the menu bar.**

Excel displays the Format menu (Figure 1-51).

FIGURE 1-51

3

• **Click AutoFormat on the Format menu.**

• **When Excel displays the AutoFormat dialog box, click the Accounting 2 format.**

Excel displays the AutoFormat dialog box with a list of available autoformats (Figure 1-52). For each autoformat, Excel provides a sample to illustrate how the body of the worksheet will appear if that autoformat is chosen.

FIGURE 1-52

4

• **Click the OK button.**

• **Select cell A10 to deselect the range A3:F8.**

Excel displays the worksheet with the range A3:F8 formatted using the autoformat, Accounting 2 (Figure 1-53).

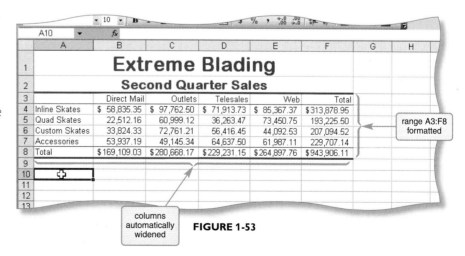

FIGURE 1-53

More About

Merging Table Formats

It is not uncommon to apply two or more of the table formats (Figure 1-52 on the previous page) to the same range. If you assign two table formats to a range, Excel does not remove the original format from the range; it simply adds the second table format to the first. Thus, if you decide to change a table format to another, select the table format None from the bottom of the list to clear the first table format.
More About

Navigation

For more information about selecting cells that contain certain entries, such as constants or formulas, visit the Excel 2003 More About Web page (scsite.com/ex2003/more) and click Using Go To Special.

The formats associated with the autoformat Accounting 2 include right-aligned column titles; numbers displayed as dollars and cents with comma separators; numbers aligned on the decimal point; the first row and total row of numbers displayed with dollar signs; and top and bottom rows displayed with borders. The width of column A has been increased so the longest row title in cell A6, Custom Skates, just fits in the column. The widths of columns B through F also have been increased so that the formatted numbers will fit in the cells.

The AutoFormat dialog box shown in Figure 1-52 on the previous page includes 17 autoformats and four buttons. Use the vertical scroll bar in the dialog box to view the autoformats that are not displayed when the dialog box first opens. Each one of these autoformats offers a different look. The one you choose depends on the worksheet you are creating. The last autoformat in the list, called None, removes all formats.

The four buttons in the AutoFormat dialog box allow you to complete the entries, modify an autoformat, or cancel changes and close the dialog box. The Close button on the title bar and the Cancel button both terminate the current activity and close the AutoFormat dialog box without making changes. The Options button allows you to deselect formats, such as fonts or borders, within an autoformat.

The worksheet now is complete. The next step is to chart the second quarter sales for the four product groups by sales channel. To create the chart, you must select the cell in the upper-left corner of the range to chart (cell A3). Rather than clicking cell A3 to select it, the next section describes how to use the Name box to select the cell.

Using the Name Box to Select a Cell

As previously noted, the Name box is located on the left side of the formula bar. To select any cell, click the Name box and enter the cell reference of the cell you want to select. The following steps show how to select cell A3.

To Use the Name Box to Select a Cell

1

• **Click the Name box in the formula bar and then type** a3 **as the cell to select.**

Even though cell A10 is the active cell, Excel displays the typed cell reference a3 in the Name box (Figure 1-54).

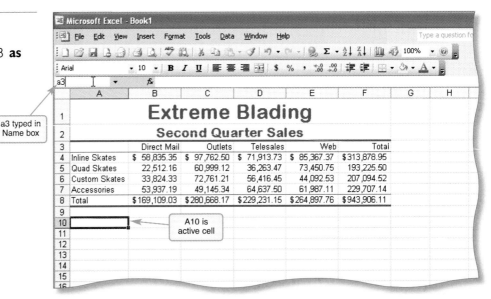

FIGURE 1-54

2

• **Press the ENTER key.**

Excel changes the active cell from cell A10 to cell A3 (Figure 1-55).

A3 is active cell

FIGURE 1-55

As you will see in later projects, in addition to using the Name box to select any cell in a worksheet, you also can use it to assign names to a cell or range of cells. Excel supports several additional ways to select a cell, as summarized in Table 1-3.

Table 1-3   Selecting Cells in Excel

KEY, BOX, OR COMMAND	FUNCTION
ALT+PAGE DOWN	Selects the cell one worksheet window to the right and moves the worksheet window accordingly.
ALT+PAGE UP	Selects the cell one worksheet window to the left and moves the worksheet window accordingly.
ARROW	Selects the adjacent cell in the direction of the arrow on the key.
CTRL+ARROW	Selects the border cell of the worksheet in combination with the arrow keys and moves the worksheet window accordingly. For example, to select the rightmost cell in the row that contains the active cell, press CTRL+RIGHT ARROW. You also can press the END key, release it, and then press the appropriate arrow key to accomplish the same task.
CTRL+HOME	Selects cell A1 or the cell one column and one row below and to the right of frozen titles and moves the worksheet window accordingly.
Find command on Edit menu or SHIFT+F5	Finds and selects a cell that contains specific contents that you enter in the Find dialog box. If necessary, Excel moves the worksheet window to display the cell. You also can press CTRL+F to display the Find dialog box.
Go To command on Edit menu or F5	Selects the cell that corresponds to the cell reference you enter in the Go To dialog box and moves the worksheet window accordingly. You also can press CTRL+G to display the Go To dialog box.
HOME	Selects the cell at the beginning of the row that contains the active cell and moves the worksheet window accordingly.
Name box	Selects the cell in the workbook that corresponds to the cell reference you enter in the Name box.
PAGE DOWN	Selects the cell down one worksheet window from the active cell and moves the worksheet window accordingly.
PAGE UP	Selects the cell up one worksheet window from the active cell and moves the worksheet window accordingly.

Adding a 3-D Clustered Column Chart to the Worksheet

As outlined in the requirements document in Figure 1-2 on page EX 6, the worksheet should include a 3-D Clustered column chart to graphically represent sales for each product group by sales channel. The 3-D Clustered column chart shown in Figure 1-56 is called an **embedded chart** because it is drawn on the same worksheet as the data.

The chart uses different colored columns to represent sales for different product groups. For the Direct Mail sales channel, for example, the light blue column represents the second quarter sales for the Inline Skates product group ($58,835.35); for the Outlets sales channel, the purple column represents the second quarter sales for Quad Skates ($60,999.12); for the Telesales sales channel, the light yellow column represents the second quarter sales for Custom Skates ($56,416.45); and for the Web sales channel, the turquoise column represents the second quarter sales for Accessories ($61,987.11). For the Outlets, Telesales, and Web sales channels, the columns follow the same color scheme to represent the comparable second quarter sales. The totals from the worksheet are not represented because the totals are not in the range specified for charting.

Excel derives the chart scale based the values in the worksheet and then displays the scale along the vertical axis (also called the **y-axis** or **value axis**) of the chart. For example, no value in the range B4:E7 is less than 0 or greater than $100,000.00, so the scale ranges from 0 to $100,000.00. Excel also determines the $20,000.00 increments of the scale automatically. For the numbers along the y-axis, Excel uses a format that includes representing the 0 value with a dash (Figure 1-56).

FIGURE 1-56

With the range to chart selected, you click the Chart Wizard button on the Standard toolbar to initiate drawing the chart. The area on the worksheet where the chart appears is called the **chart location**. As shown in Figure 1-56, the chart location in this worksheet is the range A10:F20, immediately below the worksheet data.

The following steps show how to draw a 3-D Clustered column chart that compares the second quarter sales by product group for the four sales channels.

To Add a 3-D Clustered Column Chart to the Worksheet

1

• **With cell A3 selected, position the block plus sign mouse pointer within the cell's border and drag the mouse pointer to the lower-right corner cell (cell E7) of the range to chart (A3:E7).**

Excel highlights the range to chart (Figure 1-57).

FIGURE 1-57

2

• **Click the Chart Wizard button on the Standard toolbar.**

• **When Excel displays the Chart Wizard - Step 1 of 4 - Chart Type dialog box, and with Column selected in the Chart type list, click Clustered column with a 3-D visual effect (column 1, row 2) in the Chart sub-type area.**

Excel displays the Chart Wizard - Step 1 of 4 - Chart Type dialog box as shown in Figure 1-58.

FIGURE 1-58

3

• **Click the Finish button.**

• **If the Chart toolbar appears, click its Close button.**

• **When Excel displays the chart, point to an open area in the lower-right section of the chart area so the ScreenTip, Chart Area, appears next to the mouse pointer.**

Excel draws the 3-D Clustered column chart (Figure 1-59). The chart appears in the middle of the worksheet window in a selection rectangle. The small sizing handles at the corners and along the sides of the selection rectangle indicate the chart is selected.

FIGURE 1-59

4

• **Drag the chart down and to the left to position the upper-left corner of the dotted line rectangle over the upper-left corner of cell A10. Do not release the mouse button (Figure 1-60).**

As you drag the selected chart, Excel displays a dotted line rectangle showing the new chart location and the mouse pointer changes to a cross hair with four arrowheads.

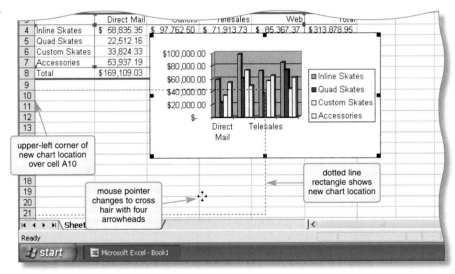

FIGURE 1-60

5

• **Release the mouse button.**

• **Point to the middle sizing handle on the right edge of the selection rectangle.**

The chart appears in a new location (Figure 1-61). The mouse pointer changes to a horizontal line with two arrowheads when it points to a sizing handle.

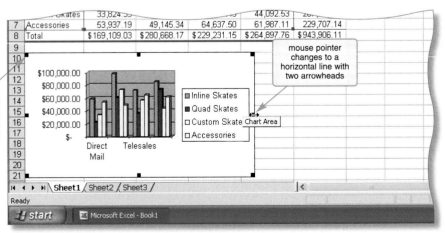

FIGURE 1-61

6

• **While holding down the ALT key, drag the sizing handle to the right edge of column F.**

While you drag, the dotted line rectangle shows the new chart location (Figure 1-62). Holding down the ALT key while you drag a chart snaps (aligns) the edge of the chart area to the worksheet gridlines.

FIGURE 1-62

7

• **If necessary, hold down the ALT key and drag the lower-middle sizing handle up to the bottom border of row 20.**

• **Click cell H20 to deselect the chart.**

The new chart location extends from the top of cell A10 to the bottom of cell F20 (Figure 1-63).

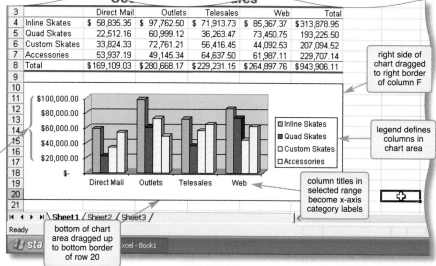

FIGURE 1-63

The embedded 3-D Clustered column chart in Figure 1-63 compares the second quarter sales for the four product groups by each sales channel. It also allows you to compare second quarter sales for the four product groups among the sales channels.

Excel automatically selects the entries in the topmost row of the chart range (row 3) as the titles for the horizontal axis (also called the **x-axis** or **category axis**) and draws a column for each of the 16 cells in the range containing numbers. The small box to the right of the column chart in Figure 1-63 contains the **legend**, which identifies the colors assigned to each bar in the chart. Excel automatically selects the entries in the leftmost column of the chart range (column A) as titles within the legend. As indicated earlier, Excel also automatically derives the chart scale on the y-axis based on the highest and lowest numbers in the chart range.

Excel offers 14 different chart types (Figure 1-58 on page EX 39). The **default chart type** is the chart Excel draws if you click the Finish button in the first Chart Wizard dialog box. When you install Excel on a computer, the default chart type is the 2-D (two-dimensional) Column chart.

Other Ways

1. On Insert menu click Chart
2. Press F11
3. In Voice Command mode, say "Chart Wizard"

More About

Printing Only the Chart

To print the embedded chart without printing the worksheet, select the chart, click File on the menu bar, click Page Setup, click the Chart tab, click the Scale to fit page in the Printed chart size area, click the Print button, and then click the OK button.

Saving a Workbook

While you are building a workbook, the computer stores it in memory. If the computer is turned off or if you lose electrical power, the workbook is lost. Hence, if you plan to use the workbook later, you must save the workbook on a floppy disk or hard disk. A saved workbook is referred to as a **file**. The following steps illustrate how to save a workbook on a floppy disk in drive A using the Save button on the Standard toolbar.

To Save a Workbook

1

- **With a floppy disk in drive A, click the Save button on the Standard toolbar.**

Excel displays the Save As dialog box (Figure 1-64). The default Save in folder is Documents (your Save in folder may be different), the default file name is Book1, and the default file type is Microsoft Office Excel Workbook.

FIGURE 1-64

2

- **Type** Extreme Blading 2nd Quarter Sales **in the File name text box.**
- **Click the Save in box arrow.**

The new file name replaces Book1 in the File name text box (Figure 1-65). A file name can be up to 255 characters and can include spaces. Excel displays a list of available drives and folders.

FIGURE 1-65

3

• **Click 3½ Floppy (A:) in the Save in list.**

Drive A becomes the selected drive (Figure 1-66). The buttons on the top and on the side of the dialog box are used to select folders, change the appearance of file names, and complete other tasks.

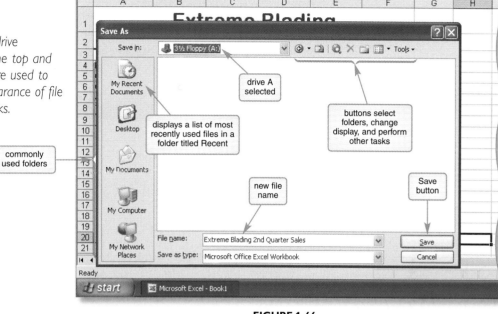

FIGURE 1-66

4

• **Click the Save button in the Save As dialog box.**

Excel saves the workbook on the floppy disk in drive A using the file name, Extreme Blading 2nd Quarter Sales. Excel automatically appends the extension .xls to the file name you entered in Step 2, which stands for Excel workbook. Although the workbook is saved on a floppy disk, it also remains in memory and is displayed on the screen (Figure 1-67). Excel displays the new file name on the title bar.

Other Ways

1. On File menu click Save As, type file name, select drive or folder, click Save button
2. Right-click workbook Control-menu icon on menu bar, click Save As on shortcut menu, type file name, select drive or folder, click Save button
3. Press CTRL+S, type file name, select drive or folder, click Save button
4. In Voice Command mode, say "File, Save As", [type desired file name], say "Save"

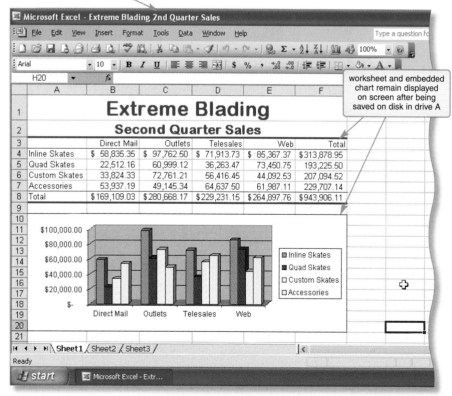

FIGURE 1-67

Microsoft Office
Excel 2003

While Excel is saving the workbook, it momentarily changes the word Ready on the status bar to Saving. It also displays a horizontal bar on the status bar indicating the amount of the workbook saved. After the save operation is complete, Excel changes the name of the workbook on the title bar from Book1 to Extreme Blading 2nd Quarter Sales (Figure 1-67 on the previous page).

The seven buttons at the top of the Save As dialog box in Figure 1-66 on the previous page and their functions are summarized in Table 1-4.

Table 1-4 Save As Dialog Box Toolbar Buttons		
BUTTON	BUTTON NAME	FUNCTION
	Default File Location	Displays contents of default file location
	Up One Level	Displays contents of folder one level up from current folder
	Search the Web	Starts browser and displays search engine
	Delete	Deletes selected file or folder
	Create New Folder	Creates new folder
	Views	Changes view of files and folders
Tools ▾	Tools	Lists commands to print or modify file names and folders

When you click the Tools button in the Save As dialog box, Excel displays the Tools menu. The General Options command on the menu allows you to save a backup copy of the workbook, create a password to limit access to the workbook, and carry out other functions that are discussed later. Saving a **backup copy** of the workbook means that each time you save a workbook, Excel copies the current version of the workbook on disk to a file with the same name, but with the words, Backup of, appended to the front of the file name. In the case of a power failure or some other problem, you can use the backup copy to restore your work.

You also can use the General Options command on the Tools menu to assign a password to a workbook so others cannot open it. A password is case-sensitive and can be up to 15 characters long. **Case-sensitive** means Excel can differentiate between uppercase and lowercase letters. If you assign a password and forget the password, you cannot access the workbook.

The five buttons on the left of the Save As dialog box in Figure 1-66 allow you to select frequently used folders. The My Recent Documents button displays a list of shortcuts (pointers) to the most recently used files in a folder titled Recent.

Printing a Worksheet

Once you have created the worksheet, you might want to print it. A printed version of the worksheet is called a **hard copy** or **printout**.

You might want a printout for several reasons. First, to present the worksheet and chart to someone who does not have access to a computer, it must be in printed form. A printout, for example, can be handed out in a management meeting about second quarter sales. In addition, worksheets and charts often are kept for reference by people other than those who prepare them. In many cases, worksheets and charts are printed and kept in binders for use by others. The following steps illustrate how to print the worksheet.

To Print a Worksheet

1

• **Ready the printer according to the printer instructions and then click the Print button on the Standard toolbar (Figure 1-68).**

Print button

FIGURE 1-68

2

• **When the printer stops printing the worksheet and the chart, retrieve the printout.**

Excel sends the worksheet to the printer, which prints it (Figure 1-69).

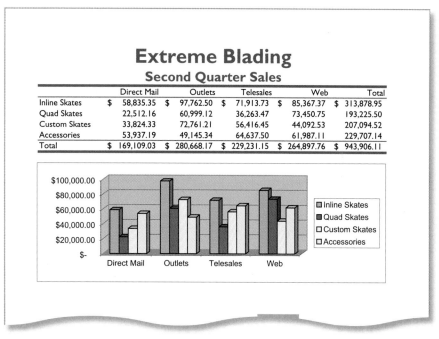

FIGURE 1-69

Prior to clicking the Print button, you can select which columns and rows in the worksheet to print. The range of cells you choose to print is called the **print area**. If you do not select a print area, as was the case in the previous set of steps, Excel automatically selects a print area on the basis of used cells. As you will see in future projects, Excel has many different print options, such as allowing you to preview the printout on the screen to see if the printout is satisfactory before sending it to the printer.

Other Ways

1. On File menu click Print, click OK button
2. Right-click workbook Control-menu icon on menu bar, click Print on shortcut menu, click OK button
3. Press CTRL+P, click OK button
4. In Voice Command mode, say "Print"

Quitting Excel

The Project 1 worksheet and embedded chart are complete. The following steps show how to quit Excel.

To Quit Excel

1

- **Point to the Close button on the right side of the title bar (Figure 1-70).**

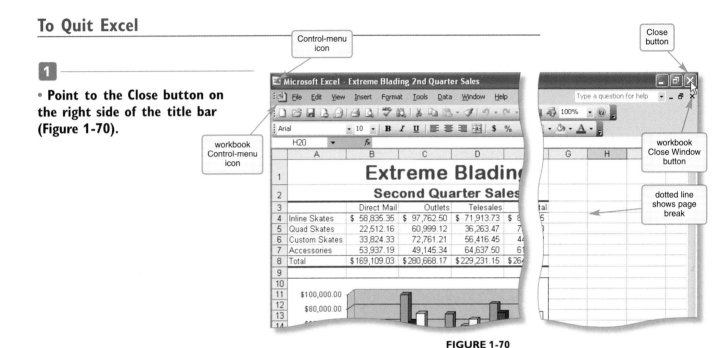

FIGURE 1-70

2

- **Click the Close button.**

If the worksheet was changed or printed, the Microsoft Excel dialog box displays the question, Do you want to save the changes you made to 'Extreme Blading 2nd Quarter Sales.xls'? (Figure 1-71). Clicking the Yes button saves the changes before quitting Excel. Clicking the No button quits Excel without saving the changes. Clicking the Cancel button closes the dialog box and returns control to the worksheet without saving the changes.

3

- **Click the No button.**

Other Ways

1. On File menu click Exit
2. Right-click Microsoft Excel button on taskbar, click Close on shortcut menu
3. Double-click Control-menu icon
4. In Voice Command mode, say "File, Exit"

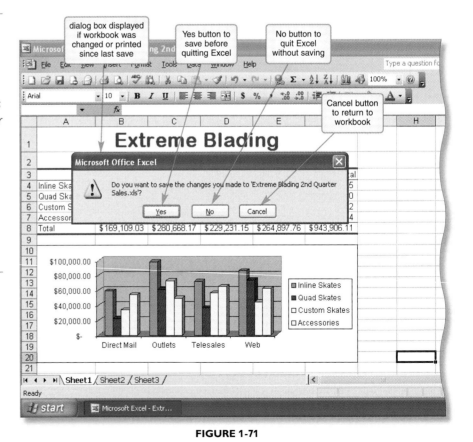

FIGURE 1-71

In Figure 1-70, you can see that the Excel window includes two Close buttons and two Control-menu icons. The Close button and Control-menu icon on the title bar can be used to quit Excel. The Close Window button and Control-menu icon on the menu bar can be used to close the workbook, but not to quit Excel.

Starting Excel and Opening a Workbook

After creating and saving a workbook, you often will have reason to retrieve it from a floppy disk. For example, you might want to review the calculations on the worksheet and enter additional or revised data. The following steps assume Excel is not running.

To Start Excel and Open a Workbook

1

• **With your floppy disk in drive A, click the Start button on the Windows taskbar, point to All Programs on the Start menu, point to Microsoft Office on the All Programs submenu, and then click Microsoft Office Excel 2003 on the Microsoft Office submenu.**

Excel starts. The Getting Started task pane lists the four most recently used files in the Open area (Figure 1-72).

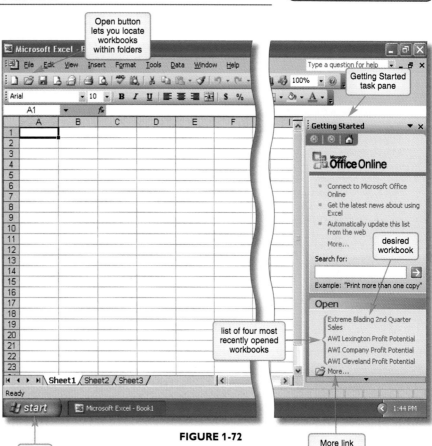

Open button lets you locate workbooks within folders

Getting Started task pane

desired workbook

list of four most recently opened workbooks

Start button

More link opens Open dialog box

FIGURE 1-72

Microsoft Office
Excel 2003

2

• **Click Extreme Blading 2nd Quarter Sales in the Open area in the Getting Started task pane.**

Excel opens the workbook Extreme Blading 2nd Quarter Sales (Figure 1-73). The Getting Started task pane closes.

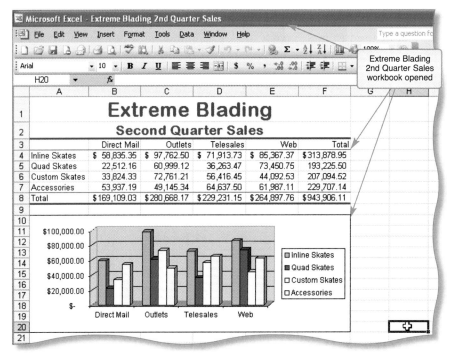

FIGURE 1-73

Other Ways

1. Click Start button, point to All Programs on Start menu, click Open Office Document on All Programs submenu, select drive A, double-click file name
2. Right-click Start button, click Explore on shortcut menu, display contents of drive A, double-click file name
3. With Excel active, in Voice Command mode, say "Open", [select file name], say "Open"

If you want to open a workbook other than one of the four most recently opened ones, click the Open button on the Standard toolbar or the More link in the Getting Started task pane. Clicking the Open button or the More link displays the Open dialog box, which allows you to navigate to a workbook stored on disk.

AutoCalculate

You easily can obtain a total, an average, or other information about the numbers in a range by using the **AutoCalculate area** on the status bar. First, select the range of cells containing the numbers you want to check. Next, right-click the AutoCalculate area to display the shortcut menu (Figure 1-74). The check mark to the left of the active function (Sum) indicates that the sum of the selected range is displayed in the AutoCalculate area on the status bar. The function of the commands on the AutoCalculate shortcut menu are described in Table 1-5.

The following steps show how to display the average second quarter sales for the Custom Skates product group.

Table 1-5   AutoCalculate Shortcut Menu Commands

COMMAND	FUNCTION
None	No value is displayed in the AutoCalculate area
Average	AutoCalculate area displays the average of the numbers in the selected range
Count	AutoCalculate area displays the number of nonblank cells in the selected range
Count Nums	AutoCalculate area displays the number of cells containing numbers in the selected range
Max	AutoCalculate area displays the highest value in the selected range
Min	AutoCalculate area displays the lowest value in the selected range
Sum	AutoCalculate area displays the sum of the numbers in the selected range

To Use the AutoCalculate Area to Determine an Average

1

• **Select the range B6:E6 and then right-click the AutoCalculate area on the status bar.**

The sum of the numbers in the range B6:E6 is displayed (207,094.52) in the AutoCalculate area, because Sum is the active function (Figure 1-74). Excel displays a shortcut menu listing the other available functions above the AutoCalculate area. If another function is active on your shortcut menu, you may see a different value in the AutoCalculate area.

FIGURE 1-74

2

• **Click Average on the shortcut menu.**

Excel displays the average of the numbers in the range B6:E6 (51,773.63) in the AutoCalculate area (Figure 1-75).

3

• **Right-click the AutoCalculate area and then click Sum on the shortcut menu.**

The AutoCalculate area displays the sum as shown earlier in Figure 1-74.

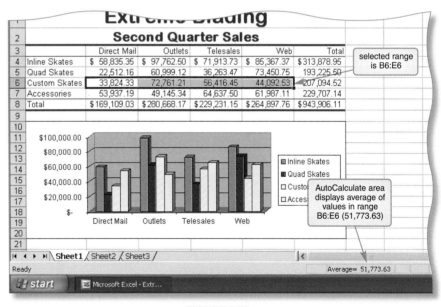

FIGURE 1-75

To change to any one of the other five functions for the range B6:E6, right-click the AutoCalculate area and then click the desired function. Clicking None at the top of the AutoCalculate shortcut menu in Figure 1-74 turns off the AutoCalculate area. Thus, if you select None, then no value will be displayed in the AutoCalculate area when you select a range.

More About

Shortcut Menus

Shortcut menus contain the most frequently used commands that relate to the object to which the mouse pointer is pointing.

Correcting Errors

You can correct errors on a worksheet using one of several methods. The method you choose will depend on the extent of the error and whether you notice it while typing the data or after you have entered the incorrect data into the cell.

Correcting Errors While You Are Typing Data into a Cell

If you notice an error while you are typing data into a cell, press the BACKSPACE key to erase the incorrect characters and then type the correct characters. If the error is a major one, click the Cancel box in the formula bar or press the ESC key to erase the entire entry and then reenter the data from the beginning.

Correcting Errors After Entering Data into a Cell

If you find an error in the worksheet after entering the data, you can correct the error in one of two ways:

1. If the entry is short, select the cell, retype the entry correctly, and then click the Enter box or press the ENTER key. The new entry will replace the old entry.
2. If the entry in the cell is long and the errors are minor, using Edit mode may be a better choice than retyping the cell entry. Use the Edit mode as described below.

   a. Double-click the cell containing the error to switch Excel to Edit mode. In **Edit mode**, Excel displays the active cell entry in the formula bar and a flashing insertion point in the active cell (Figure 1-76). With Excel in Edit mode, you can edit the contents directly in the cell — a procedure called **in-cell editing**.

   b. Make changes using in-cell editing, as indicated below.

      (1) To insert new characters between two characters, place the insertion point between the two characters and begin typing. Excel inserts the new characters at the location of the insertion point.

      (2) To delete a character in the cell, move the insertion point to the left of the character you want to delete and then press the DELETE key or place the insertion point to the right of the character you want to delete and then press the BACKSPACE key. You also can use the mouse to drag through the character or adjacent characters you want to delete and then press the DELETE key or click the Cut button on the Standard toolbar.

      (3) When you are finished editing an entry, click the Enter box or press the ENTER key.

More About

In-Cell Editing

An alternative to double-clicking the cell to edit is to select the cell and then press F2.

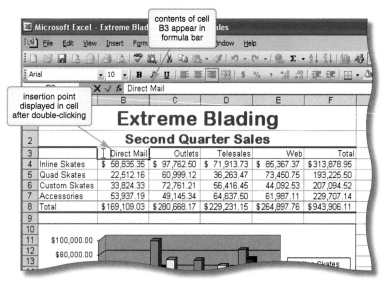

FIGURE 1-76

Correcting Errors • EX 51

When Excel enters the Edit mode, the keyboard usually is in Insert mode. In **Insert mode**, as you type a character, Excel inserts the character and moves all characters to the right of the typed character one position to the right. You can change to Overtype mode by pressing the INSERT key. In **Overtype mode**, Excel overtypes, or replaces, the character to the right of the insertion point. The INSERT key toggles the keyboard between Insert mode and Overtype mode.

While in Edit mode, you may have reason to move the insertion point to various points in the cell, select portions of the data in the cell, or switch from inserting characters to overtyping characters. Table 1-6 summarizes the more common tasks used during in-cell editing.

More About

Editing the Contents of a Cell

Rather than using in-cell editing, you can select the cell and then click the formula bar to edit the contents.

	TASK	MOUSE	KEYBOARD
1	Move the insertion point to the beginning of data in a cell.	Point to the left of the first character and click.	Press HOME
2	Move the insertion point to the end of data in a cell.	Point to the right of the last character and click.	Press END
3	Move the insertion point anywhere in a cell.	Point to the appropriate position and click the character.	Press RIGHT ARROW or LEFT ARROW
4	Highlight one or more adjacent characters.	Drag the mouse pointer through adjacent characters.	Press SHIFT+RIGHT ARROW or SHIFT+LEFT ARROW
5	Select all data in a cell.	Double-click the cell with the insertion point in the cell.	
6	Delete selected characters.	Click the Cut button on the Standard toolbar.	Press DELETE
7	Delete characters to the left of the insertion point.		Press BACKSPACE
8	Toggle between Insert and Overtype modes.		Press INSERT

Table 1-6 Summary of In-Cell Editing Tasks

Undoing the Last Cell Entry

Excel provides the Undo command on the Edit menu and the Undo button on the Standard toolbar (Figure 1-77), both of which allow you to erase recent cell entries. Thus, if you enter incorrect data in a cell and notice it immediately, click the Undo command or Undo button and Excel changes the cell entry to what it was prior to the incorrect data entry.

FIGURE 1-77

More About

The Undo Button

The Undo button can undo far more complicated worksheet activities than just removing the latest entry from a cell. In fact, most commands can be undone if you click the Undo button before you make another entry or issue another command. You cannot undo a save or print, but, as a rule, the Undo button can restore the worksheet data and settings to what they were the last time Excel was in Ready mode. With Excel, you have multiple-level undo and redo capabilities.

More About

Getting Back to Normal

If you accidentally assign unwanted formats to a range of cells, you can use the Clear command on the Edit menu to delete the formats of a selected range. Doing so changes the format to Normal style. To view the characteristics of the Normal style, click Style on the Format menu or press ALT+APOSTROPHE (').

More About

The Quick Reference

For a table that lists how to complete the tasks covered in this book using the mouse, menu, shortcut menu, and keyboard, see the Quick Reference Summary at the back of this book, or visit the Excel 2003 Quick Reference Web page (scsite.com/ex2003/qr).

Excel remembers the last 16 actions you have completed. Thus, you can undo up to 16 previous actions by clicking the Undo button arrow to display the Undo list and then clicking the action to be undone (Figure 1-77 on the previous page). You can drag through several actions in the Undo list to undo all of them at once. If no actions are available for Excel to undo, then the Undo button is dimmed and inoperative.

The Redo button, next to the Undo button on the Standard toolbar, allows you to repeat previous actions. You also can click Redo on the Edit menu, instead of using the Redo button.

Clearing a Cell or Range of Cells

If you enter data into the wrong cell or range of cells, you can erase, or clear, the data using one of the first four methods listed below. The fifth method clears the formatting from the selected cells.

To Clear Cell Entries Using the Fill Handle

1. Select the cell or range of cells and then point to the fill handle so the mouse pointer changes to a cross hair.
2. Drag the fill handle back into the selected cell or range until a shadow covers the cell or cells you want to erase. Release the mouse button.

To Clear Cell Entries Using the Shortcut Menu

1. Select the cell or range of cells to be cleared.
2. Right-click the selection.
3. Click Clear Contents on the shortcut menu.

To Clear Cell Entries Using the DELETE Key

1. Select the cell or range of cells to be cleared.
2. Press the DELETE key.

To Clear Cell Entries Using the Clear Command

1. Select the cell or range of cells to be cleared.
2. Click Edit on the menu bar and then point to Clear.
3. Click All on the Clear submenu.

To Clear Formatting Using the Clear Command

1. Select the cell or range of cells that you want to remove the formatting from.
2. Click Edit on the menu bar and then point to Clear.
3. Click Formats on the Clear submenu.

The All command on the Clear submenu is the only command that clears both the cell entry and the cell formatting. As you are clearing cell entries, always remember that you should *never press the* SPACEBAR *to clear a cell*. Pressing the SPACEBAR enters a blank character. A blank character is text and is different from an empty cell, even though the cell may appear empty.

Clearing the Entire Worksheet

If required worksheet edits are extremely extensive, you may want to clear the entire worksheet and start over. To clear the worksheet or delete an embedded chart, use the following steps.

To Clear the Entire Worksheet

1. Click the Select All button on the worksheet (Figure 1-77 on page EX 51).
2. Press the DELETE key to delete all the entries. Click Edit on the menu bar, point to Clear, and then click All on the Clear submenu to delete both the entries and formats.

The Select All button selects the entire worksheet. Instead of clicking the Select All button, you also can press CTRL+A. To clear an unsaved workbook, click the workbook's Close Window button or click the Close command on the File menu. Click the No button if the Microsoft Excel dialog box asks if you want to save changes. To start a new, blank workbook, click the New button on the Standard toolbar or click the New command on the File menu and begin working on a new workbook.

To delete an embedded chart, complete the following steps.

To Delete an Embedded Chart

1. Click the chart to select it.
2. Press the DELETE key.

Excel Help System

At any time while you are using Excel, you can get answers to questions using the **Excel Help** system. You can activate the Excel Help system by using the Type a question for help box on the menu bar, the Microsoft Excel Help button on the Standard toolbar, or by clicking Help on the menu bar (Figure 1-78). Used properly, this form of online assistance can increase your productivity and reduce your frustrations by minimizing the time you spend learning how to use Excel.

The following section shows how to get answers to your questions using the Type a question for help box. Additional information on using the Excel Help system is available in Appendix A.

Obtaining Help Using the Type a Question for Help Box on the Menu Bar

The Type a question for help box on the right side of the menu bar (see Figure 1-77 on page EX 51) lets you type free-form questions such as, how do I save or how do I create a Web page, phrases such as save a workbook or print a worksheet, or key terms such as, copy, save, or formatting. Excel responds by displaying a list of topics related to the question or terms you entered in the Search Results task pane. The following steps show how to use the Type a question for help box to obtain information on saving a workbook.

To Obtain Help Using the Type a Question for Help Box

1

• **Type** save a workbook **in the Type a question for help box on the right side of the menu bar (Figure 1-78).**

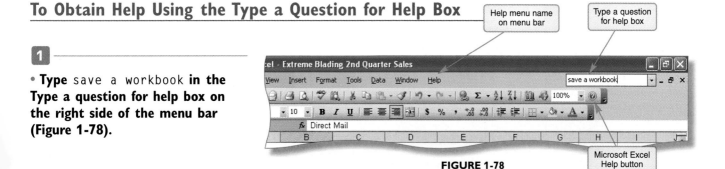

Help menu name on menu bar

Type a question for help box

Microsoft Excel Help button

FIGURE 1-78

2

• **Press the ENTER key.**

• **When Excel displays the Search Results task pane, scroll down and then click the link Save a file.**

• **If necessary, click the AutoTile button (see Figure 1-80) to tile the windows.**

Excel displays the Search Results task pane with a list of topics related to the term, save. Excel found 30 search results (Figure 1-79). When the Save a file link is clicked, Excel opens the Microsoft Excel Help window on the left side of the screen.

3

• **Click the Show All link on the right side of the Microsoft Excel Help window to expand the links in the window.**

• **Double-click the Microsoft Excel Help title bar to maximize it.**

FIGURE 1-79

The links in the Microsoft Excel Help window are expanded. Excel maximizes the window that provides Help information about saving a file (Figure 1-80).

4

• **Click the Close button on the Microsoft Excel Help window title bar.**

The Microsoft Excel Help window closes and the worksheet is active.

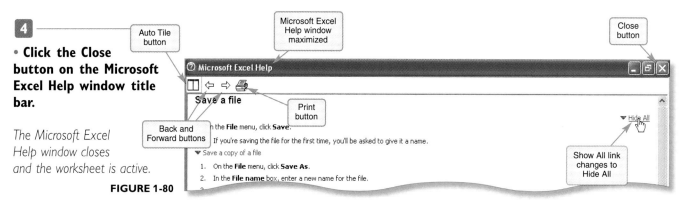

FIGURE 1-80

Use the buttons in the upper-left corner of the Microsoft Excel Help window (Figure 1-80) to navigate through the Help system, change the display, and print the contents of the window.

As you enter questions and terms in the Type a question for help box, Excel adds them to its list. Thus, if you click the Type a question for help box arrow (Figure 1-78 on the previous page), Excel will display a list of previously entered questions and terms.

Quitting Excel

The following step shows how to quit Excel.

To Quit Excel

1 **Click the Close button on the right side of the title bar, and if necessary, click the No button in the Microsoft Excel dialog box.**

Project Summary

This project presented Excel basics. First, you were introduced to starting Excel. You learned about the Excel window and how to enter text and numbers to create a worksheet. You learned how to select a range and how to use the AutoSum button to sum numbers in a column or row. Using the fill handle, you learned how to copy a cell to adjacent cells. Once the worksheet was built, you learned how to format cells one at a time using buttons on the Formatting toolbar and how to format a range using the AutoFormat command. You then learned how to use the Chart Wizard to add a 3-D Clustered column chart to the worksheet. After completing the worksheet, you learned how to save the workbook on a floppy disk, print the worksheet and chart, and then quit Excel. You also learned how to start Excel by opening an Excel document, use the AutoCalculate area, and edit data in cells. Finally, you learned how to use the Excel Help system to answer your questions.

 If you have a SAM user profile, you may have access to hands-on instruction, practice, and assessment of the skills covered in this project. Log in to your SAM account and go to your assignments page to see what your instructor has assigned.

What You Should Know

Having completed this project, you should be able to perform the tasks below. The tasks are listed in the same order they were presented in this project. For a list of the buttons, menus, toolbars, and commands introduced in this project, see the Quick Reference Summary at the back of this book and refer to the Page Number column.

1. Start Excel (EX 7)
2. Customize the Excel Window (EX 8)
3. Enter the Worksheet Titles (EX 17)
4. Enter Column Titles (EX 19)
5. Enter Row Titles (EX 20)
6. Enter Numbers (EX 22)
7. Sum a Column of Numbers (EX 23)
8. Copy a Cell to Adjacent Cells in a Row (EX 25)
9. Determine Multiple Totals at the Same Time (EX 27)
10. Change the Font Type (EX 29)
11. Bold a Cell (EX 30)
12. Increase the Font Size of a Cell Entry (EX 31)
13. Change the Font Color of a Cell Entry (EX 32)
14. Center a Cell Entry across Columns by Merging Cells (EX 33)
15. Format the Worksheet Subtitle (EX 34)
16. Use AutoFormat to Format the Body of a Worksheet (EX 34)
17. Use the Name Box to Select a Cell (EX 36)
18. Add a 3-D Clustered Column Chart to the Worksheet (EX 39)
19. Save a Workbook (EX 42)
20. Print a Worksheet (EX 45)
21. Quit Excel (EX 46)
22. Start Excel and Open a Workbook (EX 47)
23. Use the AutoCalculate Area to Determine an Average (EX 49)
24. Clear Cell Entries Using the Fill Handle (EX 52)
25. Clear Cell Entries Using the Shortcut Menu (EX 52)
26. Clear Cell Entries Using the DELETE Key (EX 52)
27. Clear Cell Entries Using the Clear Command (EX 52)
28. Clear the Entire Worksheet (EX 53)
29. Delete an Embedded Chart (EX 53)
30. Obtain Help Using the Type a Question for Help Box (EX 53)
31. Quit Excel (EX 55)

Learn It Online

Instructions: To complete the Learn It Online exercises, start your browser, click the Address bar, and then enter the Web address scsite.com/ex2003/learn. When the Excel 2003 Learn It Online page is displayed, follow the instructions in the exercises below. Each exercise has instructions for printing your results, either for your own records or for submission to your instructor.

1 Project Reinforcement TF, MC, and SA

Below Excel Project 1, click the Project Reinforcement link. Print the quiz by clicking Print on the File menu for each page. Answer each question.

2 Flash Cards

Below Excel Project 1, click the Flash Cards link and read the instructions. Type 20 (or a number specified by your instructor) in the Number of playing cards text box, type your name in the Enter your Name text box, and then click the Flip Card button. When the flash card is displayed, read the question and then click the ANSWER box arrow to select an answer. Flip through Flash Cards. If your score is 15 (75%) correct or greater, click Print on the File menu to print your results. If your score is less than 15 (75%) correct, then redo this exercise by clicking the Replay button.

3 Practice Test

Below Excel Project 1, click the Practice Test link. Answer each question, enter your first and last name at the bottom of the page, and then click the Grade Test button. When the graded practice test is displayed on your screen, click Print on the File menu to print a hard copy. Continue to take practice tests until you score 80% or better.

4 Who Wants To Be a Computer Genius?

Below Excel Project 1, click the Computer Genius link. Read the instructions, enter your first and last name at the bottom of the page, and then click the PLAY button. When your score is displayed, click the PRINT RESULTS link to print a hard copy.

5 Wheel of Terms

Below Excel Project 1, click the Wheel of Terms link. Read the instructions, and then enter your first and last name and your school name. Click the PLAY button. When your score is displayed, right-click the score and then click Print on the shortcut menu to print a hard copy.

6 Crossword Puzzle Challenge

Below Excel Project 1, click the Crossword Puzzle Challenge link. Read the instructions, and then enter your first and last name. Click the SUBMIT button. Work the crossword puzzle. When you are finished, click the Submit button. When the crossword puzzle is redisplayed, click the Print Puzzle button to print a hard copy.

7 Tips and Tricks

Below Excel Project 1, click the Tips and Tricks link. Click a topic that pertains to Project 1. Right-click the information and then click Print on the shortcut menu. Construct a brief example of what the information relates to in Excel to confirm you understand how to use the tip or trick.

8 Newsgroups

Below Excel Project 1, click the Newsgroups link. Click a topic that pertains to Project 1. Print three comments.

9 Expanding Your Horizons

Below Excel Project 1, click the Expanding Your Horizons link. Click a topic that pertains to Project 1. Print the information. Construct a brief example of what the information relates to in Excel to confirm you understand the contents of the article.

10 Search Sleuth

Below Excel Project 1, click the Search Sleuth link. To search for a term that pertains to this project, select a term below the Project 1 title and then use the Google search engine at google.com (or any major search engine) to display and print two Web pages that present information on the term.

11 Excel Online Training

Below Excel Project 1, click the Excel Online Training link. When your browser displays the Microsoft Office Online Web page, click the Excel link. Click one of the Excel courses that covers one or more of the objectives listed at the beginning of the project on page EX 4. Print the first page of the course before stepping through it.

12 Office Marketplace

Below Excel Project 1, click the Office Marketplace link. When your browser displays the Microsoft Office Online Web page, click the Office Marketplace link. Click a topic that relates to Excel. Print the first page.

Apply Your Knowledge

1 Changing the Values in a Worksheet

Instructions: Start Excel. Open the workbook Apply 1-1 Watson's Computer Discount Annual Sales from the Data Disk. See the inside back cover of this book for instructions for downloading the Data Disk or see your instructor for information on accessing the files required in this book.

Make the changes to the worksheet described in Table 1-7 so that the worksheet appears as shown in Figure 1-81. As you edit the values in the cells containing numeric data, watch the totals in row 7, the totals in column F, and the chart change.

Change the worksheet title in cell A1 to 20-point Arial Black brown, bold font and then center it across columns A through F. Change the worksheet subtitle in cell A2 to 14-point Arial Black brown, bold font and then center it across columns A through F.

Enter your name, course, laboratory assignment number, date, and instructor name in cells A21 through A25. Save the workbook using the file name, Apply 1-1 Babbage's Computer Discount Annual Sales. Print the revised worksheet and hand in the printout to your instructor.

Table 1-7 New Worksheet Data	
CELL	CHANGE CELL CONTENTS TO
A1	Babbage's Computer Discount
B4	43200.75
C4	17563.52
D5	38152.43
E5	28968.78
E6	38751.49

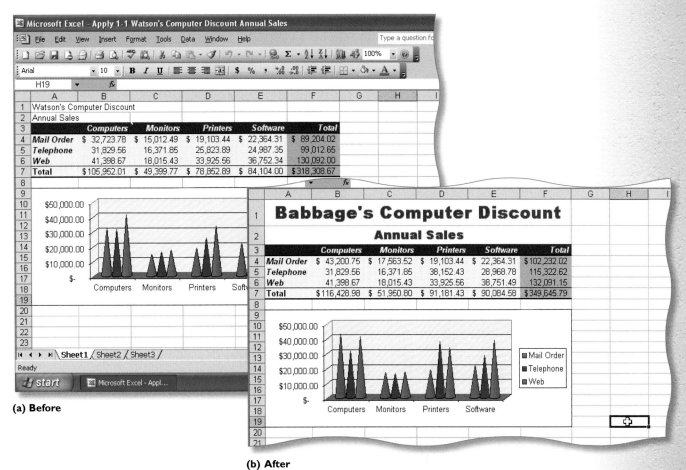

(a) Before

(b) After

FIGURE 1-81

1 Monthly Sales Analysis Worksheet

Problem: You work part-time as a spreadsheet specialist for Knotting Hill Bookstore, one of the larger bookstores in the world. Your manager has asked you to develop a monthly sales analysis worksheet similar to the one shown in Figure 1-82.

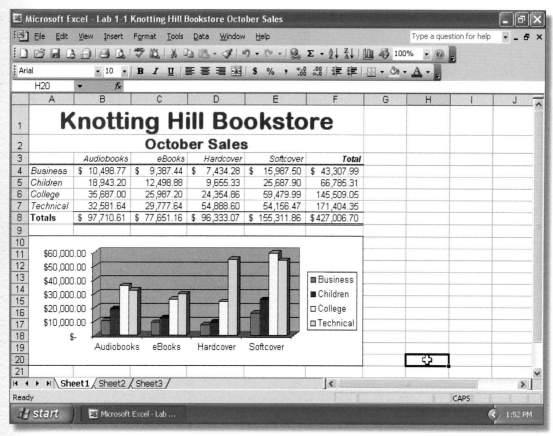

FIGURE 1-82

Instructions: Perform the following tasks.

1. Create the worksheet shown in Figure 1-82 using the sales amounts and categories in Table 1-8.

Table 1-8 Knotting Hill Bookstore October Sales				
	Audiobooks	eBooks	Hardcover	Softcover
Business	10498.77	9387.44	7434.28	15987.50
Children	18943.20	12498.88	9655.33	25687.90
College	35687.00	25987.20	24354.86	59479.99
Technical	32581.64	29777.64	54888.60	54156.47

In the Lab

2. Use the SUM function to determine the totals for the types of books, subject area, and company totals.

3. Format the worksheet title to 26-point Arial Rounded MT Bold dark blue, bold font and center it across columns A through F. Do not be concerned if the edges of the worksheet title are not displayed.

4. Format the worksheet subtitle to 16-point Arial Rounded MT Bold dark blue, bold font and center it across columns A through F.

5. Format the range A3:F8 using the AutoFormat command. Select the Accounting 3 autoformat.

6. Select the range A3:E7 and then use the Chart Wizard button on the Standard toolbar to draw a Clustered column with a 3-D visual effect chart (column 1, row 2 in the Chart sub-type list). Move and resize the chart so that it appears in the range A10:F20. If the labels along the horizontal axis (x-axis) do not appear as shown in Figure 1-82, then drag the right side of the chart so that it is displayed in the range A10:H20.

7. Enter your name, course, laboratory assignment number, date, and instructor name in cells A22 through A26.

8. Save the workbook using the file name Lab 1-1 Knotting Hill Bookstore October Sales.

9. Print the worksheet.

10. Make the following two corrections to the sales amounts: $14,785.21 for Children eBooks (cell C5), $57,752.54 for Technical Softcover books (cell E7). After you enter the corrections, the company totals in cell F8 should equal $432,889.10.

11. Print the revised worksheet. Close the workbook without saving the changes.

2 Quarterly Expense Analysis Worksheet

Problem: As the chief accountant for College Travel, Inc., you have been asked by the vice president to create a worksheet to analyze the 4th quarter expenses for the company by office and expense category (Figure 1-83 on the next page). The office locations and corresponding expenses for the 4th quarter are shown in Table 1-9.

Table 1-9 College Travel 4th Quarter Expenses				
	Atlanta	Nashville	New Orleans	Orlando
Marketing	42502.23	19231.56	32012.40	14012.00
Rent	43970.50	57510.00	29089.32	31765.23
Supplies	31892.70	18429.34	26723.15	22914.50
Travel	9512.45	12323.21	9012.56	8910.32
Wages	83463.30	72135.45	63908.55	92364.50

Instructions: Perform the following tasks.

1. Create the worksheet shown in Figure 1-83 using the data in Table 1-9.

2. Use the SUM function to determine totals expenses for the four offices, the totals for each expense category, and the company total. Add column and row headings for the totals, as appropriate.

(continued)

In the Lab

Quarterly Expense Analysis Worksheet *(continued)*

3. Change the worksheet title to 26-point Arial Black dark red, bold font, and center it across columns A through F. Format the worksheet subtitle to 16-point Arial Black dark red, bold font, and center it across columns A through F.

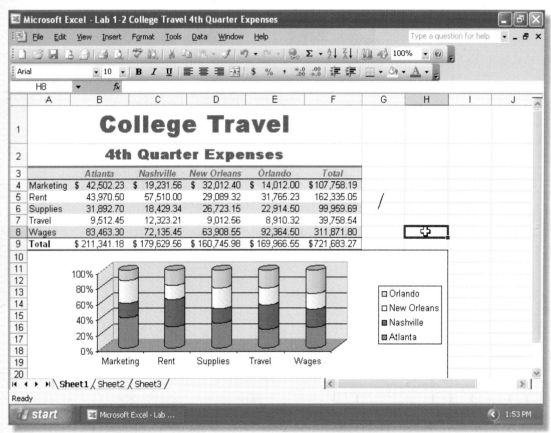

FIGURE 1-83

4. Format the range A3:F9 using the AutoFormat command on the Format menu as follows: (a) apply the autoformat Accounting 1; and (b) with the range A3:F9 still selected, apply the autoformat List 1. If you make a mistake, apply the autoformat None and then apply the autoformats again.

5. Chart the range A3:E8. Draw the 100% Stacked column with a cylindrical shape chart, as shown in Figure 1-83, by clicking the Chart Wizard button on the Standard toolbar. When Excel displays the Chart Wizard dialog box, select Cylinder in the Chart type list, and then select column 3, row 1 in the Chart sub-type list. Use the chart location A10:H20.

6. Enter your name, course, laboratory assignment number, date, and instructor name in cells A23 through A27.

7. Save the workbook using the file name, Lab 1-2 College Travel 4th Quarter Expenses. Print the worksheet.

8. Two corrections to the expenses were sent in from the accounting department. The correct expenses are $62,345.12 for the Nashville's quarterly rent (cell C5) and $18,615.42 for Orlando's quarterly travel expenses (cell E7). After you enter the two corrections, the company total in cell F9 should equal $736,223.49. Print the revised worksheet.

In the Lab

9. Use the Undo button to change the worksheet back to the original numbers in Table 1-9. Use the Redo button to change the worksheet back to the revised state.

10. Close Excel without saving the latest changes. Start Excel and open the workbook saved in step 7. Double-click cell D6 and use in-cell editing to change the New Orleans quarterly supplies expense to $29,098.32. Write the company total in cell F9 at the top of the first printout. Click the Undo button.

11. Click cell A1 and then click the Merge and Center button to split cell A1 into cells A1, B1, C1, D1, E1, and F1. To re-merge the cells into one, select the range A1:F1 and then click the Merge and Center button.

12. Hand in the two printouts to your instructor. Close the workbook without saving the changes.

3 College Expenses and Resources Worksheet

Problem: Attending college is an expensive proposition and your resources are limited. To plan for your four-year college career, you have decided to organize your anticipated resources and expenses in a worksheet. The data required to prepare your worksheet is shown in Table 1-10.

Table 1-10 College Expenses and Resources				
Expenses	Freshman	Sophomore	Junior	Senior
Room & Board	3390.00	3627.30	3881.21	4152.90
Tuition & Books	4850.00	5189.50	5552.77	5941.46
Clothes	540.00	577.80	618.25	661.52
Entertainment	635.00	679.45	727.01	777.90
Miscellaneous	325.00	347.75	372.09	398.14
Resources	Freshman	Sophomore	Junior	Senior
Savings	1700.00	1819.00	1946.33	2082.57
Parents	2390.00	2557.30	2736.31	2927.85
Job	1450.00	1551.50	1660.11	1776.32
Financial Aid	4200.00	4494.00	4808.58	5145.18

Instructions Part 1: Using the numbers in Table 1-10, create the worksheet shown in columns A through F in Figure 1-84 on the next page. Format the range A3:F9 using the AutoFormat command on the Format menu as follows: (a) select the range A3:F9 and then apply the autoformat Accounting 1; and (b) with the range A3:F9 still selected, apply the autoformat Colorful 2. Use the same autoformats for the range A11:F16.

Enter your identification on the worksheet and save the workbook using the file name Lab 1-3 Part 1 College Expenses and Resources. Print the worksheet in landscape orientation. You print in landscape orientation by invoking the Page Setup command on the File menu and then clicking Landscape in the Page sheet in the Page Setup dialog box. Click the Save button on the Standard toolbar to save the workbook with the new print settings.

In the Lab

College Expenses and Resources Worksheet *(continued)*

After reviewing the numbers, you realize you need to increase manually each of the Junior-year expenses in column D by $400. Change the Junior-year expenses to reflect this change. Manually change the financial aid for the Junior year by the amount required to cover the increase in expenses. The totals in cells F9 and F16 should equal $45,245.05. Print the worksheet. Close the workbook without saving changes. Hand in the two printouts to your instructor.

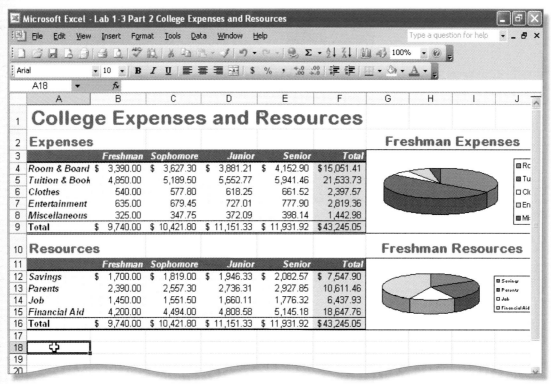

FIGURE 1-84

Instructions Part 2: Open the workbook Lab 1-3 Part 1 College Expenses and Resources. Draw a 3-D Pie chart in the range G3:J9 to show the contribution of each category of expenses for the Freshman year. Chart the range A4:B8. Add the Pie chart title as shown in cell G2 in Figure 1-84. Draw a 3-D Pie chart in the range G11:J16 to show the contribution of each category of resources for the Freshman year. Chart the range A12:B15. Add the Pie chart title shown in cell G10 in Figure 1-84. Save the workbook using the file name, Lab 1-3 Part 2 College Expenses and Resources. Print the worksheet. Hand in the printout to your instructor.

Instructions Part 3: Open the workbook Lab 1-3 Part 2 College Expenses and Resources. A close inspection of Table 1-10 shows that both expenses and resources increase 7% each year. Use the Type a question for help box on the menu bar to learn how to enter the data for the last three years using a formula and the Copy command. For example, the formula to enter in cell C4 is =B4 * 1.07. Enter formulas to replace all the numbers in the range C4:E8 and C12:E15. If necessary, reformat the tables using the autoformats, as described in Part 1. The worksheet should appear as shown in Figure 1-84, except that some of the totals will be off by 0.01 due to rounding errors. Save the worksheet using the file name, Lab 1-3 Part 3 College Expenses and Resources. Print the worksheet. Press CTRL+ACCENT MARK(`) to display the formulas. Print the formulas version. Close the workbook without saving changes. Hand in both printouts to your instructor.

Cases and Places

The difficulty of these case studies varies:
■ are the least difficult and ■■ are more difficult. The last exercise is a group exercise.

1 ■ You are employed by the Reggae Music Company. Your manager has asked you to prepare a worksheet to help her analyze monthly sales by store and by type of reggae music (Table 1-11). Use the concepts and techniques presented in this project to create the worksheet and an embedded Clustered bar chart with a 3-D visual effect.

Table 1-11	Reggae Music Company Monthly Sales			
	Boston	Kansas City	Portland	San Diego
Dancehall	6734	7821	4123	7989
Dub	5423	2134	6574	3401
Dub Poetry	3495	6291	7345	7098
Lovers Rock	6789	4523	9102	7812
Ragga	8920	9812	5637	3456
Rocksteady	2134	2190	3401	2347
Ska	5462	2923	8034	5135

2 ■ To estimate the funds you need to make it through the upcoming year, you decide to create a personal budget itemizing your expected quarterly expenses. The anticipated expenses are listed in Table 1-12. Use the concepts and techniques presented in this project to create the worksheet and an embedded 100% Stacked column chart with a conical shape that compares the quarterly cost of each expense. If necessary, reduce the size of the font in the chart so that each expense category name appears on the horizontal axis (x-axis). Use the AutoCalculate area to determine the average amount spent per quarter on each expense. Manually insert the averages with appropriate titles in an empty area on the worksheet.

Table 1-12	Quarterly Personal Budget			
	Jan - Mar	April - June	July - Sept	Oct - Dec
Mortgage	1500	1500	1500	1500
Food	900	950	950	1000
Car & Ins.	600	600	600	600
Clothes	567	433	200	459
Utilities	600	400	400	550
Miscellaneous	149	121	159	349

Cases and Places

3 ■■ The Magic Theater is a movie house that shows movies at weekday evening, weekend matinee, and weekend evening screenings. Three types of tickets are sold at each presentation: general admission, senior citizen, and children. The theater management has asked you to prepare a worksheet, based on the revenue from a typical week, that can be used to reevaluate its ticket structure. During an average week, weekday evening shows generate $7,250 from general admission ticket sales, $6,715 from senior citizen ticket sales, and $1,575 from children ticket sales. Weekend matinee shows make $6,723 from general admission ticket sales, $2,050 from senior citizen ticket sales, and $2,875 from children ticket sales. Weekend evening shows earn $9,415 from general admission ticket sales, $9,815 from senior citizen ticket sales, and $1,235 from children ticket sales. Use the concepts and techniques presented in this project to prepare a worksheet that includes total revenues for each type of ticket and for each presentation time, and a Clustered Bar chart illustrating ticket revenues.

4 ■■ Jasmine's Floral Shop on Michigan Avenue in Chicago sells floral arrangments to an exclusive clientele. The company is trying to decide whether it is feasible to open another boutique in the Chicago area. You have been asked to develop a worksheet totaling all the revenue received last year from customers living in the Chicago area. The revenue from customers living in the Chicago area by quarter is: Quarter 1, $221,565.56; Quarter 2, $182,704.34; Quarter 3, $334,116.31; and Quarter 4, $421,333.50. Create a Pie chart with a 3-D visual effect to illustrate Chicago-area revenue contribution by quarter. Use the AutoCalculate area to find the average, maximum, and minimum quarterly revenue and manually enter them and their corresponding identifiers in an empty area on the worksheet.

5 ■■ **Working Together** Visit the Registrar's office at your school and obtain data, such as age, gender, and resident status, for the students majoring in at least five different academic departments this semester. Have each member of your team divide the data into different categories. For example, separate the data by:

1. Age, divided into four different age groups
2. Gender, divided into male and female
3. Resident status, divided into resident and nonresident

After coordinating the data as a group, have each member independently use the concepts and techniques presented in this project to create a worksheet and appropriate chart to show the total students by characteristics by academic department. As a group, critique each worksheet and have each member re-do his or her worksheet based on the group recommendations. Hand in printouts of your original worksheet and final worksheet.

Microsoft
Office Excel 2003

Formulas, Functions, Formatting, and Web Queries

CASE PERSPECTIVE

Several years ago, while Alisha Wright was taking an Investment course as a sophomore in college, she persuaded six of her classmates to start a stock club geared towards researching and investing in stocks of large, well-established, and consistently profitable companies, which are referred to as blue chip stocks. They decided to call themselves the Blue Chip Stock Club. While in college, each member of the club contributed $20 per month.

Now, the club members are out of college, married, and have taken jobs around the country. They continue to invest in the stock market as a group, however, using e-mail, chat rooms, and Web cams to communicate and conduct their monthly meetings via the Internet. A few years ago, they increased their monthly contribution to $100.

At the end of each month, Alisha, the Blue Chip Stock Club's permanent treasurer, summarizes the club's financial status. Alisha plans to use Excel to create a worksheet summarizing the club's stock activities, which she can use to track and analyze the investment portfolio, answer questions posed by club members in their e-mails, and e-mail a monthly closing report to the club members. She also plans to use its Web query capabilities to access real-time stock quotes.

Alisha knows little about Excel 2003 and has asked you to show her how to create the worksheet (Figure 2-1a) and access real-time stock quotes over the Internet (Figure 2-1b).

As you read through this project, you will learn how to enter formulas and functions, how to improve the appearance of a worksheet, how to perform Web queries, and how to e-mail from within Excel.

MICROSOFT
Office Excel 2003

Formulas, Functions, Formatting, and Web Queries

PROJECT

Objectives

You will have mastered the material in this project when you can:

- Enter formulas using the keyboard and Point mode
- Recognize smart tags and option buttons
- Apply the AVERAGE, MAX, and MIN functions
- Verify a formula using Range Finder
- Format a worksheet using buttons and commands
- Add conditional formatting to a range of cells
- Change the width of a column and height of a row
- Check the spelling of a worksheet

- Preview how a printed copy of the worksheet will look
- Print a partial or complete worksheet
- Display and print the formulas version of a worksheet
- Use a Web query to get real-time data from a Web site
- Rename sheets in a workbook
- E-mail the active workbook from within Excel

Introduction

In Project 1, you learned how to enter data, sum values, format the worksheet to make it easier to read, and draw a chart. You also learned about online Help and saving, printing, and opening a workbook. This project continues to emphasize these topics and presents some new ones.

The new topics covered in this project include using formulas and functions to create the worksheet shown in Figure 2-1a. Other new topics include smart tags and option buttons, verifying formulas, adding borders, formatting numbers and text, using conditional formatting, changing the widths of columns and heights of rows, spell checking, e-mailing from within an application, renaming worksheets, and using alternative types of worksheet displays and printouts. One alternative worksheet display and printout shows the formulas in the worksheet, instead of the values. When you display the formulas in the worksheet, you see exactly what text, data, formulas, and functions you have entered into it. Finally, this project covers Web queries to obtain real-time data from a Web site (Figure 2-1b).

Excel Project 2

(a) Worksheet

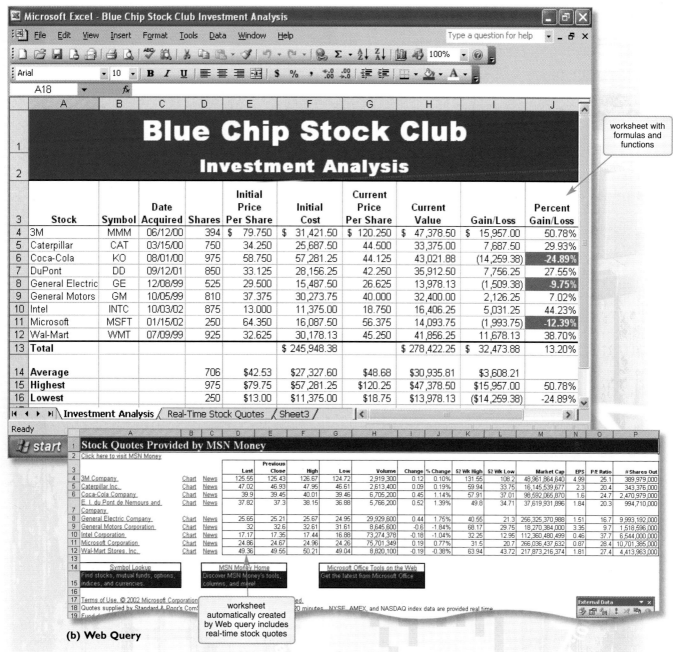

worksheet with formulas and functions

(b) Web Query

worksheet automatically created by Web query includes real-time stock quotes

FIGURE 2-1

Project Two — Blue Chip Stock Club Investment Analysis

Recall that the first step in creating an effective worksheet is to make sure you understand what is required. Requirements usually are provided by the people who will use the worksheet. The requirements document for the Blue Chip Stock Club Investment Analysis worksheet includes the following: needs, source of data, summary of calculations, Web requirements, and other facts about its development (Figure 2-2 on the next page).

REQUEST FOR NEW WORKBOOK

Date Submitted:	July 1, 2005
Submitted By:	Alisha Wright
Worksheet Title:	Blue Chip Stock Club Investment Analysis
Needs:	An easy-to-read workbook with two worksheets to provide information on the current investment portfolio and updated stock quote data. The first worksheet will summarize the club's investment portfolio (Figure 2-3). For each stock, the worksheet will include the stock name, stock symbol, date acquired, shares, initial price per share, initial cost, current price per share, current value, gain/loss, and percent gain/loss. The worksheet also will include (1) totals for initial cost, current value, and gain loss and (2) the average, highest value, and lowest value for each column of numbers. The second worksheet will use the import data capabilities of Excel to access real-time stock quotes using Web queries.
Source of Data:	The data supplied by Alisha includes the stock names, stock symbols, dates acquired, number of shares, initial price per share, and current price per share. This data is shown in Table 2-1, Blue Chip Stock Club Portfolio.
Calculations:	1. Complete the following calculations for each of the stocks: 　a. Initial Cost = Shares _ Initial Price Per Share 　b. Current Value = Shares _ Current Price Per Share 　c. Gain/Loss = Current Value − Initial Cost 　d. Percent Gain/Loss = Gain/Loss / Initial Cost 2. Compute the totals for initial cost, current value, and gain/loss. 3. Use the AVERAGE function to determine the average for the number of shares, initial price per share, initial cost per share, current price per share, current value, and gain/loss. 4. Use the MAX and MIN functions to determine the highest and lowest values for the number of shares, initial price per share, initial cost per share, current price per share, current value, gain/loss, and percent gain/loss.
Web Requirements:	Use the Web query feature of Excel to get real-time stock quotes for the stocks owned by the Blue Chip Stock Club.

Approvals

Approval Status:	X	Approved
		Rejected
Approved By:		Members of the Blue Chip Stock Club
Date:		July 6, 2005
Assigned To:		J. Quasney, Spreadsheet Specialist

FIGURE 2-2

More About

Aesthetics versus Function

In designing a worksheet, functional considerations should come first, before visual aesthetics. The function, or purpose, of a worksheet is to provide a user with direct ways to accomplish tasks. Avoid the temptation to use flashy or confusing visual elements within the worksheet, unless they will help the user more easily complete a task.

In addition, using a sketch of the worksheet can help you visualize its design. The sketch for the Blue Chip Stock Club Investment Analysis worksheet (Figure 2-3) includes a title, a subtitle, column and row headings, and the location of data values. It also uses specific characters to define the desired formatting for the worksheet as follows:

1. The row of Xs below the two leftmost columns defines the cell entries as text, such as stock names and stock symbols.
2. The rows of Zs and 9s with slashes, dollar signs, decimal points, commas, and percent signs in the remaining columns define the cell entries as numbers. The Zs indicate that the selected format should instruct Excel to suppress leading 0s. The 9s indicate that the selected format should instruct Excel to display any digits, including 0s.

3. The decimal point means that a decimal point should appear in the cell entry and indicates the number of decimal places to use.

4. The commas indicate that the selected format should instruct Excel to display a comma separator only if the number has enough digits to the left of the decimal point.

5. The slashes in the third column identify the cell entry as a date.

6. The dollar signs that are not adjacent to the Zs in the first row below the column headings and in the total row signify a fixed dollar sign. The dollar signs that are adjacent to the Zs below the total row signify a floating dollar sign, or one that appears next to the first significant digit.

7. The percent sign (%) in the far right column indicates a percent sign should appear after the number.

FIGURE 2-3

The real-time stock quotes (shown in Figure 2-1b on page EX 67) will be accessed via a Web query. The stock quotes will be returned to the active workbook on a separate worksheet. Microsoft determines the content and format of the Real-Time Stock Quotes worksheet.

Starting and Customizing Excel

With the requirements document and sketch of the worksheet complete, the next step is to use Excel to create the worksheet. To start and customize Excel, Windows must be running. If you are stepping through this project on a computer and you want your screen to match the figures in this book, then you should change your computer's resolution to 800 × 600. For more information on how to change the resolution on your computer, see Appendix B. The steps on the next page start Excel and customize the Excel window.

More About

Starting Excel

You can use a command-line switch to start Excel and control how it starts. First, click the Start button on the Windows taskbar and then click Run. Next, enter the complete path to Excel's application file including the switch (for example, "C:\Program Files\Microsoft Office\Office\Excel.exe" /e). The switch /e opens Excel without opening a new work-book; /i starts Excel with a maximized window; /p "folder" sets the active path to folder and ignores the default folder; /r "filename" opens filename in read-only mode; and /s starts Excel in safe mode.

To Start and Customize Excel

1 Click the Start button on the Windows taskbar, point to All Programs on the Start menu, point to Microsoft Office on the All Programs submenu, and then click Microsoft Office Excel 2003 on the Microsoft Office submenu.

2 If the Excel window is not maximized, double-click its title bar to maximize it.

3 If the Language bar appears, right-click it and then click Close the Language bar on the shortcut menu.

4 If the Getting Started task pane appears in the Excel window, click its Close button in the upper-right corner.

5 If the Standard and Formatting toolbars are positioned on the same row, click the Toolbar Options button and then click Show Buttons on Two Rows.

The Excel window with the Standard and Formatting toolbars on two rows appears as shown in Figure 2-1a on page EX 67.

After the Excel window is opened, Steps 3 through 5 close the Getting Started task pane, close the Language bar, and ensure that the Standard and Formatting toolbars appear on two rows.

Entering the Titles and Numbers into the Worksheet

The following steps show how to enter the worksheet title and subtitle into cells A1 and A2.

To Enter the Worksheet Title and Subtitle

1 Select cell A1. Type Blue Chip Stock Club in the cell and then press the DOWN ARROW key.

2 Type Investment Analysis in cell A2 and then press the DOWN ARROW key.

Excel displays the worksheet title in cell A1 and the worksheet subtitle in cell A2, as shown in Figure 2-4 on page EX 73.

The column titles in row 3 begin in cell A3 and extend through cell J3. The column titles in Figure 2-3 include multiple lines of text. To start a new line in a cell, press ALT+ENTER after each line, except for the last line, which is completed by clicking the Enter box, pressing the ENTER key, or pressing one of the arrow keys. When you see ALT+ENTER in a step, press the ENTER key while holding down the ALT key and then release both keys.

The stock names and the row titles Total, Average, Highest, and Lowest in the leftmost column begin in cell A4 and continue down to cell A16.

The stock club's investments are summarized in Table 2-1. This data is entered into rows 4 through 12 of the worksheet. The remainder of this section explains the steps required to enter the column titles, stock data, and row titles as shown in Figure 2-4 and then save the workbook.

Table 2-1	Blue Chip Stock Club Portfolio				
Stock	Symbol	Date Acquired	Shares	Initial Price Per Share	Current Price Per Share
3M	MMM	6/12/00	394	79.75	120.25
Caterpillar	CAT	3/15/00	750	34.25	44.50
Coca-Cola	KO	8/01/00	975	58.75	44.125
DuPont	DD	9/12/01	850	33.125	42.25
General Electric	GE	12/08/99	525	29.50	26.625
General Motors	GM	10/05/99	810	37.375	40.00
Intel	INTC	10/03/02	875	13.00	18.75
Microsoft	MSFT	1/15/02	250	64.35	56.375
Wal-Mart	WMT	7/09/99	925	32.625	45.25

To Enter the Column Titles

1 With cell A3 selected, type Stock and then press the RIGHT ARROW key.

2 Type Symbol in cell B3 and then press the RIGHT ARROW key.

3 In cell C3, type Date and then press ALT+ENTER. Type Acquired and then press the RIGHT ARROW key.

4 Type Shares in cell D3 and then press the RIGHT ARROW key.

5 In cell E3, type Initial and then press ALT+ENTER. Type Price and then press ALT+ENTER. Type Per Share and then press the RIGHT ARROW key.

6 In cell F3, type Initial and then press ALT+ENTER. Type Cost and then press the RIGHT ARROW key.

7 In cell G3, type Current and then press ALT+ENTER. Type Price and then press ALT+ENTER. Type Per Share and then press the RIGHT ARROW key.

8 In cell H3, type Current and then press ALT+ENTER. Type Value and then press the RIGHT ARROW key.

9 Type Gain/Loss in cell I3 and then press the RIGHT ARROW key.

10 In cell J3, type Percent and then press ALT+ENTER. Type Gain/Loss and then click cell A4.

The column titles appear as shown in row 3 of Figure 2-4 on page EX 73. When you press ALT+ENTER to add more lines to a cell, Excel automatically increases the height of the entire row.

The stock data in Table 2-1 includes a date on which each stock was acquired. Excel considers a date to be a number and, therefore, it displays the date right-aligned in the cell. The steps on the next page describe how to enter the stock data shown in Table 2-1.

More About

Wrapping Text

If you have a long text entry, such as a paragraph, you can instruct Excel to wrap the text in a cell, rather than pressing ALT+ENTER to end a line. To wrap text, right-click in the cell, click Format Cells on the shortcut menu, click the Alignment tab, and then click Wrap text. Excel will increase the height of the cell automatically so the additional lines will fit. If you want to control where each line ends in the cell, rather than letting Excel wrap based on the cell width, however, then you must end each line with ALT+ENTER.

More About

Two-Digit Years

When you enter a two-digit year value, Excel changes a two-digit year less than 30 to 20xx and a two-digit year of 30 and greater to 19xx. Use four-digit years to ensure that Excel interprets year values the way you intend, if necessary.

To Enter the Stock Data

1 **With cell A4 selected, type** 3M **and then press the** RIGHT ARROW **key. Type** MMM **in cell B4 and then press the** RIGHT ARROW **key.**

2 **Type** 6/12/00 **in cell C4 and then press the** RIGHT ARROW **key. Type** 394 **in cell D4 and then press the** RIGHT ARROW **key.**

3 **Type** 79.75 **in cell E4 and then press the** RIGHT ARROW **key twice. Type** 120.25 **in cell G4 and then press the** ENTER **key.**

4 **Click cell A5. Enter the data in Table 2-1 for the eight remaining stocks in rows 5 through 12.**

The stock data appears in rows 4 through 12 as shown in Figure 2-4.

To Enter the Row Titles

More About

Formatting a Worksheet

With early worksheet packages, users often skipped rows to improve the appearance of the worksheet. With Excel it is not necessary to skip rows because you can increase row heights to add white space between information.

1 **Click cell A13. Type** Total **and then press the** DOWN ARROW **key. Type** Average **in cell A14 and then press the** DOWN ARROW **key.**

2 **Type** Highest **in cell A15 and then press the** DOWN ARROW **key. Type** Lowest **in cell A16 and then press the** ENTER **key. Click cell F4.**

The row titles appear in rows 13 through 16 as shown in Figure 2-4.

With the data entered into the worksheet, the next step is to save the workbook using the file name Blue Chip Stock Club Investment Analysis. As you are building a workbook, it is a good idea to save it often so that you do not lose your work if the computer is turned off or if you lose electrical power.

To Save the Workbook

1 **With a floppy disk in drive A, click the Save button on the Standard toolbar.**

2 **When Excel displays the Save As dialog box, type** Blue Chip Stock Club Investment Analysis **in the File name text box.**

3 **If necessary, click 3½ Floppy (A:) in the Save in list. Click the Save button in the Save As dialog box.**

More About

Entering Numbers into a Range

An efficient way to enter data into a range of cells is to select a range and then enter the first number in the upper-left cell of the range. Excel responds by entering the value and moving the active cell selection down one cell. When you enter the last value in the first column, Excel moves the active cell selection to the top of the next column.

Excel saves the workbook on the floppy disk in drive A using the file name, Blue Chip Stock Club Investment Analysis.

This concludes entering the data into the worksheet. After saving the file, the worksheet remains on the screen with the file name, Blue Chip Stock Club Investment Analysis, on the title bar.

Entering Formulas

The initial cost for each stock, which appears in column F, is equal to the number of shares in column D times the initial price per share in column E. Thus, the initial cost for 3M in cell F4 is obtained by multiplying 394 (cell D4) by 79.75 (cell E4).

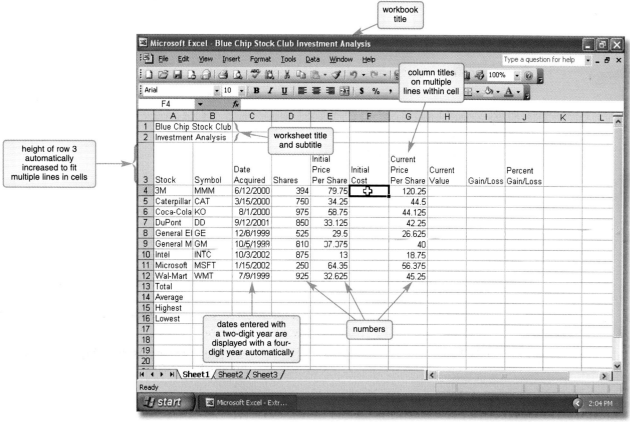

FIGURE 2-4

One of the reasons Excel is such a valuable tool is that you can assign a **formula** to a cell and Excel will calculate the result. Consider, for example, what would happen if you had to multiply 394 × 79.75 and then manually enter the product, 31421.5, in cell F4. Every time the values in cells D4 or E4 changed, you would have to recalculate the product and enter the new value in cell F4. By contrast, if you enter a formula in cell F4 to multiply the values in cells D4 and E4, Excel recalculates the product whenever new values are entered into those cells and displays the result in cell F4. The following steps enter the initial cost formula in cell F4 using the keyboard.

To Enter a Formula Using the Keyboard

1

• **With cell F4 selected, type =d4*e4 in the cell.**

Excel displays the formula in the formula bar and in cell F4 (Figure 2-5). Excel also displays colored borders around the cells referenced in the formula.

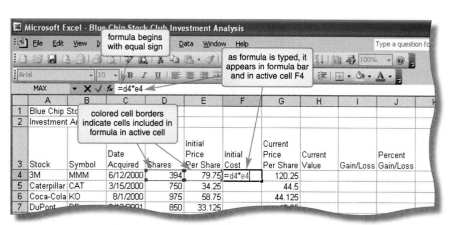

FIGURE 2-5

2

• **Press the RIGHT ARROW key twice to select cell H4.**

Instead of displaying the formula in cell F4, Excel completes the arithmetic operation indicated by the formula and displays the result, 31421.5 (Figure 2-6).

FIGURE 2-6

The **equal sign** (=) preceding d4*e4 is an important part of the formula: it alerts Excel that you are entering a formula or function and not text. Because the most common error is to reference the wrong cell in a formula mistakenly, Excel colors the borders of the cells referenced in the formula (Figure 2-5 on the previous page). The coloring helps in the reviewing process to ensure the cell references are correct. The **asterisk** (*) following d4 is the arithmetic operator that directs Excel to perform the multiplication operation. Table 2-2 describes multiplication and other valid Excel arithmetic operators.

Table 2-2   Summary of Arithmetic Operators

ARITHMETIC OPERATOR	MEANING	EXAMPLE OF USAGE	MEANING
−	Negation	−63	Negative 63
%	Percentage	=13%	Multiplies 13 by 0.01
^	Exponentiation	=5 ^ 2	Raises 5 to the second power
*	Multiplication	=17.5 * E4	Multiplies the contents of cell E4 by 17.5
/	Division	=A2 / A4	Divides the contents of cell A2 by the contents of cell A4
+	Addition	=4 + 8	Adds 4 and 8
−	Subtraction	=K15 − 13	Subtracts 13 from the contents of cell K15

You can enter the cell references in formulas in uppercase or lowercase, and you can add spaces before and after arithmetic operators to make the formulas easier to read. The formula, =d4*e4, is the same as the formulas, =d4 * e4, =D4 * e4, or =D4 * E4.

Order of Operations

When more than one arithmetic operator is involved in a formula, Excel follows the same basic order of operations that you use in algebra. Moving from left to right in a formula, the **order of operations** is as follows: first negation (−), then all percentages (%), then all exponentiations (^), then all multiplications (*) and divisions (/), and finally, all additions (+) and subtractions (−).

You can use parentheses to override the order of operations. For example, if Excel follows the order of operations, 8 * 3 + 2 equals 26. If you use parentheses, however, to change the formula to 8 * (3 + 2), the result is 40, because the parentheses instruct Excel to add 3 and 2 before multiplying by 8. Table 2-3 illustrates several examples of valid Excel formulas and explains the order of operations.

Table 2-3 Examples of Excel Formulas	
FORMULA	**MEANING**
=M5	Assigns the value in cell M5 to the active cell.
=12 + − 3^2	Assigns the sum of 12 + 9 (or 21) to the active cell.
=6 * E22 or =E22 * 6 or =(6 * E22)	Assigns six times the contents of cell E22 to the active cell.
=70% * 6	Assigns the product of 0.70 times 6 (or 4.2) to the active cell.
= − (G7 * V67)	Assigns the negative value of the product of the values contained in cells G7 and V67 to the active cell.
=5 * (P4 − G4)	Assigns the product of five times the difference between the values contained in cells P4 and G4 to the active cell.
=K5 / Y7 − D6 * L9 + W4 ^ V10	Instructs Excel to complete the following arithmetic operations, from left to right: first exponentiation (W4 ^ V10), then division (K5 / Y7), then multiplication (D6 * L9), then subtraction (K5 / Y7) − (D6 * L9), and finally addition (K5 / Y7 − D6 * L9) + (W4 ^ V10). If cells K5 = 10, D6 = 6, L9 = 2, W4 = 5, V10 = 2, and Y7 = 2, then Excel assigns the active cell the value 18; that is, 10 / 2 − 6 * 2 + 5 ^ 2 = 18.

Entering Formulas Using Point Mode

The sketch of the worksheet in Figure 2-3 on page EX 69 calls for the current value, gain/loss, and percent gain/loss of each stock to appear in columns H, I, and J, respectively. All three of these values are calculated using formulas. The formula used to calculate the current value for 3M in cell H4 multiples the number of shares in cell D4 by the current price per share in cell G4 (=D4*G4). The formula used to calculate the gain/loss for 3M in cell I4 is equal to the current value in cell H4 minus the initial cost in cell F4 (=H4 − F4). The formula used to calculate the percent gain/loss for 3M in cell J4 is equal to the gain/loss in cell I4 divided by the initial cost in cell F4 (=I4/F4).

An alternative to entering the formulas in cell H4, I4, and J4 using the keyboard is to enter the formulas using the mouse and Point mode. **Point mode** allows you to select cells for use in a formula by using the mouse. The following steps illustrate how to enter formulas using Point mode.

To Enter Formulas Using Point Mode

1

• **With cell H4 selected, type =
(equal sign) to begin the formula
and then click cell D4.**

*Excel surrounds cell D4 with a marquee
and appends D4 to the equal sign (=) in
cell H4 (Figure 2-7).*

FIGURE 2-7

2

• **Type * (asterisk) and then click cell G4.**

Excel surrounds cell G4 with a marquee and appends G4 to the asterisk (*) in cell H4. The formula =D4*G4 appears in cell H4 and in the formula bar (Figure 2-8).

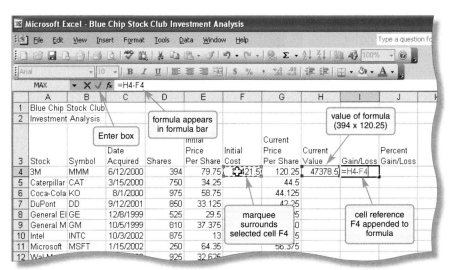

FIGURE 2-8

3

• **Click the Enter box and then click cell I4.**

• **Type = (equal sign) and then click cell H4.**

• **Type − (minus sign) and then click cell F4.**

Excel determines the result of the formula =D4*G4 and displays the result, 47378.5, in cell H4. The formula =H4–F4 appears in cell I4 and in the formula bar (Figure 2-9).

FIGURE 2-9

4

• **Click the Enter box.**

• **Click cell J4. Type = (equal sign) and then click cell I4.**

• **Type / (division sign) and then click cell F4.**

• **Click the Enter box.**

Excel calculates and then displays the gain/loss for 3M (15957) in cell I4 and the Percent gain/loss for 3M (0.507837) in cell J4 (Figure 2-10). The 0.507837 represents approximately 50.78%.

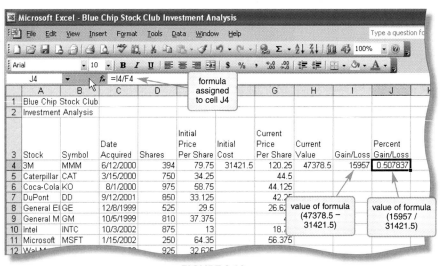

FIGURE 2-10

Depending on the length and complexity of the formula, using Point mode to enter formulas often is faster and more accurate than using the keyboard to type the entire formula. In many instances, as in the previous steps, you may want to use both the keyboard and mouse when entering a formula in a cell. You can use the keyboard to begin the formula, for example, and then use the mouse to select a range of cells.

The actual value assigned by Excel to cell J4 from the division operation in Step 4 is 0.507836990595611. While all the decimal places do not appear in Figure 2-10, Excel maintains all of them for computational purposes. Thus, if cell J4 is referenced in a formula, the value used for computational purposes is 0.507836990595611, not 0.507837. Excel displays the value in cell J4 as 0.507837 because the cell formatting is set to display only 6 digits after the decimal point. If you change the cell formatting of column J to display 15 digits after the decimal point, then Excel displays the true value 0.507836990595611. It is important to recognize this difference between the value Excel displays in a cell and the actual value to understand why the sum of data in a column sometimes is a tenth or hundredth off from the expected value.

More About

Troubling Formulas

If Excel does not accept a formula, remove the equal sign from the left side and complete the entry as text. Later, after you have entered additional data or determined the error, reinsert the equal sign to change the text back to a formula and edit the formula, as needed.

Copying Formulas Using the Fill Handle

The four formulas for 3M in cells F4, H4, I4, and J4 now are complete. You could enter the same four formulas one at a time for the eight remaining stocks, Caterpillar, Coca-Cola, DuPont, General Electric, General Motors, Intel, Microsoft, and Wal-Mart. A much easier method of entering the formulas, however, is to select the formulas in row 4 and then use the fill handle to copy them through row 12. Recall from Project 1 that the fill handle is a small rectangle in the lower-right corner of the active cell. The following steps show how to copy the formulas using the fill handle.

To Copy Formulas Using the Fill Handle

1

• **Click cell F4 and then point to the fill handle.**

• **Drag the fill handle down through cell F12 and continue to hold down the mouse button.**

A border surrounds the source and destination areas (range F4:F12) and the mouse pointer changes to a cross hair (Figure 2-11).

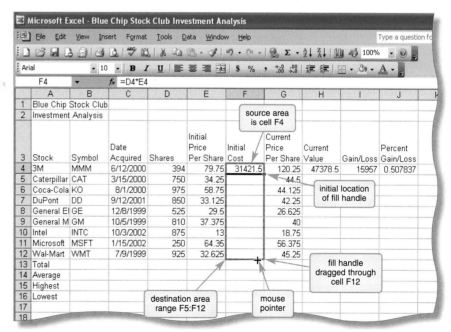

FIGURE 2-11

2

• **Release the mouse button.**

• **Select the range H4:J4 and then point to the fill handle.**

Excel copies the formula =D4*E4 to the range F5:F12 and displays the initial costs for the remaining eight stocks. Excel highlights the selected range H4:J4 (Figure 2-12). The Auto Fill Options button, which allows you to refine the copy, appears at the lower right of the destination range.

FIGURE 2-12

3

• **Drag the fill handle down through the range H5:J12.**

Excel copies the three formulas =D4*G4 in cell H4, =H4-F4 in cell I4, and =I4/F4 in cell J4 to the range H5:J12. The worksheet now displays the current value, gain/loss, and percent gain/loss for the remaining eight stocks (Figure 2-13).

FIGURE 2-13

Other Ways

1. Select source area, click Copy button on Standard toolbar, select destination area, click Paste button on Standard toolbar
2. Select source area, on Edit menu click Copy, select destination area, on Edit menu click Paste
3. Select source area, right-click copy area, click Copy on shortcut menu, select destination area, right-click paste area, click Paste on shortcut menu
4. In Voice Command mode, [select source area], say "Copy", [select destination area], say "Paste"

Recall that when you copy a formula, Excel adjusts the cell references so the new formulas contain references corresponding to the new location and performs calculations using the appropriate values. Thus, if you copy downward, Excel adjusts the row portion of cell references. If you copy across, then Excel adjusts the column portion of cell references. These cell references are called **relative references**.

Smart Tags and Option Buttons

Excel can identify certain actions to take on specific data in workbooks using **smart tags**. Data labeled with smart tags includes dates, financial symbols, people's names, and more. To use smart tags, you must turn on smart tags using the AutoCorrect Options command on the Tools menu. Once smart tags are turned on, Excel places a small purple triangle, called a **smart tag indicator**, in a cell to indicate that a smart tag is available. When you move the insertion point over the smart tag indicator, the Smart Tag Actions button appears. Clicking the Smart Tag Actions button arrow produces a list of actions you can perform on the data in that specific cell.

In addition to smart tags, Excel also displays Options buttons in a workbook while you are working on it to indicate that you can complete an operation using automatic features such as AutoCorrect, Auto Fill, error checking, and others. For example, the Auto Fill Options button shown in Figures 2-12 and 2-13 appears after a fill operation, such as dragging the fill handle. When an error occurs in a formula in a cell, Excel displays the Trace Error button next to the cell and identifies the cell with the error by placing a green triangle in the upper left of the cell.

Table 2-4 summarizes the smart tag and Options buttons available in Excel. When one of these buttons appears on your worksheet, click the button arrow to produce the list of options for modifying the operation or to obtain additional information.

Table 2-4 Smart Tag and Options Buttons in Excel

BUTTON	NAME	MENU FUNCTION
	Auto Fill Options	Gives options for how to fill cells following a fill operation, such as dragging the fill handle
	AutoCorrect Options	Undoes an automatic correction, stops future automatic corrections of this type, or causes Excel to display the AutoCorrect Options dialog box
	Insert Options	Lists formatting options following an insert of cells, rows, or columns
	Paste Options	Specifies how moved or pasted items should appear (for example, with original formatting, without formatting, or with different formatting)
	Smart Tag Actions	Lists information options for a cell containing data recognized by Excel, such as a stock symbol (see In the Lab 3, Part 4 on Page EX 139)
	Trace Error	Lists error checking options following the assignment of an invalid formula to a cell

Determining Totals Using the AutoSum Button

The next step is to determine the totals in row 13 for the initial cost in column F, current value in column H, and gain/loss in column I. To determine the total initial cost in column F, the values in the range F4 through F12 must be summed. To do so, enter the function =sum(f4:f12) in cell F13 or select cell F13 and then click the AutoSum button on the Standard toolbar twice. Similar SUM functions or the AutoSum button can be used in cells H13 and I13 to determine total current value and total gain/loss, respectively. Recall from Project 1 that when you select one cell and use the AutoSum button, you must click the AutoSum button twice. If you select a range, then you need only click the AutoSum button once.

To Determine Totals Using the AutoSum Button

1 **Select cell F13. Click the AutoSum button on the Standard toolbar twice.**

2 **Select the range H13:I13. Click the AutoSum button.**

Excel displays the three totals in row 13 as shown in Figure 2-14.

FIGURE 2-14

More About

Selecting a Range

You can select a range using the keyboard. Press F8 and then use the arrow keys to select the desired range. After you are finished, make sure to press F8 to turn the selection off or you will continue to select ranges.

Rather than using the AutoSum button to calculate column totals individually, you can select all three cells before clicking the AutoSum button to calculate all three column totals at one time. To select the nonadjacent range F13, H13, and I13, select cell F13, and then, while holding down the CTRL key, drag through the range H13:I13. Next, click the AutoSum button on the Standard toolbar.

Determining the Total Percent Gain/Loss

With the totals in row 13 determined, the next step is to copy the percent gain/loss formula in cell J12 to cell J13 as shown in the following steps.

To Determine the Total Percent Gain/Loss

1 **Select cell J12 and then point to the fill handle.**

2 **Drag the fill handle down through cell J13.**

Excel copies the formula, =I12/F12, in cell J12 to cell J13 and then adjusts the row references. The resulting formula in cell J13 is =I13/F13, which shows the club's holdings had a total gain of 0.132035 or 13.2035% (Figure 2-15).

	A	B	C	D	E	F	G	H	I	J	K	L
						fx =I12/…						
1	Blue Chip Stock Club											
2	Investment Analysis											
3	Stock	Symbol	Date Acquired	Shares	Initial Price Per Share	Initial Cost	Current Price Per Share	Current Value	Gain/Loss	Percent Gain/Loss		
4	3M	MMM	6/12/2000	394	79.75	31421.5	120.25	47378.5	15957	0.507837		
5	Caterpillar	CAT	3/15/2000	750	34.25	25687.5	44.5	33375	7687.5	0.29927		
6	Coca-Cola	KO	8/1/2000	975	58.75	57281.25	44.125	43021.88	-14259.4	-0.24894		
7	DuPont	DD	9/12/2001	850	33.125	28156.25	42.25	35912.5	7756.25	0.275472		
8	General El	GE	12/8/1999	525	29.5	15487.5	26.625	13978.13	-1509.38	-0.09746		
9	General M	GM	10/5/1999	810	37.375	30273.75	40	32400	2126.25	0.070234		
10	Intel	INTC	10/3/2002	875	13	11375	18.75	16406.25	5031.25	0.442308		
11	Microsoft	MSFT	1/15/2002	250	64.35	16087.5	56.375	14093.75	-1993.75	-0.12393		
12	Wal-Mart	WMT	7/9/1999	925	32.625	30178.13	45.25	41856.25	11678.13	0.386973		
13	Total					245948.4		278422.3	32473.88	0.132035		
14	Average											
15	Highest											
16	Lowest											

formula is =I12/F12

formula is =I13/F13

Auto Fill Options button appears after copying cell J12 to cell J13

FIGURE 2-15

More About

Formulas and Functions

For more information on entering formulas and functions, visit the Excel 2003 More About Web page (scsite.com/ex2003/more) and click Using Formulas and Functions.

The formula, I13/F13, was not copied to cell J13 when cell J4 was copied to the range J5:J12 because both cells involved in the computation (I13 and F13) were blank, or zero, at the time. A **blank cell** in Excel has a numerical value of zero, which would have resulted in an error message in cell J13. Once the totals were determined, both cells I13 and F13 (especially F13, because it is the divisor) had non-zero numerical values.

Using the AVERAGE, MAX, and MIN Functions

The next step in creating the Blue Chip Stock Club Investment Analysis worksheet is to compute the average, highest value, and lowest value for the number of shares listed in the range D4:D12 using the AVERAGE, MAX, and MIN functions in the range D14:D16. Once the values are determined for column D, the entries can be copied across to the other columns.

Excel includes prewritten formulas called functions to help you compute these statistics. A **function** takes a value or values, performs an operation, and returns a result to the cell. The values that you use with a function are called **arguments**. All functions begin with an equal sign and include the arguments in parentheses after the function name. For example, in the function =AVERAGE(D4:D12), the function name is AVERAGE, and the argument is the range D4:D12.

With Excel, you can enter functions using one of six methods: (1) the keyboard or mouse; (2) the Insert Function box in the formula bar; (3) the AutoSum button menu; (4) the Function command on the Insert menu; (5) the Name box area in the formula bar (Figure 2-16); and (6) Voice Command mode. The method you choose will depend on your typing skills and whether you can recall the function name and required arguments.

The following pages uses each of the first three methods. The keyboard and mouse method will be used to determine the average number of shares (cell D14). The Insert Function button in the formula bar method will be used to determine the highest number of shares (cell D15). The AutoSum button menu method will be used to determine the lowest number of shares (cell D16).

Determining the Average of a Range of Numbers

The **AVERAGE function** sums the numbers in the specified range and then divides the sum by the number of non-zero cells in the range. To determine the average of the numbers in the range D4:D12, use the AVERAGE function, as shown in the following steps.

To Determine the Average of a Range of Numbers Using the Keyboard and Mouse

1

- **Select cell D14.**
- **Type** =average(**in the cell.**
- **Click cell D4, the first endpoint of the range to average and drag through cell D12, the second endpoint of the range to average. Do not release the mouse button.**

A marquee surrounds the range D4:D12. When you click cell D4, Excel appends cell D4 to the left parenthesis in the formula bar and surrounds cell D4 with a marquee. When you begin dragging, Excel appends to the argument a colon (:) and the cell reference of the cell where the mouse pointer is located (Figure 2-16).

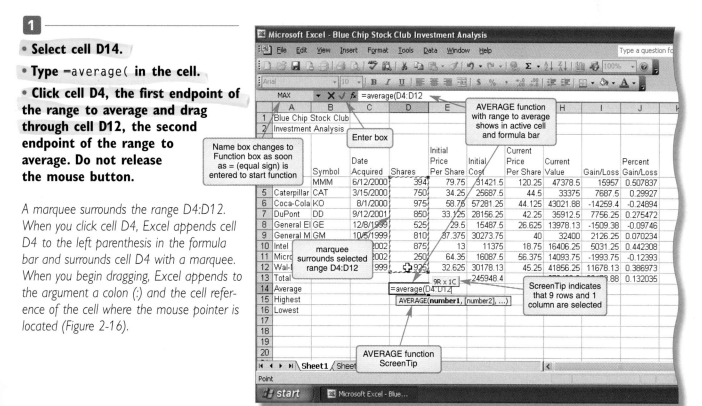

FIGURE 2-16

2

• **Release the mouse button and then click the Enter box.**

Excel computes the average of the nine numbers in the range D4:D12 and displays the result, 706, in cell D14 (Figure 2-17). Thus, the average number of shares owned in the nine companies is 706.

when cell D14 is active cell, formula bar displays AVERAGE function

right parenthesis automatically appended when Enter box is clicked or ENTER key pressed

	A	B	C	D	E	F	G	H	I	J
1	Blue Chip Stock Club									
2	Investment Analysis									
3	Stock	Symbol	Date Acquired	Shares	Initial Price Per Share	Initial Cost	Current Price Per Share	Current Value	Gain/Loss	Percent Gain/Loss
4	3M	MMM	6/12/2000	394	79.75	31421.5	120.25	47378.5	15957	0.507837
5	Caterpillar	CAT	3/15/2000	750	34.25	25687.5	44.5	33375	7687.5	0.29927
6	Coca-Cola	KO	8/1/2000	975	58.75	57281.25	44.125	43021.88	-14259.4	-0.24894
7	DuPont	DD	9/12/2001	850	33.125	28156.25	42.25	35912.5	7756.25	0.275472
8	General El	GE	12/8/1999	525	29.5	15487.5	26.625	13978.13	-1509.38	-0.09746
9	General M	GM	10/5/1999	810	37.375	30273.75	40	32400	2126.25	0.070234
10	Intel	INTC	10/3/2002	875	13	11375	18.75	16406.25	5031.25	0.442308
11	Microsoft	MSFT	1/15/2002	250	64.35	16087.5	56.375	14093.75	-1993.75	-0.12393
12	Wal-Mart	WMT	7/9/1999	925	32.625	30178.13	45.25	41856.25	11678.13	0.386973
13	Total					245948.4		278422.3	32473.88	0.132035
14	Average			706						
15	Highest									
16	Lowest									
17										
18										
19										
20										

D14 ▼ ƒx =AVERAGE(D4:D12)

average shares per stock

FIGURE 2-17

Other Ways

1. Click Insert Function box in formula bar, click AVERAGE function
2. Click AutoSum button arrow on Standard toolbar, click Average function
3. On Insert menu click Function, click AVERAGE in Select a function list
4. Type = (equal sign), click Functions box arrow, click AVERAGE
5. In Voice command mode, say "Insert Function", [select Statistical category], say "Average, OK"

More About

Entering Functions

You can drag the Function Arguments dialog box (Figure 2-19) out of the way in order to select a range. You also can click the Collapse Dialog button to the right of the Number 1 box to hide the Function Arguments dialog box. After selecting the range, click the Collapse Dialog button a second time.

The AVERAGE function requires that the argument (in this case, the range D4:D12) be included within parentheses following the function name. Excel automatically appends the right parenthesis to complete the AVERAGE function when you click the Enter box or press the ENTER key. When you use Point mode, as in the previous steps, you cannot use the arrow keys to complete the entry. While in Point mode, the arrow keys change the selected cell reference in the range you are selecting.

Determining the Highest Number in a Range of Numbers

The next step is to select cell D15 and determine the highest (maximum) number in the range D4:D12. Excel has a function called the **MAX function** that displays the highest value in a range. Although you could enter the MAX function using the keyboard and Point mode as described in the previous steps, an alternative method to entering the function is to use the Insert Function box in the formula bar, as shown in the following steps.

To Determine the Highest Number in a Range of Numbers Using the Insert Function Box

1

• **Select cell D15.**

• **Click the Insert Function box in the formula bar.**

• **When Excel displays the Insert Function dialog box, click MAX in the Select a function list.**

Excel displays the Insert Function dialog box (Figure 2-18).

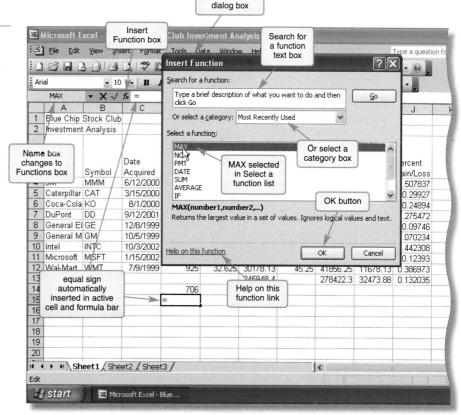

FIGURE 2-18

2

• **Click the OK button.**

• **When Excel displays the Function Arguments dialog box, type** d4:d12 **in the Number 1 box.**

Excel displays the Function Arguments dialog box with the range d4:d12 entered in the Number 1 box (Figure 2-19). The completed MAX function appears in the formula bar, and the last part of the function appears in the active cell, D15.

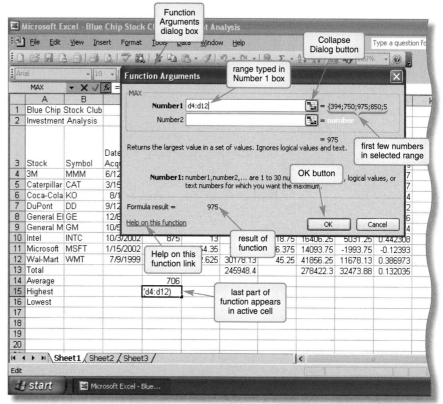

FIGURE 2-19

3

• **Click the OK button.**

Excel determines that the highest value in the range D4:D12 is 975 (value in cell D6) and displays it in cell D15 (Figure 2-20).

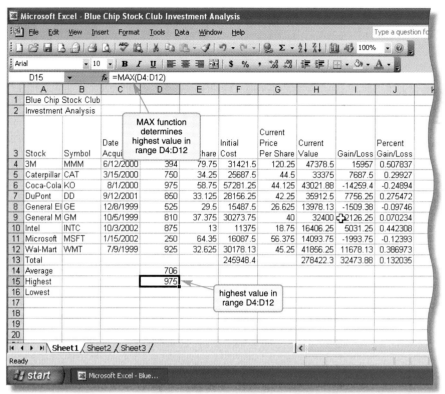

FIGURE 2-20

As shown in Figure 2-19 on the previous page, Excel displays the value the MAX function will return to cell D15 in the Function Arguments dialog box. It also lists the first few numbers in the selected range, next to the Number 1 box.

In this example, rather than entering the MAX function, you easily could scan the range D4:D12, determine that the highest number of shares is 975, and manually enter the number 975 as a constant in cell D15. Excel would display the number the same as in Figure 2-20. Because it contains a constant, however, Excel will continue to display 975 in cell D15, even if the values in the range D4:D12 change. If you use the MAX function, Excel will recalculate the highest value in the range D4:D12 each time a new value is entered into the worksheet. Manually determining the highest value in the range also would be more difficult if the club owned more stocks.

Determining the Lowest Number in a Range of Numbers

The next step is to enter the **MIN function** in cell D16 to determine the lowest (minimum) number in the range D4:D12. Although you can enter the MIN function using either of the methods used to enter the AVERAGE and MAX functions, the following steps show an alternative using the AutoSum button menu on the Standard toolbar.

To Determine the Lowest Number in a Range of Numbers Using the AutoSum Button Menu

1

• **Select cell D16.**

• **Click the AutoSum button arrow on the Standard toolbar.**

Excel displays the AutoSum button menu (Figure 2-21).

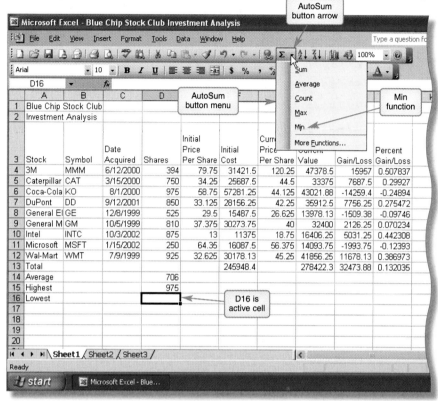

FIGURE 2-21

2

• **Click Min.**

The function =MIN(D14:D15) appears in the formula bar and in cell D16. A marquee surrounds the range D14:D15 (Figure 2-22). The range D14:D15 automatically selected by Excel is not correct.

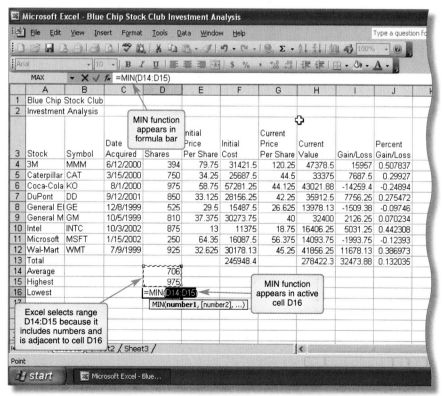

FIGURE 2-22

3

• **Click cell D4 and then drag through cell D12.**

Excel displays the function in the formula bar and in cell D14 with the new range D4:D12 (Figure 2-23).

FIGURE 2-23

4

• **Click the Enter box.**

Excel determines that the lowest value in the range D4:D12 is 250 and displays it in cell D16 (Figure 2-24).

Other Ways

1. Click Insert Function box in formula bar, click MIN function
2. On Insert menu click Function, click MIN in Select a function list
3. Type MIN function in cell
4. Type = (equal sign), click Functions box arrow, click MIN
5. In Voice command mode, say "Insert Function", [select Statistical category], say "Min, OK"

FIGURE 2-24

You can see from the previous example that using the AutoSum button menu allows you to enter one of five often-used functions easily into a cell, without having to memorize its name or the required arguments. If you need to enter a function not available on the AutoSum button menu and cannot remember its name, then click More Functions on the AutoSum button menu or click the Insert Function box in the formula bar.

Thus far, you have learned to use the SUM, AVERAGE, MAX, and MIN functions. In addition to these four functions, Excel has more than 400 additional functions that perform just about every type of calculation you can imagine. These functions are categorized in the Insert Function dialog box shown in Figure 2-18 on page EX 83. To view the categories, click the Or select a category box arrow. To obtain a description of a selected function, select its name in the Insert Function dialog box. Excel displays the description of the function below the Select a function list in the dialog box.

Copying the AVERAGE, MAX, and MIN Functions

The next step is to copy the AVERAGE, MAX, and MIN functions in the range D14:D16 to the adjacent range E14:J16. The fill handle again will be used to complete the copy. The following steps illustrate this procedure.

To Copy a Range of Cells across Columns to an Adjacent Range Using the Fill Handle

1

• **Select the range D14:D16.**

• **Drag the fill handle in the lower-right corner of the selected range through cell J16 and continue to hold down the mouse button.**

Excel displays an outline around the source and destination areas (range D14:J16) as shown in Figure 2-25.

FIGURE 2-25

2

• **Release the mouse button.**

Excel copies the three functions to the range E14:J16 (Figure 2-26). The Auto Fill Options button appears to allow you to refine the copy.

					AVERAGE, MAX, and MIN functions in range D14:D16 copied to range E14:J16		33375	7607.5	0.29927
5	Caterpillar	CAT	3/15/2000	750	34.25				
6	Coca-Cola	KO	8/1/2000	975	58.75		021.88	-14259.4	-0.24894
7	DuPont	DD	9/12/2001	850	33.125		5912.5	7756.25	0.275472
8	General El	GE	12/8/1999	525	29.5		978.13	-1509.38	-0.09746
9	General M	GM	10/5/1999	810	37.375	30273.75	40	32400	2126.25	0.070234
10	Intel	INTC	10/3/2002	875	13	11375	18.75	16406.25	5031.25	0.442308
11	Microsoft	MSFT	1/15/2002	250	64.35	16087.5	56.375	14093.75	-1993.75	-0.12393
12	Wal-Mart	WMT	7/9/1999	925	32.625	30178.13	45.25	41856.25	11678.13	0.386973
13	Total					245948.4		278422.3	32473.88	0.132035
14	Average			706	42.525	27327.6	48.68056	30935.81	3608.208	0.167974
15	Highest			975	79.75	57281.25	120.25	47378.5	15957	0.507837
16	Lowest			250	13	11375	18.75	13978.13	-14259.4	-0.24894

Auto Fill Options button

Sheet1 / Sheet2 / Sheet3 /

Ready   Average=9325.54731

start   Microsoft Excel - Blue...

FIGURE 2-26

3

• **Select cell J14 and press the DELETE key to delete the average of the percent gain/loss.**

Cell J14 is blank (Figure 2-27).

Microsoft Excel - Blue Chip Stock Club Investment Analysis

File Edit View Insert Format Tools Data Window Help   Type a question fo

Arial   10   B I U $ % ,

J14   fx

	A	B	C	D	E	F	G	H	I	J	K
1	Blue Chip Stock Club										
2	Investment Analysis										
3	Stock	Symbol	Date Acquired	Shares	Initial Price Per Share	Initial Cost	Current Price Per Share	Current Value	Gain/Loss	Percent Gain/Loss	
4	3M	MMM	6/12/2000	394	79.75	31421.5	120.25	47378.5	15957	0.507837	
5	Caterpillar	CAT	3/15/2000	750	34.25	25687.5	44.5	33375	7687.5	0.29927	
6	Coca-Cola	KO	8/1/2000	975	58.75	57281.25	44.125	43021.88	-14259.4	-0.24894	
7	DuPont	DD	9/12/2001	850	33.125	28156.25	42.25	35912.5	7756.25	0.275472	
8	General El	GE	12/8/1999	525	29.5	15487.5	26.625	13978.13	-1509.38	-0.09746	
9	General M	GM	10/5/1999	810	37.375	30273.75	40	32400	2126.25	0.070234	
10	Intel	INTC	10/3/2002	875	13	11375	18.75	16406.25	5031.25	0.442308	
11	Microsoft	MSFT	1/15/2002	250	64.35	16087.5	56.375	14093.75	-1993.75	-0.12393	
12	Wal-Mart	WMT	7/9/1999	925	32.625	30178.13	45.25	41856.25	11678.13	0.386973	
13	Total					245948.4		278422.3	32473.88	0.132035	
14	Average			706	42.525	27327.6	48.68056	30935.81	3608.208		
15	Highest			975	79.75	57281.25	120.25	47378.5	15957	0.507837	
16	Lowest			250	13	11375	18.75	13978.13	-14259.4	-0.24894	
17											

Save button

average percents in range J4:J12 mathematically invalid

FIGURE 2-27

Remember that Excel adjusts the cell references in the copied functions so each function refers to the range of numbers above it in the same column. Review the numbers in rows 14 through 16 in Figure 2-26. You should see that the functions in each column return the appropriate values, based on the numbers in rows 4 through 12 of that column.

The average of the percent gain/loss in cell J14 was deleted in Step 3 because an average of percentages of this type is mathematically invalid.

Saving a Workbook Using the Same File Name

Earlier in this project, an intermediate version of the workbook was saved using the file name, Blue Chip Stock Club Investment Analysis. The following step saves the workbook a second time using the same file name.

To Save a Workbook Using the Same File Name

1 **Click the Save button on the Standard toolbar.**

Excel saves the workbook on the floppy disk in drive A using the file name Blue Chip Stock Club Investment Analysis.

Excel automatically stores the latest version of the workbook using the same file name, Blue Chip Stock Club Investment Analysis. When you save a workbook a second time using the same file name, Excel will not display the Save As dialog box as it does the first time you save the workbook. You also can click Save on the File menu or press SHIFT+F12 or CTRL+S to save a workbook again.

If you want to save the workbook using a new name or on a different drive, click Save As on the File menu. Some Excel users, for example, use the Save button to save the latest version of the workbook on the default drive. Then, they use the Save As command to save a copy of the workbook on another drive.

Verifying Formulas Using Range Finder

One of the more common mistakes made with Excel is to include a wrong cell reference in a formula. An easy way to verify that a formula references the cells you want it to reference is to use Excel's Range Finder. **Range Finder** can be used to check which cells are referenced in the formula assigned to the active cell. Range Finder allows you to make immediate changes to the cells referenced in a formula.

To use Range Finder to verify that a formula contains the intended cell references, double-click the cell with the formula you want to check. Excel responds by highlighting the cells referenced in the formula so you can check that the cell references are correct. The following steps use Range Finder to check the formula in cell J4.

To Verify a Formula Using Range Finder

1

• **Double-click cell J4.**

Excel responds by displaying different colored borders around the cells referenced by the formula in cell J4 (Figure 2-28). The different colors allow you to see easily which cells are referenced by the formula in cell J4.

2

• **Press the ESC key to quit Range Finder.**
• **Select cell A18.**

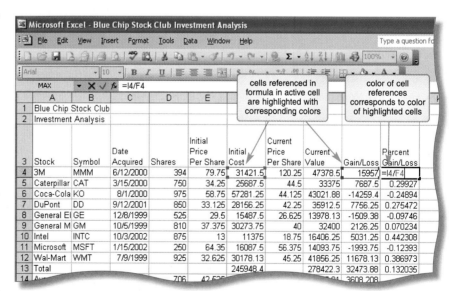

FIGURE 2-28

More About

**Checking
Formulas**

A useful command on the
Tools menu is the Error
Checking command, which
checks all formulas in a
workbook to ensure they are
referencing valid data.

Not only does Range Finder show you the cells referenced in the formula in cell J4, but it also allows you to drag the colored borders to other cells to instruct Excel to change the cell references in the formula to the newly selected cells. If you use Range Finder to change the cells referenced in a formula, press the ENTER key to complete the edit.

Formatting the Worksheet

Although the worksheet contains the appropriate data, formulas, and functions, the text and numbers need to be formatted to improve their appearance and readability.

In Project 1, the AutoFormat command was used to format the majority of the worksheet. This section describes how to change the unformatted worksheet in Figure 2-29a to the formatted worksheet in Figure 2-29b using the Formatting toolbar and Format Cells command.

(a) **Unformatted Worksheet**

(b) **Formatted Worksheet**

FIGURE 2-29

The following outlines the formatting suggested in the sketch of the worksheet in Figure 2-3 on page EX 69:

1. Worksheet title and subtitle
   a. Font type — Arial Black
   b. Font size — title 28; subtitle 18
   c. Font style — bold
   d. Alignment — center across columns A through J and center vertically
   e. Background color (range A1:J2) — blue
   f. Font color — white
   g. Border — thick box border around range A1:J2
2. Column titles
   a. Font style — bold
   b. Alignment — center
   c. Border — bottom border on row 3
3. Data
   a. Alignment — center data in column B
   b. Dates in column C — mm/dd/yy format
   c. Numbers in top row (range E4:I4) — Currency style
   d. Numbers below top row (range E5:I12) — Comma style
   e. Border — thick bottom border on row 12
4. Total line
   a. Font style of row title in cell A13 — bold
   b. Numbers — Currency style
5. Average, Highest, and Lowest lines
   a. Font style of row titles in range A14:A16 — bold
   b. Numbers — Currency style with floating dollar sign in the range E14:I16
6. Percentages in column J
   a. Numbers — Percent style with two decimal places; if a cell in range J4:J12 is less than 0, then cell appears with bold white font and background color of red
7. Column widths
   a. Column A — 13.00 characters
   b. Columns B through D — best fit
   c. Column E, G, and J — 10.00 characters
   d. Columns F, H, and I — 12.00 characters
8. Row heights
   a. Row 3 — 45.00 points
   b. Row 14 — 24.00 points
   c. Remaining rows — default

Except for vertically centering the worksheet title in row 1, the Date format assigned to the dates in column C, the Currency style assigned to the functions in rows 14 through 16, and the conditional formatting in column J, all of the listed formats can be assigned to cells using the Formatting toolbar and mouse.

Changing the Font and Centering the Worksheet Title and Subtitle

When developing presentation-quality worksheets, different fonts often are used in the same worksheet. Excel allows you to change the font of individual characters in a cell or all the characters in a cell, in a range of cells, or in the entire worksheet. To emphasize the worksheet title and subtitle in cells A1 and A2, the font type, size, and style are changed and the title and subtitle are centered as described in the following two sets of steps.

To Change the Font and Center the Worksheet Title

1

- **Click cell A1.**

- **Click the Font box arrow on the Formatting toolbar.**

Excel displays the Font list with Arial highlighted (Figure 2-30).

FIGURE 2-30

2

- **Click Arial Black (or Impact if Arial Black is not available).**

- **Click the Font Size box arrow on the Formatting toolbar and then click 28 in the Font Size list.**

- **Click the Bold button on the Formatting toolbar.**

- **Select the range A1:J1. Right-click the selection.**

Excel displays the text in cell A1 in 28-point Arial Black bold font. Excel automatically increases the height of row 1 so that the taller characters fit in the cell. Excel displays the shortcut menu for the selected range A1:J1 (Figure 2-31).

FIGURE 2-31

- **Click Format Cells on the shortcut menu.**

- **When Excel displays the Format Cells dialog box, click the Alignment tab.**

- **Click the Horizontal box arrow and select Center in the Horizontal list.**

- **Click the Vertical box arrow and select Center in the Vertical list.**

- **Click Merge cells in the Text control area.**

Excel displays the Format Cells dialog box as shown in Figure 2-32.

FIGURE 2-32

4
• **Click the OK button.**

Excel merges the cells A1 through J1 to create a new cell A1 and then centers the worksheet title horizontally across columns A through J and centers it vertically in row 1 (Figure 2-33).

FIGURE 2-33

You can change a font type, size, or style at any time while the worksheet is active. Some Excel users prefer to change fonts before they enter any data. Others change the font while they are building the worksheet or after they have entered all the data.

In Project 1, the Merge and Center button on the Formatting toolbar was used to center the worksheet title across columns. In Step 3 of the previous steps, the Alignment tab in the Format Cells dialog box is used to center the worksheet title across columns, because the project also called for vertically centering the worksheet title in row 1.

The next step is to format the worksheet subtitle in the same fashion as the worksheet title, except that the font size will be changed to 18 rather than 28.

To Change the Font and Center the Worksheet Subtitle

1. **Click cell A2. Click the Font box arrow on the Formatting toolbar.**

2. **Click Arial Black (or Impact if Arial Black is not available).**

3. **Click the Font Size box arrow on the Formatting toolbar and then click 18 in the Font Size list.**

4. **Click the Bold button on the Formatting toolbar.**

5. **Select the range A2:J2. Right-click the selection. Click Format Cells on the shortcut menu. When Excel displays the Format Cells dialog box, click the Alignment tab. Click the Horizontal box arrow and select Center in the Horizontal list. Click the Vertical box arrow and select Center in the Vertical list. Click Merge cells in the Text control area. Click the OK button.**

Excel increases the font size of the worksheet subtitle to 18, centers it horizontally across columns A through J, centers it vertically in row 2, and merges the cells A2 through J2 to create a new cell A2 (Figure 2-34 on the next page).

Other Ways

1. On Format menu click Cells, click appropriate tab, select formats, click OK button
2. Press CTRL+I, click appropriate tab, select formats, click OK button
3. In Voice Command mode, say "Format Cells, [desired tab], [desired format], OK"

Q&A

Q: What is the most popular background color?

A: Blue. Research shows that the color blue is used most often because this color connotes serenity, reflection, and proficiency.

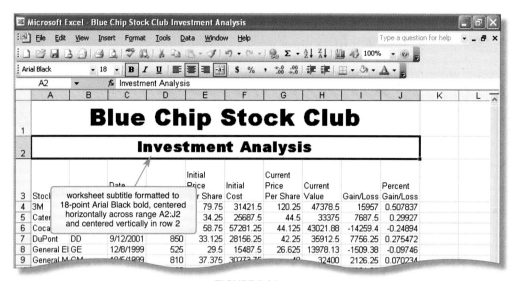

FIGURE 2-34

Some of the formatting, such as the font type, font style, and alignment, could have been done to both titles at the same time by selecting the range A1:A2 before assigning the formats. The font size, which is different, and the merging of cells, however, cannot be done to both titles at the same time.

Changing the Background and Font Colors and Applying a Box Border to the Worksheet Title and Subtitle

The final formats to be assigned to the worksheet title and subtitle are the blue background color, white font color, and thick box border (Figure 2-29b on page EX 90). The following steps complete the formatting of the worksheet titles.

To Change the Background and Font Colors and Apply a Box Border to the Worksheet Title and Subtitle

1

• **Select the range A1:A2, and then click the Fill Color button arrow on the Formatting toolbar.**

Excel displays the Fill Color palette (Figure 2-35).

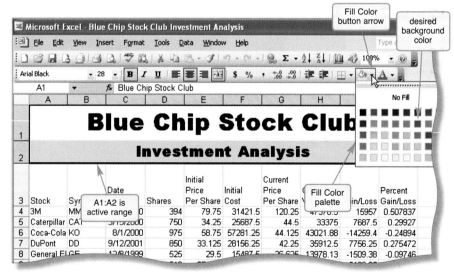

FIGURE 2-35

2

• **Click Blue (column 6, row 2) on the Fill Color palette.**

• **Click the Font Color button arrow on the Formatting toolbar.**

Excel changes the background color of cells A1 and A2 from white to blue and displays the Font Color palette (Figure 2-36).

FIGURE 2-36

3

• **Click White (column 8, row 5) on the Font Color palette.**

• **Click the Borders button arrow on the Formatting toolbar.**

Excel changes the font in the worksheet titles from black to white and displays the Borders palette (Figure 2-37).

FIGURE 2-37

4

• **Click the Thick Box Border button (column 4, row 3) on the Borders palette.**

• **Click cell B16 to deselect the range A1:A2.**

Excel displays a thick box border around the range A1:A2 (Figure 2-38).

FIGURE 2-38

> **Other Ways**
> 1. On Format menu click Cells, click appropriate tab, click desired format, click OK button
> 2. Right-click range, click Format Cells on shortcut menu, click appropriate tab, click desired format, click OK button
> 3. In Voice Command mode, say "Format Cells, [desired tab], [desired format], OK"

You can remove borders, such as the thick box border around the range A1:A2, by selecting the range and clicking the No Border button on the Borders palette. You can remove a background color by selecting the range, clicking the Fill Color button arrow on the Formatting toolbar, and then clicking the No Fill button on the Fill Color palette. The same technique allows you to change the font color back to Excel's default color, except you use the Font Color button arrow and click the Automatic button on the Font Color palette.

Applying Formats to the Column Titles

As shown in Figure 2-29b on page EX 90, the column titles are bold, centered, and have a bottom border (underline). The following steps assign these formats to the column titles.

To Bold, Center, and Apply a Bottom Border to the Column Titles

1

• **Select the range A3:J3.**

• **Click the Bold button on the Formatting toolbar.**

• **Click the Center button on the Formatting toolbar.**

• **Click the Borders button arrow on the Formatting toolbar.**

The column titles in row 3 are bold and centered (Figure 2-39). Excel displays the Borders palette. Excel also displays the column titles in columns E and G on four lines. In cell J3, the last letter of the column title appears on a line by itself.

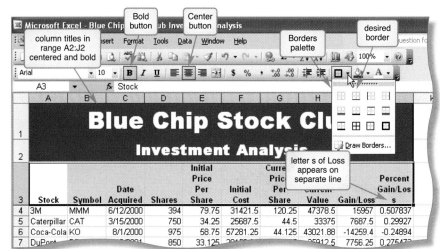

FIGURE 2-39

2

• **Click the Bottom Border button (column 2, row 1) on the Borders palette.**

Excel adds a bottom border to the range A3:J3.

You can align the contents of cells in several different ways. Left alignment, center alignment, and right alignment are the more frequently used horizontal alignments. In fact, these three horizontal alignments are used so often that Excel has Align Left, Center, and Align Right buttons on the Formatting toolbar. In addition to aligning the contents of a cell horizontally, you also can align the contents of a cell vertically, as shown earlier. In addition, you can change the orientation of a cell to display the cell contents at various angles (see the Format Cells dialog box in Figure 2-32 on page EX 92).

Centering the Stock Symbols and Formatting the Dates and Numbers in the Worksheet

With the column titles formatted, the next step is to center the stock symbols in column B and format the dates in column C. If a cell entry is short, such as the stock symbols in column B, centering the entries within their respective columns improves the appearance of the worksheet. The following steps center the data in the range B4:B12 and format the dates in the range C4:C12.

To Center Data in Cells and Format Dates

1

• **Select the range B4:B12.**
• **Click the Center button on the Formatting toolbar.**

Excel centers the stock symbols in column B.

2

• **Select the range C4:C12.**
• **Right-click the selected range and then click Format Cells on the shortcut menu.**
• **When Excel displays the Format Cells dialog box, click the Number tab, click Date in the Category list, and then click 03/14/01 in the Type list.**

Excel displays the Format Cells dialog box as shown in Figure 2-40.

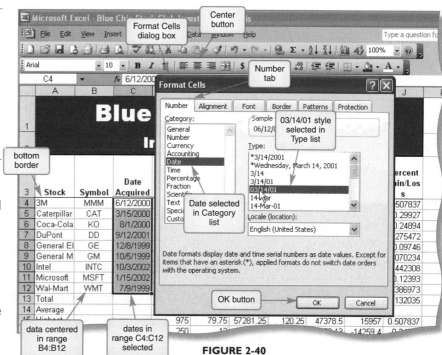

FIGURE 2-40

3

• **Click the OK button.**
• **Select cell E4 to deselect the range C4:C12.**

Excel displays the dates in column C using the date format style, mm/dd/yy (Figure 2-41).

	Stock	Symbol	Date Acquired	Shares	Initial Price Per Share	Initial Cost	Current Price Per Share	Current Value	Gain/Loss	Percent Gain/Loss
4	3M	MMM	06/12/00	394	79.75	31421.5	120.25	47378.5	15957	0.507837
5	Caterpillar	CAT	03/15/00	750	34.25	25687.5	44.5	33375	7687.5	0.29927
6	Coca-Cola	KO	08/01/00	975	58.75	57281.25	44.125	43021.88	-14259.4	-0.24894
7	DuPont	DD	09/12/01	850	33.125	28156.25	42.25	35912.5	7756.25	0.275472
8	General El	GE	12/08/99	525	29.5	15487.5	26.625	13978.13	-1509.38	-0.09746
9	General M	GM	10/05/99	810	37.375	30273.75	40	32400	2126.25	0.070234
10	Intel	INTC	10/03/02	875	13	11375	18.75	16406.25	5031.25	0.442308
11	Microsoft	MSFT	01/15/02	250	64.35	16087.5	56.375	14093.75	-1993.75	-0.12393
12	Wal-Mart	WMT	07/09/99	925	32.625	30178.13	45.25	41856.25	11678.13	0.386973
13	Total					245948.4		278422.3	32473.88	0.132035
14	Average			706	42.525	27327.6	48.68056	30935.81	3608.208	
15	Highest			975	79.75	57281.25	120.25	47378.5	15957	0.507837
16	Lowest				13	11375	18.75	13978.13	-14259.4	-0.24894

FIGURE 2-41

Rather than selecting the range B4:B12 in Step 1, you could have clicked the column B heading immediately above cell B1, and then clicked the Center button on the Formatting toolbar. In this case, all cells in column B down to cell B65536 would have been formatted to use center alignment. This same procedure could have been used to format the dates in column C.

Other Ways

1. On Format menu click Cells, click appropriate tab, click desired format, click OK button
2. Right-click range, click Format Cells on shortcut menu, click appropriate tab, click desired format, click OK button
3. In Voice Command mode, say "Format Cells, [desired tab], [desired format], OK"

Formatting Numbers Using the Formatting Toolbar

More About

Rotating and Shrinking Entries in Cells

In addition to aligning entries horizontally and vertically, you also can rotate and shrink entries to fit in a cell. To rotate or shrink entries to fit in a cell, click Format Cells on the shortcut menu, click the Alignment tab, and then select the type of control you want.

As shown in Figure 2-29b on page EX 90, the worksheet is formatted to resemble an accounting report. For example, in columns E through I, the numbers in the first row (row 4), the totals row (row 13), and the rows below the totals (rows 14 through 16) have dollar signs, while the remaining numbers (rows 5 through 12) in columns E through I do not.

To append a dollar sign to a number, you should use the Currency style format. Excel displays numbers using the **Currency style format** with a dollar sign to the left of the number, inserts a comma every three positions to the left of the decimal point, and displays numbers to the nearest cent (hundredths place). Clicking the Currency Style button on the Formatting toolbar assigns the desired Currency style format. When you use the Currency Style button to assign the Currency style format, Excel displays a **fixed dollar sign** to the far left in the cell, often with spaces between it and the first digit. To assign a **floating dollar sign** that appears immediately to the left of the first digit with no spaces, you must use the Cells command on the Format menu or the Format Cells command on the shortcut menu. The sketch of the worksheet in Figure 2-3 on page EX 69 calls for the Currency style format with a fixed dollar sign to be assigned to the numbers in the ranges E4:I4 and F13:I13, and the Currency style format with a floating dollar sign to be assigned to the numbers in the range E14:I16.

The Comma style format is used to instruct Excel to display numbers with commas and no dollar signs. The **Comma style format**, which can be assigned to a range of cells by clicking the Comma Style button on the Formatting toolbar, inserts a comma every three positions to the left of the decimal point and causes numbers to be displayed to the nearest hundredths.

The following steps show how to assign formats using the Currency Style button and the Comma Style button on the Formatting toolbar.

To Apply a Currency Style Format and Comma Style Format Using the Formatting Toolbar

1

- **Select the range E4:I4.**

- **While holding down the CTRL key, select the range F13:I13.**

- **Click the Currency Style button on the Formatting toolbar.**

Excel applies the Currency style format with fixed dollar signs to the nonadjacent ranges E4:I4 and F13:I13 as shown in Figure 2-42. Excel automatically increases the width of columns F, H, and I to best fit, so the numbers assigned the Currency style format will fit in the cells.

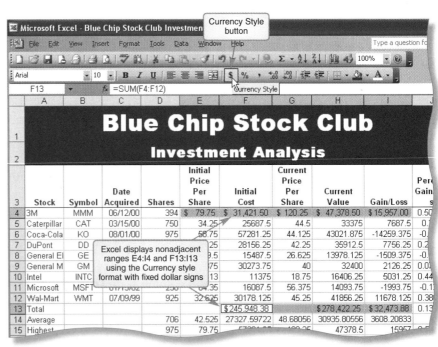

FIGURE 2-42

2

- **Select the range E5:I12.**
- **Click the Comma Style button on the Formatting toolbar.**

Excel assigns the Comma style format to the range E5:I12 (Figure 2-43).

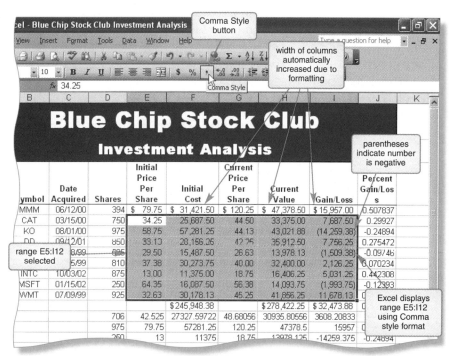

FIGURE 2-43

3

- **Click cell E4.**
- **While holding down the CTRL key, select cell G4.**
- **Click the Increase Decimal button on the Formatting toolbar.**
- **Select the range E5:E12. While holding down the CTRL key, select the range G5:G12.**
- **Click the Increase Decimal button on the Formatting toolbar.**
- **Click cell A12 to deselect the range G5:G12.**

Excel displays the initial prices and current prices with three decimal positions (Figure 2-44).

FIGURE 2-44

The Currency Style button assigns a fixed dollar sign to the numbers in the ranges E4:I4 and F13:I13. In each cell in these ranges, Excel displays the dollar sign to the far left with spaces between it and the first digit in the cell. Excel automatically rounds a number to fit the selected format.

Using the Increase Decimal button on the Formatting toolbar instructs Excel to display additional decimal places in a cell. Each time you click the Increase Decimal button, Excel adds a decimal place to the selected cell. Using the Decrease Decimal button on the Formatting toolbar instructs Excel to display fewer decimal places in a cell. Each time you click the Decrease Decimal button, Excel removes a decimal place to the selected cell.

Applying a Thick Bottom Border to the Row above the Total Row and Bolding the Total Row Titles

The following steps add a thick bottom border to row 12 and bold the total row titles.

To Apply a Thick Bottom Border to the Row above the Total Row and Bold the Total Row Titles

1 Select the range A12:J12, click the Borders button arrow on the Formatting toolbar, and then click the Thick Bottom Border button (column 2, row 2) on the Borders palette.

2 Select the range A13:A16 and then click the Bold button on the Formatting toolbar. Click cell E14 to deselect the range A13:A16.

The row immediately above the total row (row 12) has a thick bottom border, signifying the last stock in the worksheet. The row titles in the range A13:A16 are bold (Figure 2-45).

Q&A

Q: What causes the sum of a group of numbers to be a penny or two off from an expected result?

A: If the numbers being summed are the result of multiplication or division of decimal fraction numbers, or the sum or difference of numbers with different numbers of decimal places, then the numbers you see on your screen may not be the same as the numbers used in calculations. When a number has more decimal places than Excel displays on the screen, the actual number (not the displayed number) is used in the computation. This can cause the sum to be a penny or two off from an expected result. You can eliminate this problem by using the ROUND function in formulas involving decimal fraction numbers.

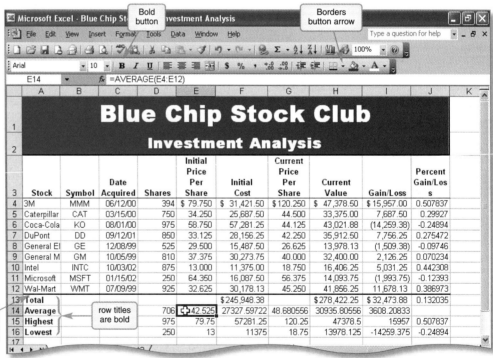

FIGURE 2-45

Formatting Numbers Using the Format Cells Command on the Shortcut Menu

The following steps show you how to use the Format Cells command on the shortcut menu to apply the Currency style format with a floating dollar sign to the numbers in the range E14:I16.

To Apply a Currency Style Format with a Floating Dollar Sign Using the Format Cells Command

1

- **Select the range E14:I16. Right-click the selected range.**

Excel displays the shortcut menu (Figure 2-46).

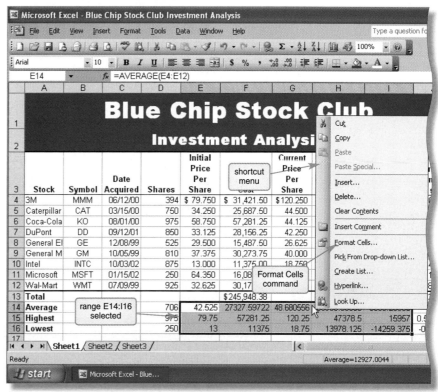

FIGURE 2-46

2

- **Click Format Cells on the shortcut menu.**

- **Click the Number tab in the Format Cells dialog box.**

- **Click Currency in the Category list and then click the third style ($1,234.10) in the Negative numbers list.**

Excel displays the Format Cells dialog box as shown in Figure 2-47.

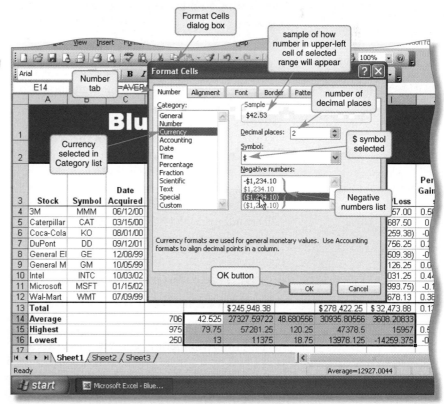

FIGURE 2-47

3

• **Click the OK button.**

Excel displays the worksheet with the numbers in rows 14 through 16 assigned the Currency style format with a floating dollar sign (Figure 2-48).

FIGURE 2-48

Other Ways

1. On Format menu click Cells, click Number tab, click Currency in Category list, select format, click OK button
2. Press CTRL+I, click Number tab, click Currency in Category list, select format, click OK button
3. Press CTRL+SHIFT+DOLLAR SIGN
4. In Voice Command mode, say "Format Cells, Number, Currency, OK"

Recall that a floating dollar sign always appears immediately to the left of the first digit, and the fixed dollar sign always appears on the left side of the cell. Cell E4, for example, has a fixed dollar sign, while cell E14 has a floating dollar sign. Also recall that, while cells E4 and E14 both were assigned a Currency style format, the Currency style was assigned to cell E4 using the Currency Style button on the Formatting toolbar and the result is a fixed dollar sign. The Currency style was assigned to cell E14 using the Format Cells dialog box and the result is a floating dollar sign.

As shown in Figure 2-47 on the previous page, you can choose from 12 categories of formats. Once you select a category, you can select the number of decimal places, whether or not a dollar sign should be displayed, and how negative numbers should appear. Selecting the appropriate negative numbers format in Step 2 on the previous page is important, because doing so adds a space to the right of the number in order to align the numbers in the worksheet on the decimal points (as do the Currency Style and Comma Style buttons). Some of the available negative number formats do not align the numbers in the worksheet on the decimal points.

The negative number format selected in the previous set of steps causes the negative entry in cell I16 to appear with parentheses surrounding the number. The third selection in the Negative numbers list (Figure 2-47) purposely was chosen to agree with the negative number format assigned to cell I6 using the Comma Style button.

Formatting Numbers Using the Percent Style Button and Increase Decimal Button

The next step is to format the percent gain/loss in column J. Currently, Excel displays the numbers in column J as a decimal fraction (for example, 0.507837 in cell J4). The following steps format the range J4:J16 to the Percent style format with two decimal places.

To Apply a Percent Style Format

1

• **Select the range J4:J16.**
• **Click the Percent Style button on the Formatting toolbar.**

Excel displays the numbers in column J as a rounded whole percent.

2

• **Click the Increase Decimal button on the Formatting toolbar twice.**

Excel displays the numbers in column J with the Percent style format with two decimal places (Figure 2-49).

FIGURE 2-49

The Percent Style button on the Formatting toolbar is used to instruct Excel to display a value as a percentage, determined by multiplying the cell entry by 100, rounding the result to the nearest percent, and adding a percent sign. For example, when cell J4 is formatted using the Percent Style and Increase Decimal buttons, Excel displays the actual value -0.507836990595611 as 50.78%.

Conditional Formatting

The next step is to emphasize the negative percentages in column J by formatting them to appear with white bold text on a red background. The Conditional Formatting command on the Format menu will be used to complete this task.

Excel lets you apply formatting that appears only when the value in a cell meets conditions that you specify. This type of formatting is called **conditional formatting**. You can apply conditional formatting to a cell, a range of cells, the entire worksheet, or the entire workbook. Usually, you apply conditional formatting to a range of cells that contains values you want to highlight, if conditions warrant. For example, you can instruct Excel to use the bold font style and change the color of the background of a cell if the value in the cell meets a condition, such as being less than 0 as shown below.

condition

cell value is less than 0

value 1   relational operator   value 2

A **condition**, which is made up of two values and a relational operator, is true or false for each cell in the range. If the condition is true, then Excel applies the formatting. If the condition is false, then Excel suppresses the formatting. What makes conditional formatting so powerful is that the cell's appearance can change as you enter new values in the worksheet.

The following steps show how to assign conditional formatting to the range J4:J12, so that any cell value less than 0 will cause Excel to display the number in the cell in white bold text with a red background.

To Apply Conditional Formatting

1

• **Select the range J4:J12.**

• **Click Format on the menu bar.**

Excel displays the Format menu (Figure 2-50).

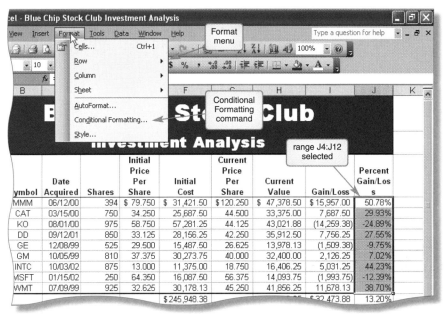

FIGURE 2-50

2

• **Click Conditional Formatting.**

• **When the Conditional Formatting dialog box appears, if necessary, click the leftmost text box arrow and then click Cell Value Is.**

• **Click the middle text box arrow and then click less than.**

• **Type 0 in the rightmost text box.**

Excel displays the Conditional Formatting dialog box as shown in Figure 2-51.

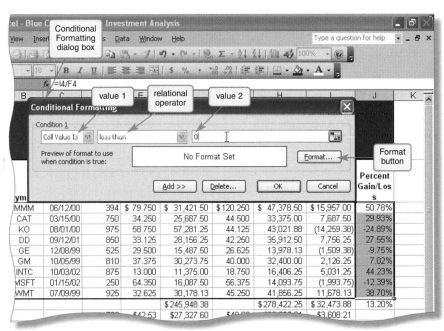

FIGURE 2-51

3

- **Click the Format button.**
- **When Excel displays the Format Cells dialog box, click the Patterns tab and then click Red (column 1, row 3).**
- **Click the Font tab and then click Bold in the Font style list.**
- **Click the Color box arrow.**

Excel displays the Format Cells dialog box as shown in Figure 2-52.

FIGURE 2-52

4

- **Click White (column 8, row 5) and then click the OK button.**

Excel displays the Conditional Formatting dialog box as shown in Figure 2-53. In the middle of the dialog box, Excel displays a preview of the format that Excel will use when the condition is true.

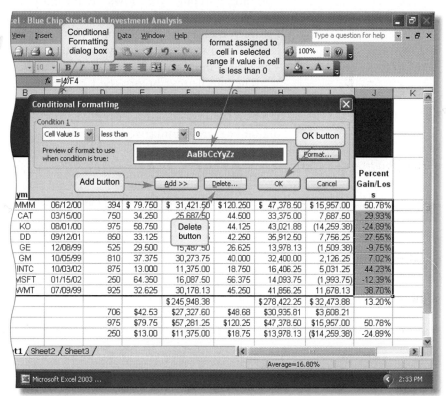

FIGURE 2-53

5

- **Click the OK button.**
- **Click cell B16 to deselect the range J4:J12.**

Excel assigns the conditional format to the range J4:J12. Excel displays any negative value in this range in bold with a red background (Figure 2-54).

FIGURE 2-54

In Figure 2-53 on the previous page, the preview box in the Conditional Formatting dialog box shows the format that will be assigned to all cells in the range J4:J12 that have a value less than 0. This preview allows you to review the format before you click the OK button. The Add button in the Conditional Formatting dialog box allows you to add two additional conditions for a total of three conditions. The Delete button allows you to delete one or more active conditions.

The middle text box in the Conditional Formatting dialog box allows you to select a relational operator, such as less than, to use in the condition. The eight different relational operators from which you can choose in the Conditional Formatting dialog box are summarized in Table 2-5.

Table 2-5 Summary of Conditional Formatting Relational Operators	
RELATIONAL OPERATOR	**DESCRIPTION**
Between	Cell value is between two numbers
Not between	Cell value is not between two numbers
Equal to	Cell value is equal to a number
Not equal to	Cell value is not equal to a number
Greater than	Cell value is greater than a number
Less than	Cell value is less than a number
Greater than or equal to	Cell value is greater than or equal to a number
Less than or equal to	Cell value is less than or equal to a number

With the conditional formatting complete, the next step is to change the column widths and row heights to make the worksheet easier to read.

Changing the Widths of Columns and Heights of Rows

When Excel starts and displays a blank worksheet on the screen, all of the columns have a default width of 8.43 characters, or 64 pixels. A **character** is defined as a letter, number, symbol, or punctuation mark in 10-point Arial font, the default font used by Excel. An average of 8.43 characters in 10-point Arial font will fit in a cell.

Another measure is pixels, which is short for picture element. A **pixel** is a dot on the screen that contains a color. The size of the dot is based on your screen's resolution. At a common resolution of 800 × 600, 800 pixels appear across the screen and 600 pixels appear down the screen for a total of 480,000 pixels. It is these 480,000 pixels that form the font and other items you see on the screen.

The default row height in a blank worksheet is 12.75 points (or 17 pixels). Recall from Project 1 that a point is equal to 1/72 of an inch. Thus, 12.75 points is equal to about 1/6 of an inch. You can change the width of the columns or height of the rows at any time to make the worksheet easier to read or to ensure that Excel displays an entry properly in a cell.

Changing the Widths of Columns

When changing the column width, you can set the width manually or you can instruct Excel to size the column to best fit. **Best fit** means that the width of the column will be increased or decreased so the widest entry will fit in the column. Sometimes, you may prefer more or less white space in a column than best fit provides. Excel thus allows you to change column widths manually.

When the format you assign to a cell causes the entry to exceed the width of a column, Excel automatically changes the column width to best fit. This happened earlier when the Currency style format was used (Figure 2-43 on page EX 99). If you do not assign a format to a cell or cells in a column, the column width will remain 8.43 characters, as is the case in columns A and B. To set a column width to best fit, double-click the right boundary of the column heading above row 1.

The following steps change the column widths: column A to 13.00 characters; columns B through D to best fit; columns E, G, and J to 10.00 characters; and columns F, H, and I to 12.00 characters.

To Change the Widths of Columns

1

• **Point to the boundary on the right side of the column A heading above row 1.**

• **When the mouse pointer changes to a split double arrow, drag to the right until the ScreenTip indicates Width: 13.00 (96 pixels). Do not release the mouse button.**

A dotted line shows the proposed right border of column A (Figure 2-55).

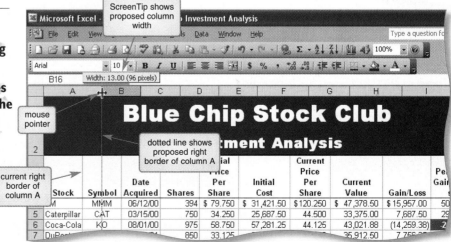

FIGURE 2-55

2

- **Release the mouse button.**
- **Drag through column headings B through D above row 1.**
- **Point to the boundary on the right side of column heading D.**

The mouse pointer becomes a split double arrow (Figure 2-56).

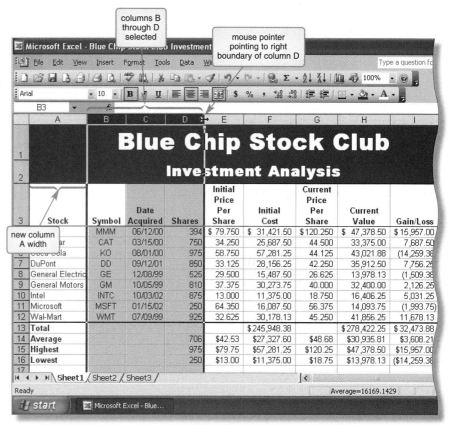

FIGURE 2-56

3

- **Double-click the right boundary of column heading D to change the width of columns B, C, and D to best fit.**
- **Click the column E heading above row 1.**
- **While holding down the CTRL key, click the column G heading and then the column J heading above row 1 so that columns E, G, and J are selected.**
- **Point to the boundary on the right side of the column J heading above row 1.**
- **Drag until the ScreenTip indicates Width: 10.00 (75 pixels). Do not release the mouse button.**

A dotted line shows the proposed right border of column J (Figure 2-57).

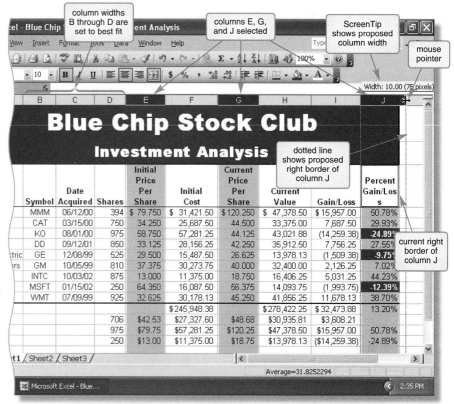

FIGURE 2-57

4

- Release the mouse button.

- Click the column F heading above row 1 to select column F.

- While holding down the CTRL key, click the column H and I headings above row 1 so that columns F, H, and I are selected.

- Point to the boundary on the right side of the column I heading above row 1.

- Drag to the right until the ScreenTip indicates Width: 12.00 (89 pixels). Do not release the mouse button.

A dotted line shows the proposed right border of column I (Figure 2-58).

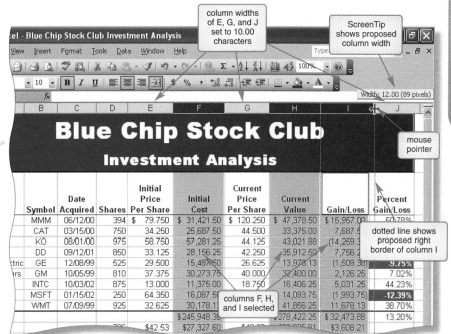

FIGURE 2-58

5

- Release the mouse button.

- Click cell B16 to deselect columns F, H, and I.

Excel displays the worksheet with the new column widths (Figure 2-59).

FIGURE 2-59

If you want to increase or decrease column width significantly, you can right-click a column heading and then use the Column Width command on the shortcut menu to change the column's width. To use this command, however, you must select one or more entire columns. As shown in the previous set of steps, you select entire columns by dragging through the column headings above row 1.

A column width can vary from zero (0) to 255 characters. If you decrease the column width to 0, the column is hidden. **Hiding cells** is a technique you can use to hide data that might not be relevant to a particular report or sensitive data that you do not want others to see. When you print a worksheet, hidden columns do not print. To instruct Excel to display a hidden column, position the mouse pointer to the right of the column heading boundary where the hidden column is located and then drag to the right.

Other Ways

1. Select cell or range of cells, on Format menu point to Column, click Width on Column sub-menu, enter desired column width, click OK button

2. Right-click column heading or drag through multiple column headings and right-click, click Column Width on shortcut menu, enter desired column width, click OK button

3. In Voice Command mode, say Format, Column, Width, [enter width], OK"

More About

Hidden Columns

Trying to unhide a range of columns using the mouse can be frustrating. An alternative is to use the keyboard, by selecting the columns to the right and left of the hidden columns and then pressing CTRL+SHIFT+RIGHT PARENTHESIS. To use the keyboard to hide a range of columns, press CTRL+0.

Changing the Heights of Rows

When you increase the font size of a cell entry, such as the title in cell A1, Excel automatically increases the row height to best fit so it can display the characters properly. Recall that Excel did this earlier when multiple lines were entered in a cell in row 3 and when the font size of the worksheet title and subtitle were increased.

You also can increase or decrease the height of a row manually to improve the appearance of the worksheet. The following steps show how to improve the appearance of the worksheet by decreasing the height of row 3 to 45.00 points and increasing the height of row 14 to 24.00 points.

To Change the Heights of Rows

1

• **Point to the boundary below row heading 3.**

• **Drag up until the ScreenTip indicates Height: 45.00 (60 pixels). Do not release the mouse button.**

Excel displays a horizontal dotted line (Figure 2-60). The distance between the dotted line and the top of row 3 indicates the proposed height for row 3.

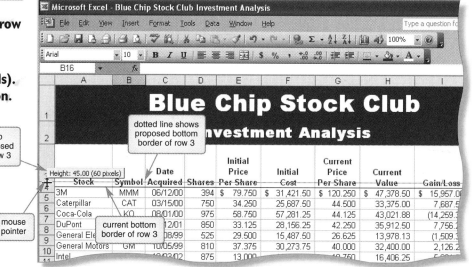

FIGURE 2-60

2

• **Release the mouse button.**

• **Point to the boundary below row heading 14.**

• **Drag down until the ScreenTip indicates Height: 24.00 (32 pixels). Do not release the mouse button.**

Excel displays a horizontal dotted line (Figure 2-61). The distance between the dotted line and the top of row 14 indicates the proposed height for row 14.

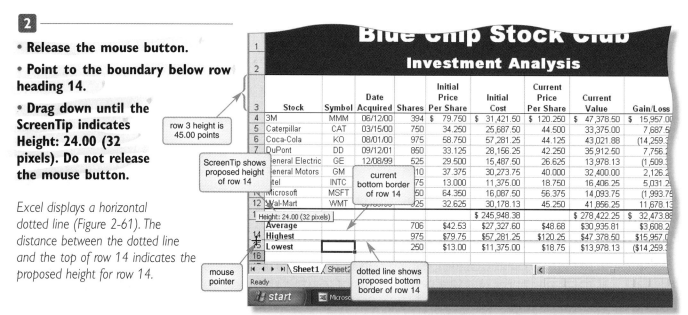

FIGURE 2-61

3

• **Release the mouse button and then select cell B16.**

The Total row and the Average row have additional white space between them, which improves the appearance of the worksheet (Figure 2-62). The formatting of the worksheet is complete.

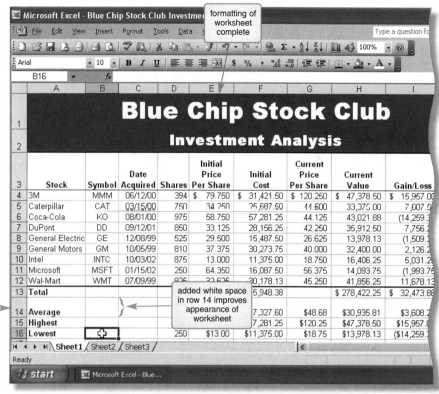

formatting of worksheet complete

row 14 height is 24.00 points

added white space in row 14 improves appearance of worksheet

FIGURE 2-62

The row height can vary between 0 and 409 points. As with column widths, when you decrease the row height to 0, the row is hidden. To instruct Excel to display a hidden row, position the mouse pointer just below the row heading boundary where the row is hidden and then drag down. To set a row height to best fit, double-click the bottom boundary of the row heading.

The task of formatting the worksheet is complete. The next step is to check the spelling of the worksheet.

Checking Spelling

Excel has a **spell checker** you can use to check the worksheet for spelling errors. The spell checker looks for spelling errors by comparing words on the worksheet against words contained in its standard dictionary. If you often use specialized terms that are not in the standard dictionary, you may want to add them to a custom dictionary using the Spelling dialog box.

When the spell checker finds a word that is not in either dictionary, it displays the word in the Spelling dialog box. You then can correct it if it is misspelled.

To illustrate how Excel responds to a misspelled word, the word, Stock, in cell A3 is misspelled purposely as the word, Stcok, as shown in Figure 2-63 on the next page.

Other Ways

1. Select cell or range of cells, on Format menu point to Row, click Height on Row submenu, enter desired height, click OK button
2. Right-click row heading or drag through multiple row headings and right-click, click Row Height on shortcut menu, enter desired row height, click OK button
3. In Voice Command mode say, Format, Row, Height, [enter height], OK"

More About

Hidden Rows

You can use the keyboard to unhide a range of rows by selecting the rows immediately above and below the hidden rows and then pressing CTRL+SHIFT+LEFT PARENTHESIS. To use the keyboard to hide a range of rows, press CTRL+9.

To Check Spelling on the Worksheet

1

• **Click cell A3 and then type** Stcok **to misspell the word Stock.**

• **Click cell A1.**

• **Click the Spelling button on the Standard toolbar.**

When the spell checker identifies the misspelled word, Stcok, in cell A3 it displays the Spelling dialog box (Figure 2-63).

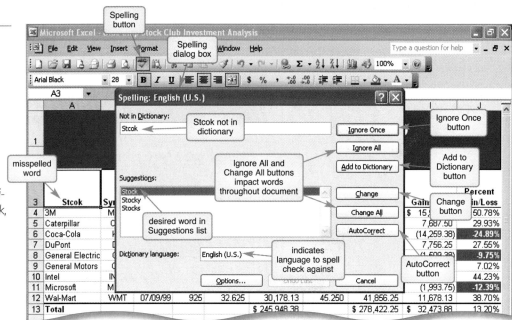

FIGURE 2-63

2

• **With the word Stock highlighted in the Suggestions list, click the Change button.**

• **As the spell checker checks the remainder of the worksheet, click the Ignore All and Change buttons as needed.**

The spell checker changes the misspelled word, Stcok, to the correct word, Stock, and continues spell checking the worksheet. When the spell checker is finished, it displays the Microsoft Office Excel dialog box with a message indicating that the spell check is complete (Figure 2-64).

3

• **Click the OK button.**

• **Click the Save button on the Standard toolbar to save the workbook.**

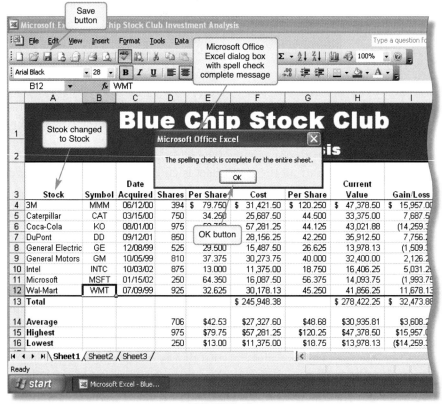

FIGURE 2-64

When the spell checker identifies that a cell contains a word not in its standard or custom dictionary, it selects that cell as the active cell and displays the Spelling dialog box. The Spelling dialog box (Figure 2-63) lists the word not found in the dictionary, a suggested correction, and a list of alternative suggestions. If one of the words in the Suggestions list is correct, click it and then click the Change button. If none of the suggestions is correct, type the correct word in the Not in Dictionary text box and then click the Change button. To change the word throughout the worksheet, click the Change All button instead of the Change button. To skip correcting the word, click the Ignore Once button. To have Excel ignore the word for the remainder of the worksheet, click the Ignore All button.

Consider these additional guidelines when using the spell checker:

- To check the spelling of the text in a single cell, double-click the cell to make the formula bar active and then click the Spelling button on the Standard toolbar.
- If you select a single cell so that the formula bar is not active and then start the spell checker, Excel checks the remainder of the worksheet, including notes and embedded charts.
- If you select a range of cells before starting the spell checker, Excel checks the spelling of the words only in the selected range.
- To check the spelling of all the sheets in a workbook, click Select All Sheets on the sheet tab shortcut menu and then start the spell checker. To instruct Excel to display the sheet tab shortcut menu, right-click any sheet tab.
- If you select a cell other than cell A1 before you start the spell checker, Excel will display a dialog box when the spell checker reaches the end of the worksheet, asking if you want to continue checking at the beginning.
- To add words to the dictionary such as your last name, click the Add to Dictionary button in the Spelling dialog box (Figure 2-63) when Excel identifies the word as not in the dictionary.
- Click the AutoCorrect button (Figure 2-63) to add the misspelled word and the correct version of the word to the AutoCorrect list. For example, suppose you misspell the word, do, as the word, dox. When the spell checker displays the Spelling dialog box with the correct word, do, in the Change to box, click the AutoCorrect button. Then, anytime in the future that you type the word, dox, Excel automatically will change it to the word, do.

Previewing and Printing the Worksheet

In Project 1, the worksheet was printed without first previewing it on the screen. By **previewing the worksheet**, however, you see exactly how it will look without generating a printout. Previewing allows you to see if the worksheet will print on one page in portrait orientation. **Portrait orientation** means the printout is printed across the width of the page. **Landscape orientation** means the printout is printed across the length of the page. Previewing a worksheet using the Print Preview command on the File menu or Print Preview button on the Standard toolbar can save time, paper, and the frustration of waiting for a printout only to discover it is not what you want.

The steps on the next page preview and then print the worksheet.

Q: Can I rely on the spell checker to find every misspelling?

A: While Excel's spell checker is a valuable tool, it is not infallible. You should proofread your workbook carefully by pointing to each word and saying it aloud as you point to it. Be mindful of misused words such as its and it's, through and though, and to and too. Nothing undermines a good impression more than a professional looking report with misspelled words.

More About

Error Checking

Always take the time to check the formulas of a worksheet before submitting it to your supervisor. You can check formulas by clicking the Error Checking command on the Tools menu. You also should test the formulas by employing data that tests the limits of formulas. Experienced spreadsheet specialists spend as much time testing a workbook as they do creating it, before placing it into production.

To Preview and Print a Worksheet

1

• **Point to the Print Preview button on the Standard toolbar (Figure 2-65).**

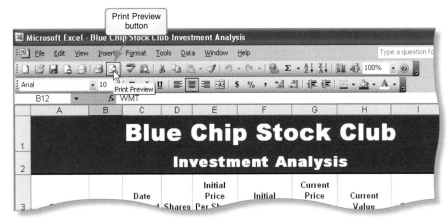

FIGURE 2-65

2

• **Click the Print Preview button.**

Excel displays a preview of the worksheet in portrait orientation, because portrait is the default orientation. In portrait orientation, the worksheet does not fit on one page (Figure 2-66).

FIGURE 2-66

3

• **Click the Setup button.**

• **When Excel displays the Page Setup dialog box, click the Page tab and then click Landscape in the Orientation area.**

Excel displays the Page Setup dialog box. The Orientation area contains two option buttons, Portrait and Landscape. The Landscape option button is selected (Figure 2-67).

FIGURE 2-67

4

• **Click the OK button.**

Excel displays the worksheet in the Preview window. In landscape orientation, the entire worksheet fits on one page (Figure 2-68).

worksheet fits on one page in landscape orientation

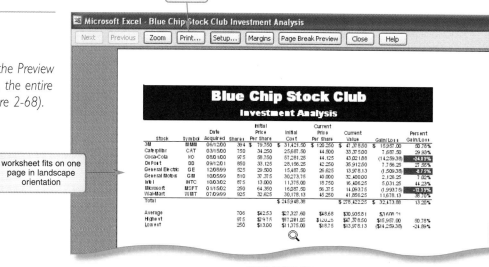

FIGURE 2-68

5

• **Click the Print button.**

Excel displays the Print dialog box as shown in Figure 2-69.

Print dialog box

All option button in Print range area instructs Excel to print entire worksheet

OK button

FIGURE 2-69

6

• **Click the OK button.**

• **Click the Save button on the Standard toolbar.**

Excel prints the worksheet (Figure 2-70). Excel saves the workbook with the landscape orientation print setting.

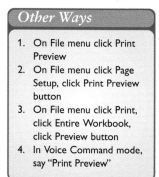

Other Ways

1. On File menu click Print Preview
2. On File menu click Page Setup, click Print Preview button
3. On File menu click Print, click Entire Workbook, click Preview button
4. In Voice Command mode, say "Print Preview"

landscape orientation

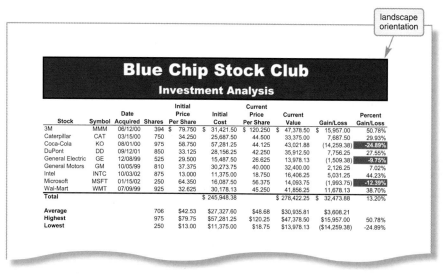

FIGURE 2-70

Once you change the orientation and save the workbook, Excel will save the orientation setting for that workbook until you change it. When you open a new workbook, Excel sets the orientation to portrait.

Several buttons are at the top of the Preview window (Figure 2-68 on the previous page). The functions of these buttons are summarized in Table 2-6.

Table 2-6	Print Preview Buttons
BUTTON	**FUNCTION**
Next	Previews the next page
Previous	Previews the previous page
Zoom	Magnifies or reduces the print preview
Print...	Prints the worksheet
Setup...	Instructs Excel to display the Print Setup dialog box
Margins	Changes the print margins
Page Break Preview	Previews page breaks
Close	Closes the Preview window
Help	Instructs Excel to display Help about the Preview window

Rather than click the Next and Previous buttons to move from page to page as described in Table 2-6, you can press the PAGE UP and PAGE DOWN keys on your keyboard. You also can click the previewed page in the Preview window when the mouse pointer shape is a magnifying glass to carry out the function of the Zoom button.

The Page Setup dialog box shown in Figure 2-67 on page EX 114 allows you to make changes to the default settings for a printout. For example, on the Page tab, you can set the page orientation, as shown in the previous set of steps; scale the printout so it fits on one page; and set the page size and print quality. Scaling, which can be used to fit a wide worksheet on one page, will be discussed later in the project. The Margins tab, Header/Footer tab, and Sheet tab in the Page Setup dialog box provide additional options that allow for even more control of the way the printout will appear. These tabs will be discussed when they are used.

When you click the Print command on the File menu or a Print button in a dialog box or Preview window, Excel displays the Print dialog box shown in Figure 2-69 on the previous page. Excel does not display the Print dialog box when you use the Print button on the Standard toolbar, as was the case in Project 1. The Print dialog box allows you to select a printer, instruct Excel what to print, and indicate how many copies of the printout you want.

More About

Printing a Section of a Worksheet

You can establish a permanent section of a worksheet to print by selecting the section, pointing to Print Area on the File menu and then clicking Set Print Area on the Print Area submenu. Later, if you wish, you can reselect the entire worksheet to print by invoking the Clear Print Area command on the Print Area submenu.

Printing a Section of the Worksheet

You might not always want to print the entire worksheet. You can print portions of the worksheet by selecting the range of cells to print and then clicking the Selection option button in the Print what area in the Print dialog box. The following steps show how to print the range A3:F16.

To Print a Section of the Worksheet

1

• **Select the range A3:F16.**

• **Click File on the menu bar and then click Print.**

• **Click Selection in the Print what area.**

Excel displays the Print dialog box (Figure 2-71). Because the Selection option button is selected, Excel will print only the selected range.

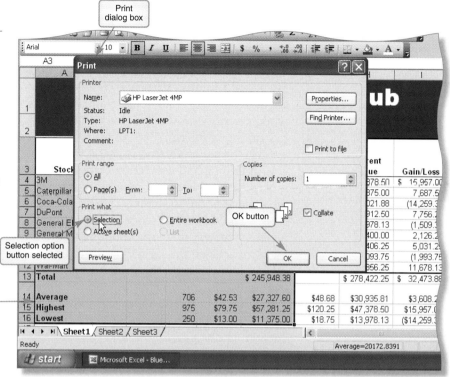

FIGURE 2-71

2

• **Click the OK button.**

• **Click cell B16 to deselect the range A3:F16.**

Excel prints the selected range of the worksheet on the printer (Figure 2-72).

Stock	Symbol	Date Acquired	Shares	Initial Price Per Share	Initial Cost
3M	MMM	06/12/00	394	$ 79.750	$ 31,421.50
Caterpillar	CAT	03/15/00	750	34.250	25,687.50
Coca-Cola	KO	08/01/00	975	58.750	57,281.25
DuPont	DD	09/12/01	850	33.125	28,156.25
General Electric	GE	12/08/99	525	29.500	15,487.50
General Motors	GM	10/05/99	810	37.375	30,273.75
Intel	INTC	10/03/02	875	13.000	11,375.00
Microsoft	MSFT	01/15/02	250	64.350	16,087.50
Wal-Mart	WMT	07/09/99	925	32.625	30,178.13
Total					$ 245,948.38
Average			706	$42.53	$27,327.60
Highest			975	$79.75	$57,281.25
Lowest			250	$13.00	$11,375.00

only selected range prints

FIGURE 2-72

The Print what area of the Print dialog box includes three option buttons (Figure 2-71). As shown in the previous steps, the Selection option button instructs Excel to print the selected range. The Active sheet(s) option button instructs Excel to print the active worksheet (the worksheet currently on the screen) or the selected worksheets. Finally, the Entire workbook option button instructs Excel to print all of the worksheets in the workbook.

Other Ways

1. Select range to print, on File menu point to Print Area, click Set Print Area, click Print button on Standard toolbar; on File menu point to Print Area, click Clear Print Area
2. Select range to print, in Voice Command mode, say "File, Print Area, Set Print Area"

Displaying and Printing the Formulas Version of the Worksheet

Microsoft Office
Excel 2003

More About

Values versus Formulas

When completing class assignments, do not enter numbers in cells that require formulas. Most instructors require their students to hand in both the values version and formulas version of the worksheet. The formulas version verifies that you entered formulas, rather than numbers, in formula-based cells.

Thus far, you have been working with the **values version** of the worksheet, which shows the results of the formulas you have entered, rather than the actual formulas. Excel also can display and print the **formulas version** of the worksheet, which shows the actual formulas you have entered, rather than the resulting values. You can toggle between the values version and formulas version by holding down the CTRL key while pressing the ACCENT MARK (`) key, which is located to the left of the number 1 key on the keyboard.

The formulas version is useful for debugging a worksheet. **Debugging** is the process of finding and correcting errors in the worksheet. Viewing and printing the formulas version instead of the values version makes it easier to see if any mistakes were made in the formulas.

When you change from the values version to the formulas version, Excel increases the width of the columns so the formulas and text do not overflow into adjacent cells on the right. The formulas version of the worksheet thus usually is significantly wider than the values version. To fit the wide printout on one page, you can use landscape orientation and the Fit to option in the Page sheet in the Page Setup dialog box. The following steps change the view of the worksheet from the values version to the formulas version of the worksheet and then print the formulas version on one page.

To Display the Formulas in the Worksheet and Fit the Printout on One Page

1

• Press CTRL+ACCENT MARK (`).

• When Excel displays the formulas version of the worksheet, click the right horizontal scroll arrow until column J appears.

• If the Formula Auditing toolbar appears, click its Close button.

Excel changes the display of the worksheet from values to formulas (Figure 2-73). It displays the formulas in the worksheet showing unformatted numbers, formulas, and functions that were assigned to the cells. Excel automatically increases the column widths.

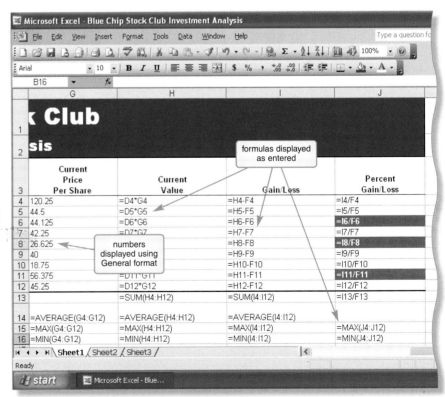

FIGURE 2-73

2

- **Click File on the menu bar and then click Page Setup.**

- **When Excel displays the Page Setup dialog box, click the Page tab.**

- **If necessary, click Landscape to select it and then click Fit to in the Scaling area.**

Excel displays the Page Setup dialog box with the Landscape and Fit to option buttons selected (Figure 2-74).

FIGURE 2-74

3

- **Click the Print button in the Page Setup dialog box.**

- **When Excel displays the Print dialog box, click the OK button.**

- **After viewing and printing the formulas version, press CTRL+ACCENT mark (`) to instruct Excel to display the values version.**

Excel prints the formulas in the worksheet on one page in landscape orientation (Figure 2-75). Excel displays the values version of the worksheet.

FIGURE 2-75

Although the formulas version of the worksheet was printed in the previous example, you can see from Figure 2-73 that you can review the formulas on the screen.

Other Ways

1. On Tools menu click Options, click View tab, click Formulas check box, click OK button
2. In Voice Command mode, say "Tools, Options, View, Formulas, OK"

Office
Excel 2003

About**

The Fit To Option

Do not take the Fit To option lightly. Most applications involve worksheets that extend well beyond the 8½"-by-11" page. Most users, however, want the information to print on one page, at least with respect to the width of the worksheet. The Fit To option thus is a valuable tool for Excel users.

Changing the Print Scaling Option Back to 100%

Depending on your printer driver, you may have to change the Print Scaling option back to 100% after using the Fit to option. The following steps reset the Print Scaling option so future worksheets print at 100%, instead of being resized to print on one page.

To Change the Print Scaling Option Back to 100%

1 Click File on the menu bar and then click Page Setup.

2 Click the Page tab in the Page Setup dialog box. Click Adjust to in the Scaling area.

3 If necessary, type 100 in the Adjust to box.

4 Click the OK button.

The print scaling is set to normal.

The Adjust to box allows you to specify the percentage of reduction or enlargement in the printout of a worksheet. The default percentage is 100%. When you click the Fit to option, this percentage automatically changes to the percentage required to fit the printout on one page.

Importing External Data from a Web Source Using a Web Query

One of the major features of Excel is its capability of importing external data from Web sites. To import external data from a Web site, you must have access to the Internet. You then can import data stored on a Web site using a **Web query**. When you run a Web query, Excel imports the external data in the form of a worksheet. As described in Table 2-7, three Web queries are available when you first install Excel. All three Web queries relate to investment and stock market activities.

About**

Web Queries

Most Excel specialists that build Web queries use the worksheet returned from the Web query as an engine to supply data to another worksheet in the workbook. With 3-D cell references, you can create a worksheet similar to the Blue Chip Stock Club worksheet to feed the Web query stock symbols and get refreshed stock prices in return.

Table 2-7 Excel Web Queries	
QUERY	EXTERNAL DATA RETURNED
MSN MoneyCentral Investor Currency Rates	Currency rates
MSN MoneyCentral Investor Major Indices	Major indices
MSN MoneyCentral Investor Stock Quotes	Up to 20 stocks of your choice

The data returned by the stock-related Web queries is real time in the sense that it is no more than 20 minutes old during the business day. The following steps show how to get the most recent stock quotes for the nine stocks owned by the Blue Chip Stock Club — 3M, Caterpillar, Coca-Cola, DuPont, General Electric, General Motors, Intel, Microsoft, and Wal-Mart. Although you can have a Web query return data to a blank workbook, the following steps have the data returned to a blank worksheet in the Blue Chip Stock Club Investment Analysis workbook.

To Import Data from a Web Source Using a Web Query

1

• **With the Blue Chip Stock Club Investment Analysis workbook open, click the Sheet2 tab at the bottom of the window.**

• **With cell A1 active, click Data on the menu bar, and then point to Import External Data on the Data menu.**

Excel displays the Data menu and Import External Data submenu as shown in Figure 2-76.

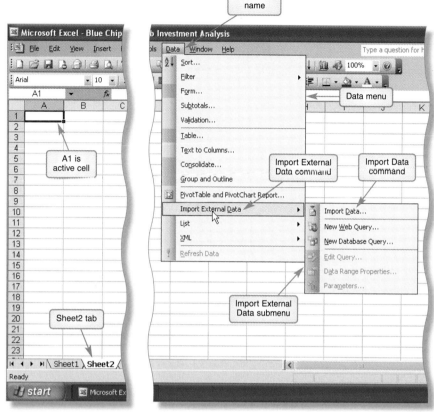

FIGURE 2-76

2

• **Click Import Data on the Import External Data submenu.**

Excel displays the Select Data Source dialog box (Figure 2-77). If your screen is different, ask your instructor for the folder location of the Web queries.

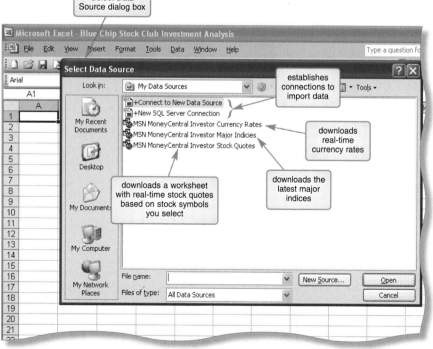

FIGURE 2-77

3

• **Double-click MSN MoneyCentral Investor Stock Quotes.**

• **When Excel displays the Import Data dialog box, if necessary, click Existing worksheet to select it.**

Excel displays the Import Data dialog box (Figure 2-78).

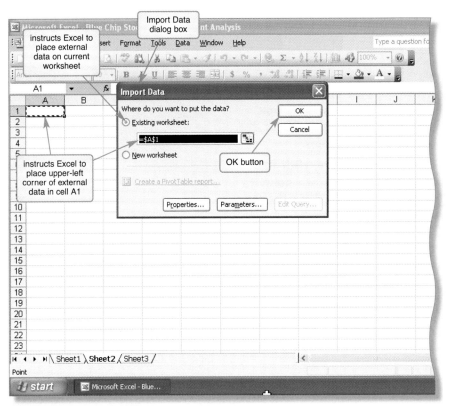

FIGURE 2-78

4

• **Click the OK button.**

• **When Excel displays the Enter Parameter Value dialog box, type the eight stock symbols** mmm cat ko dd ge gm intc msft wmt **in the text box.**

• **Click Use this value/reference for future refreshes to select it.**

Excel displays the Enter Parameter Value dialog box (Figure 2-79). You can enter up to 20 stock symbols separated by spaces (or commas).

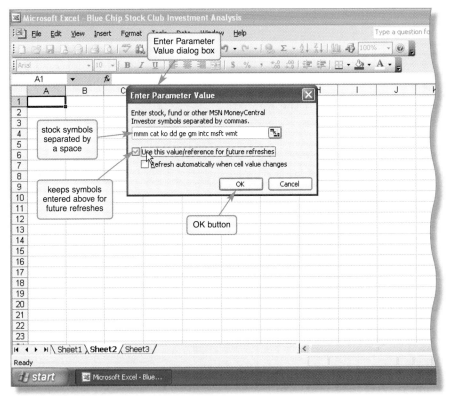

FIGURE 2-79

5

- **Click the OK button.**

Once your computer connects to the Internet, a message appears informing you that Excel is getting external data. After a short period, Excel displays a new worksheet with the desired data (Figure 2-80). The complete worksheet is shown in Figure 2-1b on page EX 67.

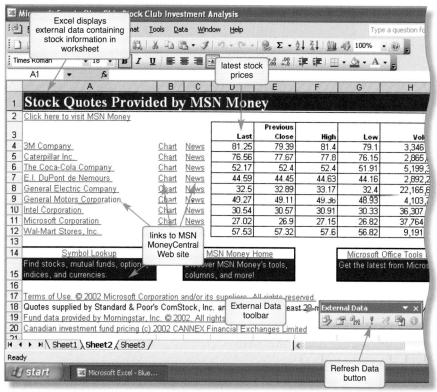

FIGURE 2-80

Other Ways

1. Press ALT+D, D, D
2. In Voice Command mode say, "Data, Import, External Data, Import Data"

As shown in Figure 2-80, Excel displays the data returned from the Web query in an organized, formatted worksheet, which has a worksheet title, column titles, and a row of data for each stock symbol entered. Other than the first column, which contains the stock name and stock symbol, you have no control over the remaining columns of data returned. The latest price of each stock appears in column D.

Once Excel displays the worksheet, you can refresh the data as often as you want. To refresh the data for all the stocks, click the Refresh All button on the External Data toolbar (Figure 2-81). Because the Use this value/reference for future refreshes check box was selected in Step 4 of the previous steps (Figure 2-79), Excel will continue to use the same stock symbols each time it refreshes. You can change the symbols by clicking the Query Parameters button on the External Data toolbar.

If the External Data toolbar does not appear, right-click any toolbar and then click External Data. Instead of using the External Data toolbar, you also can invoke any Web query command by right-clicking any cell in the returned worksheet to display a shortcut menu with several of the same commands as the External Data toolbar.

This section gives you an idea of the potential of Web queries by having you use just one of Excel's Web queries. To reinforce the topics covered here, work through In the Lab 3 on page EX 136.

The workbook is nearly complete. The final step is to change the names of the sheets located on the sheet tabs at the bottom of the Excel window.

FIGURE 2-81

Changing the Worksheet Names

The sheet tabs at the bottom of the window allow you to view any worksheet in the workbook. You click the sheet tab of the worksheet you want to view in the Excel window. By default, Excel presets the names of the worksheets to Sheet1, Sheet2, and so on. The worksheet names become increasingly important as you move towards more sophisticated workbooks, especially those in which you reference cells between worksheets. The following steps show how to rename worksheets by double-clicking the sheet tabs.

To Change the Worksheet Names

1

• **Double-click the sheet tab labeled Sheet2 in the lower-left corner of the window.**

• **Type** Real-Time Stock Quotes **as the worksheet name and then press the ENTER key.**

The new worksheet name appears on the sheet tab (Figure 2-82).

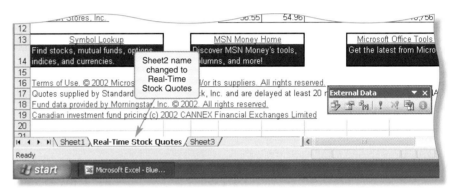

FIGURE 2-82

2

• **Double-click the sheet tab labeled Sheet1 in the lower-left corner of the window.**

• **Type** Investment Analysis **as the worksheet name and then press the ENTER key.**

Excel changes the worksheet name from Sheet1 to Investment Analysis (Figure 2-83).

FIGURE 2-83

Worksheet names can be up to 31 characters (including spaces) in length. Longer worksheet names, however, mean that fewer sheet tabs will show. To view more sheet tabs, you can drag the tab split box (Figure 2-83) to the right. This will reduce the size of the scroll bar at the bottom of the screen. Double-click the tab split box to reset it to its normal position.

You also can use the tab scrolling buttons to the left of the sheet tabs (Figure 2-83) to move between worksheets. The leftmost and rightmost scroll buttons move to the first or last worksheet in the workbook. The two middle scroll buttons move one worksheet to the left or right.

E-Mailing a Workbook from within Excel

The most popular service on the Internet is electronic mail, or **e-mail**, which is the electronic transmission of messages and files to and from other computers using the Internet. Using e-mail, you can converse with friends across the room or on another continent. One of the features of e-mail is the ability to attach Office files, such as Word documents or Excel workbooks, to an e-mail message and send it to a coworker. In the past, if you wanted to e-mail a workbook, you saved the workbook, closed the file, started your e-mail program, and then attached the workbook to the e-mail message before sending it. With Excel you have the capability of e-mailing a worksheet or workbook directly from within Excel. For these steps to work properly, you must have an e-mail address and one of the following as your e-mail program: Microsoft Outlook, Microsoft Outlook Express, Microsoft Exchange Client, or another 32-bit e-mail program compatible with Messaging Application Programming Interface. The following steps show how to e-mail the Blue Chip Stock Club Investment Analysis workbook from within Excel to Alisha Wright at the e-mail address wright_alisha@hotmail.com.

More About

Obtaining an E-Mail Account

Several Web sites that allow you to sign up for free e-mail are available. For more information on signing up for free e-mail, visit the Excel 2003 More About Web page (scsite.com/ex2003/more) and click Signing Up for E-mail.

To E-Mail a Workbook from within Excel

1

- **With the Blue Chip Stock Club Investment Analysis workbook open, click File on the menu bar and then point to Send To.**

Excel displays the File menu and Send To submenu as shown in Figure 2-84.

FIGURE 2-84

2

- **Click Mail Recipient (as Attachment) on the Send To submenu.**

- **When the e-mail Message window appears, type** wright_alisha@hotmail.com **in the To text box.**

- **Type the message shown in the message area in Figure 2-85.**

Excel displays the e-mail Message window. The workbook is included as an attachment (Figure 2-85).

3

- **Click the Send button.**

The e-mail with the attached workbook is sent to wright_alisha@hotmail.com.

FIGURE 2-85

Other Ways

1. Click E-mail button on Standard toolbar
2. On File menu point to Send To, click Mail Recipient on Send To submenu
3. In Voice Command mode, say "File, Send To, Mail Recipient as Attachment"

Because the workbook was sent as an attachment, Alisha Wright can double-click the attachment in the e-mail to open it in Excel, or she can save it on disk and then open it at a later time. The worksheet also could have been sent as part of the text portion of the e-mail by using the E-mail button on the Standard toolbar or by clicking the Mail Recipient command on the Send To submenu. In this case, the recepient would be able to read the worksheet in the e-mail message, but would not be able to open it in Excel.

When you send an e-mail from within Excel, you can choose from many other available options. The Options button on the toolbar, for example, allows you to send the e-mail to a group of people in a particular sequence and get responses along the route.

More About

Microsoft Certification

The Microsoft Office Specialist Certification program provides an opportunity for you to obtain a valuable industry credential — proof that you have the Excel 2003 skills required by employers. For more information, see Appendix E or visit the Excel 2003 Certification Web page (scsite.com/ex2003/cert).

Saving the Workbook and Quitting Excel

After completing the workbook and e-mailing a copy of the workbook, the final steps are to save the workbook and quit Excel.

To Save the Workbook and Quit Excel

1 Click the Save button on the Standard toolbar.

2 Click the Close button on the upper-right corner of the title bar.

Project Summary

In creating the Blue Chip Stock Club Investment Analysis workbook, you learned how to enter formulas, calculate an average, find the highest and lowest numbers in a range, verify formulas using Range Finder, change fonts, draw borders, align text, format numbers, change column widths and row heights, and add conditional formatting to a range of numbers. You learned how to spell check a worksheet, preview a worksheet, print a worksheet, print a section of a worksheet, and display and print the formulas version of the worksheet using the Fit to option. You also learned how to complete a Web query to generate a worksheet using external data obtained from the Web and rename sheet tabs. Finally, you learned how to send an e-mail directly from within Excel with the opened workbook as an attachment.

 If you have a SAM user profile, you may have access to hands-on instruction, practice, and assessment of the skills covered in this project. Log in to your SAM account and go to your assignments page to see what your instructor has assigned.

What You Should Know

Having completed this project, you should be able to perform the tasks below. The tasks are listed in the same order they were presented in this project. For a list of the buttons, menus, toolbars, and commands introduced in this project, see the Quick Reference Summary at the back of this book and refer to the Page Number column.

1. Start and Customize Excel   (EX 70)
2. Enter the Worksheet Title and Subtitle   (EX 70)
3. Enter the Column Titles   (EX 71)
4. Enter the Stock Data   (EX 72)
5. Enter the Row Titles   (EX 72)
6. Save the Workbook   (EX 72)
7. Enter a Formula Using the Keyboard   (EX 73)
8. Enter Formulas Using Point Mode   (EX 75)
9. Copy Formulas Using the Fill Handle   (EX 77)
10. Determine Totals Using the AutoSum Button   (EX 79)
11. Determine the Total Percent Gain/Loss   (EX 80)
12. Determine the Average of a Range of Numbers Using the Keyboard and Mouse   (EX 81)
13. Determine the Highest Number in a Range of Numbers Using the Insert Function Box   (EX 83)
14. Determine the Lowest Number in a Range of Numbers Using the AutoSum Button Menu   (EX 85)
15. Copy a Range of Cells across Columns to an Adjacent Range Using the Fill Handle   (EX 87)

16. Save a Workbook Using the Same File Name   (EX 89)
17. Verify a Formula Using Range Finder   (EX 89)
18. Change the Font and Center the Worksheet Title   (EX 92)
19. Change the Font and Center the Worksheet Subtitle   (EX 93)
20. Change the Background and Font Colors and Apply a Box Border to the Worksheet Title and Subtitle   (EX 94)
21. Bold, Center, and Apply a Bottom Border to the Column Titles   (EX 96)
22. Center Data in Cells and Format Dates   (EX 97)
23. Apply a Currency Style Format and Comma Style Format Using the Formatting Toolbar   (EX 98)
24. Apply a Thick Bottom Border to the Row above the Total Row and Bold the Total Row Titles   (EX 100)
25. Apply a Currency Style Format with a Floating Dollar Sign Using the Format Cells Command   (EX 101)
26. Apply a Percent Style Format   (EX 103)
27. Apply Conditional Formatting   (EX 104)

(continued)

What You Should Know *(continued)*

28. Change the Widths of Columns   (EX 107)
29. Change the Heights of Rows   (EX 110)
30. Check Spelling on the Worksheet   (EX 112)
31. Preview and Print a Worksheet   (EX 114)
32. Print a Section of the Worksheet   (EX 117)
33. Display the Formulas in the Worksheet and Fit the Printout on One Page   (EX 118)
34. Change the Print Scaling Option Back to 100%   (EX 120)
35. Import Data from a Web Source Using a Web Query   (EX 121)
36. Change the Worksheet Names   (EX 124)
37. E-Mail a Workbook from within Excel   (EX 125)
38. Save the Workbook and Quit Excel   (EX 126)

More About

The Quick Reference

For a table that lists how to complete the tasks covered in this book using the mouse, menu, shortcut menu, and keyboard, see the Quick Reference Summary at the back of this book or visit the Excel 2003 Quick Reference Web page (scsite.com/ex2003/qr).

Learn It Online

Instructions: To complete the Learn It Online exercises, start your browser, click the Address bar, and then enter the Web address scsite.com/ex2003/learn. When the Excel 2003 Learn It Online page is displayed, follow the instructions in the exercises below. Each exercise has instructions for printing your results, either for your own records or for submission to your instructor.

1 Project Reinforcement TF, MC, and SA

Below Excel Project 2, click the Project Reinforcement link. Print the quiz by clicking Print on the File menu for each page. Answer each question.

2 Flash Cards

Below Excel Project 2, click the Flash Cards link and read the instructions. Type 20 (or a number specified by your instructor) in the Number of playing cards text box, type your name in the Enter your Name text box, and then click the Flip Card button. When the flash card is displayed, read the question and then click the ANSWER box arrow to select an answer. Flip through Flash Cards. If your score is 15 (75%) correct or greater, click Print on the File menu to print your results. If your score is less than 15 (75%) correct, then redo this exercise by clicking the Replay button.

3 Practice Test

Below Excel Project 2, click the Practice Test link. Answer each question, enter your first and last name at the bottom of the page, and then click the Grade Test button. When the graded practice test is displayed on your screen, click Print on the File menu to print a hard copy. Continue to take practice tests until you score 80% or better.

4 Who Wants To Be a Computer Genius?

Below Excel Project 2, click the Computer Genius link. Read the instructions, enter your first and last name at the bottom of the page, and then click the PLAY button. When your score is displayed, click the PRINT RESULTS link to print a hard copy.

5 Wheel of Terms

Below Excel Project 2, click the Wheel of Terms link. Read the instructions, and then enter your first and last name and your school name. Click the PLAY button. When your score is displayed, right-click the score and then click Print on the shortcut menu to print a hard copy.

6 Crossword Puzzle Challenge

Below Excel Project 2, click the Crossword Puzzle Challenge link. Read the instructions, and then enter your first and last name. Click the SUBMIT button. Work the crossword puzzle. When you are finished, click the Submit button. When the crossword puzzle is redisplayed, click the Print Puzzle button to print a hard copy.

7 Tips and Tricks

Below Excel Project 2, click the Tips and Tricks link. Click a topic that pertains to Project 2. Right-click the information and then click Print on the shortcut menu. Construct a brief example of what the information relates to in Excel to confirm you understand how to use the tip or trick.

8 Newsgroups

Below Excel Project 2, click the Newsgroups link. Click a topic that pertains to Project 2. Print three comments.

9 Expanding Your Horizons

Below Excel Project 2, click the Expanding Your Horizons link. Click a topic that pertains to Project 2. Print the information. Construct a brief example of what the information relates to in Excel to confirm you understand the contents of the article.

10 Search Sleuth

Below Excel Project 2, click the Search Sleuth link. To search for a term that pertains to this project, select a term below the Project 2 title and then use the Google search engine at google.com (or any major search engine) to display and print two Web pages that present information on the term.

11 Excel Online Training

Below Excel Project 2, click the Excel Online Training link. When your browser displays the Microsoft Office Online Web page, click the Excel link. Click one of the Excel courses that covers one or more of the objectives listed at the beginning of the project on page EX 66. Print the first page of the course before stepping through it.

12 Office Marketplace

Below Excel Project 2, click the Office Marketplace link. When your browser displays the Microsoft Office Online Web page, click the Office Marketplace link. Click a topic that relates to Excel. Print the first page.

Apply Your Knowledge

1 Profit Analysis Worksheet

Instructions Part 1: Start Excel. Open the workbook Apply 2-1 e-cove Profit Analysis from the Data Disk. See the inside back cover of this book for instructions for downloading the Data Disk or see your instructor for information on accessing the files required in this book. The purpose of this exercise is to open a partially completed workbook, enter formulas and functions, copy the formulas and functions, and then format the worksheet titles and numbers. As shown in Figure 2-86, the completed worksheet analyzes profits by item. Use the following formulas:

Total Sales (cell F3) = Units Sold * (Unit Cost + Unit Profit) or =C3 * (D3 + E3)

Total Profit (cell G3) = Units Sold * Unit Profit or = C3 * E3

% Total Profit (cell H3) = Total Profit / Total Sales or = G3 / F3

FIGURE 2-86

Use the fill handle to copy the three formulas in the range F3:H3 to the range F4:H11. After the copy is complete, click the Auto Fill Options button and then click the Fill Without Formatting command to maintain the bottom double border in the range F11:H11. Determine totals for the units sold, total sales, and total profit in row 12. In the range C13:C15, determine the lowest value, highest value, and average value, respectively, for the values in the range C3:C11. Use the fill handle to copy the three functions to the range D13:H15. Delete the average from cell H15, because an average of percentages of this type is mathematically invalid.

Apply Your Knowledge

Format the worksheet as follows:

(1) cell A1 – change to Impact font (or a font of your choice) with a dark red (column 1, row 2) background
(2) cells D3:G3 and F12:G12 – apply Currency style format with fixed dollar signs
(3) cells C3, C4:G11, and C13:C15 – apply Comma style format
(4) cells C3:C15 – format numbers to appear with no decimal places
(5) cells H3:H14 – apply Percent style format with three decimal places
(6) cells D13:G15 – apply Currency style format with floating dollar signs

Enter your name, course, laboratory assignment number (Apply 2-1), date, and instructor name in the range A20:A24. Preview and print the worksheet in landscape orientation. Save the workbook using the file name, Apply 2-1 e-cove Profit Analysis Complete.

Use Range Finder to verify the formula in cell G3. Print the range A2:F15. Press CTRL+ACCENT MARK (`) to change the display from the values version of the worksheet to the formulas version. Print the formulas version in landscape orientation on one page with gridlines showing (Figure 2-87) by (1) using the Fit to option in the Page sheet in the Page Setup dialog box and (2) clicking Gridlines on the Sheet sheet in the Page Setup dialog box. Press CTRL+ACCENT MARK (`) to change the display of the worksheet back to the values version. Do not save the workbook. Hand in the three printouts to your instructor.

Instructions Part 2: In column E, use the keyboard to add manually $3.00 to the profit of each product with a unit profit less than $40.00 and $4.00 to the profits of all other products. You should end up with $11,352,596.55 in cell G12. Print the worksheet. Do not save the workbook. Hand in the printout to your instructor.

Report

e-cove Auction
Profit Analysis

Item Number	Item Description	Units Sold	Unit Cost	Unit Profit	Total Sales	Total Profit	% Total Profit
A4T5	FTP Software	32435	92.95	19.75	=C3*(D3+E3)	=C3*E3	=G3/F3
C812	Game Software	16534	175.99	45.65	=C4*(D4+E4)	=C4*E4	=G4/F4
H4TT	Hard Disk	32102	110.6	62.5	=C5*(D5+E5)	=C5*E5	=G5/F5
K890	Monitor	34391	121.35	38.75	=C6*(D6+E6)	=C6*E6	=G6/F6
MM34	PDA	23910	200.23	95.15	=C7*(D7+E7)	=C7*E7	=G7/F7
NK34	Printer	45219	50.65	12.85	=C8*(D8+E8)	=C8*E8	=G8/F8
R567	Stereo Speakers	63213	34.2	14.35	=C9*(D9+E9)	=C9*E9	=G9/F9
SH67	System Unit	52109	43	12.75	=C10*(D10+E10)	=C10*E10	=G10/F10
Z345	Tax Software	76145	38.25	13	=C11*(D11+E11)	=C11*E11	=G11/F11
Totals		=SUM(C3:C11)			=SUM(F3:F11)	=SUM(G3:G11)	
Lowest		=MIN(C3:C11)	=MIN(D3:D11)	=MIN(E3:E11)	=MIN(F3:F11)	=MIN(G3:G11)	=MIN(H3:H11)
Highest		=MAX(C3:C11)	=MAX(D3:D11)	=MAX(E3:E11)	=MAX(F3:F11)	=MAX(G3:G11)	=MAX(H3:H11)
Average		=AVERAGE(C3:C11)	=AVERAGE(D3:D11)	=AVERAGE(E3:E11)	=AVERAGE(F3:F11)	=AVERAGE(G3:G11)	

FIGURE 2-87

In the Lab

1 Weekly Payroll Worksheet

Problem: Illiana Custom Homes has hired you as an intern in its software applications department. Because you took an Excel course last semester, the assistant manager has asked you to prepare a weekly payroll report for the six employees listed in Table 2-8.

Table 2-8 Illiana Custom Homes Weekly Payroll Data			
Employee	**Rate**	**Hours**	**Dep.**
Jedi, Hubert	24.90	40.00	3
Kaden, Hadef	33.50	38.75	5
Pancer, Dion	12.90	66.00	8
Rifken, Felix	29.75	27.25	3
Sanchez, Maria	21.35	45.00	5
Scarff, Heidi	17.85	39.75	1

Microsoft Excel - Lab 2-1 Illiana Custom Homes Weekly Payroll Report

File Edit View Insert Format Tools Data Window Help   Type a question for help

Arial   10   B I U $ %

A15

Illiana Custom Homes
Weekly Payroll Report

	Employee	Rate	Hours	Dep.	Gross Pay	Fed. Tax	State Tax	Net Pay	% Taxes
3	Employee	Rate	Hours	Dep.	Gross Pay	Fed. Tax	State Tax	Net Pay	% Taxes
4	Jedi, Hubert	$24.90	40.00	3	$ 996.00	$ 176.12	$ 31.87	$ 788.00	20.883%
5	Kaden, Hadef	33.50	38.75	5	1,298.13	221.17	41.54	1,035.42	20.237%
6	Pancer, Dion	12.90	66.00	8	851.40	108.74	27.24	715.41	15.972%
7	Rifken, Felix	29.75	27.25	3	810.69	139.06	25.94	645.68	20.354%
8	Sanchez, Maria	21.35	45.00	5	960.75	153.69	30.74	776.32	19.197%
9	Scarff, Heidi	17.85	39.75	1	709.54	134.22	22.71	552.62	22.116%
10	Totals		256.75		$5,626.50	$ 933.00	$ 180.05	$4,513.45	19.782%
11	Average	$23.38	42.79	4	$937.75	$155.50	$30.01	$752.24	
12	Highest	$33.50	66.00	8	$1,298.13	$221.17	$41.54	$1,035.42	22.116%
13	Lowest	$12.90	27.25	1	$709.54	$108.74	$22.71	$552.62	15.972%

Sheet1 / Sheet2 / Sheet3 /

Ready

start   Microsoft Excel - Lab ...   2:57 PM

FIGURE 2-88

Instructions Part 1: Perform the following tasks to create a worksheet similar to the one shown in Figure 2-88.

1. Enter the worksheet titles Illiana Custom Homes in cell A1 and Weekly Payroll Report in cell A2. Enter the column titles in row 3, the data in Table 2-8 in columns A through D, and the row titles in the range A10:A13.

In the Lab

2. Use the following formulas to determine the gross pay, federal tax, state tax, and net pay for the first employee:
   a. Gross Pay (cell E4) = Rate*Hours or =B4 * C4
   b. Fed. Tax (cell F4) = 20% * (Gross Pay – Dep. * 38.46) or =20% *(E4 – D4 * 38.46)
   c. State Tax (cell G4) = 3.2% * Gross Pay or =3.2% * E4
   d. Net Pay (cell H4) = Gross Pay – (Fed. Tax + State Tax) or =E4 – (F4 + G4)
   e. % Taxes (I4) = (Fed. Tax + State Tax) / Gross Pay or =(F4 + G4) / E4
   Copy the formulas for the first employee to the remaining employees.
3. Calculate totals for hours, gross pay, federal tax, state tax, net pay, and % taxes paid in row 10.
4. Use the appropriate functions to determine the average, highest, and lowest values of each column in rows 11 through 13. Delete the value in cell I11.
5. Use Range Finder to verify each of the formulas entered in row 4.
6. Select the range A1:A2 and change its background color to red. Change the worksheet title to 26-point Broadway white, bold font (or a font of your choice). Center the worksheet title across columns A through I. Vertically center the worksheet title. Format the worksheet subtitle in a similar fashion, except change its font size to 18. Assign the range A1:A2 a border (column 4, row 4 on the Borders palette). Assign the Comma style format with two decimal places to the ranges B5:H9 and C4:C13. Assign a Currency style format with a fixed dollar sign to the ranges B4, E4:H4, and E10:H10. Assign a Currency style format with a floating dollar sign to the ranges B11:B13 and E11:H13. Assign the Number style format with 0 decimals to the range D4:D13 and center the range. Assign a Percent style format with three decimal places to the range I4:I13. Bold, italicize, and assign a bottom border (column 2, row 1 on the Borders palette) to the range A3:I3. Align right the column titles in the range B3:I3. Bold and italicize the range A10:A13. Assign a top and thick bottom border (column 1, row 3 on the Borders palette) to the range A10:I10.
7. Change the width of column A to 18.00 characters. If necessary, change the widths of columns B through H to best fit. Change the heights of row 1 to 39.75 points and rows 2, 3, and 11 to 30.00 points.
8. Use the Conditional Formatting command on the Format menu to display white, bold font on a blue background for any rate in the range B4:B9 greater than $25.00.
9. Enter your name, course, laboratory assignment number (Lab 2-1), date, and instructor name in the range A15:A19.
10. Spell check the worksheet. Save the workbook using the file name Lab 2-1 Illiana Custom Homes Weekly Payroll Report. Preview and then print the worksheet.
11. Press CTRL+ACCENT MARK (`) to change the display from the values version to the formulas version. Print the formulas version of the worksheet in landscape orientation using the Fit to option in the Page sheet in the Page Setup dialog box. After the printer is finished, press CTRL+ACCENT MARK (`) to reset the worksheet to the values version. Reset the Scaling option to 100% by clicking the Adjust to option button in the Page sheet in the Page Setup dialog box and then setting the percent value to 100%. Hand in the printouts to your instructor.

Instructions Part 2: Use the keyboard to increase manually the number of hours worked for each employee by 12 hours. The total net pay in cell H10 should equal $5,806.00. If necessary, increase the width of column F to best fit to view the new federal tax total. Preview and print the worksheet with the new values. Do not save the workbook. Hand in the printout to your instructor.

2 Accounts Receivable Balance Sheet

Problem: You are a spreadsheet specialist in the Accounting department of Fife's Finer Furniture, a popular Virginia Beach-based furniture company with several outlets in major cities across the United States. You have been asked to use Excel to generate a report (Figure 2-89) that summarizes the monthly accounts receivable balance. A graphic breakdown of the data also is desired. The customer accounts receivable data in Table 2-9 is available for test purposes.

Table 2-9	Fife's Finer Furniture Accounts Receivable Data				
Customer ID	Customer Name	Beginning Balance	Purchases	Payments	Credits
A421	Sri, Oranu	32548.30	3291.50	6923.00	785.25
H861	Agarwall, Bikash	9351.55	4435.10	5000.00	75.00
K190	Amigo, Julio	5909.50	750.30	2350.00	0.00
M918	Wang, Shiela	18761.60	5560.00	1875.00	905.25
P415	Davis, Jasmine	14098.20	1596.10	3250.00	236.45
R623	Smith, John	18433.60	200.20	1375.00	196.00
U111	Gupta, Arjun	13462.75	2026.00	750.00	25.00

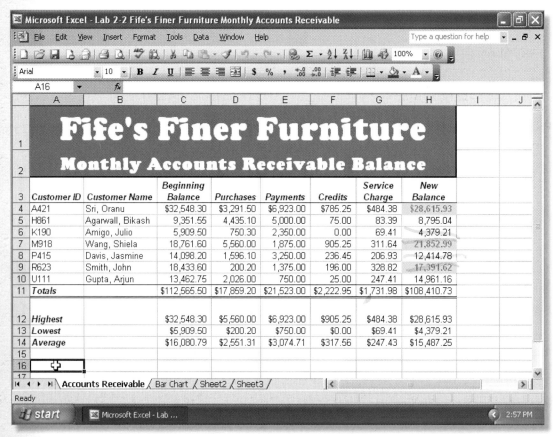

FIGURE 2-89

In the Lab

Instructions Part 1: Create a worksheet similar to the one shown in Figure 2-89. Include the six columns of customer data in Table 2-9 in the report, plus two additional columns to compute a service charge and a new balance for each customer. Assume no negative unpaid monthly balances. Perform the following tasks.

1. Enter and format the worksheet title, worksheet subtitle, column titles and row titles. Use a font type of your choice for the worksheet titles. The Cooper Black font is shown in Figure 2-89. Bold and italicize the column titles in row 3. Add a bottom border to the column titles in row 3. Center the column titles in the range B3:H3. Bold and italicize the titles in the range A11:A14. Add a top and double bottom border to the range A11:H11.

2. Enter the data in Table 2-9.

3. Use the following formulas to determine the service charge in column G and the new balance in column H for the first customer. Copy the two formulas down through the remaining customers.
   a. Service Charge (cell G4) = 1.95% * (Beginning Balance – Payments – Credits) or = 0.0195 * (C4 - E4 - F4)
   b. New Balance (H4) = Beginning Balance + Purchases – Payments – Credits + Service Charge or C4 + D4 - E4 - F4 + G4

4. Determine the totals in row 11.

5. Determine the maximum, minimum, and average values in cells C12:C14 for the range C4:C10 and then copy the range C12:C14 to D12:H14.

6. Change the width of column A to 11.00 characters. Change the widths of columns B through H to best fit. Change the heights of row 3 to 27.75 and row 12 to 30.00 points.

7. Assign the Currency style with a floating dollar sign to the cells containing numeric data in the ranges C4:H4 and C11:H14. Assign the Comma style (currency with no dollar sign) to the range C5:H10.

8. Use conditional formatting to change the formatting to green bold font on a yellow background in any cell in the range H4:H10 that contains a value greater than or equal to 15000.

9. Change the widths of columns C through H to best fit again, if necessary.

10. Change the worksheet name from Sheet1 to Accounts Receivable.

11. Enter your name, course, laboratory assignment number (Lab 2-2), date, and instructor name in the range A16:A20.

12. Spell check the worksheet. Preview and then print the worksheet in landscape orientation. Save the workbook using the file name Lab 2-2 Fife's Finer Furniture Monthly Accounts Receivable.

13. Print the range A3:D14. Print the formulas version on one page. Close the workbook without saving the changes. Hand in the three printouts to your instructor.

Instructions Part 2: This part requires that you use the Chart Wizard button on the Standard toolbar to draw a 3-D Bar chart. If necessary, use the Type a question for help box on the menu bar to obtain information on drawing a Bar chart on a separate sheet in the workbook.

With the Lab 2-2 Fife's Finer Furniture Monthly Accounts Receivable workbook open, draw the 3-D Bar chart showing each customer's total new balance as shown in Figure 2-90 on the next page. Use the CTRL key and mouse to select the nonadjacent chart ranges B4:B10 and H4:H10. The customer names in the range B4:B10 will identify the bars, while the data series in the range H4:H10 will determine the length of the bars. Click the Chart Wizard button on the Standard toolbar. When the Chart Wizard - Step 1 of 4 - Chart Type dialog box is displayed, select the Bar Chart type and Chart sub-type Clustered bar with a 3-D visual effect (column 1, row 2). Click the Next button twice to display the Chart Wizard - Step 3 of 4 - Chart Options dialog box. Add the chart title Accounts Receivable. Click the Next button and select As new sheet to draw the bar chart on a new worksheet.

(continued)

In the Lab

Accounts Receivable Balance Sheet *(continued)*

Change the worksheet name from Chart1 to Bar Chart. Drag the Accounts Receivable tab to the left of the Bar Chart tab to reorder the sheets in the workbook. Save the workbook using the same file name as in Part 1. Preview and print the chart. Hand in the printout to your instructor.

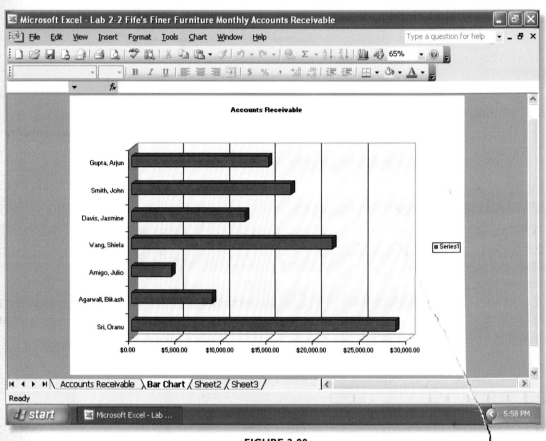

FIGURE 2-90

Instructions Part 3: With the Lab 2-2 Fife's Finer Furniture Monthly Accounts Receivable workbook open, click the Accounts Receivable tab. Change the following purchases: account number K190 to $6,500.00; account number R623 to $3,000.00. The total new balance in cell H11 should equal $116,960.23. Select both sheets by holding down the SHIFT key and then clicking the Bar Chart tab. Preview and print the selected sheets. Hand in the printouts to your instructor. Save the worksheet using the file name Lab 2-2 Fife's Finer Furniture Monthly Accounts Receivable 2.

Instructions Part 4: With your instructor's permission, e-mail the workbook created in this exercise with the changes indicated in Part 2 as an attachment to your instructor. Close the workbook without saving the changes.

3 Equity Web Queries

Problem: Esmeralda Dominga, president of Pro Cards, Inc., recently attended a Microsoft Office seminar at the local community college and learned that Excel can connect to the Web, download real-time stock data into a worksheet, and then refresh the data as often as needed. Because you have had courses in Excel and the Internet, she has hired you as a consultant to develop a stock analysis workbook. Her portfolio is listed in Table 2-10.

Instructions Part 1: If necessary, connect to the Internet. Open a new Excel workbook and select cell A1. Perform a Web query to obtain multiple stock quotes (Figure 2-91), using the stock symbols in Table 2-10. Enter your name, course, laboratory assignment number (Lab 2-3a), date, and instructor name in the range A22:A26. Rename the worksheet Multiple Quotes. Save the workbook using the file name Lab 2-3 Esmeralda Dominga Equities Online. Preview and then print the worksheet in landscape orientation using the Fit to option.

Table 2-10 Esmeralda Dominga's Stock Portfolio	
Company	**Stock Symbol**
International Business Machines	IBM
Oracle	ORCL
Johnson & Johnson	JNJ
Boeing	BA
Home Depot	HD
Citigroup	C

Click the following links and print the Web page that appears in the browser window: Click here to visit MSN Money; Oracle Corporation; Chart to the right of Home Depot, Inc., and News to the right of Citigroup Inc. Hand in the printouts to your instructor.

FIGURE 2-91

Instructions Part 2: Create a worksheet listing the major indices and their current values on Sheet 2 of the Lab 2-3 Esmeralda Dominga Equities Online workbook (Figure 2-92 on the next page). To create this worksheet, double-click MSN MoneyCentral Investor Major Indices in the Select Data Source dialog box. Enter your name, course, laboratory assignment number (Lab 2-3b), date, and instructor name below the last entry in column A. Rename the worksheet Major Indices. Save the workbook using the same file name as in Part 1. Preview and then print the worksheet in landscape orientation using the Fit to option. Hand in the printout to your instructor.

(continued)

Equity Web Queries *(continued)*

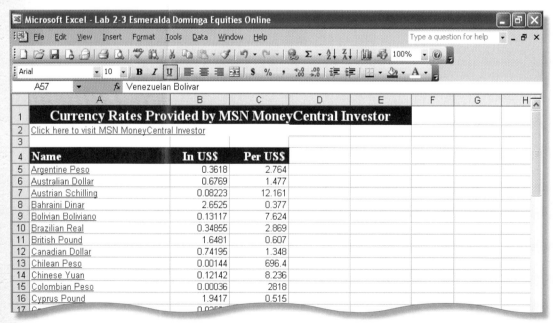

FIGURE 2-92

Instructions Part 3: Create a worksheet listing the latest currency rates on Sheet 3 of the Lab 2-3 Esmeralda Dominga Equities Online workbook (Figure 2-93). To create this worksheet, double-click MSN MoneyCentral Investor Currency Rates in the Select Data Source dialog box. Enter your name, course, laboratory assignment number (Lab 2-3c), date, and instructor name below the last entry in column A. Rename the sheet Currency Rates. Save the workbook using the same file name as in Part 1. Preview and then print the worksheet in portrait orientation using the Fit to option. Hand in the printout to your instructor.

FIGURE 2-93

Instructions Part 4: Excel recognizes certain types of data in a cell, such as stock symbols. To indicate that it recognizes the data, Excel then inserts a smart tag indicator (a small purple triangle) in the lower-right corner of those cells. If you click the cell with the smart tag indicator, Excel displays the Smart Tag Actions button. If you click the Smart Tag Actions button arrow, Excel displays a menu (Figure 2-94) that can be used to gain instant access to information about the data. To ensure Excel options are set to label data with smart tags, click AutoCorrect Options on the Tools menu and then click the Smart Tags tab when the AutoCorrect dialog box appears. If necessary, select the three check boxes, Label data with smart tags, Smart tag lists (MSN MoneyCentral Financial Symbols), and Embed smart tags in this workbook.

With a new workbook opened, enter the column title, Stock Symbols, in cell A1 as shown in Figure 2-94. Enter the three stock symbols, JPM (J.P. Morgan Chase), MCD (McDonald's Corporation), and SBC (SBC Communications) in the range A2:A4. Save the workbook using the file name Lab 2-3 Smart Tags.

Click cell A4. When Excel displays the Smart Tag Actions button, click the arrow to display the Smart Tag Actions list (Figure 2-94). One at a time, click the first three commands below Financial Symbol: SBC. Print the Web pages that your browser displays when you click these three commands and then print the worksheet. Repeat these steps, clicking the first three commands in the Smart Tag Actions list for the stock symbols in cells A2 and A3. Hand in the printouts to your instructor.

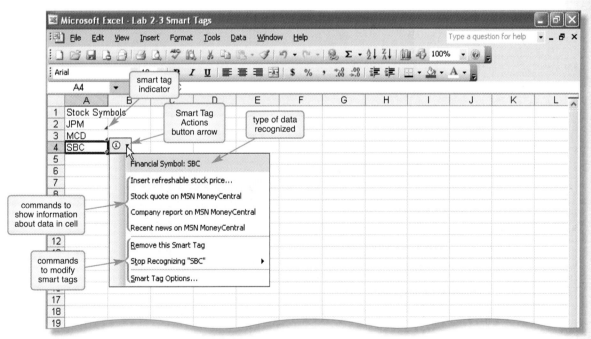

FIGURE 2-94

Cases and Places

The difficulty of these case studies varies:
■ are the least difficult and ■■ are more difficult. The last exercise is a group exercise.

1 ■ You are the cochairman of the fund-raising committee for the school's band. You want to compare various fund-raising ideas to determine which will give you the best profit. You obtain information from six businesses about their products (Table 2-11). Using the formulas in Table 2-12 and the general worksheet layout in Table 2-11, produce a worksheet to share the information with your committee. Use the concepts and techniques presented in this project to create and format the worksheet.

Table 2-11   Band Fund-Raising Data and Worksheet Layout

Company	Product	Cost Per Unit	Margin	Selling Price	Profit Per 3000 Sales
T&S	T-shirts	$2.50	60%	Formula A	Formula B
Aunt Mame's	Coffee	2.00	55%		
Wong Lo	Green Tea	1.75	65%		
Pen & Pencil	Pens	1.60	50%		
Gum-It	Gum	1.75	53%		
Dip-N-Donuts	Donuts	2.60	45%		
Minimum	Formula C				
Maximum	Formula D				

Table 2-12   Band Fund-Raising Formulas

Formula A = Cost Per Unit / (1 − Margin)

Formula B = 3000 * (Selling Price − Cost Per Unit)

Formula C = MIN function

Formula D = MAX function

Cases and Places

2 ■■ To determine the effectiveness of their endangered species recovery plan, the Fish and Wildlife Department traps and releases red wolves in selected sections of the state and records how many are pregnant. To obtain a representative sample, the department tries to trap and release approximately 20% of the population. The sample for eight sections is shown in Table 2-13. Use the following formula to determine the total red wolf population for each section:

Wolves in a Section = 5 * (Wolves Caught + Pregnant Wolves) – 5 * Death Rate * (Wolves Caught + Pregnant Wolves)

Use the concepts and techniques presented in this project to create the worksheet. Determine appropriate totals. Finally, estimate the total state red wolf population if 925 sections are in the state.

Table 2-13	Red Wolf Catch Data		
Section	Wolves Caught	Wolves Pregnant	Annual Death Rate
1	7	3	51%
2	8	6	67%
3	7	1	51%
4	6	4	61%
5	3	1	60%
6	4	2	54%
7	4	2	44%
8	4	1	53%

Cases and Places

3 ■■ You are a spreadsheet specialist consultant for Super Store Furniture. The owners of the store want to know the profit potential of their furniture inventory. The data and the format of the desired report are shown in Table 2-14. The required formulas are shown in Table 2-15.

Use the concepts and techniques developed in this project to create and format the worksheet and chart. Hand in a printout of the values version and formulas version of the worksheet. The company just received a shipment of 100 additional loveseats and 250 end tables. Update the appropriate cells in the Units on Hands column. The additional inventory yields a total profit potential of $3,878,742.96.

Table 2-14 Super Store Profit Potential Data and Worksheet Layout

Item	Units On Hand	Unit Cost	Total Cost	Average Unit Price	Total Value	Potential Profit
Rugs	983	$89.00	Formula A	Formula B	Formula C	Formula D
Sofas	1,980	678.00				
Loveseats	2,187	189.00				
End Tables	2,354	65.45				
Lamps	2,346	23.85				
Total	—		—		—	—
Average	Formula E					
Lowest	Formula F					
Highest	Formula G					

Table 2-15 Super Store Profit Potential Formulas

Formula A = Units on Hand * Unit Cost

Formula B = Unit Cost * (1 / (1 − .65))

Formula C = Units on Hand * Average Unit Price

Formula D = Total Value − Total Cost

Formula E = AVERAGE function

Formula F = MIN function

Formula G = MAX function

Cases and Places

4 ■■ LUV Steel Company pays a 3.25% commission to its salespeople to stimulate sales. The company also pays each employee a base salary. The management has projected each employee's sales for the next quarter. This information — employee name, employee base salary, and projected sales — is as follows: Meeks, Tyrone, $12,500.00, $542,413.00; Mandinka, Al-Jabbar, $10,250.00, $823,912.00; Silverstein, Aaron, $9,150.00, $362,750.00; Chronowski, John, $6,950.00, $622,165.00; Putin, Nikita, $9,500.00, $750,450.00.

With this data, you have been asked to develop a worksheet calculating the amount of commission and the projected quarterly salary for each employee. The following formulas can be used to obtain this information:

Commission Amount = 3.25% × Projected Sales

Quarterly Salary = Base Salary + Commission Amount

Include a total, average value, highest value, and lowest value for employee base salary, commission amount, and quarterly salary. Use the concepts and techniques presented in this project to create and format the worksheet.

Create a 3-D Pie chart on a separate sheet illustrating the portion each employee's quarterly salary contributes to the total quarterly salary. Use the Microsoft Excel Help system to create a professional looking 3-D Pie chart with title and data labels.

5 ■■ **Working Together** Have each member of your team select six stocks — two technology stocks, two bank stocks, and two retail stocks. Each member should submit the stock names, stock symbols, and an approximate 12-month-old price. Create a worksheet that lists the stock names, symbols, price, and number of shares for each stock (use 500 shares as number of shares for all stocks). Format the worksheet so that it has a professional appearance and is as informative as possible.

Have the group do research on the use of 3-D references, which is a reference to a range that spans two or more worksheets in a workbook (use Microsoft Excel Help). Use what the group learns to create a Web query on the Sheet2 worksheet by referencing the stock symbols on the Sheet1 worksheet. Change the cells that list current price per share numbers on the Sheet1 worksheet to use 3-D cell references that refer to the worksheet created by the Web query on the Sheet2 worksheet. Present your workbook and findings to the class.

MICROSOFT
Office Access 2003

MICROSOFT

Office Access 2003

Creating and Using a Database

PROJECT

1

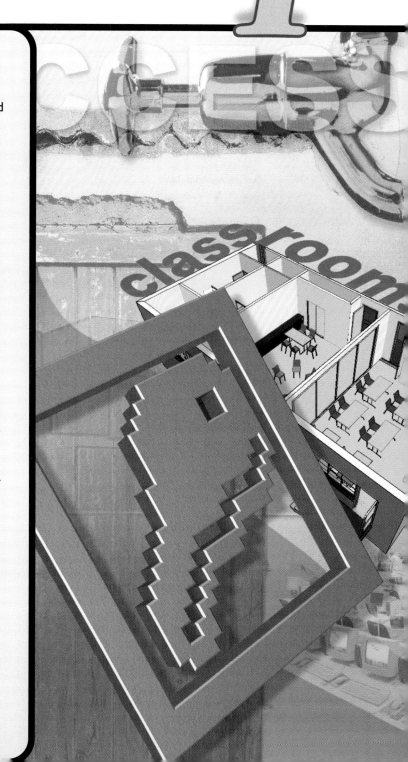

CASE PERSPECTIVE

Ashton James College (AJC) has a solid reputation in the community, delivers quality computer courses, and has a faculty of highly professional, dedicated instructors. Its graduates are among the top achievers in the state. Recently, at the urging of area businesses that depend on the college-educated workforce, AJC has begun to offer corporate computer training through its Continuing Education department. The programs have proved to be very popular, and the client list is growing rapidly.

AJC employs several trainers to teach these corporate courses. It assigns each client to a specific trainer. The trainer contacts the client to determine the particular course the client requires. The trainer then customizes a program for that particular client. The trainer will schedule all the necessary training sessions.

To ensure that operations run smoothly, Ashton James College needs to maintain data on its trainers and their clients. The AJC administration wants to organize the data in a database, managed by a database management system such as Access. In this way, AJC can keep its data current and accurate while program administrators analyze the data for trends and produce a variety of useful reports. Your task is to help the director of continuing education at Ashton James College, Dr. Robert Gernaey, create and use the database.

As you read through this project, you will learn how to use Access to create a database.

Creating and Using a Database

PROJECT

Objectives

You will have mastered the material in this project when you can:

- Describe databases and database management systems
- Start Access
- Describe the features of the Access desktop
- Create a database
- Create a table and add records
- Close a table
- Close a database and quit Access
- Open a database
- Print the contents of a table
- Create and use a simple query
- Create and use a simple form
- Create and print a custom report
- Design a database to eliminate redundancy

What Is Microsoft Office Access 2003?

Microsoft Office Access 2003 is a powerful database management system (DBMS) that functions in the Windows environment and allows you to create and process data in a database. Some of the key features are:

- **Data entry and update**   Access provides easy mechanisms for adding, changing, and deleting data, including the capability of making mass changes in a single operation.
- **Queries (questions)**   Access makes it possible to ask complex questions concerning the data in the database and then receive instant answers.
- **Forms**   Access allows the user to produce attractive and useful forms for viewing and updating data.
- **Reports**   Access report creation tools make it easy to produce sophisticated reports for presenting data.
- **Web support**   Access allows you to save objects, reports, and tables in HTML format so they can be viewed using a browser. You also can import and export documents in XML format. Access's capability of creating data access pages allows real-time access to data in the database via the Internet.

What Is New in Access?

This latest version of Access has many new features to make you more productive. You can view information on dependencies between various database objects. You can enable error checking for many common errors in forms and reports. You can add smart tags to fields in tables, queries, forms, or data access pages. Access now has a command to backup a database. Many wizards provide more options for sorting data. You can export to, import from, or link to a Windows SharePoint Services list. Access now offers enhanced XML support.

Project One — Ashton James College Database

Creating, storing, sorting, and retrieving data are important tasks. In their personal lives, many people keep a variety of records such as names, addresses, and telephone numbers of friends and business associates, records of investments, records of expenses for tax purposes, and so on. For effective use of this data, users must have quick access to it. Businesses also must be able to store and access information quickly and easily.

The term **database** describes a collection of data organized in a manner that allows access, retrieval, and use of that data. A **database management system**, such as Access, is a software tool that allows you to use a computer to create a database; add, change, and delete data in the database; sort the data in the database; retrieve data in the database; and create forms and reports using the data in the database.

In Access, a database consists of a collection of tables. Figure 1-1 shows a sample database for Ashton James College, which consists of two tables. The Client table contains information about the clients to which Ashton James College provides services. The college assigns each client to a specific trainer. The Trainer table contains information about the trainers to whom these clients are assigned.

Client table

fields

records

CLIENT NUMBER	NAME	ADDRESS	CITY	STATE	ZIP CODE	AMOUNT PAID	CURRENT DUE	TRAINER NUMBER
BS27	Blant and Sons	4806 Park	Lake Hammond	TX	76653	$21,876.00	$892.50	42
CE16	Center Services	725 Mitchell	San Julio	TX	78364	$26,512.00	$2,672.00	48
CP27	Calder Plastics	7300 Cedar	Lake Hammond	TX	76653	$8,725.00	$0.00	48
EU28	Elba's Furniture	1445 Hubert	Tallmadge	TX	77231	$4,256.00	$1,202.00	53
FI28	Farrow-Idsen	829 Wooster	Cedar Ridge	TX	79342	$8,287.50	$925.50	42
FL93	Fairland Lawn	143 Pangborn	Lake Hammond	TX	76653	$21,625.00	$0.00	48
HN83	Hurley National	3827 Burgess	Tallmadge	TX	77231	$0.00	$0.00	48
MC28	Morgan-Alyssa	923 Williams	Crumville	TX	76745	$24,761.00	$1,572.00	42
PS82	PRIM Staffing	72 Crestview	San Julio	TX	78364	$11,682.25	$2,827.50	53
TE26	Telton-Edwards	5672 Anderson	Dunston	TX	77893	$8,521.50	$0.00	48

clients of trainer Belinda Perry

Trainer table

TRAINER NUMBER	LAST NAME	FIRST NAME	ADDRESS	CITY	STATE	ZIP CODE	HOURLY RATE	YTD EARNINGS
42	Perry	Belinda	261 Porter	Burdett	TX	76734	$23.00	$27,620.00
48	Stevens	Michael	3135 Gill	Rockwood	TX	78884	$21.00	$23,567.50
53	Gonzalez	Manuel	265 Maxwell	Camino	TX	76574	$24.00	$29,885.00
67	Danville	Marty	1827 Maple	Dunston	TX	77893	$20.00	$0.00

trainer Belinda Perry

FIGURE 1-1

More About

Databases in Access 2003

In some DBMSs, every table, query, form, or report is stored in a separate file. This is not the case in Access 2003, in which a database is stored in a single file on disk. The file contains all the tables, queries, forms, reports, and programs created for this database.

The rows in the tables are called **records**. A record contains information about a given person, product, or event. A row in the Client table, for example, contains information about a specific client.

The columns in the tables are called fields. A **field** contains a specific piece of information within a record. In the Client table, for example, the fourth field, City, contains the city where the client is located.

The first field in the Client table is the Client Number. Ashton James College assigns a number to each client. As is common to the way in which many organizations format client numbers, Ashton James College calls it a *number*, although it actually contains letters. The AJC client numbers consist of two uppercase letters followed by a two-digit number.

These numbers are unique; that is, no two clients are assigned the same number. Such a field can be used as a **unique identifier**. This simply means that a given client number will appear only in a single record in the table. Only one record exists, for example, in which the client number is CP27. A unique identifier also is called a **primary key**. Thus, the Client Number field is the primary key for the Client table.

The next seven fields in the Client table are Name, Address, City, State, Zip Code, Amount Paid, and Current Due. The Amount Paid field contains the amount that the client has paid Ashton James College year-to-date (YTD), but before the current period. The Current Due field contains the amount due to AJC for the current period.

For example, client BS27 is Blant and Sons. The address is 4806 Park in Lake Hammond, Texas. The Zip code is 76653. The client has paid $21,876.00 for training services so far this year. The amount due for the current period is $892.50.

AJC assigns each client a single trainer. The last field in the Client table, Trainer Number, gives the number of the client's trainer.

The first field in the Trainer table, Trainer Number, is the number Ashton James College assigns to the trainer. These numbers are unique, so Trainer Number is the primary key of the Trainer table.

The other fields in the Trainer table are Last Name, First Name, Address, City, State, Zip Code, Hourly Rate, and YTD Earnings. The Hourly Rate field gives the trainer's hourly billing rate, and the YTD Earnings field contains the total amount that AJC has paid the trainer for services so far this year.

For example, Trainer 42 is Belinda Perry. Her address is 261 Porter in Burdett, Texas. The Zip code is 76734. Her hourly billing rate is $23.00, and her YTD earnings are $27,620.00.

The trainer number appears in both the Client table and the Trainer table. It relates clients and trainers. For example, in the Client table, you see that the trainer number for client BS27 is 42. To find the name of this trainer, look for the row in the Trainer table that contains 42 in the Trainer Number field. After you have found it, you know the client is assigned to Belinda Perry. To find all the clients assigned to Belinda Perry, however, you must look through the Client table for all the clients that contain 42 in the Trainer Number field. Her clients are BS27 (Blant and Sons), FI28 (Farrow-Idsen), and MC28 (Morgan-Alyssa).

The last trainer in the Trainer table, Marty Danville, has not been assigned any clients yet; therefore, his trainer number, 67, does not appear on any row in the Client table.

Figure 1-1 on page AC 5 shows the data that must be maintained in the database. The first step is to create the database and the tables it contains. In the process, you must define the fields included in the two tables, as well as the type of data each field will contain. Then, you must add the appropriate records to the tables. Finally, you will print the contents of the tables. After you have completed these tasks, you will create a query, a form, and a report.

Starting Access

If you are stepping through this project on a computer, and you want your screen to agree with the figures in this book, then you should change your computer's resolution to 800 × 600. For more information on how to change the resolution on your computer, see Appendix D. To start Access, Windows must be running. The following steps show how to start Access.

More About

The Access Help System

Need Help? It is no further than the Type a question for help box on the menu bar in the upper-right corner of the window. Click the box that contains the text, Type a question for help (Figure 1-3 on the next page), type help, and then press the ENTER key. Access responds with a list of topics you can click to learn about obtaining help on any Access-related topic. To find out what is new in Access 2003, type what is new in Access in the Type a question for help box.

To Start Access

1

• **Click the Start button on the Windows taskbar, point to All Programs on the Start menu and then point to Microsoft Office on the All Programs submenu.**

Windows displays the Start menu, the All Programs submenu, and the Microsoft Office submenu (Figure 1-2).

FIGURE 1-2

• Click Microsoft Office Access 2003.

Access starts. After several seconds, the Access window appears (Figure 1-3).

• If the Access window is not maximized, double-click its title bar to maximize it.

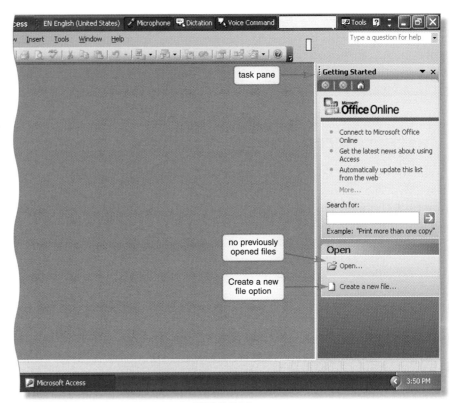

FIGURE 1-3

The screen in Figure 1-3 illustrates how the Access window looks the first time you start Access after installation on most computers. Access displays a task pane on the right side of the screen at startup. A **task pane** is a separate window that enables users to carry out some Access tasks more efficiently. When you start Access, it displays the Getting Started task pane, which is a small window that provides commonly used links and commands that allow you to open files, create new files, or search Office-related topics on the Microsoft Web site. The task pane is used only to create a new database and then it is closed.

If the Office Speech Recognition software is installed and active on your computer, then when you start Access the Language bar is displayed on the screen. The **Language bar** allows you to speak commands and dictate text. It usually is located on the right side of the Windows taskbar next to the notification area and changes to include the speech recognition functions available in Access. In this book, the Language bar is closed. For additional information about the Language bar, see the next page and Appendix B. The following steps show how to close the Language bar if it appears on the screen.

To Close the Language Bar

1

• **Right-click the Language bar to display a list of commands.**

The Language bar shortcut menu appears (Figure 1-4).

2

• **Click Close the Language bar.**
• **Click the OK button.**

The Language bar disappears.

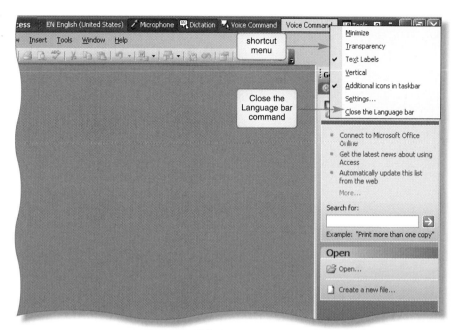

FIGURE 1-4

Speech Recognition

With the **Office Speech Recognition software** installed and a microphone, you can speak the names of toolbar buttons, menus, menu commands, list items, alerts, and dialog box controls, such as OK and Cancel. You also can dictate field entries, such as text and numbers. To indicate whether you want to speak commands or dictate cell entries, you use the Language bar. The Language bar can be in one of three states: (1) **restored**, which means it is displayed somewhere in the Access window (Figure 1-5a); (2) **minimized**, which means it is displayed on the Windows taskbar (Figure 1-5b); or (3) **hidden**, which means you do not see it on the screen. If the Language bar is hidden and you want it to display, then do the following:

1. Right-click an open area on the Windows taskbar at the bottom of the screen.
2. Point to Toolbars and then click Language bar on the Toolbars submenu.

(a) Language Bar in Access Window with Microphone Enabled

(b) Language Bar Minimized on Windows Taskbar

FIGURE 1-5

If the Language bar command is dimmed on the Toolbars submenu or if the Speech command is dimmed on the Tools menu, the Office Speech Recognition software is not installed.

Creating a New Database

In Access, all the tables, reports, form, and queries that you create are stored in a single file called a database. Thus, before creating any of these objects, you first must create the database that will hold them. You can use either the Database Wizard or the Blank database option in the task pane to create a new database. The Database Wizard can guide you by suggesting some commonly used databases. If you choose to create a database using the Database Wizard, you would use the following steps.

To Create a Database Using the Database Wizard

1. Click the New button on the Database toolbar and then click the On my computer link in the New File task pane.
2. When Access displays the Template dialog box, click the Databases tab, and then click the database that is most appropriate for your needs.
3. Follow the instructions in the Database Wizard dialog box to create the database.

Because you already know the tables and fields you want in the Ashton James College database, you would use the Blank database option in the task pane rather than the Database Wizard. The following steps illustrate how to use the Blank database option to create a database on a floppy disk in drive A.

To Create a New Database

1

• **Insert a formatted floppy disk in drive A.**

• **Click the New button on the Database toolbar to display the task pane.**

• **Click the Blank database option in the task pane, and then click the Save in box arrow.**

Access displays the File New Database dialog box and the Save in list appears (Figure 1-6a). Your File name text box may display db1.mdb, rather than db1.

FIGURE 1-6a

2

- **Click 3½ Floppy (A:).**

- **Click the File name text box.**

- **Use the BACKSPACE key or the DELETE key to delete db1 and then type** Ashton James College **as the file name.**

The file name is changed to Ashton James College (Figure 1-6b).

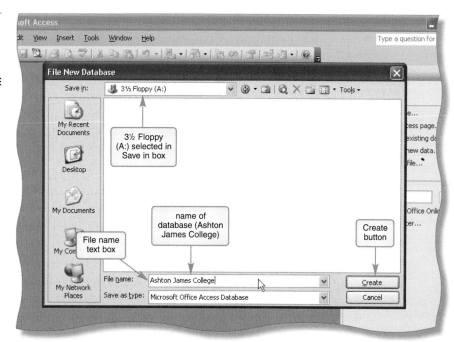

FIGURE 1-6b

3

- **Click the Create button to create the database.**

The Ashton James College database is created. The Ashton James College : Database window appears in the Microsoft Access window (Figure 1-7). The task pane does not appear.

FIGURE 1-7

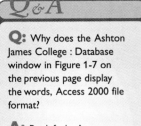

The Access Window

The Access window (Figure 1-7 on the previous page) contains a variety of features that play important roles when you are working with a database.

Title Bar

The **title bar** is the top bar in the Microsoft Access window. It includes the title of the application, Microsoft Access. The icon on the left is the Control-menu icon. Clicking this icon displays a menu from which you can close the Access window. The button on the right is the Close button. Clicking the Close button closes the Access window.

Menu Bar

The **menu bar** is displayed below the title bar. It is a special toolbar that displays the menu names. Each menu name represents a menu of commands that you can use to retrieve, store, print, and manipulate data. When you point to a menu name on the menu bar, the area of the menu bar is displayed as a selected button. Access shades selected buttons in light orange and surrounds them with a blue outline. To display a menu, such as the Edit menu, click the Edit menu name on the menu bar (Figures 1-8a and 1-8b). A **menu** is a list of commands. If you point to a command on the menu with an arrow to its right, a **submenu** is displayed from which you can choose a command.

Q: Why does the Ashton James College : Database window in Figure 1-7 on the previous page display the words, Access 2000 file format?

A: By default, Access creates a new database in Access 2000 format. A file in Access 2000 format can be opened in Access 2000, Access 2002, or Access 2003. This allows you to share your database with users who do not have Access 2003. You can open a file in Access 2002-2003 only in Access 2002 or later. Certain features of Access 2003 are not available if the database is in Access 2000 file format.

(a)

(b)

FIGURE 1-8

When you click a menu name on the menu bar, Access displays a **short menu** listing the most recently used commands (Figure 1-8a). If you wait a few seconds or click the arrows at the bottom of the short menu, the full menu appears. The **full menu** lists all the commands associated with a menu (Figure 1-8b). You also can display a full menu immediately by double-clicking the menu name on the menu bar. In this book, always have Access display the full menu using one of the following techniques.

1. Click the menu name on the menu bar and then wait a few seconds.
2. Click the menu name and then click the arrows at the bottom of the short menu.

3. Click the menu name and then point to the arrows at the bottom of the short menu.
4. Double-click the menu name.

Both short and full menus display some **dimmed commands** that appear gray, or dimmed, instead of black, which indicates they are not available for the current selection. A command with a medium blue shading to the left of it on a full menu is called a **hidden command** because it does not display on a short menu. As you use Access, it automatically personalizes the short menus for you based on how often you use commands. That is, as you use hidden commands, Access *unhides* them and places them on the short menu.

Toolbars

Below the menu bar is a toolbar. A **toolbar** contains buttons that allow you to perform certain tasks more quickly than using the menu bar. Each button contains a picture, or **icon**, depicting its function. When you move the mouse pointer over a button, the name of the button appears below it in a **ScreenTip**. The toolbar shown in Figure 1-7 on page AC 11 is the Database toolbar. The specific toolbar or toolbars that appear will vary, depending on the task on which you are working. Access routinely displays the toolbar or toolbars you will need for the task. If you want to change these or simply to determine what toolbars are available for the given task, consult Appendix D.

Taskbar

The Windows **taskbar** at the bottom of the screen displays the Start button, any active windows, and the current time.

Status Bar

Immediately above the Windows taskbar is the **status bar**. It contains special information that is appropriate for the task on which you are working. Currently, it contains the word, Ready, which means Access is ready to accept commands.

Database Window

The **Database window**, referred to in Figure 1-7 as the Ashton James College : Database window, is a special window that allows you to access easily and rapidly a variety of objects such as tables, queries, forms, and reports. To do so, you will use the various components of the window.

Shortcut Menus

Rather than use toolbars to accomplish a given task, you also can use **shortcut menus**, which are menus that display the actions available for a particular item. To display the shortcut menu for an item, right-click the item; that is, point to the item and then click the right mouse button. Figures 1-9a and 1-9b on the next page illustrate the use of toolbars and shortcut menus to perform the same task, namely to print the contents of the Client table. In the figure, the tables you will create in this project already have been created.

FIGURE 1-9

Before the action illustrated in Figure 1-9a, you would have to select the Client table by clicking it. Then, you would point to the Print button on the toolbar as shown in the figure. When you point to a button on a toolbar, the ScreenTip appears, indicating the purpose of the button, in this case Print. When you click the button, the corresponding action takes place. In this case, Access will print the contents of the Client table.

To use a shortcut menu to perform the same task, you would right-click the Client table, which produces the shortcut menu shown in Figure 1-9b. You then would click the desired command, in this case the Print command, on the shortcut menu. The corresponding action then takes place.

You can use whichever option you prefer. Many professionals who use Access will use a combination. If it is simplest to use the shortcut menu, which often is the case, they will use the shortcut menu. If it is simpler just to click a toolbar button, they will do that. The steps in this text follow this approach; that is, using a combination of both options. The text indicates how to accomplish the task using the other approach, as well. Thus, if the steps use a shortcut menu, the Other Ways box at the end of the steps will indicate how you could accomplish the task using a toolbar button. If the steps use a button, the Other Ways box will indicate how you could accomplish the task with a shortcut menu.

AutoCorrect

Not visible in the Access window, the **AutoCorrect** feature of Access works behind the scenes, correcting common mistakes when you complete a text entry in a cell. AutoCorrect makes three types of corrections for you:

1. Corrects two initial capital letters by changing the second letter to lowercase.
2. Capitalizes the first letter in the names of days.
3. Replaces commonly misspelled words with their correct spelling. For example, it will change the misspelled word *recieve* to *receive* when you complete the entry. AutoCorrect will correct the spelling automatically of more than 400 commonly misspelled words.

Creating a Table

An Access database consists of a collection of tables. After you have created the database, you must create each of the tables within it. In this project, for example, you must create both the Client and Trainer tables shown in Figure 1-1 on page AC 5.

To create a table, you describe the structure of the table to Access by describing the fields within the table. For each field, you indicate the following:

1. **Field name** — Each field in the table must have a unique name. In the Client table (Figure 1-10a and 1-10b on the next page), for example, the field names are Client Number, Name, Address, City, State, Zip Code, Amount Paid, Current Due, and Trainer Number.

> ### More About
> #### AutoCorrect
> Using the Office AutoCorrect feature, you can create entries that will replace abbreviations with spelled-out names and phrases automatically. For example, you can create the abbreviated entry *dbms* for *database management system*. Whenever you type dbms followed by a space or punctuation mark, Access automatically replaces dbms with database management system. AutoCorrect works with text in a datasheet or in a form. To specify AutoCorrect rules and exceptions to the rules, click Tools on the menu bar and then click AutoCorrect Options.

> ### More About
> #### Creating a Table: The Table Wizard
> Access includes a Table Wizard that guides you by suggesting some commonly used tables and fields. To use the Table Wizard, click Tables on the Objects bar and then click Create table by using wizard. Follow the directions in the Table Wizard dialog boxes. After you create the table, you can modify it at any time by opening the table in Design view.

Structure of Client table

FIELD NAME	DATA TYPE	FIELD SIZE	PRIMARY KEY?	DESCRIPTION
Client Number	Text	4	Yes	Client Number (Primary Key)
Name	Text	20		Client Name
Address	Text	15		Street Address
City	Text	15		City
State	Text	2		State (Two-Character Abbreviation)
Zip Code	Text	5		Zip Code (Five-Character Version)
Amount Paid	Currency			Amount Paid by Client This Year
Current Due	Currency			Current Due from Client This Period
Trainer Number	Text	2		Number of Client's Trainer

FIGURE 1-10a

Client table

CLIENT NUMBER	NAME	ADDRESS	CITY	STATE	ZIP CODE	AMOUNT PAID	CURRENT DUE	TRAINER NUMBER
BS27	Blant and Sons	4806 Park	Lake Hammond	TX	76653	$21,876.00	$892.50	42
CE16	Center Services	725 Mitchell	San Julio	TX	78364	$26,512.00	$2,672.00	48
CP27	Calder Plastics	7300 Cedar	Lake Hammond	TX	76653	$8,725.00	$0.00	48
EU28	Elba's Furniture	1445 Hubert	Tallmadge	TX	77231	$4,256.00	$1,202.00	53
FI28	Farrow-Idsen	829 Wooster	Cedar Ridge	TX	79342	$8,287.50	$925.50	42
FL93	Fairland Lawn	143 Pangborn	Lake Hammond	TX	76653	$21,625.00	$0.00	48
HN83	Hurley National	3827 Burgess	Tallmadge	TX	77231	$0.00	$0.00	48
MC28	Morgan-Alyssa	923 Williams	Crumville	TX	76745	$24,761.00	$1,572.00	42
PS82	PRIM Staffing	72 Crestview	San Julio	TX	78364	$11,682.25	$2,827.50	53
TE26	Telton-Edwards	5672 Anderson	Dunston	TX	77893	$8,521.50	$0.00	48

FIGURE 1-10b

Q: Do all database management systems use the same data types?

A: No. Different database management systems have different available data types. Even data types that are essentially the same can have different names. The Access 2003 Text data type, for example, is referred to as Character in some systems and Alpha in others.

More About

Primary Keys

In some cases, the primary key consists of a combination of fields rather than a single field. For more information about determining primary keys in such situations, visit the Access 2003 More About Web page (scsite.com/ac2003/more) and click Primary Keys.

2. **Data type** — Data type indicates to Access the type of data the field will contain. Some fields can contain only numbers. Others, such as Amount Paid and Current Due, can contain numbers and dollar signs. Still others, such as Name and Address, can contain letters.

3. **Description** — Access allows you to enter a detailed description of the field.

You also can assign field widths to text fields (fields whose data type is Text). This indicates the maximum number of characters that can be stored in the field. If you do not assign a width to such a field, Access assumes the width is 50.

You also must indicate which field or fields make up the primary key; that is, the unique identifier, for the table. In the Ashton James College database, the Client Number field is the primary key of the Client table and the Trainer Number field is the primary key of the Trainer table.

The rules for field names are:

1. Names can be up to 64 characters in length.

2. Names can contain letters, digits, and spaces, as well as most of the punctuation symbols.

3. Names cannot contain periods, exclamation points (!), accent graves (`), or square brackets ([ ]).

4. The same name cannot be used for two different fields in the same table.

Each field has a **data type**. This indicates the type of data that can be stored in the field. The data types you will use in this project are:

1. **Text** — The field can contain any characters. A maximum number of 255 characters is allowed in a field whose data type is Text.

2. **Number** — The field can contain only numbers. The numbers either can be positive or negative. Fields are assigned this type so they can be used in arithmetic operations. Fields that contain numbers but will not be used for arithmetic operations usually are assigned a data type of Text. The Trainer Number field, for example, is a text field because the trainer numbers will not be involved in any arithmetic.

3. **Currency** — The field can contain only monetary data. The values will appear with currency symbols, such as dollar signs, commas, decimal points, and with two digits following the decimal point. Like numeric fields, you can use currency fields in arithmetic operations. Access assigns a size to currency fields automatically.

Table 1-1 shows the other data types that are available.

Table 1-1	Additional Data Types
DATA TYPE	DESCRIPTION
Memo	Field can store a variable amount of text or combinations of text and numbers where the total number of characters may exceed 255.
Number	Field can store numeric data that can be used in mathematical calculations.
Date/Time	Field can store dates and times.
AutoNumber	Field can store a unique sequential number that Access assigns to a record. Access will increment the number by 1 as each new record is added.
Yes/No	Field can store only one of two values. The choices are Yes/No, True/False, or On/Off.
OLE Object	Field can store an OLE object, which is an object linked to or embedded in the table.
Hyperlink	Field can store text that can be used as a hyperlink address.
Lookup Wizard	Field can store a value from another table or from a list of values by using a list box or combo box. Choosing this data type starts the Lookup Wizard, which assists in the creation of the field. The field then is a Lookup field. The data type is set based on the values you selected in the wizard. If the values are text for example, the field is assigned the Text data type.

The field names, data types, field widths, primary key information, and descriptions for the Client table are shown in Figure 1-10a on page AC 15.

With the information in Figures 1-10a and 1-10b, you are ready to begin creating the table. The following steps illustrate how to create a table.

To Create a Table

1

• **Click the New button on the Database window toolbar.**

The New Table dialog box appears (Figure 1-11).

FIGURE 1-11

2

• **Click Design View and then click the OK button.**

The Table1 : Table window appears (Figure 1-12).

FIGURE 1-12

3

• **Double-click the title bar of the Table1 : Table window to maximize the window.**

Access displays the maximized Table1 : Table window (Figure 1-13).

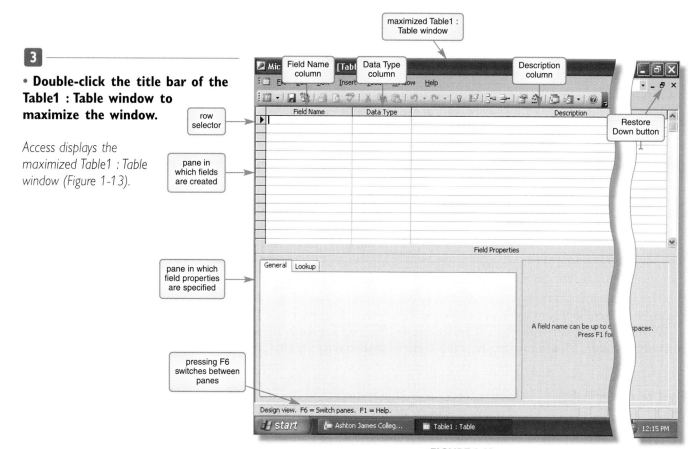

FIGURE 1-13

Defining the Fields

The next step in creating the table is to define the fields by specifying the required details in the Table window, which include entries in the Field Name, Data Type, and Description columns and additional information in the Field Properties pane in the lower portion of the Table window. You press the F6 key to move from the upper **pane** (portion of the screen), the one where you define the fields, to the lower pane, the one where you define field properties. As you define the fields, the **row selector** (Figure 1-13), the small box or bar that, when you click it, selects the entire row, indicates the field you currently are describing. It is positioned on the first field, indicating Access is ready for you to enter the name of the first field in the Field Name column.

The following steps show how to define the fields in the table.

To Define the Fields in a Table

1

• **Type** Client Number **(the name of the first field) in the Field Name column, and then press the TAB key.**

The words, Client Number, appear in the Field Name column and the insertion point advances to the Data Type column, indicating you can enter the data type (Figure 1-14). The word, Text, one of the possible data types, currently appears. The arrow indicates a list of data types is available by clicking the arrow.

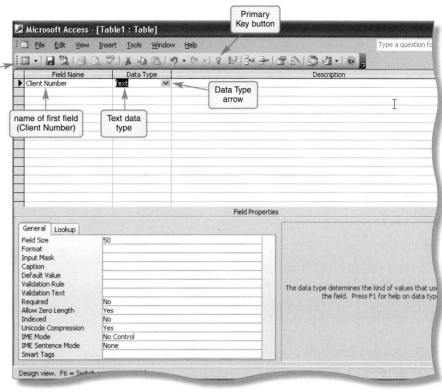

FIGURE 1-14

2

• **Because Text is the correct data type, press the TAB key to move the insertion point to the Description column, type** Client Number (Primary Key) **as the description, and then click the Primary Key button on the Table Design toolbar.**

The Client Number field is the primary key as indicated by the key symbol that appears in the row selector (Figure 1-15). A ScreenTip, which is a description of the button, appears.

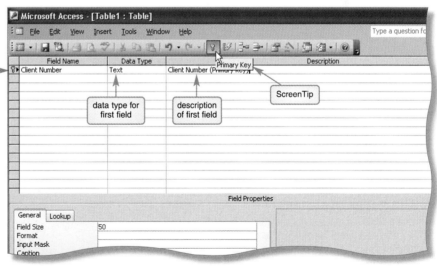

FIGURE 1-15

3

• **Press the F6 key.**

The current entry in the Field Size property box (50) is selected (Figure 1-16).

FIGURE 1-16

Microsoft Office
Access 2003

4

• **Type** 4 **as the size of the Client Number field.**

• **Press the** F6 **key to return to the Description column for the Client Number field, and then press the TAB key to move to the Field Name column in the second row.**

The insertion point moves to the second row just below the field name Client Number (Figure 1-17).

FIGURE 1-17

5

• **Use the techniques illustrated in Steps 1 through 4 to make the entries from the Client table structure shown in Figure 1-10a on page AC 15 up through and including the name of the Amount Paid field.**

• **Click the Data Type box arrow.**

The additional fields are entered (Figure 1-18). A list of available data types appears in the Data Type column for the Amount Paid field.

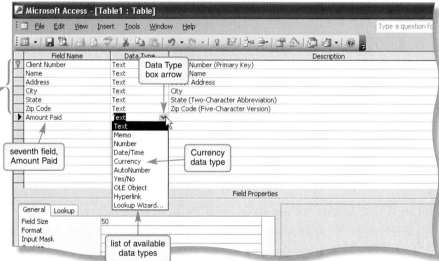

FIGURE 1-18

6

• **Click Currency and then press the TAB key.**

• **Make the remaining entries from the Client table structure shown in Figure 1-10a.**

All the fields are entered (Figure 1-19).

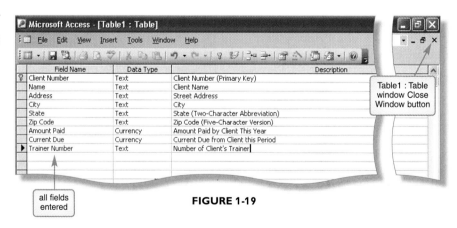

FIGURE 1-19

The description of the table is now complete.

Correcting Errors in the Structure

When creating a table, check the entries carefully to ensure they are correct. If you make a mistake and discover it before you press the TAB key, you can correct the error by repeatedly pressing the BACKSPACE key until the incorrect characters are removed. Then, type the correct characters. If you do not discover a mistake until later, you can click the entry, type the correct value, and then press the ENTER key.

If you accidentally add an extra field to the structure, select the field by clicking the row selector (the leftmost column on the row that contains the field to be deleted). After you have selected the field, press the DELETE key. This will remove the field from the structure.

If you forget a field, select the field that will follow the field you want to add by clicking the row selector, and then press the INSERT key. The remaining fields move down one row, making room for the missing field. Make the entries for the new field in the usual manner.

If you made the wrong field a primary key field, click the correct primary key entry for the field and then click the Primary Key button on the Table Design toolbar.

As an alternative to these steps, you may want to start over. To do so, click the Close Window button for the Table1 : Table window and then click the No button in the Microsoft Office Access dialog box. The initial Microsoft Access window is displayed and you can repeat the process you used earlier.

Closing and Saving a Table

The Client table structure now is complete. The final step is to close and save the table within the database. At this time, you should give the table a name.

Table names are from 1 to 64 characters in length and can contain letters, numbers, and spaces. The two table names in this project are Client and Trainer.

The following steps close and save the table.

To Close and Save a Table

1

• **Click the Close Window button for the Table1 : Table window (see Figure 1-19). (Be sure not to click the Close button on the Microsoft Access title bar, because this would close Microsoft Access.)**

The Microsoft Office Access dialog box appears (Figure 1-20).

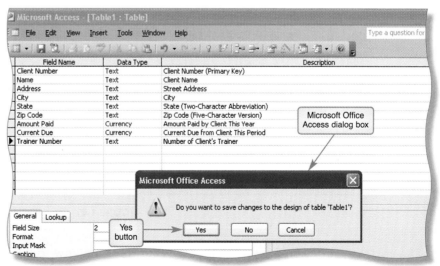

FIGURE 1-20

2

• **Click the Yes button in the Microsoft Office Access dialog box, and then type** Client **as the name of the table.**

The Save As dialog box appears (Figure 1-21). The table name is entered.

3

• **Click the OK button in the Save As dialog box.**

The table is saved. The window containing the table design no longer is displayed.

FIGURE 1-21

Other Ways

1. On File menu click Save
2. Press CTRL+S
3. In Voice Command mode, say "Save"

Adding Records to a Table

Creating a table by building the structure and saving the table is the first step in a two-step process. The second step is to add records to the table. To add records to a table, the table must be open. When making changes to tables, you work in Datasheet view. In **Datasheet view**, the table is represented as a collection of rows and columns called a **datasheet**. It looks very much like the tables shown in Figure 1-1 on page AC 5.

You often add records in phases. You may, for example, not have enough time to add all the records in one session. To illustrate this process, this project begins by adding the first two records in the Client table (Figure 1-22). The remaining records are added later.

Client table (first 2 records)

CLIENT NUMBER	NAME	ADDRESS	CITY	STATE	ZIP CODE	AMOUNT PAID	CURRENT DUE	TRAINER NUMBER
BS27	Blant and Sons	4806 Park	Lake Hammond	TX	76653	$21,876.00	$892.50	42
CE16	Center Services	725 Mitchell	San Julio	TX	78364	$26,512.00	$2,672.00	48

FIGURE 1-22

The following steps illustrate how to open the Client table and then add records.

To Add Records to a Table

1

• **Right-click the Client table in the Ashton James College : Database window.**

The shortcut menu for the Client table appears (Figure 1-23). The Ashton James College : Database window is maximized because the previous window, the Client : Table window, was maximized. (If you wanted to restore the Database window to its original size, you would click the Restore Window button.)

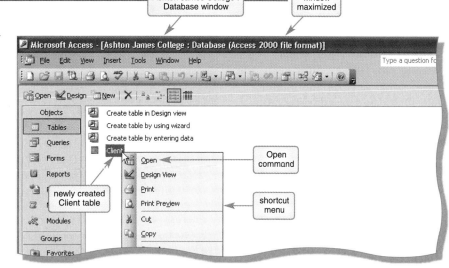

FIGURE 1-23

2

• **Click Open on the shortcut menu.**

*Access displays the Client : Table window (Figure 1-24). The window contains the Datasheet view for the Client table. The **record selector**, the small box or bar that, when clicked, selects the entire record, is positioned on the first record. The status bar at the bottom of the window also indicates that the record selector is positioned on record 1.*

FIGURE 1-24

3

• **Type BS27 as the first client number (see Figure 1-22). Be sure you type the letters in uppercase as shown in the table in Figure 1-22 so they are entered in the database correctly.**

The client number is entered, but the insertion point is still in the Client Number field (Figure 1-25). The pencil icon in the record selector column indicates that the record is being edited but changes to the record are not saved yet. Microsoft Access also creates a row for a new record.

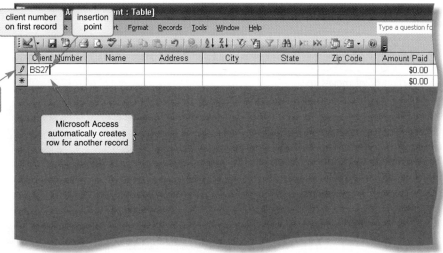

FIGURE 1-25

4

• **Press the TAB key to complete the entry for the Client Number field.**

• **Type the following entries, pressing the TAB key after each one:** Blant and Sons **as the name,** 4806 Park **as the address,** Lake Hammond **as the city,** TX **as the state, and** 76653 **as the Zip code.**

The Name, Address, City, State, and Zip Code fields are entered (Figure 1-26).

FIGURE 1-26

5

• **Type** 21876 **as the Amount Paid amount and then press the TAB key. (You do not need to type dollar signs or commas. In addition, because the digits to the right of the decimal point are both zeros, you do not need to type either the decimal point or the zeros.)**

• **Type** 892.50 **as the current due amount and then press the TAB key.**

• **Type** 42 **as the trainer number to complete data entry for the record.**

The fields have shifted to the left (Figure 1-27). The Amount Paid and Current Due values appear with dollar signs and decimal points. The insertion point is positioned in the Trainer Number field.

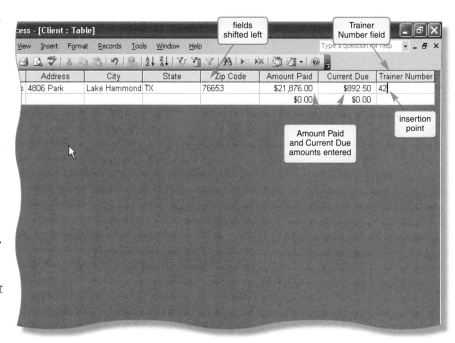

FIGURE 1-27

6

• **Press the TAB key.**

The fields shift back to the right, the record is saved, and the insertion point moves to the client number field on the second row (Figure 1-28).

FIGURE 1-28

7

- **Use the techniques shown in Steps 3 through 6 to add the data for the second record shown in Figure 1-22 on page AC 22.**

The second record is added and the insertion point moves to the Client Number field on the third row (Figure 1-29).

first two records entered in Client table

Client : Table window Close Window button

FIGURE 1-29

As soon as you have entered or modified a record and moved to another record, the original record is saved. This is different from other applications. The rows entered in a spreadsheet, for example, are not saved until the entire spreadsheet is saved.

Correcting Errors in the Data

Check your entries carefully to ensure they are correct. If you make a mistake and discover it before you press the TAB key, correct it by pressing the BACKSPACE key until the incorrect characters are removed and then typing the correct characters.

If you discover an incorrect entry later, correct the error by clicking the incorrect entry and then making the appropriate correction. If the record you must correct is not on the screen, use any technique, such as the UP ARROW and DOWN ARROW keys to move to it. If the field you want to correct is not visible on the screen, use the horizontal scroll bar along the bottom of the screen to shift all the fields until the one you want appears. Then make the correction.

If you add an extra record accidentally, select the record by clicking the record selector that immediately precedes the record. Then, press the DELETE key. This will remove the record from the table. If you forget a record, add it using the same procedure as for all the other records. Access will place it in the correct location in the table automatically.

If you cannot determine how to correct the data, you are, in effect, stuck on the record. Access neither allows you to move to any other record until you have made the correction, nor allows you to close the table. If you encounter this situation, simply press the ESC key. Pressing the ESC key will remove from the screen the record you are trying to add. You then can move to any other record, close the table, or take any other action you desire.

More About

Correcting Errors in the Data

You also can undo changes to a field by clicking the Undo typing button on the Table Datasheet toolbar. If you already have moved to another record and want to delete the record you just added, click Edit on the menu bar and then click Undo Saved Record.

Closing a Table and Database and Quitting Access

It is a good idea to close a table as soon as you have finished working with it. It keeps the screen from getting cluttered and prevents you from making accidental changes to the data in the table. If you no longer will work with the database, you should close the database as well. With the creation of the Client table complete, you also can quit Access at this point.

The steps on the next page close the table and the database and then quit Access.

To Close a Table and Database and Quit Access

1

• **Click the Close Window button for the Client : Table window.**

The datasheet for the Client table no longer appears (Figure 1-30).

2

• **Click the Close Window button for the Ashton James College : Database window.**

The Ashton James College : Database window no longer appears.

3

• **Click the Close button for the Microsoft Access window.**

The Microsoft Access window closes and the Windows desktop appears.

FIGURE 1-30

Opening a Database

To work with any of the tables, reports, or forms in a database, the database must be open. The following steps open the database from within Access.

To Open a Database

1

• **Start Access following the steps on pages AC 7 and AC 8.**

• **If the task pane appears, click its Close button.**

• **Click the Open button on the Database toolbar.**

The Open dialog box appears (Figure 1-31).

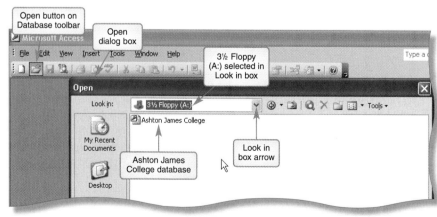

FIGURE 1-31

2

• **Be sure 3½ Floppy (A:) folder appears in the Look in box. If not, click the Look in box arrow and click 3½ Floppy (A:).**

• **Click Ashton James College.**

Access displays the Open dialog box (Figure 1-32). The 3½ Floppy (A:) folder appears in the Look in box and the files on the floppy disk in drive A are displayed. (Your list may be different.)

3

• **Click the Open button in the Open dialog box.**

• **If a Security Warning dialog box appears, click the Open button.**

The database opens and the Ashton James College : Database window appears.

FIGURE 1-32

Adding Additional Records

You can add records to a table that already contains data using a process almost identical to that used to add records to an empty table. The only difference is that you place the insertion point after the last data record before you enter the additional data. To do so, use the **Navigation buttons**, which are buttons used to move within a table, found near the lower-left corner of the screen shown in Figure 1-34 on the next page. The purpose of each of the Navigation buttons is described in Table 1-2.

Table 1-2 Navigation Buttons in Datasheet View	
BUTTON	**PURPOSE**
First Record	Moves to the first record in the table
Previous Record	Moves to the previous record
Next Record	Moves to the next record
Last Record	Moves to the last record in the table
New Record	Moves to the end of the table to a position for entering a new record

The steps on the next page add the remaining records (Figure 1-33 on the next page) to the Client table.

Other Ways

1. On File menu click Open
2. In Getting Started task pane, click name of database
3. Press CTRL + O
4. In Voice Command mode, say "Open"

Q&A

Q: Why click the New Record button? Could you just click the Client Number on the first open record and then add the record?

A: You could click the Client Number on the first open record, provided that record appears on the screen. With only two records in the table, this is not a problem. Once a table contains more records than will fit on the screen, it is easier to click the New Record button.

Client table (last 8 records)

CLIENT NUMBER	NAME	ADDRESS	CITY	STATE	ZIP CODE	AMOUNT PAID	CURRENT DUE	TRAINER NUMBER
CP27	Calder Plastics	7300 Cedar	Lake Hammond	TX	76653	$8,725.00	$0.00	48
EU28	Elba's Furniture	1445 Hubert	Tallmadge	TX	77231	$4,256.00	$1,202.00	53
FI28	Farrow-Idsen	829 Wooster	Cedar Ridge	TX	79342	$8,287.50	$925.50	42
FL93	Fairland Lawn	143 Pangborn	Lake Hammond	TX	76653	$21,625.00	$0.00	48
HN83	Hurley National	3827 Burgess	Tallmadge	TX	77231	$0.00	$0.00	48
MC28	Morgan-Alyssa	923 Williams	Crumville	TX	76745	$24,761.00	$1,572.00	42
PS82	PRIM Staffing	72 Crestview	San Julio	TX	78364	$11,682.25	$2,827.50	53
TE26	Telton-Edwards	5672 Anderson	Dunston	TX	77893	$8,521.50	$0.00	48

FIGURE 1-33

To Add Additional Records to a Table

1

• **Right-click the Client table in the Ashton James College : Database window, and then click Open on the shortcut menu.**

• **When the Client table appears, maximize the window by double-clicking its title bar.**

The datasheet appears (Figure 1-34).

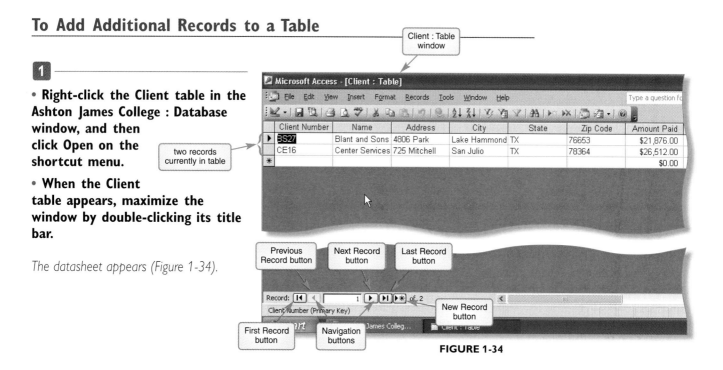

FIGURE 1-34

2

• **Click the New Record button.**

Access places the insertion point in position to enter a new record (Figure 1-35).

FIGURE 1-35

3
_____

• **Add the records from Figure 1-33 using the same techniques you used to add the first two records.**

all 10 records entered

The additional records are added (Figure 1-36).

4
_____

• **Click the Close Window button for the datasheet.**

The window containing the table closes and the Ashton James College : Database window appears.

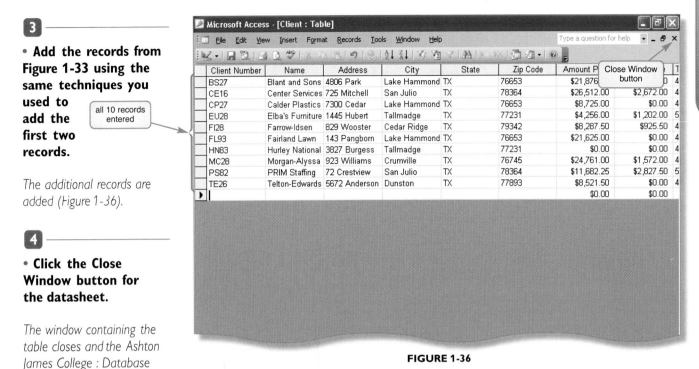

Client Number	Name	Address	City	State	Zip Code	Amount P	Close Window button	T
BS27	Blant and Sons	4806 Park	Lake Hammond	TX	76653	$21,876		4
CE16	Center Services	725 Mitchell	San Julio	TX	78364	$26,512.00	$2,672.00	4
CP27	Calder Plastics	7300 Cedar	Lake Hammond	TX	76653	$8,725.00	$0.00	4
EU28	Elba's Furniture	1445 Hubert	Tallmadge	TX	77231	$4,256.00	$1,202.00	5
FI28	Farrow-Idsen	829 Wooster	Cedar Ridge	TX	79342	$8,287.50	$925.50	4
FL93	Fairland Lawn	143 Pangborn	Lake Hammond	TX	76653	$21,625.00	$0.00	4
HN83	Hurley National	3827 Burgess	Tallmadge	TX	77231	$0.00	$0.00	4
MC28	Morgan-Alyssa	923 Williams	Crumville	TX	76745	$24,761.00	$1,572.00	4
PS82	PRIM Staffing	72 Crestview	San Julio	TX	78364	$11,682.25	$2,827.50	5
TE26	Telton-Edwards	5672 Anderson	Dunston	TX	77893	$8,521.50	$0.00	4
						$0.00	$0.00	

FIGURE 1-36

Previewing and Printing the Contents of a Table

When working with a database, you often will need to print a copy of the table contents. Figure 1-37 shows a printed copy of the contents of the Client table. (Yours may look slightly different, depending on your printer.) Because the Client table is wider substantially than the screen, it also will be wider than the normal printed page in portrait orientation. **Portrait orientation** means the printout is across the width of the page. **Landscape orientation** means the printout is across the length of the page. Thus, to print the wide database table, use landscape orientation. If you are printing the contents of a table that fit on the screen, you will not need landscape orientation. A convenient way to change to landscape orientation is to preview what the printed copy will look like by using Print Preview. This allows you to determine whether landscape orientation is necessary and, if it is, to change the orientation easily to landscape. In addition, you also can use Print Preview to determine whether any adjustments are necessary to the page margins.

Client   9/15/05

Client Number	Name	Address	City	State	Zip Code	Amount Paid	Current Due	Trainer Number
BS27	Blant and Sons	4806 Park	Lake Hammond	TX	76653	$21,876.00	$892.50	42
CE16	Center Service	725 Mitchell	San Julio	TX	78364	$26,512.00	$2,672.00	48
CP27	Calder Plastics	7300 Cedar	Lake Hammond	TX	76653	$8,725.00	$0.00	48
EU28	Elba's Furniture	1445 Hubert	Tallmadge	TX	77231	$4,256.00	$1,202.00	53
FI28	Farrow-Idsen	829 Wooster	Cedar Ridge	TX	79342	$8,287.50	$925.50	42
FL93	Fairland Lawn	143 Pangborn	Lake Hammond	TX	76653	$21,625.00	$0.00	48
HN83	Hurley National	3827 Burgess	Tallmadge	TX	77231	$0.00	$0.00	48
MC28	Morgan-Alyssa	923 Williams	Crumville	TX	76745	$24,761.00	$1,572.00	42
PS82	PRIM Staffing	72 Crestview	San Julio	TX	78364	$11,682.25	$2,827.50	53
TE26	Telton-Edwards	5672 Anderson	Dunston	TX	77893	$8,521.50	$0.00	48

FIGURE 1-37

The following steps illustrate using Print Preview to preview and then print the Client table.

To Preview and Print the Contents of a Table

1

• **Right-click the Client table.**

The shortcut menu for the Client table appears (Figure 1-38).

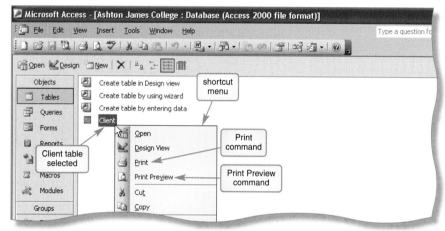

FIGURE 1-38

2

• **Click Print Preview on the shortcut menu.**

• **Point to the approximate position shown in Figure 1-39.**

The preview of the report appears. The mouse pointer shape changes to a magnifying glass, indicating you can magnify a portion of the report.

FIGURE 1-39

3

• **Click the magnifying glass mouse pointer in the approximate position shown in Figure 1-39.**

The portion surrounding the mouse pointer is magnified (Figure 1-40). The last field that appears is the Zip Code field. The Amount Paid, Current Due, and Trainer Number fields do not appear. To display the additional fields, you will need to switch to landscape orientation.

FIGURE 1-40

4

• **Click the Setup button on the Print Preview toolbar.**

Access displays the Page Setup dialog box (Figure 1-41).

FIGURE 1-41

5

• **Click the Page tab.**

The Page sheet appears (Figure 1-42). The Portrait option button currently is selected. (Option button refers to the round button that indicates choices in a dialog box. When the corresponding option is selected, the button contains within it a solid circle. Clicking an option button selects it, and deselects all others.)

FIGURE 1-42

6

• **Click Landscape, and then click the OK button.**

The orientation is changed to landscape as shown by the report that appears on the screen (Figure 1-43). The last field that is displayed is the Trainer Number field; so all fields currently appear. If they did not, you could decrease the left and right margins; that is, the amount of space left by Access on the left and right edges of the report.

FIGURE 1-43

7

• **Click the Print button to print the report, and then click the Close button on the Print Preview toolbar.**

The report prints. It looks like the report shown in Figure 1-37 on page AC 29. The Print Preview window closes and the Ashton James College : Database window appears.

Creating Additional Tables

A database typically consists of more than one table. The Ashton James College database contains two, the Client table and the Trainer table. You need to repeat the process of creating a table and adding records for each table in the database. In the Ashton James College database, you need to create and add records to the Trainer table. The structure and data for the table are given in Figure 1-44.

Structure of Trainer table

FIELD NAME	DATA TYPE	FIELD SIZE	PRIMARY KEY?	DESCRIPTION
Trainer Number	Text	2	Yes	Trainer Number (Primary Key)
Last Name	Text	10		Last Name of Trainer
First Name	Text	8		First Name of Trainer
Address	Text	15		Street Address
City	Text	15		City
State	Text	2		State (Two-Character Abbreviation)
Zip Code	Text	5		Zip Code (Five-Character Version)
Hourly Rate	Currency			Hourly Rate of Trainer
YTD Earnings	Currency			YTD Earnings of Trainer

Trainer table

TRAINER NUMBER	LAST NAME	FIRST NAME	ADDRESS	CITY	STATE	ZIP CODE	HOURLY RATE	YTD EARNINGS
42	Perry	Belinda	261 Porter	Burdett	TX	76734	$23.00	$27,620.00
48	Stevens	Michael	3135 Gill	Rockwood	TX	78884	$21.00	$23,567.50
53	Gonzalez	Manuel	265 Maxwell	Camino	TX	76574	$24.00	$29,885.00
67	Danville	Marty	1827 Maple	Dunston	TX	77893	$20.00	$0.00

FIGURE 1-44

The following steps show how to create the table.

More About

Printing the Contents of a Table

You can change the margins, paper size, paper source, or the printer that will be used to print the report. To change the margins, select the Margins sheet in the Page Setup dialog box and then enter the appropriate margin size. To change the paper size, paper source, or the printer, select the Page sheet in the Page Setup dialog box, click the appropriate down arrow, and then select the desired option.

To Create an Additional Table

1

• **Make sure the Ashton James College database is open.**

• **Click the New button on the Database window toolbar, click Design View, and then click the OK button.**

• **Enter the data for the fields for the Trainer table from Figure 1-44. Be sure to click the Primary Key button when you enter the Trainer Number field.**

The entries appear (Figure 1-45).

FIGURE 1-45

2

• **Click the Close Window button, click the Yes button in the Microsoft Office Access dialog box when asked if you want to save the changes, and then type** Trainer **as the name of the table.**

The Save As dialog box appears (Figure 1-46). The table name is entered.

3

• **Click the OK button.**

The table is saved in the Ashton James College database. The window containing the table structure no longer appears.

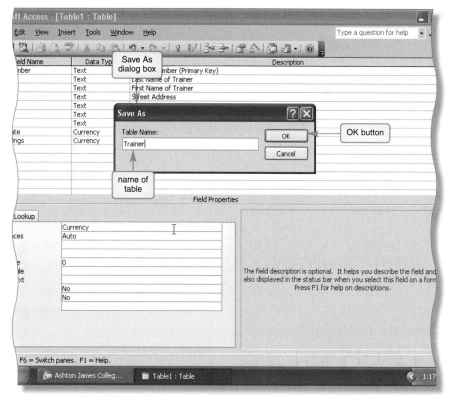

FIGURE 1-46

Adding Records to the Additional Table

Now that you have created the Trainer table, use the steps on the next page to add records to it.

To Add Records to an Additional Table

1

• **Right-click the Trainer table, and then click Open on the shortcut menu. Enter the Trainer data from Figure 1-44 on page AC 32 into the Trainer table.**

The datasheet displays the entered records (Figure 1-47).

2

• **Click the Close Window button for the Trainer : Table window.**

Access closes the table and removes the datasheet from the screen.

FIGURE 1-47

The records are now in the table.

Using Queries

Queries are simply questions, the answers to which are in the database. Access contains a powerful query feature. Through the use of this feature, you can ask a wide variety of complex questions. For simple requests, however, such as listing the number, name, and trainer number of all clients, you do not need to use the query feature, but instead can use the Simple Query wizard.

The following steps use the Simple Query wizard to create a query to display the number, name, and trainer number of all clients.

To Use the Simple Query Wizard to Create a Query

1

• **With the Tables object selected and the Client table selected, click the New Object button arrow on the Database toolbar.**

A list of objects that can be created is displayed (Figure 1-48).

FIGURE 1-48

2

• **Click Query on the New Object list.**

The New Query dialog box appears (Figure 1-49).

FIGURE 1-49

3

• **Click Simple Query Wizard, and then click the OK button.**

Access displays the Simple Query Wizard dialog box (Figure 1-50). It contains a list of available fields and a list of selected fields. Currently no fields are selected for the query.

FIGURE 1-50

4

• **Click the Add Field button to add the Client Number field.**

• **Click the Add Field button a second time to add the Name field.**

• **Click the Trainer Number field, and then click the Add Field button to add the Trainer Number field.**

The fields are selected (Figure 1-51).

FIGURE 1-51

Microsoft Office
Access 2003

5

• **Click the Next button, and then type** Client-Trainer Query **as the name for the query.**

The Simple Query Wizard dialog box displays the new query name (Figure 1-52).

FIGURE 1-52

6

• **Click the Finish button to complete the creation of the query.**

Access displays the query results (Figure 1-53). The results contain all records, but only contain the Client Number, Name, and Trainer Number fields.

7

• **Click the Close Window button for the Client-Trainer Query : Select Query window.**

Access closes the query and the Ashton James College : Database window appears.

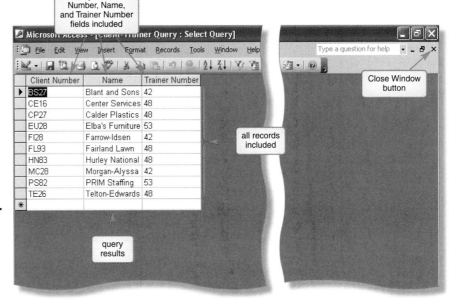

FIGURE 1-53

The query is complete. You can use it at any time you like in the future without needing to repeat the above steps.

Using a Query

After you have created and saved a query, you can use it at any time in the future by opening it. To open a saved query, click the Queries object on the Objects bar, right-click the query, and then click Open on the shortcut menu. To print the results, click the Print button on the toolbar. If you want to change the design of the query, click Design View on the shortcut menu rather than Open. To print the query without first opening it, click Print on the shortcut menu.

You often want to restrict the records that are included. For example, you might only want to include those clients whose trainer number is 42. In such a case, you need to enter the 42 as a **criterion**, which is a condition that the records to be included must satisfy. To do so, you will open the query in Design view, enter the criterion below the appropriate field, and then run the query. The following steps show how to enter a criterion to include only clients of trainer 42 and then run the query.

To Use a Query

1

• **If necessary, click the Queries object. Right-click the Client-Trainer Query.**

The shortcut menu for the Client-Trainer Query is displayed (Figure 1-54).

FIGURE 1-54

2

• **Click Design View on the shortcut menu.**

The query appears in Design view (Figure 1-55).

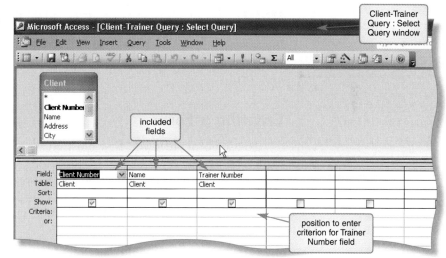

FIGURE 1-55

3

• **Click the Criteria row in the Trainer Number column of the grid, and then type 42 as the criterion.**

The criterion is typed (Figure 1-56).

FIGURE 1-56

4

• Click the Run button on the Query Design toolbar.

Access displays the results (Figure 1-57). Only the clients of trainer 42 are included.

5

• **Close the window containing the query results by clicking its Close Window button.**

• **When asked if you want to save your changes, click the No button.**

The results no longer appear. The changes to the query are not saved.

FIGURE 1-57

Other Ways

1. On Query menu click Run
2. In Voice Command mode, say "Run"

Q&A

Q: If you saved the query, what would happen the next time you ran the query?

A: You would see only clients of trainer 42.

Using a Form to View Data

In creating tables, you have used Datasheet view; that is, the data on the screen appeared as a table. You also can use **Form view**, in which you see data contained in a form.

Creating a Form

To use Form view, you first must create a form. The simplest way to create a form is to use the New Object button on the Database toolbar. The following steps illustrate using the New Object button to create a form for the Client table.

To Use the New Object Button to Create a Form

1

• **Make sure the Ashton James College database is open, the Database window appears, and the Client table is selected.**

• **If necessary, click the Tables object on the Objects bar.**

• **Click the New Object button arrow on the Database toolbar.**

A list of objects that can be created appears (Figure 1-58).

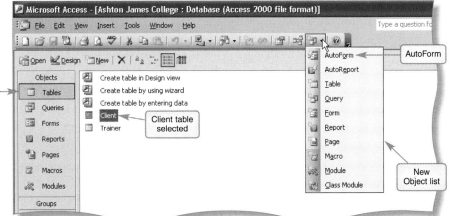

FIGURE 1-58

2

- **Click AutoForm on the New Object list.**

After a brief delay, the form appears (Figure 1-59). If you do not move the mouse pointer after clicking the New Object button, the ScreenTip for the Properties button may appear when the form opens. Access displays the Formatting toolbar when a form is created. (When you close the form, this toolbar no longer appears.)

FIGURE 1-59

Other Ways

1. On Insert menu click AutoForm
2. In Voice Command mode, say "New Object, AutoForm"
3. In Voice Command mode, say "Insert, AutoForm"

Closing and Saving the Form

Closing a form is similar to closing a table. The only difference is that you will be asked if you want to save the form unless you previously have saved it. The following steps close the form and save it as Client.

To Close and Save a Form

1

- **Click the Close Window button for the Client window (see Figure 1-59).**

Access displays the Microsoft Office Access dialog box (Figure 1-60).

FIGURE 1-60

2

- **Click the Yes button.**

The Save As dialog box appears (Figure 1-61). The name of the table (Client) becomes the name of the form automatically. This name could be changed, if desired.

3

- **Click the OK button.**

The form is saved as part of the database and the form closes. The Ashton James College : Database window is redisplayed.

FIGURE 1-61

Opening the Saved Form

After you have saved a form, you can use it at any time in the future by opening it. Opening a form is similar to opening a table. Before opening the form, however, the Forms object, rather than the Tables object, must be selected.

The following steps show how to open the Client form.

To Open a Form

1

• **With the Ashton James College database open and the Database window on the screen, click Forms on the Objects bar, and then right-click the Client form.**

The list of forms appears (Figure 1-62). The shortcut menu for the Client form appears.

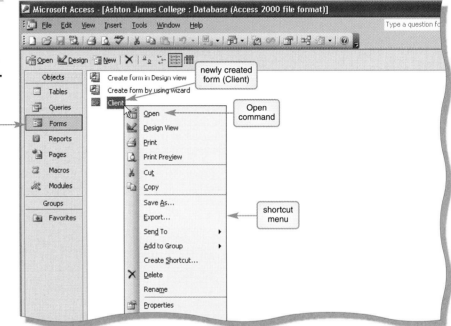

FIGURE 1-62

2

• **Click Open on the shortcut menu.**

The Client form appears (Figure 1-63).

Other Ways

1. Click Forms object, double-click desired form
2. Click Forms object, click desired form, click Open button on Database window toolbar
3. Click Forms object, click desired form, press ALT+O
4. In Voice Command mode, say "Forms, [click desired form], Open"

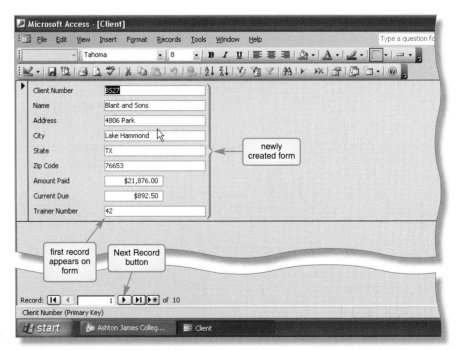

FIGURE 1-63

Using the Form

You can use the form just as you used Datasheet view. You use the Navigation buttons to move between records. You can add new records or change existing ones. To delete the record appearing on the screen, after selecting the record by clicking its record selector, press the DELETE key. Thus, you can perform database operations using either Form view or Datasheet view.

Because you can see only one record at a time in Form view, to see a different record, such as the fifth record, you must use the Navigation buttons to move to it. The following step illustrates moving from record to record in Form view.

To Use a Form

1

• **Click the Next Record button four times.**

Access displays the fifth record on the form (Figure 1-64).

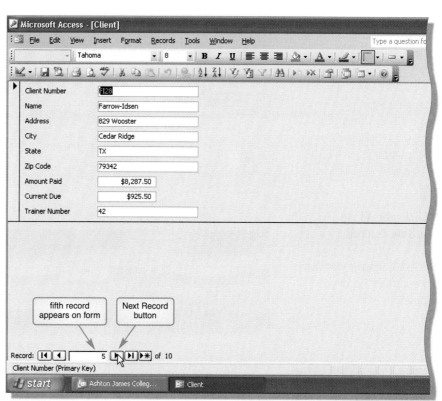

fifth record appears on form

Next Record button

FIGURE 1-64

Switching Between Form View and Datasheet View

In some cases, after you have seen a record in Form view, you will want to switch to Datasheet view to see the collection of records. The steps on the next page show how to switch from Form view to Datasheet view.

To Switch from Form View to Datasheet View

1

• **Click the View button arrow on the Form View toolbar.**

The list of available views appears (Figure 1-65).

FIGURE 1-65

2

• **Click Datasheet View.**

The table appears in Datasheet view (Figure 1-66). The record selector is positioned on the fifth record.

3

• **Click the Close Window button.**

The Client window closes and the datasheet no longer appears.

FIGURE 1-66

Other Ways

1. On View menu click Datasheet View
2. In Voice Command mode, say "View, Datasheet View"

Creating a Report

Earlier in this project, you printed a table using the Print button. The report you produced was shown in Figure 1-37 on page AC 29. While this type of report presented the data in an organized manner, the format is very rigid. You cannot select the fields to appear, for example; the report automatically includes all the fields and they appear in precisely the same order as in the table. A way to change the title of the table is not available. Therefore, it will be the same as the name of the table.

In this section, you will create the report shown in Figure 1-67. This report features significant differences from the one in Figure 1-37. The portion at the top of the report in Figure 1-67, called a **page header**, contains a custom title. The contents of this page header appear at the top of each page. The **detail lines**, which are the lines that are printed for each record, contain only those fields you specify and in the order you specify.

Client Amount Report

Client Number	Name	Amount Paid	Current Due
BS27	Blant and Sons	$21,876.00	$892.50
CE16	Center Services	$26,512.00	$2,672.00
CP27	Calder Plastics	$8,725.00	$0.00
EU28	Elba's Furniture	$4,256.00	$1,202.00
FI28	Farrow-Idsen	$8,287.50	$925.50
FL93	Fairland Lawn	$21,625.00	$0.00
HN83	Hurley National	$0.00	$0.00
MC28	Morgan-Alyssa	$24,761.00	$1,572.00
PS82	PRIM Staffing	$11,682.25	$2,827.50
TE26	Telton-Edwards	$8,521.50	$0.00

FIGURE 1-67

The following steps show how to create the report in Figure 1-67.

To Create a Report

1

• **Click Tables on the Objects bar, and then make sure the Client table is selected.**

• **Click the New Object button arrow on the Database toolbar.**

The list of available objects appears (Figure 1-68).

FIGURE 1-68

2

• **Click Report.**

Access displays the New Report dialog box (Figure 1-69).

FIGURE 1-69

3

• **Click Report Wizard, and then click the OK button.**

Access displays the Report Wizard dialog box (Figure 1-70). As you click the Next button in this dialog box, a series of options helps you create the report.

FIGURE 1-70

4

• **Click the Add Field button to add the Client Number field.**

• **Click the Add Field button to add the Name field.**

• **Add the Amount Paid and Current Due fields just as you added the Client Number and Name fields.**

The fields for the report appear in the Selected Fields box (Figure 1-71).

FIGURE 1-71

5

• **Click the Next button.**

The Report Wizard dialog box displays options to specify any grouping that is to take place (Figure 1-72).

FIGURE 1-72

6

• **Because you will not specify any grouping, click the Next button in the Report Wizard dialog box.**

• **Click the Next button a second time because you will not need to change the sort order for the records.**

The Report Wizard dialog box displays options for changing the layout and orientation of the report (Figure 1-73).

FIGURE 1-73

7

• **Make sure that Tabular is selected as the Layout and Portrait is selected as the Orientation, and then click the Next button.**

The Report Wizard dialog box displays options you can select for the style of the report (Figure 1-74).

FIGURE 1-74

8

• **Be sure the Corporate style is selected, click the Next button, and then type** Client Amount Report **as the new title.**

The Report Wizard dialog box displays the new title of the report (Figure 1-75).

FIGURE 1-75

9

• **Click the Finish button.**

Access displays a preview of the report (Figure 1-76). Your report may look slightly different, depending on your printer.

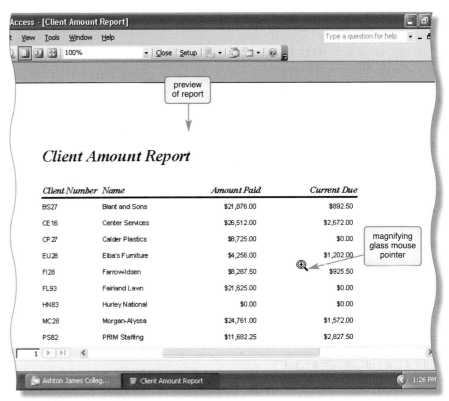

FIGURE 1-76

10

• **Click the magnifying glass mouse pointer anywhere within the report to see the entire report.**

The entire report appears (Figure 1-77).

11

• **Click the Close Window button in the Client Amount Report window.**

The report no longer appears. It has been saved automatically using the name Client Amount Report.

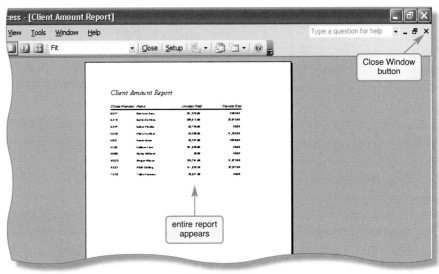

FIGURE 1-77

Other Ways

1. On Objects bar click Reports, double-click Create report by using wizard
2. On Objects bar click Reports, click New on Database window toolbar
3. On Insert menu click Report
4. In Voice Command mode, say "Insert, Report"

Printing the Report

With the report created, you can preview the report to determine if you need to change the orientation or the page margins. You also can print the report. If you want to print specific pages or select other print options, use the Print command on the File menu. The following steps on the next page show how to print a report using the shortcut menu.

To Print a Report

1

• **If necessary, click Reports on the Objects bar in the Database window.**

• **Right-click the Client Amount Report.**

The Client Amount Report is selected and the shortcut menu appears (Figure 1-78).

2

• **Click Print on the shortcut menu.**

The report prints. It should look similar to the one shown in Figure 1-67 on page AC 43.

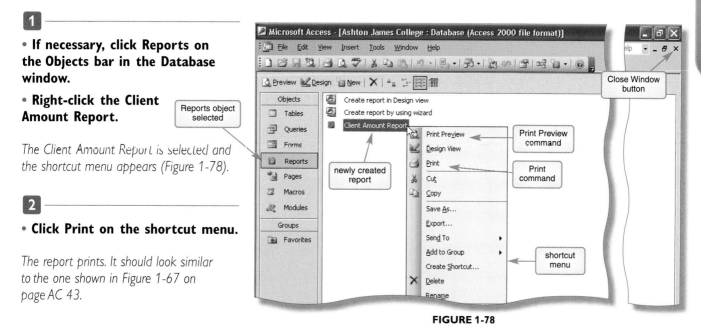

FIGURE 1-78

Closing the Database

After you have finished working with a database, you should close it. The following step closes the database by closing its Database window.

To Close a Database

1 Click the Close Window button for the Ashton James College : Database window.

Access Help System

At any time while you are using Access, you can get answers to questions by using the Access Help system. You can activate the Access Help system by using the Type a question for help box on the menu bar, by clicking the Microsoft Access Help button on the toolbar, or by clicking Help on the menu bar (Figure 1-79 on the next page). Used properly, this form of online assistance can increase your productivity and reduce your frustrations by minimizing the time you spend learning how to use Access.

The section on the next page shows how to get answers to your questions using the Type a question for help box. Additional information about using the Access Help system is available in Appendix A.

More About

The Access Help System

The best way to become familiar with the Access Help system is to use it. Appendix A includes detailed information on the Access Help system and exercises that will help you gain confidence in using it.

Obtaining Help Using the Type a Question for Help Box on the Menu Bar

The Type a question for help box on the right side of the menu bar lets you type in free-form questions, such as *how do I save* or *how do I create a Web page* or, you can type in terms, such as *copy*, *save*, or *formatting*. Access responds by displaying a list of topics related to what you entered. The following steps show how to use the Type a question for help box to obtain information on removing a primary key.

To Obtain Help Using the Type a Question for Help Box

1

• **Click the Type a question for help box on the right side of the menu bar.**

• **Type** how do I remove a primary key **in the box (Figure 1-79).**

FIGURE 1-79

2

• **Press the ENTER key.**

Access displays the Search Results task pane, which includes a list of topics relating to the question, how do I remove a primary key (Figure 1-80). Your list may be different.

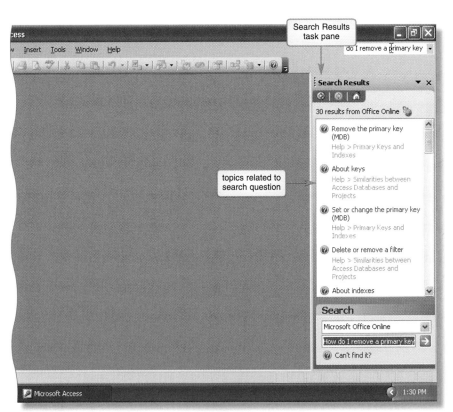

FIGURE 1-80

3

• **Point to the Remove the primary key (MDB) topic.**

The mouse pointer changes to a hand indicating it is pointing to a link (Figure 1-81).

FIGURE 1-81

4

• **Click Remove the primary key (MDB).**

Access displays a Microsoft Office Access Help window that provides Help information about removing the primary key (Figure 1-82). Your window may be in a different position.

5

• **Click the Close button on the Microsoft Office Access Help window title bar.**

The Microsoft Access Help window closes.

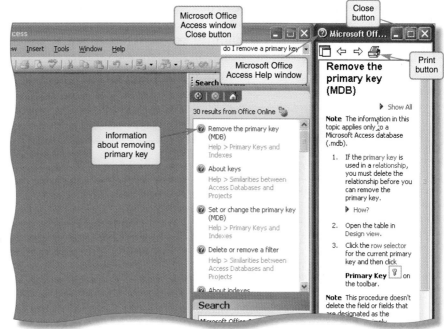

FIGURE 1-82

Use the buttons in the upper-left corner of the Microsoft Office Access Help window (Figure 1-82) to navigate through the Help system, and change the appearance and print the contents of the window.

As you enter questions and terms in the Type a question for help box, Access adds them to its list. Thus, if you click the Type a question for help box arrow, a list of previously asked questions and terms will appear.

Quitting Access

After you close a database, you can open another database, create a new database, or simply quit Access and return to the Windows desktop. The following step quits Access.

To Quit Access

1 **Click the Close button in the Microsoft Access window (see Figure 1-82 on the previous page).**

Designing a Database

More About

Database Design: Design Method

A variety of methods have been developed for designing complex databases given a set of input and output requirements. For more information about database design methods, visit the Access 2003 More About Web page (scsite.com/ac2003/more) and click Database Design.

Database design refers to the arrangement of data into tables and fields. In the example in this project, the design is specified, but in many cases, you will have to determine the design based on what you want the system to accomplish.

With large, complex databases, the database design process can be extensive. Major sections of advanced database textbooks are devoted to this topic. Often, however, you should be able to design a database effectively by keeping one simple principle in mind: design to remove redundancy. **Redundancy** means storing the same fact in more than one place.

To illustrate, you need to maintain the following information shown in Figure 1-83. In the figure, all the data is contained in a single table. Notice that the data for a given trainer (number, name, address, and so on) occurs on more than one record.

duplicate trainer names

Client table

CLIENT NUMBER	NAME	ADDRESS	...	CURRENT DUE	TRAINER NUMBER	LAST NAME	FIRST NAME	...
BS27	Blant and Sons	4806 Park	...	$892.50	42	Perry	Belinda	...
CE16	Center Services	725 Mitchell	...	$2,672.00	48	Stevens	Michael	...
CP27	Calder Plastics	7300 Cedar	...	$0.00	48	Stevens	Michael	...
EU28	Elba's Furniture	1445 Hubert	...	$1,202.00	53	Gonzalez	Manuel	...
FI28	Farrow-Idsen	829 Wooster	...	$925.50	42	Perry	Belinda	...
FL93	Fairland Lawn	143 Pangborn	...	$0.00	48	Stevens	Michael	...
HN83	Hurley National	3827 Burgess	...	$0.00	48	Stevens	Michael	...
MC28	Morgan-Alyssa	923 Williams	...	$1,572.00	42	Perry	Belinda	...
PS82	PRIM Staffing	72 Crestview	...	$2,827.50	53	Gonzalez	Manuel	...
TE26	Telton-Edwards	5672 Anderson	...	$0.00	48	Stevens	Michael	...

FIGURE 1-83

More About

The Quick Reference

For a table that lists how to complete tasks covered in this book using the mouse, menu, shortcut menu, and keyboard, see the Quick Reference Summary at the back of this book, or visit the Access 2003 Quick Reference Web page (scsite.com/ac2003/qr).

Storing this data on multiple records is an example of redundancy, which causes several problems, including:

1. Redundancy wastes space on the disk. The name of trainer 42 (Belinda Perry), for example, should be stored only once. Storing this fact several times is wasteful.

2. Redundancy makes updating the database more difficult. If, for example, Belinda Perry's name changes, her name would need to be changed in several different places.

3. A possibility of inconsistent data exists. If, for example, you change the name of Belinda Perry on client FI28's record to Belinda Martin, but do not change it on client BS27's record, the data is inconsistent. In both cases, the trainer number is 42, but the names are different.

The solution to the problem is to place the redundant data in a separate table, one in which the data no longer will be redundant. If, for example, you place the data for trainers in a separate table (Figure 1-84), the data for each trainer will appear only once.

More About

Database Design: Normalization

A special technique, called normalization, identifies and eliminates redundancy. For more information about normalization, visit the Access 2003 More About Web page (scsite.com/ac2003/more) and click Normalization.

trainer data is in separate table

Trainer table

TRAINER NUMBER	LAST NAME	FIRST NAME	ADDRESS	CITY	STATE	ZIP CODE	HOURLY RATE	YTD EARNINGS
42	Perry	Belinda	261 Porter	Burdett	TX	76734	$23.00	$27,620.00
48	Stevens	Michael	3135 Gill	Rockwood	TX	78884	$21.00	$23,567.50
53	Gonzalez	Manuel	265 Maxwell	Camino	TX	76574	$24.00	$29,885.00

Client table

CLIENT NUMBER	NAME	ADDRESS	CITY	STATE	ZIP CODE	AMOUNT PAID	CURRENT DUE	TRAINER NUMBER
BS27	Blant and Sons	4806 Park	Lake Hammond	TX	76653	$21,876.00	$892.50	42
CE16	Center Services	725 Mitchell	San Julio	TX	78364	$26,512.00	$2,672.00	48
CP27	Calder Plastics	7300 Cedar	Lake Hammond	TX	76653	$8,725.00	$0.00	48
EU28	Elba's Furniture	1445 Hubert	Tallmadge	TX	77231	$4,256.00	$1,202.00	53
FI28	Farrow-Idsen	829 Wooster	Cedar Ridge	TX	79342	$8,287.50	$925.50	42
FL93	Fairland Lawn	143 Pangborn	Lake Hammond	TX	76653	$21,625.00	$0.00	48
HN83	Hurley National	3827 Burgess	Tallmadge	TX	77231	$0.00	$0.00	48
MC28	Morgan-Alyssa	923 Williams	Crumville	TX	76745	$24,761.00	$1,572.00	42
PS82	PRIM Staffing	72 Crestview	San Julio	TX	78364	$11,682.25	$2,827.50	53
TE26	Telton-Edwards	5672 Anderson	Dunston	TX	77893	$8,521.50	$0.00	48

FIGURE 1-84

Notice that you need to have the trainer number in both tables. Without it, no way exists to tell which trainer is associated with which client. The remaining trainer data, however, was removed from the Client table and placed in the Trainer table. This new arrangement corrects the problems of redundancy in the following ways:

1. Because the data for each trainer is stored only once, space is not wasted.
2. Changing the name of a trainer is easy. You have only to change one row in the Trainer table.
3. Because the data for a trainer is stored only once, inconsistent data cannot occur.

Designing to omit redundancy will help you to produce good and valid database designs.

More About

Microsoft Certification

The Microsoft Office Specialist Certification program provides an opportunity for you to obtain a valuable industry credential — proof that you have the Access 2003 skills required by employers. For more information, see Appendix E, or visit the Access 2003 Certification Web page (scsite.com/ac2003/cert).

Microsoft Office
Access 2003

Project Summary

In Project 1, you learned about databases and database management systems. You learned how to create a database and how to create the tables within a database. You saw how to define the fields in a table by specifying the characteristics of the fields. You learned how to open a table, how to add records to it, and how to close it. You also printed the contents of a table. You learned how to use the Simple Query wizard to create a query that included columns from a table as well as how to enter a criterion to restrict the rows that were included. You created a form to view data on the screen and also created a custom report. You learned how to use Microsoft Access Help. Finally, you learned how to design a database to eliminate redundancy.

 If you have a SAM user profile, you may have access to hands-on instruction, practice, and assessment of the skills covered in this project. Log in to your SAM account and go to your assignments page to see what your instructor has assigned.

What You Should Know

Having completed this project, you should be able to perform the tasks below. The tasks are listed in the same order they were presented in this project. For a list of the buttons, menus, toolbars, and commands introduced in this project, see the Quick Reference Summary at the back of this book and refer to the Page Number column.

1. Start Access   (AC 7)
2. Close the Language Bar   (AC 9)
3. Create a New Database   (AC 10)
4. Create a Table   (AC 17)
5. Define the Fields in a Table   (AC 19)
6. Close and Save a Table   (AC 21)
7. Add Records to a Table   (AC 23)
8. Close a Table and Database and Quit Access (AC 26)
9. Open a Database   (AC 26)
10. Add Additional Records to a Table   (AC 28)
11. Preview and Print the Contents of a Table (AC 30)
12. Create an Additional Table   (AC 33)
13. Add Records to an Additional Table   (AC 34)

14. Use the Simple Query Wizard to Create a Query (AC 34)
15. Use a Query   (AC 37)
16. Use the New Object Button to Create a Form (AC 38)
17. Close and Save a Form   (AC 39)
18. Open a Form   (AC 40)
19. Use a Form   (AC 41)
20. Switch from Form View to Datasheet View (AC 42)
21. Create a Report   (AC 43)
22. Print a Report   (AC 47)
23. Close a Database   (AC 47)
24. Obtain Help Using the Type a Question for Help Box   (AC 48)
25. Quit Access   (AC 50)

Learn It Online

Instructions: To complete the Learn It Online exercises, start your browser, click the Address bar, and then enter the Web address scsite.com/ac2003/learn. When the Access 2003 Learn It Online page is displayed, follow the instructions in the exercises below. Each exercise has instructions for printing your results, either for your own records or for submission to your instructor.

1 Project Reinforcement TF, MC, and SA

Below Access Project 1, click the Project Reinforcement link. Print the quiz by clicking Print on the File menu for each page. Answer each question.

2 Flash Cards

Below Access Project 1, click the Flash Cards link and read the instructions. Type 20 (or a number specified by your instructor) in the Number of playing cards text box, type your name in the Enter your Name text box, and then click the Flip Card button. When the flash card is displayed, read the question and then click the ANSWER box arrow to select an answer. Flip through Flash Cards. If your score is 15 (75%) correct or greater, click Print on the File menu to print your results. If your score is less than 15 (75%) correct, then redo this exercise by clicking the Replay button.

3 Practice Test

Below Access Project 1, click the Practice Test link. Answer each question, enter your first and last name at the bottom of the page, and then click the Grade Test button. When the graded practice test is displayed on your screen, click Print on the File menu to print a hard copy. Continue to take practice tests until you score 80% or better.

4 Who Wants To Be a Computer Genius?

Below Access Project 1, click the Computer Genius link. Read the instructions, enter your first and last name at the bottom of the page, and then click the PLAY button. When your score is displayed, click the PRINT RESULTS link to print a hard copy.

5 Wheel of Terms

Below Access Project 1, click the Wheel of Terms link. Read the instructions, and then enter your first and last name and your school name. Click the PLAY button. When your score is displayed, right-click the score and then click Print on the shortcut menu to print a hard copy.

6 Crossword Puzzle Challenge

Below Access Project 1, click the Crossword Puzzle Challenge link. Read the instructions, and then enter your first and last name. Click the SUBMIT button. Work the crossword puzzle. When you are finished, click the Submit button. When the crossword puzzle is redisplayed, click the Print Puzzle button to print a hard copy.

7 Tips and Tricks

Below Access Project 1, click the Tips and Tricks link. Click a topic that pertains to Project 1. Right-click the information and then click Print on the shortcut menu. Construct a brief example of what the information relates to in Access to confirm you understand how to use the tip or trick.

8 Newsgroups

Below Access Project 1, click the Newsgroups link. Click a topic that pertains to Project 1. Print three comments.

9 Expanding Your Horizons

Below Access Project 1, click the Expanding Your Horizons link. Click a topic that pertains to Project 1. Print the information. Construct a brief example of what the information relates to in Access to confirm you understand the contents of the article.

10 Search Sleuth

Below Access Project 1, click the Search Sleuth link. To search for a term that pertains to this project, select a term below the Project 1 title and then use the Google search engine at google.com (or any major search engine) to display and print two Web pages that present information on the term.

11 Access Online Training

Below Access Project 1, click the Access Online Training link. When your browser displays the Microsoft Office Online Web page, click the Access link. Click one of the Access courses that covers one or more of the objectives listed at the beginning of the project on page AC 4. Print the first page of the course before stepping through it.

12 Office Marketplace

Below Access Project 1, click the Office Marketplace link. When your browser displays the Microsoft Office Online Web page, click the Office Marketplace link. Click a topic that relates to Access. Print the first page.

Apply Your Knowledge

1 Changing Data, Creating Queries, and Creating Reports

Instructions: Start Access. Open the database Begon Pest Control from the Data Disk. See the inside back cover for instructions for downloading the Data Disk or see your instructor for information about accessing the files required in this book.

Begon Pest Control is a company that performs pest control services for commercial businesses. Begon has a database that keeps track of its technicians and customers. The database has two tables. The Customer table contains data on the customers who use the services of Begon. The Technician table contains data on the individuals employed by Begon. The structure and data are shown for the Customer table in Figure 1-85 and for the Technician table in Figure 1-86.

Structure of Customer table

FIELD NAME	DATA TYPE	FIELD SIZE	PRIMARY KEY?	DESCRIPTION
Customer Number	Text	4	Yes	Customer Number (Primary Key)
Name	Text	20		Customer Name
Address	Text	15		Street Address
City	Text	15		City
State	Text	2		State (Two-Character Abbreviation)
Zip Code	Text	5		Zip Code (Five-Character Version)
Balance	Currency			Amount Owed by Customer
Technician Number	Text	3		Number of Customer's Technician

Customer table

CUSTOMER NUMBER	NAME	ADDRESS	CITY	STATE	ZIP CODE	BALANCE	TECHNICIAN NUMBER
AT23	Atlas Repair	220 Beard	Kady	TN	42514	$335.00	203
AZ01	AZ Auto	412 Beechwood	Conradt	TN	42547	$300.00	210
BL35	Blanton Shoes	443 Chedder	Kady	TN	42514	$290.00	210
CJ45	C Joe Diner	87 Fletcher	Carlton	TN	52764	$0.00	214
CM90	Cramden Co.	234 Fairlawn	Conradt	TN	42546	$355.00	203
HI25	Hill Crafts	245 Beard	Kady	TN	42514	$334.00	210
KL50	Klean n Dri	378 Stout	Carlton	TN	52764	$365.00	210
MC10	Moss Carpet	109 Fletcher	Carlton	TN	52764	$398.00	203
PV83	Prime Video	734 Lanton	Conradt	TN	42547	$0.00	214
SE05	Servete Mfg Co.	879 Redfern	Kady	TN	42515	$343.00	210

FIGURE 1-85

Apply Your Knowledge

Structure of Technician table

FIELD NAME	DATA TYPE	FIELD SIZE	PRIMARY KEY?	DESCRIPTION
Technician Number	Text	3	Yes	Technician Number (Primary Key)
Last Name	Text	10		Last Name of Technician
First Name	Text	8		First Name of Technician
Address	Text	15		Street Address
City	Text	15		City
State	Text	2		State (Two-Character Abbreviation)
Zip Code	Text	5		Zip Code (Five-Character Version)
Hourly Rate	Currency			Hourly Pay Rate

Technician table

TECHNICIAN NUMBER	LAST NAME	FIRST NAME	ADDRESS	CITY	STATE	ZIP CODE	HOURLY RATE
203	Estevez	Miguel	467 Clay	Kady	TN	42517	$11.50
210	Hillsdale	Rachel	78 Parkton	Conradt	TN	42547	$11.75
214	Liu	Chou	897 North	Carlton	TN	52764	$11.65
220	Short	Chris	111 Maple	Conradt	TN	42547	$11.50

FIGURE 1-86

Instructions: Perform the following tasks:

1. Open the Customer table and change the Technician Number for customer KL50 to 214.
2. Print the Customer table.
3. Use the Simple Query Wizard to create a new query to display and print the customer number, name, and technician number for records in the Customer table as shown in Figure 1-87 on the next page.
4. Save the query as Customer-Technician Query and then close the query.
5. Open the Customer-Technician Query in Design View and restrict the query results to only those customers whose technician number is 210.
6. Print the query but do not save the changes.
7. Create the report shown in Figure 1-88 on the next page for the Customer table.
8. Print the report.

(continued)

Microsoft Office
Access 2003

Apply Your Knowledge

Changing Data, Creating Queries, and Creating Reports *(continued)*

Microsoft Access - [Customer-Technician Query :

File Edit View Insert Format Records Tools

Customer Numb	Name	Technician Num
AT23	Atlas Repair	203
AZ01	AZ Auto	210
BL35	Blanton Shoes	210
CJ45	C Joe Diner	214
CM90	Cramden Co.	203
HI25	Hill Crafts	210
KL50	Klean n Dri	214
MC10	Moss Carpet	203
PV83	Prime Video	214
SE05	Servete Mfg Co.	210

FIGURE 1-87

Customer Amount Report

Customer Number	Name	Balance
AT23	Atlas Repair	$335.00
AZ01	AZ Auto	$300.00
BL35	Blanton Shoes	$290.00
CJ45	C Joe Diner	$0.00
CM90	Cramden Co.	$355.00
HI25	Hill Crafts	$334.00
KL50	Klean n Dri	$365.00
MC10	Moss Carpet	$398.00
PV83	Prime Video	$0.00
SE05	Servete Mfg Co.	$343.00

FIGURE 1-88

In the Lab

1 Creating the Birds2U Database

Problem: Birds2U is a new online retailer. The company specializes in products for bird and nature enthusiasts. The database consists of two tables. The Item table contains information on items available for sale. The Supplier table contains information on the companies that supply the items.

Instructions: Perform the following tasks:

1. Create a new database in which to store all the objects related to the items for sale. Call the database Birds2U.
2. Create the Item table using the structure shown in Figure 1-89. Use the name Item for the table.
3. Add the data shown in Figure 1-89 to the Item table.
4. Print the Item table.

Structure of Item table

FIELD NAME	DATA TYPE	FIELD SIZE	PRIMARY KEY?	DESCRIPTION
Item Code	Text	4	Yes	Item Code (Primary Key)
Description	Text	20		Description of Item
On Hand	Number			Number of Units On Hand
Cost	Currency			Cost of Item
Selling Price	Currency			Selling Price of Item
Supplier Code	Text	2		Code of Item's Supplier

Item table

ITEM CODE	DESCRIPTION	ON HAND	COST	SELLING PRICE	SUPPLIER CODE
BA35	Bat House	14	$43.50	$45.50	21
BB01	Bird Bath	2	$82.10	$86.25	13
BE19	Bee Box	7	$39.80	$42.50	21
BL06	Bluebird House	9	$14.35	$15.99	13
BU24	Butterfly Box	6	$36.10	$37.75	21
GF12	Globe Feeder	12	$14.80	$16.25	05
HF01	Hummingbird Feeder	5	$11.35	$14.25	05
PM05	Purple Martin House	3	$67.10	$69.95	13
SF03	Suet Feeder	7	$8.05	$9.95	05
WF10	Window Feeder	10	$14.25	$15.95	05

FIGURE 1-89

5. Create the Supplier table using the structure shown in Figure 1-90 on the next page. Use the name Supplier for the table.
6. Add the data shown in Figure 1-90 to the Supplier table.
7. Print the Supplier table.
8. Create a form for the Supplier table. Use the name Supplier for the form.
9. Open the form you created and change the address for Supplier Code 17 to 56 Beechwood.
10. Create and print the report shown in Figure 1-91 on the next page for the Item table.

(continued)

In the Lab

Creating the Birds2U Database *(continued)*

Structure of Supplier table

FIELD NAME	DATA TYPE	FIELD SIZE	PRIMARY KEY?	DESCRIPTION
Supplier Code	Text	2	Yes	Supplier Code (Primary Key)
Name	Text	20		Supplier Name
Address	Text	15		Street Address
City	Text	15		City
State	Text	2		State (Two-Character Abbreviation)
Zip Code	Text	5		Zip Code (Five-Character Version)
Telephone Number	Text	12		Telephone Number (999-999-9999 Version)

Supplier table

SUPPLIER CODE	NAME	ADDRESS	CITY	STATE	ZIP CODE	TELEPHONE NUMBER
05	All Birds Supply	234 Southward	Elgin	AZ	85165	602-555-6756
13	Bird Casa Ltd	38 Junction	Grandber	TX	78628	512-555-3402
17	Lawn Fixtures	56 Beecham	Holligan	CA	95418	707-555-4545
21	Natural Woods	67 Main	Ghostman	MI	49301	610-555-3333

FIGURE 1-90

Inventory Report

Item Code	Description	On Hand	Cost
BA35	Bat House	14	$43.50
BB01	Bird Bath	2	$82.10
BE19	Bee Box	7	$39.80
BL06	Bluebird House	9	$14.35
BU24	Butterfly Box	6	$36.10
GF12	Globe Feeder	12	$14.80
HF01	Hummingbird Feeder	5	$11.35
PM05	Purple Martin House	3	$67.10
SF03	Suet Feeder	7	$8.05
WF10	Window Feeder	10	$14.25

FIGURE 1-91

In the Lab

2 Creating the Babbage Bookkeeping Database

Problem: Babbage Bookkeeping is a local company that provides bookkeeping services to several small businesses in the area. The database consists of two tables. The Client table contains information on the businesses that use Babbage's services. The Bookkeeper table contains information on the bookkeeper assigned to the business.

Instructions: Perform the following tasks:

1. Create a new database in which to store all the objects related to the bookkeeping data. Call the database Babbage Bookkeeping.
2. Create and print the Client table using the structure and data shown in Figure 1-92. Then, create and print the Bookkeeper table using the structure and data shown in Figure 1-93 on the next page.

Structure of Client table

FIELD NAME	DATA TYPE	FIELD SIZE	PRIMARY KEY?	DESCRIPTION
Client Number	Text	3	Yes	Client Number (Primary Key)
Name	Text	20		Name of Client
Address	Text	15		Street Address
City	Text	15		City
Zip Code	Text	5		Zip Code (Five-Character Version)
Balance	Currency			Amount Currently Owed for Services
Bookkeeper Number	Text	2		Number of Client's Bookkeeper

Client table

CLIENT NUMBER	NAME	ADDRESS	CITY	ZIP CODE	BALANCE	BOOKKEEPER NUMBER
A54	Afton Mills	612 Revere	Grant City	58120	$315.50	22
A62	Atlas Suppliers	227 Dandelion	Empeer	58216	$525.00	24
B26	Blake-Scripps	557 Maum	Grant City	58120	$229.50	24
D76	Dege Grocery	446 Linton	Portage	59130	$485.75	34
G56	Grand Cleaners	337 Abelard	Empeer	58216	$265.00	22
H21	Hill Shoes	247 Fulton	Grant City	58121	$228.50	24
J77	Jones Plumbing	75 Getty	Portage	59130	$0.00	24
M26	Mohr Crafts	665 Maum	Empeer	58216	$312.50	22
S56	SeeSaw Ind.	31 Liatris	Portage	59130	$362.50	34
T45	Tate Repair	824 Revere	Grant City	58120	$254.00	24

FIGURE 1-92

(continued)

Creating the Babbage Bookkeeping Database *(continued)*

Structure of Bookkeeper table

FIELD NAME	DATA TYPE	FIELD SIZE	PRIMARY KEY?	DESCRIPTION
Bookkeeper Number	Text	2	Yes	Bookkeeper Number (Primary Key)
Last Name	Text	10		Last Name of Bookkeeper
First Name	Text	8		First Name of Bookkeeper
Address	Text	15		Street Address
City	Text	15		City
Zip Code	Text	5		Zip Code (Five-Character Version)
Hourly Rate	Currency			Hourly Rate
YTD Earnings	Currency			Year-to-Date Earnings

Bookkeeper table

BOOKKEEPER NUMBER	LAST NAME	FIRST NAME	ADDRESS	CITY	ZIP CODE	HOURLY RATE	YTD EARNINGS
22	Lewes	Johanna	26 Cotton	Portage	59130	$14.50	$18,245.00
24	Rodriguez	Mario	79 Marsden	Grant City	58120	$13.50	$17,745.50
34	Wong	Choi	263 Topper	Empeer	58216	$14.00	$16,750.25

FIGURE 1-93

3. Change the Bookkeeper Number for client J77 to 34.
4. Use the Simple Query Wizard to create a new query to display and print the Client Number, Name, and Bookkeeper Number for all clients where the bookkeeper number is 24.
5. Create and print the report shown in Figure 1-94 for the Client table.

Balance Due Report

Client Number	Name	Balance
A54	Afton Mills	$315.50
A62	Atlas Suppliers	$525.00
B26	Blake-Scripps	$229.50
D76	Dege Grocery	$485.75
G56	Grand Cleaners	$265.00
H21	Hill Shoes	$228.50
J77	Jones Plumbing	$0.00
M26	Mohr Crafts	$312.50
S56	SeeSaw Ind.	$362.50
T45	Tate Repair	$254.00

FIGURE 1-94

In the Lab

3 Creating the City Guide Database

Problem: The local chamber of commerce publishes a guide for newcomers. To help finance the guide, the chamber includes advertisements from local businesses. Advertising representatives receive a commission based on the advertising revenues they generate. The database consists of two tables. The Advertiser table contains information on the businesses that advertise in the guide. The Ad Rep table contains information on the advertising representative assigned to the account.

Instructions Part 1: Using the data shown in Figures 1-95 and 1-96 on the next page create the City Guide database, the Advertiser table, and the Ad Rep table. Note that the Ad Rep table uses the number data type. Print the tables. Then, create a form for the Advertiser table.

Structure of Advertiser table

FIELD NAME	DATA TYPE	FIELD SIZE	PRIMARY KEY?	DESCRIPTION
Advertiser Number	Text	4	Yes	Advertiser Number (Primary Key)
Name	Text	20		Name of Advertiser
Address	Text	15		Street Address
Zip Code	Text	5		Zip Code (Five-Character Version)
Telephone Number	Text	8		Telephone Number (999-9999 Version)
Balance	Currency			Amount Currently Owed
Amount Paid	Currency			Amount Paid Year-to-Date
Ad Rep Number	Text	2		Number of Advertising Representative

Data for Advertiser table

ADVERTISER NUMBER	NAME	ADDRESS	ZIP CODE	TELEPHONE NUMBER	BALANCE	AMOUNT PAID	AD REP NUMBER
A228	Adam's Music	47 Berton	19363	555-0909	$90.00	$565.00	26
B103	Barbecue Joint	483 Cantor	19363	555-8990	$185.00	$825.00	29
C048	Chloe's Salon	10 Main	19362	555-2334	$0.00	$375.00	29
C135	Creative Toys	26 Jefferson	19362	555-1357	$130.00	$865.00	32
D217	Dog Groomers	33 Maple	19362	555-2468	$290.00	$515.00	26
G346	Gold's Clothes	196 Lincoln	19364	555-3579	$0.00	$805.00	29
M321	Meat Shoppe	234 Magnolia	19363	555-6802	$215.00	$845.00	29
P124	Palace Theatre	22 Main	19364	555-8024	$65.00	$180.00	26
S111	Suds n Spuds	10 Jefferson	19365	555-5791	$465.00	$530.00	32
W456	Western Wear	345 Oaktree	19363	555-7913	$105.00	$265.00	26

FIGURE 1-95

(continued)

Creating the City Guide Database *(continued)*

Structure for Ad Rep table

FIELD NAME	DATA TYPE	FIELD SIZE	PRIMARY KEY?	DESCRIPTION
Ad Rep Number	Text	2	Yes	Advertising Rep Number (Primary Key)
Last Name	Text	10		Last Name of Advertising Rep
First Name	Text	8		First Name of Advertising Rep
Address	Text	15		Street Address
City	Text	15		City
Zip Code	Text	5		Zip Code (Five-Character Version)
Comm Rate	Number	Double		Commission Rate on Advertising Sales
Commission	Currency			Year-to-Date Total Commissions

Data for Ad Rep table

AD REP NUMBER	LAST NAME	FIRST NAME	ADDRESS	CITY	ZIP CODE	COMM RATE	COMMISSION
26	Febo	Jen	57 Barton	Crescent	19111	0.09	$6,500.00
29	Martinson	Kyle	87 Pearl	Newton	19124	0.08	$6,250.00
32	Rogers	Elena	45 Magret	San Luis	19362	0.09	$7,000.00

FIGURE 1-96

Instructions Part 2: Correct the following error. The ad rep assigned to the Meat Shoppe account should be Elena Rogers. Use the form you created to make the correction, and then print the form showing the corrected record. To print the form, open the form, click File on the menu bar, and then click Print. Click Selected Records(s) as the Print Range. Click the OK button.

Instructions Part 3: Create a query to find which accounts Kyle Martinson represents. Print the results. Prepare an advertiser status report that lists the advertiser's number, name, balance currently owed, and amount paid to date.

Cases and Places

The difficulty of these case studies varies:
■ are the least difficult and ■■ are more difficult. The last exercise is a group exercise.

1 ■ To help finance your college education, you formed a small business. You provide dog-walking services to local residents. Dog walkers are paid by the walk for each dog they walk. The business has grown rapidly and you now have several other students working for you. You realize that you need to computerize your business.

Design and create a database to store the data that College Dog Walkers needs to manage its business. Then create the necessary tables and enter the data from the Case 1-1 College Dog Walkers Word document on the Data Disk. Print the tables. See the inside back cover of this book for instructions for downloading the Data Disk or see your instructor for information on accessing the files required in this book.

2 ■ The Health and Physical Education department at your college recognized early that personal training would be a growth field. One of your friends graduated from the program and has started a company, InPerson Fitness Company. The company specializes in personal training in the comfort of the customer's home. It designs exercise programs for clients based on each person's health history, abilities, and fitness objectives. The company is expanding rapidly and you have been hired to computerize the business.

Design and create a database to store the data that InPerson Fitness needs to manage its business. Then create the necessary tables and enter the data from the Case 1-2 InPerson Fitness Word document on the Data Disk. Print the tables. See the inside back cover of this book for instructions for downloading the Data Disk or see your instructor for information on accessing the files required in this book.

3 ■■ Regional Books is a local bookstore that specializes in books that are of local interest. These are books that are set in the region or are written by authors who live in the area. The owner has asked you to create and update a database that she can use to keep track of the books she has in stock.

Design and create a database to store the book data. To create the Books table, use the Table Wizard and select the Books table. You do not need to select all the fields the Table Wizard provides and you can rename the fields in the table. (**Hint**: See More About Creating a Table: The Table Wizard on page AC 15.) Enter the data from the Case 1-3 Regional Books Word document on the Data Disk. Print the tables. Prepare a sample query and a sample report to illustrate to the owner the types of tasks that can be done with a database management system. See the inside back cover of this book for instructions for downloading the Data Disk or see your instructor for information on accessing the files required in this book.

Cases and Places

4 ■■ The Campus Housing office at the local university provides a listing of available off-campus rentals by private owners. The office would like to make this listing available on the campus Web site. The administrator has asked you to create and update a database that can store information about available off-campus housing. The housing list is in the Case 1-4 Campus Housing Word document on the Data Disk. A listing that has 0 bedrooms is either an efficiency apartment or a room for rent in a home. Distance indicates the rental unit's distance in miles from the university. Parking signifies whether reserved parking is available with the unit.

Design and create a database to meet the needs of the Campus Housing office. Then create the necessary tables, enter the data from the Case 1-4 Campus Housing Word document on the Data Disk. Print the tables. Prepare a sample form, sample query, and sample report to illustrate to the office the types of tasks that can be done with a database management system. See the inside back cover of this book for instructions for downloading the Data Disk or see your instructor for information on accessing the files required in this book.

5 ■■ **Working Together** Conducting a job search requires careful preparation. In addition to preparing a resume and cover letter, you will need to research the companies for which you are interested in working and contact these companies to let them know of your interest and qualifications. Microsoft Access can help you manage the job search process. The Database Wizard includes a Contact Management template that can create a database that will help you keep track of your job contacts.

Have each member of your team explore the features of the Database Wizard and determine individually which fields should be included in a Contact Management database. As a group, review your choices and decide on one common design. Prepare a short paper for your instructor that explains why your team chose those particular fields to include in the database.

After agreeing on the database design, assign one member to create the database using the Database Wizard. Every other team member should research a company and add the data to the database. Print the alphabetical contact listing that the Database Wizard creates. Turn in the short paper and the report to your instructor.

Querying a Database Using the Select Query Window

PROJECT

2

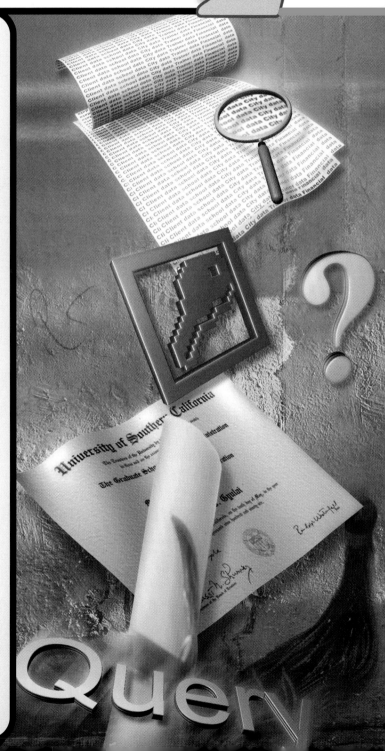

CASE PERSPECTIVE

Dr. Gernaey and his colleagues are eager for Ashton James College (AJC) to obtain the benefits they anticipated when they set up the database of client and trainer data. One immediate benefit they expect is the capability of easily asking questions such as the following concerning the data in the database and rapidly getting the answers.

1. What are the name, the amount paid, and the current due of client CP27?

2. Which clients' names begin with Fa?

3. Which clients are located in Lake Hammond?

4. Which clients have a current due of $0.00?

5. Which clients have an amount paid that is more than $20,000.00?

6. Which clients of trainer 48 have an amount paid that is more than $20,000.00?

7. In what cities are all the clients located?

8. How many hours has each trainer worked so far this year?

9. What is the client number and name of each client, and what is the number and name of the trainer to whom each client is assigned?

AJC needs to find information about clients located in a specific city, but they want to enter a different city each time they ask the question. A parameter query would enable this. They also have a special way they want to summarize their data and a crosstab query will present the data in the desired form.

Your task is to assist the administration of AJC in obtaining answers to these and other questions using Access query features.

As you read through this project, you will learn how to query a database and use the Select Query window.

MICROSOFT
Office Access 2003

Querying a Database Using the Select Query Window

Objectives:

You will have mastered the material in this project when you can:

- Create and run queries
- Print query results
- Include fields in the design grid
- Use text and numeric data in criteria
- Create and use parameter queries
- Save a query and use the saved query

- Use compound criteria in queries
- Sort data in queries
- Join tables in queries
- Perform calculations in queries
- Use grouping in queries
- Create crosstab queries

Introduction

A database management system such as Access offers many useful features, among them the capability of answering questions such as those posed by the administration of Ashton James College (Figure 2-1). The answers to these questions, and many more, are found in the database, and Access can find the answers quickly. When you pose a question to Access, or any other database management system, the question is called a query. A **query** is simply a question represented in a way that Access can understand.

Thus, to find the answer to a question, you first create a corresponding query using the techniques illustrated in this project. After you have created the query, you instruct Access to run the query; that is, to perform the steps necessary to obtain the answer. Access then will display the answer in Datasheet view.

Project Two — Querying the Ashton James College Database

The steps in this project obtain answers to the questions posed by the administration of Ashton James College. These include the questions shown in Figure 2-1, as well as many other questions that may be deemed important.

- What are the name, the amount paid, and the current due for client CP27?
- Which clients' names begin with Fa?
- In what cities are all the clients located?
- Which clients are located in Lake Hammond?
- Which clients of trainer 48 have an amount paid that is more than $20,000.00?

Client table

CLIENT NUMBER	NAME	ADDRESS	CITY	STATE	ZIP CODE	AMOUNT PAID	CURRENT DUE	TRAINER NUMBER
BS27	Blant and Sons	4806 Park	Lake Hammond	TX	76653	$21,876.00	$892.50	42
CE16	Center Services	725 Mitchell	San Julio	TX	78364	$26,512.00	$2,672.00	48
CP27	Calder Plastics	7300 Cedar	Lake Hammond	TX	76653	$8,725.00	$0.00	48
EU28	Elba's Furniture	1445 Hubert	Tallmadge	TX	77231	$4,256.00	$1,202.00	53
FI28	Farrow-Idsen	829 Wooster	Cedar Ridge	TX	79342	$8,287.50	$925.50	42
FL93	Fairland Lawn	143 Pangborn	Lake Hammond	TX	76653	$21,625.00	$0.00	48
HN83	Hurley National	3827 Burgess	Tallmadge	TX	77231	$0.00	$0.00	48
MC28	Morgan-Alyssa	923 Williams	Crumville	TX	76745	$24,761.00	$1,572.00	42
PS82	PRIM Staffing	72 Crestview	San Julio	TX	78364	$11,682.25	$2,827.50	53
TE26	Telton-Edwards	5672 Anderson	Dunston	TX	77893	$8,521.50	$0.00	48

CLIENT NUMBER	NAME	AMOUNT PAID	CURRENT DUE
FI28	Farrow-Idsen	$8,287.50	$925.50
FL93	Fairland Lawn	$21,625.00	$0.00

CLIENT NUMBER	NAME	ADDRESS
BS27	Blant and Sons	4806 Park
CP27	Calder Plastics	7300 Cedar
FL93	Fairland Lawn	143 Pangborn

CLIENT NUMBER	NAME	AMOUNT PAID	CURRENT DUE
CP27	Calder Plastics	$8,725.00	$0.00

CITY
Cedar Ridge
Crumville
Dunston
Lake Hammond
Tallmadge

CLIENT NUMBER	NAME	AMOUNT PAID	CURRENT DUE	TRAINER NUMBER
CE16	Center Services	$26,512.00	$2,672.00	48
FL93	Fairland Lawn	$21,625.00	$0.00	48

FIGURE 2-1

More About

Queries: Query Languages

Before the advent of query languages in the mid-1970s, obtaining answers to questions concerning data in a database was very difficult, requiring that someone write lengthy (several hundred line) programs in languages such as COBOL. Query languages made it easy to obtain answers to such questions.

More About

The Access Help System

Need Help? It is no further than the Type a question for help box on the menu bar in the upper-right corner of the window. Click the box that contains the text, Type a question for help (Figure 2-5), type help, and then press the ENTER key. Access responds with a list of topics you can click to learn about obtaining help on any Access-related topic. To find out what is new in Access 2003, type what is new in Access in the Type a question for help box.

Opening the Database

If you are stepping through this project on a computer, and you want your screen to agree with the figures in this book, then you should change your computer's resolution to 800 × 600. For more information on how to change the resolution on your computer, see Appendix D. Before creating queries, first you must open the database. The following steps summarize the procedure to complete this task, once you have started Access.

To Open a Database

1 Click the Open button on the Database toolbar.

2 If necessary, click the Look in box arrow and then click 3½ Floppy (A:). Click Ashton James College, the database created in Project 1. (If you did not complete the steps in Project 1, see your instructor for a copy of the database.)

3 Click the Open button in the Open dialog box. If a Security Warning dialog box appears, click the Open button.

The database opens and the Ashton James College : Database window appears.

Creating and Running Queries

You create a query by making entries in a special window called a **Select Query window**. Once the database is open, the first step in creating a query is to select the table for which you are creating a query in the Database window. Then, you use the New Object button to design the new query in the Select Query window. It typically is easier to work with the Select Query window if it is maximized. Thus, as a standard practice, maximize the Select Query window as soon as you have created it. In addition, it often is useful to resize both panes within the window. This enables you to resize the field list that appears in the upper pane so more fields appear.

The following steps initiate creating a query.

To Create a Query

1

• **Be sure the Ashton James College database is open, the Tables object is selected, and the Client table is selected.**

• **Click the New Object button arrow on the Database toolbar.**

The list of available objects appears (Figure 2-2).

FIGURE 2-2

2

• **Click Query.**

Access displays the New Query dialog box
(Figure 2-3).

FIGURE 2-3

3

• **With Design View
selected, click the OK
button.**

The Query1 : Select
Query window appears
(Figure 2-4).

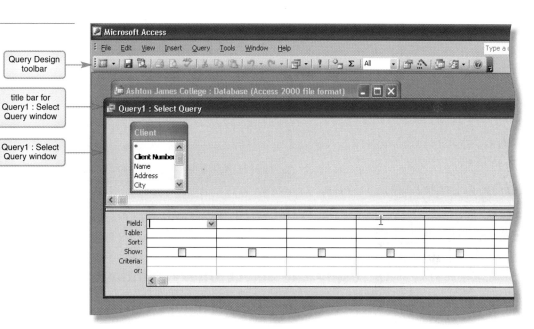

FIGURE 2-4

4

• **Maximize the Query1 : Select
Query window by double-clicking
its title bar, and then drag the line
separating the two panes to the
approximate position shown in
Figure 2-5.**

The Query1 : Select Query
window is maximized. The
upper pane contains a field list
for the Client table. The lower
pane contains the **design grid**,
which is the area where you
specify fields to be included, sort
order, and the criteria the records you are
looking for must satisfy. The mouse pointer
shape indicates you can drag the line.

FIGURE 2-5

Microsoft Office
Access 2003

5

• **Drag the lower edge of the field box down far enough so all fields in the Client table are displayed (Figure 2-6).**

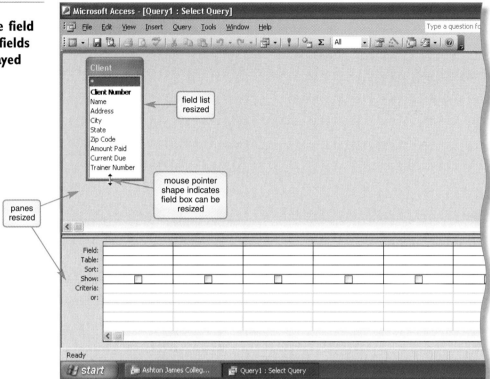

FIGURE 2-6

Other Ways

1. Click Queries object, double-click Create query in Design view
2. On Insert menu click Query
3. In Voice Command mode, say "Insert, Query"

More About

Queries: Query-by-Example

Query-by-Example, often referred to as QBE, was a query language first proposed in the mid-1970s. In this approach, users asked questions by filling in a table on the screen. The approach to queries taken by several DBMSs is based on Query-by-Example. For more information, visit the Access 2003 More About Web page (scsite.com/ac2003/more) and click QBE.

Using the Select Query Window

Once you have created a new Select Query window, you are ready to create the actual query by making entries in the design grid in the lower pane of the window. You enter the names of the fields you want included in the Field row in the grid. You also can enter criteria, such as the fact that the client number must be a specific number, such as CP27, in the Criteria row of the grid. When you do so, only the record or records that match the criterion will be included in the answer.

Displaying Selected Fields in a Query

Only the fields that appear in the design grid will be included in the results of the query. Thus, to include only certain fields, place only these fields in the grid, and no others. If you place the wrong field in the grid inadvertently, click Edit on the menu bar and then click Delete to remove it. Alternatively, you could click Clear Grid on the Edit menu to clear the entire design grid and then start over.

The following step creates a query to show the client number, name, and trainer number for all clients by including only those fields in the design grid.

To Include Fields in the Design Grid

1

• If necessary, maximize the Query1 : Select Query window containing the field list for the Client table in the upper pane of the window and an empty design grid in the lower pane.

• Double-click the Client Number field in the field list to include it in the query.

• Double-click the Name field to include it in the query, and then double-click the Trainer Number field to include it as well.

The Client Number, Name, and Trainer Number fields are included in the query (Figure 2-7).

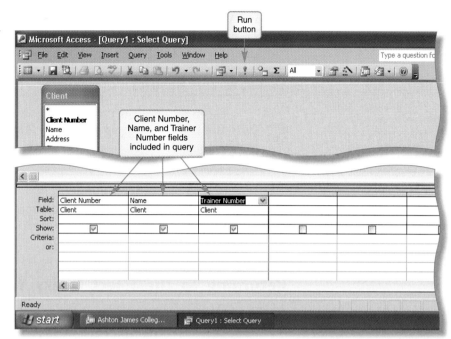

FIGURE 2-7

Running a Query

Once you have created the query, you run the query to produce the results using the Run button on the Query Design toolbar. Access performs the steps necessary to obtain and display the answer. The set of records that makes up the answer will be displayed in Datasheet view. Although it looks like a table that is stored on your disk, it really is not. The records are constructed from data in the existing Client table. If you were to change the data in the Client table and then rerun this same query, the results would reflect the changes. The following step runs the query.

To Run the Query

1

• Click the Run button on the Query Design toolbar (see Figure 2-7).

The query is executed and the results appear (Figure 2-8).

FIGURE 2-8

More About

Queries: SQL

The most widespread of
all the query languages is a
language called SQL. In SQL,
users type commands such
as SELECT CURRENT DUE
FROM CUSTOMER WHERE
CITY = "Tallmadge" to find
the current due amounts
of all customers located in
Tallmadge. Many database
management systems, including Access, offer SQL as one
option for querying databases.
For more information, visit
the Access 2003 More
About Web page
(scsite.com/ac2003/more)
and click SQL.

Printing the Results of a Query

To print the results of a query, use the same techniques you learned in Project 1 on page AC 29 to print the data in the table. The following step prints the current query results.

To Print the Results of a Query

1 **Click the Print button on the Query Datasheet toolbar (see Figure 2-8 on the previous page).**

The results print.

If the results of a query require landscape orientation, switch to landscape orientation before you click the Print button as indicated in Project 1 on page AC 31.

Returning to the Select Query Window

You can examine the results of a query on your screen to see the answer to your question. You can scroll through the records, if necessary, just as you scroll through the records of any other table. You also can print a copy of the table. In any case, once you are finished working with the results, you can return to the Select Query window to ask another question. The following steps illustrate how to return to the Select Query window.

To Return to the Select Query Window

1

• **Click the View button arrow on the Query Datasheet toolbar.**

The Query View list appears (Figure 2-9).

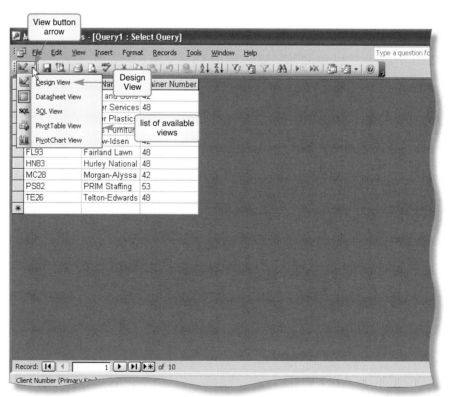

FIGURE 2-9

2

• **Click Design View.**

The Query1 : Select Query window is redisplayed (Figure 2-10).

FIGURE 2-10

Other Ways

1. On View menu click Design View
2. In Voice Command mode, say "View, Design View"

Notice that the icon on the View button is the Design View icon. This indicates that the next time you want to display the window in Design view, you need only click the View button.

Closing a Query

To close a query, close the Select Query window. When you do so, Access displays the Microsoft Office Access dialog box asking if you want to save your query for future use. If you think you will need to create the same exact query often, you should save the query. For now, you will not save any queries. You will see how to save them later in the project. The following steps close a query without saving it.

To Close the Query

1

• **Click the Close Window button for the Query1 : Select Query window (see Figure 2-10).**

Access displays the Microsoft Office Access dialog box (Figure 2-11). Clicking the Yes button saves the query and clicking the No button closes the query without saving.

2

• **Click the No button in the Microsoft Office Access dialog box.**

The Query1 : Select Query window closes. The query is not saved.

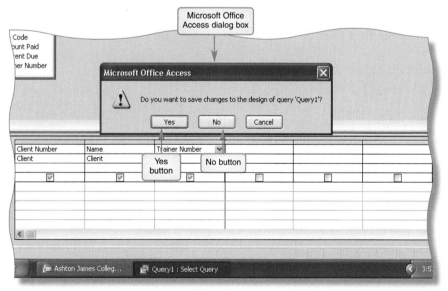

FIGURE 2-11

Other Ways

1. On File menu click Close
2. In Voice Command mode, say "File, Close"

Including All Fields in a Query

If you want to include all fields in a query, you could select each field individually. A simpler way to include all fields is available, however. By selecting the asterisk (*) in the field list, you are indicating that all fields are to be included. The following steps use the asterisk to include all fields.

To Include All Fields in a Query

1

• **Be sure you have a maximized Query1 : Select Query window with resized upper and lower panes, an expanded field list for the Client table in the upper pane, and an empty design grid in the lower pane. (See Steps 1 through 5 on pages AC 68 through AC 70 to create the query and resize the window.)**

• **Double-click the asterisk at the top of the field list.**

The maximized Query1 : Select Query window displays two resized panes. The table name, Client, followed by a period and an asterisk is added to the design grid, indicating all fields are included (Figure 2-12).

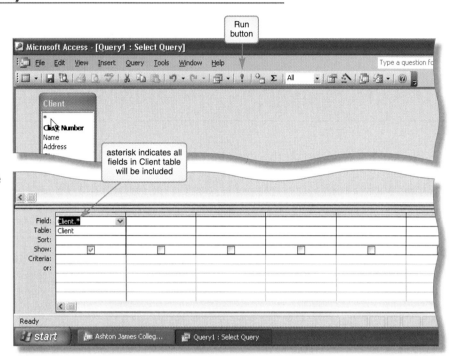

FIGURE 2-12

2

• **Click the Run button.**

The results appear and all fields in the Client table are included (Figure 2-13).

3

• **Click the View button on the Query Datasheet toolbar to return to the Query1 : Select Query window.**

The Query1 : Select Query window replaces the datasheet.

FIGURE 2-13

Other Ways

1. Drag asterisk from field list to design grid
2. Click column in grid, click arrow, click Client.*

Clearing the Design Grid

If you make mistakes as you are creating a query, you can fix each one individually. Alternatively, you simply may want to clear the query; that is, clear out the entries in the design grid and start over. One way to clear out the entries is to close the Select Query window and then start a new query just as you did earlier. A simpler approach, however, is to use the Clear Grid command on the Edit menu. The following steps clear the design grid.

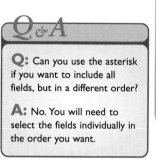

To Clear the Design Grid

1

• **Click Edit on the menu bar.**

The Edit menu appears (Figure 2-14).

2

• **Click Clear Grid.**

Access clears the design grid so you can enter your next query.

FIGURE 2-14

Entering Criteria

When you use queries, usually you are looking for those records that satisfy some criterion. You might want the name, amount paid, and current due amounts of the client whose number is CP27, for example, or of those clients whose names start with the letters, Fa. To enter criteria, enter them in the Criteria row in the design grid below the field name to which the criterion applies. For example, to indicate that the client number must be CP27, you first must add the Client Number field to the design grid. You then would type CP27 in the Criteria row below the Client Number field.

The next examples illustrate the types of criteria that are available.

Using Text Data in Criteria

To use **text data** (data in a field whose data type is Text) in criteria, simply type the text in the Criteria row below the corresponding field name. The steps on the next page query the Client table and display the client number, name, amount paid, and current due amount of client CP27.

To Use Text Data in a Criterion

1

• **One by one, double-click the Client Number, Name, Amount Paid, and Current Due fields to add them to the query.**

The Client Number, Name, Amount Paid, and Current Due fields are added to the design grid (Figure 2-15).

FIGURE 2-15

2

• **Click the Criteria row for the Client Number field and then type** CP27 **as the criterion.**

The criterion is entered (Figure 2-16). When the mouse pointer is in the Criteria box, its shape changes to an I-beam.

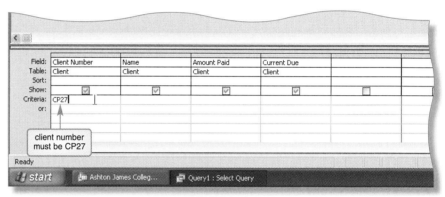

FIGURE 2-16

3

• **Click the Run button to run the query.**

The results appear (Figure 2-17). Only client CP27 is included. (The extra blank row contains $0.00 in the Amount Paid and Current Due fields. Unlike text fields, which are left blank, number and currency fields in the extra row contain 0. Because the Amount Paid and Current Due fields are currency fields, the values are displayed as $0.00.)

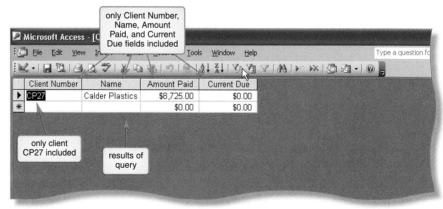

FIGURE 2-17

Using Wildcards

Two special wildcards are available in Microsoft Access. **Wildcards** are symbols that represent any character or combination of characters. The first of the two wildcards, the **asterisk** (*), represents any collection of characters. Thus Fa* represents the letters, Fa, followed by any collection of characters. The other wildcard symbol is the **question mark** (?), which represents any individual character. Thus t?m represents the letter, T, followed by any single character followed by the letter, m, such as Tim or Tom.

The following steps use a wildcard to find the number, name, and address of those clients whose names begin with Fa. Because you do not know how many characters will follow the Fa, the asterisk is appropriate.

To Use a Wildcard

1

• **Click the View button on the Query Datasheet toolbar to return to the Query1 : Select Query window.**

• **If necessary, click the Criteria row below the Client Number field.**

• **Use the DELETE or BACKSPACE key as necessary to delete the current entry (CP27).**

• **Click the Criteria row below the Name field.**

• **Type Fa* as the criterion.**

The criterion is entered (Figure 2-18).

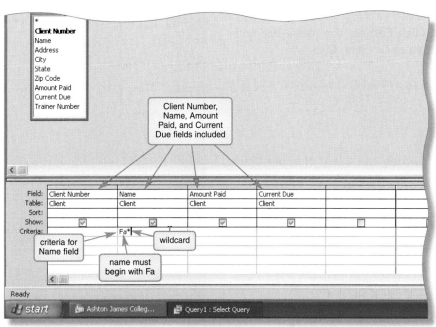

FIGURE 2-18

2

• **Click the Run button to run the query.**

• **If instructed to do so, print the results by clicking the Print button on the Query Datasheet toolbar.**

The results appear (Figure 2-19). Only the clients whose names start with Fa are included.

FIGURE 2-19

Criteria for a Field Not in the Result

In some cases, you may have criteria for a particular field that should not appear in the results of the query. For example, you may want to see the client number, name, address, and amount paid for all clients located in Lake Hammond. The criteria involve the City field, which is not one of the fields to be included in the results.

To enter a criterion for the City field, it must be included in the design grid. Normally, this also would mean it would appear in the results. To prevent this from happening, remove the check mark from its Show check box in the Show row of the grid. The steps on the next page illustrate the process by displaying the client number, name, and amount paid for clients located in Lake Hammond.

Q&A

Q: Can you add records or edit records in Query Datasheet view?

A: Yes. If the data in the query result is based on one table, you can add and edit records just as you did when the table was displayed in Table Datasheet view.

To Use Criteria for a Field Not Included in the Results

1

• **Click the View button on the Query Datasheet toolbar to return to the Query1 : Select Query window.**

• **Click Edit on the menu bar and then click Clear Grid.**

Access clears the design grid so you can enter the next query.

2

• **Include the Client Number, Name, Address, Amount Paid, and City fields in the query.**

• **Type** Lake Hammond **as the criterion for the City field.**

The fields are included in the grid, and the criterion for the City field is entered (Figure 2-20).

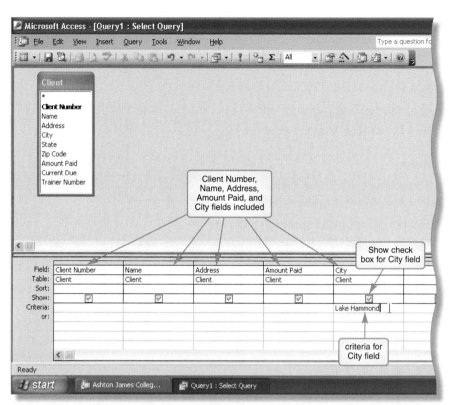

FIGURE 2-20

3

• **Click the Show check box to remove the check mark.**

The check mark is removed from the Show check box for the City field (Figure 2-21), indicating it will not show in the result. Because the City field is a text field, Access has added quotation marks before and after Lake Hammond automatically.

FIGURE 2-21

4

• **Click the Run button to run the query.**

• **If instructed to do so, print the results by clicking the Print button.**

The results appear (Figure 2-22). The City field does not appear. The only clients included are those located in Lake Hammond.

FIGURE 2-22

Creating a Parameter Query

Rather than giving a specific criterion when you first create the query, on occasion, you may want to be able to enter part of the criterion when you run the query and then have the appropriate results appear. For example, to include all the clients located in Tallmadge, you could enter Tallmadge as a criterion in the City field. From that point on, every time you ran the query, only the clients in Tallmadge would appear.

A better way is to allow the user to enter the city at the time the query is run. Thus a user could run the query, enter Tallmadge as the city and then see all the clients in Tallmadge. Later, the user could run the same query, but enter Lake Hammond as the city, and then see all the clients in Lake Hammond. To do this, you create a **parameter query**, which is a query that prompts for input whenever it is run. You enter a parameter, rather than a specific value as the criterion. You create one by enclosing a value in a criterion in square brackets. It is important that the value in the brackets does not match the name of any field. If you enter a field name in square brackets, Access assumes you want that particular field and will not prompt the user for input. For example, you could place [Enter City] as the criterion in the City field.

The following steps create a parameter query that will prompt the user to enter a city, and then display the client number, name, address, and amount paid for all clients located in that city.

Q&A

Q: What actions could you take to find clients located in Lake Hammond rather than Tallmadge?

A: Either create a new query or modify the existing query by replacing Tallmadge with Lake Hammond as the criterion.

More About

Parameter Queries

Parameter queries are especially useful in cases where the same query is run frequently with slight changes to one or more of the query's criteria. By using parameters rather than specific values, you can enter the values for the criterion as the query is run, rather than having to change the query design.

To Create and Run a Parameter Query

1

• **Click the View button on the Query Datasheet toolbar to return to the Query1 : Select Query window.**

• **Erase the current criterion in the City column, and then type** [Enter City] **as the new criterion.**

The criterion is entered (Figure 2-23).

FIGURE 2-23

2

• **Click the Run button to run the query.**

Access displays the Enter Parameter Value dialog box (Figure 2-24). The value (Enter City) previously entered in brackets appears in the dialog box.

FIGURE 2-24

3

• **Type** Tallmadge **in the Enter City text box and then click the OK button.**

The results appear (Figure 2-25). Only clients whose city is Tallmadge are included. The city name is not displayed in the results.

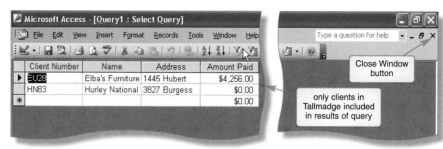

FIGURE 2-25

Each time you run this query, you will be asked to enter a city. Only clients in the city you enter will be included in the results.

Saving a Query

In many cases, you will construct a query you will want to use again. By saving the query, you will eliminate the need to repeat all your entries. The following steps illustrate the process by saving the query you just have created and assigning it the name Client-City Query. You can save with either the query design or the query results appearing on the screen.

To Save a Query

1

• **Click the Close Window button for the Query1 : Select Query window containing the query results.**

• **Click the Yes button in the Microsoft Office Access dialog box when asked if you want to save the changes to the design of the query.**

• **Type** Client-City Query **in the Query Name text box.**

The Save As dialog box appears with the query name you typed (Figure 2-26).

2

• **Click the OK button to save the query.**

Access saves the query and closes the Query1 : Select Query window.

FIGURE 2-26

Using a Saved Query

Once you have saved a query, you can use and manipulate it at any time in the future by opening it. When you right-click the query in the Database window, Access displays a shortcut menu containing commands that allow you to open, print, and change the design of the query. You also can print the results by clicking the Print button on the toolbar. If you want to print the query results without first opening the query, you would click Print on the shortcut menu.

The query is run against the current database. Thus, if changes have been made to the data since the last time you ran it, the results of the query may be different. The following steps use the query named Client-City Query.

More About

Saved Queries

Forms and reports can be based on either tables or saved queries. To create a report or form based on a query, click the Query tab, select the query, click the New Object button arrow, and then click the appropriate command (Report or Form). From that point on, the process is the same as for a table.

To Use a Saved Query

1

• **Click Queries on the Objects bar, and then right-click Client-City Query.**

The shortcut menu for Client-City Query appears (Figure 2-27).

2

• **Click Open on the shortcut menu, type** Tallmadge **in the Enter City text box, and then click the OK button.**

The results appear. They look like the results shown in Figure 2-25.

3

• **Click the Close Window button for the Client-City Query : Select Query window containing the query results.**

FIGURE 2-27

You can use the query at any time by following the above steps. Each time you do so, you will be prompted to enter a city. Only the clients in that city will be displayed in the results.

Using Numeric Data in Criteria

To enter a number in a criterion, type the number without any dollar signs or commas. The steps on the next page display all clients whose current due amount is $0.00.

To Use a Number in a Criterion

1

• **Click the Tables object on the Objects bar and ensure the Client table is selected.**

• **Click the New Object button arrow on the Database toolbar, click Query, and then click the OK button in the New Query dialog box.**

• **Drag the line separating the two panes to the approximate position shown in Figure 2-28, and drag the lower edge of the field box down far enough so all fields in the Client table appear.**

• **Include the Client Number, Name, Amount Paid, and Current Due fields in the query.**

• **Type 0 as the criterion for the Current Due field. You should not enter a dollar sign or decimal point in the criterion.**

The fields are selected and the criterion is entered (Figure 2-28).

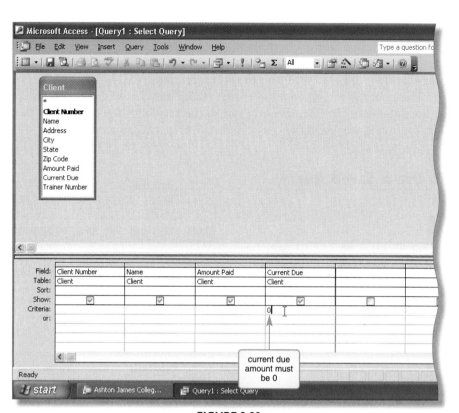

FIGURE 2-28

2

• **Click the Run button to run the query.**

• **If instructed to print the results, click the Print button.**

The results appear (Figure 2-29). Only those clients that have a current due amount of $0.00 are included.

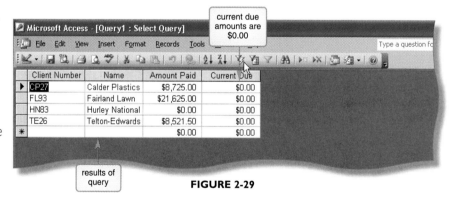

FIGURE 2-29

Using Comparison Operators

Unless you specify otherwise, Access assumes that the criteria you enter involve equality (exact matches). In the last query, for example, you were requesting those clients whose current due amount is equal to 0 (zero). If you want something other than an exact match, you must enter the appropriate **comparison operator**. The comparison operators are > (greater than), < (less than), >= (greater than or equal to), <= (less than or equal to), and NOT (not equal to).

The following steps use the > operator to find all clients whose amount paid is more than $20,000.00.

To Use a Comparison Operator in a Criterion

1

• **Click the View button on the Query Datasheet toolbar to return to the Query1 : Select Query window.**

• **Erase the 0 in the Current Due column.**

• **Type >20000 as the criterion for the Amount Paid field. Remember that you should not enter a dollar sign, a comma, or decimal point in the criterion.**

The fields are selected and the criterion is entered (Figure 2-30).

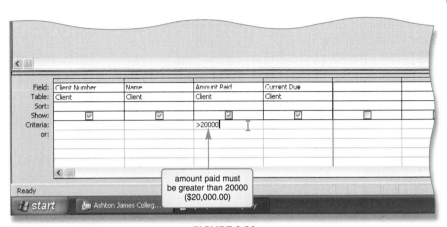

FIGURE 2-30

2

• **Click the Run button to run the query.**

• **If instructed to print the results, click the Print button.**

The results appear (Figure 2-31). Only those clients who have an amount paid greater than $20,000.00 are included.

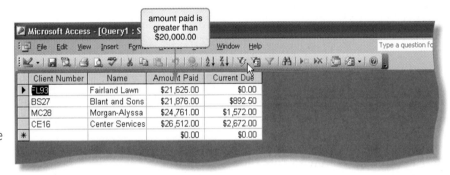

FIGURE 2-31

Using Compound Criteria

Often you will have more than one criterion that the data for which you are searching must satisfy. This type of criterion is called a **compound criterion**. Two types of compound criteria exist.

In an **AND criterion**, each individual criterion must be true in order for the compound criterion to be true. For example, an AND criterion would allow you to find those clients that have an amount paid greater than $20,000.00 and whose trainer is trainer 48.

Conversely, an **OR criterion** is true provided either individual criterion is true. An OR criterion would allow you to find those clients that have an amount paid greater than $20,000.00 or whose trainer is trainer 48. In this case, any client whose amount paid is greater than $20,000.00 would be included in the answer whether or not the client's trainer is trainer 48. Likewise, any client whose trainer is trainer 48 would be included whether or not the client had an amount paid greater than $20,000.00.

Using AND Criteria

To combine criteria with AND, place the criteria on the same line. The following steps use an AND criterion to find those clients whose amount paid is greater than $20,000.00 and whose trainer is trainer 48.

To Use a Compound Criterion Involving AND

1

• **Click the View button on the Query Datasheet toolbar to return to the Query1 : Select Query window.**

• **Include the Trainer Number field in the query.**

• **Type** 48 **as the criterion for the Trainer Number field.**

Criteria have been entered for the Amount Paid and Trainer Number fields (Figure 2-32).

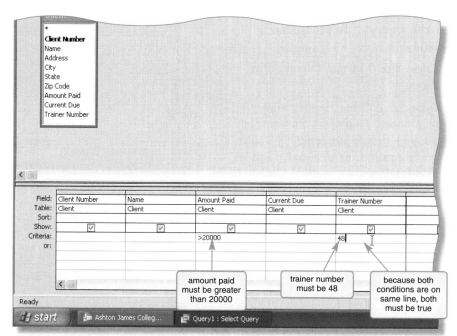

FIGURE 2-32

2

• **Click the Run button to run the query.**

• **If instructed to print the results, click the Print button.**

The results appear (Figure 2-33). Only the clients whose amount paid is greater than $20,000.00 and whose trainer number is 48 are included.

FIGURE 2-33

Using OR Criteria

To combine criteria with OR, the criteria must go on separate lines in the Criteria area of the grid. The following steps use an OR criterion to find those clients whose amount paid is greater than $20,000.00 or whose trainer is trainer 48 (or both).

To Use a Compound Criterion Involving OR

1

• **Click the View button on the Query Datasheet toolbar to return to the Query1 : Select Query window.**

2

• **If necessary, click the Criteria entry for the Trainer Number field and then use the BACKSPACE key or the DELETE key to erase the entry ("48").**

• **Click the or row (below the Criteria row) for the Trainer Number field and then type 48 as the entry.**

The criteria are entered for the Amount Paid and Trainer Number fields on different lines (Figure 2-34).

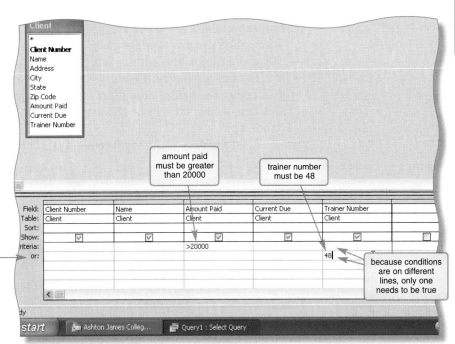

FIGURE 2-34

3

• **Click the Run button to run the query.**

• **If instructed to print the results, click the Print button.**

The results appear (Figure 2-35). Only those clients whose amount paid is greater than $20,000.00 or whose trainer number is 48 are included.

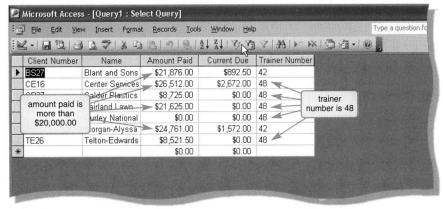

FIGURE 2-35

Sorting Data in a Query

In some queries, the order in which the records appear really does not matter. All you need be concerned about are the records that appear in the results. It does not matter which one is first or which one is last.

In other queries, however, the order can be very important. You may want to see the cities in which clients are located and would like them arranged alphabetically. Perhaps you want to see the clients listed by trainer number. Further, within all the clients of any given trainer, you might want them to be listed by amount paid.

> *More About*
>
> ### Sorting Data in a Query
>
> When sorting data in a query, the records in the underlying tables (the tables on which the query is based) are not actually rearranged. Instead, the DBMS will determine the most efficient method of simply displaying the records in the requested order. The records in the underlying tables remain in their original order.

To order the records in the answer to a query in a particular way, you **sort** the records. The field or fields on which the records are sorted is called the **sort key**. If you are sorting on more than one field (such as sorting by amount paid within trainer number), the more important field (Trainer Number) is called the **major key** (also called the **primary sort key**) and the less important field (Amount Paid) is called the **minor key** (also called the **secondary sort key**).

To sort in Microsoft Access, specify the sort order in the Sort row of the design grid below the field that is the sort key. If you specify more than one sort key, the sort key on the left will be the major sort key and the one on the right will be the minor key.

The following steps sort the cities in the Client table.

To Sort Data in a Query

1

• **Click the View button on the Query Datasheet toolbar to return to the Query1 : Select Query window.**

• **Click Edit on the menu bar and then click Clear Grid.**

2

• **Include the City field in the design grid.**

• **Click the Sort row below the City field, and then click the Sort row arrow that appears.**

The City field is included (Figure 2-36). A list of available sort orders appears.

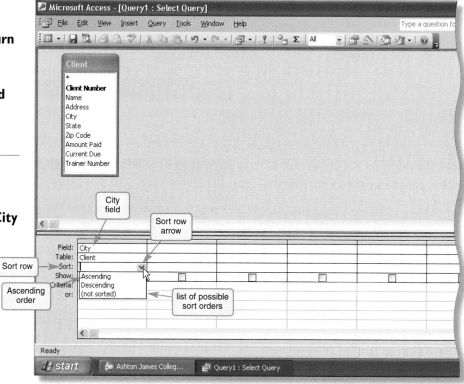

FIGURE 2-36

3

• **Click Ascending.**

Ascending is selected as the order (Figure 2-37).

FIGURE 2-37

4

• **Click the Run button to run the query.**

• **If instructed to print the results, click the Print button.**

The results contain the cities from the Client table (Figure 2-38). The cities appear in alphabetical order. Duplicates, also called **identical rows***, are included.*

FIGURE 2-38

Omitting Duplicates

When you sort data, duplicates normally are included. In Figure 2-38, for example, San Julio appeared twice, Lake Hammond appeared three times, and Tallmadge appeared twice. To sort to eliminate duplicates, use the Properties button on the Query Design toolbar or the Properties command on the shortcut menu to display the item's property sheet. A **property sheet** is a window containing the various properties of the object. To omit duplicates, you will use the property sheet to change the Unique Values property.

The following steps produce a sorted list of the cities in the Client table in which each city is listed only once.

To Omit Duplicates

1

• **Click the View button on the Query Datasheet toolbar to return to the Query1 : Select Query window.**

• **Click the second field in the design grid (the empty field following City). You must click the second field or you will not get the correct results and will have to repeat this step.**

• **Click the Properties button on the Query Design toolbar.**

Access displays the Query Properties sheet (Figure 2-39). (If your sheet looks different, you clicked the wrong place and will have to repeat the step.)

FIGURE 2-39

2

• **Click the Unique Values property box, and then click the arrow that appears to produce a list of available choices for Unique Values.**

• **Click Yes and then close the Query Properties sheet by clicking its Close button.**

• **Click the Run button to run the query.**

• **If instructed to print the results, click the Print button.**

The results appear (Figure 2-40). The cities are sorted alphabetically. Each city is included only once.

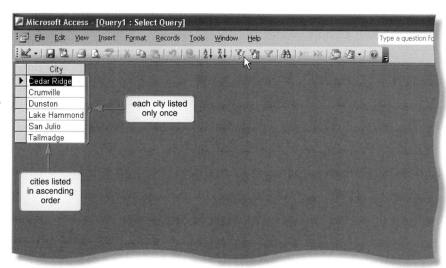

FIGURE 2-40

Other Ways
1. On View menu click Properties
2. Right-click second field in design grid, click Properties on shortcut menu
3. In Voice Command mode, say "Properties"

Sorting on Multiple Keys

The next example lists the number, name, trainer number, and amount paid for all clients. The data is to be sorted by amount paid (low to high) within trainer number, which means that the Trainer Number field is the major key and the Amount Paid field is the minor key.

The following steps accomplish this sorting by specifying the Trainer Number and Amount Paid fields as sort keys.

To Sort on Multiple Keys

1

• **Click the View button on the Query Datasheet toolbar to return to the Query1 : Select Query window.**

• **Click Edit on the menu bar and then click Clear Grid.**

2

• **Include the Client Number, Name, Trainer Number, and Amount Paid fields in the query in this order.**

• **Select Ascending as the sort order for both the Trainer Number field and the Amount Paid field (Figure 2-41).**

FIGURE 2-41

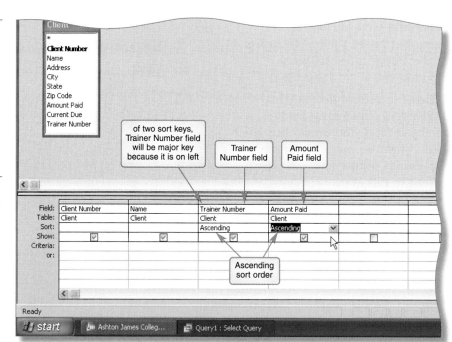

3

• **Click the Run button to run the query.**

• **If instructed to print the results, click the Print button.**

The results appear (Figure 2-42). The clients are sorted by trainer number. Within the collection of clients having the same trainer, the clients are sorted by amount paid.

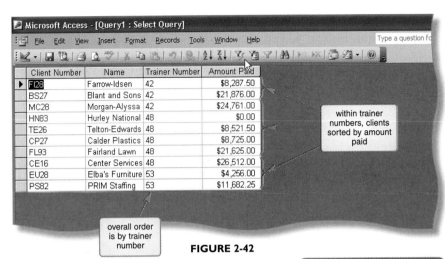

FIGURE 2-42

It is important to remember that the major sort key must appear to the left of the minor sort key in the design grid. If you attempted to sort by amount paid within trainer number, but placed the Amount Paid field to the left of the Trainer Number field, your results would be incorrect.

Creating a Top-Values Query

Rather than show all the results of a query, you may want to show only a specified number of records or a percentage of records. Creating a **top-values query** allows you to quantify the results. When you sort records, you can limit results to those records having the highest (descending sort) or lowest (ascending sort) values. To do so, first create a query that sorts the data in the desired order. Next, use the Top Values box on the Query Design toolbar to change the number of records to be included from All to the desired number. The following steps show the first four records that were included in the results of the previous query.

To Create a Top-Values Query

1

• **Click the View button on the Query Datasheet toolbar to return to the Query1 : Select Query window.**

• **Click the Top Values box on the Query Design toolbar, and then type 4 as the new value.**

The value in the Top Values box is changed from All to 4 (Figure 2-43).

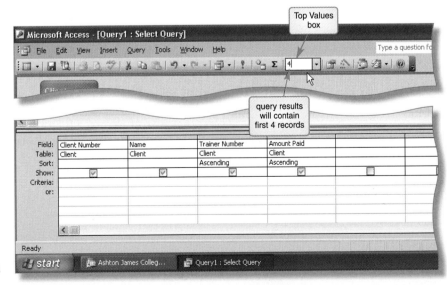

FIGURE 2-43

2

• **Click the Run button to run the query.**

• **If instructed to print the results, click the Print button.**

The results appear (Figure 2-44). Only the first four records are included.

3

• **Close the query by clicking the Close Window button for the Query1 : Select Query window.**

• **When asked if you want to save your changes, click the No button.**

The Query1 : Select Query window closes. The query is not saved.

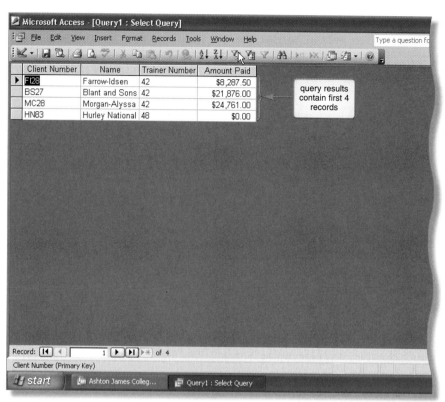

FIGURE 2-44

When you run a top-values query, it is important to change the value in the Top Values box back to All. If you do not change the Top Values value back to all, the previous value will remain in force. Consequently, you may very well not get all the records you should in the next query.

A good practice whenever you use a top-values query is to close the query as soon as you are done. That way, you will begin your next query from scratch, which guarantees that the value is set back to All.

Joining Tables

The Ashton James College database needs to satisfy a query that requires values from the Client table and the Trainer table. Specifically, the query needs to list the number and name of each client along with the number and name of the client's trainer. The client's name is in the Client table, whereas the trainer's name is in the Trainer table. Thus, this query cannot be satisfied using a single table. You need to **join** the tables; that is, to find records in the two tables that have identical values in matching fields (Figure 2-45). In this example, you need to find records in the Client table and the Trainer table that have the same value in the Trainer Number fields.

Give me the number and
name of each client along
with the number and name
of each client's trainer.

Client table

CLIENT NUMBER	NAME	...	TRAINER NUMBER
BS27	Blant and Sons	...	42
CE16	Center Services	...	48
CP27	Calder Plastics	...	48
EU28	Elba's Furniture	...	53
FI28	Farrow-Idsen	...	42
FL93	Fairland Lawn	...	48
HN83	Hurley National	...	48
MC28	Morgan-Alyssa	...	42
PS82	PRIM Staffing	...	53
TE26	Telton-Edwards	...	48

Trainer table

TRAINER NUMBER	LAST NAME	FIRST NAME	...
42	Perry	Belinda	...
48	Stevens	Michael	...
53	Gonzalez	Manuel	...
67	Danville	Marty	...

Trainer table

CLIENT NUMBER	NAME	...	TRAINER NUMBER	LAST NAME	FIRST NAME	...
BS27	Blant and Sons	...	42	Perry	Belinda	...
CE16	Center Services	...	48	Stevens	Michael	...
CP27	Calder Plastics	...	48	Stevens	Michael	...
EU28	Elba's Furniture	...	53	Gonzalez	Manuel	...
FI28	Farrow-Idsen	...	42	Perry	Belinda	...
FL93	Fairland Lawn	...	48	Stevens	Michael	...
HN83	Hurley National	...	48	Stevens	Michael	...
MC28	Morgan-Alyssa	...	42	Perry	Belinda	...
PS82	PRIM Staffing	...	53	Gonzalez	Manuel	...
TE26	Telton-Edwards	...	48	Stevens	Michael	...

FIGURE 2-45

To join tables in Access, first you bring field lists for both tables to the upper pane of the Select Query window. Access will draw a line, called a **join line**, between matching fields in the two tables indicating that the tables are related. You then can select fields from either table. Access will join the tables automatically.

The first step is to select the Trainer table in the Database window and create a new query. Then, add the Client table to the query. A join line will appear connecting the Trainer Number fields in the two field lists. This join line indicates how the tables are related; that is, linked through these matching fields. (If you fail to give the matching fields the same name, Access will not insert the line. You can insert it manually, however, by clicking one of the two matching fields and dragging the mouse pointer to the other matching field.)

The steps on the next page create a new query, add the Client table and then select the appropriate fields.

Q: Assuming you want the Trainer Number field to be the major key and the Amount Paid field to be the minor key as in the previous steps, how could you display the Amount Paid field before the Trainer Number field?

A: Include the Trainer Number field, the Amount Paid field, and then the Trainer Number field a second time. Select Ascending as the sort order for the first Trainer Number field and for the Amount Paid field. Remove the check mark from the Show check box for the first Trainer Number field. Thus, the first Trainer Number field will be part of the sort key, but will not appear in the results. The second Trainer Number field will appear in the results after the Amount Paid field.

To Join Tables

1

• **With the Tables object selected and the Trainer table selected, click the New Object button arrow on the Database toolbar.**

• **Click Query, and then click the OK button.**

• **Drag the line separating the two panes to the approximate position shown in Figure 2-46, and then drag the lower edge of the field list box down far enough so all fields in the Trainer table appear.**

• **Click the Show Table button on the Query Design toolbar.**

Access displays the Show Table dialog box (Figure 2-46).

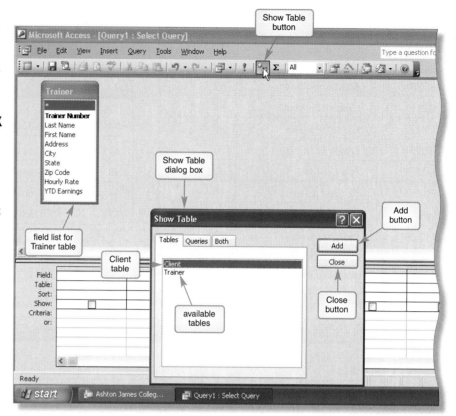

FIGURE 2-46

2

• **Be sure the Client table is selected, and then click the Add button.**

• **Close the Show Table dialog box by clicking the Close button.**

• **Expand the size of the field list so all the fields in the Client table appear.**

The field lists for both tables appear (Figure 2-47). A join line connects the two field lists.

FIGURE 2-47

3

• **Include the Trainer Number, Last Name, and First Name fields from the Trainer table as well as the Client Number and Name fields from the Client table.**

• **Select Ascending as the sort order for both the Trainer Number field and the Client Number field.**

The fields from both tables are selected (Figure 2-48).

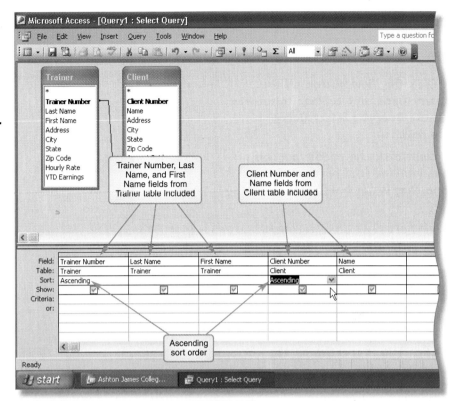

FIGURE 2-48

4

• **Click the Run button to run the query.**

• **If instructed to print the results, click the Print button.**

The results appear (Figure 2-49). They contain data from both the Trainer and Client tables. The records are sorted by trainer number and within trainer number by client number.

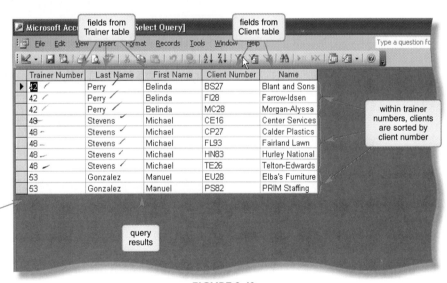

FIGURE 2-49

Changing Join Properties

Normally records that do not match will not appear in the results of a join query. A trainer such as Marty Danville, for whom no clients currently exist, for example, would not appear. To cause such a record to be displayed, you need to change the **join properties**, which are the properties that indicate which records appear in a join, of the query as the steps on the next page illustrate.

Other Ways

1. On Query menu click Show Table
2. Right-click any open area in upper pane, click Show Table on shortcut menu
3. In Voice Command mode, say "Show Table"

To Change Join Properties

1

• **Click the View button on the Query Datasheet toolbar to return to the Query1 : Select Query window.**

• **Right-click the middle portion of the join line (the portion of the line that is not bold).**

The shortcut menu appears (Figure 2-50). (If Join Properties does not appear on your shortcut menu, you did not point to the appropriate portion of the join line. You will need to right-click again.)

FIGURE 2-50

2

• **Click Join Properties on the shortcut menu.**

Access displays the Join Properties dialog box (Figure 2-51).

FIGURE 2-51

3

• **Click option button 2 to include all records from the Trainer table regardless of whether or not they match any clients.**

• **Click the OK button.**

• **Run the query by clicking the Run button.**

• **If instructed to print the results, click the Print button.**

The results appear (Figure 2-52).

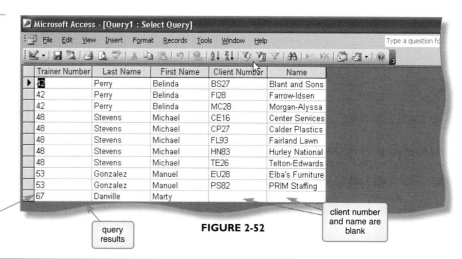

FIGURE 2-52

With the change to the join properties, trainer 67 is included, even though the trainer does not have any clients.

Restricting Records in a Join

Sometimes you will want to join tables, but you will not want to include all possible records. In such cases, you will relate the tables and include fields just as you did before. You also will include criteria. For example, to include the same fields as in the previous query, but only those clients whose amount paid is more than $20,000.00, you will make the same entries as before, but also include >20000 as a criterion for the Amount Paid field.

The following steps modify the query from the previous example to restrict the records that will be included in the join.

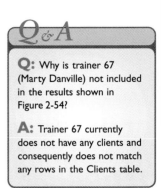

Q: Why is trainer 67 (Marty Danville) not included in the results shown in Figure 2-54?

A: Trainer 67 currently does not have any clients and consequently does not match any rows in the Clients table.

To Restrict the Records in a Join

1

• **Click the View button on the Query Datasheet toolbar to return to the Query1 : Select Query window.**

• **Add the Amount Paid field to the query.**

• **Type >20000 as the criterion for the Amount Paid field and then click the Show check box for the Amount Paid field to remove the check mark.**

The Amount Paid field appears in the design grid (Figure 2-53). A criterion is entered for the Amount Paid field, and the Show check box is empty, indicating that the field will not appear in the results of the query.

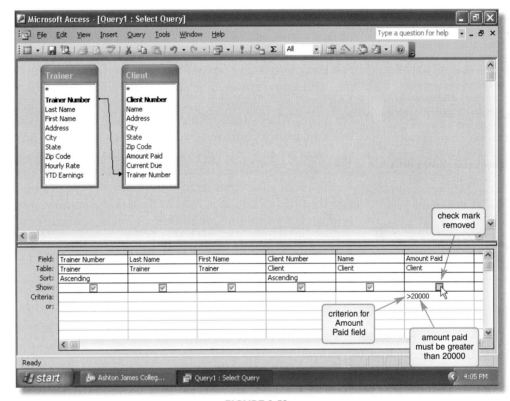

FIGURE 2-53

2

• **Click the Run button to run the query.**

• **If instructed to print the results, click the Print button.**

The results appear (Figure 2-54). Only those clients with an amount paid greater than $20,000.00 are displayed in the result. The Amount Paid field does not appear.

FIGURE 2-54

Calculations

Many types of calculations are available for use in queries. For example, you can add the values in two fields together, or you can calculate the sum or average of the values in one field.

Using Calculated Fields

Suppose that Ashton James College wants to know the number of hours worked by each trainer. This poses a problem because the Trainer table does not include a field for hours worked. You can calculate it, however, because the number of hours worked is equal to the YTD earnings divided by the hourly rate. A field that can be computed from other fields is called a **calculated field**.

To include calculated fields in queries, you enter a name for the calculated field, a colon, and then the expression in one of the columns in the Field row. Any fields included in the expression must be enclosed in square brackets ([ ]). For the number of hours worked, for example, you will type Hours Worked:[YTD Earnings]/[Hourly Rate] as the expression.

You can type the expression directly into the Field row. You will not be able to see the entire entry, however, because the Field row is not large enough. The preferred way is to select the column in the Field row and then use the Zoom command on its shortcut menu. When Access displays the Zoom dialog box, you can enter the expression.

You are not restricted to division in calculations. You can use addition (+), subtraction (-), or multiplication (*). You also can include parentheses in your calculations to indicate which calculations should be done first.

The following steps remove the Client table from the query (it is not needed), and then use a calculated field to display the number, last name, hourly rate, year-to-date earnings, and number of hours worked for all trainers.

To Use a Calculated Field in a Query

1

• **Click the View button on the Query Datasheet toolbar to return to the Query1 : Select Query window.**

• **Right-click any field in the Client table field list.**

• **Click Remove Table on the shortcut menu to remove the Client table from the Query1 : Select Query window.**

• **Click Edit on the menu bar and then click Clear Grid. Include the Trainer Number, Last Name, Hourly Rate, and YTD Earnings.**

• **Right-click the Field row in the first open column in the design grid.**

The shortcut menu appears (Figure 2-55).

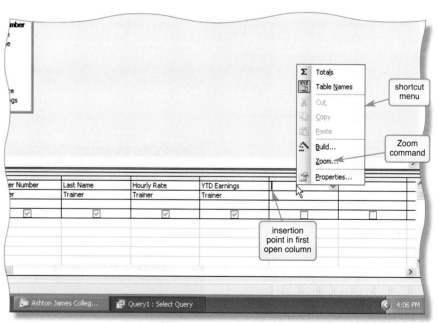

FIGURE 2-55

2

- **Click Zoom on the shortcut menu.**

- **Type** Hours Worked:[YTD Earnings]/[Hourly Rate] **in the Zoom dialog box that appears.**

Access displays the Zoom dialog box (Figure 2-56). The expression you typed appears within the dialog box.

FIGURE 2-56

3

- **Click the OK button.**

A portion of the expression you entered appears in the fifth field in the design grid (Figure 2-57).

FIGURE 2-57

4

- **Click the Run button to run the query.**

- **If instructed to print the results, click the Print button.**

The results appear (Figure 2-58). Microsoft Access has calculated and displayed the number of hours worked for each trainer.

FIGURE 2-58

Other Ways

1. Press SHIFT+F2

Instead of clicking Zoom on the shortcut menu, you can click Build. Access displays the Expression Builder dialog box that provides assistance in creating the expression. If you know the expression you will need, however, usually it is easier to enter it using the Zoom command.

More About

Calculated Fields

Because it is easy to compute values in a query, it is not necessary to store calculated fields, also called computed fields, in a database. It is not necessary, for example, to store the total amount (the amount paid amount plus the current due amount), because it can be calculated whenever it is required.

Changing Format and Caption

You can change the way items appear in the results of a query by changing their format. You also can change the heading at the top of a column in the results by changing the caption. Just as when you omitted duplicates, you will make this change by using the field's property sheet. In the property sheet, you can change the desired property, such as the format, the number of decimal places, or the caption. The following steps change the format of Hours Worked to Fixed and the number of decimal places to 1, thus guaranteeing that the number on each row will contain exactly one decimal place. They also change the caption of the Hourly Rate field to Rate.

To Change a Format and a Caption

1

• **Click the View button on the Query Datasheet toolbar to return to the Query1 : Select Query window.**

• **If necessary, click the Hours Worked field in the design grid, and then click the Properties button on the Query Design toolbar.**

• **Click the Format box, click the Format box arrow, and then click Fixed.**

• **Click the Decimal Places box, and then type 1 as the number of decimal places.**

Access displays the Field Properties sheet (Figure 2-59). The format is changed to Fixed and the number of decimal places is set to 1.

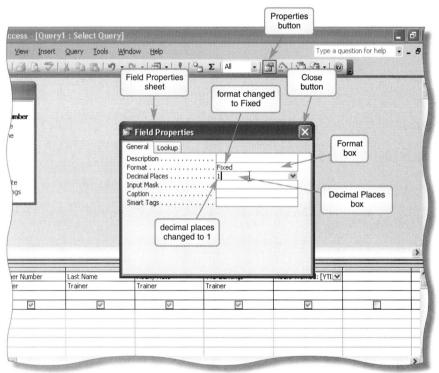

FIGURE 2-59

2

• **Close the Field Properties sheet by clicking its Close button.**

• **Click the Hourly Rate field in the design grid, and then click the Properties button on the Query Design toolbar.**

• **Click the Caption box, and then type Rate as the caption.**

Access displays the Field Properties sheet (Figure 2-60). The caption is changed to Rate.

FIGURE 2-60

3

• **Click the Run button to run the query.**

• **If instructed to print the results, click the Print button.**

The results appear (Figure 2-61). The Hourly Rate caption is changed to Rate. The numbers in the Hours Worked column all contain exactly one decimal place.

4

• **Click the Close Window button for the Query1 : Select Query window.**

• **When asked if you want to save your changes, click the No button.**

The Query1 : Select Query window closes. The query is not saved.

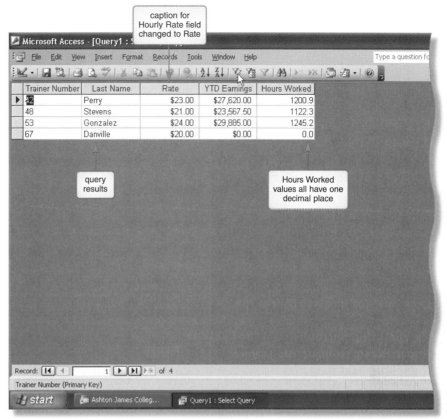

caption for Hourly Rate field changed to Rate

query results

Hours Worked values all have one decimal place

FIGURE 2-61

If you had saved the query, the changes you made to the properties would be saved along with the query.

Calculating Statistics

Microsoft Access supports the built-in statistics: COUNT, SUM, AVG (average), MAX (largest value), MIN (smallest value), STDEV (standard deviation), VAR (variance), FIRST, and LAST. These statistics are called aggregate functions. An **aggregate function** is a function that performs some mathematical function against a group of records. To use any of these aggregate functions in a query, you include it in the Total row in the design grid. The Total row routinely does not appear in the grid. To include it, click the Totals button on the Query Design toolbar.

The steps on the next page create a new query for the Client table and then calculate the average amount paid for all clients.

To Calculate Statistics

1

• **With the Tables object selected and the Client table selected, click the New Object button arrow on the Database toolbar.**

• **Click Query, and then click the OK button.**

• **Drag the line separating the two panes to the approximate position shown in Figure 2-62, and drag the lower edge of the field list box down far enough so all fields in the Client table appear.**

• **Click the Totals button on the Query Design toolbar, and then double-click the Amount Paid field.**

The Total row now is included in the design grid (Figure 2-62). The Amount Paid field is included, and the entry in the Total row is Group By.

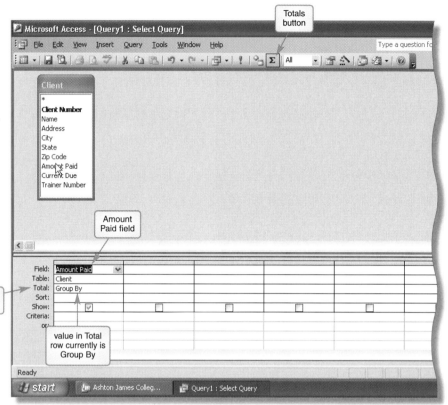

FIGURE 2-62

2

• **Click the Total row in the Amount Paid column, and then click the Total row arrow that appears.**

The list of available options appears (Figure 2-63).

FIGURE 2-63

3

• **Click Avg.**

Avg is selected (Figure 2-64).

FIGURE 2-64

4

• **Click the Run button to run the query.**

• **If instructed to print the results, click the Print button.**

The result appears (Figure 2-65), showing the average amount paid for all clients.

average amount paid by all clients

FIGURE 2-65

Other Ways

1. On View menu click Totals
2. Right-click any open area in upper pane, click Totals on shortcut menu
3. In Voice Command mode, say "Totals"

Using Criteria in Calculating Statistics

Sometimes calculating statistics for all the records in the table is appropriate. In other cases, however, you will need to calculate the statistics for only those records that satisfy certain criteria. To enter a criterion in a field, first you select Where as the entry in the Total row for the field and then enter the criterion in the Criteria row. The following steps use this technique to calculate the average amount paid for clients of trainer 48.

To Use Criteria in Calculating Statistics

1

• **Click the View button on the Query Datasheet toolbar to return to the Query1 : Select Query window.**

2

• **Include the Trainer Number field in the design grid.**

• **Produce the list of available options for the Total row entry just as you did when you selected Avg for the Amount Paid field.**

• **Use the vertical scroll bar to move through the options until the Where option appears.**

The list of available options appears (Figure 2-66). The Group By entry in the Trainer Number field may not be highlighted on your screen depending on where you clicked in the Total row.

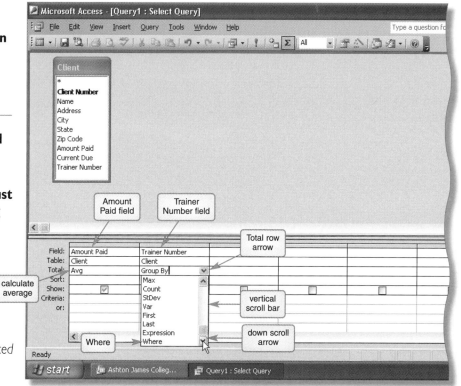

FIGURE 2-66

3

• **Click Where.**

• **Type** 42 **as the criterion for the Trainer Number field.**

Where is selected as the entry in the Total row for the Trainer Number field and 42 is entered in the Criteria row (Figure 2-67).

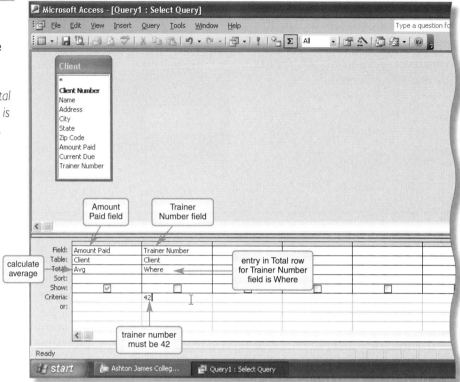

FIGURE 2-67

4

• **Click the Run button to run the query.**

• **If instructed to print the results, click the Print button.**

The results appear (Figure 2-68), giving the average amount paid for clients of trainer 42.

FIGURE 2-68

Grouping

Another way statistics often are used is in combination with grouping; that is, statistics are calculated for groups of records. You may, for example, need to calculate the average amount paid for the clients of each trainer. You will want the average for the clients of trainer 42, the average for clients of trainer 48, and so on.

Grouping means creating groups of records that share some common characteristic. In grouping by Trainer Number, for example, the clients of trainer 42 would form one group, the clients of trainer 48 would be a second, and the clients of trainer 53 form a third group. The calculations then are made for each group. To indicate grouping in Access, select Group By as the entry in the Total row for the field to be used for grouping.

The following steps calculate the average amount paid for clients of each trainer.

To Use Grouping

1

• **Click the View button on the Query Datasheet toolbar to return to the Query1 : Select Query window.**

• **Click Edit on the menu bar and then click Clear Grid.**

• **Include the Trainer Number field.**

• **Include the Amount Paid field, and then click Avg as the calculation in the Total row.**

The Trainer Number and Amount Paid fields are included (Figure 2-69). Group By currently is the entry in the Total row for the Trainer Number field, which is correct; thus, it was not changed.

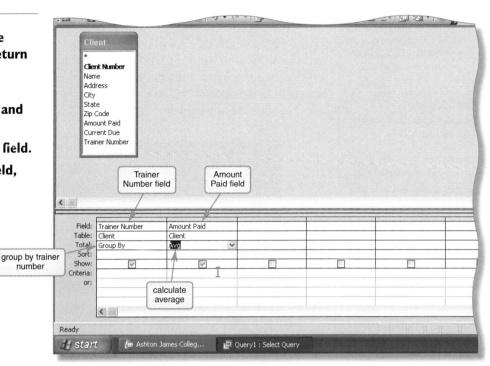

FIGURE 2-69

2

• **Click the Run button to run the query.**

• **If instructed to print the results, click the Print button.**

The results appear (Figure 2-70), showing each trainer's number along with the average amount paid for the clients of that trainer. Because the results are grouped by trainer number, a single row exists for each trainer summarizing all the clients of that trainer.

3

• **Close the query by clicking the Close Window button for the Query1 : Select Query window.**

• **When asked if you want to save your changes, click the No button.**

The Query1 : Select Query window closes. The query is not saved.

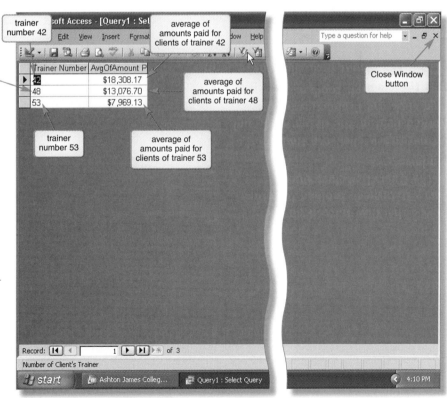

FIGURE 2-70

More About

Microsoft Certification

The Microsoft Office Specialist Certification program provides an opportunity for you to obtain a valuable industry credential — proof that you have the Access 2003 skills required by employers. For more information, see Appendix E, or visit the Access 2003 Certification Web page (scsite.com/ac2003/cert).

Crosstab Queries

Crosstab queries are useful for summarizing data. A **crosstab query** calculates a statistic (for example, sum, average, or count) for data that is grouped by two different types of information. One of the types will appear down the side of the resulting datasheet, and the other will appear across the top. Figure 2-71 shows a crosstab in which the total of amount paid is grouped by both city and trainer number with cities down the left-hand side and trainer numbers across the top. For example, the entry in the row labeled Cedar Ridge and in the column labeled 42 represents the total of the amount paid for all clients of trainer 42 who live in Cedar Ridge.

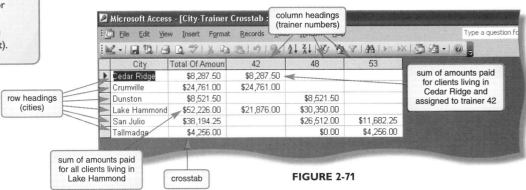

FIGURE 2-71

The following steps use the Crosstab Query wizard to create a crosstab query.

To Create a Crosstab Query

1

• **With the Tables object selected and the Client table selected, click the New Object button arrow.**

• **Click Query, click Crosstab Query Wizard in the New Query dialog box, and then click the OK button.**

Access displays the Crosstab Query Wizard dialog box (Figure 2-72).

FIGURE 2-72

2

• **With the Tables option button selected and the Client table selected, click the Next button.**

• **Click the City field, and then click the Add Field button.**

The Crosstab Query Wizard dialog box displays options for selecting field values as row headings (Figure 2-73). The City field is selected as the field whose values will provide the row headings.

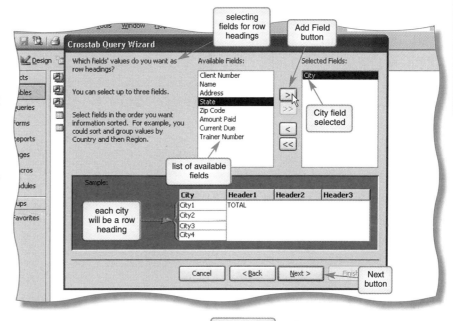

FIGURE 2-73

3

• **Click the Next button, and then click the Trainer Number field.**

The Crosstab Query Wizard dialog box displays options for selecting field values as column headings (Figure 2-74). The Trainer Number field is selected as the field whose values will provide the column headings.

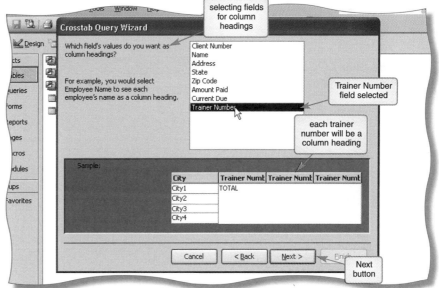

FIGURE 2-74

4

• **Click the Next button, click the Amount Paid field, and then click Sum.**

The Crosstab Query Wizard dialog box displays options for selecting fields for calculations for column and row intersections (Figure 2-75). The Amount Paid field is selected as the field whose value will be calculated for each row and column intersection. Because Sum is the selected function, the calculation will be the total amount paid.

FIGURE 2-75

5

• **Click the Next button, and then type** City-Trainer Crosstab **as the name of the query.**

The Crosstab Query Wizard dialog box displays options for naming and viewing the query and modifying the design (Figure 2-76). The name is entered.

6

• **Click the Finish button.**

• **If instructed to print the results, click the Print button.**

The results now can appear. They look like the results shown in Figure 2-71 on page AC 104.

7

• **Close the query by clicking its Close Window button.**

The query no longer appears.

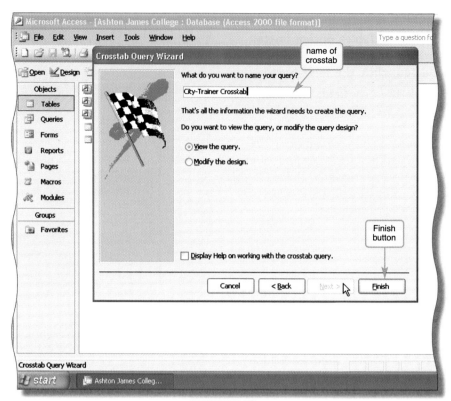

FIGURE 2-76

The query containing the crosstab now can be run just like any other query.

Closing a Database and Quitting Access

The following steps close the database and quit Access.

To Close a Database and Quit Access

1. **Click the Close Window button for the Ashton James College : Database window.**

2. **Click the Close button for the Microsoft Access window.**

Project Summary

In Project 2, you created and ran a variety of queries. You saw how to select fields in a query. You used text data and wildcards in criteria. You created a parameter query, which allowed users to enter a criterion when they run the query. You learned how to save a query for future use and how to use a query you have saved. You also used comparison operators in criteria involving numeric data. You combined criteria with both AND and OR. You saw how to sort the results of a query, how to join tables, how to restrict the records in a join, and how to change join properties. You created computed fields and calculated statistics. You changed formats and captions. You learned how to use grouping. Finally, you learned how to create a crosstab query.

What You Should Know

Having completed this project, you should be able to perform the tasks below. The tasks are listed in the same order they were presented in this project. For a list of the buttons, menus, toolbars, and commands introduced in this project, see the Quick Reference Summary at the back of this book and refer to the Page Number column.

1. Open a Database   (AC 68)
2. Create a Query   (AC 68)
3. Include Fields in the Design Grid   (AC 71)
4. Run the Query   (AC 71)
5. Print the Results of a Query   (AC 72)
6. Return to the Select Query Window   (AC 72)
7. Close the Query   (AC 73)
8. Include All Fields in a Query   (AC 74)
9. Clear the Design Grid   (AC 75)
10. Use Text Data in a Criterion   (AC 76)
11. Use a Wildcard   (AC 77)
12. Use Criteria for a Field Not Included in the Results   (AC 78)
13. Create and Run a Parameter Query   (AC 79)
14. Save a Query   (AC 80)
15. Use a Saved Query   (AC 81)
16. Use a Number in a Criterion   (AC 82)
17. Use a Comparison Operator in a Criterion   (AC 83)
18. Use a Compound Criterion Involving AND   (AC 84)
19. Use a Compound Criterion Involving OR   (AC 85)
20. Sort Data in a Query   (AC 86)
21. Omit Duplicates   (AC 87)
22. Sort on Multiple Keys   (AC 88)
23. Create a Top-Values Query   (AC 89)
24. Join Tables   (AC 92)
25. Change Join Properties   (AC 94)
26. Restrict the Records in a Join   (AC 95)
27. Use a Calculated Field in a Query   (AC 96)
28. Change a Format and a Caption   (AC 98)
29. Calculate Statistics   (AC 100)
30. Use Criteria in Calculating Statistics   (AC 101)
31. Use Grouping   (AC 103)
32. Create a Crosstab Query   (AC 104)
33. Close a Database and Quit Access   (AC 106)

Learn It Online

Instructions: To complete the Learn It Online exercises, start your browser, click the Address bar, and then enter the Web address scsite.com/ac2003/learn. When the Access 2003 Learn It Online page is displayed, follow the instructions in the exercises below. Each exercise has instructions for printing your results, either for your own records or for submission to your instructor.

1 Project Reinforcement TF, MC, and SA

Below Access Project 2, click the Project Reinforcement link. Print the quiz by clicking Print on the File menu for each page. Answer each question.

Flash Cards

Below Access Project 2, click the Flash Cards link and read the instructions. Type 20 (or a number specified by your instructor) in the Number of playing cards text box, type your name in the Enter your Name text box, and then click the Flip Card button. When the flash card is displayed, read the question and then click the ANSWER box arrow to select an answer. Flip through Flash Cards. If your score is 15 (75%) correct or greater, click Print on the File menu to print your results. If your score is less than 15 (75%) correct, then redo this exercise by clicking the Replay button.

3 Practice Test

Below Access Project 2, click the Practice Test link. Answer each question, enter your first and last name at the bottom of the page, and then click the Grade Test button. When the graded practice test is displayed on your screen, click Print on the File menu to print a hard copy. Continue to take practice tests until you score 80% or better.

4 Who Wants To Be a Computer Genius?

Below Access Project 2, click the Computer Genius link. Read the instructions, enter your first and last name at the bottom of the page, and then click the PLAY button. When your score is displayed, click the PRINT RESULTS link to print a hard copy.

5 Wheel of Terms

Below Access Project 2, click the Wheel of Terms link. Read the instructions, and then enter your first and last name and your school name. Click the PLAY button. When your score is displayed, right-click the score and then click Print on the shortcut menu to print a hard copy.

6 Crossword Puzzle Challenge

Below Access Project 2, click the Crossword Puzzle Challenge link. Read the instructions, and then enter your first and last name. Click the SUBMIT button. Work the crossword puzzle. When you are finished, click the Submit button. When the crossword puzzle is redisplayed, click the Print Puzzle button to print a hard copy.

7 Tips and Tricks

Below Access Project 2, click the Tips and Tricks link. Click a topic that pertains to Project 2. Right-click the information and then click Print on the shortcut menu. Construct a brief example of what the information relates to in Access to confirm you understand how to use the tip or trick.

8 Newsgroups

Below Access Project 2, click the Newsgroups link. Click a topic that pertains to Project 2. Print three comments.

9 Expanding Your Horizons

Below Access Project 2, click the Expanding Your Horizons link. Click a topic that pertains to Project 2. Print the information. Construct a brief example of what the information relates to in Access to confirm you understand the contents of the article.

10 Search Sleuth

Below Access Project 2, click the Search Sleuth link. To search for a term that pertains to this project, select a term below the Project 2 title and then use the Google search engine at google.com (or any major search engine) to display and print two Web pages that present information on the term.

11 Access Online Training

Below Access Project 2, click the Access Online Training link. When your browser displays the Microsoft Office Online Web page, click the Access link. Click one of the Access courses that covers one or more of the objectives listed at the beginning of the project on page AC 66. Print the first page of the course before stepping through it.

12 Office Marketplace

Below Access Project 2, click the Office Marketplace link. When your browser displays the Microsoft Office Online Web page, click the Office Marketplace link. Click a topic that relates to Access. Print the first page.

Apply Your Knowledge

1 Querying the Begon Pest Control Database

Instructions: Start Access. Open the Begon Pest Control database that you modified in Apply Your Knowledge 1 in Project 1 on page AC 54. (If you did not complete this exercise, see your instructor for a copy of the modified database.) Perform the following tasks:

1. Create a query for the Customer table and add the Name and Address fields to the design grid.
2. Find only those records where the client has an address on Fletcher. Run the query and change the address for the client on 109 Fletcher to 190 Fletcher. Print the results. Return to Design view and clear the grid.
3. Add the Customer Number, Name, City, and Balance fields to the design grid. Sort the records in ascending order by City and descending by Balance. Run the query and print the results. Return to Design view.
4. Modify the query to allow the user to enter a different city each time the query is run. Run the query to find all customers who live in Kady. Print the query results. Save the query as Customer-City Query.
5. Open the Customer-City Query in Design view. Run the query to find all customers who live in Carlton but restrict retrieval to the top two records. Print the results. Close the query without saving it.
6. Create a new query for the Technician table and then join the Technician and Customer tables. Add the Technician Number, First Name and Last Name fields from the Technician table and the Customer Number, and Name fields from the Customer table. Sort the records in ascending order by Technician Number and Customer Number. All technicians should appear in the result even if they currently have no customers. Run the query and print the results.
7. Restrict the records retrieved in task 6 above to only those customers who have a balance greater than $350.00. Run the query and print the results. Close the query without saving it.
8. Create and print the crosstab shown in Figure 2-77. The crosstab groups total of customers' balances by city and technician number.

City	Total Of Balance	203	210	214
Carlton	$763.00	$398.00		$365.00
Conradt	$655.00	$355.00	$300.00	$0.00
Kady	$1,302.00	$335.00	$967.00	

FIGURE 2-77

In the Lab

1 Querying the Birds2U Database

Problem: The management of Birds2U has determined a number of questions it wants the database management system to answer. You must obtain the answers to the questions posed by management.

Instructions: Use the database created in the In the Lab 1 of Project 1 on page AC 57 for this assignment or see your instructor for information on accessing the files required for this book. Perform the following tasks:

1. Open the Birds2U database and create a new query to display and print the Item Code, Description, On Hand, and Selling Price for all records in the Item table.
2. Display and print the Item Code, Description, Cost, and Supplier Code fields for all products where the Supplier Code is 13.

(continued)

In the Lab

1 Querying the Birds2U Database *(continued)*

3. Display and print the Item Code and Description fields for all items where the description includes the letters "bird."
4. Display and print the Item Code and Description fields for all items with a cost less than $15.00.
5. Display and print the Item Code and Description fields for all products that have a selling price greater than $50.00.
6. Display and print all fields for those items with a selling price greater than $30.00 and where the number on hand is at least 5.
7. Display and print all fields for those items that have a supplier code of 13 or a selling price less than $16.00.
8. Include the Item Code, Description, On Hand, and Selling Price in the design grid. Change the caption for the On Hand column to In Stock and sort the records in descending order by selling price. Run the query and print the results. Run the query again but this time limit retrieval to the top 3 records.
9. Join the Supplier table and the Item table. Display the Supplier Code and Name from the Supplier table and the Item Code, Description, On Hand, and Cost from the Item table. Sort the records in ascending order by Supplier Code and by Item Code. All suppliers should display in the result even if they currently supply no items. Run the query and print the results. Save the query as Suppliers and Items.
10. Restrict the records retrieved in task 9 above to only those products where number on hand is less than 5. Run the query and print the results. Close the query and do not save the changes.
11. Create a new query for the Item table and include the Item Code and Description fields in the design grid. Calculate the on-hand value (on hand * cost) for all records in the table. Run the query and print the results.
12. Display and print the average selling price of all items.
13. Display and print the average selling price of items grouped by supplier code.

2 Querying the Babbage Bookkeeping Database

Problem: Babbage Bookkeeping has determined a number of questions it wants the database management system to answer. You must obtain the answers to the questions posed by the bookkeeping service.

Instructions: Use the database created in the In the Lab 2 of Project 1 on page AC 59 for this assignment or see your instructor for information on accessing the files required for this book. Perform the following tasks:

1. Open the Babbage Bookkeeping database and create a new query for the Client table.
2. Display and print the Name and Balance fields for all clients where the bookkeeper number is 24.
3. Display and print the Client Number, Name, and Balance fields for all clients located in Empeer with a balance greater than $300.00.
4. Display and print the Client Number, Name, and Address fields for all clients with an address on Maum.
5. Display and print the cities in ascending order. Each city should appear only once.
6. Create a query that will allow the user to enter the city to search when the query is run. The query results should display the Client Number, Name, and Bookkeeper Number. Test the query by searching for those records where the client is located in Portage. Save the query as Client-City Query.
7. Include the Client Number, Name, and Balance fields in the design grid. Sort the records in descending order by the Balance field. Display and print the top half of the records.

In the Lab

8. Display and print the Client Number, Name, and Balance fields for all clients where the bookkeeper number is 24 or 34 and the balance is greater than $300.00. (*Hint:* Use Microsoft Access Help to solve this problem.)

9. Display and print the First Name, Last Name, and Hourly Rate fields from the Bookkeeper table and the Client Number, Name, and Balance fields from the Client table. Sort the records in ascending order by bookkeeper's last name and client's name.

10. Create a new query for the Bookkeeper table and include the Bookkeeper Number, First Name, Last Name, and Hourly Rate in the design grid. Calculate the number of hours each bookkeeper has worked (YTD Earnings/ Hourly Rate). Display hours worked as an integer (0 decimal places). Run the query and print the results.

11. Display and print the following statistics: the total balance for all clients; the total balance for clients of bookkeeper 22; and the total balance for each bookkeeper.

12. Create the crosstab shown in Figure 2-78. The crosstab groups total of clients' balances by city and bookkeeper number. Save the crosstab as City-Bookkeeper Crosstab. Print the crosstab.

	Microsoft Access - [City-Bookkeeper Crosstab : Crosstab Query]			
File	Edit	View	Insert	Format	Records	Tools	Window	Help
City	Total Of Balance	22	24	34
Empeer	$1,102.50	$577.50	$525.00	
Grant City	$1,027.50	$315.50	$712.00	
Portage	$848.25			$848.25

FIGURE 2-78

3 Querying the City Guide Database

Problem: The chamber of commerce has determined a number of questions it wants the database management system to answer. You must obtain the answers to the questions posed by the chamber.

Instructions: Use the database created in the In the Lab 3 of Project 1 on page AC 61 for this exercise or see your instructor for information on accessing the files required for this book. Print the answers to each question.

Instructions Part 1: Create a new query for the Advertiser table and include the Advertiser Number, Name, Balance, and Amount Paid fields in the design grid. Answer the following questions: (1) Which advertisers' names begin with C? (2) Which advertisers are located on Main? (3) Which advertisers have a current balance of $0.00? (4) Which advertisers have a balance greater than $150.00 and have an amount paid greater than $800.00? (5) Which five advertisers have the highest balances? (6) For each advertiser, what is the total of the current balance and the amount paid?

Instructions Part 2: Join the Ad Rep table and the Advertiser table. Include the Ad Rep Number, First Name, and Last Name from the Ad Rep table and the Advertiser Number, Name, and Balance from the Advertiser table in the design grid. Sort the records in ascending order by Ad Rep Number and Advertiser Number. Perform the following: (1) Calculate the pending commission (comm rate * balance) for each ad rep. The pending commission should display as currency. (2) Restrict retrieval to only those records where the pending commission is greater than $20.00.

Instructions Part 3: Calculate the following statistics: (1) What is the average balance for advertisers assigned to ad rep 26? (2) What is the total amount paid of all advertisers? (3) What is the total balance for each ad rep?

Cases and Places

The difficulty of these case studies varies:
■ are the least difficult and ■■ are more difficult. The last exercise is a group exercise.

1 ■ Use the College Dog Walkers database you created in Cases and Places 1 in Project 1 on page AC 63 for this assignment or see your instructor for information on accessing the files required for this book. Perform the following: (a) Display and print the number and name of all customers who live on Easton. (b) Display and print the number, name, telephone number, and balance for all customers who have a balance of at least $40.00. (c) Display and print the number, name, balance, walker first name, and walker last name for all customers. Sort the records in ascending order by walker last name. (d) Display and print the average balance of all customers. (e) Display and print the average balance of customers grouped by walker. (f) Display and print the total balance of all customers.

2 ■ Use the InPerson Fitness Company database you created in Cases and Places 2 in Project 1 on page AC 63 for this assignment or see your instructor for information on accessing the files required for this book. Perform the following: (a) Display and print the number, client name, and balance for all clients of a particular trainer. The owner should be able to enter a different trainer number each time the query is run. (b) Display and print the number, client name, and total of balance due and amount paid. (c) Display and print the number, client name, and balance of all clients whose amount paid is greater than $400.00. (d) Display and print the trainer number, trainer name, client number, client name, client address, and client telephone number for all clients. Sort the data ascending by trainer number and client number. (e) Display and print the total amount paid and total balance grouped by trainer.

3 ■■ Use the Regional Books database you created in Cases and Places 3 in Project 1 on page AC 63 for this assignment or see your instructor for information on accessing the files required for this book. Perform the following: (a) List the book code, title, and on-hand value (units on hand * price) of all books. (b) List the book code, title, and price of all paperback books. (c) List the book code, title, price, and publisher name for all books where there are less than 3 books on hand. (d) Display and print the book code, title, and author for all books. (e) Find the lowest priced book and the highest priced book.

4 ■■ Use the Campus Housing database you created in Cases and Places 4 in Project 1 on page AC 64 for this assignment or see your instructor for information on accessing the files required for this book. Display and print the following: (a) List all rental units that are located two miles or less from campus. (b) List all rental units that have parking and allow pets. (c) List all three-bedroom apartments that rent for less than $1,000.00 a month. (d) Find the average rent for two-bedroom apartments. (e) List the owners of all units that are efficiencies or rooms for rent. (f) List the different lease terms in ascending order. Each lease term should display only once.

5 ■■ **Working Together** Create an additional query for each of the four databases described in the Cases and Places. Each team must create a parameter query, a top values query, a crosstab query, and an aggregate query. Select the database to use to create each specific query type. Use all four databases, that is, one database per specific query type. Run each of the queries and print the results. Write a one-page paper that lists the queries the team created and explains why the team chose those queries.

$$
\begin{array}{r}
2 \\
77 \\
76 \\
88 \\
\hline
243
\end{array}
$$

$$3\overline{)243} = 81$$

$$
\begin{array}{r}
81 \\
16.5 \\
\hline
97.5
\end{array}
$$

$$2\overline{)97.5}$$

Power Point
Project Require...

Pres By/gru
Intro + loop-

@ Least 6 slices
a sign on each slide

- Title Slides
- clip art at least ov pick

- e_ slide must have Transitions
- Blend from into

@ least on slide has t
have build/or effect.

$$
\begin{array}{r}
2.5 \quad 15 \quad 10 \quad 5 \\
2.5 \\
3. .5 \\
2. .5 \\
\hline
16.5
\end{array}
$$

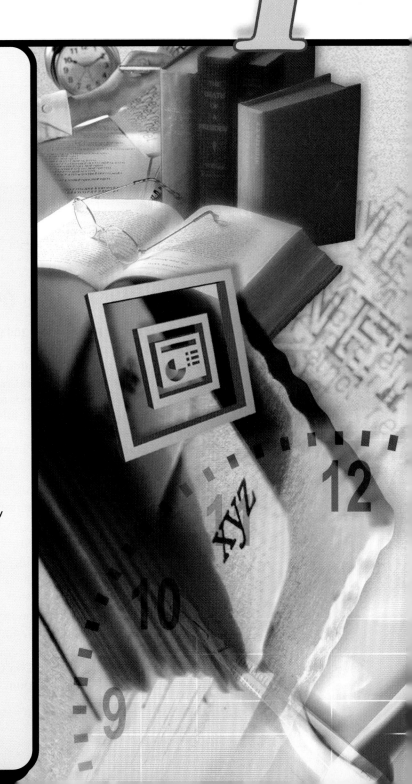

MICROSOFT
Office PowerPoint 2003

Using a Design Template and Text Slide Layout to Create a Presentation

PROJECT

1

CASE PERSPECTIVE

Do you use the 168 hours in each week effectively? From attending class, doing homework, attending school events, exercising, eating, watching television, and sleeping, juggling the demands of school and personal lives can be daunting. Odds are that one of every three students will fail a course at one point in their college career due to poor study habits.

The ability to learn effectively is the key to college success. What matters is not how long people study but how well they use their time in the classroom and while preparing for class assignments and tests. Students with good academic skills maximize their time and, consequently, achieve the highest grades on exams and homework assignments. They ultimately earn higher incomes than their less organized peers because good academic practices carry over to the working environment.

Advisers in the Academic Skills Center at your college are aware of this fact and are developing seminars to help students succeed. Their first presentation focuses on getting organized, enhancing listening skills, and taking tests effectively. Dr. Traci Johnson, the dean of the Academic Skills Center, has asked you to help her create a PowerPoint slide show to use at next month's lunchtime study skills session (Figure 1-1 on page PPT 5). In addition, she would like handouts of the slides to distribute to these students.

As you read through this project, you will learn how to use PowerPoint to create, save, and print a slide show that is composed of single- and multi-level bulleted lists.

MICROSOFT
Office PowerPoint 2003

Using a Design Template and Text Slide Layout to Create a Presentation

PROJECT

Objectives

You will have mastered the material in this project when you can:

- Start and customize PowerPoint
- Describe the PowerPoint window
- Select a design template
- Create a title slide and text slides with single- and multi-level bulleted lists
- Change the font size and font style

- Save a presentation
- End a slide show with a black slide
- View a presentation in slide show view
- Quit PowerPoint and then open a presentation
- Display and print a presentation in black and white
- Use the PowerPoint Help system

What Is Microsoft Office PowerPoint 2003?

Microsoft Office PowerPoint 2003 is a complete presentation graphics program that allows you to produce professional-looking presentations (Figure 1-1). A PowerPoint **presentation** also is called a **slide show**.

PowerPoint contains several features to simplify creating a slide show. For example, you can instruct PowerPoint to create a predesigned presentation, and then you can modify the presentation to fulfill your requirements. You quickly can format a slide show using one of the professionally designed presentation design templates. To make your presentation more impressive, you can add tables, charts, pictures, video, sound, and animation effects. Additional PowerPoint features include the following:

- **Word processing** create bulleted lists, combine words and images, find and replace text, and use multiple fonts and type sizes.
- **Outlining** develop your presentation using an outline format. You also can import outlines from Microsoft Word or other word processing programs.
- **Charting** create and insert charts into your presentations. The two chart types are: standard, which includes bar, line, pie, and xy (scatter) charts; and custom, which shows such objects as floating bars and colored lines.
- **Drawing** form and modify diagrams using shapes such as arcs, arrows, cubes, rectangles, stars, and triangles.
- **Inserting multimedia** insert artwork and multimedia effects into your slide show. The Microsoft Clip Organizer contains hundreds of media files, including pictures, photos, sounds, and movies.

Strategies for College Success

Presented by
Lakemore Academic Skills Center

(a) Slide 1 (Title Slide)

Get Organized
- ☐ Time management skills help balance academic, work, and social events
- ☐ Create a schedule each week that accounts for all activities
- ☐ Plan two hours of study time for each one hour of class time

(b) Slide 2 (Single-Level Bulleted List)

Listen Actively
- ☐ Sit in the front row to focus attention
  - ■ Do not tolerate distractions
- ☐ Make mental summaries of material
- ☐ Be prepared for class
  - ■ Review notes from books, previous class
  - ■ Preview material to be covered that day

(c) Slide 3 (Multi-Level Bulleted List)

Excel on Exams
- ☐ Review test material throughout week
  - ■ Cramming before exam is ineffective
    - ☐ Facts remain only in short-term memory
- ☐ Review entire test before answering
  - ■ Start with the material you know
    - ☐ Think positively and stay focused

(d) Slide 4 (Multi-Level Bulleted List)

FIGURE 1-1

- **Web support** save presentations or parts of a presentation in HTML format so they can be viewed and manipulated using a browser. You can publish your slide show to the Internet or to an intranet.
- **E-mailing** send your entire slide show as an attachment to an e-mail message.
- **Using Wizards** create a presentation quickly and efficiently by answering prompts for specific content criteria. For example, the **AutoContent Wizard** gives prompts for the type of slide show you are planning, such as communicating serious news or motivating a team, and the type of output, such as an on-screen presentation or black and white overheads.

PowerPoint gives you the flexibility to make presentations using a projection device attached to a personal computer (Figure 1-2a) and using overhead transparencies (Figure 1-2b). In addition, you can take advantage of the World Wide Web and run virtual presentations on the Internet (Figure 1-2c). PowerPoint also can create paper printouts of the individual slides, outlines, and speaker notes.

This latest version of PowerPoint has many new features to make you more productive. It saves the presentation to a CD; uses pens, highlighters, arrows, and pointers for emphasis; and includes a thesaurus and other research tools.

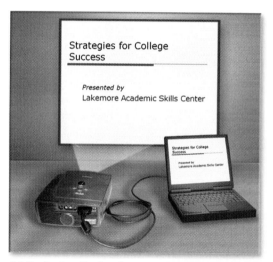

(a) Projection Device Connected to a Personal Computer

(b) Overhead Transparencies

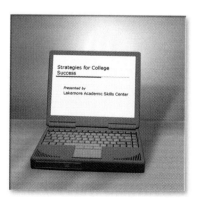

(c) PowerPoint Presentation on the World Wide Web

FIGURE 1-2

Project One — Strategies for College Success

PowerPoint allows you to produce slides to use in an academic, business, or other environment. In Project 1, you create the presentation shown in Figures 1-1a through 1-1d. The objective is to produce a presentation, called Strategies for College Success, to be displayed using a projection device. As an introduction to PowerPoint, this project steps you through the most common type of presentation, which is a **text slide** consisting of a bulleted list. A **bulleted list** is a list of paragraphs, each preceded by a bullet. A **bullet** is a symbol such as a heavy dot (•) or other character that precedes text when the text warrants special emphasis.

Starting and Customizing PowerPoint

If you are stepping through this project on a computer and you want your screen to agree with the figures in this book, then you should change your computer's resolution to 800 × 600. To change the resolution on your computer, see Appendix D.

To start PowerPoint, Windows must be running. The quickest way to begin a new presentation is to use the Start button on the **Windows taskbar** at the bottom of the screen. The following steps show how to start PowerPoint and a new presentation.

To Start PowerPoint

1

• **Click the Start button on the Windows taskbar, point to All Programs on the Start menu, point to Microsoft Office on the All Programs submenu, and then point to Microsoft Office PowerPoint 2003 on the Microsoft Office submenu.**

Windows displays the commands on the Start menu above the Start button, the All Programs submenu, and the Microsoft Office submenu (Figure 1-3).

FIGURE 1-3

2

• **Click Microsoft Office PowerPoint 2003.**

PowerPoint starts. While PowerPoint is starting, the mouse pointer changes to the shape of an hourglass. After several seconds, PowerPoint displays a blank presentation titled Presentation1 in the PowerPoint window (Figure 1-4).

3

• **If the PowerPoint window is not maximized, double-click its title bar to maximize it.**

FIGURE 1-4

More About

Task Panes

When you first start PowerPoint, a small window called a task pane may be docked on the right side of the screen. You can drag a task pane title bar to float the pane in your work area or dock it on either the left or right side or the top or bottom of a screen, depending on your personal preference.

The screen shown in Figure 1-4 illustrates how the PowerPoint window looks the first time you start PowerPoint after installation on most computers. If the Office Speech Recognition software is installed and active on your computer, then, when you start PowerPoint, the Language bar is displayed on the screen. The **Language bar** contains buttons that allow you to speak commands and dictate text. It usually is located on the right side of the Windows taskbar next to the notification area, and it changes to include the speech recognition functions available in PowerPoint. In this book, the Language bar is closed because it takes up computer resources, and with the Language bar active, the microphone can be turned on accidentally by clicking the Microphone button, causing your computer to act in an unstable manner. For additional information about the Language bar, see page PPT 16 and Appendix B.

As shown in Figure 1-4, PowerPoint displays a task pane on the right side of the screen. A **task pane** is a separate window that enables users to carry out some PowerPoint tasks more efficiently. When you start PowerPoint, it displays the Getting Started task pane, which is a small window that provides commonly used links and commands that allow you to open files, create new files, or search Office-related topics on the Microsoft Web site. In this book, the Getting Started task pane is hidden to allow the maximum screen size to appear in PowerPoint.

At startup, PowerPoint also displays two toolbars on a single row. A **toolbar** contains buttons, boxes, and menus that allow you to perform frequent tasks quickly. To allow for more efficient use of the buttons, the toolbars should appear on two separate rows, instead of sharing a single row. The following steps show how to close the Language bar, close the Getting Started task pane, and instruct PowerPoint to display the toolbars on two separate rows.

To Customize the PowerPoint Window

1

• **If the Language bar appears, right-click it to display a list of commands.**

The Language bar shortcut menu appears (Figure 1-5).

FIGURE 1-5

2

• **Click the Close the Language bar command.**

• **If necessary, click the OK button in the Language Bar dialog box.**

• **Click the Getting Started task pane Close button in the upper-right corner of the task pane.**

• **If the Standard and Formatting toolbars are positioned on the same row, click the Toolbar Options button on the Standard toolbar.**

The Language bar disappears. PowerPoint closes the Getting Started task pane and increases the size of the PowerPoint window. PowerPoint also displays the Toolbar Options list showing the buttons that do not fit on the toolbars when the toolbars are displayed on one row (Figure 1-6).

FIGURE 1-6

3

• **Click Show Buttons on Two Rows.**

PowerPoint displays the buttons on two separate rows (Figure 1-7). The Toolbar Options list shown in Figure 1-6 on the previous page is empty because all the buttons are displayed on two rows.

FIGURE 1-7

As you work through creating a presentation, you will find that certain PowerPoint operations result in displaying a task pane. Besides the Getting Started task pane shown in Figure 1-4 on page PPT 8, PowerPoint provides 15 additional task panes: Help, Search Results, Clip Art, Research, Clipboard, New Presentation, Template Help, Shared Workspace, Document Updates, Slide Layout, Slide Design, Slide Design - Color Schemes, Slide Design - Animation Schemes, Custom Animation, and Slide Transition. These task panes are discussed when they are used. You can show or hide a task pane by clicking the Task Pane command on the View menu. You can activate additional task panes by clicking the down arrow to the left of the Close button on the task pane title bar (Figure 1-4) and then selecting a task pane in the list. To switch between task panes that you opened during a session, use the Back and Forward buttons on the left side of the task pane title bar.

The PowerPoint Window

The basic unit of a PowerPoint presentation is a **slide**. A slide contains one or many **objects**, such as a title, text, graphics, tables, charts, and drawings. An object is the building block for a PowerPoint slide. PowerPoint assumes the first slide in a new presentation is the **title slide**. The title slide's purpose is to introduce the presentation to the audience.

In PowerPoint, you have the option of using the PowerPoint default settings or establishing your own. A **default setting** is a particular value for a variable that PowerPoint assigns initially. It controls the placement of objects, the color scheme, the transition between slides, and other slide attributes, and it remains in effect unless you cancel or override it. **Attributes** are the properties or characteristics of an object. For example, if you underline the title of a slide, the title is the object, and the underline is the attribute. When you start PowerPoint, the default **slide layout** is **landscape orientation**, where the slide width is greater than its height. In landscape orientation, the slide size is preset to 10 inches wide and 7.5 inches high. You can change the slide layout to **portrait orientation**, so the slide height is greater than its width, by clicking Page Setup on the File menu. In portrait orientation, the slide width is 7.5 inches, and the height is 10 inches.

When a PowerPoint window is open, its name appears in an icon on the Windows taskbar. The **active application** is the one displaying in the foreground of the desktop. That application's corresponding icon on the Windows taskbar is displayed recessed.

PowerPoint Views

PowerPoint has three main views: normal view, slide sorter view, and slide show view. A **view** is the mode in which the presentation appears on the screen. You may use any or all views when creating a presentation, but you can use only one at a time. You also can select one of these views to be the default view. Change views by clicking one of the view buttons located at the lower-left of the PowerPoint window above the Drawing toolbar (Figure 1-7). The PowerPoint window display varies depending on the view. Some views are graphical while others are textual.

You generally will use normal view and slide sorter view when you are creating a presentation. **Normal view** is composed of three working areas that allow you to work on various aspects of a presentation simultaneously (Figure 1-7). The left side of the screen has a tabs pane that consists of an **Outline tab** and a **Slides tab** that alternate between views of the presentation in an outline of the slide text and a thumbnail, or miniature, view of the slides. You can type the text of the presentation on the Outline tab and easily rearrange bulleted lists, paragraphs, and individual slides. As you type, you can view this text in the **slide pane**, which shows a large view of the current slide on the right side of the window. You also can enter text, graphics, animations, and hyperlinks directly in the slide pane. The **notes pane** at the bottom of the window is an area where you can type notes and additional information. This text can consist of notes to yourself or remarks to share with your audience.

In normal view, you can adjust the width of the slide pane by dragging the **splitter bar** and the height of the notes pane by dragging the pane borders. After you have created at least two slides, **scroll bars**, **scroll arrows**, and **scroll boxes** will be displayed below and to the right of the windows, and you can use them to view different parts of the panes.

Slide sorter view is helpful when you want to see all the slides in the presentation simultaneously. A thumbnail version of each slide is displayed, and you can rearrange their order, add transitions and timings to switch from one slide to the next in a presentation, add and delete slides, and preview animations.

Slide show view fills the entire screen and allows you to see the slide show just as your audience will view it. Transition effects, animation, graphics, movies, and timings are shown as they will appear during an actual presentation.

More About

Sizing Panes

The three panes in normal view allow you to work on all aspects of your presentation simultaneously. You can drag the splitter bar and the pane borders to make each area larger or smaller.

Table 1-1 identifies the view buttons and provides an explanation of each view.

Table 1-1	View Buttons and Functions	
BUTTON	BUTTON NAME	FUNCTION
▣	Normal View	Shows three panes: the tabs pane with either the Outline tab or the Slides tab, the slide pane, and the notes pane.
▤	Slide Sorter View	Shows thumbnail versions of all slides in a presentation. You then can copy, cut, paste, or otherwise change the slide position to modify the presentation. Slide sorter view also is used to add timings, to select animated transitions, and to preview animations.
▦	Slide Show View	Shows the slides as an electronic presentation on the full screen of your computer's monitor. Looking much like a slide projector display, this view can show you the effect of transitions, build effects, slide timings, and animations.

Placeholders, Text Areas, Mouse Pointer, and Scroll Bars

The PowerPoint window contains elements similar to the document windows in other Microsoft Office applications. Other features are unique to PowerPoint. The main elements are the placeholders, text areas, mouse pointer, and scroll bars.

PLACEHOLDERS **Placeholders** are boxes that are displayed when you create a new slide. All layouts except the Blank slide layout contain placeholders. Depending on the particular slide layout selected, placeholders are displayed for the slide title, body text, charts, tables, organization charts, media clips, and clip art. You type titles, body text, and bulleted lists in **text placeholders**; you place graphic elements in chart placeholders, table placeholders, organizational chart placeholders, and clip art placeholders. A placeholder is considered an **object**, which is a single element of a slide.

TEXT AREAS **Text areas** are surrounded by a dotted outline. The title slide in Figure 1-7 on page PPT 10 has two text areas that contain the text placeholders where you will type the main heading, or title, of a new slide and the subtitle, or other object. Other slides in a presentation may use a layout that contains text areas for a title and bulleted lists.

MOUSE POINTER The **mouse pointer** can become one of several different shapes depending on the task you are performing in PowerPoint and the pointer's location on the screen. The different shapes are discussed when they appear.

SCROLL BARS When you add a second slide to a presentation, a **vertical scroll bar** appears on the right side of the slide pane. PowerPoint allows you to use the scroll bar to move forward or backward through the presentation.

The **horizontal scroll bar** also may be displayed. It is located on the bottom of the slide pane and allows you to display a portion of the slide when the entire slide does not fit on the screen.

Status Bar, Menu Bar, Standard Toolbar, Formatting Toolbar, and Drawing Toolbar

The status bar is displayed at the bottom of the screen above the Windows taskbar (Figure 1-7). The menu bar, Standard toolbar, and Formatting toolbar are displayed at the top of the screen just below the title bar. The Drawing toolbar is displayed above the status bar.

STATUS BAR   Immediately above the Windows taskbar at the bottom of the screen is the status bar. The **status bar** consists of a message area and a presentation design template identifier (Figure 1-7). Generally, the message area shows the current slide number and the total number of slides in the slide show. For example, in Figure 1-7 the message area shows Slide 1 of 1. Slide 1 is the current slide, and of 1 indicates the slide show contains only one slide. The template identifier shows Default Design, which is the template PowerPoint uses initially.

MENU BAR   The **menu bar** is a special toolbar that includes the PowerPoint menu names (Figure 1-8a). Each **menu name** represents a menu of commands that you can use to perform tasks such as retrieving, storing, printing, and manipulating objects in a presentation. When you point to a menu name on the menu bar, the area of the menu bar containing the name changes to a button. To display a menu, such as the Edit menu, click the Edit menu name on the menu bar. A **menu** is a list of commands. If you point to a command on a menu that has an arrow to its right edge, a **submenu** shows another list of commands.

(a) Menu Bar and Toolbars

FIGURE 1-8

When you click a menu name on the menu bar, PowerPoint displays a **short menu** listing the most recently used commands (Figure 1-8b). If you wait a few seconds or click the arrows at the bottom of the short menu, it expands into a full menu. A **full menu** lists all the commands associated with a menu (Figure 1-8c). You also can display a full menu immediately by double-clicking the menu name on the menu bar. In this book, always have PowerPoint show the full menu by using one of the following techniques:

1. Click the menu name on the menu bar and then wait a few seconds.
2. Click the menu name on the menu bar and then click the arrows at the bottom of the short menu.
3. Click the menu name on the menu bar and then point to the arrows at the bottom of the short menu.
4. Double-click the menu name on the menu bar.

(b) Short Menu

(c) Full Menu

FIGURE 1-8 *(continued)*

Both short and full menus display some **dimmed commands** that appear gray, or dimmed, instead of black, which indicates they are not available for the current selection. A command with a dark gray shading to the left of it on a full menu is a **hidden command** because it does not appear on a short menu. As you use PowerPoint, it automatically personalizes the short menus for you based on how often you use commands. That is, as you use hidden commands, PowerPoint *unhides* them and places them on the short menu.

The menu bar can change to include other menu names depending on the type of work you are doing in PowerPoint. For example, if you are adding a chart to a slide, Data and Chart menu names are added to the menu bar with commands that reflect charting options.

STANDARD, FORMATTING, AND DRAWING TOOLBARS The **Standard toolbar** (Figure 1-9a), **Formatting toolbar** (Figure 1-9b), and **Drawing toolbar** (Figure 1-9c on the next page) contain buttons and boxes that allow you to perform frequent tasks more quickly than when using the menu bar. For example, to print a slide show, you click the Print button on the Standard toolbar. Each button has an image on the button face that helps you remember the button's function. Also, when you move the mouse pointer over a button or box, the name of the button or box appears below it in a ScreenTip. A **ScreenTip** is a short on-screen note associated with the object to which you are pointing. For examples of ScreenTips, see Figures 1-3 and 1-13 on pages PPT 7 and PPT 19.

Figure 1-9 illustrates the Standard, Formatting, and Drawing toolbars and describes the functions of the buttons. Each of the buttons and boxes will be explained in detail when they are used.

More About

Hiding Toolbars

To display more of the PowerPoint window, you can hide a toolbar you no longer need. To hide a toolbar, right-click any toolbar and then click the check mark next to the toolbar you want to hide on the shortcut menu.

(a) Standard Toolbar

(b) Formatting Toolbar

FIGURE 1-9

(c) Drawing Toolbar

FIGURE 1-9 *(continued)*

PowerPoint has several additional toolbars you can display by pointing to Toolbars on the View menu and then clicking the respective name on the Toolbars submenu. You also may display a toolbar by pointing to a toolbar and right-clicking to display a shortcut menu, which lists the available toolbars. A **shortcut menu** contains a list of commands or items that relate to the item to which you are pointing when you right-click.

Speech Recognition

With the **Office Speech Recognition software** installed and a microphone, you can speak the names of toolbar buttons, menus, menu commands, list items, alerts, and dialog box controls, such as OK and Cancel. You also can dictate words to fill the placeholders. To indicate whether you want to speak commands or dictate placeholder entries, you use the Language bar. The Language bar can be in one of four states: (1) **restored**, which means it is displayed somewhere in the PowerPoint window (Figure 1-10a); (2) **minimized**, which means it is displayed on the Windows taskbar (Figure 1-10b); (3) **hidden**, which means you do not see it on the screen but it will be displayed the next time you start your computer; (4) **closed**, which means it is hidden permanently until you enable it. If the Language bar is hidden or closed and you want it to display, then do the following:

1. Right-click an open area on the Windows taskbar at the bottom of the screen.
2. Point to Toolbars and then click Language bar on the Toolbars submenu.

(a) Language Bar Restored

FIGURE 1-10

(b) Language Bar Minimized on Windows Taskbar

FIGURE 1-10 *(continued)*

If the Language bar command is dimmed on the Toolbars submenu or if the Speech command is dimmed on the Tools menu, the Office Speech Recognition software is not installed.

In this book, the Language bar does not appear in the figures. If you want to close the Language bar so that your screen is identical to what you see in the book, right-click the Language bar and then click Close the Language bar on the shortcut menu.

Additional information about the speech recognition capabilities of PowerPoint is available in Appendix B.

Choosing a Design Template

A **design template** provides consistency in design and color throughout the entire presentation. It determines the color scheme, font and font size, and layout of a presentation. PowerPoint has three Slide Design task panes that allow you to choose and change the appearance of slides in your presentation. The **Slide Design task pane** shows a variety of styles. You can alter the colors used in the design templates by using the **Slide Design – Color Schemes task pane**. In addition, you can animate elements of your presentation by using the **Slide Design – Animation Schemes task pane**.

In this project, you will select a particular design template by using the Slide Design task pane. The top section of the task pane, labeled Used in This Presentation, shows the template currently used in the slide show. PowerPoint uses the **Default Design** template until you select a different style. When you place your mouse over a template, the name of the template appears. Once a PowerPoint slide show has been created on the computer, the next section of the task pane displayed is the Recently Used templates. This area shows the four templates you have used in your newest slide shows. The Available For Use area shows additional templates. The templates are displayed in alphabetical order in the two columns.

You want to change the template for this presentation from the Default Design to Profile. The steps on the next page apply the Profile design template.

To Choose a Design Template

1

• **Point to the Slide Design button on the Formatting toolbar (Figure 1-11).**

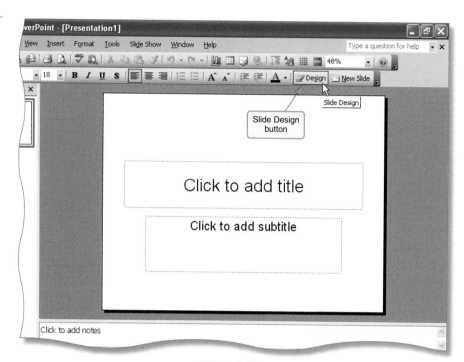

FIGURE 1-11

2

• **Click the Slide Design button and then point to the down scroll arrow in the Apply a design template list.**

The Slide Design task pane appears (Figure 1-12). The Apply a design template list shows thumbnail views of numerous design templates. Your list may look different depending on your computer. The Default Design template is highlighted in the Used in This Presentation area. Other templates display in the Available For Use area and possibly in the Recently Used area. The Close button in the Slide Design task pane can be used to close the task pane if you do not want to apply a new template.

FIGURE 1-12

3

• **Click the down scroll arrow to scroll through the list of design templates until Profile appears in the Available For Use area. Point to the Profile template.**

The Profile template is selected, as indicated by the blue box around the template and the arrow button on the right side (Figure 1-13). PowerPoint provides 45 templates in the Available For Use area. Additional templates are available on the Microsoft Office Online Web site. A ScreenTip shows the template's name. Your system may display the ScreenTip, Profile.pot, which indicates the design template's file extension (.pot).

FIGURE 1-13

4

• **Click Profile.**

• **Point to the Close button in the Slide Design task pane.**

The template is applied to Slide 1, as shown in the slide pane and Slides tab (Figure 1-14).

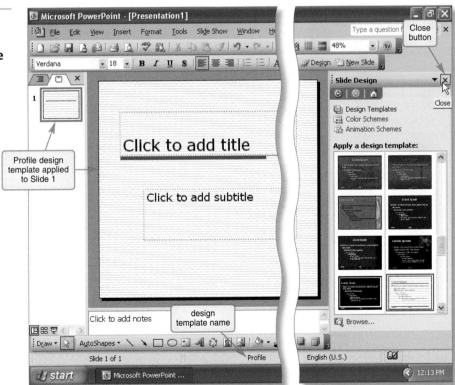

FIGURE 1-14

5

• **Click the Close button.**

Slide 1 is displayed in normal view with the Profile design template (Figure 1-15).

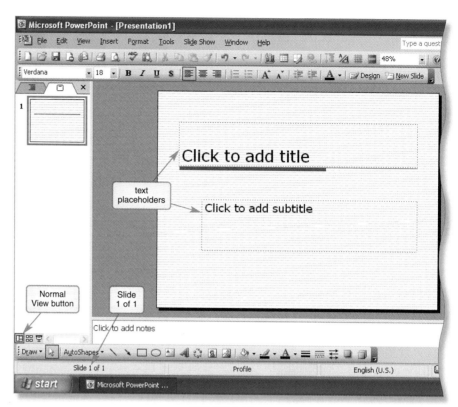

FIGURE 1-15

Creating a Title Slide

With the exception of a blank slide, PowerPoint assumes every new slide has a title. To make creating a presentation easier, any text you type after a new slide appears becomes title text in the title text placeholder.

Entering the Presentation Title

The presentation title for Project 1 is Strategies for College Success. To enter text in your slide, you type on the keyboard or speak into the microphone. As you begin entering text in the title text placeholder, the title text is displayed immediately in the Slide 1 thumbnail in the Slides tab. The following steps create the title slide for this presentation.

To Enter the Presentation Title

1

- **Click the label, Click to add title, located inside the title text placeholder.**

*The insertion point is in the title text placeholder (Figure 1-16). The **insertion point** is a blinking vertical line (|), which indicates where the next character will display. The mouse pointer changes to an I-beam. A **selection rectangle** appears around the title text placeholder. The placeholder is selected as indicated by the border and sizing handles displaying on the edges.*

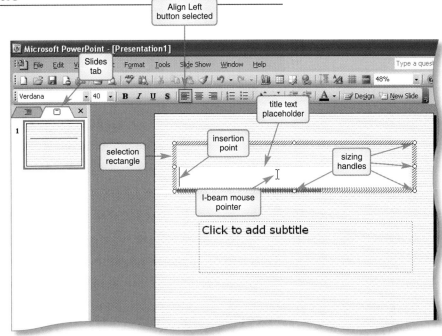

FIGURE 1-16

2

- **Type** Strategies for College Success **in the title text placeholder. Do not press the ENTER key.**

The title text, Strategies for College Success, appears on two lines in the title text placeholder and in the Slides tab (Figure 1-17). The insertion point appears after the final letter s in Success. The title text is displayed aligned left in the placeholder with the default text attributes of the Verdana font and font size 40.

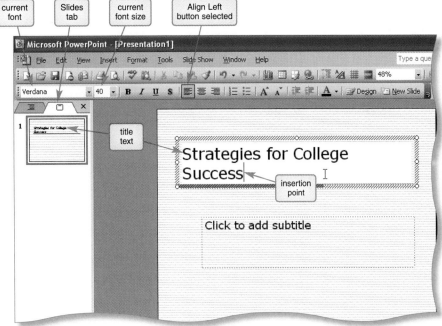

FIGURE 1-17

Other Ways

1. In Dictation mode, say "Strategies for College Success"

PowerPoint **line wraps** text that exceeds the width of the placeholder. One of PowerPoint's features is **text AutoFit**. If you are creating a slide and need to squeeze an extra line in the text placeholder, PowerPoint will prompt you to resize the existing text in the placeholder so the spillover text will fit on the slide.

Correcting a Mistake When Typing

If you type the wrong letter, press the BACKSPACE key to erase all the characters back to and including the one that is incorrect. If you mistakenly press the ENTER key after typing the title and the insertion point is on the new line, simply press the BACKSPACE key to return the insertion point to the right of the letter s in the word Success.

When you install PowerPoint, the default setting allows you to reverse up to the last 20 changes by clicking the Undo button on the Standard toolbar. The ScreenTip that appears when you point to the Undo button changes to indicate the type of change just made. For example, if you type text in the title text placeholder and then point to the Undo button, the ScreenTip that appears is Undo Typing. For clarity, when referencing the Undo button in this project, the name displaying in the ScreenTip is referenced. Another way to reverse changes is to click the Undo command on the Edit menu. As with the Undo button, the Undo command reflects the last type of change made to the presentation.

You can reapply a change that you reversed with the Undo button by clicking the Redo button on the Standard toolbar. Clicking the Redo button reverses the last undo action. The ScreenTip name reflects the type of reversal last performed.

Entering the Presentation Subtitle

The next step in creating the title slide is to enter the subtitle text into the subtitle text placeholder. Complete the following steps to enter the presentation subtitle.

To Enter the Presentation Subtitle

1

• **Click the label, Click to add subtitle, located inside the subtitle text placeholder.**

The insertion point appears in the subtitle text placeholder (Figure 1-18). The mouse pointer changes to an I-beam, indicating the mouse is in a text placeholder. The selection rectangle indicates the placeholder is selected.

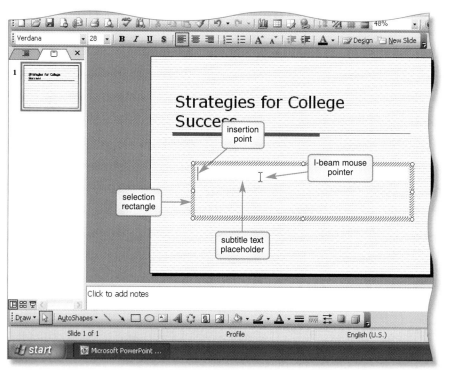

FIGURE 1-18

2

• **Type** Presented by **and then press the ENTER key.**

• **Type** Lakemore Academic Skills Center **but do not press the ENTER key.**

The subtitle text appears in the subtitle text placeholder and the Slides tab (Figure 1-19). The insertion point appears after the letter r in Center. A red wavy line appears below the word, Lakemore, to indicate a possible spelling error.

FIGURE 1-19

After pressing the ENTER key in Step 2, PowerPoint created a new line, which is the second paragraph in the placeholder. A **paragraph** is a segment of text with the same format that begins when you press the ENTER key and ends when you press the ENTER key again.

Other Ways

1. In Dictation mode, say "Presented by, New Line, Lakemore Academic Skills Center"

Text Attributes

This presentation uses the Profile design template. Each design template has its own text attributes. A **text attribute** is a characteristic of the text, such as font, font size, font style, or text color. You can adjust text attributes any time before, during, or after you type the text. Recall that a design template determines the color scheme, font and font size, and layout of a presentation. Most of the time, you use the design template's text attributes and color scheme. Occasionally, you may want to change the way a presentation looks, however, and still keep a particular design template. PowerPoint gives you that flexibility. You can use the design template and change the font and the font's color, effects, size, and style. Text may have one or more font styles and effects simultaneously. Table 1-2 on the next page explains the different text attributes available in PowerPoint.

More About

Text Attributes

The Microsoft Web site contains a comprehensive glossary of typography terms. The information includes a diagram illustrating text attributes. For more information, visit the PowerPoint 2003 More About Web page (scsite.com/ppt2003/more) and then click Attributes.

Table 1-2	Design Template Text Attributes
ATTRIBUTE	**DESCRIPTION**
Color	Defines the color of text. Printing text in color requires a color printer or plotter.
Effects	Effects include underline, shadow, emboss, superscript, and subscript. Effects can be applied to most fonts.
Font	Defines the appearance and shape of letters, numbers, and special characters.
Size	Specifies the height of characters on the screen. Character size is gauged by a measurement system called points. A single point is about 1/72 of an inch in height. Thus, a character with a point size of 18 is about 18/72 (or 1/4) of an inch in height.
Style	Font styles include regular, bold, italic, and bold italic.

The next two sections explain how to change the font size and font style attributes.

Changing the Style of Text to Italic

Text font styles include plain, italic, bold, shadowed, and underlined. PowerPoint allows you to use one or more text font styles in a presentation. The following steps add emphasis to the first line of the subtitle text by changing regular text to italic text.

To Change the Text Font Style to Italic

1

• **Triple-click the paragraph, Presented by, in the subtitle text placeholder, and then point to the Italic button on the Formatting toolbar.**

The paragraph, Presented by, is highlighted (Figure 1-20). The Italic button is surrounded by a blue box. You select an entire paragraph quickly by triple-clicking any text within the paragraph.

FIGURE 1-20

2

• **Click the Italic button.**

The text is italicized on the slide and the slide thumbnail (Figure 1-21).

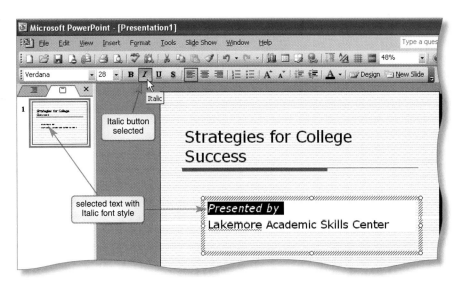

FIGURE 1-21

Other Ways

1. Right-click selected text, click Font on shortcut menu, click Italic in Font style list
2. On Format menu click Font, click Italic in Font style list
3. Press CTRL+I
4. In Voice Command mode, say "Italic"

To remove the italic style from text, select the italicized text and then click the Italic button. As a result, the Italic button is not selected, and the text does not have the italic font style.

Changing the Font Size

The Profile design template default font size is 40 point for title text and 28 point for body text. A point is 1/72 of an inch in height. Thus, a character with a point size of 40 is 40/72 (or 5/9) of an inch in height. Slide 1 requires you to increase the font size for the paragraph, Lakemore Academic Skills Center. The following steps illustrate how to increase the font size.

To Increase Font Size

1

• **Position the mouse pointer in the paragraph, Lakemore Academic Skills Center, and then triple-click.**

PowerPoint selects the entire paragraph (Figure 1-22).

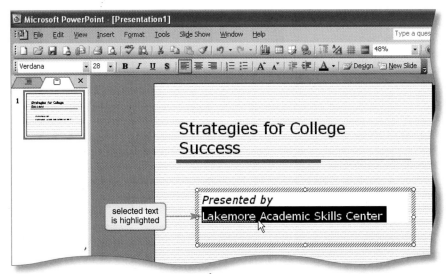

FIGURE 1-22

2

• **Point to the Font Size box arrow on the Formatting toolbar.**

The ScreenTip shows the words, Font Size (Figure 1-23). The Font Size box is surrounded by a box and indicates that the subtitle text is 28 point.

FIGURE 1-23

3

• **Click the Font Size box arrow, click the Font Size box scroll bar, and then point to 32 in the Font Size list.**

When you click the Font Size box, a list of available font sizes is displayed in the Font Size list (Figure 1-24). The font sizes displayed depend on the current font, which is Verdana. Font size 32 is highlighted.

FIGURE 1-24

4

• **Click 32.**

The font size of the subtitle text, Lakemore Academic Skills Center, increases to 32 point (Figure 1-25). The Font Size box on the Formatting toolbar shows 32, indicating the selected text has a font size of 32.

Other Ways

1. Click Increase Font Size button on Formatting toolbar
2. On Format menu click Font, click new font size in Size box, or type font size between 1 and 4000, click OK button
3. Right-click selected text, click Font on shortcut menu, type new font size in Size box, click OK button
4. In Voice Command mode, say "Font Size, [font size]"

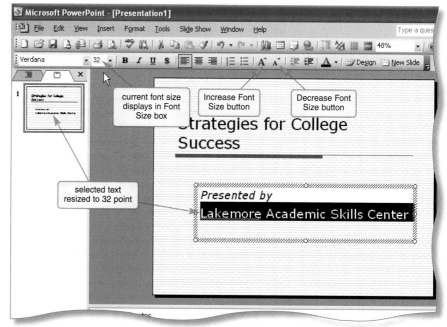

FIGURE 1-25

The Increase Font Size button on the Formatting toolbar (Figure 1-25) increases the font size in preset increments each time you click the button. If you need to decrease the font size, click the Font Size box arrow and then select a size smaller than 32. The Decrease Font Size button on the Formatting toolbar (Figure 1-25) also decreases the font size in preset increments each time you click the button.

Saving the Presentation on a Floppy Disk

While you are building a presentation, the computer stores it in memory. It is important to save the presentation frequently because the presentation will be lost if the computer is turned off or you lose electrical power. Another reason to save your work is that if you run out of lab time before completing your project, you may finish the project later without starting over. Therefore, always save any presentation you will use later on a floppy disk or hard disk. A saved presentation is referred to as a **file**. Before you continue with Project 1, save the work completed thus far. The following steps illustrate how to save a presentation on a floppy disk in drive A using the Save button on the Standard toolbar.

To Save a Presentation on a Floppy Disk

1

• **With a formatted floppy disk in drive A, click the Save button on the Standard toolbar.**

The Save As dialog box is displayed (Figure 1-26). The default folder, My Documents, appears in the Save in box. Strategies for College Success appears highlighted in the File name text box because PowerPoint uses the words in the title text placeholder as the default file name. Presentation appears in the Save as type box. The buttons on the top and on the side are used to select folders and change the appearance of file names and other information.

FIGURE 1-26

2

• **Type** College Success **in the File name text box. Do not press the ENTER key after typing the file name.**

• **Click the Save in box arrow.**

The name, College Success, appears in the File name text box (Figure 1-27). A file name can be up to 255 characters and can include spaces. The Save in list shows a list of locations in which to save a presentation. Your list may look different depending on the configuration of your system. Clicking the Cancel button closes the Save As dialog box.

FIGURE 1-27

3

• **Click 3½ Floppy (A:) in the Save in list.**

Drive A becomes the selected drive (Figure 1-28).

FIGURE 1-28

4

• **Click the Save button in the Save As dialog box.**

PowerPoint saves the presentation on the floppy disk in drive A. The title bar shows the file name used to save the presentation, College Success (Figure 1-29).

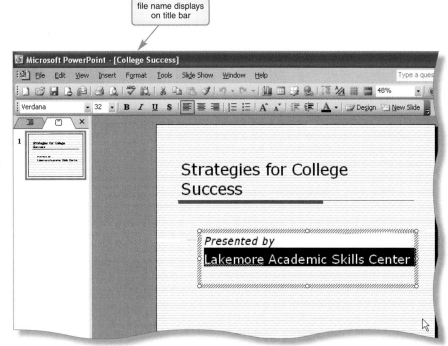

file name displays on title bar

FIGURE 1-29

PowerPoint automatically appends the extension .ppt to the file name, College Success. The **.ppt** extension stands for **P**ower**P**oint. Although the slide show, College Success, is saved on a floppy disk, it also remains in memory and is displayed on the screen.

It is a good practice to save periodically while you are working on a project. By doing so, you protect yourself from losing all the work you have done since the last time you saved.

The seven buttons at the top and to the right in the Save As dialog box in Figure 1-28 and their functions are summarized in Table 1-3.

Other Ways

1. On File menu click Save As, type file name, select drive or folder, click Save button
2. On File menu click Save As, click My Computer button, select drive or folder, click Save button
3. Press CTRL+S or press SHIFT+F12, type file name, select drive or folder, click OK button
4. In Voice Command mode, say "File, Save As, [type desired file name], Save"

Table 1-3	Save As Dialog Box Toolbar Buttons	
BUTTON	**BUTTON NAME**	**FUNCTION**
	Default File Location	Displays contents of default file location
	Up One Level	Displays contents of folder one level up from current folder
	Search the Web	Starts browser and displays search engine
	Delete	Deletes selected file or folder
	Create New Folder	Creates new folder
	Views	Changes view of files and folders
Tools	Tools	Lists commands to print or modify file names and folders

More About

Passwords

The most common word used for a password is the word, password. When choosing a password for your files, experts recommend using a combination of letters and numbers and making the word at least eight characters. Avoid using your name and the names of family members or pets.

When you click the Tools button in the Save As dialog box, PowerPoint displays a list. The Save Options command in the list allows you to save the presentation automatically at a specified time interval and to reduce the file size. The Security Options command allows you to modify the security level for opening files that may contain harmful computer viruses and to assign a password to limit access to the file. A password is case-sensitive and can be up to 15 characters long. **Case-sensitive** means PowerPoint can differentiate between uppercase and lowercase letters. If you assign a password and then forget the password, you cannot access the file.

The file buttons on the left of the Save As dialog box in Figure 1-28 on page PPT 28 allow you to select frequently used folders. The My Recent Documents button displays a list of shortcuts (pointers) to the most recently used files in a folder titled Recent. You cannot save presentations to the Recent folder.

Adding a New Slide to a Presentation

With the title slide for the presentation created, the next step is to add the first text slide immediately after the title slide. Usually, when you create a presentation, you add slides with text, graphics, or charts. When you add a new slide, PowerPoint uses the Title and Text slide layout. Some placeholders allow you to double-click the placeholder and then access other objects, such as media clips, charts, diagrams, and organization charts.

The following steps add a new Text slide layout with a bulleted list. The default PowerPoint setting will display the Slide Layout task pane each time a new slide is added. Your system may not display this task pane if the setting has been changed.

To Add a New Text Slide with a Bulleted List

1

• **Click the New Slide button on the Formatting toolbar.**

The Slide Layout task pane opens. The Title and Text slide layout is selected. Slide 2 of 2 appears on the status bar (Figure 1-30).

FIGURE 1-30

2

• **If necessary, click the Show when inserting new slides check box to remove the check mark, and then click the Close button on the Slide Layout task pane.**

Slide 2 appears in both the slide pane and Slides tab retaining the attributes of the Profile design template (Figure 1-31). The vertical scroll bar appears in the slide pane. The bullet appears as an outline square.

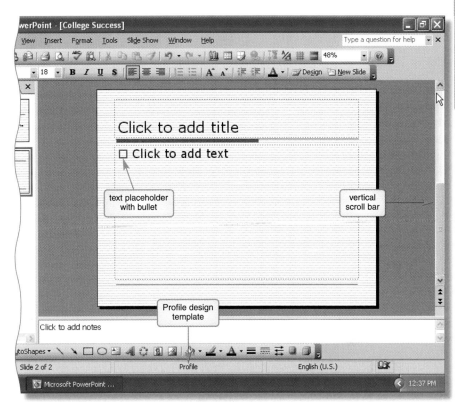

FIGURE 1-31

Slide 2 appears with a title text placeholder and a text placeholder with a bullet. You can change the layout for a slide at any time during the creation of a presentation by clicking Format on the menu bar and then clicking Slide Layout. You also can click View on the menu bar and then click Task Pane. You then can double-click the slide layout of your choice from the Slide Layout task pane.

Creating a Text Slide with a Single-Level Bulleted List

The information in the Slide 2 text placeholder is presented in a bulleted list. All the bullets appear on one level. A **level** is a position within a structure, such as an outline, that indicates the magnitude of importance. PowerPoint allows for five paragraph levels. Each paragraph level has an associated bullet. The bullet font is dependent on the design template.

Entering a Slide Title

PowerPoint assumes every new slide has a title. The title for Slide 2 is Get Organized. The step on the next page shows how to enter this title.

To Enter a Slide Title

1

• **Click the title text placeholder and then type** Get Organized **in the placeholder. Do not press the ENTER key.**

The title, Get Organized, appears in the title text placeholder and in the Slides tab (Figure 1-32). The insertion point appears after the d in Organized. The selection rectangle indicates the title text placeholder is selected.

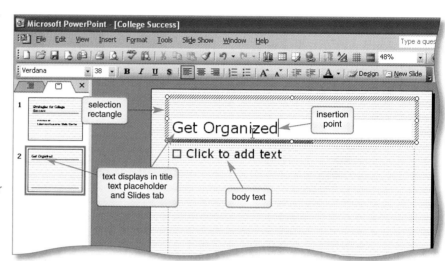

FIGURE 1-32

Selecting a Text Placeholder

Before you can type text into the text placeholder, you first must select it. The following step selects the text placeholder on Slide 2.

To Select a Text Placeholder

1

• **Click the bulleted paragraph labeled, Click to add text.**

The insertion point appears immediately to the right of the bullet on Slide 2 (Figure 1-33). The mouse pointer may change shape if you move it away from the bullet. The selection rectangle indicates the text placeholder is selected.

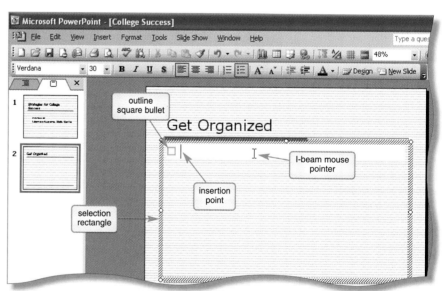

FIGURE 1-33

Typing a Single-Level Bulleted List

As discussed previously, a bulleted list is a list of paragraphs, each of which is preceded by a bullet. A paragraph is a segment of text ended by pressing the ENTER key. The next step is to type the single-level bulleted list, which consists of three entries (Figure 1-1b on page PPT 5). The following steps illustrate how to type a single-level bulleted list.

To Type a Single-Level Bulleted List

1

• **Type** Time management skills help balance academic, work, and social events **and then press the ENTER key.**

The paragraph, Time management skills help balance academic, work, and social events, appears (Figure 1-34). The font size is 30. The insertion point appears after the second bullet. When you press the ENTER key, PowerPoint ends one paragraph and begins a new paragraph. With the Title and Text slide layout, PowerPoint places an outline square bullet in front of the new paragraph.

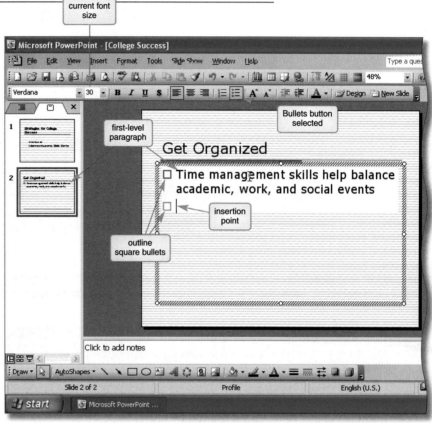

FIGURE 1-34

2

• **Type** Create a schedule each week that accounts for all activities **and then press the** ENTER **key.**

• **Type** Plan two hours of study time for each one hour of class time **but do not press the** ENTER **key.**

• **Point to the New Slide button on the Formatting toolbar.**

The insertion point is displayed after the e in time (Figure 1-35). Three new first-level paragraphs are displayed with outline square bullets in both the text placeholder and the Slides tab. When you press the ENTER *key, PowerPoint adds a new paragraph at the same level as the previous paragraph.*

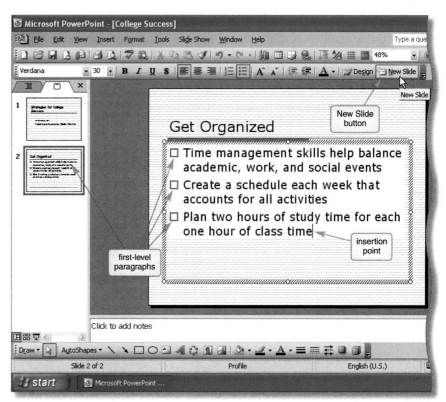

FIGURE 1-35

Notice that you did not press the ENTER key after typing the last paragraph in Step 2. If you press the ENTER key, a new bullet appears after the last entry on this slide. To remove an extra bullet, press the BACKSPACE key.

Creating a Text Slide with a Multi-Level Bulleted List

Slides 3 and 4 in Figure 1-1 on page PPT 5 contain more than one level of bulleted text. A slide that consists of more than one level of bulleted text is called a **multi-level bulleted list slide**. Beginning with the second level, each paragraph indents to the right of the preceding level and is pushed down to a lower level. For example, if you increase the indent of a first-level paragraph, it becomes a second-level paragraph. This lower-level paragraph is a subset of the higher-level paragraph. It usually contains information that supports the topic in the paragraph immediately above it. You increase the indent of a paragraph by clicking the Increase Indent button on the Formatting toolbar.

When you want to raise a paragraph from a lower level to a higher level, you click the Decrease Indent button on the Formatting toolbar.

Creating a text slide with a multi-level bulleted list requires several steps. Initially, you enter a slide title in the title text placeholder. Next, you select the body text placeholder. Then, you type the text for the multi-level bulleted list, increasing and decreasing the indents as needed. The next several sections explain how to add a slide with a multi-level bulleted list.

Adding New Slides and Entering Slide Titles

When you add a new slide to a presentation, PowerPoint keeps the same layout used on the previous slide. PowerPoint assumes every new slide has a title. The title for Slide 3 is Listen Actively. The following steps show how to add a new slide (Slide 3) and enter a title.

To Add a New Slide and Enter a Slide Title

1

• **Click the New Slide button.**

Slide 3 of 3 appears in the slide pane and Slides tab (Figure 1-36).

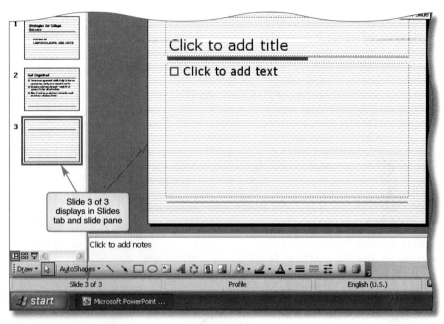

FIGURE 1-36

2

• **Type** Listen Actively **in the title text placeholder. Do not press the ENTER key.**

Slide 3 shows the Title and Text slide layout with the title, Listen Actively, in the title text placeholder and in the Slides tab (Figure 1-37). The insertion point appears after the y in Actively.

FIGURE 1-37

Slide 3 is added to the presentation with the desired title.

Other Ways

1. Press SHIFT+CTRL+M
2. In Dictation mode, say "New Slide, Listen Actively"

Typing a Multi-Level Bulleted List

The next step is to select the body text placeholder and then type the multi-level bulleted list, which consists of six entries (Figure 1-1c on page PPT 5). The following steps show how to create a list consisting of three levels.

To Type a Multi-Level Bulleted List

1

• **Click the bulleted paragraph labeled, Click to add text.**

The insertion point appears immediately to the right of the bullet on Slide 3. The mouse pointer may change shape if you move it away from the bullet.

2

• **Type** Sit in the front row to focus attention **and then press the ENTER key.**

• **Point to the Increase Indent button on the Formatting toolbar.**

The paragraph, Sit in the front row to focus attention, appears (Figure 1-38). The font size is 30. The insertion point appears to the right of the second bullet.

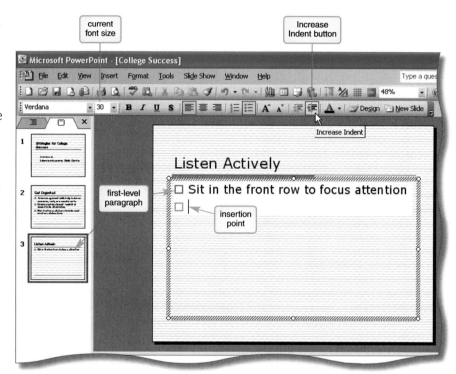

FIGURE 1-38

3

• **Click the Increase Indent button.**

The second paragraph indents below the first and becomes a second-level paragraph (Figure 1-39). The bullet to the left of the second paragraph changes from an outline square to a solid square, and the font size for the paragraph now is 26. The insertion point appears to the right of the solid square.

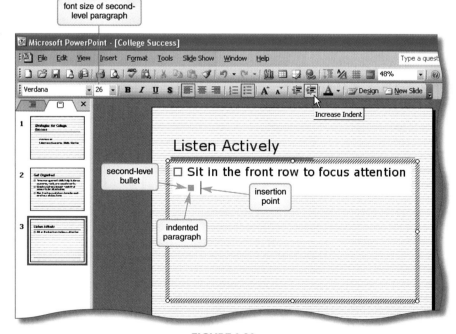

FIGURE 1-39

4

• **Type** Do not tolerate distractions **and then press the ENTER key.**

• **Point to the Decrease Indent button on the Formatting toolbar.**

The first second-level paragraph appears with a solid orange square bullet in both the slide pane and the Slides tab (Figure 1-40). When you press the ENTER key, PowerPoint adds a new paragraph at the same level as the previous paragraph.

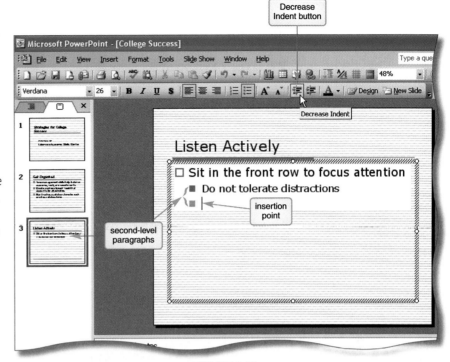

FIGURE 1-40

5

• **Click the Decrease Indent button.**

The second-level paragraph becomes a first-level paragraph (Figure 1-41). The bullet of the new paragraph changes from a solid orange square to an outline square, and the font size for the paragraph is 30. The insertion point appears to the right of the outline square bullet.

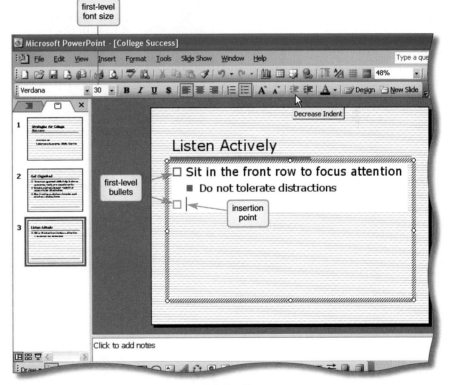

FIGURE 1-41

The steps on the next page complete the text for Slide 3.

Other Ways

1. In Dictation mode, say, "Sit in the front row to focus attention, New Line, Increase Indent, Do not tolerate distractions, New Line, Decrease Indent"

To Type the Remaining Text for Slide 3

1 **Type** Make mental summaries of material **and then press the ENTER key.**

2 **Type** Be prepared for class **and then press the ENTER key.**

3 **Click the Increase Indent button on the Formatting toolbar.**

4 **Type** Review notes from books, previous class **and then press the ENTER key.**

5 **Type** Preview material to be covered that day **but do not press the ENTER key.**

Other Ways

1. In Dictation mode, say "Make mental summaries of material, New Line, Be prepared for class, Increase Indent, Review notes from books comma previous class, New Line, Preview material to be covered that day"

Slide 3 is displayed as shown in Figure 1-42. The insertion point appears after the y in day.

FIGURE 1-42

In Step 4 above, you did not press the ENTER key after typing the last paragraph. If you press the ENTER key, a new bullet appears after the last entry on this slide. To remove an extra bullet, press the BACKSPACE key.

Slide 4 is the last slide in this presentation. It also is a multi-level bulleted list and has three levels. The following steps create Slide 4.

To Create Slide 4

1 **Click the New Slide button on the Formatting toolbar.**

2 **Type** Excel on Exams **in the title text placeholder.**

3 **Press CTRL+ENTER to move the insertion point to the body text placeholder.**

4 **Type** Review test material throughout week **and then press the ENTER key.**

5 **Click the Increase Indent button on the Formatting toolbar. Type** Cramming before exams is ineffective **and then press the ENTER key.**

The title and first two levels of bullets are added to Slide 4 (Figure 1-43).

Other Ways

1. In Dictation mode, say "New Slide, Excel on Exams, [type CTRL+ENTER], Review test material throughout week, New Line, Increase Indent, Cramming before exams is ineffective"

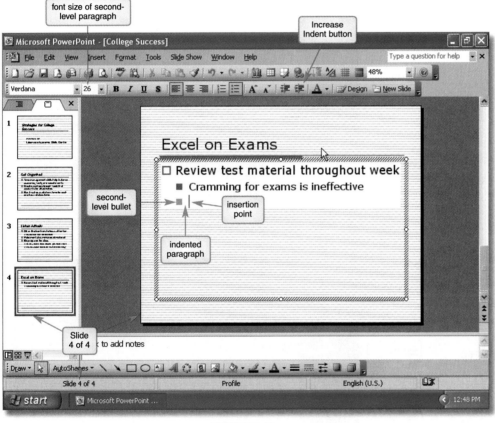

FIGURE 1-43

Creating a Third-Level Paragraph

The next line in Slide 4 is indented an additional level, to the third level. The steps on the next page create an additional level.

To Create a Third-Level Paragraph

1

• **Click the Increase Indent button on the Formatting toolbar.**

The second-level paragraph becomes a third-level paragraph (Figure 1-44). The bullet to the left of the new paragraph changes from a solid square to an outline square, and the font size for the paragraph is 23. The insertion point appears after the outline square bullet.

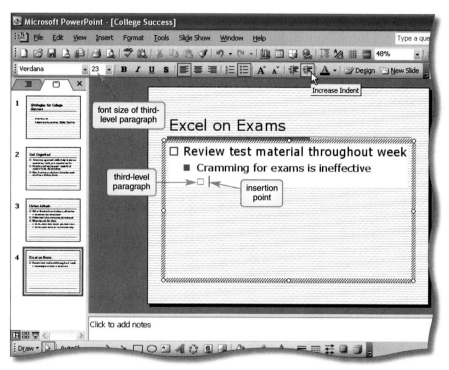

FIGURE 1-44

2

• **Type** Facts remain only in short-term memory **and then press the ENTER key.**

• **Point to the Decrease Indent button on the Formatting toolbar.**

The first third-level paragraph, Facts remain only in short-term memory, is displayed with the bullet for a second third-level paragraph (Figure 1-45).

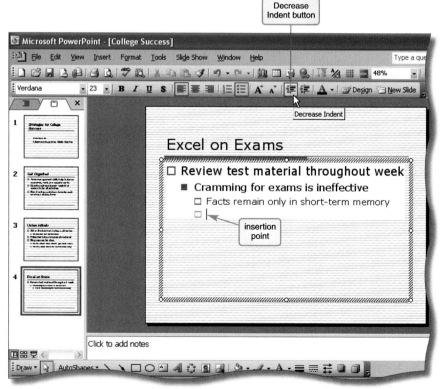

FIGURE 1-45

3

• **Click the Decrease Indent button two times.**

The insertion point appears at the first level (Figure 1-46).

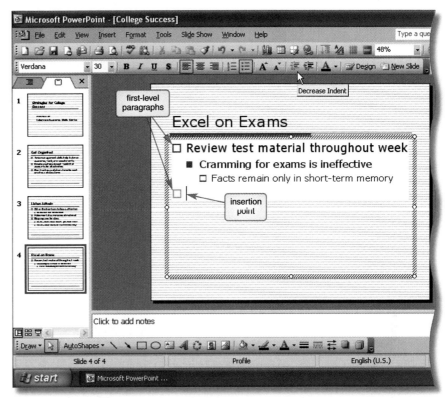

FIGURE 1-46

The title text and three levels of paragraphs discussing preparing for exams are complete. The next three paragraphs concern strategies for taking tests. As an alternative to clicking the Increase Indent button, you can press the TAB key. Likewise, instead of clicking the Decrease Indent button, you can press the SHIFT+TAB keys. The following steps illustrate how to type the remaining text for Slide 4.

To Type the Remaining Text for Slide 4

1 **Type** Review entire test before answering **and then press the ENTER key.**

2 **Press the TAB key to increase the indent to the second level.**

3 **Type** Start with the material you know **and then press the ENTER key.**

4 **Press the TAB key to increase the indent to the third level.**

5 **Type** Think positively and stay focused **but do not press the ENTER key.**

The Slide 4 title text and body text are displayed in the slide pane and Slides tabs (Figure 1-47 on the next page). The insertion point appears after the d in focused.

Other Ways

1. In Dictation mode, say "Tab, Facts remain only in short-term memory, New Line, [type backspace]"

Other Ways

1. In Dictation mode, say "Review entire test before answering, New Line, Tab, Start with the material you know, New Line, Tab, Think positively and stay focused"

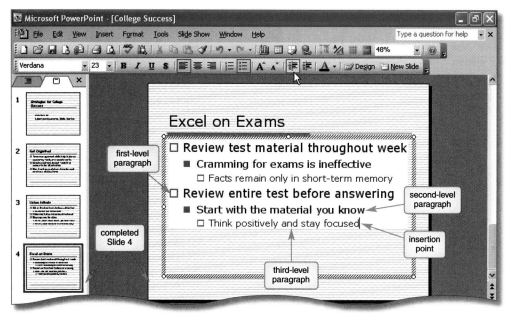

FIGURE 1-47

All the slides are created for the College Success slide show. This presentation consists of a title slide, one text slide with a single-level bulleted list, and two text slides with a multi-level bulleted list.

Ending a Slide Show with a Black Slide

After the last slide in the slide show appears, the default PowerPoint setting is to end the presentation with a black slide. This black slide appears only when the slide show is running and concludes the slide show gracefully so your audience never sees the PowerPoint window. A **black slide** ends all slide shows unless the option setting is deselected. The following steps verify that the End with black slide option is activated.

To End a Slide Show with a Black Slide

1

• **Click Tools on the menu bar and then point to Options (Figure 1-48).**

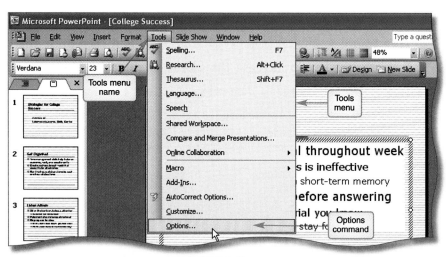

FIGURE 1-48

2

• **Click Options.**

• **If necessary, click the View tab when the Options dialog box appears.**

• **Verify that the End with black slide check box is selected.**

• **If a check mark does not show, click End with black slide.**

• **Point to the OK button.**

The Options dialog box appears (Figure 1-49). The View sheet contains settings for the overall PowerPoint display and for a particular slide show.

3

• **Click the OK button.**

The End with black slide option will cause the slide show to end with a black slide until it is deselected.

FIGURE 1-49

With all aspects of the presentation complete, it is important to save the additions and changes you have made to the College Success presentation.

Saving a Presentation with the Same File Name

Saving frequently cannot be overemphasized. When you first saved the presentation, you clicked the Save button on the Standard toolbar, and the Save dialog box appeared. When you want to save the changes made to the presentation after your last save, you again click the Save button. This time, however, the Save dialog box does not appear because PowerPoint updates the document called College Success.ppt on the floppy disk. The steps on the next page illustrate how to save the presentation again.

Q & A

Q: Can PowerPoint recover files lost during power failures?

A: Yes. If PowerPoint's AutoRecover feature is turned on, files that were open when PowerPoint stopped responding may be displayed in the Document Recovery task pane. This task pane allows you to open the files, view the contents, and compare versions. You then can save the most complete version of your presentation.

To Save a Presentation with the Same File Name

1 **Be certain your floppy disk is in drive A.**

2 **Click the Save button on the Standard toolbar.**

PowerPoint overwrites the old College Success.ppt document on the floppy disk in drive A with the revised presentation document. Slide 4 is displayed in the PowerPoint window.

Moving to Another Slide in Normal View

When creating or editing a presentation in normal view, you often want to display a slide other than the current one. You can move to another slide using several methods. In the Outline tab, you can point to any of the text in a particular slide to display that slide in the slide pane, or you can drag the scroll box on the vertical scroll bar up or down to move through the text in the presentation. In the slide pane, you can click the Previous Slide or Next Slide button on the vertical scroll bar. Clicking the Next Slide button advances to the next slide in the presentation. Clicking the Previous Slide button backs up to the slide preceding the current slide. You also can drag the scroll box on the vertical scroll bar. When you drag the scroll box, the **slide indicator** shows the number and title of the slide you are about to display. Releasing the mouse button shows the slide.

A slide's **Zoom setting** affects the portion of the slide displaying in the slide pane. PowerPoint defaults to a setting of approximately 50 percent so the entire slide is displayed. This percentage depends on the size and type of your monitor. If you want to display a small portion of the current slide, you would zoom in by clicking the **Zoom box arrow** and then clicking the desired magnification. You can display the entire slide in the slide pane by clicking **Fit** in the Zoom list. The Zoom setting affects the action of the vertical and horizontal scroll bars. If Zoom is set so the entire slide is not visible in the slide pane, clicking the up scroll arrow on the vertical scroll bar shows the next portion of the slide, not the previous slide.

Using the Scroll Box on the Slide Pane to Move to Another Slide

Before continuing with Project 1, you want to display the title slide. The following steps show how to move from Slide 4 to Slide 1 using the scroll box on the slide pane vertical scroll bar.

To Use the Scroll Box on the Slide Pane to Move to Another Slide

1

• **Position the mouse pointer on the scroll box.**

• **Press and hold down the mouse button.**

Slide: 4 of 4 Excel on Exams appears in the slide indicator (Figure 1-50). When you click the scroll box, the Slide 4 thumbnail has no gray border in the Slides tab.

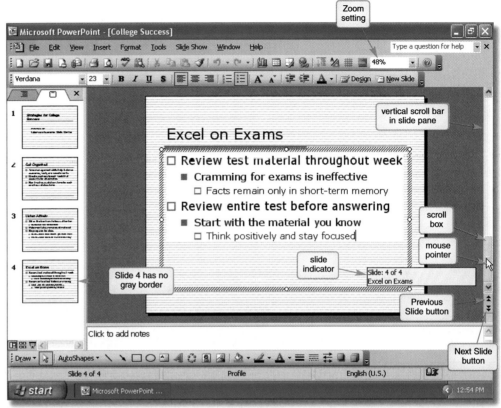

FIGURE 1-50

2

• **Drag the scroll box up the vertical scroll bar until Slide: 1 of 4 Strategies for College Success appears in the slide indicator.**

Slide: 1 of 4 Strategies for College Success appears in the slide indicator (Figure 1-51). Slide 4 still is displayed in the PowerPoint window.

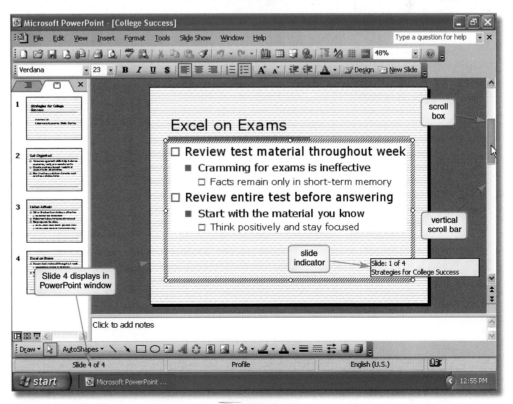

FIGURE 1-51

3

• **Release the mouse button.**

Slide 1, titled Strategies for College Success, appears in the PowerPoint window (Figure 1-52). The Slide 1 thumbnail has a gray border in the Slides tab, indicating it is selected.

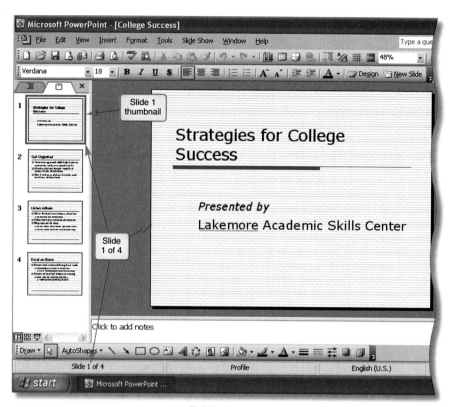

FIGURE 1-52

Other Ways

1. Click Next Slide button or Previous Slide button to move forward or back one slide
2. Press PAGE DOWN or PAGE UP to move forward or back one slide
3. In Voice Command mode, say "Next page" or "Previous page"

Viewing the Presentation in Slide Show View

The Slide Show button, located in the lower-left of the PowerPoint window above the status bar, allows you to show a presentation using a computer. The computer acts like a slide projector, displaying each slide on a full screen. The full-screen slide hides the toolbars, menus, and other PowerPoint window elements. When making a presentation, you use **slide show view**. You can start slide show view from normal view or slide sorter view.

Starting Slide Show View

Slide show view begins when you click the Slide Show button in the lower-left of the PowerPoint window above the status bar. PowerPoint then shows the current slide on the full screen without any of the PowerPoint window objects, such as the menu bar or toolbars. The following steps show how to start slide show view.

To Start Slide Show View

1

• **Point to the Slide Show button in the lower-left corner of the PowerPoint window above the status bar (Figure 1-53).**

FIGURE 1-53

2

• **Click the Slide Show button.**

A starting slide show message may display momentarily, and then the title slide fills the screen (Figure 1-54). The PowerPoint window is hidden.

Strategies for College Success

Presented by
Lakemore Academic Skills Center

title slide in slide show view

FIGURE 1-54

Other Ways

1. On View menu click Slide Show
2. Press F5
3. In Voice Command mode, say "View show"

Advancing Through a Slide Show Manually

After you begin slide show view, you can move forward or backward through the slides. PowerPoint allows you to advance through the slides manually or automatically. The steps on the next page illustrate how to move manually through the slides.

To Move Manually Through Slides in a Slide Show

1

• **Click each slide until the Excel on Exams slide (Slide 4) is displayed.**

Slide 4 is displayed (Figure 1-55). Each slide in the presentation shows on the screen, one slide at a time. Each time you click the mouse button, the next slide appears.

Slide 4 displays in slide show view

Excel on Exams

☐ Review test material throughout week
 ■ Cramming before exams is ineffective
  ☐ Facts remain only in short-term memory
☐ Review entire test before answering
 ■ Start with the material you know
  ☐ Think positively and stay focused

FIGURE 1-55

2

• **Click Slide 4.**

The black slide appears (Figure 1-56). The message at the top of the slide announces the end of the slide show. If you wanted to end the presentation at this point and return to normal view, you would click the black slide.

End of slide show, click to exit.

message

FIGURE 1-56

Using the Popup Menu to Go to a Specific Slide

Slide show view has a shortcut menu, called the Popup menu, that appears when you right-click a slide in slide show view. This menu contains commands to assist you during a slide show. For example, clicking the Next command moves to the next slide. Clicking the Previous command moves to the previous slide. Pointing to the Go to Slide command and then clicking the desired slide allows you to move to any slide in the presentation. The Go to Slide submenu contains a list of the slides in the presentation. You can go to the requested slide by clicking the name of that slide. The following steps illustrate how to go to the title slide (Slide 1) in the College Success presentation.

To Display the Popup Menu and Go to a Specific Slide

1

• **With the black slide displaying in slide show view, right-click the slide.**

• **Point to Go to Slide on the Popup menu, and then point to 1 Strategies for College Success in the Go to Slide submenu.**

The Popup menu appears on the black slide, and the Go to Slide submenu shows a list of slides in the presentation (Figure 1-57). Your screen may look different because the Popup menu appears near the location of the mouse pointer at the time you right-click.

2

• **Click 1 Strategies for College Success.**

The title slide, Strategies for College Success (shown in Figure 1-54 on page PPT 47), is displayed.

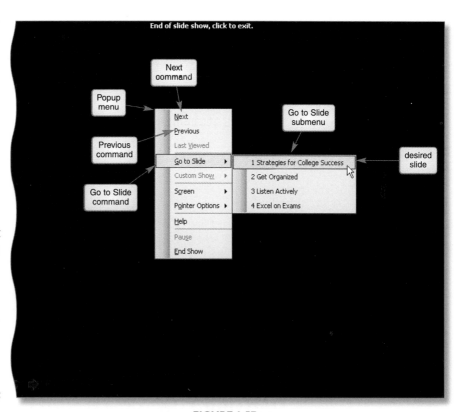

FIGURE 1-57

Additional Popup menu commands allow you to change the mouse pointer to a ballpoint or felt tip pen or highlighter that draws in various colors, make the screen black or white, create speaker notes, and end the slide show. Popup menu commands are discussed as they are used.

Using the Popup Menu to End a Slide Show

The End Show command on the Popup menu ends slide show view and returns to the same view as when you clicked the Slide Show button. The steps on the next page show how to end slide show view and return to normal view.

To Use the Popup Menu to End a Slide Show

1

• **Right-click the title slide and then point to End Show on the Popup menu.**

The Popup menu appears on Slide 1 (Figure 1-58).

2

• **Click End Show.**

• **If the Microsoft Office PowerPoint dialog box appears, click the Yes button.**

PowerPoint ends slide show view and returns to normal view (shown in Figure 1-59 below). Slide 1 is displayed because it is the last slide displayed in slide show view.

FIGURE 1-58

Quitting PowerPoint

The College Success presentation now is complete. When you quit PowerPoint, you are prompted to save any changes made to the presentation since the last save. The program then closes all PowerPoint windows, quits, and returns control to the desktop. The following steps quit PowerPoint.

To Quit PowerPoint

1

• **Point to the Close button on the PowerPoint title bar (Figure 1-59).**

FIGURE 1-59

2

• **Click the Close button.**

PowerPoint closes and the Windows desktop is displayed (Figure 1-60). If you made changes to the presentation since your last save, a Microsoft Office PowerPoint dialog box appears asking if you want to save changes. Clicking the Yes button saves the changes to the presentation before quitting PowerPoint. Clicking the No button quits PowerPoint without saving the changes. Clicking the Cancel button cancels the exit and returns control to the presentation.

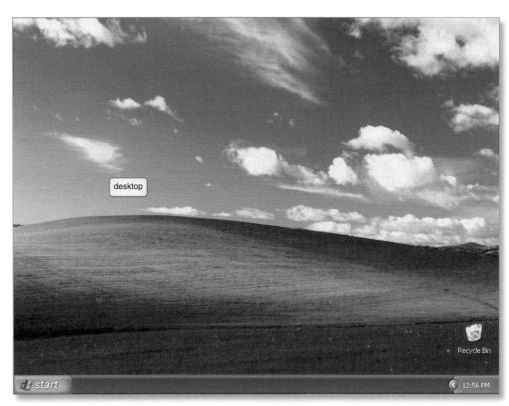

FIGURE 1-60

Other Ways

1. On File menu click Exit
2. Right-click Microsoft PowerPoint button on taskbar, click Close on shortcut menu
3. Double-click PowerPoint Control-menu icon; or click PowerPoint Control-menu icon, on Control menu click Close
4. In Voice Command mode, say "File, Exit"

Starting PowerPoint and Opening a Presentation

Once you have created and saved a presentation, you may need to retrieve it from the floppy disk to make changes. For example, you may want to replace the design template or modify some text. The steps on the next page assume PowerPoint is not running.

To Start PowerPoint and Open an Existing Presentation

1

• **With your floppy disk in drive A, click the Start button on the taskbar, point to All Programs, point to Microsoft Office, and then click Microsoft Office PowerPoint 2003 on the Microsoft Office submenu.**

• **When the Getting Started task pane opens, point to the Open link in the Open area.**

PowerPoint starts. The Getting Started task pane opens (Figure 1-61).

FIGURE 1-61

2

• **Click the Open link. Click the Look in box arrow, click 3½ Floppy (A:), and then double-click College Success.**

PowerPoint opens the presentation College Success and shows the first slide in the PowerPoint window (Figure 1-62). The presentation is displayed in normal view because PowerPoint opens a presentation in the same view in which it was saved. The Getting Started task pane disappears.

Other Ways

1. Right-click Start button, click Explore, display contents of drive A, double-click file name
2. Click Open button on Standard toolbar, select file name, click Open button in Open Office Document dialog box
3. On File menu click Open, select file name, click Open button in Open dialog box
4. In Voice Command mode, say "Open, [file name], Open"

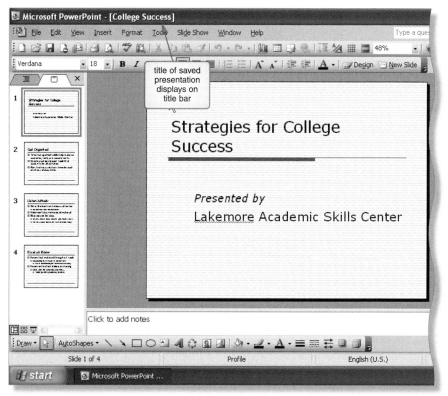

FIGURE 1-62

When you start PowerPoint and open the College Success file, the application name and file name are displayed on a recessed button on the Windows taskbar. When more than one application is open, you can switch between applications by clicking the appropriate application button. If you want to open a presentation other than a recent one, click the Open button on the Standard toolbar or in the Getting Started task pane. Either button lets you navigate to a slide show stored on a disk.

Checking a Presentation for Spelling and Consistency

After you create a presentation, you should check it visually for spelling errors and style consistency. In addition, you can use PowerPoint's Spelling and Style tools to identify possible misspellings and inconsistencies.

Checking a Presentation for Spelling Errors

PowerPoint checks the entire presentation for spelling mistakes using a standard dictionary contained in the Microsoft Office group. This dictionary is shared with the other Microsoft Office applications such as Word and Excel. A **custom dictionary** is available if you want to add special words such as proper names, cities, and acronyms. When checking a presentation for spelling errors, PowerPoint opens the standard dictionary and the custom dictionary file, if one exists. When a word appears in the Spelling dialog box, you perform one of the actions listed in Table 1-4.

Q & A

Q: Can I rely on the spelling checker?

A: While PowerPoint's Spelling checker is a valuable tool, it is not infallible. You should proofread your presentation carefully by pointing to each word and saying it aloud as you point to it. Be mindful of commonly misused words such as its and it's, through and though, and to and too.

Table 1-4 Summary of Spelling Checker Actions	
ACTION	DESCRIPTION
Ignore the word	Click the Ignore button when the word is spelled correctly but not found in the dictionaries. PowerPoint continues checking the rest of the presentation.
Ignore all occurrences of the word	Click the Ignore All button when the word is spelled correctly but not found in the dictionaries. PowerPoint ignores all occurrences of the word and continues checking the rest of the presentation.
Select a different spelling	Click the proper spelling of the word from the list in the Suggestions box. Click the Change button. PowerPoint corrects the word and continues checking the rest of the presentation.
Change all occurrences of the misspelling to a different spelling	Click the proper spelling of the word from the list in the Suggestions box. Click the Change All button. PowerPoint changes all occurrences of the misspelled word and continues checking the rest of the presentation.
Add a word to the custom dictionary	Click the Add button. PowerPoint opens the custom dictionary, adds the word, and continues checking the rest of the presentation.
View alternative spellings	Click the Suggest button. PowerPoint lists suggested spellings. Click the correct word from the Suggestions box or type the proper spelling. Then click the Change button. PowerPoint continues checking the rest of the presentation.
Add spelling error to AutoCorrect list	Click the AutoCorrect button. PowerPoint adds the spelling error and its correction to the AutoCorrect list. Any future misspelling of the word is corrected automatically as you type.
Close	Click the Close button to close the Spelling checker and return to the PowerPoint window.

The standard dictionary contains commonly used English words. It does not, however, contain proper names, abbreviations, technical terms, poetic contractions, or antiquated terms. PowerPoint treats words not found in the dictionaries as misspellings.

Starting the Spelling Checker

The following steps illustrate how to start the Spelling checker and check the entire presentation.

To Start the Spelling Checker

1

• **Point to the Spelling button on the Standard toolbar (Figure 1-63).**

FIGURE 1-63

2

• **Click the Spelling button.**

• **When the Spelling dialog box appears, point to the Ignore button.**

PowerPoint starts the Spelling checker and displays the Spelling dialog box (Figure 1-64). The word, Lakemore, appears in the Not in Dictionary box. Depending on the custom dictionary, Lakemore may not be recognized as a misspelled word.

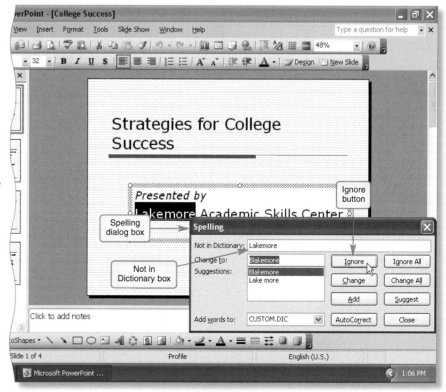

FIGURE 1-64

3

• **Click the Ignore button.**
• **When the Microsoft Office PowerPoint dialog box appears, point to the OK button.**

PowerPoint ignores the word, Lakemore, and continues searching for additional misspelled words. PowerPoint may stop on additional words depending on your typing accuracy. When PowerPoint has checked all slides for misspellings, the Microsoft Office PowerPoint dialog box informs you that the spelling check is complete (Figure 1-65).

FIGURE 1-65

4

• **Click the OK button.**
• **Click the slide to remove the highlight from the word, Lakemore.**

PowerPoint closes the Spelling checker and returns to the current slide, Slide 1 (Figure 1-66), or to the slide where a possible misspelled word displayed.

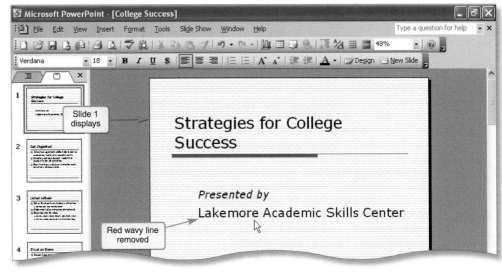

FIGURE 1-66

The red wavy line below the word, Lakemore, is gone because you instructed PowerPoint to ignore that word, which does not appear in the standard dictionary. You also could have added that word to the dictionary so it would not be flagged as a possible misspelled word in subsequent presentations you create using that word.

Other Ways

1. On Tools menu click Spelling
2. Press ALT+T, press S; when finished, press ENTER
3. Press F7
4. In Voice Command mode, say "Spelling"

Correcting Errors

After creating a presentation and running the Spelling checker, you may find that you must make changes. Changes may be required because a slide contains an error, the scope of the presentation shifts, or the style is inconsistent. This section explains the types of errors that commonly occur when creating a presentation.

Types of Corrections Made to Presentations

You generally make three types of corrections to text in a presentation: additions, deletions, and replacements.

- Additions are necessary when you omit text from a slide and need to add it later. You may need to insert text in the form of a sentence, word, or single character. For example, you may want to add the presenter's middle name on the title slide.
- Deletions are required when text on a slide is incorrect or no longer is relevant to the presentation. For example, a slide may look cluttered. Therefore, you may want to remove one of the bulleted paragraphs to add more space.
- Replacements are needed when you want to revise the text in a presentation. For example, you may want to substitute the word, their, for the word, there.

Editing text in PowerPoint basically is the same as editing text in a word processing package. The following sections illustrate the most common changes made to text in a presentation.

Deleting Text

You can delete text using one of three methods. One is to use the BACKSPACE key to remove text just typed. The second is to position the insertion point to the left of the text you wish to delete and then press the DELETE key. The third method is to drag through the text you wish to delete and then press the DELETE key. (Use the third method when deleting large sections of text.)

Replacing Text in an Existing Slide

When you need to correct a word or phrase, you can replace the text by selecting the text to be replaced and then typing the new text. As soon as you press any key on the keyboard, the highlighted text is deleted and the new text is displayed.

PowerPoint inserts text to the left of the insertion point. The text to the right of the insertion point moves to the right (and shifts downward if necessary) to accommodate the added text.

Displaying a Presentation in Black and White

Printing handouts of a presentation allows you to use them to make overhead transparencies. The Color/Grayscale button on the Standard toolbar shows the presentation in black and white before you print. Table 1-5 identifies how PowerPoint objects display in black and white.

Table 1-5 Appearance in Black and White View	
OBJECT	**APPEARANCE IN BLACK AND WHITE VIEW**
Bitmaps	Grayscale
Embossing	Hidden
Fills	Grayscale
Frame	Black
Lines	Black
Object shadows	Grayscale
Pattern fills	Grayscale
Slide backgrounds	White
Text	Black
Text shadows	Hidden

The following steps show how to display the presentation in black and white.

To Display a Presentation in Black and White

1

• **Click the Color/Grayscale button on the Standard toolbar and then point to Pure Black and White in the list.**

The Color/Grayscale list is displayed (Figure 1-67). Pure Black and White alters the slides' appearance so that only black lines display on a white background. Grayscale shows varying degrees of gray.

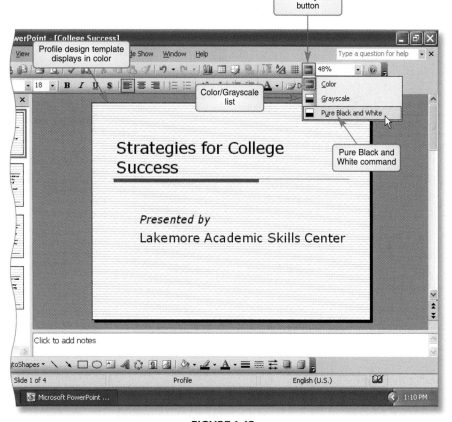

FIGURE 1-67

2

• **Click Pure Black and White.**

Slide 1 is displayed in black and white in the slide pane (Figure 1-68). The four thumbnail slides are displayed in color in the Slides tab. The Grayscale View toolbar appears. The Color/Grayscale button on the Standard toolbar changes from color bars to black and white.

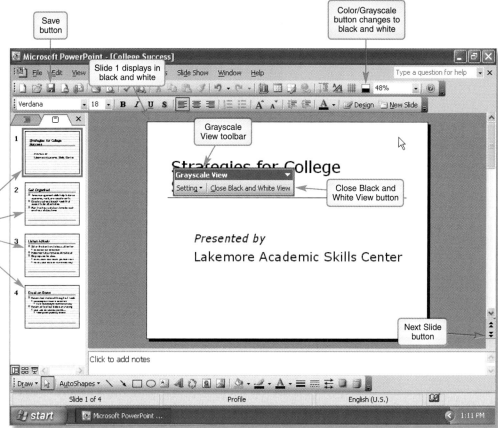

FIGURE 1-68

3

• **Click the Next Slide button three times to view all slides in the presentation in black and white.**

• **Point to the Close Black and White View button on the Grayscale View toolbar (Figure 1-69).**

FIGURE 1-69

4

- **Click the Close Black and White View button.**

Slide 4 is displayed with the default Profile color scheme (Figure 1-70).

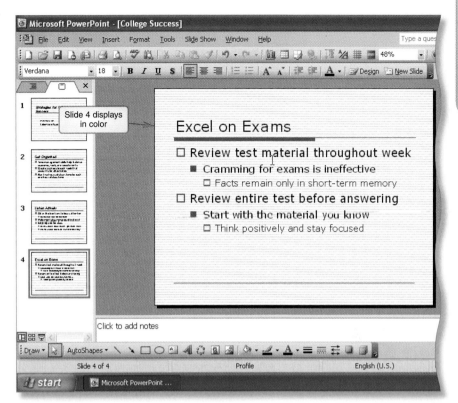

FIGURE 1-70

After you view the text objects in the presentation in black and white, you can make any changes that will enhance printouts produced from a black and white printer or photocopier.

Printing a Presentation

After you create a presentation, you often want to print it. A printed version of the presentation is called a **hard copy**, or **printout**. The first printing of the presentation is called a **rough draft**. The rough draft allows you to proofread the presentation to check for errors and readability. After correcting errors, you print the final copy of the presentation.

Saving Before Printing

Before printing a presentation, you should save your work in the event you experience difficulties with the printer. You occasionally may encounter system problems that can be resolved only by restarting the computer. In such an instance, you will need to reopen the presentation. As a precaution, always save the presentation before you print. The steps on the next page save the presentation before printing.

To Save a Presentation Before Printing

1 Verify that the floppy disk is in drive A.

2 Click the Save button on the Standard toolbar.

All changes made after your last save now are saved on the floppy disk.

Printing the Presentation

After saving the presentation, you are ready to print. Clicking the Print button on the Standard toolbar causes PowerPoint to print all slides in the presentation. The following steps illustrate how to print the presentation slides.

To Print a Presentation

1

• **Ready the printer according to the printer instructions.**

• **Click the Print button on the Standard toolbar.**

The printer icon in the tray status area on the Windows taskbar indicates a print job is processing (Figure 1-71). This icon may not display on your system, or it may display on your status bar. After several moments, the slide show begins printing on the printer. When the presentation is finished printing, the printer icon in the tray status area on the Windows taskbar no longer is displayed.

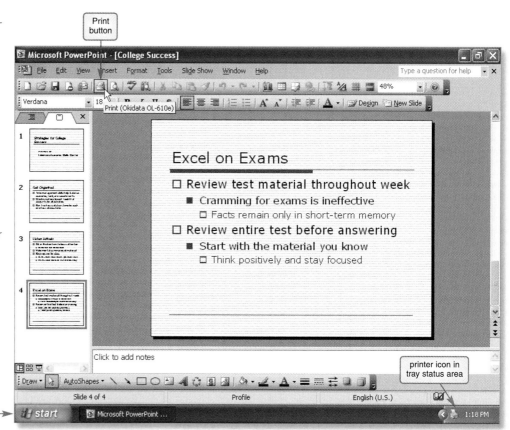

FIGURE 1-71

2

• **When the printer stops, retrieve the printouts of the slides.**

The presentation, College Success, prints on four pages (Figures 1-72a through 1-72d).

(a) Slide 1

(b) Slide 2

(c) Slide 3

(d) Slide 4

FIGURE 1-72

You can click the printer icon next to the clock in the tray status area on the Windows taskbar to obtain information about the presentations printing on your printer and to delete files in the print queue that are waiting to be printed.

Making a Transparency

With the handouts printed, you now can make overhead transparencies using one of several devices. One device is a printer attached to your computer, such as an inkjet printer or a laser printer. Transparencies produced on a printer may be in black and white or color, depending on the printer. Another device is a photocopier. Because each of these devices requires a special transparency film, check the user's manual for the film requirement of your specific device, or ask your instructor.

PowerPoint Help System

You can get answers to PowerPoint questions at any time by using the PowerPoint Help system. You can activate the PowerPoint Help system by using the Type a question for help box on the menu bar, by using the Microsoft PowerPoint Help button on the Standard toolbar, or by clicking Help on the menu bar (Figure 1-73). Used properly, this form of online assistance can increase your productivity and reduce your frustrations by minimizing the time you spend learning how to use PowerPoint.

The following section shows how to get answers to your questions using the Type a question for help box. Additional information on using the PowerPoint Help system is available in Appendix A and Table 1-6 on page PPT 65.

Obtaining Help Using the Type a Question for Help Box on the Menu Bar

The Type a question for help box on the right side of the menu bar lets you type free-form questions such as, *how do I save* or *how do I create a Web page*, or you can type terms such as, *copy*, *save*, or *format*. PowerPoint responds by displaying a list of topics related to what you typed. The following steps show how to use the Type a question for help box to obtain information on formatting bullets.

To Obtain Help Using the Type a Question for Help Box

1

• **Type** bullet **in the Type a question for help box on the right side of the menu bar (Figure 1-73).**

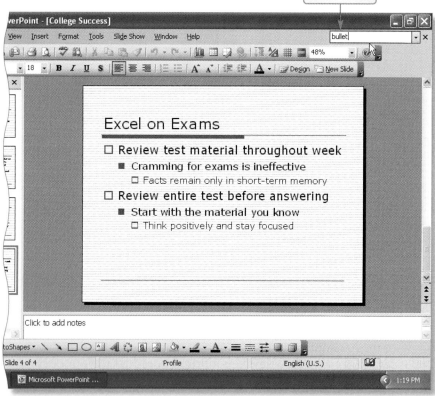

FIGURE 1-73

2

- **Press the ENTER key.**

- **When PowerPoint displays the Search Results task pane, scroll down and then point to the topic, Change the bullet style in a list.**

PowerPoint displays the Search Results task pane with a list of topics relating to the term, bullet. PowerPoint found 30 results from Microsoft Office Online. The mouse pointer changes to a hand, which indicates it is pointing to a link (Figure 1-74).

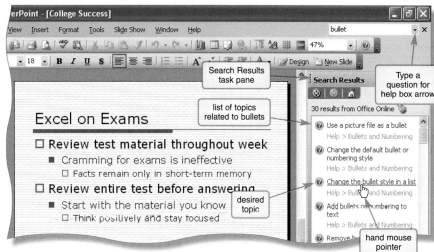

FIGURE 1-74

3

- **Click Change the bullet style in a list.**

- **When the Microsoft Office PowerPoint Help window is displayed, double-click its title bar to maximize it.**

A Microsoft Office PowerPoint Help window provides Help information about changing the bullet style in a list (Figure 1-75).

FIGURE 1-75

4

- **Click the Show All link.**

Directions for changing a bullet style for a single list are displayed. Options include change the bullet character, change the bullet size, and change the bullet color (Figure 1-76).

FIGURE 1-76

5

• **Drag the scroll box down the vertical scroll bar until Change the bullet color is displayed.**

PowerPoint displays specific details of changing the color of the bullets on a slide (Figure 1-77).

6

• **Click the Close button on the Microsoft Office PowerPoint Help window title bar.**

• **Click the Close button on the Search Results task pane.**

The PowerPoint Help window closes, and the PowerPoint presentation is displayed.

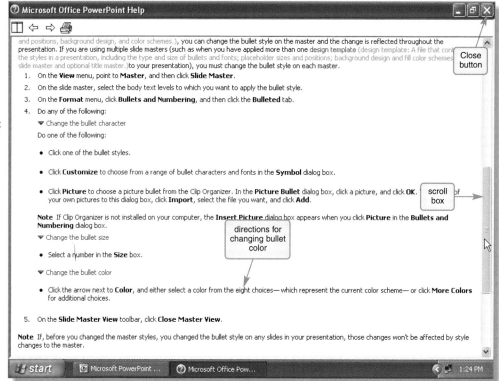

FIGURE 1-77

Other Ways

1. Click Microsoft Office PowerPoint Help button on Standard toolbar; or on Help menu click Microsoft Office PowerPoint Help
2. Press F1

Use the buttons in the upper-left corner of the Microsoft Office PowerPoint Help window (Figure 1-75 on the previous page) to navigate through the Help system, change the display, and print the contents of the window.

As you enter questions and terms in the Type a question for help box, PowerPoint adds them to its list. Thus, if you click the Type a question for help box arrow (Figure 1-74 on the previous page), PowerPoint will display a list of previously asked questions and terms.

Table 1-6 summarizes the major categories of Help available to you. Because of the way the PowerPoint Help system works, be certain to review the rightmost column of Table 1-6 if you have difficulties activating the desired category of Help. Additional information on using the PowerPoint Help system is available in Appendix A.

Quitting PowerPoint

Project 1 is complete. The final task is to close the presentation and quit PowerPoint. The following steps quit PowerPoint.

To Quit PowerPoint

1 Click the Close button on the title bar.

2 If prompted to save the presentation before quitting PowerPoint, click the Yes button in the Microsoft Office PowerPoint dialog box.

Table 1-6	PowerPoint Help System	
TYPE	DESCRIPTION	HOW TO ACTIVATE
Microsoft Office PowerPoint Help	Displays PowerPoint Help task pane. Answers questions or searches for terms that you type in your own words.	Click the Microsoft Office PowerPoint Help button on the Standard toolbar or click Microsoft Office PowerPoint Help on the Help menu.
Office Assistant	Similar to the Type a question for help box. The Office Assistant answers questions that you type in your own words, offers tips, and provides help for a variety of PowerPoint features.	Click the Office Assistant icon. If the Office Assistant does not display, click Show the Office Assistant on the Help menu.
Type a question for help box	Answers questions or searches for terms that you type in your own words.	Type a question or term in the Type a question for help box on the menu bar and then press the ENTER key.
Table of Contents	Groups Help topics by general categories. Use when you know only the general category of the topic in question.	Click the Microsoft Office PowerPoint Help button on the Standard toolbar or click Microsoft Office PowerPoint Help on the Help menu, and then click the Table of Contents link on the PowerPoint Help task pane.
Microsoft Office Online	Used to access technical resources and download free product enhancements on the Web.	Click Microsoft Office Online on the Help menu.
Detect and Repair	Automatically finds and fixes errors in the application.	Click Detect and Repair on the Help menu.

Project Summary

In creating the Strategies for College Success slide show in this project, you gained a broad knowledge of PowerPoint. First, you were introduced to starting PowerPoint and creating a presentation consisting of a title slide and single- and multi-level bulleted lists. You learned about PowerPoint design templates, objects, and attributes.

This project illustrated how to create an interesting introduction to a presentation by changing the text font style to italic and increasing font size on the title slide. Completing these tasks, you saved the presentation. Then, you created three text slides with bulleted lists, two with multi-level bullets, to explain effective academic skills. Next, you learned how to view the presentation in slide show view. Then, you learned how to quit PowerPoint and how to open an existing presentation. You used the Spelling checker to search for spelling errors. You learned how to display the presentation in black and white. You also learned how to print hard copies of the slides in order to make handouts and overhead transparencies. Finally, you learned how to use the PowerPoint Help system to answer your questions.

 If you have a SAM user profile, you may have access to hands-on instruction, practice, and assessment of the skills covered in this project. Log in to your SAM account and go to your assignments page to see what your instructor has assigned.

What You Should Know

Having completed this project, you should be able to perform the tasks below. The tasks are listed in the same order they were presented in this project. For a list of the buttons, menus, toolbars, and commands introduced in this project, see the Quick Reference Summary at the back of this book and refer to the Page Number column.

1. Start PowerPoint   (PPT 7)
2. Customize the PowerPoint Window   (PPT 9)
3. Choose a Design Template   (PPT 18)
4. Enter the Presentation Title   (PPT 21)
5. Enter the Presentation Subtitle   (PPT 22)
6. Change the Text Font Style to Italic   (PPT 24)
7. Increase Font Size   (PPT 25)
8. Save a Presentation on a Floppy Disk   (PPT 27)
9. Add a New Text Slide with a Bulleted List (PPT 30)
10. Enter a Slide Title   (PPT 32)
11. Select a Text Placeholder   (PPT 32)
12. Type a Single-Level Bulleted List   (PPT 33)
13. Add a New Slide and Enter a Slide Title (PPT 35)
14. Type a Multi-Level Bulleted List   (PPT 36)
15. Type the Remaining Text for Slide 3   (PPT 38)
16. Create Slide 4   (PPT 39)
17. Create a Third-Level Paragraph   (PPT 40)
18. Type the Remaining Text for Slide 4   (PPT 41)
19. End a Slide Show with a Black Slide   (PPT 42)

20. Save a Presentation with the Same File Name (PPT 44)
21. Use the Scroll Box on the Slide Pane to Move to Another Slide   (PPT 45)
22. Start Slide Show View   (PPT 47)
23. Move Manually Through Slides in a Slide Show (PPT 48)
24. Display the Popup Menu and Go to a Specific Slide   (PPT 49)
25. Use the Popup Menu to End a Slide Show (PPT 50)
26. Quit PowerPoint   (PPT 50)
27. Start PowerPoint and Open an Existing Presentation   (PPT 52)
28. Start the Spelling Checker   (PPT 54)
29. Display a Presentation in Black and White (PPT 57)
30. Save a Presentation Before Printing   (PPT 60)
31. Print a Presentation   (PPT 60)
32. Obtain Help Using the Type a Question for Help Box   (PPT 62)
33. Quit PowerPoint   (PPT 64)

Learn It Online

Instructions: To complete the Learn It Online exercises, start your browser, click the Address bar, and then enter the Web address scsite.com/ppt2003/learn. When the PowerPoint 2003 Learn It Online page is displayed, follow the instructions in the exercises below. Each exercise has instructions for printing your results, either for your own records or for submission to your instructor.

1 Project Reinforcement TF, MC, and SA

Below PowerPoint Project 1, click the Project Reinforcement link. Print the quiz by clicking Print on the File menu for each page. Answer each question.

2 Flash Cards

Below PowerPoint Project 1, click the Flash Cards link and read the instructions. Type 20 (or a number specified by your instructor) in the Number of playing cards text box, type your name in the Enter your Name text box, and then click the Flip Card button. When the flash card is displayed, read the question and then click the ANSWER box arrow to select an answer. Flip through Flash Cards. If your score is 15 (75%) correct or greater, click Print on the File menu to print your results. If your score is less than 15 (75%) correct, then redo this exercise by clicking the Replay button.

3 Practice Test

Below PowerPoint Project 1, click the Practice Test link. Answer each question, enter your first and last name at the bottom of the page, and then click the Grade Test button. When the graded practice test is displayed on your screen, click Print on the File menu to print a hard copy. Continue to take practice tests until you score 80% or better.

4 Who Wants To Be a Computer Genius?

Below PowerPoint Project 1, click the Computer Genius link. Read the instructions, enter your first and last name at the bottom of the page, and then click the PLAY button. When your score is displayed, click the PRINT RESULTS link to print a hard copy.

5 Wheel of Terms

Below PowerPoint Project 1, click the Wheel of Terms link. Read the instructions, and then enter your first and last name and your school name. Click the PLAY button. When your score is displayed, right-click the score and then click Print on the shortcut menu to print a hard copy.

6 Crossword Puzzle Challenge

Below PowerPoint Project 1, click the Crossword Puzzle Challenge link. Read the instructions, and then enter your first and last name. Click the SUBMIT button. Work the crossword puzzle. When you are finished, click the Submit button. When the crossword puzzle is redisplayed, click the Print Puzzle button to print a hard copy.

7 Tips and Tricks

Below PowerPoint Project 1, click the Tips and Tricks link. Click a topic that pertains to Project 1. Right-click the information and then click Print on the shortcut menu. Construct a brief example of what the information relates to in PowerPoint to confirm you understand how to use the tip or trick.

8 Newsgroups

Below PowerPoint Project 1, click the Newsgroups link. Click a topic that pertains to Project 1. Print three comments.

9 Expanding Your Horizons

Below PowerPoint Project 1, click the Expanding Your Horizons link. Click a topic that pertains to Project 1. Print the information. Construct a brief example of what the information relates to in PowerPoint to confirm you understand the contents of the article.

10 Search Sleuth

Below PowerPoint Project 1, click the Search Sleuth link. To search for a term that pertains to this project, select a term below the Project 1 title and then use the Google search engine at google.com (or any major search engine) to display and print two Web pages that present information on the term.

11 PowerPoint Online Training

Below PowerPoint Project 1, click the PowerPoint Online Training link. When your browser displays the Microsoft Office Online Web page, click the PowerPoint link. Click one of the PowerPoint courses that covers one or more of the objectives listed at the beginning of the project on page PPT 4. Print the first page of the course before stepping through it.

12 Office Marketplace

Below PowerPoint Project 1, click the Office Marketplace link. When your browser displays the Microsoft Office Online Web page, click the Office Marketplace link. Click a topic that relates to PowerPoint. Print the first page.

Apply Your Knowledge

1 Searching on the World Wide Web

Instructions: Start PowerPoint. Open the presentation Apply 1-1 Internet Searching from the Data Disk. See the inside back cover of this book for instructions for downloading the Data Disk or see your instructor for information on accessing the files required for this book. The two slides in the presentation give information on tools to search the Web. Make the following changes to the slides so they appear as shown in Figure 1-78.

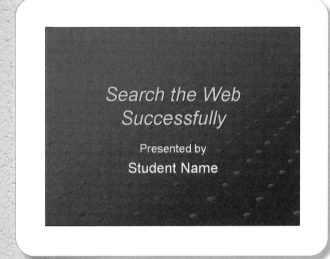

Search the Web
Successfully

Presented by
Student Name

Two Search Tools

• Subject Directory
  ▪ Categorized lists of links arranged by subject and displayed in series of menus
• Search Engine
  ▪ Requires search text: a word, words, phrase
    • Carefully craft keywords to limit search

(a) Slide 1 (Title Slide)   **(b) Slide 2 (Multi-Level Bulleted List)**

FIGURE 1-78

Change the design template to Digital Dots. On the title slide, use your name in place of Student Name and change the font size to 40. Italicize the title text.

On Slide 2, increase the indent of the second and fourth paragraphs, Categorized lists of links arranged by subject and displayed in series of menus, and Requires search text: a word, words, phrase, to second-level paragraphs. Then change the last paragraph, Carefully craft keywords to limit search, to a third-level paragraph.

Display the revised presentation in black and white, and then print the two slides.

Save the presentation using the file name, Apply 1-1 Search Tools. Hand in the hard copy to your instructor.

In the Lab

Note: These labs require you to create presentations based on notes. When you design these slide shows, use the 7 × 7 rule, which states that each line should have a maximum of seven words, and each slide should have a maximum of seven lines.

1 Common Cold Concerns Presentation

Problem: The common cold is one of the most frequent health problems; more than one billion cases are reported each year. Although no remedy cures the runny nose or sore throat that accompany this illness, students can reduce their chances of catching a cold and feel better when they are sick. Dr. Larry Hopper is the head physician at your campus's health clinic. He has asked you to prepare a short PowerPoint presentation and handouts to educate students about how to thwart the common cold. He hands you the outline shown in Figure 1-79 and asks you to create the presentation shown in Figures 1-80a through 1-80f on the following pages.

I.) Coping with the Common Cold
Presented by
Larry Hopper, M.D.

II.) Cold Facts
- We have more than 1 billion colds annually
- No remedy cures the common cold
- You can reduce the chances of catching a cold
- You can feel better when you are sick

III.) When You Are Feeling Sick
- Get plenty of rest
- Drink lots of fluids
- Consume chicken soup

IV.) If Your Throat Is Sore
- Gargle with warm salt water
- Let a lozenge dissolve slowly in your mouth
  - Choose one with menthol and mild anesthetic

V.) If Your Nose Is Stuffy
- Try a decongestant
  - Shrinks blood vessels
  - Do not take for more than three days
- Try an antihistamine
  - Relieves a runny nose, itching, and sneezing
  - Has a drying effect

VI.) Avoid a Cold
- Stay away from other people with colds
- Wash your hands frequently
- Keep your hands away from your mouth and nose
- Dispose of tissues promptly

FIGURE 1-79

(continued)

Common Cold Concerns Presentation *(continued)*

**Coping with the
Common Cold**

Presented by
Larry Hopper, M.D.

(a) Slide 1

Cold Facts

- We have more than 1 billion colds annually
- No remedy cures the common cold
- You can reduce the chances of catching a cold
- You can feel better when you are sick

(b) Slide 2

When You Are Feeling Sick

- Get plenty of rest
- Drink lots of fluids
- Consume chicken soup

(c) Slide 3

If Your Throat Is Sore

- Gargle with warm salt water
- Let a lozenge dissolve slowly in your mouth
  - Choose one with menthol and mild anesthetic

(d) Slide 4

FIGURE 1-80

In the Lab

If Your Nose Is Stuffy

- Try a decongestant
  - Shrinks blood vessels
  - Do not take for more than three days
- Try an antihistamine
  - Relieves a runny nose, itching, and sneezing
  - Has a drying effect

Avoid a Cold

- Stay away from other people with colds
- Wash your hands frequently
- Keep your hands away from your mouth and nose
- Dispose of tissues promptly

(e) Slide 5

(f) Slide 6

FIGURE 1-80 *(continued)*

Instructions: Perform the following tasks.

1. Create a new presentation using the Network design template (row 14, column 2).
2. Using the typed notes illustrated in Figure 1-79 on page PPT 69, create the title slide shown in Figure 1-80a using your name in place of Larry Hopper. Italicize the title paragraph, Coping with the Common Cold, and increase the font size to 60. Increase the font size of the first paragraph of the subtitle text, Presented by, to 36. Italicize your name.
3. Using the typed notes in Figure 1-79, create the five text slides with bulleted lists shown in Figures 1-80b through 1-80f.
4. Click the Spelling button on the Standard toolbar. Correct any errors.
5. Drag the scroll box to display Slide 1. Click the Slide Show button to start slide show view. Then click to display each slide.
6. Save the presentation using the file name, Lab 1-1 Common Cold Concerns.
7. Display and print the presentation in black and white. Close the presentation. Hand in the hard copy to your instructor.

2 Computers 4 U Repair Store Presentation

Problem: Computers 4 U is a computer repair store near your campus. The co-owners, Elliott Dane and Lynn Verone, specialize in repairing computer systems and building custom computers. Elliott and Lynn want to attract new customers, and they have asked you to help them design a PowerPoint advertising campaign. Having graduated from your college, they are familiar with the hardware and software students need for their classes. They have typed information on their services for you (Figure 1-81), and they have asked you to create the presentation shown in Figures 1-82a through 1-82d.

1) Computers 4 U
Complete Repairs and Service
Elliott Dane and Lynn Verone

2) Hardware and Software
- Convenient in-store appointments
- On-site service
  - 24 hours a day
- Plan for future computer purchases
- Arrange financing for new systems

3) Complete Supplies
- Toner cartridges
  - All major printer brands in-stock
- Paper
  - Wide variety of patterns and colors
- Labels
  - Complete selection of sizes

4) Convenient Location
- Bremen Mall
  - 15800 South Wabash Street
  - Napier, Washington
  - 555-1123

FIGURE 1-81

In the Lab

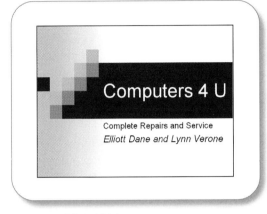

(a) Slide 1 (Title Slide)

(c) Slide 3

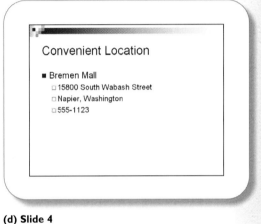

(b) Slide 2

(d) Slide 4

FIGURE 1-82

Instructions: Perform the following tasks.

1. Create a new presentation using the Pixel design template (row 16, column 1).
2. Using the typed notes illustrated in Figure 1-81, create the title slide shown in Figure 1-82a using your name in place of Elliott Dane. Italicize both names. Increase the font size of the title paragraph, Computers 4 U, to 68. Decrease the font size of the first paragraph of the subtitle text, Complete Repairs and Service, to 30.
3. Using the typed notes in Figure 1-81, create the three text slides with bulleted lists shown in Figures 1-82b through 1-82d.
4. Click the Spelling button on the Standard toolbar. Correct any errors.
5. Save the presentation using the file name, Lab 1-2 Computers 4 U.
6. Display the presentation in black and white.
7. Print the black and white presentation. Close the presentation. Hand in the hard copy to your instructor.

In the Lab

3 Community Center Course Update

Problem: The Rivercrest Community Center has updated its winter classes and has included activities for town residents of all ages. For children, the new classes are Skateboarding Fundamentals, Tumbling for Toddlers, and Basketball Boot Camp. For adults, the new offerings are Yoga and Spinning. Seniors can enroll in Self-Defense and Flexibility.

Instructions Part 1: Using the outline in Figure 1-83, create the presentation shown in Figure 1-84. Use the Radial design template. On the title slide, type your name in place of Janice Jackson, increase the font size of the title paragraph, Rivercrest Community Center, to 50, and change the text font style to italic. Increase the font size of the subtitle paragraph, New Winter Classes, to 40. Create the three text slides with multi-level bulleted lists shown in Figures 1-84b through 1-84d.

Correct any spelling mistakes, and then view the slide show. Save the presentation using the file name, Lab 1-3 Part One Winter Classes. Display and print the presentation in black and white.

---

1. Rivercrest Community Center
New Winter Classes
Janice Jackson, Director

2. Children's Classes
- Skateboarding Fundamentals
  - Emphasizes safety and control
- Tumbling for Toddlers
  - Learn coordination while having fun
- Basketball Boot Camp
  - Features game strategies and conditioning

3. Adults' Classes
- Yoga
  - Enjoy a mind-body experience
    - Release external tensions and chaos
- Spinning
  - Learn proper bike set-up
  - Involves series of cycling techniques

4. Seniors' Classes
- Self-defense
  - Learn to avoid dangerous situations
- Flexibility
  - Improve range of motion, balance, posture
    - Helps to prevent falls
  - Instill your body with grace and movement

FIGURE 1-83

In the Lab

Rivercrest Community Center

New Winter Classes
Janice Jackson, Director

(a) Slide 1 (Title Slide)

Children's Classes

- Skateboarding Fundamentals
  - Emphasizes safety and control
- Tumbling for Toddlers
  - Learn coordination while having fun
- Basketball Boot Camp
  - Features game strategies and conditioning

(b) Slide 2

Adults' Classes

- Yoga
  - Enjoy a mind-body experience
    - Release external tensions and chaos
- Spinning
  - Learn proper bike set-up
  - Involves series of cycling techniques

(c) Slide 3

Seniors' Classes

- Self-defense
  - Learn to avoid dangerous situations
- Flexibility
  - Improve range of motion, balance, posture
    - Helps to prevent falls
  - Instill your body with grace and movement

(d) Slide 4

FIGURE 1-84

(continued)

Community Center Course Update *(continued)*

Instructions Part 2: The Rivercrest Community Center wants to update this presentation to promote the summer class schedule. Modify the presentation created in Part 1 to create the presentation shown in Figure 1-85. Change the design template to Glass Layers.

On the title slide, remove the italics from the title paragraph, Rivercrest Community Center, decrease the font size to 44, and center the text. Change the first subtitle paragraph to New Summer Classes. Then change your title in the second subtitle paragraph to Executive Director and decrease the font size to 28.

On Slide 2, delete the first-level paragraph regarding the basketball boot camp and replace it with the paragraph, Swimming Safely. Delete the last paragraph on the slide and replace it with the paragraph, Practice proper breathing and strokes.

On Slide 3, change the first subtitle paragraph to Yoga and Tai Chi. Then change the first first-level paragraph under Spinning to, Learn proper bike set-up and form.

On Slide 4, change the second-level paragraph under Self-Defense to, Learn to escape from an attacker.

Correct any spelling mistakes, and then view the slide show. Save the presentation using the file name, Lab 1-3 Part Two Summer Classes. Display and print the presentation in black and white. Close the presentation. Hand in both presentation printouts to your instructor.

In the Lab

(a) Slide 1

(b) Slide 2

(c) Slide 3

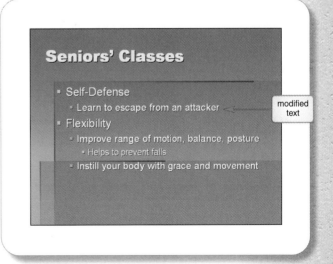

(d) Slide 4

FIGURE 1-85

Cases and Places

The difficulty of these case studies varies:
■ are the least difficult and ■■ are more difficult. The last exercise is a group exercise.

Note: Remember to use the 7 × 7 rule as you design the presentations: a maximum of seven words on a line and a maximum of seven lines on one slide.

1 ■ The dispatcher at the Imperial Grove Police Station is noticing an increase in the number of calls made to the emergency 911 telephone number. These calls, unfortunately, are not always emergencies. Community residents have been calling the number to obtain information on everything from the times of movies at the local theatre to the names of the local city trustees. Police Chief Gina Colatta wants to inform homeowners of the importance of using the 911 service correctly. She created the outline shown in Figure 1-86 and asks you to help her prepare an accompanying PowerPoint presentation to show at the local mall and food stores. Using the concepts and techniques introduced in this project, together with Chief Colatta's outline, develop a slide show with a title slide and three text slides with bulleted lists. Print the slides so they can be distributed to residents at the conclusion of the presentation.

1) 911 – A Call for Help
    Presented by
    Chief Gina Colatta
    Imperial Grove Police Department

2) What It Is For
    When you need an emergency response
        Fire
        Police
        Emergency Medical Personnel
    When disaster occurs
        Tornadoes, earthquakes, floods

3) How to Help
    Do not call for general information
        Consult local telephone directories
    If you call by mistake:
        Tell the dispatcher you have misdialed
    Wait if you hear a recording

4) Other Information
    Tell the telephone company if you change your name or address
        This info displays on the dispatcher's screen
        The dispatcher relies on this information
    Be certain your house number can be seen from the street

FIGURE 1-86

Cases and Places

2 ▪ Your school is planning a job fair to occur during the week of midterm exams. The Placement Office has invited 100 companies and local businesses to promote its current and anticipated job openings. The Placement Office director, Latasha Prince, hands you the outline shown in Figure 1-87 and asks you to prepare a presentation and handouts to promote the event. Use this list to design and create a presentation with a title slide and three text slides with bulleted lists.

1. Brookville College Career Fair
   Presented by
   Brookville College Placement Office
   Latasha Prince, Director

2. Who Is Coming?
   National corporations
      Progressive companies looking for high-quality candidates
   Local companies
      Full-time and part-time
       - Hundreds of jobs

3. When Is It?
   Midterm week
      Monday through Friday
   Brookville College Cafeteria
   Convenient hours
      9:00 a.m. to 8:00 p.m.

4. How Should I Prepare?
   Bring plenty of resumes
      More than 100 companies expected
   Dress neatly
   View the Placement Office Web site
      Up-to-date information
      Company profiles

FIGURE 1-87

Cases and Places

3 ■■ In-line skating is a popular recreational sport throughout the world. In 1989, three million skaters spent $20 million on these skates and protective gear. In 1994, sales soared when nearly 14 million skaters spent $250 million. Today, the more than 27 million in-line skaters are purchasing more than $300 million in equipment yearly. Females account for 52 percent of skaters, and youths ranging in age from 7 to 17 are 58 percent of the total skaters. In-line skaters can participate more safely if they follow these steps: Wear full protective gear, including a helmet, wrist guards, and knee and elbow pads; practice basic skills, including braking, turning, and balancing, in a parking lot or other flat surface; always skate under control; and avoid hills until mastering speed control. The public relations director of your local park district has asked you to prepare a slide show emphasizing these safety tips and illustrating the in-line skating popularity surge. You decide to develop a slide show to run at the sporting goods store. Prepare a short presentation aimed at encouraging skaters to practice safe skating.

4 ■■ About 25 percent of the population suffers from the flu each year from October through May. Flu-related symptoms generally last for two weeks and include sudden headaches, chills, dry coughs, high fevers, and body aches. Serious complications are common, and an estimated 20,000 Americans die each year from the disease. Annual flu shots can help prevent the illness, and they are recommended for high-risk individuals such as the elderly and healthcare workers. Some drugs will help shorten the duration of the illness and decrease its severity if given within 48 hours after symptoms appear. General health tips include eating a balanced diet, getting enough rest, staying home when ill, exercising frequently, and washing hands frequently with warm, soapy water. Your campus' health services department wants to develop a presentation for students informing them about the flu and giving advice to stay healthy. Using the techniques introduced in the project, create a presentation about the flu.

5 ■■ **Working Together** Volunteers can make a contribution to society while they gain much fulfillment in return. Community organizations and non-for-profit businesses frequently seek volunteers for various projects. Have each member of your team visit or telephone several local civic groups to determine volunteer opportunities. Gather data about:

1) Required duties
2) Number of required hours
3) Contact person
4) Address
5) Telephone number

After coordinating the data, create a presentation with at least one slide showcasing the charitable organization. As a group, critique each slide. Hand in a hard copy of the final presentation.

Using the Outline Tab and Clip Art to Create a Slide Show

PROJECT

2

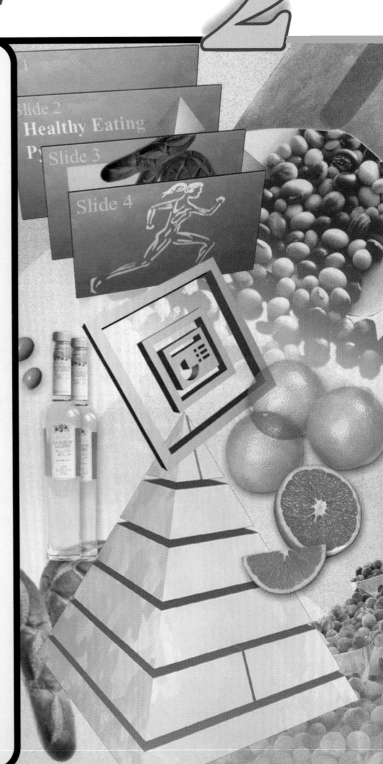

CASE PERSPECTIVE

For some students, the Healthy Eating Pyramid developed by the Harvard School of Public Health is as foreign as the Great Pyramid of Egypt. Eating a balanced diet seems as impossible as solving a quadratic formula. Obesity, hypertension, heart disease, and diabetes are soaring as a consequence of poor eating and lack of exercise, as two of every three Americans are classified as overweight or obese. Moreover, 25 percent of the U.S. population leads a completely sedentary lifestyle.

Cultural and social factors contribute to this unhealthy existence, so health care and fitness professionals need to educate adults and adolescents about adopting nutritious meals and daily exercise as the basis of a healthy lifestyle. Jessica Cantero, the Fitness Director at your college, realizes that students need to understand and apply simple measures they can take to help promote a healthy body. She wants to develop a series of workshops to motivate students to control their weight, exercise moderately, and release stress.

She knows that PowerPoint slide shows enhance speakers' presentations, so she asks you to assist her in developing a slide show to accompany her first workshop. This presentation will include nutritional information based on the Healthy Eating Pyramid, daily exercise guidelines, relaxation principles, and the advantages of maintaining a healthy lifestyle.

As you read through this project, you will learn how to use PowerPoint to add clip art and animation to increase the presentation's visual interest. You also will e-mail the completed presentation to Jessica.

Using the Outline Tab and Clip Art to Create a Slide Show

PROJECT

2

Objectives

You will have mastered the material in this project when you can:

- Start and customize a new slide show from an outline
- Add a slide and create a closing slide on the Outline tab
- Create text slides with multi-level bulleted lists on the Outline tab
- Save and review a presentation
- Insert and move clip art and change its size
- Add a header and footer to outline pages
- Animate clip art
- Add an animation scheme and run an animated slide show
- Print a presentation outline
- E-mail a slide show from within PowerPoint

Introduction

At some time during either your academic or business life, you probably will make a presentation. The presentation may be informative by providing detailed information about a specific topic. Other presentations may be persuasive by selling a proposal or a product to a client, convincing management to approve a new project, or influencing the board of directors to accept the new fiscal budget. As an alternative to creating your presentation in the slide pane in normal view, as you did in Project 1, PowerPoint provides an outlining feature to help you organize your thoughts. When the outline is complete, it becomes the foundation for your presentation.

Project Two — Healthy Eating, Healthy Living

Project 2 uses PowerPoint to create the five-slide Healthy Eating, Healthy Living presentation shown in Figures 2-1a through 2-1e. You create the presentation from the outline shown in Figure 2-2 on page PPT 84.

Healthy Eating
Healthy Living

Nutrition and Fitness Basics
Clark College Fitness Center

(a) Slide 1

Nutrition Guidelines

- Healthy Eating Pyramid
  - Eat more vegetable oils, whole grains
  - Eat less pasta, white bread

(b) Slide 2

Recommended Exercise

- 30 minutes of daily moderate-intensity activity
  - Brisk walking
  - Bicycling
  - Gardening

(c) Slide 3

Relaxation Techniques

- Quiet the mind and body
  - Visualize a tranquil setting
  - Concentrate on positive thoughts
- Build strength and refresh the body
  - Practice yoga or Pilates basics
  - Improve balance through core training

(d) Slide 4

Healthy Living Benefits

- Lowers cholesterol, blood pressure
- Reduces heart disease risk
- Helps prevent adult-onset diabetes
  - Affects 8% of adults
- Maintains body weight
  - Helps avoid excess gain

(e) Slide 5

FIGURE 2-1

I. Healthy Eating Healthy Living
   A. Nutrition and Fitness Basics
   B. Clark College Fitness Center
II. Nutrition Guidelines
   A. Healthy Eating Pyramid
      1. Eat more vegetable oils, whole grains
      2. Eat less pasta, white bread
III. Recommended Exercise
   A. 30 minutes of daily moderate-intensity activity
      1. Brisk walking
      2. Bicycling
      3. Gardening
IV. Relaxation Techniques
   A. Quiet the mind and body
      1. Visualize a tranquil setting
      2. Concentrate on positive thoughts
   B. Build strength and refresh the body
      1. Practice yoga or Pilates basics
      2. Improve balance through core training
V. Healthy Living Benefits
   A. Lowers cholesterol, blood pressure
   B. Reduces heart disease risk
   C. Helps prevent adult-onset diabetes
      1. Affects 8% of adults
   D. Maintains body weight
      1. Helps avoid excess gain

FIGURE 2-2

You can create your presentation outline using the Outline tab. When you create an outline, you type all the text at one time, as if you were typing an outline on a sheet of paper. This technique differs from creating a presentation in the slide pane in normal view, where you type text as you create each individual slide and the text is displayed both in the slide pane and on the Outline tab. PowerPoint creates the presentation as you type the outline by evaluating the outline structure and displaying a miniature view of the slide. Regardless of how you build a presentation, PowerPoint automatically creates the three views discussed in Project 1: normal, slide sorter, and slide show.

The first step in creating a presentation on the Outline tab is to type a title for the outline. The **outline title** is the subject of the presentation and later becomes the presentation title text. Then, you type the remainder of the outline, indenting appropriately to establish a structure, or hierarchy. Once the outline is complete, you make your presentation more persuasive by adding **clips**, which are media files of art, animation, sound, and movies. This project uses outlining to create the presentation and clip art to support the text visually.

Starting and Customizing PowerPoint

Project 1 introduced you to starting a presentation document, choosing a layout, and applying a design template. The following steps summarize how to start a new presentation, customize the PowerPoint window, choose a layout, and apply a design template. To start and customize PowerPoint, Windows must be running. If you are stepping through this project on a computer and you want your screen to match the figures in this book, then you should change your computer's resolution to 800 × 600. For more information on how to change the resolution on your computer, see Appendix B.

More About

Outlining

Outlining helps you plan, organize, and design your presentation. When you start to create an outline, you often begin to see new possibilities and find new ways to divide and group your ideas. You also find gaps where additional information is needed. A final glance at an outline can tell you if your plan is appropriate. For more information on outlining, visit the PowerPoint 2003 More About Web page (scsite.com/ppt2003/more) and click Outlining.

To Start and Customize PowerPoint

1 Click the Start button on the Windows taskbar, point to All Programs on the Start menu, point to Microsoft Office on the All Programs submenu, and then click Microsoft Office PowerPoint 2003 on the Microsoft Office submenu.

2 If the PowerPoint window is not maximized, double-click its title bar to maximize it.

3 If the Language bar appears, right-click it and then click Close the Language bar on the shortcut menu.

4 If the Getting Started task pane appears in the PowerPoint window, click its Close button in the upper-right corner.

5 If the Standard and Formatting toolbars are positioned on the same row, click the Toolbar Options button and then click Show Buttons on Two Rows.

6 Click the Slide Design button on the Formatting toolbar. When the Slide Design task pane is displayed, click the down scroll arrow in the Apply a design template list, and then click the Axis template in the Available For Use area.

7 Click the Close button in the Slide Design task pane.

If the Axis template is not displayed in the Slide Design task pane, ask your instructor about installing additional templates. The PowerPoint window with the Standard and Formatting toolbars on two rows appears as shown in Figure 2-3. PowerPoint displays the Title Slide layout and the Axis template on Slide 1 in normal view.

FIGURE 2-3

Using the Outline Tab

The **Outline tab** provides a quick, easy way to create a presentation. **Outlining** allows you to organize your thoughts in a structured format. An outline uses indentation to establish a **hierarchy**, which denotes levels of importance to the main topic. An outline is a summary of thoughts, presented as headings and subheadings, often used as a preliminary draft when you create a presentation.

The three panes — tabs, slide, and notes — shown in normal view also display when you click the Outline tab. The notes pane is displayed below the slide pane. In the tabs pane, the slide text appears along with a slide number and a slide icon. Body text is indented below the title text. Objects, such as pictures, graphs, or tables, do not display. The slide icon is blank when a slide does not contain objects. The attributes for text on the Outline tab are the same as in normal view except for color and paragraph style.

PowerPoint formats a title style and five levels of body text in an outline. The outline begins with the slide title, which is not indented. The title is the main topic of the slide. Body text supporting the main topic begins on the first level and also is not indented. If desired, additional supporting text can be added on the second through fifth levels. Each level is indented. Levels four and five generally are used for very detailed scientific and engineering presentations. Business and sales presentations usually focus on summary information and use the first, second, and third levels.

PowerPoint initially displays in normal view when you start a new presentation. To type the outline, click the Outline tab in the tabs pane. The following steps show how to change to the Outline tab and display the Outlining toolbar.

To Change to the Outline Tab and Display the Outlining Toolbar

1

• **Click the Outline tab located in the tabs pane.**

The Outline tab is selected. The tabs pane increases and the slide pane decreases in size. The tabs pane consists of the Outline tab and the Slides tab (Figure 2-4).

FIGURE 2-4

2

• **Click View on the menu bar and then point to Toolbars.**

• **Point to Outlining on the Toolbars submenu.**

The View menu and Toolbars submenu are displayed (Figure 2-5).

FIGURE 2-5

3

• **Click Outlining.**

The Outlining toolbar is displayed (Figure 2-6).

FIGURE 2-6

You can create and edit your presentation on the Outline tab. This tab also makes it easy to sequence slides and to relocate title text and body text from one slide to another. In addition to typing text to create a new presentation on the Outline tab, PowerPoint can produce slides from an outline created in Microsoft Word or another word processing application if you save the outline as an RTF file or as a plain text file. The file extension **RTF** stands for **R**ich **T**ext **F**ormat.

Table 2-1 describes the buttons on the Outlining toolbar.

Table 2-1	Buttons on the Outlining Toolbar	
BUTTON	**BUTTON NAME**	**DESCRIPTION**
	Promote	Moves the selected paragraph to the next-higher level (up one level, to the left).
	Demote	Moves the selected paragraph to the next-lower level (down one level, to the right).
	Move Up	Moves a selected paragraph and its collapsed (temporarily hidden) subordinate text above the preceding displayed paragraph.
	Move Down	Moves a selected paragraph and its collapsed (temporarily hidden) subordinate text down, below the following displayed paragraph.
	Collapse	Hides all but the titles of selected slides. Collapsed text is represented by a gray line.
	Expand	Displays the titles and all collapsed text of selected slides.
	Collapse All	Displays only the title of each slide. Text other than the title is represented by a gray line below the title.
	Expand All	Displays the titles and all the body text for each slide.
	Summary Slide	Creates a new slide from the titles of the slides you select in slide sorter or normal view. The summary slide creates a bulleted list from the titles of the selected slides. PowerPoint inserts the summary slide in front of the first selected slide.
	Show Formatting	Shows or hides character formatting (such as bold and italic) in normal view. In slide sorter view, switches between showing all text and objects on each slide and displaying titles only.
	Toolbar Options	Allows you to select the particular buttons you want to display on the toolbar.

Creating a Presentation on the Outline Tab

The Outline tab enables you to view title and body text, add and delete slides, drag and drop slide text, drag and drop individual slides, promote and demote text, save a presentation, print an outline, print slides, copy and paste slides or text to and from other presentations, apply a design template, and import an outline. When you **drag and drop** slide text or individual slides, you change the order of the text or the slides by selecting the text or slide you want to move or copy and then dragging the text or slide to its new location.

Developing a presentation on the Outline tab is quick because you type the text for all slides on one screen. Once you type the outline, the presentation fundamentally is complete. If you choose, you then can enhance your presentation with objects in the slide pane.

Creating a Title Slide on the Outline Tab

Recall from Project 1 that the title slide introduces the presentation to the audience. In addition to introducing the presentation, Project 2 uses the title slide to capture the audience's attention by using a design template with an interesting title. The following steps show how to create a title slide on the Outline tab.

To Create a Title Slide on the Outline Tab

1

• **Click the Slide 1 slide icon on the Outline tab.**

The Slide 1 slide icon is selected. You also could click anywhere in the tabs pane to select the slide icon (Figure 2-7).

FIGURE 2-7

2

• **Type** Healthy Eating **and then press the SHIFT+ENTER keys.**

• **Type** Healthy Living **and then press the ENTER key.**

• **Point to the Demote button on the Outlining toolbar.**

The Demote ScreenTip is displayed (Figure 2-8). Pressing the SHIFT+ENTER keys moves the insertion point to the next line and maintains the same first level. The insertion point is in position for typing the title for Slide 2. The first-level font is Arial and the font size is 40 point.

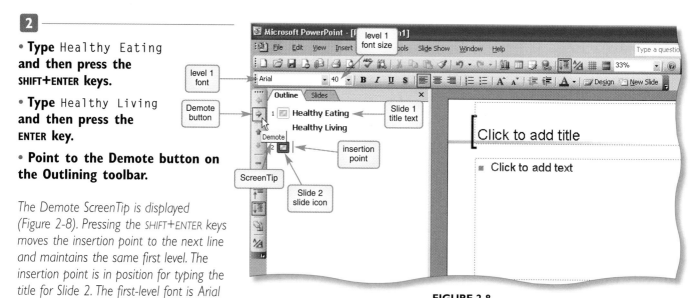

FIGURE 2-8

3

- **Click the Demote button on the Outlining toolbar.**

- **Type** Nutrition and Fitness Basics **and then press the ENTER key.**

- **Type** Clark College Fitness Center **and then press the ENTER key.**

The paragraphs, Nutrition and Fitness Basics and Clark College Fitness Center, are subtitles on the title slide (Slide 1) and demote to the second level (Figure 2-9). The second level is indented to the right below the first-level paragraph. The second-level font is Arial and the font size is 32 point.

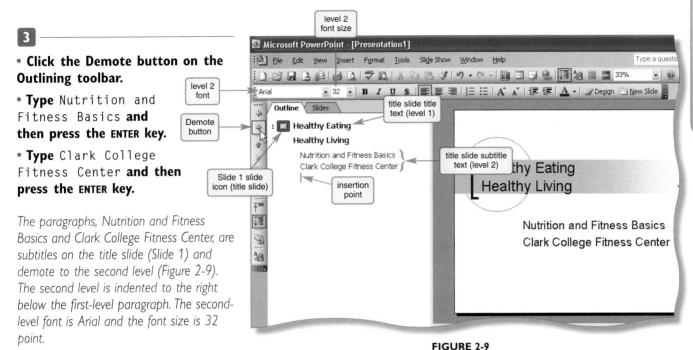

FIGURE 2-9

The title slide text for the Healthy Eating, Healthy Living presentation is complete. The next section explains how to add a slide on the Outline tab.

Adding a Slide on the Outline Tab

Recall from Project 1 that when you add a new slide in normal view, PowerPoint defaults to a Text slide layout with a bulleted list. This action occurs on the Outline tab as well. One way to add a new slide on the Outline tab is to promote a paragraph to the first level by clicking the Promote button on the Outlining toolbar until the insertion point or the paragraph is displayed at the first level. A slide icon is displayed when the insertion point or paragraph reaches this level. The following step shows how to add a slide on the Outline tab.

To Add a Slide on the Outline Tab

1

- **Click the Promote button on the Outlining toolbar.**

The Slide 2 slide icon is displayed, indicating a new slide is added to the presentation (Figure 2-10). The insertion point is in position to type the title for Slide 2 at the first level.

FIGURE 2-10

After you add a slide, you are ready to type the slide text. The next section explains how to create text slides with multi-level bulleted lists on the Outline tab.

Creating Text Slides with Multi-Level Bulleted Lists on the Outline Tab

To create a text slide with multi-level bulleted lists, you demote or promote the insertion point to the appropriate level and then type the paragraph text. Recall from Project 1 that when you demote a paragraph, PowerPoint adds a bullet to the left of each level. Depending on the design template, each level has a different bullet font. Also recall that the design template determines font attributes, including the bullet font.

The first text slide you create in Project 2 describes the basic nutritional guidelines comprising the Healthy Eating Pyramid. The slide title is displayed as a first-level paragraph on the Outline tab and in the slide pane, and the Pyramid name and food suggestions are displayed as second- and third-level paragraphs. The following steps explain how to create a text slide with a multi-level bulleted list on the Outline tab.

To Create a Text Slide with a Multi-Level Bulleted List on the Outline Tab

1

• **Type** Nutrition Guidelines **and then press the** ENTER **key.**

• **Click the Demote button on the Outlining toolbar to demote to the second level.**

The title for Slide 2, Nutrition Guidelines, is displayed and the insertion point is in position to type the first bulleted paragraph (Figure 2-11). A bullet is displayed to the left of the insertion point.

FIGURE 2-11

2 ———————————

• **Type** Healthy Eating Pyramid **and then press the ENTER key.**

• **Click the Demote button on the Outlining toolbar to demote to the third level.**

• **Type** Eat more vegetable oils, whole grains **and then press the ENTER key.**

• **Type** Eat less pasta, white bread **and then press the ENTER key.**

Slide 2 is displaycd with three levels: the title, Nutrition Guidelines, on the first level; the Pyramid name on the second level; and two bulleted paragraphs and the insertion point on the third level (Figure 2-12).

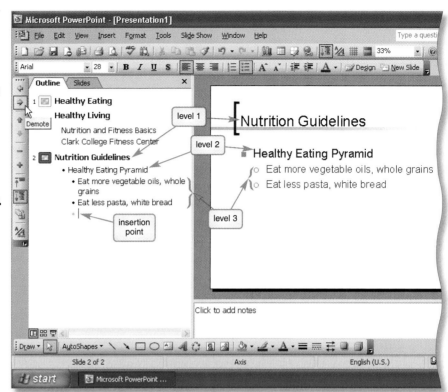

FIGURE 2-12

Slide 2 is complete. The text on this slide abides by the 7 × 7 rule. As you learned in Project 1, this rule recommends that each line should have a maximum of seven words, and each slide should have a maximum of seven lines. All slides in this slide show use the 7 × 7 rule.

The remaining three slides in the presentation contain multi-level bulleted lists. Slide 3 provides information about exercise guidelines, Slide 4 gives details about relaxation procedures, and Slide 5 lists the benefits of adhering to a healthy lifestyle. It is easy and efficient to type the text for these slides on the Outline tab because you can view all the text you type in the outline in the tabs pane to check organization.

Creating a Second Text Slide with a Multi-Level Bulleted List

The next slide, Slide 3, provides details about daily exercise. Experts recommend exercising moderately for 30 minutes each day. The steps on the next page show how to create this slide.

Q & A

Q: How many levels should a slide have?

A: Three. Graphic designers recommend limiting the levels to three although PowerPoint gives you five levels of body text to use on each slide. Details on all five levels may overwhelm audiences. If you find yourself needing more than three levels, consider combining content in one level or using two different slides.

To Create a Second Text Slide with a Multi-Level Bulleted List

1 Click the Promote button on the Outlining toolbar two times so that Slide 3 is added after Slide 2.

2 Type Recommended Exercise and then press the ENTER key.

3 Click the Demote button on the Outlining toolbar to demote to the second level.

4 Type 30 minutes of daily moderate-intensity activity and then press the ENTER key.

5 Click the Demote button to demote to the third level.

6 Type Brisk walking and then press the ENTER key.

7 Type Bicycling and then press the ENTER key.

8 Type Gardening and then press the ENTER key.

The completed Slide 3 is displayed (Figure 2-13).

FIGURE 2-13

Creating a Third Text Slide with a Multi-Level Bulleted List

Slide 4 describes recommended relaxation techniques that should be practiced in conjunction with eating nutritional meals and exercising daily. The following steps show how to create this slide.

To Create a Third Text Slide with a Multi-Level Bulleted List

1 Click the Promote button on the Outlining toolbar two times so that Slide 4 is added after Slide 3.

2 Type Relaxation Techniques and then press the ENTER key.

3 Click the Demote button on the Outlining toolbar to demote to the second level.

4 **Type** `Quiet the mind and body` **and then press the ENTER key.**

5 **Click the Demote button to demote to the third level.**

6 **Type** `Visualize a tranquil setting` **and then press the ENTER key.**

7 **Type** `Concentrate on positive thoughts` **and then press the ENTER key.**

8 **Click the Promote button to promote to the second level.**

9 **Type** `Build strength and refresh the body` **and then press the ENTER key.**

10 **Click the Demote button to demote to the third level.**

11 **Type** `Practice yoga or Pilates basics` **and then press the ENTER key.**

12 **Type** `Improve balance through core training` **and then press the ENTER key.**

The completed Slide 4 is displayed (Figure 2-14).

FIGURE 2-14

Creating a Closing Slide on the Outline Tab

The last slide in a presentation is the closing slide. A **closing slide** gracefully ends a presentation. Often used during a question and answer session, the closing slide usually remains on the screen to reinforce the message delivered during the presentation. Professional speakers design the closing slide with one or more of these methods:

1. List important information. Tell the audience what to do next.
2. Provide a memorable illustration or example to make a point.
3. Appeal to emotions. Remind the audience to take action or accept responsibility.
4. Summarize the main point of the presentation.
5. Cite a quotation that directly relates to the main point of the presentation. This technique is most effective if the presentation started with a quotation.

The last text slide you create in Project 2 describes the benefits of practicing a healthy lifestyle. The steps on the next page show how to create this closing slide.

To Create a Closing Slide on the Outline Tab

1 **Click the Promote button on the Outlining toolbar two times to add Slide 5 after Slide 4. Type** Healthy Living Benefits **and then press the ENTER key.**

2 **Click the Demote button on the Outlining toolbar to demote to the second level. Type** Lowers cholesterol, blood pressure **and then press the ENTER key.**

3 **Type** Reduces heart disease risk **and then press the ENTER key.**

4 **Type** Helps prevent adult-onset diabetes **and then press the ENTER key.**

5 **Click the Demote button to demote to the third level. Type** Affects 8% of adults **and then press the ENTER key.**

6 **Click the Promote button to promote to the second level. Type** Maintains body weight **and then press the ENTER key.**

7 **Click the Demote button. Type** Helps avoid excess gain **but do not press the ENTER key.**

The completed Slide 5 is displayed (Figure 2-15).

FIGURE 2-15

The outline now is complete and you should save the presentation. The next section explains how to save the presentation.

Saving a Presentation

Recall from Project 1 that it is wise to save your presentation frequently. With all the text for your presentation created, save the presentation using the following steps.

To Save a Presentation

1 Insert a formatted floppy disk in drive A and then click the Save button on the Standard toolbar.

2 Type Nutrition and Fitness in the File name text box. Do not press the ENTER key after typing the file name. Click the Save in box arrow.

3 Click 3½ Floppy (A:) in the Save in list.

4 Click the Save button in the Save As dialog box.

The presentation is saved with the file name, Nutrition and Fitness, on the floppy disk in drive A. PowerPoint uses the first text line in a presentation as the default file name. The file name is displayed on the title bar.

Reviewing a Presentation in Slide Sorter View

In Project 1, you displayed slides in slide show view to evaluate the presentation. Slide show view, however, restricts your evaluation to one slide at a time. The Outline tab is best for quickly reviewing all the text for a presentation. Recall from Project 1 that slide sorter view allows you to look at several slides at one time, which is why it is the best view to use to evaluate a presentation for content, organization, and overall appearance. The following step shows how to change from the Outline tab to slide sorter view.

To Change the View to Slide Sorter View

1

• **Click the Slide Sorter View button at the lower left of the PowerPoint window.**

PowerPoint displays the presentation in slide sorter view (Figure 2-16). Slide 5 is selected because it was the current slide on the Outline tab. The Slide Sorter View button is selected.

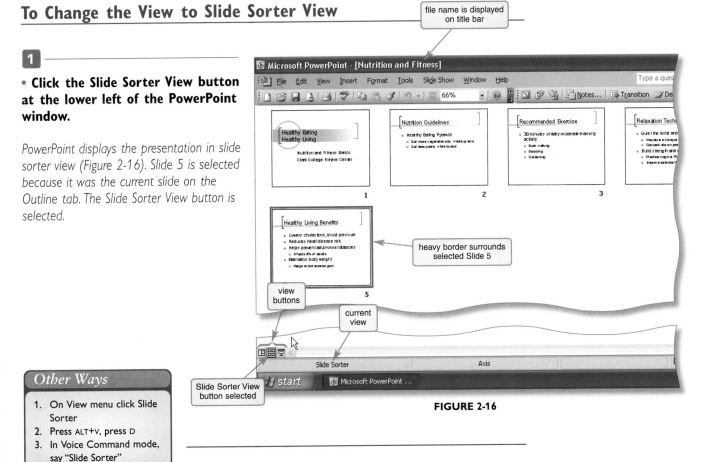

FIGURE 2-16

You can review the five slides in this presentation all in one window. Notice the slides have a significant amount of space and look plain. These observations indicate a need to add visual interest to the slides by using clips. The next several sections explain how to improve the presentation by changing slide layouts and adding clip art.

You can make changes to text in normal view and on the Outline tab. It is best, however, to change the view to normal view when altering the slide layouts so you can see the results of your changes. The following steps show how to change the view from slide sorter view to normal view.

To Change the View to Normal View

1

- **Click the Slide 2 slide thumbnail.**
- **Point to the Normal View button at the lower left of the PowerPoint window.**

Slide 2 is selected, as indicated by the thick blue border around that slide (Figure 2-17).

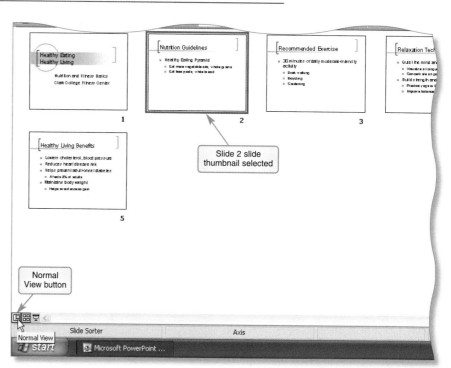

FIGURE 2-17

2

- **Click the Normal View button.**

The Normal View button is selected at the lower left of the PowerPoint window. The Slide 2 slide icon is selected in the tabs pane, and Slide 2 is displayed in the slide pane (Figure 2-18).

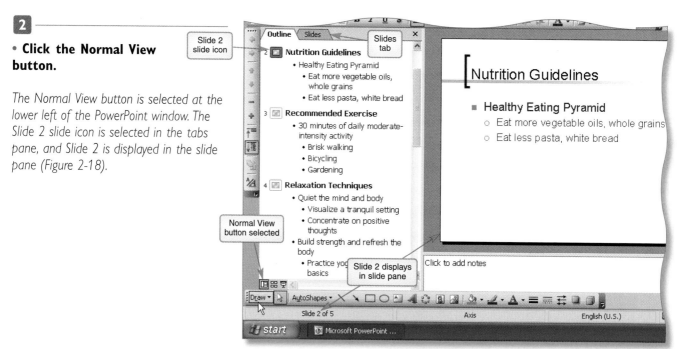

FIGURE 2-18

3

• **Click the Slides tab in the tabs pane.**

The tabs pane reduces in size. Slide thumbnails of the five slides are displayed (Figure 2-19).

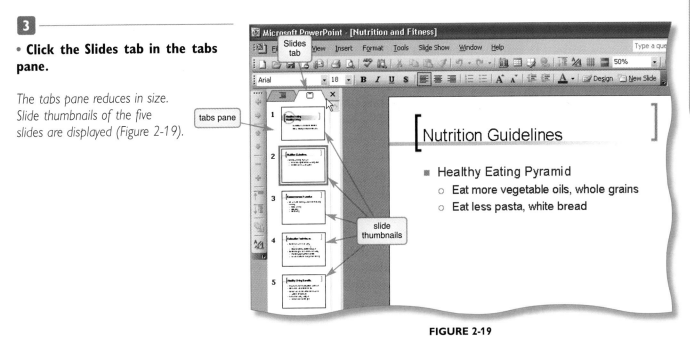

FIGURE 2-19

Switching between slide sorter view and normal view helps you review your presentation and assess whether the slides have an attractive design and adequate content.

Changing Slide Layout

When you developed this presentation, PowerPoint applied the Title Slide layout for Slide 1 and the Title and Text layout for the other four slides in the presentation. These layouts are the default styles. A **layout** specifies the arrangement of placeholders on a slide. These placeholders are arranged in various configurations and can contain text, such as the slide title or a bulleted list, or they can contain content, such as clips, pictures, charts, tables, and shapes. The placement of the text, in relationship to content, depends on the slide layout. The content placeholders may be to the right or left of the text, above the text, or below the text. You can specify a particular slide layout when you add a new slide to a presentation or after you have created the slide.

Using the **Slide Layout task pane**, you can choose a slide layout. The layouts in this task pane are arranged in four areas: Text Layouts, Content Layouts, Text and Content Layouts, and Other Layouts. The two layouts you have used in this project — Title Slide and Title and Text — are included in the Text Layouts area, along with the Title Only and Title and 2-Column Text layouts. The Content Layouts area contains a blank slide and a variety of placeholder groupings for charts, tables, clip art, pictures, diagrams, and media clips. The Text and Content Layouts have placeholders for a title, a bulleted list, and content. The Other Layouts area has layouts with placeholders for a title and one object, such as clip art, charts, media clips, tables, organization charts, and charts.

When you change the layout of a slide, PowerPoint retains the text and objects and repositions them into the appropriate placeholders. Using slide layouts eliminates the need to resize objects and the font size because PowerPoint automatically sizes the objects and text to fit the placeholders. If the objects are in **landscape orientation**, meaning their width is greater than their height, PowerPoint sizes them to the width of the placeholders. If the objects are in **portrait orientation**, meaning their height is greater than their width, PowerPoint sizes them to the height of the placeholders.

Adding clips to Slides 2 and 3 requires two steps. First, change the slide layout to Title, Text, and Content or to Title, 2 Content and Text. Then, insert clip art into the content placeholders. The following steps show how to change the slide layout on Slide 2 from Title and Text to Title, Text, and Content.

To Change the Slide Layout to Title, Text, and Content

1

• **Click Format on the menu bar and then point to Slide Layout (Figure 2-20).**

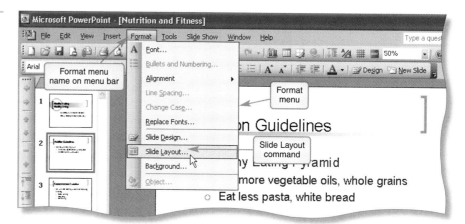

FIGURE 2-20

2

• **Click Slide Layout.**

• **Click the down arrow in the Apply slide layout area and scroll down until the Text and Content Layouts area displays.**

• **Point to the Title, Text, and Content layout in the Text and Content Layouts area.**

The Slide Layout task pane is displayed (Figure 2-21). The Title, Text, and Content layout is selected, as indicated by the blue box around the template, the ScreenTip, and the down arrow on the right side.

FIGURE 2-21

3

• **Click Title, Text, and Content.**

The layout is applied to Slide 2 (Figure 2-22). PowerPoint moves the text placeholder containing the bulleted list to the left side of the slide and automatically resizes the text. The content placeholder on the right side of the slide has the message, Click icon to add content.

FIGURE 2-22

4

• **Click the Close button in the Slide Layout task pane.**

Slide 2 is displayed in normal view with the new slide layout applied (Figure 2-23).

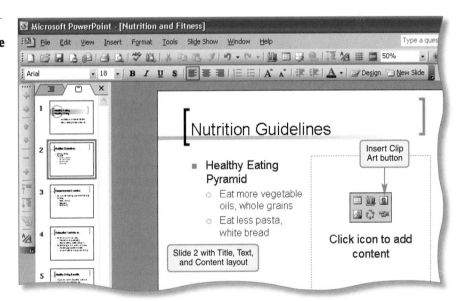

FIGURE 2-23

PowerPoint reduced the second-level text in the Slide 2 text placeholder from a font size of 32 point to 28 point so all the words fit into the placeholder.

Adding Clip Art to a Slide

Clip art helps the visual appeal of the Nutrition and Fitness slide show and offers a quick way to add professional-looking graphic images to a presentation without creating the images yourself. This art is contained in the **Microsoft Clip Organizer**, a collection of drawings, photographs, sounds, videos, and other media files shared with Microsoft Office applications.

Other Ways

1. Right-click slide anywhere except text placeholders, click Slide Layout on shortcut menu, double-click desired slide layout
2. Press ALT+O, press L, press ARROW keys to select desired slide layout, press ENTER
3. In Voice Command mode, say "Format, Slide Layout, Title Text and Content, Close"

Q: Can I add clips to the Clip Organizer?

A: Yes. You can add media files and objects created in Microsoft Office programs. The media files are stored in a new subcollection in the My Collections clip collection folder. The objects can be pictures, WordArt, and AutoShapes, and you can store them in any desired collection folder.

You can add clip art to your presentation in two ways. One way is by selecting one of the slide layouts that includes a content placeholder with instructions to open the Microsoft Clip Organizer to add content. You will add art to Slides 2 and 3 in this manner. Double-clicking a button in the content placeholder activates the instructions to open the Select Picture dialog box, which allows you to enter keywords to search for clips.

The second method is by clicking the Insert Clip Art button on the Drawing toolbar to open the Clip Art task pane. The **Clip Art task pane** allows you to search for clips by using descriptive keywords, file names, media file formats, and clip collections. Specific file formats could be for clip art, photographs, movies, and sounds. Clips are organized in hierarchical **clip collections**, which combine topic-related clips into categories, such as Academic, Business, and Technology. You also can create your own collections for frequently used clips. You will insert clip art into Slides 4 and 5 using this process. You then will arrange the clips on the slides without using a placeholder for content.

Table 2-2 shows four categories from the Office Collections in the Microsoft Clip Organizer and keywords of various clip art files in those categories. Clip art images have one or more keywords associated with various entities, activities, labels, and emotions. In most instances, the keywords give the name of the clip and related categories. For example, an image of a cow in the Animals category has the keywords animals, cattle, cows, dairies, farms, and Holsteins. You can enter these keywords in the Search text box to find clips when you know one of the words associated with the image. Otherwise, you may find it necessary to scroll through several categories to find an appropriate clip.

Table 2-2 Microsoft Clip Organizer Category and Keyword Examples	
CATEGORY	**CLIP ART KEYWORDS**
Academic	Books, knowledge, information, schools, school buses, apple for the teacher, professors
Business	Computers, inspirations, ideas, currencies, board meetings, conferences, teamwork, profits
Nature	Lakes, flowers, plants, seasons, wildlife, weather, trees, sunshine, rivers, leaves
Technology	Computers, diskettes, microchips, cellular telephones, e-commerce, office equipment, data exchanges

Depending on the installation of the Microsoft Clip Organizer on your computer, you may not have the clip art used in this project. Contact your instructor if you are missing clips used in the following steps. If you have an open connection to the Internet, clips from the Microsoft Web site will display automatically as the result of your search results.

Inserting Clip Art into a Content Placeholder

With the Title, Text, and Content layout applied to Slide 2, you insert clip art into the content placeholder. The following steps show how to insert clip art of a cornucopia into the content placeholder on Slide 2.

To Insert Clip Art into a Content Placeholder

1

• **Point to the Insert Clip Art button in the content placeholder.**

The Insert Clip Art button is selected (Figure 2-24). A ScreenTip describes its function.

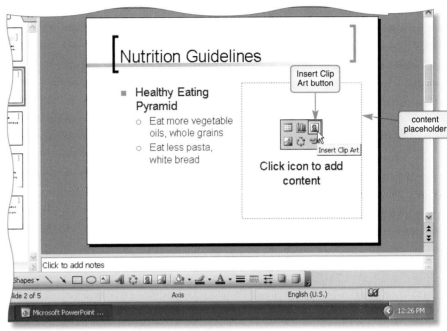

FIGURE 2-24

2

• **Click the Insert Clip Art button.**

• **Type** food **in the Search text text box and then point to the Go button.**

The Select Picture dialog box is displayed (Figure 2-25). The clips displaying on your computer may vary.

FIGURE 2-25

3

• **Click the Go button.**

• **If necessary, scroll down the list to display the cornucopia clip shown in Figure 2-26.**

• **Click the clip to select it.**

The Microsoft Clip Organizer searches for and displays all pictures having the keyword, food (Figure 2-26). The desired clip of a cornucopia is displayed with a blue box around it. Your clips may be different depending on the clips installed on your computer and if you have an open connection to the Internet, in which case you may need to obtain an appropriate clip from the Internet.

FIGURE 2-26

4

• **Click the OK button.**

• **If the Picture toolbar is displayed, click the Close button on the Picture toolbar.**

The selected clip is inserted into the top content placeholder on Slide 2 (Figure 2-27). PowerPoint sizes the clip automatically to fit the placeholder.

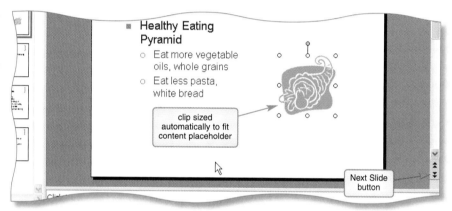

FIGURE 2-27

Slide 2 is complete. The next step is to change the Slide 3 layout and then add two clips. This slide uses the Title, 2 Content and Text slide layout so the two clips display vertically on the left side of the slide and the bulleted list is displayed on the right side. The following steps show how to change the slide layout and then add clip art to Slide 3.

To Change the Slide Layout to Title, 2 Content and Text and Insert Clip Art

1 Click the Next Slide button on the vertical scroll bar to display Slide 3.

2 Click Format on the menu bar and then click Slide Layout.

3 Scroll to display the Title, 2 Content and Text slide layout located in the Text and Content Layouts area of the Slide Layout task pane.

4 Click the Title, 2 Content and Text slide layout and then click the Close button in the Slide Layout task pane.

5 Click the Insert Clip Art button in the top content placeholder. **Type** woman in the Search text text box and then click the Go button.

6 If necessary, scroll down the list to display the desired clip of a woman walking and then click the clip to select it. Click the OK button.

The selected clip is inserted into the content placeholder on Slide 3 (Figure 2-28). The slide has the Title, 2 Content and Text slide layout.

FIGURE 2-28

Inserting a Second Clip into a Slide

Another clip on Slide 3 is required to fill the bottom content placeholder. This clip should be the image of roses. The following steps show how to insert the roses clip into the bottom placeholder on Slide 3.

To Insert a Second Clip into a Slide

1 Click the Insert Clip Art button in the bottom content placeholder.

2 **Type** flowers **in the Search text text box and then click the Go button.**

3 If necessary, scroll down the list to display the desired clip of yellow roses, click the clip to select it, and then click the OK button.

The selected clip is inserted into the bottom content placeholder on Slide 3 (Figure 2-29). PowerPoint automatically sizes the clip to fit the placeholder.

FIGURE 2-29

Slide 3 is complete. Your next step is to add a clip to Slide 4 without changing the slide layout.

Inserting Clip Art into a Slide without a Content Placeholder

PowerPoint does not require you to use a content placeholder to add clips to a slide. You can insert clips on any slide regardless of its slide layout. On Slides 2 and 3, you added clips that enhanced the message in the text. Recall that the slide layout on Slide 4 is Title and Text. Because this layout does not contain a content placeholder, you can use the Insert Clip Art button on the Drawing toolbar to start the Microsoft Clip Organizer. The clip for which you are searching has a house located by a lake. A few of its keywords are house, buildings, homes, and lakes. The following steps show how to insert this clip into a slide that does not have a content placeholder.

To Insert Clip Art into a Slide without a Content Placeholder

1

• **Click the Next Slide button on the vertical scroll bar to display Slide 4.**

• **Click Tools on the menu bar and then click AutoCorrect Options.**

• **If necessary, when the AutoCorrect dialog box displays, click the AutoFormat As You Type tab.**

• **Click Automatic layout for inserted objects in the Apply as you work area if a check mark does not display.**

• **Click OK.**

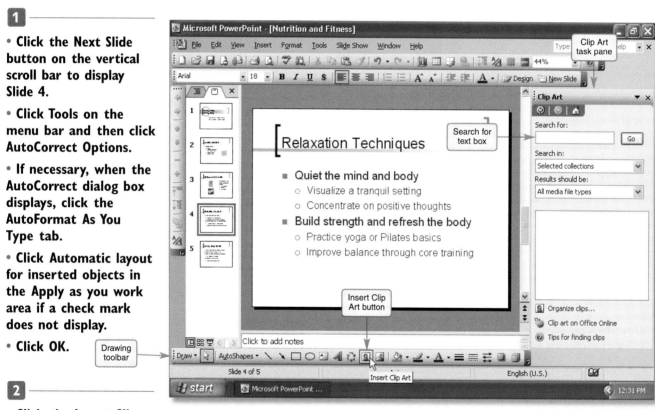

FIGURE 2-30

2

• **Click the Insert Clip Art button on the Drawing toolbar.**

• **If the Add Clips to Organizer dialog box displays asking if you want to catalog media files, click Don't show this message again, or, if you want to catalog later, click the Later button.**

The Clip Art task pane is displayed (Figure 2-30).

3

• **Click the Search for text box.**

• **Type** house **and then press the ENTER key.**

• **If necessary, scroll to display the desired clip of a house located beside a lake.**

• **Point to this image.**

The clip of a lake and house is displayed with any other clips sharing the house keyword (Figure 2-31). Your clips may be different. The clip's keywords, size in pixels (260 x 223), file size (33 KB), and file type (WMF) are displayed.

FIGURE 2-31

4

• **Click the desired clip.**

• **Click the Close button on the Clip Art task pane title bar.**

PowerPoint inserts the clip into Slide 4 (Figure 2-32). The slide layout changes automatically to Title, Text, and Content. The Automatic Layout Options button is displayed. If your slide layout does not change, then continue this project using the Moving Clip Art section on page PPT 108.

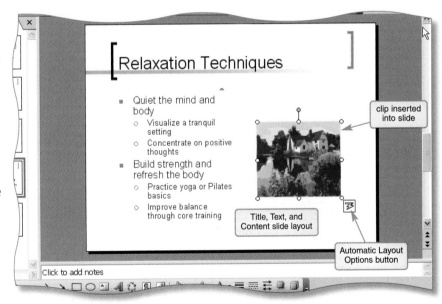

FIGURE 2-32

In addition to clip art, you can insert pictures into a presentation. These may include scanned photographs, line art, and artwork from compact discs. To insert a picture into a presentation, the picture must be saved in a format that PowerPoint can recognize. Table 2-3 (on the next page) identifies some of the formats PowerPoint recognizes.

You can import files saved with the .emf, .gif, .jpg, .png, .bmp, .rle, .dib, and .wmf formats directly into PowerPoint presentations. All other file formats require separate filters that are shipped with the PowerPoint installation software and must be installed. You can download additional filters from the Microsoft Office Online Web site.

Table 2-3   Primary File Formats PowerPoint Recognizes

FORMAT	FILE EXTENSION
Computer Graphics Metafile	.cgm
CorelDRAW	.cdr, .cdt, .cmx, and .pat
Encapsulated PostScript	.eps
Enhanced Metafile	.emf
FlashPix	.fpx
Graphics Interchange Format	.gif
Hanako	.jsh, .jah, and .jbh
Joint Photographic Experts Group (JPEG)	.jpg
Kodak PhotoCD	.pcd
Macintosh PICT	.pct
PC Paintbrush	.pcx
Portable Network Graphics	.png
Tagged Image File Format	.tif
Windows Bitmap	.bmp, .rle, .dib
Microsoft Windows Metafile	.wmf
WordPerfect Graphics	.wpg

Smart Tags

A **smart tag** is a button that PowerPoint automatically displays on the screen when performing a certain action. The Automatic Layout Options button in Figure 2-32 on the previous page is a smart tag. In addition to the Automatic Layout Options button, PowerPoint provides three other smart tags. Table 2-4 summarizes the smart tags available in PowerPoint.

Table 2-4   Smart Tags in PowerPoint

SMART TAG BUTTON		MENU FUNCTION
	AutoCorrect Options	Undoes an automatic correction, stops future automatic corrections of this type, or displays the AutoCorrect Options dialog box.
	Paste Options	Specifies how moved or pasted items should display, e.g., with original formatting, without formatting, or with different formatting.
	AutoFit Options	Undoes automatic text resizing to fit the current placeholder or changes single-column layouts to two-column layouts, inserts a new slide, or splits the text between two slides.
	Automatic Layout Options	Adjusts the slide layout to accommodate an inserted object.

Clicking a smart tag button shows a menu that contains commands relative to the action performed at the location of the smart tag. For example, if you want PowerPoint to undo the layout change when you add a clip to a slide, click the Automatic Layout Options button to display the Smart Tag Actions menu, and then click Undo Automatic Layout on the Smart Tag Actions menu to display the initial layout.

Using the Automatic Layout Options Button to Undo a Layout Change

The Title and Text layout used in Slide 4 did not provide a content placeholder for the clip you inserted, so PowerPoint automatically changed the layout to Title, Text, and Content. If your slide layout did not change, then disregard this section and continue the project on the next page with the Moving Clip Art section. Because the text now violates the 7 × 7 rule with this layout and because you want to place the clip in a location other than the areas specified, you should change the layout to the Title and Text layout.

The Automatic Layout Options button is displayed because PowerPoint changed the layout automatically. If you move your mouse pointer near the changed object or text, the Automatic Layout Options button is displayed as an arrow, indicating that a list of options is available that allow you to undo the new layout, stop the automatic layout of inserted objects, or alter the AutoCorrect Options settings. The following steps show how to undo the layout change.

To Use the Automatic Layout Options Button to Undo a Layout Change

1

• **If your slide layout automatically changed to Title, Text, and Content, click the Automatic Layout Options button.**

• **Point to Undo Automatic Layout.**

The Automatic Layout Options list is displayed (Figure 2-33). Clicking Undo Automatic Layout will reverse the layout change.

FIGURE 2-33

2

• **Click Undo Automatic Layout.**

The layout reverts to Title and Text (Figure 2-34).

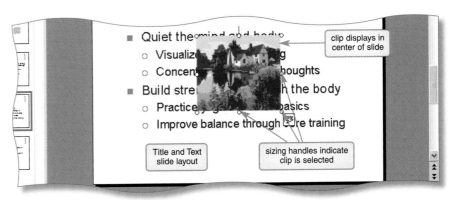

FIGURE 2-34

The desired clip is displayed in the center of Slide 4, which has the original Title and Text slide layout. The next step is to move the clip to the top-right corner of the slide.

Moving Clip Art

After you insert a clip into a slide, you may want to reposition it. The house clip on Slide 4 overlays the bulleted list. You want to move the clip away from the text to the upper-right corner of the slide. The following steps show how to move the clip to the upper-right corner of the slide.

To Move Clip Art

1

• **With the clip selected, point to the clip and then press and hold down the mouse button.**

• **Drag the clip to the upper-right corner of the slide.**

• **Release the mouse button.**

When you drag a clip, a dotted box is displayed. The dotted box indicates the clip's new position. When you release the left mouse button, the clip of the house is displayed in the new location and the dotted line disappears (Figure 2-35). Sizing handles display at the corners and along its edges.

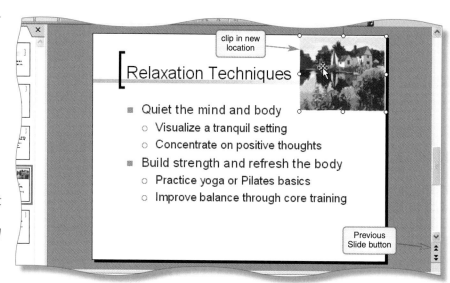

FIGURE 2-35

Changing the Size of Clip Art

Sometimes it is necessary to change the size of clip art. For example, on Slide 2 much space appears around the clip. To make this object fit onto the slide, you increase its size. To change the size of a clip by an exact percentage, use the Format Picture command on the shortcut menu. The Format Picture dialog box contains six tabbed sheets with several formatting options. The **Size sheet** contains options for changing a clip's size. You either enter the exact height and width in the Size and rotate area, or enter the height and width as a percentage of the original clip in the Scale area. When a check mark is displayed in the **Lock aspect ratio check box**, the height and width settings change to maintain the original aspect ratio. **Aspect ratio** is the relationship between an object's height and width. For example, a 3-by-5-inch object scaled to 50 percent would become a 1½-by-2½-inch object. The following steps describe how to increase the size of the clip using the Format Picture dialog box.

To Change the Size of Clip Art

1

• **Click the Previous Slide button on the vertical scroll bar two times to display Slide 2.**

• **Right-click the clip.**

• **Point to Format Picture on the shortcut menu.**

Sizing handles display at the clip's corners and along its edges (Figure 2-36).

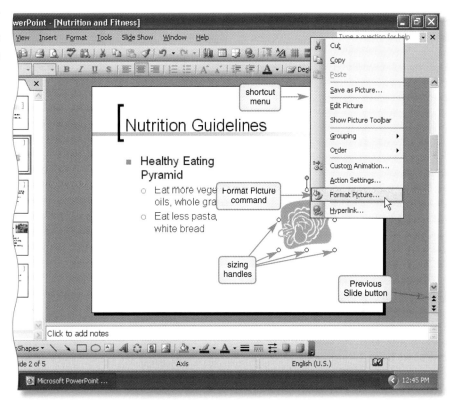

FIGURE 2-36

2

• **Click Format Picture.**

• **Click the Size tab when the Format Picture dialog box is displayed.**

The Size sheet in the Format Picture dialog box is displayed (Figure 2-37). The Height and Width text boxes in the Scale area display the current percentage of the clip, 100%. Check marks are displayed in the Lock aspect ratio and Relative to original picture size check boxes.

FIGURE 2-37

3

• **Click and hold down the mouse button on the Height box up arrow in the Scale area until 135% is displayed.**

Both the Height and Width text boxes in the Scale area display 135% (Figure 2-38). PowerPoint automatically changes the Height and Width text boxes in the Size and rotate area to reflect changes in the Scale area.

FIGURE 2-38

4

• **Click the OK button.**

• **Drag the clip to the right of the bulleted list.**

PowerPoint closes the Format Picture dialog box and displays the enlarged clip in the desired location (Figure 2-39).

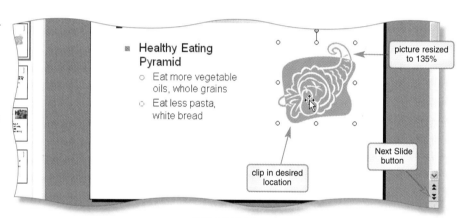

FIGURE 2-39

Inserting, Moving, and Sizing a Clip into a Slide

With Slides 1 through 4 complete, the final step is to add the stethoscope clip to the closing slide, Slide 5. The following steps show how to add a stethoscope to Slide 5 without changing the Title and Text layout, size the clip, and then move it to the lower-right corner of the slide.

To Insert, Move, and Size a Clip into a Slide

1 Click the Next Slide button on the vertical scroll bar three times to display Slide 5.

2 Click the Insert Clip Art button on the Drawing toolbar. Delete the word, house, in the Search for text box, type stethoscope, and then press the ENTER key. Click the stethoscope shown in Figure 2-40 or another appropriate clip. Click the Close button on the Clip Art task pane title bar.

3 If the layout changes, click the Automatic Layout Options button and then click Undo Automatic Layout.

4 Right-click the stethoscope and then click Format Picture on the shortcut menu. Click the Size tab in the Format Picture dialog box, click and hold down the mouse button on the Height box up arrow in the Scale area until 160% is displayed, and then click the OK button.

5 Drag the stethoscope to the lower-right corner of the slide.

The stethoscope is inserted, moved, and sized into Slide 5 (Figure 2-40).

FIGURE 2-40

Saving the Presentation Again

To preserve the work completed, perform the following step to save the presentation again.

To Save a Presentation

1 Click the Save button on the Standard toolbar.

The changes made to the presentation after the previous save are saved on the floppy disk.

A default setting in PowerPoint allows for **fast saves,** which saves only the changes made since the last time you saved. To save a full copy of the complete presentation, click Tools on the menu bar, click Options on the Tools menu, and then click the Save tab. Remove the check mark in the Allow fast saves check box by clicking the check box and then click the OK button.

Adding a Header and Footer to Outline Pages

A printout of the presentation outline often is used as an audience handout. Distributing a copy of the outline provides the audience with paper on which to write notes or comments. Another benefit of distributing a copy of the outline is to help the audience see the text on the slides when lighting is poor or the room is too large. To help identify the source of the printed outline, add a descriptive header and footer. A **header** is displayed at the top of the sheet of paper or slide, and a **footer** is displayed at the bottom. Both contain specific information, such as the presenter's name or the company's telephone number. In addition, the current date and time and the slide or page number can display beside the header or footer information.

Using the Notes and Handouts Sheet to Add Headers and Footers

You add headers and footers to outline pages by clicking the Notes and Handouts sheet in the Header and Footer dialog box and entering the information you want to print. The following steps show how to add the current date, header information, the page number, and footer information to the printed outline.

To Use the Notes and Handouts Sheet to Add Headers and Footers

1

• **Click View on the menu bar and then point to Header and Footer (Figure 2-41).**

FIGURE 2-41

2

• **Click Header and Footer.**

• **Click the Notes and Handouts tab when the Header and Footer dialog box is displayed.**

The Notes and Handouts sheet in the Header and Footer dialog box is displayed (Figure 2-42). Check marks display in the Date and time, Header, Page number, and Footer check boxes. The Fixed option button is selected.

FIGURE 2-42

3

• **Click the Update automatically option button and then click the Header text box.**

• **Type** Healthy Eating, Healthy Living **in the Header text box.**

• **Click the Footer text box.**

• **Type** Clark College Fitness Center **in the Footer text box (Figure 2-43).**

FIGURE 2-43

4

• **Click the Apply to All button.**

PowerPoint applies the header and footer text to the outline, closes the Header and Footer dialog box, and displays Slide 5 (Figure 2-44). You cannot see header and footer text until you print the outline (shown in Figure 2-60 on page PPT 124).

FIGURE 2-44

Applying Animation Schemes

PowerPoint provides many animation effects to add interest and make a slide show presentation look professional. **Animation** includes special visual and sound effects applied to text or content. For example, each line on the slide can swivel as it is displayed on the screen. Or an object can zoom in from the top of the screen to the bottom. PowerPoint provides a variety of **preset animation schemes** that determine slide transitions and effects for the title and body text. A **slide transition** is a special effect used to progress from one slide to the next in a slide show. PowerPoint also allows you to set your own **custom animation** effects by defining your own animation types and speeds and sound effects on a slide. The following pages discuss how to add these animation effects to the presentation.

Adding an Animation Scheme to a Slide Show

PowerPoint has preset animation schemes with visual effects that vary the slide transitions and the methods in which the slide title and bullets or paragraphs display on the slides. Not all animation schemes have the slide transition element or effects for both the title and body text. These schemes are grouped in three categories: Subtle, Moderate, and Exciting. The name of the animation scheme characterizes the visual effects used. For example, the Unfold animation scheme in the Moderate category uses the Push Right slide transition effect, the Fly In effect for the title text, and the Unfold effect for the body text. The Pinwheel scheme in the Exciting category does not use a slide transition effect, but it uses the Pinwheel effect for the title text and the Peek In effect for the body text.

In this presentation, you apply the Float animation scheme to all slides. This effect is added easily by using the Slide Design task pane, which you used earlier in this project to select a design template. The following steps show how to apply the Float animation scheme to the Nutrition and Fitness presentation.

To Add an Animation Scheme to a Slide Show

1

• **Click Slide Show on the menu bar and then point to Animation Schemes (Figure 2-45).**

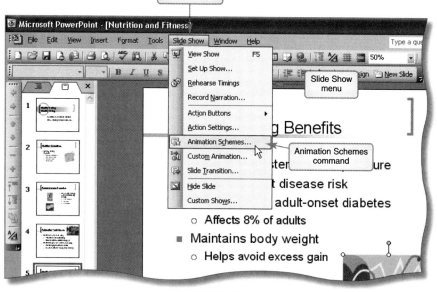

FIGURE 2-45

2

• **Click Animation Schemes.**

• **Scroll down the Apply to selected slides list and then point to Float in the Exciting category.**

The Slide Design task pane is displayed (Figure 2-46). The list of possible slide transition effects is displayed in the Apply to selected slides area. The Float ScreenTip shows that the Float animation scheme uses the Comb Horizontal slide transition, the Float effect for the title text, and the Descend effect for the body text.

FIGURE 2-46

3

• **Click Float.**

• **Point to the Apply to All Slides button.**

PowerPoint applies the Float animation effect to Slide 5, as indicated by the animation icon on the left side of the Slide 5 slide thumbnail on the Slides tab (Figure 2-47). The Float animation effect is previewed because the AutoPreview check box is selected.

FIGURE 2-47

4

• **Click Apply to All Slides.**

• **Click the Close button in the Slide Design task pane.**

The Float animation effect is applied to all slides in the presentation (Figure 2-48).

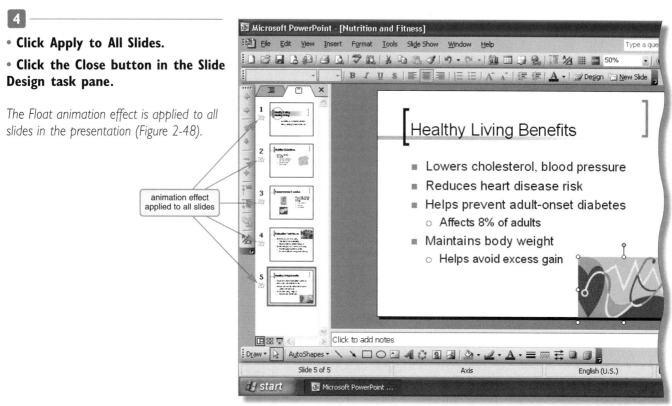

animation effect
applied to all slides

FIGURE 2-48

Animating Clip Art

To add visual interest to a presentation, you can **animate** certain content. On Slide 5, for example, having the stethoscope appear in a diamond pattern on the screen will provide an interesting effect. Animating clip art takes several steps as described in the following sections.

Adding Animation Effects

PowerPoint allows you to animate clip art along with animating text. Because Slide 5 lists the benefits of maintaining a healthy lifestyle, you want to emphasize these facts by having the clip appear on the screen in a diamond pattern. One way of animating clip art is to select options in the Custom Animation dialog box. The following steps show how to add the Diamond animation effect to the clip on Slide 5.

To Animate Clip Art

1

• **Right-click the clip and then point to Custom Animation on the shortcut menu.**

The shortcut menu is displayed (Figure 2-49). The clip is selected, as indicated by the sizing handles that display at the corners and along its edges.

FIGURE 2-49

2

• **Click Custom Animation.**
• **Point to the Add Effect button.**

The Custom Animation task pane is displayed (Figure 2-50). Two animation effects have been applied to the title and body of the slide previously.

FIGURE 2-50

3

• **Click the Add Effect button, point to Entrance, and then point to Diamond in the Entrance effects list.**

A list of possible effects for the Entrance option is displayed (Figure 2-51). Your list may vary. You can apply a variety of effects to the clip, including how it enters and exits the slide.

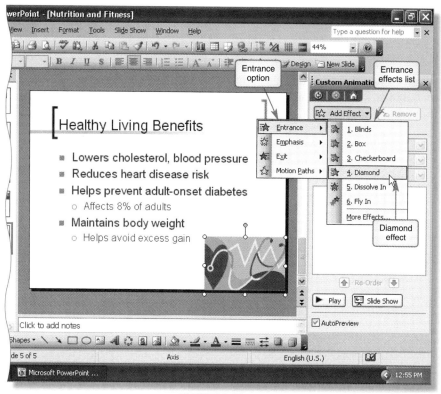

FIGURE 2-51

4

• **Click Diamond.**

The animation effect is applied to the stethoscope, as indicated by the number 1 icon displaying to the left of the clip and the corresponding 1 displaying in the Custom Animation list (Figure 2-52). You will see this effect when you click the mouse on that slide during your slide show.

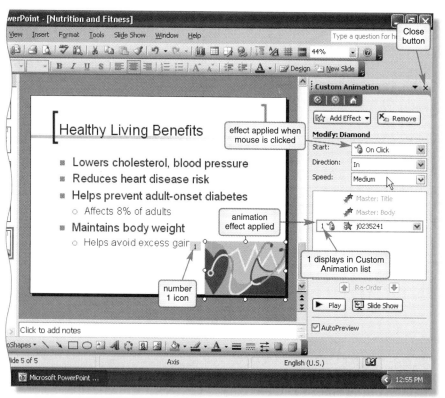

FIGURE 2-52

5

• **Click the Close button on the Custom Animation task pane title bar (Figure 2-53).**

The stethoscope clip will appear in the presentation using the Diamond animation effect during the slide show.

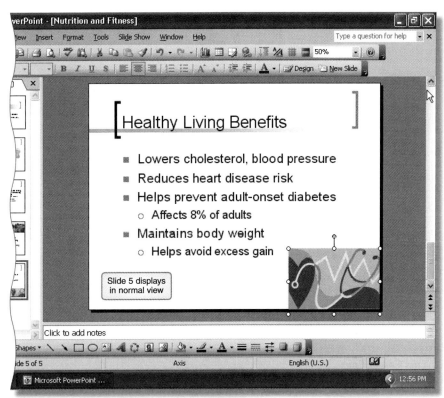

FIGURE 2-53

When you run the slide show, the bulleted-list paragraphs are displayed, and then the clip art will begin displaying on the slide in a diamond shape at the position where you inserted it into Slide 5.

Animation effects are complete for this presentation. You now can review the presentation in slide show view and correct any spelling errors.

Saving the Presentation Again

The presentation is complete. The following step shows how to save the finished presentation on a floppy disk before running the slide show.

To Save a Presentation

1 **Click the Save button on the Standard toolbar.**

PowerPoint saves the presentation on your floppy disk by saving the changes made to the presentation since the last save.

Running an Animated Slide Show

Project 1 introduced you to using slide show view to look at your presentation one slide at a time. This project introduces you to running a slide show with preset and custom animation effects. When you run a slide show with slide transition effects, PowerPoint displays the slide transition effect when you click the mouse button to advance to the next slide. When a slide has text animation effects, each paragraph level is displayed in the sequence specified by the animation settings in the Custom Animation dialog box. The following steps show how to run the animated Nutrition and Fitness presentation.

To Run an Animated Slide Show

1

• **Click the Slide 1 slide thumbnail on the Slides tab.**

• **Click the Slide Show button at the lower left of the PowerPoint window.**

• **When Slide 1 is displayed in slide show view, click the slide anywhere.**

PowerPoint applies the Comb Horizontal slide transition effect and shows the title slide title text, Healthy Eating, Healthy Living (Figure 2-54), using the Float animation effect. When you click the slide, the first paragraph in the subtitle text placeholder, Nutrition and Fitness Basics, is displayed using the Descend animation effect.

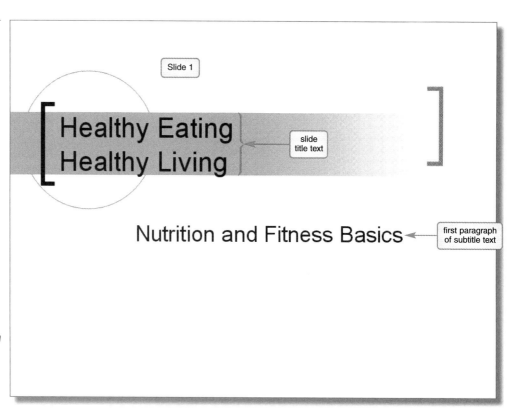

FIGURE 2-54

2

• **Click the slide again.**

PowerPoint displays the second paragraph in the subtitle text placeholder, Clark College Fitness Center, using the Float animation effect (Figure 2-55). If the Popup Menu buttons are displayed when you move the mouse pointer, do not click them.

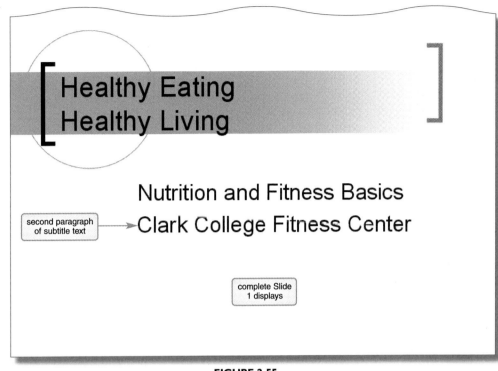

FIGURE 2-55

3

• **Continue clicking to finish running the slide show and return to normal view.**

Each time a new slide is displayed, PowerPoint first displays the Comb Horizontal slide transition effect and only the slide title using the Float effect. Then, PowerPoint builds each slide based on the animation settings. When you click the slide after the last paragraph is displayed on the last slide of the presentation, PowerPoint displays a blank slide. When you click again, PowerPoint exits slide show view and returns to normal view (Figure 2-56).

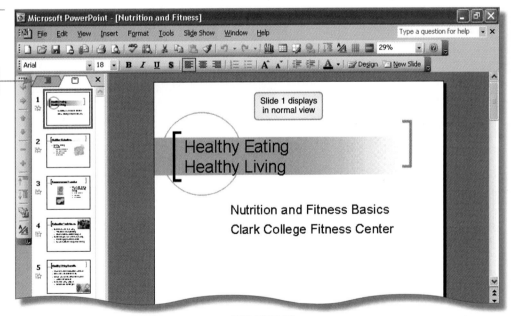

FIGURE 2-56

Other Ways

1. On Slide Show menu click View Show, click slide until slide show ends
2. Press ALT+D, press V, press ENTER until slide show ends
3. In Voice Command mode, say "Slide Show, View Show"

With the presentation complete and animation effects tested, the last step is to print the presentation outline and slides.

Printing a Presentation Created on the Outline Tab

Microsoft Office
PowerPoint 2003

When you click the Print button on the Standard toolbar, PowerPoint prints a hard copy of the presentation component last selected in the Print what box in the Print dialog box. To be certain to print the component you want, such as the presentation outline, use the Print command on the File menu. When the Print dialog box is displayed, you can select the appropriate presentation component in the Print what box. The next two sections explain how to use the Print command on the File menu to print the presentation outline and the presentation slides.

Printing an Outline

During the development of a lengthy presentation, it often is easier to review your outline in print rather than on the screen. Printing your outline also is useful for audience handouts or when your supervisor or instructor wants to review your subject matter before you develop your presentation fully.

Recall that the Print dialog box shows print options. When you want to print your outline, select Outline View in the Print what list in the Print dialog box. The outline, however, prints as last viewed on the Outline tab. This means that you must select the Zoom setting to display the outline text as you want it to print. If you are uncertain of the Zoom setting, you should return to the Outline tab and review it before printing. The following steps show how to print an outline from normal view.

To Print an Outline

1

• **Click the Outline tab.**

• **Ready the printer according to the printer manufacturer's instructions.**

• **Click File on the menu bar and then point to Print.**

The File menu is displayed (Figure 2-57). The Expand All button on the Outlining toolbar is selected, so the entire outline will print. If you want to print only the slide titles, you would click the Collapse All button.

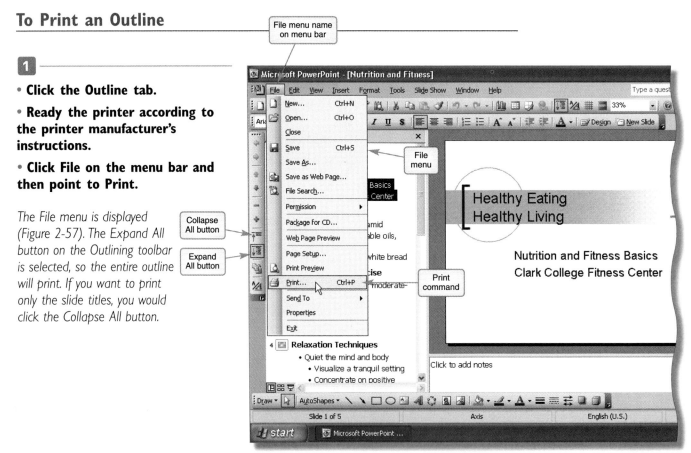

FIGURE 2-57

2

• **Click Print on the File menu.**

• **When the Print dialog box is displayed, click the Print what box arrow and then point to Outline View.**

The Print dialog box is displayed (Figure 2-58). Outline View is displayed highlighted in the Print what list.

FIGURE 2-58

3

• **Click Outline View in the list (Figure 2-59).**

FIGURE 2-59

4

• **Click the OK button.**

To cancel the print request, click the Cancel button.

5

• **When the printer stops, retrieve the printout of the outline.**

PowerPoint displays the five slides in outline form (Figure 2-60). The words, Healthy Eating, Healthy Living, and the current date display in the header, and the words, Clark College Fitness Center, and the page number display in the footer.

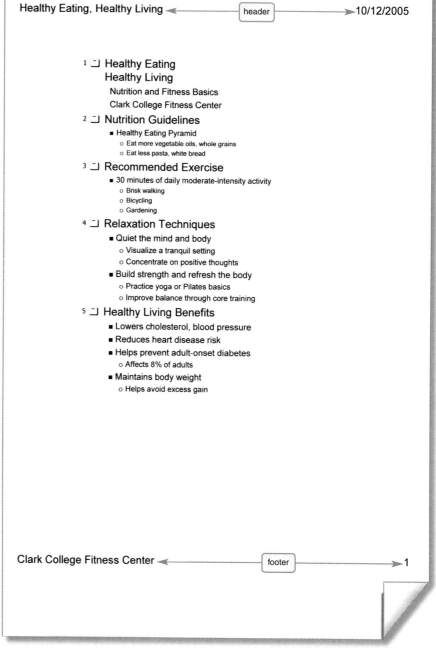

Healthy Eating, Healthy Living ← header → 10/12/2005

1. Healthy Eating
   Healthy Living
   Nutrition and Fitness Basics
   Clark College Fitness Center
2. Nutrition Guidelines
   - Healthy Eating Pyramid
     o Eat more vegetable oils, whole grains
     o Eat less pasta, white bread
3. Recommended Exercise
   - 30 minutes of daily moderate-intensity activity
     o Brisk walking
     o Bicycling
     o Gardening
4. Relaxation Techniques
   - Quiet the mind and body
     o Visualize a tranquil setting
     o Concentrate on positive thoughts
   - Build strength and refresh the body
     o Practice yoga or Pilates basics
     o Improve balance through core training
5. Healthy Living Benefits
   - Lowers cholesterol, blood pressure
   - Reduces heart disease risk
   - Helps prevent adult-onset diabetes
     o Affects 8% of adults
   - Maintains body weight
     o Helps avoid excess gain

Clark College Fitness Center ← footer → 1

FIGURE 2-60

Other Ways

1. On File menu click Print Preview, click Outline View in Print what list, click Print button on Print Preview toolbar
2. Press ALT+F, press P, press TAB, press W, press DOWN ARROW until Outline View is selected, press ENTER, press ENTER
3. In Voice Command mode, say "File, Print, Print What, Outline View, OK"

The **Print what list** in the Print dialog box contains options for printing slides, handouts, notes, and an outline. The Handouts area allows you to specify whether you want one, two, three, four, six, or nine slide images to display on each page. Printing handouts is useful for reviewing a presentation because you can analyze several slides displayed simultaneously on one page. Additionally, many businesses distribute handouts of the slide show before a presentation so the attendees can refer to a copy. To print handouts, click Handouts in the Print what box, click the Slides per page box arrow in the Handouts area, and then click 1, 2, 3, 4, 6, or 9. You can change the order in which the Nutrition and Fitness slides display on a page by clicking the Horizontal option button for Order in the Handouts area, which shows Slides 1 and 2, 3 and 4, and 5 and 6 adjacent to each other, or the Vertical option button for Order, which shows Slides 1 and 4, 2 and 5, and 3 and 6 adjacent to each other.

You also can click the Preview button if you want to see how your printout will look. After viewing the preview, click the Close button on the Preview window toolbar to return to normal view.

Printing Presentation Slides

At this point, you may want to check the spelling in the entire presentation and instruct PowerPoint to ignore any words spelled correctly. After correcting errors, you will want to print a final copy of your presentation. If you made any changes to your presentation since your last save, be certain to save your presentation before you print.

The following steps show how to print the presentation.

To Print Presentation Slides

1 Ready the printer according to the printer manufacturer's instructions.

2 Click File on the menu bar and then click Print.

3 When the Print dialog box is displayed, click the Print what box arrow.

4 Click Slides in the list.

5 Click the OK button. When the printer stops, retrieve the slide printouts.

The printouts should resemble the slides in Figures 2-61a through 2-61e.

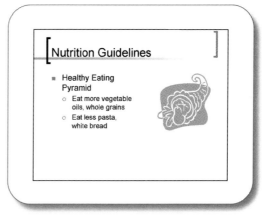

(a) Slide 1   (b) Slide 2

FIGURE 2-61

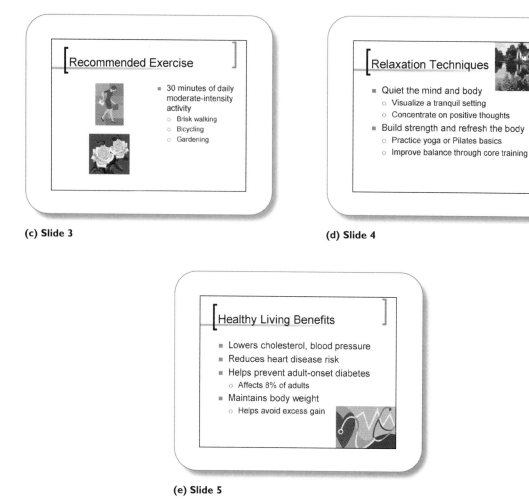

(c) Slide 3

(d) Slide 4

(e) Slide 5

FIGURE 2-61 *(continued)*

E-Mailing a Slide Show from within PowerPoint

More About

**The Quick
Reference**

For more information, see
the Quick Reference
Summary at the back of this
book, or visit the PowerPoint
2003 Quick Reference Web
page (scsite.com/
ppt2003/qr).

Billions of e-mail messages are sent throughout the world each day. Computer users
use this popular service on the Internet to send and receive plain text e-mail or to
send and receive e-mail content that includes objects, links to other Web pages, and
file attachments. These attachments can include Office files, such as PowerPoint slide
shows or Word documents. Using Microsoft Office, you can e-mail the presentation
directly from within PowerPoint.

For these steps to work properly, users need an e-mail address and a 32-bit
e-mail program compatible with a Messaging Application Programming Interface,
such as Outlook, Outlook Express, or Microsoft Exchange Client. Free e-mail
accounts are available at hotmail.com. The following steps show how to e-mail the
slide show from within PowerPoint to Jessica Cantero. Assume her e-mail address is
jessica_cantero@hotmail.com. If you do not have an E-mail button on the Standard
toolbar, then this activity is not available to you.

To E-Mail a Slide Show from within PowerPoint

1

• **Click the E-mail (as Attachment) button on the Standard toolbar. See your instructor if the Choose Profile dialog box displays.**

• **When the e-mail Message window is displayed, type** jessica_cantero @hotmail.com **in the To text box.**

• **Select the text in the Subject text box and then type** Nutrition and Fitness slide show **in the Subject text box.**

• **Click the message body.**

PowerPoint displays the e-mail Message window (Figure 2-62). The insertion point is in the message body so you can type a message to Jessica Cantero.

FIGURE 2-62

2

• **Type** Attached is the PowerPoint presentation you can use for your first workshop. **in the message body.**

• **Point to the Send button.**

The message is intended to help the recipient of the e-mail understand the purpose of your e-mail (Figure 2-63).

3

• **Click the Send button on the Standard toolbar.**

The e-mail with the attached presentation is sent to jessica_cantero@hotmail.com.

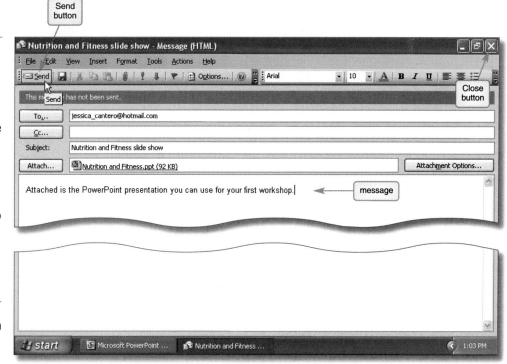

FIGURE 2-63

More About

E-Mail Messages

The first e-mail message was sent in 1969 from Professor Leonard Kleinrock to a colleague at Stanford University. Researchers estimate the number of messages sent daily will jump from the current 31 billion to 60 billion by 2006. For more information on e-mail messages, visit the PowerPoint 2003 More About Web page (scsite.com/ppt2003/more) and click E-Mail.

Because the slide show was sent as an attachment, Jessica Cantero can save the attachment and then open the presentation in PowerPoint. You can choose many more options when you send e-mail from within PowerPoint. For example, the Background command on the Format menu changes the colors of the message background and lets you add a picture to use as the background. In addition, the Security button on the Standard toolbar allows you to send secure messages that only your intended recipient can read.

Saving and Quitting PowerPoint

If you made any changes to your presentation since your last save, you should save it again before quitting PowerPoint. The following steps show how to save changes to the presentation and quit PowerPoint.

To Save Changes and Quit PowerPoint

1 Click the Close button on the Microsoft PowerPoint window title bar.

2 If prompted, click the Yes button in the Microsoft PowerPoint dialog box.

PowerPoint saves any changes made to the presentation since the last save and then quits PowerPoint.

Project Summary

In creating the Healthy Eating, Healthy Living slide show in this project, you increased your knowledge of PowerPoint. You created a slide presentation on the Outline tab where you entered all the text in the form of an outline. You arranged the text using the Promote and Demote buttons. Once the outline was complete, you changed slide layouts and added clip art. After adding clip art to slides without using a content placeholder, you moved and sized the clips. You added preset animation effects and applied animation effects to a clip. You learned how to run an animated slide show demonstrating slide transition and animation effects. Finally, you printed the presentation outline and slides using the Print command on the File menu and e-mailed the presentation.

 If you have a SAM user profile, you may have access to hands-on instruction, practice, and assessment of the skills covered in this project. Log in to your SAM account and go to your assignments page to see what your instructor has assigned.

What You Should Know

Having completed this project, you should be able to perform the tasks below. The tasks are listed in the same order they were presented in this project. For a list of the buttons, menus, toolbars, and commands introduced in this project, see the Quick Reference Summary at the back of this book and refer to the Page Number column.

1. Start and Customize PowerPoint   (PPT 85)
2. Change to the Outline Tab and Display the Outlining Toolbar   (PPT 86)
3. Create a Title Slide on the Outline Tab   (PPT 88)
4. Add a Slide on the Outline Tab   (PPT 89)
5. Create a Text Slide with a Multi-Level Bulleted List on the Outline Tab   (PPT 90)
6. Create a Second Text Slide with a Multi-Level Bulleted List   (PPT 92)
7. Create a Third Text Slide with a Multi-Level Bulleted List   (PPT 92)
8. Create a Closing Slide on the Outline Tab (PPT 94)
9. Save a Presentation   (PPT 95)
10. Change the View to Slide Sorter View   (PPT 95)
11. Change the View to Normal View   (PPT 96)
12. Change the Slide Layout to Title, Text, and Content   (PPT 98)
13. Insert Clip Art into a Content Placeholder (PPT 101)
14. Change the Slide Layout to Title, 2 Content and Text and Insert Clip Art   (PPT 102)
15. Insert a Second Clip into a Slide   (PPT 103)

16. Insert Clip Art into a Slide without a Content Placeholder   (PPT 104)
17. Use the Automatic Layout Options Button to Undo a Layout Change   (PPT 107)
18. Move Clip Art   (PPT 108)
19. Change the Size of Clip Art   (PPT 109)
20. Insert, Move, and Size a Clip into a Slide (PPT 110)
21. Save a Presentation   (PPT 111)
22. Use the Notes and Handouts Sheet to Add Headers and Footers   (PPT 112)
23. Add an Animation Scheme to a Slide Show (PPT 114)
24. Animate Clip Art   (PPT 117)
25. Save a Presentation   (PPT 119)
26. Run an Animated Slide Show   (PPT 120)
27. Print an Outline   (PPT 122)
28. Print Presentation Slides   (PPT 125)
29. E-Mail a Slide Show from within PowerPoint (PPT 127)
30. Save Changes and Quit PowerPoint   (PPT 128)

Learn It Online

Instructions: To complete the Learn It Online exercises, start your browser, click the Address bar, and then enter the Web address scsite.com/ppt2003/learn. When the PowerPoint 2003 Learn It Online page is displayed, follow the instructions in the exercises below. Each exercise has instructions for printing your results, either for your own records or for submission to your instructor.

1 Project Reinforcement TF, MC, and SA

Below PowerPoint Project 2, click the Project Reinforcement link. Print the quiz by clicking Print on the File menu for each page. Answer each question.

Flash Cards

Below PowerPoint Project 2, click the Flash Cards link and read the instructions. Type 20 (or a number specified by your instructor) in the Number of playing cards text box, type your name in the Enter your Name text box, and then click the Flip Card button. When the flash card is displayed, read the question and then click the ANSWER box arrow to select an answer. Flip through Flash Cards. If your score is 15 (75%) correct or greater, click Print on the File menu to print your results. If your score is less than 15 (75%) correct, then redo this exercise by clicking the Replay button.

3 Practice Test

Below PowerPoint Project 2, click the Practice Test link. Answer each question, enter your first and last name at the bottom of the page, and then click the Grade Test button. When the graded practice test is displayed on your screen, click Print on the File menu to print a hard copy. Continue to take practice tests until you score 80% or better.

4 Who Wants To Be a Computer Genius?

Below PowerPoint Project 2, click the Computer Genius link. Read the instructions, enter your first and last name at the bottom of the page, and then click the PLAY button. When your score is displayed, click the PRINT RESULTS link to print a hard copy.

5 Wheel of Terms

Below PowerPoint Project 2, click the Wheel of Terms link. Read the instructions, and then enter your first and last name and your school name. Click the PLAY button. When your score is displayed, right-click the score and then click Print on the shortcut menu to print a hard copy.

6 Crossword Puzzle Challenge

Below PowerPoint Project 2, click the Crossword Puzzle Challenge link. Read the instructions, and then enter your first and last name. Click the SUBMIT button. Work the crossword puzzle. When you are finished, click the Submit button. When the crossword puzzle is redisplayed, click the Print Puzzle button to print a hard copy.

7 Tips and Tricks

Below PowerPoint Project 2, click the Tips and Tricks link. Click a topic that pertains to Project 2. Right-click the information and then click Print on the shortcut menu. Construct a brief example of what the information relates to in PowerPoint to confirm you understand how to use the tip or trick.

8 Newsgroups

Below PowerPoint Project 2, click the Newsgroups link. Click a topic that pertains to Project 2. Print three comments.

9 Expanding Your Horizons

Below PowerPoint Project 2, click the Expanding Your Horizons link. Click a topic that pertains to Project 2. Print the information. Construct a brief example of what the information relates to in PowerPoint to confirm you understand the contents of the article.

10 Search Sleuth

Below PowerPoint Project 2, click the Search Sleuth link. To search for a term that pertains to this project, select a term below the Project 2 title and then use the Google search engine at google.com (or any major search engine) to display and print two Web pages that present information on the term.

11 PowerPoint Online Training

Below PowerPoint Project 2, click the PowerPoint Online Training link. When your browser displays the Microsoft Office Online Web page, click the PowerPoint link. Click one of the PowerPoint courses that covers one or more of the objectives listed at the beginning of the project on page PPT 82. Print the first page of the course before stepping through it.

12 Office Marketplace

Below PowerPoint Project 2, click the Office Marketplace link. When your browser displays the Microsoft Office Online Web page, click the Office Marketplace link. Click a topic that relates to PowerPoint. Print the first page.

Apply Your Knowledge

1 Hiking for Family Fitness

Instructions: Start PowerPoint. Open the presentation Apply 2-1 Hiking Adventure from the Data Disk. See the inside back cover of this book for instructions for downloading the Data Disk or see your instructor for information on accessing the files required for this book. The four slides in the presentation give information on helping families plan for a hike through forest preserves and parks. Make the following changes to the slides so they appear as shown in Figure 2-64.

(a) Slide 1

(b) Slide 2

(c) Slide 3

(d) Slide 4

FIGURE 2-64

Change the design template to Layers. On the title slide, replace the words, Student Name, with your name. Then add the current date, page number, and your name to the notes and handouts footer.

On Slide 1, increase the font size of the Family Hiking paragraph to 72 point and then italicize this text. Insert the leaves clip shown in Figure 2-64a. Scale the clip art to 118% and then drag the clip to the bottom-right corner of the slide. Apply the Box Entrance custom animation effect to the clip.

(continued)

Apply Your Knowledge

Hiking for Family Fitness *(continued)*

On Slide 2, change the slide layout to Title and Text over Content. Insert the backpacking clip shown in Figure 2-64b on the previous page. Change the size of the clip to 167% and then drag the clip to the bottom center of the slide.

On Slide 3, insert the toaster clip shown in Figure 2-64c. Undo the Automatic Layout if necessary, increase the clip size to 207%, and then drag it to the bottom-right corner of the slide. Apply the Blinds Entrance custom animation effect to the clip.

On Slide 4, change the slide layout to Title and Content over Text. Insert the snowflake clip shown in Figure 2-64d and then change the size of the clip to 120%. Apply the Spin Emphasis custom animation effect to the clip. Increase the font size of the level 2 body text paragraphs to 24 point and the level 3 body text paragraphs to 20 point.

Apply the Descend animation scheme in the Moderate category list to all slides.

Save the presentation using the file name, Apply 2-1 Family Hiking. Print the presentation with all four slides on one page and the outline, and then hand in the hard copies to your instructor.

In the Lab

1 An Apple a Day Presentation

Problem: The adage, "An apple a day keeps the doctor away" may be good health advice for many people. Dozens of varieties of apples can be used in pies, applesauce, juice, salads, and side dishes. Your Health 101 instructor has assigned a research paper and a five-minute presentation on the topic of the health benefits of eating apples. You generate the outline shown in Figure 2-65 to prepare the presentation. You use the outline to create the presentation shown in Figures 2-66a through 2-66d.

I. An Apple a Day...
    A. ...May Keep the Doctor Away
    B. Nick Saunders
    C. Health 101

II. Healthy Apple Facts
    A. Contains cancer-fighting antioxidants
        1. More than a 1,500 milligram megadose of Vitamin C
        2. Fight bad cholesterol
    B. Complex carbohydrates give longer, more even energy boost
    C. Contains boron
        1. Helps harden bones

III. Apple Nutrients
    A. Pectin
        1. Aids digestion
        2. May help reduce cancer, heart disease
    B. Fiber
        1. Equal to bran cereal

IV. Cook or Baking Quantities
    A. 3 medium-sized apples equal 1 pound
    B. 6-8 medium-sized apples fill a 9-inch pie
    C. 1 pound makes 1½ cups applesauce

FIGURE 2-65

In the Lab

(a) Slide 1

(b) Slide 2

(c) Slide 3

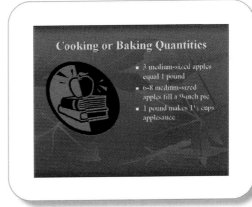

(d) Slide 4

FIGURE 2-66

Instructions: Perform the following tasks.

1. Use the Outline tab to create a new presentation. Apply the Maple design template.
2. Using the outline shown in Figure 2-65, create the title slide shown in Figure 2-66a. Use your name instead of the text, Nick Saunders. Decrease the font size of the class name to 24 point. Insert the caduceus clip art. Scale the clip to 150% and then drag the clip to the lower-left corner of the slide. Add the Blinds Entrance custom animation effect to the clip.
3. Insert a new slide. Change the slide layout on Slide 2 to Title and 2-Column Text. Using the outline in Figure 2-65, type the text for Slide 2. Insert the doctor clip art shown in Figure 2-66b. Scale the clip to 200% and then drag the clip between the two columns of text.
4. Using the outline shown in Figure 2-65, create the Slides 3 and 4 with the bulleted lists shown in Figures 2-66c and 2-66d.
5. Change the slide layout on Slide 3 to Title, Text, and Content. Insert the medicine clip art shown in Figure 2-66c. Scale the clip art to 210% and then center it in the space beside the text. Add the Diamond Entrance custom animation effect to the clip.
6. On Slide 4, change the slide layout to Title, Content and Text. Insert the apple clip art shown in Figure 2-66d, scale it to 200%, and then center it in the space beside the text. Add the Box Entrance custom animation effect.

(continued)

An Apple a Day Presentation *(continued)*

7. Add your name to the outline header and your school's name to the outline footer.
8. Apply the Title arc animation scheme in the Exciting category to all slides in the presentation.
9. Save the presentation using the file name, Lab 2-1 Apples.
10. Display and print the presentation with two slides on one page and the outline. Close the presentation. Hand in the hard copy to your instructor.

2 Financial Planning Advice

Problem: Credit card debt is at an all-time high, and many people are nearing retirement age with inadequate savings. Many students at your school have asked their instructors and members of the Accounting Club for advice on helping them gain financial security. To assist these students, the Accounting Club members have decided to prepare a PowerPoint presentation to show to these students. They have given you the outline shown in Figure 2-67. You create the text for the presentation on the Outline tab, and you decide to add animation effects to the slide show. The completed slides are shown in Figures 2-68a through 2-68d.

1. It Figures: Your Financial Future
    Build a Secure Fiscal Plan
    Midwest College Accounting Club

2. Prepare for Retirement Now
    Eliminate all debt
    Follow the 20/80 rule
        Live on 20 percent
        Save 80 percent
    Develop a financial plan

3. Realize Importance of Financial Planning
    Establish a monthly budget
    Develop an investment strategy
        Savings
        Low-risk investments
        High-risk investments

4. Use a Certified Financial Planner
    Helps prepare taxes
    Gives insurance advice
    Develops debt-reduction strategies
    Assists with estate planning

FIGURE 2-67

(a) Slide 1

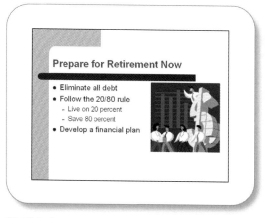

(b) Slide 2

FIGURE 2-68

In the Lab

(c) Slide 3

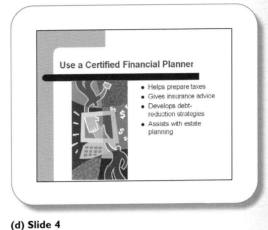

(d) Slide 4

FIGURE 2-68 *(continued)*

Instructions: Perform the following tasks.

1. Use the Outline tab to create a new presentation from the outline shown in Figure 2-67. Apply the Capsules design template.
2. On the title slide, italicize the title text, It Figures: Your Financial Future. Increase the font size of the text, Build a Secure Fiscal Plan, to 36 point. Using Figure 2-68a as a reference, insert the dollar clip art shown, scale it to 105%, and then drag it to the upper-right corner of the slide.
3. On Slide 2, insert the clip art shown in Figure 2-68b and then, if necessary, click the AutoCorrect Options button to undo the layout change. Scale the clip to 230% and then drag it to the right of the text.
4. On Slide 3, change the slide layout to Title, Text, and Content. Insert the clip art shown in Figure 2-68c. Scale the clip to 160% and then move it to the location shown in the figure.
5. On Slide 4, change the slide layout to Title, Content and Text. Insert the clip art shown in Figure 2-68d, scale the clip to 195%, and then move it to the location shown in the figure.
6. Add the current date and your name to the outline header. Include Accounting Club and the page number in the outline footer.
7. Apply the Compress animation scheme in the Moderate category to all slides.
8. Animate the clip on Slide 1 using the Spin Emphasis custom animation effect, the clip on Slide 2 using the Fly In Entrance effect, and the clip on Slide 3 using the Box Entrance effect. Do not animate the clip on Slide 4.
9. Save the presentation using the file name, Lab 2-2 Financial Future.
10. Display and print the presentation with two slides on one page and the outline. Close the presentation. Hand in the hard copy to your instructor.

In the Lab

3 Strength Training for New Fitness Center Members

Problem: Strength training offers many positive benefits: it builds power, provides energy, decreases fatigue, and improves mood, self-confidence, and self-esteem. Additional advantages are helping to prevent osteoporosis, burn calories, and balance the body. Mary Halen, the director of your campus fitness center, wants new members to view a presentation on strength training. She gives you the outline shown in Figure 2-69. You create the text for the presentation on the Outline tab and then search for appropriate clip art to add to the slides. You are unable to find images that are part of the Microsoft Clip Organizer, so you connect to the Internet, obtain clips from the Microsoft Office Online Web site, and create the slides shown in Figure 2-70. The clips you find may vary from the clips shown in Figures 2-70a through 2-70d. You refine the presentation using an animation scheme and custom animation effects and then e-mail the presentation to Mary.

Gain More Than Muscles with Strength Training
    Presented by
    Mary Halen
    Central College Fitness Center

Build Power
    Increase performance in many sports
        Tennis and golf
    Increase endurance
        Running and swimming

Feel Energized
    Improve mood, confidence, and esteem
        Expand beyond sports into personal life
    Burn calories
        Even while resting
        Increase body's metabolism for up to 12 hours after exercising

Improve Health
    Help prevent osteoporosis
        Strengthen bones
        Build bone density
    Balance body by making both sides strong
        Normally one side is stronger than the other
        Balanced body is less prone to injuries

FIGURE 2-69

(a) Slide 1

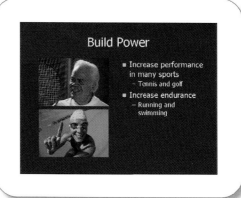

(b) Slide 2

FIGURE 2-70

In the Lab

(c) Slide 3

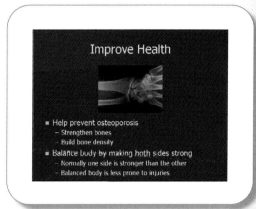

(d) Slide 4

FIGURE 2-70 *(continued)*

Instructions: Perform the following tasks.

1. Create a new presentation using the Slit design template and the outline in Figure 2-69.

2. On the title slide, insert and size both clip art images shown in Figure 2-70a. Add the Fly In Entrance custom animation effect and change the speed to Medium.

3. On Slide 2, change the slide layout to Title, 2 Content and Text. Insert the clips shown in Figure 2-70b. Add the Fly In Entrance custom animation effect for the top image and change the direction to From Top. Add the Fly In Entrance custom animation effect for the bottom image. Size the clips if necessary.

4. On Slide 3, insert the clip shown in Figure 2-70c. Add the Spin Emphasis custom animation effect. Size the clip if necessary.

5. Change the slide layout on Slide 4 (Figure 2-70d) to Title and Content over Text. Insert the clip art image shown. Add the Box Entrance custom animation effect. Size the clip if necessary.

6. Display your name and the current date in the outline header, and display the page number and the name of your school in the outline footer.

7. Apply the Unfold animation scheme in the Moderate category to all slides.

8. Save the presentation using the file name, Lab 2-3 Strength Training.

9. Display and print the presentation with all four slides on one page and the outline. Close the presentation. Hand in the hard copy to your instructor.

10. E-mail the presentation to Mary using the address mary_halen@hotmail.com.

Cases and Places

The difficulty of these case studies varies:
■ are the least difficult and ■■ are more difficult. The last exercise is a group exercise.

Note: Remember to use the 7 × 7 rule as you design the presentations: a maximum of seven words on a line and a maximum of seven lines on one slide.

1 ■ One of the easiest methods of exercising is walking. Active walkers know that walking enhances the body and spirit. Paula Pearson, the director of recreation at your community's park district, wants to organize a walking club, and she has asked you to help her promote the idea. She hands you the outline shown in Figure 2-71 and asks you to create a slide show. Using the concepts and techniques introduced in this project, together with Paula's outline, develop slides for a presentation. Include clip art, animation effects, and an animation scheme. Print the outline and slides as handouts so they can be distributed to presentation attendees.

---

1. Walk On
  Walk Your Way to Health
      Presented by
      Paula Pearson
      West Haven Park District

2. Walking Benefits
  - Enhances both body and spirit
  - Prolongs life, according to leading researchers

3. Training Techniques
  - Try interval training
      Increase walking speed for 30 seconds
      Return to normal speed for one minute

4. Walking Techniques
  - Walk with a friend
      Adds motivation
      Helps pass the time
      Gives motivation to walk in inclement weather
  - Swing arms
      Increases heart rate, burns more calories

FIGURE 2-71

Cases and Places

2 The community theater company in the town of Northern Shores is seeking subscribers and volunteers for the upcoming season. The public relations director has supplied the outline shown in Figure 2-72. You have been asked to help with the recruiting efforts. You decide to develop a presentation that includes information about the newly renovated theater, volunteer opportunities, and upcoming performances. Using the concepts and techniques introduced in this project, together with the outline, develop slides for a presentation. Include clip art, animation effects, and an animation scheme. Display the presentation title in the outline header and your name in the outline footer. Print the outline and slides as handouts.

A. Northern Shores Center for the Performing Arts
    The area's newest and finest theater company

B. Northern Shores Theater Venue
    Newly renovated building
        More than $7 million spent
        Improved sight lines and acoustics
        Full symphony orchestra pit
    Comfortable seating
        Accommodations for the disabled

C. Volunteer Opportunities
    Developing and distributing promotional materials
    Ushering at performances
    Participating in social activities throughout the year
    Assisting with Children's Theater

D. Upcoming Performances
    February 14 - Music for the Heart
    March 17 - Irish Favorites
    July 1 - Americana Folk Tales
    December 16 - Holiday Spectacular

FIGURE 2-72

Cases and Places

3 ■■ Many students on your campus visit the Health Clinic asking for antibiotics prescriptions. The doctors and nurses spend much time explaining that antibiotics are not necessarily the best medicine for the illnesses. You work in the clinic part time and volunteer to create a PowerPoint presentation that answers many of the students' common questions. You speak with the doctors on staff and learn that antibiotics are credited with changing modern medicine. They are used to kill bacteria, not viruses, and can control infectious diseases. Many bacteria, however, have become resistant to these drugs. Antibiotics are prescribed for bacterial infections, not viruses such as flu, colds, most coughs, and sore throats. Students can take antibiotics prudently by taking all doses of the medications exactly as prescribed. They should not stop taking drugs early, even if they feel fine. Antibiotic resistance occurs when the medications are taken unnecessarily. When the illness persists, additional drugs may be required to kill the germ. Some bacteria refuse to die, and super strains have been bred by overuse and misuse of antibiotics. Using this information, develop a slide show. Choose an appropriate design template and add clip art, animation effects, and an animation scheme. Print the presentation slides and outline to distribute as handouts for patients.

4 ■■ The Healthy Eating Pyramid shows that a balanced diet contains daily servings of fruit and vegetables. Although fruit and vegetables are less costly than snack foods, many adults and children buy junk food rather than the vitamin-laden fruit and vegetable alternatives. Your school cafeteria manager has asked you to prepare a PowerPoint presentation explaining the ABCs of fruits and vegetables to students. Using the techniques introduced in the project, create a presentation about the virtues of eating these foods. Include clip art, animation effects, and an animation scheme to add interest. Print the outline and slides as handouts so they can be distributed to cafeteria diners.

5 ■■ **Working Together** Prospective employees often focus on salary and job responsibilities when they consider job offers. One area they often neglect, however, is benefit packages. Career counselors emphasize that these benefits can contribute significantly to salary levels and should be given serious consideration. Have each member of your team visit or telephone several local businesses, your campus placement center, or companies' Web sites to determine benefit packages. Gather data about:
1) Retirement plans
2) Stock options
3) Life insurance coverage
4) Health coverage
5) Tuition reimbursement
6) Signing bonuses
7) On-site fitness facilities

After coordinating the data, create a presentation with at least one slide showcasing each company's benefit packages. As a group, critique each slide. Hand in a hard copy of the final presentation.

MICROSOFT
Office PowerPoint 2003

Creating a Presentation on the Web Using PowerPoint

CASE PERSPECTIVE

A home office can be the key to redefining the way we work. More than 54 percent of American households have a home office, and more than 46 million Americans work at home at least part time. These offices range from a desk and chair in the kitchen to a separate room complete with storage and ergonomic furniture.

Many people attempt to create an effective workspace only to realize that the space lacks comfort, connectivity, and convenience. The most important step in developing the home office is planning. Start by developing a budget, analyzing electrical needs such as the placement of outlets, and listing computer hardware and office equipment. Decisions need to be made about the optimal type of lighting, whether to buy modular or built-in furniture, and the arrangement of work materials to increase efficiency and minimize body strain.

Making these decisions can be daunting. Professional space planners know how to make functional and ergonomic workspaces. By analyzing their clients' unique needs, they can design environments that help workers be productive and comfortable. They arrange the equipment and furniture based on the clients' tasks and the rooms' dimensions and constraints.

Comfort @ Home, Inc., is a local business specializing in assisting home workers to develop the best office design for their needs. Kendra Linder, the owner of this business, wants to provide community residents with the guidelines for an effective home office design. She decides the most effective way to disseminate this information is to create a PowerPoint slide show (Figure 1 on the next page) and then have you publish the presentation on the World Wide Web.

As you read through this Web feature, you will learn how to create and display a Web page from a PowerPoint presentation, edit the results using a browser, and then publish the presentation.

Objectives

You will have mastered the material in this project when you can:

- Preview and save a presentation as a Web page
- Create a new folder using file management tools
- View a Web page using a browser
- Edit the Web page content through a browser
- Publish a presentation as a Web page

Introduction

The graphic design power of PowerPoint allows you to create vibrant presentations that convey information in a clear, interesting manner. Some of these presentations are created for small, specific audiences, such as a subcommittee planning a department retreat. In this case, the presentation may be shown in an office conference room. Other presentations are designed for large, general audiences, such as workers at a corporation's various offices across the country learning about a new insurance benefits package. These employees can view the presentation on their company's **intranet**, which is an internal network that uses Internet technologies. On a grand scale, you can inform the entire world about the contents of your presentation by posting your slide show to the World Wide Web. To publish to the World Wide Web, you need a **File Transfer Protocol (FTP)** program to copy your presentation and related files to an **Internet service provider (ISP)** computer.

PowerPoint provides you with two ways to create a Web page. First, you can start a new presentation, as you did in Projects 1 and 2 when you produced the Strategies for College Success and the Healthy

Eating, Healthy Living presentations. PowerPoint provides a Web Presentation template in the **AutoContent Wizard** option when you start PowerPoint. The wizard provides design and content ideas to help you develop an effective slide show for an intranet or for the Internet by opening a sample presentation that you can alter by adding your own text and graphics.

Second, the Save as Web Page command on the File menu allows you to **publish** presentations, which is the process of making existing presentations available to others on the World Wide Web or on a company's intranet. If you have access to a Web server, you can publish Web pages by saving them to a Web folder or to an FTP location. To learn more about publishing Web pages to a Web folder or FTP location using Microsoft Office applications, refer to Appendix C.

The Publish command allows you to create a Web page from a single slide or from a multiple-slide presentation. This Web Feature illustrates opening the Home Office presentation on the Data Disk (Figure 1a) and then saving the presentation as

FIGURE 1

a Web page using the Save as Web Page command. You will save the Web pages and associated folders on a floppy disk rather than to a Web server. At times, this saving process may be slow and requires patience. See the inside back cover of this book for instructions for downloading the Data Disk or see your instructor for information on accessing the files required in this book.

Then, you will edit the presentation, save it again, and view it again in your default browser. Finally, you will publish your presentation, and PowerPoint will start your default browser and open your file so you can view the presentation (Figures 1b through 1e).

Using Web Page Preview and Saving a PowerPoint Presentation as a Web Page

PowerPoint makes it easy to create a presentation and then preview how it will display on an intranet or on the World Wide Web. This action opens the presentation in your default Web browser without saving files. By previewing your slide show, you can decide which features look good and which need modification. The left side of the window includes the navigation frame, which is the outline of the presentation. The outline contains a table of contents consisting of each slide's title text. You can click the Expand/Collapse Outline button below the navigation frame to view the complete slide text. The right side of the window shows the complete slide in the slide frame. The speaker notes, if present, are displayed in the notes frame below the slide frame. Once the preview is acceptable, you then can save the presentation as a Web page.

Previewing the Presentation as a Web Page

Because you are converting the Home Office presentation on the Data Disk to a Web page, the first step in this project is to open the Home Office file. At any time while developing a presentation, you can preview it as a Web page by using the Web Page Preview command on the File menu. When you use the Web Page Preview command, your browser starts and the presentation is displayed as a Web page. The steps on the next page show how to use the Web Page Preview command.

More About

Home Office Planning

Assistance for designing an effective home office is available on various Web sites. Furniture companies, space planners, and ergonomics experts provide helpful advice for developing comfortable and useful workspaces. For more information on home office planning, visit the PowerPoint 2003 More About Web page (scsite.com/ppt2003/more) and click Offices.

More About

Viewing a Presentation

Saving the presentation in Web page format is an excellent vehicle for distributing the slide show to many viewers. Another method of sharing your file is by broadcasting, which allows audience members to view the slide show in real time on their computers while you control precisely what they see. You also can record a broadcast so viewers can watch the presentation at their convenience.

To Preview the Presentation as a Web Page

- **Insert the Data Disk in drive A.**
- **Start PowerPoint and then open the presentation, Home Office, on the Data Disk in drive A.**
- **Click File on the menu bar.**

PowerPoint starts and opens the slide show, Home Office, in normal view. The presentation is composed of four slides. PowerPoint displays the File menu (Figure 2).

FIGURE 2

- **Click Web Page Preview.**

PowerPoint starts your browser. The browser displays a Web page preview of Slide 1 of the Home Office presentation in the slide frame in the browser window (Figure 3). The navigation frame contains the table of contents, which consists of the title text of each slide. The speaker notes are displayed in the notes frame. The Microsoft PowerPoint button on the taskbar no longer is selected. Windows displays a selected browser button on the taskbar, indicating it is active.

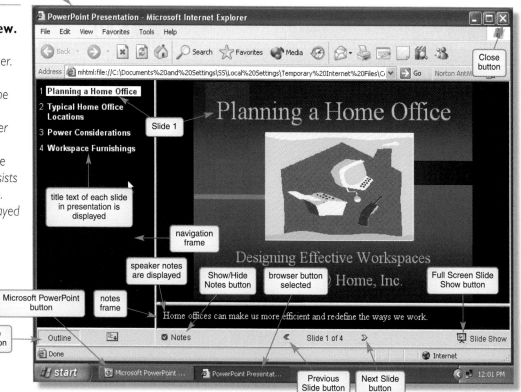

FIGURE 3

3

• **Click the Full Screen Slide Show button.**

Slide 1 fills the entire screen (Figure 4). The Slide 1 title text and clip art are displayed. The Web Page preview in the browser is nearly identical to the display of the presentation in PowerPoint.

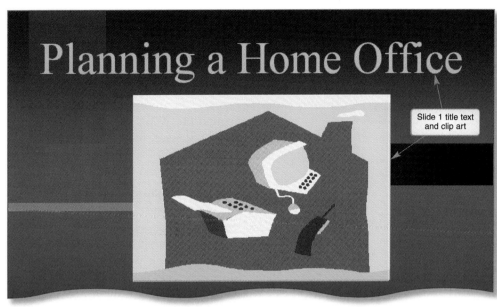

FIGURE 4

4

• **Click to display the first line of the subtitle text.**

The first line of the Slide 1 subtitle text is displayed.

5

• **Continue clicking each slide in the presentation.**
• **When the black slide is displayed, click it.**

Each of the four slides in the Home Office presentation is displayed. The message on the black slide, End of slide show, click to exit., indicates the conclusion of the slide show.

6

• **Click the Close button on the right side of the browser title bar.**

The browser closes, PowerPoint becomes active, and PowerPoint displays Slide 1 (Figure 5).

FIGURE 5

Q: On what days are audience members most attentive?

A: Sundays, Mondays, and Tuesdays. Researchers believe these days are the best for delivering presentations because the viewers are more relaxed than at the middle and end of the week. As you choose to show or hide your outline and notes, consider your audience's attention span. You may need to provide more information via the outline and notes on the days when your audience is less focused.

More About

Browsers

In 1993, computer science students at the University of Illinois developed Mosaic, one of the first graphical Web browsers. Marc Andreessen and a friend worked 18 hours a day for 6 weeks to develop this browser. This success led to the organization of the Netscape Communications Corporation. For more information on graphical Web browsers, visit the PowerPoint 2003 More About Web page (scsite.com/ppt2003/more) and click Browsers.

The Web page preview shows that PowerPoint can produce professional-looking Web pages from presentations. You can alter the browser window by choosing to display or hide the navigation and notes frames. To hide the navigation frame, click the Show/Hide Outline button below the outline. Later, if you want to redisplay the navigation frame, click the Show/Hide Outline button again. Similarly, the Show/Hide Notes button below the slide frame allows you to display or conceal the speaker notes, if present, on a particular slide.

To advance through the Web page, you also can click the Next Slide button below the slide frame. Likewise, to display a slide appearing earlier in the slide show, click the Previous Slide button.

Saving a PowerPoint Presentation as a Web Page to a New Folder

Once the preview of a PowerPoint slide show is acceptable, you can save it as a Web page so you can view it in a Web browser. Microsoft Internet Explorer and Netscape Navigator are the two more common browsers installed on computers today.

You can save the presentation in one of two Web page formats. One format is called **Single File Web Page**, which saves all the Web page components in a single file with an .mht extension. This format is useful for e-mailing presentations in **hypertext markup language (HTML)**, which is a language browsers can interpret. The second format, called **Web Page**, saves the Web page in a file and some of its components in a folder. This format is useful if you need access to the components, such as clip art, that comprise the Web page. Both formats convert the slide show contents into HTML.

You can save and then view the presentation in two ways. First, you can save the entire presentation as a Web page, quit PowerPoint, open your browser, and open the Web page in your browser. Second, you can combine these steps by saving the presentation as a Web page, publishing the presentation, and then viewing the presentation as a Web page. In this case, PowerPoint will start the browser and display your presentation automatically. Later in this feature, the Publish button will be used to explain further how you can customize a Web page.

Experienced users organize their storage devices by creating folders and then save related files to a common folder. PowerPoint allows you to create folders in the Save As dialog box before saving a file. The following steps create a new folder on the Data Disk in drive A and then save the Home Office presentation in the Web Page format to the new folder.

To Save a Presentation in Web Page Format to a New Folder

1

- **With the Home Office presentation open, click the Next Slide button twice to view Slide 3.**

- **Click the notes pane and then type** More than 46 million Americans work at home at least part time; more than 54 percent of American households have a home office. **as the note.**

- **Click File on the menu bar.**

PowerPoint displays the File menu (Figure 6). The last four words of the speaker notes you typed appear in the notes pane.

FIGURE 6

2

- **Click Save as Web Page.**

- **When the Save As dialog box is displayed, type** Home Office Web Page **in the File name text box.**

- **Click the Save as type box arrow and then click Web Page.**

PowerPoint displays the Save As dialog box (Figure 7). The default file format type is Single File Web Page.

FIGURE 7

3

• **If necessary, click the Save in box arrow and select 3½ Floppy (A:).**

• **Click the Create New Folder button.**

• **When the New Folder dialog box is displayed, type** Web Feature **in the Name text box.**

PowerPoint displays the New Folder dialog box (Figure 8).

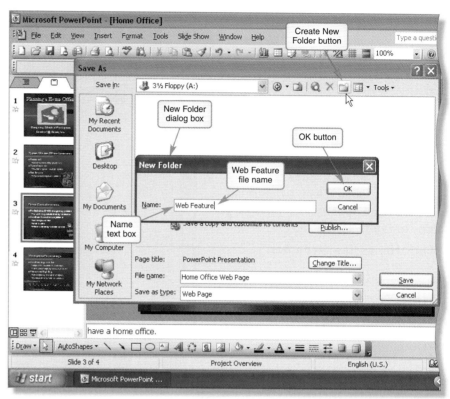

FIGURE 8

4

• **Click the OK button in the New Folder dialog box.**

PowerPoint automatically selects the new Web Feature folder in the Save in box.

5

• **Click the Save button.**

• **After all files are saved, click the Close button on the right side of the title bar to close PowerPoint.**

PowerPoint saves the presentation in HTML format on the Data Disk in drive A in the Web Feature folder using the file name Home Office Web Page.htm. PowerPoint closes (Figure 9).

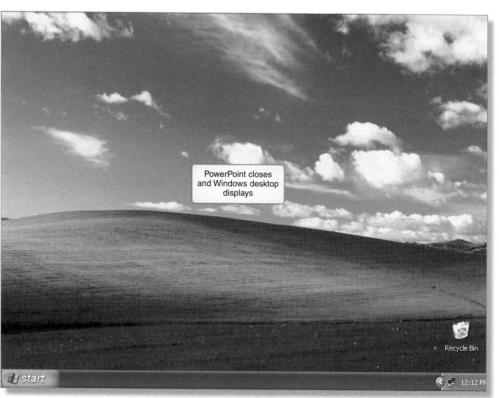

FIGURE 9

The Save As dialog box that displays when you use the Save as Web Page command is slightly different from the Save As dialog box that displays when you use the Save As command. The Publish button in the Save As dialog box in Figure 7 on page PPT 147 is an alternative to the Save button and allows you to customize the Web page further. In the previous set of steps, the Save button was used to complete the save. Later in this feature, the Publish button will be used to explain further how you can customize a Web page.

File Management Tools in PowerPoint

Creating a new folder allows you to organize your work. PowerPoint automatically inserts the new folder name in the Save in box when you click the OK button in the New Folder dialog box (Figure 8). Once you create a folder, you can right-click it while the Save As dialog box is active and perform many file manager tasks directly in PowerPoint. For example, once the shortcut menu is displayed, you can rename the selected folder, delete it, copy it, display its properties, and perform other file management functions.

If you have access to a Web server that allows you to save files to a Web folder, then you can save the Web page directly to the Web server by clicking the My Network Places button in the lower-left corner of the Save As dialog box (Figure 7). If you have access to a Web server that allows you to save to an FTP site, then you can select the FTP site under FTP locations in the Save in box just as you select any folder in which to save a file. To save a presentation to a Web server, see Appendix C.

After PowerPoint saves the presentation in Step 5, it displays the HTML file — not the presentation — in the PowerPoint window. PowerPoint can continue to display the presentation in HTML format because within the HTML file that was created, PowerPoint also saved the formats to display the HTML file. This is referred to as **round tripping** the HTML file back to the application in which it was created.

Viewing the Web Page Using Your Browser

With the Home Office Web page saved to the folder, Web Feature, on the Data Disk in drive A, the next step is to view it using a browser, such as Microsoft Internet Explorer or Netscape, as shown in the steps on the next page.

More About

Saving Files

PowerPoint provides many file formats for saving presentations. One useful format that allows viewers to see, but not alter, a presentation is the PowerPoint Show (.pps) format. A slide show saved as a PowerPoint Show always will open as a slide show presentation.

More About

Viewing Web Presentations

Several PowerPoint features do not work when a presentation is viewed as a Web page. These features include embossed and shadow effects for fonts, text that is animated by the letter or word rather than by the paragraph, and special effects on charts. In addition, music will not play throughout a Web presentation because moving to another slide stops the sound.

To View the Web Page Using Your Browser

1

• **If necessary, insert the Data Disk in drive A.**

• **Click the Start button on the taskbar, point to All Programs, and then click Internet Explorer.**

• **When the Internet Explorer window displays, type** a:\web feature\home office web page.htm **in the Address bar and then press the ENTER key.**

The browser displays Slide 1 in the Web page, Home Office Web Page.htm (Figure 10).

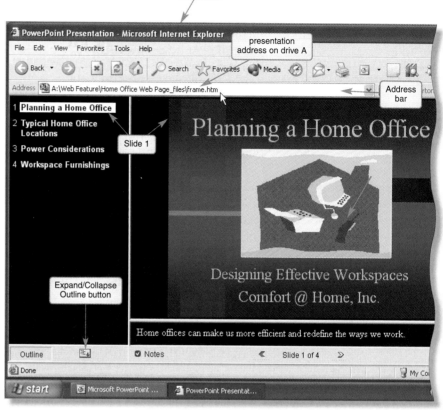

FIGURE 10

2

• **Click the Expand/ Collapse Outline button at the bottom of the window.**

The text of each slide in an outline appears in the navigation frame (Figure 11). To display only the title of each slide, you would click the Expand/Collapse Outline button again.

FIGURE 11

3

• **Click the Next Slide button three times to view all four slides.**

The browser displays each of the slides in the Home Office presentation. Slide 4 is displayed in the browser (Figure 12).

FIGURE 12

Figures 11 and 12 show that a Web page is an ideal medium for distributing information to a large group of people. The Web page can be made available to anyone with a computer, browser, and the address. The Web page also can be e-mailed easily because it resides in a single file, rather than in a file and folder.

If you want, you can use the Print command on the File menu in your browser to print the slides one at a time. You also can view the HTML source PowerPoint created by clicking Source on the View menu in Internet Explorer or Page Source on the View menu in Netscape.

Editing a Web Page through a Browser

You may want to modify your Web page by making small changes to the text or art on some slides. In this presentation, you want to change the title text in Slide 1 to reflect the fact that a home office can provide comfort as well as efficiency. You can modify the presentation using PowerPoint directly in the browser window. Your computer may indicate other editing options, such as using Windows Notepad. The steps on the next page modify the Title Slide title text.

More About

Printing

If your printer seems to print slowly, Microsoft suggests clearing at least two megabytes of space on your hard drive and also closing any unnecessary programs that are running simultaneously.

To Edit a Web Page through a Browser

1

• **Click the Edit with Microsoft Office PowerPoint button on the Standard Buttons toolbar.**

• **Select the words, Planning a Home Office, in the title text placeholder.**

When you click the Edit button, PowerPoint opens a new presentation with the same file name as the Web presentation file name, as indicated by the title bar and the selected Microsoft PowerPoint - [Home Office Web Page] button on the Windows taskbar (Figure 13). A selection rectangle appears around the title text placeholder. The four words are highlighted.

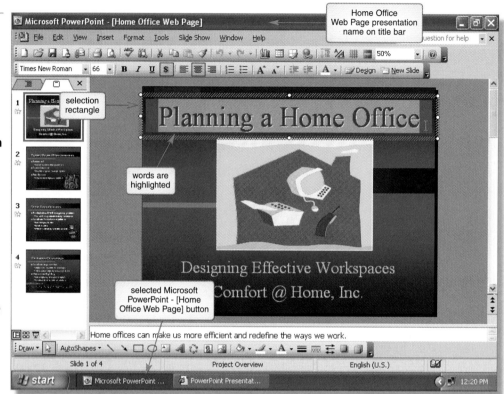

FIGURE 13

2

• **Type** The Comforts of Home **in the title text placeholder.**

The title text is modified (Figure 14).

FIGURE 14

• **Click the Save button on the Standard toolbar.**

It takes several minutes for PowerPoint to save the changes to the Home Office Web Page.htm file on the Data Disk in drive A. The buttons on the taskbar indicate that the PowerPoint presentation and the browser are open.

• **Click the PowerPoint Presentation - Microsoft Internet Explorer button on the taskbar.**

• **Click the Previous Slide button three times to display Slide 1.**

The browser displays the revised title text on Slide 1 (Figure 15). If the revised text does not display, click the Refresh button on the Standard Buttons toolbar.

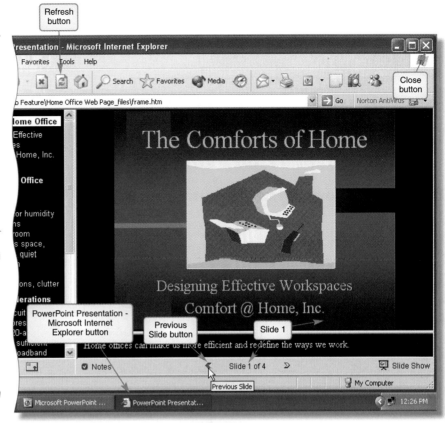

FIGURE 15

• **Click the Close button on the browser title bar.**

• **Click the Save button to save the revised PowerPoint Home Office Web Page.**

The browser closes, and the PowerPoint window displays in normal view with the modified Slide 1 of the Home Office Web Page presentation active (Figure 16).

FIGURE 16

Publishing a Web Page

PowerPoint allows you to publish the presentation by saving the pages to a Web folder or to an FTP location. When you publish your presentation, it is available for other computer users to view on the Internet or by other means. Publishing a Web page of a presentation is an alternative to distributing printed copies of the slides. The following section uses the Publish button in the Save As dialog box, rather than the Save button, to illustrate PowerPoint's additional publishing capabilities.

To Publish a PowerPoint Presentation

1

• **Click File on the menu bar and then click Save as Web Page.**

• **Click the Save as type box arrow and then click Single File Web Page.**

• **Type** Home Office Single File Web Page **in the File name text box.**

• **If necessary, click the Save in box arrow, select 3½ Floppy (A:) in the Save in list, and then select the folder, Web Feature.**

The Save As dialog box is displayed (Figure 17). When you use the Publish button, PowerPoint will save the Web page in a single file.

FIGURE 17

2

• **Click the Publish button.**

• **If the Office Assistant appears, click No, don't provide help now.**

• **If necessary, click Open published Web page in browser to select it.**

The Publish as Web Page dialog box is displayed (Figure 18). PowerPoint defaults to publishing the complete presentation, although you can choose to publish one or a range of slides. The Open published Web page in browser check box is selected, which means the Home Office Single File Web Page presentation will open in your default browser when you click the Publish button.

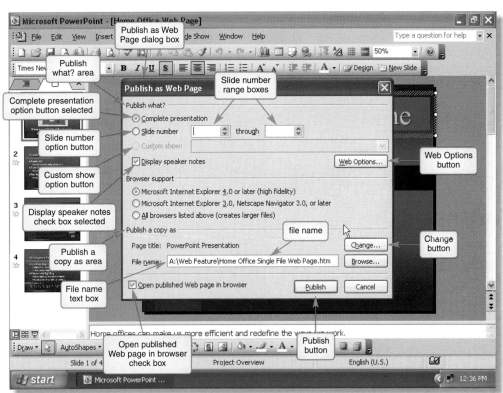

FIGURE 18

3

• **Click the Publish button.**

PowerPoint saves the presentation as a single file, Home Office Single File Web Page.mht, in the Web Feature folder on the Data Disk in drive A. After a few minutes, PowerPoint opens your default Web browser in a separate window (Figure 19). If the browser does not open, click the PowerPoint Presentation - Microsoft Internet Explorer button on the Windows taskbar.

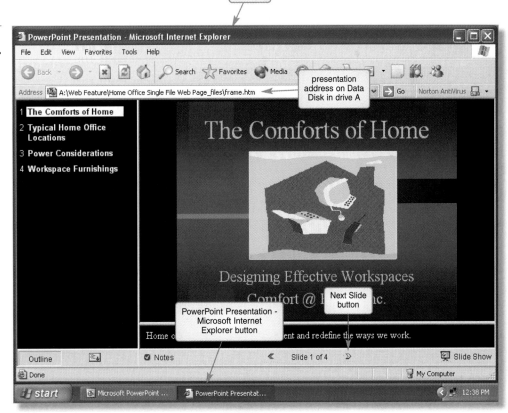

FIGURE 19

4

• **Click the Next Slide button three times to view the four slides.**

• **Click the Close button in the upper-right corner of the browser window.**

• **Click File on the menu bar, click Print, click the Print what arrow, click Handouts, click Vertical in the Handouts area, and then click the OK button.**

• **Click the Save button to save the revised Home Office Web Page.**

The browser closes, and PowerPoint prints the four slides as a handout (Figure 20). PowerPoint takes a few minutes to save the file to the Data Disk.

FIGURE 20

Publishing provides customizing options that are not available when you simply save the entire presentation and then start your browser. The Publish as Web Page dialog box provides several options to customize your Web page. For example, you can change the page title that displays on the browser's title bar and in the history list. People visiting your Web site can store a link to your Web page, which will display in their favorites list. To change the page title, you click the Change button in the Publish a copy as area (Figure 18 on the previous page) and then type a new title.

The Publish what? area of the Publish as Web Page dialog box allows you to publish parts of your presentation. PowerPoint defaults to publishing the complete presentation, but you can select specific slides by clicking the Slide number option button and then entering the range of desired slide numbers in the range boxes. In addition, you can publish a custom show you have created previously. A **custom show** is a subset of your presentation that contains slides tailored for a specific audience. For example, you may want to show Slides 1, 2, and 4 to one group and Slides 1, 3, and 4 to another group.

You can choose to publish only the publication slides and not the accompanying speaker notes. By default, the Display speaker notes check box is selected in the Publish what? area. You typed speaker notes for Slide 1 of this presentation, so the speaker notes will appear in the browser window. If you do not want to make your notes available to users, click the Display speaker notes check box to remove the check mark.

The Web Options button in the Publish what? area allows you to select options to determine how your presentation will look when viewed in a Web browser. You can choose options such as allowing slide animation to show, selecting the screen size, and having the notes and outline panes display when viewing the presentation in a Web browser.

The Web page now is complete. The next step is to make your Web presentation available to others on your network, an intranet, or the World Wide Web. Ask your instructor how you can post your presentation.

> **More About**
>
> **Publishing Web Presentations**
>
> Once a presentation is published, viewers can view the slide show and then offer comments about the document. Saving the presentation as an .htm or .mht Web-based format provides the most flexibility for these reviewers. The .mht format combines multiple pictures and slides into a single file called a Web archive. A Web archive works in the same manner as a Web page does in .htm format. For more information on publishing Web presentations, visit the PowerPoint 2003 More About Web page (scsite.com/ppt2003/more) and click Publishing.

Web Feature Summary

This Web feature introduced you to creating a Web page by viewing an existing presentation as a Web page in your default browser. The presentation then was saved as an HTML file. Next, you modified Slide 1. You then reviewed the Slide 1 change using your default browser and then published the slide show. With the Home Office presentation converted to a Web page, you can post the file to an intranet or to the World Wide Web.

 If you have a SAM user profile, you may have access to hands-on instruction, practice, and assessment of the skills covered in this project. Log in to your SAM account and go to your assignments page to see what your instructor has assigned.

What You Should Know

Having completed this project, you should be able to perform the tasks below. The tasks are listed in the same order they were presented in this project. For a list of the buttons, menus, toolbars, and commands introduced in this project, see the Quick Reference Summary at the back of this book and refer to the Page Number column.

1. Preview the Presentation as a Web Page (PPT 144)

2. Save a Presentation in Web Page Format to a New Folder   (PPT 147)

3. View the Web Page Using Your Browser (PPT 150)

4. Edit a Web Page through a Browser (PPT 152)

5. Publish a PowerPoint Presentation   (PPT 154)

1 Creating a Web Page from the College Success Presentation

Problem: Dr. Traci Johnson, the dean of the Academic Skills Center at Lakemore College, wants to expand the visibility of the College Success presentation you created for the Academic Skills Center in Project 1. Dr. Johnson believes the World Wide Web would be an excellent vehicle to help students throughout the campus and at other colleges, and she has asked you to help transfer the presentation to the Internet.

Instructions: Start PowerPoint and then perform the following steps with a computer.

1. Open the College Success presentation shown in Figure 1-1 on page PPT 5 that you created in Project 1. (If you did not complete Project 1, see your instructor for a copy of the presentation.)
2. Use the Save as Web Page command on the File menu to save the presentation in Web page format. Create a new folder called College Success Exercise and then save the Web page with the file name, Lab WF 1-1 Lakemore.
3. View the presentation in a browser.
4. Edit the Web page by using the words, Achieve Your Academic Personal Best, as the Slide 1 title text.
5. Change the last paragraph to the words, Turn off cellular telephone, on Slide 3.
6. View the modified Web page in a browser.
7. Print the modified presentation as a handout with the slides arranged vertically.
8. Ask your instructor for instructions on how to post your Web page so others may have access to it.

2 Creating a Web Page from the Nutrition and Fitness Presentation

Problem: The Nutrition and Fitness presentation you developed in Project 2 for Jessica Cantero, the Fitness director at your college, is generating much interest. Students are registering for the first workshop and are inquiring about additional seminars. Jessica has asked you to post the presentation to the school's intranet.

Instructions: Start PowerPoint and then perform the following steps with a computer.

1. Open the Nutrition and Fitness presentation shown in Figures 2-1a through 2-1e on page PPT 83 that you created in Project 2. (If you did not complete Project 2, see your instructor for a copy of the presentation.)
2. Use the Save as Web Page command on the File menu to save the presentation in Web Page format. Create a new folder called Healthy Exercise and then save the Web page using the file name, Lab WF 1-2 Nutrition.
3. View the presentation in a browser.
4. Modify Slide 1 by italicizing both subtitle lines.
5. On Slide 1, type Workshops are scheduled each Monday at 7 p.m. and Friday at noon. as the note.
6. Modify Slide 3 by changing the word, Bicycling, to the word, Golfing.
7. On Slide 4, type Yoga has been practiced actively for more than 5,000 years. as the note.
8. View the modified Web page in a browser.
9. Print the modified presentation as a handout with the slides arranged horizontally.
10. Ask your instructor for instructions on how to post your Web page so others may have access to it.

In the Lab

3 Creating a Personal Presentation

Problem: You have decided to apply for a position as a tutor in your college's academic assistance center. You are preparing to send your resume and cover letter to the dean of this area in your school, and you want to develop a unique way to publicize your academic skills and personality traits. You decide to create a personalized PowerPoint presentation emphasizing your scholarly achievements and your interpersonal communication skills. You refer to this presentation in your cover letter and inform the executive director that she can view this presentation because you have saved the presentation as a Web page and posted the pages on your school's Web server.

Instructions: Start PowerPoint and then perform the following steps with a computer.

1. Prepare a presentation highlighting your scholarly skills and personality strengths. Create a title slide and at least three additional slides. Use appropriate clip art and an animation scheme.
2. Use the Save as Web Page command to convert and publish the presentation as a single file Web page. Save the Web page in a folder named Tutoring Web File using the file name, Lab WF 1-3 Tutor Position.
3. View the presentation in a browser.
4. Print the Web page.
5. Ask your instructor for instructions on how to post your Web page so others may have access to it.

Appendix A

Microsoft Office Help System

Using the Microsoft Office Help System

This appendix shows you how to use the Microsoft Office Help system. At anytime while you are using one of the Microsoft Office 2003 applications, you can interact with its Help system and display information on any topic associated with the application. To illustrate the use of the Office Help system, you will use the Microsoft Word application in this appendix. The Help systems in other Office applications respond in a similar fashion.

As shown in Figure A-1, five methods for accessing Word's Help system are available:

1. Microsoft Office Word Help button on the Standard toolbar
2. Microsoft Office Word Help command on the Help menu
3. Function key F1 on the keyboard
4. Type a question for help box on the menu bar
5. Office Assistant

FIGURE A-1

(a) Word Help Task Pane

(b) Search Results Task Pane

(c) Microsoft Office Word Help Window

All five methods result in the Word Help system displaying a task pane on the right side of the Word window. The first three methods cause the **Word Help task pane** to display (Figure A-1a on the previous page). This task pane includes a Search text box in which you can enter a word or phrase on which you want help. Once you enter the word or phrase, the Word Help system displays the Search Results task pane (Figure A-1b on the previous page). With the Search Results task pane displayed, you can select specific Help topics.

As shown in Figure A-1, methods 4 and 5 bypass the Word Help task pane and display the **Search Results task pane** (Figure A-1b) with a list of links that pertain to the selected topic. Thus, any of the five methods for accessing the Word Help system results in displaying the Search Results task pane. Once the Word Help system displays this task pane, you can choose links that relate to the word or phrase on which you searched. In Figure A-1, for example, header was the searched topic (About headers and footers), which resulted in the Word Help system displaying the Microsoft Office Word Help window with information about headers and footers (Figure A-1c on the previous page).

Navigating the Word Help System

The quickest way to access the Word Help system is through the Type a question for help box on the right side of the menu bar at the top of the screen. Here you can type words, such as ruler, font, or column, or phrases, such as justify a paragraph, or how do I display formatting marks. The Word Help system responds by displaying a list of links in the Search Results task pane.

Here are two tips regarding the words or phrases you enter to initiate a search: (1) check the spelling of the word or phrase; and (2) keep your search very specific, with fewer than seven words, to return the most accurate results.

Assume for the following example that you want to know more about tables. The following steps show how to use the Type a question for help box to obtain useful information about tables by entering the keyword table. The steps also show you how to navigate the Word Help system.

To Obtain Help Using the Type a Question for Help Box

1

• **Click the Type a question for help box on the right side of the menu bar, type** table, **and then press the ENTER key (Figure A-2).**

The Word Help system displays the Search Results task pane on the right side of the window. The Search Results task pane contains a list of 30 links (Figure A-2). If you do not find what you are looking for, you can modify or refine the search in the Search area at the bottom of the task pane. The topics displayed in your Search Results task pane may be different.

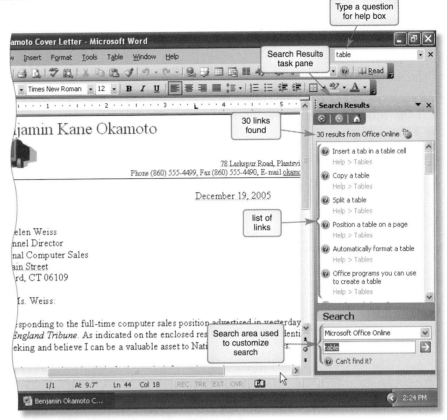

FIGURE A-2

2

Scroll down the list of links in the Search Results task pane and then click the About tables link.

• **When Word displays the Microsoft Office Help Word window, click its Auto Tile button in the upper-left corner of the window (Figure A-4 on the next page), if necessary, to tile the windows.**

Word displays the Microsoft Office Word Help window with the desired information about tables (Figure A-3). With the Microsoft Office Word Help window and Microsoft Word window tiled, you can read the information in one window and complete the task in the other window.

FIGURE A-3

3

• **Double-click the Microsoft Office Word Help window title bar.**

• **Click the Show All link in the upper-right corner of the window.**

• **After reviewing the information, click the Hide All link that replaced the Show All link.**

The Microsoft Office Word Help window is maximized so it fills the entire screen (Figure A-4). If you are connected to the Internet, you can give Microsoft your opinion as to whether the information was helpful by clicking the Yes or No button at the bottom of the page. The Show All link expands the coverage of information and the Hide all link condenses the information displayed on the topic in the Microsoft Office Word Help window.

4

• **Click the Restore Down button on the right side of the Microsoft Office Word Help window title bar to return to the tiled state shown in Figure A-3 on the previous page.**

• **Click the Close button on the Microsoft Office Word Help window title bar.**

The Microsoft Office Word Help window is closed and the Word document is active.

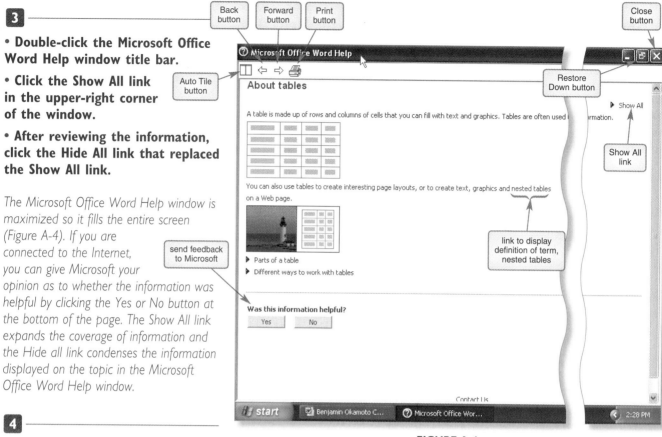

FIGURE A-4

Use the four buttons in the upper-left corner of the Microsoft Office Word Help window (Figure A-4) to tile or untile, navigate through the Help system, or print the contents of the window. As you click links in the Search Results task pane, the Word Help system displays new pages of information. The Word Help System remembers the links you visited and allows you to redisplay the pages visited during a session by clicking the Back and Forward buttons (Figure A-4).

If none of the links presents the information you want, you can refine the search by entering another word or phrase in the Search text box in the Search Results task pane (Figure A-2 on the previous page). If you have access to the Web, then the scope is global for the initial search. **Global** means all of the categories listed in the Search box of the Search area in Figure A-2 are searched. For example, you can, restrict the scope to **Offline Help,** which results in a search of related links only on your hard disk.

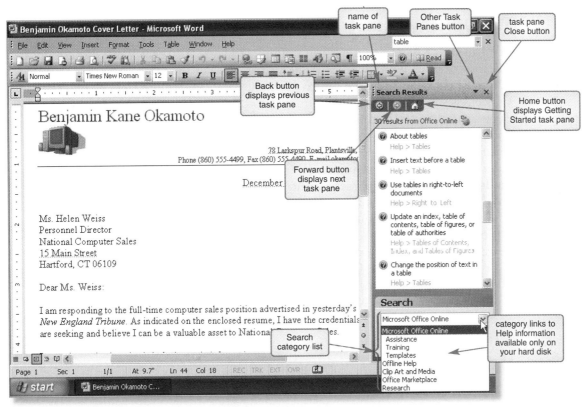

FIGURE A-5

Figure A-5 shows several additional features of the Search Results task pane. The Other Task Panes button and Close button on the Search Results task pane title bar allow you to display other task panes and close the Search Results task pane. The three buttons below the Search Results task pane title bar allow you to navigate between task panes (Back button and Forward button) and display the Getting Started task pane (Home button).

As you enter words and phrases in the Type a question for help box, the Word Help system adds them to the Type a question for help list. To display the list of previously typed words and phrases, click the Type a question for help box arrow (Figure A-6).

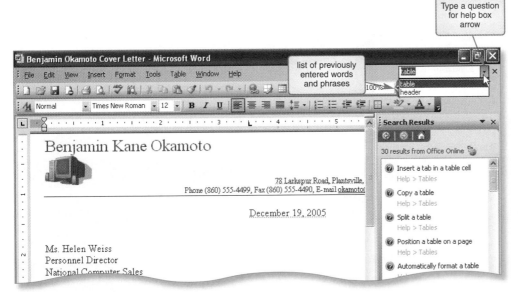

FIGURE A-6

The Office Assistant

The **Office Assistant** is an icon (middle of Figure A-7) that Word displays in the Microsoft Office Word window while you work. For the Office Assistant to display, you must click the Show the Office Assistant command on the Help menu. The Office Assistant has multiple functions. First, it will respond in the same way as the Type a question for help box with a list of topics that relate to the word or phrase you enter in the text box in the Office Assistant balloon. The entry can be in the form of a word or phrase as if you were talking to a person. For example, if you want to learn more about printing a file, in the balloon text box, you can type any of the following words or phrases: print, print a document, how do I print a file, or anything similar.

In the example in Figure A-7, the phrase, print a document, is entered into the Office Assistant balloon text box. The Office Assistant responds by displaying the Search Results task pane with a list of links from which you can choose. Once you click a link in the Search Results task pane, the Word Help system displays the information in the Microsoft Office Word Help window (Figure A-7).

FIGURE A-7

In addition, the Office Assistant monitors your work and accumulates tips during a session on how you might increase your productivity and efficiency. The accumulation of tips must be enabled. You enable the accumulation of tips by right-clicking the Office Assistant, clicking Options on the shortcut menu, and then selecting the types of tips you want accumulated. You can view the tips at anytime. The accumulated tips appear when you activate the Office Assistant balloon. Also, if at anytime you see a light bulb above the Office Assistant, click it to display the most recent tip. If the Office Assistant is hidden, then the light bulb shows on the Microsoft Office Word Help button on the Standard toolbar.

You hide the Office Assistant by invoking the Hide the Office Assistant command on the Help menu or by right-clicking the Office Assistant and then clicking Hide on the shortcut menu. The Hide the Office Assistant command shows on the Help menu only when the Office Assistant is active in the Word window. If the Office Assistant begins showing up on your screen without you instructing it to show, then right-click the Office Assistant, click Options on the shortcut menu, click the Use the Office Assistant check box to remove the check mark, and then click the OK button.

If the Office Assistant is active in the Word window, then Word displays all program and system messages in the Office Assistant balloon.

You may or may not want the Office Assistant to display on the screen at all times. As indicated earlier, you can hide it and then show it later through the Help menu. For more information about the Office Assistant, type office assistant in the Type a question for help box and then click the links in the Search Results task pane.

Question Mark Button in Dialog Boxes and Help Icon in Task Panes

You use the Question Mark button with dialog boxes. It is located in the upper-right corner on the title bar of the dialog boxes, next to the Close button. For example, in Figure A-8 on the next page, the Print dialog box appears on the screen. If you click the Question Mark button in the upper-right corner of the dialog box, the Microsoft Office Word Help window is displayed and provides information about the options in the Print dialog box.

Some task panes include a Help icon. It can be located in various places within the task pane. For example, in the Clip Art task pane shown in Figure A-8, the Help icon appears at the bottom of the task pane and the Tips for finding clips link appears to the right of the Help icon. When you click the link, the Microsoft Office Word Help window is displayed and provides tips for finding clip art.

FIGURE A-8

Other Help Commands on the Help Menu

Thus far, this appendix has discussed the first two commands on the Help menu:
(1) the Microsoft Office Word Help command (Figure A-1 on page APP 1) and
(2) the Show the Office Assistant command (Figure A-7 on page APP 6). Several
additional commands are available on the Help menu as shown in Figure A-9.
Table A-1 summarizes these commands.

other commands on Help menu

FIGURE A-9

Table A-1   Summary of Other Help Commands on the Help Menu

COMMAND ON HELP MENU	FUNCTION
Microsoft Office Online	Activates the browser, which displays the Microsoft Office Online Home page. The Microsoft Office Online Home page contains links that can improve Office productivity.
Contact Us	Activates the browser, which displays Microsoft contact information and a list of useful links.
WordPerfect Help	Displays the Help for WordPerfect Users dialog box, which includes information about carrying out commands in Word.
Check for Updates	Activates the browser, which displays a list of updates to Office 2003. These updates can be downloaded and installed to improve the efficiency of Office or to fix an error in one or more of the Office applications.
Detect and Repair	Detects and repairs errors in the Word program.
Activate Product	Activates Word if it has not already been activated.
Customer Feedback Options	Gives or denies Microsoft permission to collect anonymous information about the hardware.
About Microsoft Office Word	Displays the About Microsoft Word dialog box. The dialog box lists the owner of the software and the product identification. You need to know the product identification if you call Microsoft for assistance. The three buttons below the OK button are the System Info button, Tech Support button, and Disabled Items button. The System Info button displays system information, including hardware resources, components, software environment, and applications. The Tech Support button displays technical assistance information. The Disabled Items button displays a list of disabled items that prevents Word from functioning properly.

1 Using the Type a Question for Help Box

Instructions: Perform the following tasks using the Word Help system.

1. Use the Type a question for help box on the menu bar to get help on adding a bullet.
2. Click Add bullets or numbering in the list of links in the Search Results task pane. If necessary, tile the windows. Double-click the Microsoft Office Word Help window title bar to maximize it. Click the Show All link. Read and print the information. At the top of the printout, write down the number of links the Word Help system found.
3. Click the Restore Down button on the Microsoft Office Word Help title bar to restore the Microsoft Office Word Help window.
4. One at a time, click two additional links in the Search Results task pane and print the information. Hand in the printouts to your instructor. Use the Back and Forward buttons to return to the original page.
5. Use the Type a question for help box to search for information on adjusting line spacing. Click the Adjust line or paragraph spacing link in the Search Results task pane. Maximize the Microsoft Office Word Help window. Read and print the contents of the window. One at a time, click the links on the page and print the contents of the window. Close the Microsoft Office Word Help window.
6. For each of the following words and phrases, click one link in the Search Results task pane, click the Show All link, and then print the page: page zoom; date; print preview; office clipboard; word count; and themes.

2 Expanding on the Word Help System Basics

Instructions: Use the Word Help system to understand the topics better and answer the questions listed below. Answer the questions on your own paper, or hand in the printed Help information to your instructor.

1. Show the Office Assistant. Right-click the Office Assistant and then click Animate! on the shortcut menu. Repeat invoking the Animate! command to see various animations.
2. Right-click the Office Assistant, click Options on the shortcut menu, click the Reset my tips button, and then click the OK button. If necessary, repeatedly click the Office Assistant and then click off the Office Assistant until a light bulb appears above the Office Assistant. When you see the light bulb, it indicates that the Office Assistant has a tip to share with you.
3. Use the Office Assistant to find help on undoing. Click the Undo mistakes link and then print the contents of the Microsoft Office Word Help window. Close the window. Hand in the printouts to your instructor. Hide the Office Assistant.
4. Press the F1 key. Search for information on Help. Click the first two links in the Search Results task pane. Read and print the information for both links.
5. Display the Help menu. One at a time, click the Microsoft Office Online, Contact Us, and Check for Updates commands. Print the contents of each Internet Explorer window that displays and then close the window. Hand in the printouts to your instructor.
6. Click About Microsoft Office Word on the Help menu. Click the Tech Support button, print the contents of the Microsoft Office Word Help window, and then close the window. Click the System Info button. If necessary, click the plus sign to the left of Components in the System Summary list to display the Components category. Click CD-ROM and then print the information. Click Display and then print the information. Hand in the printouts to your instructor.

Appendix B

Speech and Handwriting Recognition and Speech Playback

Introduction

This appendix discusses the Office capability that allows users to create and modify worksheets using its alternative input technologies available through **text services**. Office provides a variety of text services, which enable you to speak commands and enter text in an application. The most common text service is the keyboard. Other text services include speech recognition and handwriting recognition.

The Language Bar

The **Language bar** allows you to use text services in the Office applications. You can utilize the Language bar in one of three states: (1) in a restored state as a floating toolbar in the Word window (Figure B-1a or Figure B-1b if Text Labels are enabled); (2) in a minimized state docked next to the notification area on the Windows taskbar (Figure B-1c); or (3) hidden (temporarily closed and out of the way). If the Language bar is hidden, you can activate it by right-clicking the Windows taskbar, pointing to Toolbars on the shortcut menu (Figure B-1d), and then clicking Language bar on the Toolbars submenu. If you want to close the Language bar, right-click the Language bar and then click Close the Language bar on the shortcut menu (Figure B-1e).

(b) Language Bar with Text Labels Enabled

(c) Minimized Language Bar Docked on Windows Taskbar next to Notification Area

FIGURE B-1

(a) Language Bar with Text Labels Disabled

(d) Windows Taskbar Shortcut Menu and Toolbars Submenu

(e) Language Bar Shortcut Menu

When Windows was installed on your computer, the installer specified a default language. For example, most users in the United States select English (United States) as the default language. You can add more than 90 additional languages and varying dialects such as Basque, English (Zimbabwe), French (France), French (Canada), German (Germany), German (Austria), and Swahili. With multiple languages available, you can switch from one language to another while working in Word. If you change the language or dialect, then text services may change the functions of the keys on the keyboard, adjust speech recognition, and alter handwriting recognition. If a second language is activated, then a Language icon appears immediately to the right of the move handle on the Language bar and the language name is displayed on the Word status bar. This appendix assumes that English (United States) is the only language installed. Thus, the Language icon does not appear in the examples in Figure B-1 on the previous page.

Buttons on the Language Bar

The Language bar shown in Figure B-2a contains seven buttons. The number of buttons on your Language bar may be different. These buttons are used to select the language, customize the Language bar, control the microphone, control handwriting, and obtain help.

The first button on the left is the Microphone button, which enables and disables the microphone. When the microphone is enabled, text services adds two buttons and a balloon to the Language bar (Figure B-2b). These additional buttons and the balloon will be discussed shortly.

The second button from the left is the Speech Tools button. The Speech Tools button displays a menu of commands (Figure B-2c) that allow you to scan the current document looking for words to add to the speech recognition dictionary; hide or show the balloon on the Language bar; train the Speech Recognition service so that it can interpret your voice better; add and delete specific words to and from its dictionary, such as names and other words not understood easily; and change the user profile so more than one person can use the microphone on the same computer.

The third button from the left on the Language bar is the Handwriting button. The Handwriting button displays the Handwriting menu (Figure B-2d), which lets you choose the Writing Pad (Figure B-2e), Write Anywhere (Figure B-2f), or the on-screen keyboard (Figure B-2g). The On-Screen Symbol Keyboard command on the Handwriting menu displays an on-screen keyboard that allows you to enter special symbols that are not available on a standard keyboard. You can choose only one form of handwriting at a time.

The fourth button indicates which one of the handwriting forms is active. For example, in Figure B-2a, the Writing Pad is active. The handwriting recognition capabilities of text services will be discussed shortly.

The fifth button from the left on the Language bar is the Help button. The Help button displays the Help menu. If you click the Language Bar Help command on the Help menu, the Language Bar Help window appears (Figure B-2h). On the far right of the Language bar are two buttons stacked above and below each other. The top button is the Minimize button and the bottom button is the Options button. The Minimize button minimizes the Language bar so that it appears on the Windows taskbar. The next section discusses the Options button.

Customizing the Language Bar

The down arrow icon immediately below the Minimize button in Figure B-2a is called the Options button. The Options button displays a menu of text services options (Figure B-2i). You can use this menu to hide the Speech Tools, Handwriting, and Help buttons on the Language bar by clicking their names to remove the check mark to the left of each button. You also can show the Correction, Speak Text, and Pause Speaking buttons on the Language bar by clicking their names to place a check mark to the left of the respective command. When you select text and then click the Correction button, a list of correction alternatives is displayed in the Word window. You can use the Corrections button to correct both speech recognition and handwriting recognition errors. The Speak Text and Pause Speaking buttons are discussed at the end of this Appendix. The Settings command on the Options menu displays a dialog box that lets you customize the Language bar. This command will be discussed shortly. The Restore Defaults command redisplays hidden buttons on the Language bar.

FIGURE B-2

If you right-click the Language bar, a shortcut menu appears (Figure B-3a on the next page). This shortcut menu lets you further customize the Language bar. The Minimize command on the shortcut menu docks the Language bar on the Windows taskbar. The Transparency command in Figure B-3a toggles the Language bar between being solid and transparent. You can see through a transparent Language bar (Figure B-3b). The Text Labels command toggles on text labels on the Language bar (Figure B-3c) and off (Figure B-3b). The Vertical command displays the Language bar vertically on the screen (Figure B-3d).

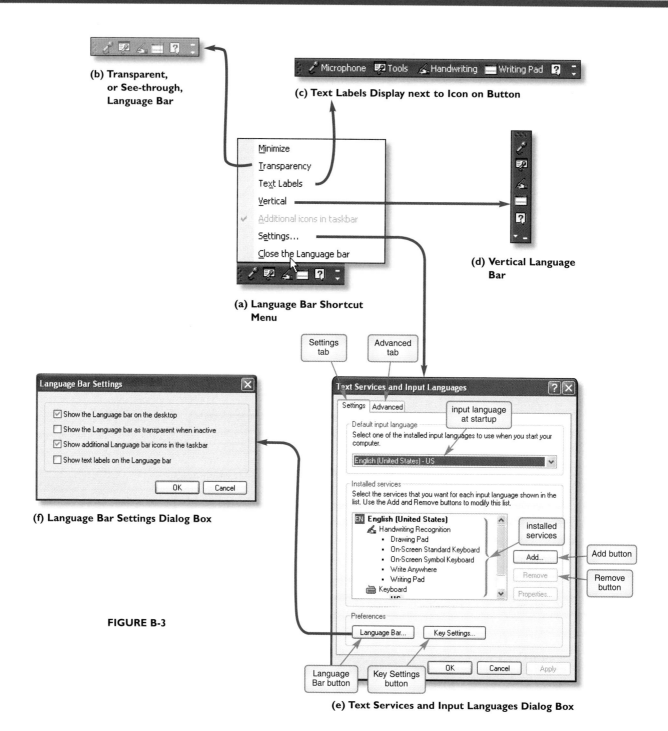

(b) Transparent, or See-through, Language Bar

(c) Text Labels Display next to Icon on Button

(a) Language Bar Shortcut Menu

(d) Vertical Language Bar

FIGURE B-3

(f) Language Bar Settings Dialog Box

(e) Text Services and Input Languages Dialog Box

The Settings command in Figure B-3a displays the Text Services and Input Languages dialog box (Figure B-3e). The Text Services and Input Languages dialog box allows you to add additonal languages, add and remove text services, modify keys on the keyboard, modify the Language bar, and extend support of advanced text services to all programs, including Notepad and other programs that normally do not support text services (through the Advanced tab). If you want to remove any one of the services in the Installed services list, select the service, and then click the Remove button. If you want to add a service, click the Add button. The Key Settings button allows you to modify the keyboard. If you click the Language Bar button in the Text Services and Input Languages dialog box, the Language Bar Settings dialog box appears (Figure B-3f). This dialog box contains Language bar options, some of which are the same as the commands on the Language bar shortcut menu shown in Figure B-3a.

The Close the Language bar command on the shortcut menu shown in Figure B-3a closes or hides the Language bar. If you close the Language bar and want to redisplay it, see Figure B-1d on page APP 11.

Speech Recognition

The **Speech Recognition service** available with Office enables your computer to recognize human speech through a microphone. The microphone has two modes: dictation and voice command (Figure B-4). You switch between the two modes by clicking the Dictation button and the Voice Command button on the Language bar. These buttons appear only when you turn on Speech Recognition by clicking the Microphone button on the Language bar (Figure B-5a on the next page). If you are using the Microphone button for the very first time in Word, it will require that you check your microphone settings and step through voice training before activating the Speech Recognition service.

The Dictation button places the microphone in Dictation mode. In **Dictation mode**, whatever you speak is entered as text at the location of the insertion point. The Voice Command button places the microphone in Voice Command mode. In **Voice Command mode**, whatever you speak is interpreted as a command. If you want to turn off the microphone, click the Microphone button on the Language bar or in Voice Command mode say, "Mic off" (pronounced mike off). It is important to remember that minimizing the Language bar does not turn off the microphone.

(a) Enter Text in Dictation Mode

(b) Enter Commands in Voice Command Mode

FIGURE B-4

The Language bar speech message balloon shown in Figure B-5b displays messages that may offer help or hints. In Voice Command mode, the name of the last recognized command you said appears. If you use the mouse or keyboard instead of the microphone, a message will appear in the Language bar speech message balloon indicating the word you could say. In Dictation mode, the message, Dictating, usually appears. The Speech Recognition service, however, will display messages to inform you that you are talking too soft, too loud, too fast, or to ask you to repeat what you said by displaying, What was that?

Getting Started with Speech Recognition

For the microphone to function properly, you should follow these steps:

1. Make sure your computer meets the minimum requirements.
2. Start Word. Activate Speech Recognition by clicking Tools on the menu bar and then clicking Speech.
3. Set up and position your microphone, preferably a close-talk headset with gain adjustment support.
4. Train Speech Recognition.

(a) Microphone Off

(b) Microphone On

FIGURE B-5

The following sections describe these steps in more detail.

SPEECH RECOGNITION SYSTEM REQUIREMENTS For Speech Recognition to work on your computer, it needs the following:

1. Microsoft Windows 98 or later or Microsoft Windows NT 4.0 or later
2. At least 128 MB RAM
3. 400 MHz or faster processor
4. Microphone and sound card

SETUP AND POSITION YOUR MICROPHONE Set up your microphone as follows:

1. Connect your microphone to the sound card in the back of the computer.
2. Position the microphone approximately one inch out from and to the side of your mouth. Position it so you are not breathing into it.
3. On the Language bar, click the Speech Tools button and then click Options on the Speech Tools menu (Figure B-6a).
4. When text services displays the Speech input settings dialog box (Figure B-6b), click the Advanced Speech button. When text services displays the Speech Properties dialog box (Figure B-6c), click the Speech Recognition tab.
5. Click the Configure Microphone button. Follow the Microphone Wizard directions as shown in Figures B-6d, B-6e, and B-6f. The Next button will remain dimmed in Figure B-6e until the volume meter consistently stays in the green area.
6. If someone else installed Speech Recognition, click the New button in the Speech Properties dialog box and enter your name. Click the Train Profile button and step through the Voice Training dialog boxes. The Voice Training dialog boxes will require that you enter your gender and age group. It then will step you through voice training.

You can adjust the microphone further by clicking the Settings button in the Speech Properties dialog box (Figure B-6c). The Settings button displays the Recognition Profile Settings dialog box that allows you to adjust the pronunciation sensitivity and accuracy versus recognition response time.

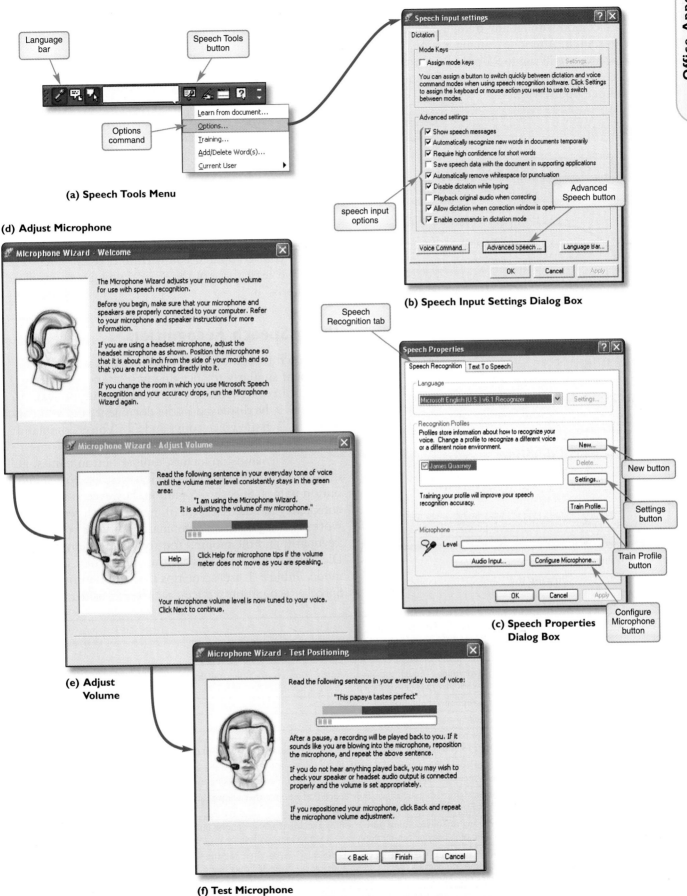

(a) Speech Tools Menu

(b) Speech Input Settings Dialog Box

(c) Speech Properties Dialog Box

(d) Adjust Microphone

(e) Adjust Volume

(f) Test Microphone

FIGURE B-6

TRAIN THE SPEECH RECOGNITION SERVICE The Speech Recognition service will understand most commands and some dictation without any training at all. It will recognize much more of what you speak, however, if you take the time to train it. After one training session, it will recognize 85 to 90 percent of your words. As you do more training, accuracy will rise to 95 percent. If you feel that too many mistakes are being made, then continue to train the service. The more training you do, the more accurately it will work for you. Follow these steps to train the Speech Recognition service:

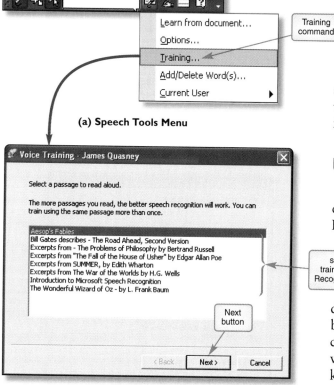

(a) Speech Tools Menu

(b) Voice Training Dialog Box

FIGURE B-7

1. Click the Speech Tools button on the Language bar and then click Training (Figure B-7a).
2. When the Voice Training dialog box appears (Figure B-7b), click one of the sessions and then click the Next button.
3. Complete the training session, which should take less than 15 minutes.

If you are serious about using a microphone to speak to your computer, you need to take the time to go through at least three of the eight training sessions listed in Figure B-7b.

Using Speech Recognition

Speech recognition lets you enter text into a document similarly to speaking into a tape recorder. Instead of typing, you can dictate text that you want to be displayed in the document, and you can issue voice commands. In Voice Command mode, you can speak menu names, commands on menus, toolbar button names, and dialog box option buttons, check boxes, list boxes, and button names. Speech recognition, however, is not a completely hands-free form of input. Speech recognition works best if you use a combination of your voice, the keyboard, and the mouse. You soon will discover that Dictation mode is far less accurate than Voice Command mode. Table B-1 lists some tips that will improve the Speech Recognition service's accuracy considerably.

Table B-1	Tips to Improve Speech Recognition
NUMBER	**TIP**
1	The microphone hears everything. Though the Speech Recognition service filters out background noise, it is recommended that you work in a quiet environment.
2	Try not to move the microphone around once it is adjusted.
3	Speak in a steady tone and speak clearly.
4	In Dictation mode, do not pause between words. A phrase is easier to interpret than a word. Sounding out syllables in a word will make it more difficult for the Speech Recognition service to interpret what you are saying.
5	If you speak too loudly or too softly, it makes it difficult for the Speech Recognition service to interpret what you said. Check the Language bar speech message balloon for an indication that you may be speaking too loudly or too softly.
6	If you experience problems after training, adjust the recognition options that control accuracy and rejection by clicking the Settings button shown in Figure B-6c on the previous page.
7	When you are finished using the microphone, turn it off by clicking the Microphone button on the Language bar or in Voice Command mode, say "Mic off." Leaving the microphone on is the same as leaning on the keyboard.
8	If the Speech Recognition service is having difficulty with unusual words, then add the words to its dictionary by using the Learn from document and Add/Delete Word(s) commands on the Speech Tools menu (Figure B-8a). The last names of individuals and the names of companies are good examples of the types of words you should add to the dictionary.
9	Training will improve accuracy; practice will improve confidence.

The last command on the Speech Tools menu is the Current User command (Figure B-8a). The Current User command is useful for multiple users who share a computer. It allows them to configure their own individual profiles, and then switch between users as they use the computer.

For additional information about the Speech Recognition service, enter speech recognition in the Type a question for help box on the menu bar.

Handwriting Recognition

Using the Office **Handwriting Recognition service**, you can enter text and numbers into Word by writing instead of typing. You can write using a special handwriting device that connects to your computer or you can write on the screen using your mouse. Four basic methods of handwriting are available by clicking the Handwriting button on the Language bar: Writing Pad; Write Anywhere; Drawing Pad; and On-Screen Keyboard. Although the on-screen keyboard does not involve handwriting recognition, it is part of the Handwriting menu and, therefore, will be discussed in this section.

If your Language bar does not include the Handwriting button, then for installation instructions, enter install handwriting recognition in the Type a question for help box on the menu bar.

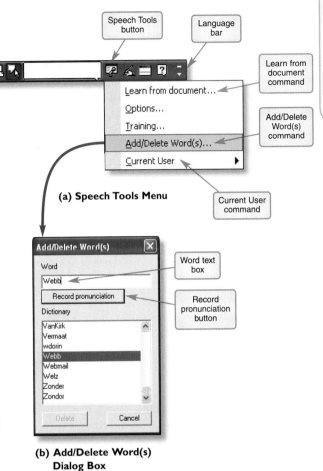

(a) Speech Tools Menu

(b) Add/Delete Word(s) Dialog Box

FIGURE B-8

Writing Pad

To display the Writing Pad, click the Handwriting button on the Language bar and then click Writing Pad (Figure B-9). The **Writing Pad** resembles a notepad with one or more lines on which you can use freehand to print or write in cursive. With the Text button enabled, you can form letters on the line by moving the mouse while holding down the mouse button. To the right of the notepad is a rectangular toolbar. Use the buttons on this toolbar to adjust the Writing Pad, select cells, and activate other handwriting applications.

FIGURE B-9

Consider the example in Figure B-9 on the previous page. With the insertion point at the top of the document, the word, Computers, is written in cursive on the **Pen line** in the Writing Pad. As soon as the word is complete, the Handwriting Recognition service automatically converts the handwriting to typed characters and inserts the text at the location of the insertion point. With the Ink button enabled, instead of the Text button, the text is inserted in handwritten form in the document.

You can customize the Writing Pad by clicking the Options button on the left side of the Writing Pad title bar and then clicking the Options command (Figure B-10a). Invoking the Options command causes the Handwriting Options dialog box to be displayed. The Handwriting Options dialog box contains two sheets: Common and Writing Pad. The Common sheet lets you change the pen color and pen width, adjust recognition, and customize the toolbar area of the Writing Pad. The Writing Pad sheet allows you to change the background color and the number of lines that are displayed in the Writing Pad. Both sheets contain a Restore Default button to restore the settings to what they were when the software was installed initially.

FIGURE B-10

When you first start using the Writing Pad, you may want to remove the check mark from the Automatic recognition check box in the Common sheet in the Handwriting Options dialog box (Figure B-10b). With the check mark removed, the Handwriting Recognition service will not interpret what you write in the Writing Pad until you click the Recognize Now button on the toolbar (Figure B-9 on the previous page). This allows you to pause and adjust your writing.

The best way to learn how to use the Writing Pad is to practice with it. Also, for more information, enter handwriting recognition in the Type a question for help box on the menu bar.

Write Anywhere

Rather than use Writing Pad, you can write anywhere on the screen by invoking the Write Anywhere command on the Handwriting menu (Figure B-11) that appears when you click the Handwriting button on the Language bar. In this case, the entire window is your writing pad.

In Figure B-11, the word, Report, is written in cursive using the mouse button. Shortly after the word is written, the Handwriting Recognition service interprets it, assigns it to the location of the insertion point, and erases what was written.

It is recommended that when you first start using the Write Anywhere service that you remove the check mark from the Automatic recognition check box in the Common sheet in the Handwriting Options dialog box (Figure B-10b). With the check mark removed, the Handwriting Recognition service will not interpret what you write on the screen until you click the Recognize Now button on the toolbar (Figure B-11).

FIGURE B-11

Write Anywhere is more difficult to use than the Writing Pad, because when you click the mouse button, Word may interpret the action as moving the insertion point rather than starting to write. For this reason, it is recommended that you use the Writing Pad.

Drawing Pad

With the Drawing Pad, you can insert a freehand drawing or sketch in a Word document. To display the Drawing Pad, click the Handwriting button on the Language bar and then click Drawing Pad (Figure B-12). Create a drawing by dragging the mouse in the Drawing Pad. In Figure B-12, the mouse was used to draw a tic-tac-toe game. When you click the Insert Drawing button on the Drawing Pad toolbar, Word inserts the drawing in the document at the location of the insertion point. Other buttons on the toolbar allow you to erase a drawing, erase your last drawing stroke, copy the drawing to the Office Clipboard, or activate the Writing Pad.

FIGURE B-12

The best way to learn how to use the Drawing Pad is to practice with it. Also, for more information, enter drawing pad in the Type a question for help box on the menu bar.

On-Screen Keyboard

The On-Screen Standard Keyboard command on the Handwriting menu (Figure B-13) displays an on-screen keyboard. The **on-screen keyboard** lets you enter data at the location of the insertion point by using your mouse to click the keys. The on-screen keyboard is similar to the type found on hand-held computers or PDAs.

The On-Screen Symbol Keyboard command on the Handwriting menu (Figure B-13) displays a special on-screen key-board that allows you to enter symbols that are not on your key-board, as well as Unicode charac-ters. **Unicode characters** use a coding scheme capable of representing all the world's current languages.

FIGURE B-13

Speech Playback

Using **speech playback**, you can have your computer read back the text in a document. Word provides two buttons for speech playback: Speak Text and Pause Speaking. To show the Speak Text button on the Language bar, click the Options button on the Language bar (Figure B-14) and then click Speak Text on the Options menu. Similarly, click the Options button on the Language bar and then click Pause Speaking on the Options menu to show the Pause Speaking button on the Language bar.

To use speech playback, position the insertion point where you want the computer to start reading back the text in the document and then click the Speak Text button on the Language bar (Figure B-14). The computer reads from the location of the insertion point until the end of the document or until you click the Pause Speaking button on the Language bar. An alternative is to select the text you want the computer to read and then click the Speak Text button on the Language bar. After the computer reads back the selected text, it stops speech playback.

When you click the Speak Text button on the Language bar, it changes to a Stop Speaking button. Click the Stop Speaking button on the Language bar to stop the speech playback. If you click the Pause Speaking button on the Language bar to stop speech playback, the Pause Speaking button changes to a Resume Speaking button that you click when you want the computer to continue reading the document from the location at which it stopped reading.

FIGURE B-14

Customizing Speech Playback

You can customize speech playback through the
Speech Properties dialog box. Click the Speech Tools button on
the Language bar and then click Options on the Speech Tools
menu (Figure B-6a on page APP 17). When text services displays
the Speech input settings dialog box (Figure B-6b), click the
Advanced Speech button. When text services displays the
Speech Properties dialog box, click the Text To Speech tab
(Figure B-15). The Text To Speech sheet has two areas: Voice
selection and Voice speed. The Voice selection area lets you
choose between two male voices and one female
voice. You can click the Preview Voice button to
hear a sample of the voice. The Voice speed area
contains a slider. Drag the slider to slow down
or speed up the pace of the speaking voice.

FIGURE B-15

Appendix C

Publishing Office Web Pages to a Web Server

With the Office applications, you use the Save as Web Page command on the File menu to save the Web page to a Web server using one of two techniques: Web folders or File Transfer Protocol. A **Web folder** is an Office shortcut to a Web server. **File Transfer Protocol** (**FTP**) is an Internet standard that allows computers to exchange files with other computers on the Internet.

You should contact your network system administrator or technical support staff at your ISP to determine if their Web server supports Web folders, FTP, or both, and to obtain necessary permissions to access the Web server. If you decide to publish Web pages using a Web folder, you must have the Office Server Extensions (OSE) installed on your computer.

Using Web Folders to Publish Office Web Pages

When publishing to a Web folder, someone first must create the Web folder before you can save to it. If you are granted permission to create a Web folder, you must obtain the URL of the Web server, a user name, and possibly a password that allows you to access the Web server. You also must decide on a name for the Web folder. Table C-1 explains how to create a Web folder.

Office adds the name of the Web folder to the list of current Web folders. You can save to this folder, open files in the folder, rename the folder, or perform any operations you would to a folder on your hard disk. You can use your Office program or Windows Explorer to access this folder. Table C-2 explains how to save to a Web folder.

Using FTP to Publish Office Web Pages

When publishing a Web page using FTP, you first must add the FTP location to your computer before you can save to it. An FTP location, also called an **FTP site**, is a collection of files that reside on an FTP server. In this case, the FTP server is the Web server.

To add an FTP location, you must obtain the name of the FTP site, which usually is the address (URL) of the FTP server, and a user name and a password that allows you to access the FTP server. You save and open the Web pages on the FTP server using the name of the FTP site. Table C-3 explains how to add an FTP site.

Office adds the name of the FTP site to the FTP locations list in the Save As and Open dialog boxes. You can open and save files using this list. Table C-4 explains how to save to an FTP location.

Table C-1   Creating a Web Folder

1. Click File on the menu bar and then click Save As (or Open).
2. When the Save As dialog box (or Open dialog box) appears, click My Network Places on the My Places bar, and then click the Create New Folder button on the toolbar.
3. When the Add Network Place Wizard dialog box appears, click the Next button. If necessary, click Choose another network location. Click the Next button. Click the View some examples link, type the Internet or network address, and then click the Next button. Click Log on anonymously to deselect the check box, type your user name in the User name text box, and then click the Next button. Enter the name you want to call this network place and then click the Next button. Click the Finish button.

Table C-2   Saving to a Web Folder

1. Click File on the menu bar and then click Save As.
2. When the Save As dialog box appears, type the Web page file name in the File name text box. Do not press the ENTER key.
3. Click My Network Places on the My Places bar.
4. Double-click the Web folder name in the Save in list.
5. If the Enter Network Password dialog box appears, type the user name and password in the respective text boxes and then click the OK button.
6. Click the Save button in the Save As dialog box.

Table C-3   Adding an FTP Location

1. Click File on the menu bar and then click Save As (or Open).
2. In the Save As dialog box, click the Save in box arrow and then click Add/Modify FTP Locations in the Save in list; or in the Open dialog box, click the Look in box arrow and then click Add/Modify FTP Locations in the Look in list.
3. When the Add/Modify FTP Locations dialog box appears, type the name of the FTP site in the Name of FTP site text box. If the site allows anonymous logon, click Anonymous in the Log on as area; if you have a user name for the site, click User in the Log on as area and then enter the user name. Enter the password in the Password text box. Click the OK button.
4. Close the Save As or the Open dialog box.

Table C-4   Saving to an FTP Location

1. Click File on the menu bar and then click Save As.
2. When the Save As dialog box appears, type the Web page file name in the File name text box. Do not press the ENTER key.
3. Click the Save in box arrow and then click FTP Locations.
4. Double-click the name of the FTP site to which you wish to save.
5. When the FTP Log On dialog box appears, enter your user name and password and then click the OK button.
6. Click the Save button in the Save As dialog box.

Appendix D

Changing Screen Resolution and Resetting the Word Toolbars and Menus

This appendix explains how to change your screen resolution in Windows to the resolution used in this book. It also describes how to reset the Word toolbars and menus to their installation settings.

Changing Screen Resolution

The **screen resolution** indicates the number of pixels (dots) that your computer uses to display the letters, numbers, graphics, and background you see on your screen. The screen resolution usually is stated as the product of two numbers, such as 800 × 600 (pronounced 800 by 600). An 800 x 600 screen resolution results in a display of 800 distinct pixels on each of 600 lines, or about 480,000 pixels. The figures in this book were created using a screen resolution of 800 × 600.

The screen resolutions most commonly used today are 800 × 600 and 1024 x 768, although some Office specialists operate their computers at a much higher screen resolution, such as 2048 x 1536. The following steps show how to change the screen resolution from 1024 × 768 to 800 × 600.

To Change the Screen Resolution

1

• **If necessary, minimize all applications so that the Windows desktop appears.**

• **Right-click the Windows desktop.**

Windows displays the Windows desktop shortcut menu (Figure D-1).

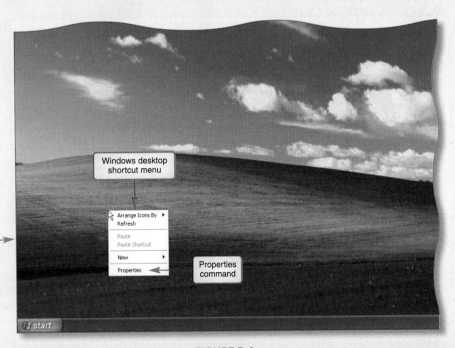

Windows desktop shortcut menu

Windows desktop shown at 1024 ◊ 768 screen resolution

Arrange Icons By
Refresh

Paste
Paste Shortcut

New

Properties

Properties command

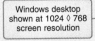
start

FIGURE D-1

2

• **Click Properties on the shortcut menu.**

• **When Windows displays the Display Properties dialog box, click the Settings tab.**

Windows displays the Settings sheet in the Display Properties dialog box (Figure D-2). The Settings sheet shows a preview of the Windows desktop using the current screen resolution (1024 x 768). The Settings sheet also shows the screen resolution and the color quality settings.

FIGURE D-2

3

• **Drag the slider in the Screen resolution area to the left so that the screen resolution changes to 800 x 600.**

The screen resolution in the Screen resolution area changes to 800 × 600 (Figure D-3). The Settings sheet shows a preview of the Windows desktop using the new screen resolution (800 × 600).

FIGURE D-3

4

- Click the OK button.
- If Windows displays the Monitor Settings dialog box, click the Yes button.

Windows changes the screen resolution from 1024 × 768 to 800 × 600 (Figure D-4).

800 ◊ 600
screen resolution

FIGURE D-4

As shown in the previous steps, as you decrease the screen resolution, Windows displays less information on your screen, but the information increases in size. The reverse also is true: as you increase the screen resolution, Windows displays more information on your screen, but the information decreases in size.

Resetting the Word Toolbars and Menus

Word customization capabilities allow you to create custom toolbars by adding and deleting buttons and personalize menus based on their usage. Each time you start Word, the toolbars and menus are displayed using the same settings as the last time you used it. The figures in this book were created with the Word toolbars and menus set to the original, or installation, settings.

Resetting the Standard and Formatting Toolbars

The steps on the next page show how to reset the Standard and Formatting toolbars.

To Reset the Standard and Formatting Toolbars

1

• **Start Word.**

• **Click the Toolbar Options button on the Standard toolbar and then point to Add or Remove Buttons on the Toolbar Options menu.**

Word displays the Toolbar Options menu and the Add or Remove Buttons submenu (Figure D-5).

FIGURE D-5

2

• **Point to Standard on the Add or Remove Buttons submenu.**

• **When Word displays the Standard submenu, scroll down and then point to Reset Toolbar.**

The Standard submenu indicates the buttons and boxes that are displayed on the Standard toolbar (Figure D-6). To remove a button from the Standard toolbar, click a button name with a check mark to the left of the name to remove the check mark.

3

• **Click Reset Toolbar.**

• **If a Microsoft Word dialog box is displayed, click the Yes button.**

Word resets the Standard toolbar to its original settings.

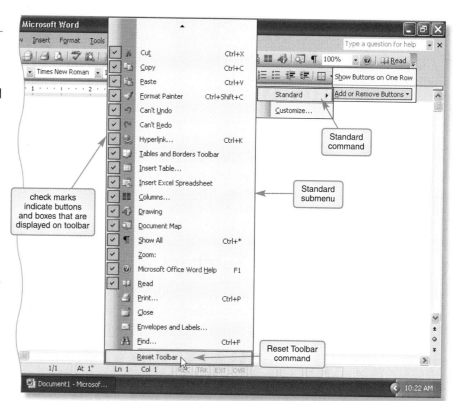

FIGURE D-6

4

• **Reset the Formatting toolbar by following Steps 1 through 3 and replacing any reference to the Standard toolbar with the Formatting toolbar.**

Not only can you use the Standard submenu shown in Figure D-6 to reset the Standard toolbar to its original settings, but you also can use it to customize the Standard toolbar by adding and deleting buttons. To add or delete buttons, click the button name on the Standard submenu to add or remove the check mark. Buttons with a check mark to the left currently are displayed on the Standard toolbar; buttons without a check mark are not displayed on the Standard toolbar. You can complete the same tasks for the Formatting toolbar, using the Formatting submenu to add and delete buttons from the Formatting toolbar.

Resetting the Word Menus

The following steps show how to reset the Word menus to their original settings.

To Reset the Word Menus

1

• **Click the Toolbar Options button on the Standard toolbar and then point to Add or Remove Buttons on the Toolbar Options menu.**

Word displays the Toolbar Options menu and the Add or Remove Buttons submenu (Figure D-7).

FIGURE D-7

2

• **Click Customize on the Add or Remove Buttons submenu.**

• **When Word displays the Customize dialog box, click the Options tab.**

The Customize dialog box contains three sheets used for customizing the Word toolbars and menus (Figure D-8).

3

• **Click the Reset menu and toolbar usage data button.**

• **When Word displays the Microsoft Word dialog box, click the Yes button.**

• **Click the Close button in the Customize dialog box.**

Word resets the menus to the original settings.

FIGURE D-8

Other Ways

1. On View menu point to Toolbars, click Customize on Toolbars submenu, click Options tab, click Reset menu and toolbar usage data button, click Yes button, click Close button

2. Right-click toolbar, click Customize on shortcut menu, click Options tab, click Reset menu and toolbar usage data button, click Yes button, click Close button

3. In Voice Command mode, say "View, Toolbars, Customize, Options, Reset menu and toolbar usage data, Yes, Close"

Using the Options sheet in the Customize dialog box, as shown in Figure D-8 on the previous page, you can select options to personalize menus and toolbars. For example, you can select or deselect a check mark that instructs Word to display the Standard and Formatting toolbars on two rows. You also can select whether Word always displays full menus or displays short menus followed by full menus, after a short delay. Other options available on the Options sheet including settings to instruct Word to display toolbars with large icons; to use the appropriate font to display font names in the Font list; and to display a ScreenTip when a user points to a toolbar button. Clicking the Help button in the upper-right corner of the Customize dialog box displays Help topics that will assist you in customizing toolbars and menus.

Using the Commands sheet in the Customize dialog box, you can add buttons to toolbars and commands to menus. Recall that the menu bar at the top of the Word window is a special toolbar. To add buttons to a toolbar, click a category name in the Categories list and then drag the command name in the Commands list to a toolbar. To add commands to a menu, click a category name in the Categories list, drag the command name in the Commands list to a menu name on the menu bar, and then, when the menu is displayed, drag the command to the desired location in the list of menu commands.

Using the Toolbars sheet in the Customize dialog box, you can add new toolbars and reset existing toolbars and the menu. To add a new toolbar, click the New button, enter a toolbar name in the New Toolbar dialog box, and then click the OK button. Once the new toolbar is created, you can use the Commands sheet to add or remove buttons, as you would with any other toolbar. If you add one or more buttons to an existing toolbar and want to reset the toolbar to its original settings, click the toolbar name in the Toolbars list so a check mark is displayed to the left of the name and then click the Reset button. If you add commands to one or more menus and want to reset the menus to their default settings, click Menu Bar in the Toolbars list on the Toolbars sheet so a check mark is displayed to the left of the name and then click the Reset button. When you have finished, click the Close button to close the Customize dialog box.

Appendix E

Microsoft Office Specialist Certification

What Is Microsoft Office Specialist Certification?

Microsoft Office Specialist certification provides a framework for measuring your proficiency with the Microsoft Office 2003 applications, such as Microsoft Office Word 2003, Microsoft Office Excel 2003, Microsoft Office Access 2003, Microsoft Office PowerPoint 2003, and Microsoft Office Outlook 2003. The levels of certification are described in Table E-1.

Table E-1 Levels of Microsoft Office Specialist Certification

LEVEL	DESCRIPTION	REQUIREMENTS	CREDENTIAL AWARDED
Microsoft Office Specialist	Indicates that you have an understanding of the basic features in a specific Microsoft Office 2003 application	Pass any ONE of the following: Microsoft Office Word 2003 Microsoft Office Excel 2003 Microsoft Office Access 2003 Microsoft Office PowerPoint 2003 Microsoft Office Outlook 2003	Candidates will be awarded one certificate for each of the Specialist-level exams they have passed: Microsoft Office Word 2003 Microsoft Office Excel 2003 Microsoft Office Access 2003 Microsoft Office PowerPoint 2003 Microsoft Office Outlook 2003
Microsoft Office Expert	Indicates that you have an understanding of the advanced features in a specific Microsoft Office 2003 application	Pass any ONE of the following: Microsoft Office Word 2003 Expert Microsoft Office Excel 2003 Expert	Candidates will be awarded one certificate for each of the Expert-level exams they have passed: Microsoft Office Word 2003 Expert Microsoft Office Excel 2003 Expert
Microsoft Office Master	Indicates that you have a comprehensive understanding of the features of four of the five primary Microsoft Office 2003 applications	Pass the following: Microsoft Office Word 2003 Expert Microsoft Office Excel 2003 Expert Microsoft Office PowerPoint 2003 And pass ONE of the following: Microsoft Office Access 2003 or Microsoft Office Outlook 2003	Candidates will be awarded the Microsoft Office Master certificate for fulfilling the requirements.

Why Should You Be Certified?

Being Microsoft Office certified provides a valuable industry credential — proof that you have the Office 2003 applications skills required by employers. By passing one or more Microsoft Office Specialist certification exams, you demonstrate your proficiency in a given Office 2003 application to employers. With more than 400 million people in 175 nations and 70 languages using Office applications, Microsoft is targeting Office 2003 certification to a wide variety of companies. These companies include temporary employment agencies that want to prove the expertise of their workers, large corporations looking for a way to measure the skill set of employees, and training companies and educational institutions seeking Microsoft Office 2003 teachers with appropriate credentials.

The Microsoft Office Specialist Certification Exams

You pay $50 to $100 each time you take an exam, whether you pass or fail. The fee varies among testing centers. The **Microsoft Office Expert** exams, which you can take up to 60 minutes to complete, consist of between 40 and 60 tasks that you perform on a personal computer in a simulated environment. The tasks require you to use the application just as you would in doing your job. The **Microsoft Office Specialist** exams contain fewer tasks, and you will have slightly less time to complete them. The tasks you will perform differ on the two types of exams. After passing designated Expert and Specialist exams, candidates are awarded the **Microsoft Office Master** certificate (see the requirements in Table E-1 on the previous page).

How to Prepare for the Microsoft Office Specialist Certification Exams

The Shelly Cashman Series offers several Microsoft-approved textbooks that cover the required objectives of the Microsoft Office Specialist certification exams. For a listing of the textbooks, visit the Shelly Cashman Series Microsoft Office Specialist Center at scsite.com/winoff2003/cert. Click the link Shelly Cashman Series Microsoft Office 2003-Approved Microsoft Office Textbooks (Figure E-1). After using any of the books listed in an instructor-led course, you should be prepared to take the indicated Microsoft Office Specialist certification exam.

How to Find an Authorized Testing Center

To locate a testing center, call 1-800-933-4493 in North America, or visit the Shelly Cashman Series Microsoft Office Specialist Center at scsite.com/winoff2003/cert. Click the link Locate an Authorized Testing Center Near You (Figure E-1). At this Web site, you can look for testing centers around the world.

Shelly Cashman Series Microsoft Office Specialist Center

The Shelly Cashman Series Microsoft Office Specialist Center (Figure E-1) lists more than 15 Web sites you can visit to obtain additional information about certification. The Web page (scsite.com/winoff2003/cert) includes links to general information about certification, choosing an application for certification, preparing for the certification exam, and taking and passing the certification exam.

FIGURE E-1

Index

MICROSOFT
Office 2003

Quick Reference Summary

In the Microsoft Office 2003 applications, you can accomplish a task in a number of ways. The following four tables (one each for Microsoft Office Word 2003, Microsoft Office Excel 2003, Microsoft Office Access 2003, and Microsoft Office PowerPoint 2003,) provide a quick reference to each task presented in this textbook. The first column identifies the task. The second column indicates the page number on which the task is discussed in the book. The subsequent four columns list the different ways the task in column one can be carried out. You can invoke the commands listed in the MOUSE, MENU BAR, and SHORTCUT MENU columns using Voice commands.

Table 1 Microsoft Office Word 2003 Quick Reference Summary

TASK	PAGE NUMBER	MOUSE	MENU BAR	SHORTCUT MENU	KEYBOARD SHORTCUT
1.5 Line Spacing	WD 87	Line Spacing button arrow on Formatting toolbar	Format | Paragraph | Indents and Spacing tab	Paragraph | Indents and Spacing tab	CTRL+5
AutoCorrect Entry, Create	WD 91		Tools | AutoCorrect Options | AutoCorrect tab		
AutoCorrect Options	WD 90	AutoCorrect Options button			
Blank Line Above Paragraph	WD 87		Format | Paragraph | Indents and Spacing tab	Paragraph | Indents and Spacing tab	CTRL+0 (zero)
Bold	WD 44	Bold button on Formatting toolbar	Format | Font | Font tab	Font | Font tab	CTRL+B
Capitalize Letters	WD 87		Format | Font | Font tab	Font | Font tab	CTRL+SHIFT+A
Case of Letters	WD 87				SHIFT+F3
Center	WD 38	Center button on Formatting toolbar	Format | Paragraph | Indents and Spacing tab	Paragraph | Indents and Spacing tab	CTRL+E
Center Vertically	WD 38		File | Page Setup | Layout tab		
Clip Art, Insert	WD 46		Insert | Picture | Clip Art		
Close Document	WD 59	Close button on menu bar	File | Close		CTRL+W
Count Words	WD 100	Recount button on Word Count toolbar	Tools | Word Count		
Custom Dictionary	WD 121		Tools | Options | Spelling and Grammar tab		
Double-Space Text	WD 80	Line Spacing button on Formatting toolbar	Format | Paragraph | Indents and Spacing tab	Paragraph | Indents and Spacing tab	CTRL+2
Double-Underline	WD 87		Format | Font | Font tab	Font | Font tab	CTRL+SHIFT+D
E-Mail Document	WD 123	E-mail button on Standard toolbar	File | Send To | Mail Recipient		
Find	WD 117	Select Browse Object button on vertical scroll bar	Edit | Find		CTRL+F
Find and Replace	WD 116	Double-click left side of status bar	Edit | Replace		CTRL+H
First-Line Indent	WD 88	Drag First Line Indent marker on ruler	Format | Paragraph | Indents and Spacing tab	Paragraph | Indents and Spacing tab	
Font	WD 36	Font box arrow on Formatting toolbar	Format | Font | Font tab	Font | Font tab	CTRL+SHIFT+F
Font Size	WD 17	Font Size box arrow on Formatting toolbar	Format | Font | Font tab	Font | Font tab	CTRL+SHIFT+P
Footnote, Create	WD 94		Insert | Reference | Footnote		
Footnote, Delete	WD 99	Delete note reference mark			
Footnote, Edit	WD 99	Double-click note reference mark	View | Footnotes		
Footnotes to Endnotes, Convert	WD 99		Insert | Reference | Footnote		
Formatting Marks	WD 21	Show/Hide ¶ button on Standard toolbar	Tools | Options | View tab		CTRL+SHIFT+*

Table 1 Microsoft Office Word 2003 Quick Reference Summary *(continued)*

TASK	PAGE NUMBER	MOUSE	MENU BAR	SHORTCUT MENU	KEYBOARD SHORTCUT
Full Menu	WD 13	Double-click menu name	Click menu name and wait		
Go To	WD 111	Select Browse Object button on vertical scroll bar	Edit | Go To		CTRL+G
Hanging Indent, Create	WD 105	Drag Hanging Indent marker on ruler	Format | Paragraph | Indents and Spacing tab	Paragraph | Indents and Spacing tab	CTRL+T
Hanging Indent, Remove	WD 87	Drag Hanging Indent marker on ruler	Format | Paragraph | Indents and Spacing tab	Paragraph | Indents and Spacing tab	CTRL+SHIFT+T
Header, Display	WD 81		View | Header and Footer		
Help	WD 60 and Appendix A	Microsoft Office Word Help button on Standard toolbar	Help | Microsoft Office Word Help		F1
Hyperlink, Create	WD 108	Insert Hyperlink button on Standard toolbar		Hyperlink	Web address then ENTER or SPACEBAR
Indent, Decrease	WD 87	Decrease Indent button on Formatting toolbar	Format | Paragraph | Indents and Spacing tab	Paragraph | Indents and Spacing tab	CTRL+SHIFT+M
Indent, Increase	WD 87	Increase Indent button on Formatting toolbar	Format | Paragraph | Indents and Spacing tab	Paragraph | Indents and Spacing tab	CTRL+M
Italicize	WD 41	Italic button on Formatting toolbar	Format | Font | Font tab	Font | Font tab	CTRL+I
Justify Paragraph	WD 87	Justify button on Formatting toolbar	Format | Paragraph | Indents and Spacing tab	Paragraph | Indents and Spacing tab	CTRL+J
Left-Align	WD 86	Align Left button on Formatting toolbar	Format | Paragraph | Indents and Spacing tab	Paragraph | Indents and Spacing tab	CTRL+L
Margins	WD 78	In print layout view, drag margin boundary on ruler	File | Page Setup | Margins tab		
Move Selected Text	WD 113	Drag and drop	Edit | Cut; Edit | Paste	Cut; Paste	CTRL+X; CTRL+V
Open Document	WD 55	Open button on Standard toolbar	File | Open		CTRL+O
Page Break	WD 103		Insert | Break		CTRL+ENTER
Page Numbers, Insert	WD 83	Insert Page Number button on Header and Footer toolbar	Insert | Page Numbers		
Paste Options, Menu	WD 115	Paste Options button			
Print Document	WD 53	Print button on Standard toolbar	File | Print		CTRL+P
Quit Word	WD 54	Close button on title bar	File | Exit		ALT+F4
Redo Action	WD 39	Redo button on Standard toolbar	Edit | Redo		
Repeat Command	WD 39		Edit | Repeat		
Research Task Pane	WD 124	ALT+click word in document	Tools | Research		
Research Task Pane, Insert text from	WD 125			Right-click selected text in task pane, click Copy; right-click document, click Paste	Select text in task pane, CTRL+C; click document. CTRL+V
Resize Graphic	WD 50	Drag sizing handle	Format | Picture | Size tab	Format Picture | Size tab	
Restore Graphic	WD 51	Format Picture button on Picture toolbar	Format | Picture | Size tab	Format Picture | Size tab	
Right-Align	WD 37	Align Right button on Formatting toolbar	Format | Paragraph | Indents and Spacing tab	Paragraph | Indents and Spacing tab	CTRL+R
Ruler, Show or Hide	WD 11		View | Ruler		
Save Document - New Name or Format	WD 52		File | Save As		F12
Save Document - Same Name	WD 52	Save button on Standard toolbar	File | Save		CTRL+S
Save New Document	WD 28	Save button on Standard toolbar	File | Save		CTRL+S
Select Document	WD 113	Point to left and triple-click	Edit | Select All		CTRL+A
Select Graphic	WD 49	Click graphic			
Select Group of Words	WD 43	Drag through words			CTRL+SHIFT+ARROW
Select Line	WD 40	Point to left of line and click			SHIFT+DOWN ARROW
Select Multiple Paragraphs	WD 33	Point to left of first paragraph and drag down			CTRL+SHIFT+DOWN ARROW
Select Paragraph	WD 113	Triple-click paragraph			

Table 1 Microsoft Office Word 2003 Quick Reference Summary

TASK	PAGE NUMBER	MOUSE	MENU BAR	SHORTCUT MENU	KEYBOARD SHORTCUT
Select Sentence	WD 112	CTRL+click sentence			CTRL+SHIFT+ARROW
Select Word	WD 58	Double-click word			CTRL+SHIFT+ARROW
Single-Space Text	WD 87	Line Spacing button arrow on Formatting toolbar	Format | Paragraph | Indents and Spacing tab	Paragraph | Indents and Spacing tab	CTRL+1
Small Uppercase Letters	WD 87		Format | Font | Font tab	Font | Font tab	CTRL+SHIFT+K
Sort Paragraphs	WD 109		Table | Sort		
Spelling and Grammar Check At Once	WD 119	Spelling and Grammar button on Standard toolbar	Tools | Spelling and Grammar	Spelling	F7
Spelling Check as You Type	WD 26	Double-click Spelling and Grammar Status icon on status bar		Right-click flagged word, click word on shortcut menu	
Style, Modify	WD 96	Styles and Formatting button on Formatting toolbar	Format | Styles and Formatting		
Subscript	WD 87		Format | Font | Font tab	Font | Font tab	CTRL+=
Superscript	WD 87		Format | Font | Font tab	Font | Font tab	CTRL+SHIFT+PLUS SIGN
Synonym	WD 118		Tools | Language | Thesaurus	Synonyms | desired word	SHIFT+F7
Task Pane, Display Different	WD 10	Other Task Panes button on task pane			
Toolbar, Dock	WD 82	Double-click toolbar title bar			
Toolbar, Float	WD 82	Drag toolbar move handle			
Toolbar, Show Entire	WD 14	Double-click toolbar move handle	Tools | Customize | Options tab		
Underline	WD 42	Underline button on Formatting toolbar	Format | Font | Font tab	Font | Font tab	CTRL+U
Underline Words	WD 87		Format | Font | Font tab	Font | Font tab	CTRL+SHIFT+W
Undo	WD 39	Undo button on Standard toolbar	Edit | Undo		CTRL+Z
Zoom	WD 21	Zoom box arrow on Formatting toolbar	View | Zoom		

Table 2 Microsoft Excel 2003 Quick Reference Summary

TASK	PAGE NUMBER	MOUSE	MENU BAR	SHORTCUT MENU	KEYBOARD SHORTCUT
AutoFormat	EX 34		Format | AutoFormat		ALT+O | A
AutoSum	EX 23	AutoSum button on Standard toolbar	Insert | Function		ALT+=
Bold	EX 30	Bold button on Formatting toolbar	Format | Cells | Font tab	Format Cells | Font tab	CTRL+B
Borders	EX 96	Borders button on Formatting toolbar	Format | Cells | Border tab	Format Cells | Border tab	CTRL+1 | B
Center	EX 97	Center button on Formatting toolbar	Format | Cells | Alignment tab	Format Cells | Alignment tab	CTRL+1 | A
Center Across Columns	EX 33	Merge and Center button on Formatting toolbar	Format | Cells | Alignment tab	Format Cells | Alignment tab	CTRL+1 | A
Chart	EX 39	Chart Wizard button on Standard toolbar	Insert | Chart		F11
Clear Cell	EX 52	Drag fill handle back	Edit | Clear | All	Clear Contents	DELETE
Close Workbook	EX 46	Close button on menu bar or workbook Control-menu icon	File | Close		CTRL+W
Color Background	EX 94	Fill Color button on Formatting toolbar	Format | Cells | Patterns tab	Format Cells | Patterns tab	CTRL+1 | P
Column Width	EX 107	Drag column heading boundary	Format | Column | Width	Column Width	ALT+O | C | W
Comma Style Format	EX 108	Comma Style button on Formatting toolbar	Format | Cells | Number tab | Accounting	Format Cells | Number tab | Accounting	CTRL+1 | N

Table 2 Microsoft Excel 2003 Quick Reference Summary (continued)

TASK	PAGE NUMBER	MOUSE	MENU BAR	SHORTCUT MENU	KEYBOARD SHORTCUT
Conditional Formatting	EX 104		Format | Conditional Formatting		ALT+O | D
Currency Style Format	EX 98	Currency Style button on Formatting toolbar	Format | Cells | Number | Currency	Format Cells | Number | Currency	CTRL+1 | N
Decimal Place, Decrease	EX 100	Decrease Decimal button on Formatting toolbar	Format | Cells | Number tab | Currency	Format Cells | Number tab | Currency	CTRL+1 | N
Decimal Place, Increase	EX 99	Increase Decimal button on Formatting toolbar	Format | Cells | Number tab | Currency	Format Cells | Number tab | Currency	CTRL+1 | N
E-Mail from Excel	EX 125	E-mail button on Standard toolbar	File | Send To | Mail Recipient		ALT+F | D | A
Fit to Print	EX 118		File | Page Setup | Page tab		ALT+F | U | P
Font Color	EX 32	Font Color button on Formatting toolbar	Format | Cells | Font tab	Format Cells | Font tab	CTRL+1 | F
Font Size	EX 31	Font Size box arrow on Formatting toolbar	Format | Cells | Font tab	Format Cells | Font tab	CTRL+1 | F
Font Type	EX 29	Font box arrow on Formatting toolbar	Format | Cells | Font tab	Format Cells | Font tab	CTRL+1 | F
Formula Assistance	EX 83	Insert Function box in formula bar	Insert | Function		CTRL+A after you type function name
Formulas Version	EX 118		Tools | Options | View tab | Formulas		CTRL+ACCENT MARK
Full Screen	EX 11		View | Full Screen		ALT+V | U
Function	EX 81	Insert Function box in formula bar	Insert | Function		SHIFT+F3
Go To	EX 37	Click cell	Edit | Go To		F5
Help	EX 53 and Appendix A	Microsoft Excel Help button on Standard toolbar	Help | Microsoft Excel Help		F1
Hide Column	EX 109	Drag column heading boundary	Format | Column | Hide	Hide	CTRL+0 (zero) to hide CTRL+SHIFT+) to display
Hide Row	EX 111	Drag row heading boundary	Format | Row | Hide	Hide	CTRL+9 to hide CTRL+SHIFT+(to display
In-Cell Editing	EX 50	Double-click cell			F2
Language Bar	EX 15 and Appendix B		Tools | Speech | Speech Recognition	Toolbars | Language bar	ALT+T | H | H
Merge Cells	EX 33	Merge and Center button on Formatting toolbar	Format | Cells | Alignment tab	Format Cells | Font tab | Alignment tab	ALT+O | E | A
Name Cells	EX 37	Click Name box in formula bar, type name	Insert | Name | Define		ALT+I | N | D
New Workbook	EX 53	New button on Standard toolbar	File | New		CTRL+N
Open Workbook	EX 47	Open button on Standard toolbar	File | Open		CTRL+O
Percent Style Format	EX 103	Percent Style button on Formatting toolbar	Format | Cells | Number tab | Percentage	Format Cells | Number tab | Percentage	CTRL+1 | N
Preview Worksheet	EX 114	Print Preview button on Standard toolbar	File | Print Preview		ALT+F | V
Print Worksheet	EX 113	Print button on Standard toolbar	File | Print		CTRL+P
Quit Excel	EX 46	Close button on title bar	File | Exit		ALT+F4
Range Finder	EX 89	Double-click cell			
Redo	EX 52	Redo button on Standard toolbar	Edit | Redo		ALT+E | R
Row Height	EX 110	Drag row heading boundary	Format | Row | Height	Row Height	ALT+O | R | E

Table 2 Microsoft Excel 2003 Quick Reference Summary

TASK	PAGE NUMBER	MOUSE	MENU BAR	SHORTCUT MENU	KEYBOARD SHORTCUT
Save Workbook, New Name	EX 42		File | Save As		ALT+F | A
Save Workbook, Same Name	EX 89	Save button on Standard toolbar	File | Save		CTRL+S
Select All of Worksheet	EX 53	Select All button on worksheet			CTRL+A
Select Cell	EX 16	Click cell			Use arrow keys
Shortcut Menu	EX 92	Right-click object			SHIFT+F10
Spell Check	EX 112	Spelling button on Standard toolbar	Tools | Spelling		F7
Split Cell	EX 33	Merge and Center button on Formatting toolbar	Format | Cells | Alignment tab	Format Cells | Alignment tab	ALT+O | E | A
Stock Quotes	EX 121		Data | Import External Data | Import Data		ALT+D | D | D
Task Pane	EX 8		View | Task Pane		ALT+V | K
Toolbar, Reset	Appendix D	Toolbar Options button on toolbar, Add or Remove Buttons, Customize, Toolbars tab		Customize | Toolbars	ALT+V | T | C | B
Toolbar, Show Entire	EX 13	Double-click move handle			
Undo	EX 51	Undo button on Standard toolbar	Edit | Undo		CTRL+Z
Unhide Column	EX 109	Drag hidden column heading boundary to right	Format | Column | Unhide	Unhide	ALT+O | C | U
Unhide Row	EX 111	Drag hidden row heading boundary down	Format | Row | Unhide	Unhide	ALT+O | R | U

Table 3 Microsoft Office Access 2003 Quick Reference Summary

TASK	PAGE NUMBER	MOUSE	MENU BAR	SHORTCUT MENU	KEYBOARD SHORTCUT
Add Record	AC 23	New Record button	Insert | New Record		
Add Table to Query	AC 92	Show Table button	Query | Show Table	Show Table	
Calculate Statistics	AC 100	Totals button	View | Totals	Totals	
Clear Query	AC 75		Edit | Clear Grid		
Close Database	AC 26	Close Window button	File | Close		
Close Form	AC 39	Close Window button	File | Close		
Close Query	AC 73	Close Window button	File | Close		
Close Table	AC 21	Close Window button	File | Close		
Create Calculated Field	AC 96			Zoom	SHIFT+F2
Create Database	AC 10	New button	File | New		CTRL+N
Create Form	AC 38	New Object button arrow | AutoForm	Insert | AutoForm		
Create Query	AC 68	New Object button arrow | Query	Insert | Query		
Create Report	AC 43	New Object button arrow | Report	Insert | Report		
Create Table	AC 17	Tables object | Create table in Design view or Create table by using wizard	Insert | Table		

Table 3 Microsoft Office Access 2003 Quick Reference Summary *(continued)*

TASK	PAGE NUMBER	MOUSE	MENU BAR	SHORTCUT MENU	KEYBOARD SHORTCUT
Crosstab Query	AC 104	New Object button arrow | Query	Insert | Query		
Exclude Duplicates	AC 87	Properties button	View | Properties | Unique Values Only	Properties | Unique Values Only	
Exclude Field from Query Results	AC 78	Show check box			
Field Size	AC 19	Field Size property box			
Field Type	AC 20	Data Type box arrow | appropriate type			Appropriate letter
Format a Calculated Field	AC 98	Properties button	View | Properties	Properties	
Group in Query	AC 103	Totals button	View | Totals		
Include All Fields in Query	AC 74	Double-click asterisk in field list			
Include Field in Query	AC 71	Double-click field in field list			
Join Properties	AC 94		View | Join Properties	Join Properties	
Key Field	AC 19	Primary Key button	Edit | Primary Key	Primary Key	
Move to First Record	AC 27	First Record button			CTRL+UP ARROW
Move to Last Record	AC 27	Last Record button			CTRL+DOWN ARROW
Move to Next Record	AC 27	Next Record button			DOWN ARROW
Move to Previous Record	AC 27	Previous Record button			UP ARROW
Open Database	AC 26	Open button	File | Open		CTRL+O
Open Table	AC 26	Tables object | Open button		Open	Use ARROW keys to move highlight to name, then press ENTER key
Preview Table	AC 30	Print Preview button	File | Print Preview	Print Preview	
Print Report	AC 47	Print button	File | Print	Print	CTRL+P
Print Results of Query	AC 72	Print button	File | Print	Print	CTRL+P
Print Table	AC 30	Print button	File | Print	Print	CTRL+P
Quit Access	AC 50	Close button	File | Exit		ALT+F4
Return to Select Query Window	AC 72	View button arrow	View | Design View		
Run Query	AC 71	Run button	Query | Run		
Save Form	AC 39	Save button	File | Save		CTRL+S
Save Query	AC 80	Save button	File | Save		CTRL+S
Save Table	AC 21	Save button	File | Save		CTRL+S
Select Fields for Report	AC 44	Add Field button or Add All Fields button			
Simple Query Wizard	AC 34	New Object button arrow | Query,	Insert | Query		
Sort Data in Query	AC 86	Sort row | Sort row arrow | type of sort			
Switch Between Form and Datasheet Views	AC 41	View button arrow	View | Datasheet View		
Top-Values Query	AC 89	Top Values button	View | Properties	Properties	
Use AND Criterion	AC 84				Place criteria on same line
Use OR Criterion	AC 85				Place criteria on separate lines

Table 4 Microsoft PowerPoint 2003 Quick Reference Summary

TASK	PAGE NUMBER	MOUSE	MENU BAR	SHORTCUT MENU	KEYBOARD SHORTCUT
Animate Text	PPT 114		Slide Show | Custom Animation | Add Effect button		ALT+D | M
Black Slide, End Show	PPT 42		Tools | Options | End with black slide		ALT+T | O | E
Check Spelling	PPT 54	Spelling button on Standard toolbar	Tools | Spelling		F7
Clip Art, Add Animation Effects	PPT 117		Slide Show | Custom Animation		ALT+D | M
Clip Art, Change Size	PPT 109	Format Picture button on Picture toolbar | Size tab	Format | Picture | Size tab	Format Picture | Size tab	ALT+O | I | Size tab
Clip Art, Insert	PPT 101, PPT 104	Insert Clip Art button on Drawing toolbar	Insert | Picture | Clip Art		ALT+I | P | C
Clip Art, Move	PPT 108	Drag			
Delete Text	PPT 56	Cut button on Standard toolbar	Edit | Cut	Cut	CTRL+X or BACKSPACE or DELETE
Demote a Paragraph on Outline tab	PPT 90	Demote button on Outlining toolbar			TAB or ALT+SHIFT+RIGHT ARROW
Design Template	PPT 18	Slide Design button on Formatting toolbar	Format | Slide Design	Slide Design	ALT+O | D
Display a Presentation in Black and White	PPT 57	Color/Grayscale button on Standard toolbar	View | Color/Grayscale | Pure Black and White		ALT+V | C | U
Edit Web Page through Browser	PPT 152	Edit button on Internet Explorer Standard Buttons toolbar	File on browser menu bar | Edit with Microsoft PowerPoint in browser window		ALT+F | D in browser window
E-Mail from PowerPoint	PPT 127	E-mail button on Standard toolbar	File | Send To | Mail Recipient		ALT+F | D | A
End Slide Show	PPT 50			End Show	ESC
Font	PPT 24	Font box arrow on Formatting toolbar	Format | Font	Font	ALT+O | F
Font Color	PPT 24	Font Color button arrow on Formatting toolbar, desired color	Format | Font	Font | Color	ALT+O | F | ALT+C | DOWN ARROW
Font Size, Decrease	PPT 27	Decrease Font Size button on Formatting toolbar	Format | Font	Font | Size	CTRL+SHIFT+LEFT CARET (<)
Font Size, Increase	PPT 25	Increase Font Size button on Formatting toolbar	Format | Font	Font | Size	CTRL+SHIFT+RIGHT CARET (>)
Header and Footer, Add to Outline Page	PPT 112		View | Header and Footer | Notes and Handouts tab		ALT+V | H | Notes and Handouts tab
Help	PPT 62 and Appendix A	Microsoft PowerPoint Help button on Standard toolbar	Help | Microsoft PowerPoint Help		F1
Italicize	PPT 24	Italic button on Formatting toolbar	Format | Font | Font style	Font | Font style	CTRL+I
Language Bar	PPT 16	Language Indicator button in tray	Tools | Speech | Speech Recognition		ALT+T | H | H
Move a Paragraph Down	PPT 87	Move Down button on Outlining toolbar			ALT+SHIFT+DOWN ARROW
Move a Paragraph Up	PPT 87	Move Up button on Outlining toolbar			ALT+SHIFT+UP ARROW

Table 4 Microsoft PowerPoint 2003 Quick Reference Summary

TASK	PAGE NUMBER	MOUSE	MENU BAR	SHORTCUT MENU	KEYBOARD SHORTCUT
New Slide	PPT 30	New Slide button on Formatting toolbar	Insert | New Slide		CTRL+M
Next Slide	PPT 45	Next Slide button on vertical scroll bar			PAGE DOWN
Normal View	PPT 96	Normal View button at lower-left PowerPoint window	View | Normal		ALT+V | N
Open Presentation	PPT 52	Open button on Standard toolbar	File | Open		CTRL+O
Paragraph Indent, Decrease	PPT 37	Decrease Indent button on Formatting toolbar			SHIFT+TAB or ALT+ SHIFT+LEFT ARROW
Paragraph Indent, Increase	PPT 36	Increase Indent button on Formatting toolbar			TAB or ALT+SHIFT+ RIGHT ARROW
Preview Presentation as Web Page	PPT 144		File | Web Page Preview		ALT+F | B
Previous Slide	PPT 45	Previous Slide button on vertical scroll bar			PAGE UP
Print a Presentation	PPT 60	Print button on Standard toolbar	File | Print		CTRL+P
Print on Outline	PPT 122		File | Print | Print what box arrow | Outline View		CTRL+P | TAB | TAB | DOWN ARROW | Outline View
Promote a Paragraph on Outline tab	PPT 89	Promote button on Outlining toolbar			SHIFT+TAB or ALT+ SHIFT+LEFT ARROW
Publish a Presentation	PPT 154		File | Save as Web Page | Publish | Publish		ALT+F | G | ALT+P | ALT+P
Quit PowerPoint	PPT 50	Close button on title bar or double-click control icon on title bar	File | Exit		ALT+F4 or CTRL+Q
Redo Action	PPT 22	Redo button on Standard toolbar	Edit | Redo		CTRL+Y or ALT+E | R
Save a Presentation	PPT 27	Save button on Standard toolbar	File | Save		CTRL+S
Save as Web Page	PPTW 147		File | Save as Web Page		ALT+F | G
Slide Layout	PPT 98		Format | Slide Layout	Slide Layout	ALT+O | L
Slide Show View	PPT 47	Slide Show button at lower-left PowerPoint window	View | Slide Show		F5 or ALT+V | W
Slide Sorter View	PPT 95	Slide Sorter View button at lower-left PowerPoint window	View | Slide Sorter		ALT+V | D
Spelling Check	PPT 54	Spelling button on Standard toolbar	Tools | Spelling	Spelling	F7
Task Pane	PPT 11		View | Task Pane		ALT+V | K
Toolbar, Reset	Appendix D	Toolbar Options button on toolbar, Add or Remove Buttons, Customize, Toolbars tab		Customize | Toolbars tab	ALT+V | T | C | B
Toolbar, Show Entire	PPT 9	Double-click move handle			
Undo Action	PPT 22	Undo button on Standard toolbar	Edit | Undo		CTRL+Z or ALT+E | U
Zoom Percentage, Increase	PPT 44	Zoom Box arrow on Standard toolbar	View | Zoom		ALT+V | Z